ADVANCE REA

MW00560708

Polymath

the Life and Professions of Dr. Alex Comfort Author of the Joy of Sex

by

Eric Laursen

ADVANCE READING COPY

Polymath: The Life and Professions of Dr. Alex Comfort, Author of *The Joy Of Sex*

ISBN 978-1-84935-496-7
E-ISBN 978-1-84935-497-4
Library of Congress Control Number: 2022948750

AK Press
370 Ryan Avenue #100
Chico, CA 95973
USA
www.akpress.org
akpress@akpress.org

AK Press
33 Tower Street
Edinburgh, EH6, 7BN
Scotland
www.akuk.com
akuk@akpress.org

The addresses above would be delighted to provide you with the latest AK Press catalog, featuring several thousand books, pamphlets, audio and video products, and stylish apparel published and distributed by AK Press. Alternatively, visit our websites for the complete catalog, latest news and updates, events, and secure ordering.

Cover design by John Yates | www.stealworks.com
Cover photograph of Alex Comfort courtesy of Nick Comfort
Author photograph of Eric Laursen by Matthew Cavanaugh
Printed in the United States of America on acid-free, recycled paper

In memory of Robert Laursen
October 4, 1924–October 9, 2019

Contents

PREFACE

Understanding the Human

Mitchell Beazley, a two-year-old London publishing and book-packaging house, was trying to break out of its niche producing atlases and wine guides when a prominent British biologist approached them with something new and daring: a detailed, explicitly illustrated sex manual, geared for mainstream audiences. The authors, who chose to remain anonymous, were a couple who lived "somewhere in the Mediterranean.... One of them is a practicing physician," the biologist said; he had merely edited their manuscript.

This being 1971 and the height of the sexual revolution, the publishers were intrigued. Unlike the usual run of such books—poorly written, full of misinformation, bearing a distinct aura of sleaze—this one was erudite and urbane yet informal and often witty. It was organized, entertainingly, as a cookbook, "a Cordon Bleu Guide to Lovemaking." For perhaps the first time, here was a sex manual that a respectable but adventurous couple needn't feel embarrassed to consult, something a mainstream publisher might actually have a chance peddling to respectable bookshops.

The biologist who brought the manuscript to Mitchell Beazley soon revealed himself to be the author: Alex Comfort, an accomplished, fifty-one-year-old, Cambridge-educated poet, novelist, political thinker, and broadcaster, and, as a scientist, a leader in the study of human aging. And this was not his first book on sex. He had been writing and advocating for greater sexual freedom, better and more frank sex education, and an end to the legal persecution of sexual minorities for more than two decades.

Comfort had also lived much of what he wrote about in his book. Almost a dozen years earlier, he had experienced a midlife sexual reawakening when he commenced an affair with a family friend. They turned her London flat into the scene of a long course in sexual experiment, complete with Polaroid photographs, a detailed notebook, and extensive delving into lovemaking texts from ancient India, Japan, and Renaissance Italy. Distressed by the raft of dubious sex primers hitting the market in the late '60s—especially David Reuben's *Everything You Always Wanted to Know about Sex but Were Afraid to Ask*, which he dismissed as "eccentric porn"—Comfort decided to write his own.

He seemed the unlikeliest person to produce such a book. Middle-aged, scholarly, and physically unprepossessing, he was missing four fingers of his left hand (lost in a childhood scientific experiment with explosives). Yet Alex Comfort was a captivating talker with an encyclopedic mind, a polymath who had already carved out a position—in print and on radio and TV—as one of the most stimulating public intellectuals and controversialists in postwar Britain. A longtime anarchist and peace activist, he had made headlines in 1961 when, with Bertrand Russell and thirty-two other organizers, he was imprisoned for his role in calling a mass sit-down demonstration for nuclear disarmament in Trafalgar Square.

The Joy of Sex, as his book came to be titled, vaulted Comfort into another category entirely, making him, along with Havelock Ellis, Alfred Kinsey, and Masters and Johnson, a key figure in the transformation of cultural attitudes about sex. The book was the fruit of a long personal and intellectual journey, blending elements of Comfort's anarcho-pacifist philosophy, his knowledge of the human body and medical practice, his many years of research into the sexual practices of different cultures, his own personal experience, and the communication skills he had honed as a writer and broadcaster.

The combination produced one of the biggest best sellers of the second half of the twentieth century, moving more than twelve million copies (to date) in various editions and a host of languages following its appearance in 1972. It remains one of the most recognized titles in publishing history. Long before the term "sex positive" gained currency, Comfort's book revolutionized the field of sex advice, establishing that writing about what happens in the bedroom (and elsewhere), not to mention how it's presented in print, could be fun and engaging, dispensing with both the porn shop air and the clinical tone of the counseling that doctors tended to provide.

Virtually every mainstream sex guide produced in its wake, of which there have been many, borrows something of the authorial voice, the attitude of toleration and self-discovery, and even some of the organizational structure Comfort created for his book, even when the authors deplore the more dated attitudes it expressed. In this respect, every sex-curious heterosexual couple in the years since who have turned to a book for advice on how to get more out of their experience in bed have been reading Alex Comfort, an achievement acknowledged by later sexual advisers from Dr. Ruth Westheimer to Dan Savage.

For millions of readers, however, *The Joy of Sex* will always carry an embarrassing after-odor of the late 1960s and early '70s, grouped with such publishing artifacts as the poetry of Rod McKuen, *Jonathan Livingston Seagull*, and self-help guides like *Your Erroneous Zones*. Years after it was published, its author occasionally referred to it as "a bit of an albatross, because it was entirely a side project. It was purely the luck of the draw that it sold better" than the fifty-odd other books he had published since the age of eighteen. These included poetry, fiction, drama, and travel narratives; scientific papers and popular titles on human aging, geriatric medical care and psychiatry, and the practice of medicine; and books on sociology, social biology, sexual behavior, and the ethics of political activism, from an anarchist perspective. They included translations from French and Sanskrit, works of political theory and analysis, and studies of the intersection of biology and religion and physics and the mind. Accompanying these were thousands of articles and pamphlets, book and art reviews, lectures, radio and television scripts, and lyrics for protest songs. In a remarkably productive life, he left his mark on a half-dozen-odd different fields: gerontology (the study of aging), geriatrics (the health and care of the aged), sexology, the study of mollusks, literature, anarchism, grassroots political activism, and phenomenology.

All of it, Comfort insisted, fit together as one large project. "My interest is human biology," he said in a 1974 *New York Times* interview. "Poetry, religion, sex, are really forms of human behavior. I am interested in the whole spectrum of the biology of man."[1] He was inspired to write novels because the novel had "both drawn upon and contributed directly to psychology, social anthropology, and even physics and biology," he wrote. Becoming a poet fed into the project as well, because good poetry could take complicated ideas, ones that needed pages of dense text to explain in prose, and make them empathic, communicable as feelings and emotions. Scientific discovery didn't depend entirely on logic and method, he argued, but also on imagination and inspiration, just as did poetry and art, making them all part of the same general area of understanding.

Comfort's interest in the human ("man" was the term he grew up with and used throughout his career) was always colored by the anarcho-pacifist perspective he arrived at in his twenties, during World War II and the immediate postwar years. Asked forty years later by an old comrade why he hadn't written much on anarchism recently, he replied, "Because it is a general background to all my thinking (fish don't write essays on water)." Anarchism for him was an ethical position that resisted false distinctions between the individual and the collective, insisting that no society is healthy when individuals do not accept a broad-ranging responsibility to each other, even—or especially—when that means disobeying and opposing the State.

This ethic of responsibility infused his most famous book. He encouraged couples to explore their fantasies rather than suppress them, provided they weren't violent or abusive, and in this way take responsibility for each other's pleasure. "The true nature of *The Joy of Sex*," wrote the British journalist, broadcaster, and cultural historian Matthew Sweet, "was one that few noticed at the time and few have remarked on since. It was a book about personal responsibility and freedom from convention; a book founded on the idea that political and erotic repression shared a common pathology. *The Joy of Sex* was the anarchist manifesto that conquered 1970s suburbia—a radical text that found a place on the shelves of millions of readers who didn't know Kropotkin from Kermit the Frog."[2]

His friends habitually described Comfort as a polymath, commonly defined as one whose knowledge embraces a wide range of complex subjects and, more importantly, often calls on several of them at once to address complex problems. He was admired for this quality, but as the century grew older it marked him as something of a throwback to the earlier decades and even the Victorian era, when an English person armed with a strong classical education seemingly could roam at will through the sciences, law, politics, and literature without being accused of trespassing in any of them. Stereotypically they were men, and Bertrand Russell, Thomas Huxley and his grandsons Aldous and Julian, Alfred North Whitehead, H. G. Wells, Winston Churchill, and the geneticist J. B. S. Haldane were well-known examples in Comfort's early years. (He got to know Russell, Haldane, and Julian Huxley personally.) In his last decade, and somehow fittingly, he wanted most to be remembered for his poetry.

By the time he wrote *The Joy of Sex*, however, figures like Russell were either dead or receding into the past, and to be this type of Renaissance figure had become a liability. In an age of specialization, publishers and academic employers didn't know what to do with him. As one of the world's foremost gerontologists and best-selling authors, he complained that he couldn't secure a permanent, paid academic post, and publishers found his choice of subjects and genres bewildering, except when he wrote about sex.

There was nothing archaic about the fields in which he chose to work and write, however. Gerontology was still struggling to establish itself as a coherent and respectable branch of science when he first tackled it in the '50s. His first book on the subject, *The Biology of Senescence*, was instrumental in separating the plausible theories of aging from the plethora of crackpot explanations and rejuvenation "treatments" and establishing what was really known about the subject at the time. Geriatric care was a neglected and decidedly not prestigious branch of medicine and psychiatry in America when he moved to the United States and began training specialists and proselytizing for greater attention to be paid to a growing population of elderly.

Sexology still barely existed as a respectable area of study in the late 1940s, when Comfort started writing about and campaigning for sex education that was free of prejudices and misinformation about teenage sexuality, sexual minorities, and the specifics of what couples do in bed. As an anarchist, he was an important figure in shifting the movement away from increasingly fruitless attempts at mass labor mobilization and toward an emphasis on direct action that would define protest politics in the postwar decades. He also explored the connection between anarchism and fields like biology, psychology, anthropology, and sociology, continuing a line of inquiry begun by the earlier anarchist scientists Peter Kropotkin and Élisée and Élie Reclus.

Comfort turned to phenomenology late in his career and published two provocative books on the biological origins of religion and how the human "I" is created in the mind in light of the new science of quantum physics, areas that would attract greater attention from scientists and philosophers in the twenty-first century. When he attempted, with his fiction of the '40s and '50s, to import the continental novel of ideas (Sartre, Camus, Mann, Musil) into English literature, the results were not entirely successful, and the project didn't catch on, but it may not be the last such effort. When he and other poets tried to bring something of the Romantic tradition back to English poetry in the '40s after a decade dominated by the more cerebral work of W. H Auden and his companions, again the project failed, but much of the work they produced endures and remains captivating.

Did Comfort spread himself too thin? Would his impact in any of the fields in which he worked have been greater if he had gone further and deeper in one or two and hadn't felt compelled to enter so many? Asked late in life, he declined to answer. The more relevant question is whether he could have lived any other way. He seemed to have an internal signal always to look for solutions in one field by bringing in data and insights from one of the others: by connecting physics to biology, anarchism to social biology, sex to sociology. This was the only way he could see to fully understand the "biology of man," or simply, the human.

"IT WAS VERY DIFFICULT to know Alex," Leonard Hayflick, a biogerontologist and longtime friend, admitted. "He was one of the brightest persons I've ever met, and his mind worked so fast! Certainly, I couldn't always keep up with him. But it built a shell around him that prevented him from being known easily. People would know several sides of him but not the whole thing, because he was so damn brilliant."[3] Being active in so many fields, his friendships tended to be compartmentalized and to omit anything highly intimate.

Yet, Alex was a warm person with a wide circle of colleagues and acquaintances in nearly every part of the world, many of whom admired and loved him. He was a brilliant conversationalist and—in smaller settings—a sometimes devastating public speaker with a penchant for satire. His bottomless inventory of limericks, appropriate for every conceivable occasion, was legendary. But his son recalled that he never had a close friend to whom he could open up about his deepest feelings. Many people with whom he had long relationships—scientists, writers (including George Orwell), publishers, political organizers—only met him in person once or twice and kept in touch with him largely by correspondence. He chalked this up to an intense pace of work—he produced his first novels and poetry collections while still qualifying as a doctor—and impatience at wasting time. Additionally, he suffered from migraines much of his adult life that brought on spells of depression.

But this separateness also stemmed from Alex's upbringing by an intellectually gifted mother who trained him to be a scholar from nearly his first days. Learning came easily, and he quickly found that it was the easiest way for an unathletic boy from an unfashionable middle-class background to gain favor. It also, as Hayflick recalled, "built a shell around him." His closest friends were likely his two wives—Ruth, the mother of his only child, journalist Nicholas Comfort; and Jane, his second—but both relationships were fraught with difficulties. Ruth was a serene and reserved person who loved him but often found him exhausting. Jane, a warm, sexually alive, but emotionally fragile person, he could never make really happy. For twelve difficult years he split his time between the two women, keeping all three of them generally dissatisfied, before divorcing Ruth and marrying Jane.

Alex was conscious of this lack, this difficulty in fully connecting with other people, which underscored his feeling of separateness from them. Accordingly, he set about understanding the human and communicating that understanding. It was how he achieved his own sentimental education. Sexual liberation fit naturally into this program because he felt that sex was one of the critical spaces in which people learn to be social and to practice mutual aid, which to him was part of what it meant to be human in a world without God and with the certainty of the individual's death:

> For Freedom and Beauty are not fixed stars,
> but cut by man only from his own flesh,
> but lit by man, only for his sojourn
>
> because our shout into the cup of sky
> brings back no echo, brings back no echo ever:
> because man's mind lives at his stature's length
>
> because the stars have for us no earnest of winning
> because there is no resurrection
> because all things are against us, we are ourselves.[4]

CHAPTER 1

Nonconformists (1920–1932)

In Monken Hadley Common, a small boy stands by a fence bordering the bridge dividing the common from the railroad tracks near Barnet Station. Placing himself properly, he can see through Hadley Tunnel to where four lines of the Great Northern Railway join into two and pass through the tunnel as trains from as far away as York head into London and their terminal point at King's Cross Station. He makes sure to be at his post by the fence, or at Barnet Station, promptly at 11:00 a.m. any day he can, and the trains are familiar to him: Gresley Pacifics, with "big, round, bland faces, a look of severity and hard work"; Ivatt Atlantics, with their "young, moustached faces, like the Laughing Cavalier"; and his favorites, the Robinson Director class 4-4-0's, with un-English names like Mons and Zeebrugge, sporting "broad, round, hingeless" faces and "a little wheel instead of latch handles, set like a pig's nose in the middle."

Even when he can't contrive to see the locomotives close-up, he can catch a fleeting glimpse or at least recognize them by ear—while shopping with his mother, playing in the garden of the family's house in Barnet, or from his window in the rear bedroom—because each has a distinct whistle, and nowhere in his neighborhood are the trains far from earshot. "Even at night," he would remember years later, "I was in bed listening to the trains—first a rushing, like the wind, which came and went; then a rumbling underground as they went through the tunnel; and then a burst of sound as they came out and ran on down the bank toward London." If half asleep, he recalled, he would come "fully awake" at the sound of a 4-4-0 going by.

The boy spends hours at a stretch watching the trains, carefully noting locomotive serial numbers as they come and go, and at home he draws diagrams of engine types and collects photographs of engines and cars in a schoolboy notebook. His father gives him the small, color-illustrated train cards from packets of cigarettes, and these too he pastes into his notebook, annotated with serial numbers and whimsical nicknames: Knight of the Golden Fleece, Hercules, Great Bear. It's not just a matter of observing and noting for the precocious boy. It's a deliberate program to absorb, study, and understand—the first of many he will take up during his life.

THE GREAT NORTHERN RAILWAY "figured very largely" in his childhood, Alex Comfort later told a radio audience.[1] But "locospotting," later known as trainspotting, was not yet a national craze when he developed his fascination with locomotives in the late 1920s and '30s. That would come during Britain's years of austerity during and after World War II, when anything—even the rush of watching a massive, noisy behemoth roaring by—could be satisfactory entertainment.

In those earlier decades, Alex was part of a small but growing underground, disproportionately boys, nurtured by hobbyist publications that began to appear in the 1890s and ABC books that taught children to spell using pictures of trains, both encouraging them to feel a part of their country's great imperial-industrial project.[2] Schedules could be obtained for free and provided a handy place to jot down sightings, much as birdwatchers maintain life lists. But, for the really dedicated, the sound of a whistle and exhaust was enough to know which train was passing through.

Whence the cult of the steam locomotive? Alex later traced it to two things. "[It was] a lack in our society of minor gods, demi-gods, numinous things, which we miss all our lives but which we supply most readily in childhood; and secondly, the purely fortuitous way in which the demands of mechanical design give the locomotive a superficial resemblance to a half-human, half-animal being. . . . Locomotives seem to serve us, when we are children, as the masks and the ritual figures serve for less mechanical people. They are, I suppose, ancestor figures—half ancestors, half playmates."

Locospotting could be dangerous—practitioners sometimes scrambled onto precarious perches to catch a glimpse—but that was part of the appeal. In the interwar years, the British Empire was very much alive, if a bit shaken, still presided over by a king-emperor. London, in and around which Alex would live for most of his life, was its hub and heart, and the great British rail systems were its veins and arteries. Railroads bound the Crown's territories together from India to East Africa to

British Guiana. The Great Northern and the other lines that crisscrossed the island made Britain the centerpiece of a vast circulatory system of goods and services, raw materials, administration, migration, occupational travel, and social interchange. The locomotives that drove the trains—those demigods with their mass, their clamor, and their speed—plugged a small boy from a quiet suburb into the mythos and global enterprise that the empire advertised.

At the same time, and in the right spot, when no train was passing, Alex could close his eyes and imagine that none of it existed. Barnet, where he grew up, perched right on the northern edge of Greater London, was an ancient rural parish still containing, in Alex's day, dwellings that could be described as cottages. Fanny Trollope and her son Anthony had lived there more than ninety years earlier, and much of the place looked as it had in their day. Alex's family had lived in this eastern end of the Home Counties surrounding London for centuries. While some had moved to America and Australia, the bulk of them remained there, mainly in Kent and Essex, their occupations changing as the region became less rural and more commercial.

The region was also tying itself more firmly into London's commuter belt, in part because of the railroads and partly owing to the changes sweeping through the English economy and society. London was losing its place as the largest city in the world but was still growing and still a magnet for people from throughout the British Isles and the empire beyond. Alex's parents had met just before World War I, not in his father's home town of South Woodford, another northern suburb, but in London itself. Alexander Charles Comfort was taking night courses toward a degree in classics at Birkbeck College, which had been established in the early nineteenth century to provide part-time education to artisans and craftspeople and was now part of the University of London. Daisy Elizabeth Fenner (Elizabeth to everyone) had won a scholarship to Birkbeck and was studying modern languages full-time. He was an administrator at the London County Council (LCC), in education; she had been a schoolteacher in South London. Both were the first in their families to attend university and earn degrees. They also waited longer to marry than was traditional in much of society at the time—he at 33 and she at 32—and they decided to wed on their lunch break in 1915.

As it was wartime, they waited even longer to have their first (and only) child. Alexander Comfort was born on February 10, 1920, in Palmer's Green, North London. The couple were by now living in Barnet, at Havengore, a still fairly new, Arts and Crafts house they had leased and furnished in part with items made by students from LCC schools.[3] In 1925 they bought the freehold and thus became homeowners. Alex would have the back bedroom, overlooking a backyard that stretched into the distance, but the house had a somewhat gloomy interior, with heavy oak timbers and, after Elizabeth opted for a popular look of the 1930s, dark brown woodwork, picked out to give it a wood-grain look while the walls were painted with a dark cream distemper. The house also possessed hidden dangers due to Alexander's penchant for do-it-yourself home improvement. He wired a double power outlet into the lighting circuit in the downstairs bathroom, creating a risk of fire until a later owner found and dismantled the wiring decades later.[4]

The community Alex was born into still occupied a netherworld between self-contained rural England and the gravitational force of London. Barnet, Hertfordshire, had hosted a weekly market since King John's time and a horse fair since that of Elizabeth I. As London grew in Victorian days, so did Barnet sprout new housing developments, including the one that contained Havengore, perfect for young families looking for quiet and space to grow. The Great Northern carried commuters like Alexander Comfort in to King's Cross Station, but since Barnet was not yet on the tube—it wouldn't be connected to the Underground until 1940—its people still shopped primarily at the big stores in neighboring Finchley, which also boasted pubs and a large cinema. Families could still explore the wild park of Monken Hadley Common, through which the Great Northern passed. Barnet itself would not become a borough of London until 1965.

Judged by all the usual statistics, the little Comfort family offered a fine specimen of the life that millions of middle-class English strove to make for themselves in the early twentieth century. When the LCC's new headquarters building was completed in 1922, Alexander Comfort moved into an office in the grandiose Edwardian Baroque structure on the south bank of the Thames, next to Westminster Bridge. He was soon moving up in the LCC schools hierarchy, doing seemingly a little of everything, from working with head teachers to distributing educational films (silent at the time), but with an emphasis on project-managing construction of schools and other facilities in the fast-growing county system. In later years he was especially proud of his role in helping set up and manage Coram's Fields, the much-admired, seven-acre children's park and service center in Bloomsbury.[5]

The Comforts soon started taking regular holidays in Hartland, a pretty seaside town in northwest Devon, next door to Cornwall. Often Alexander transported Elizabeth and their young son in the sidecar of his

Douglas motorcycle. The town boasted a stately home that had been an Augustinian monastery before the Reformation, with gardens laid out by the great English landscape designer Gertrude Jekyll. Hartland lacked the sandy beaches and balmy weather of the English Riviera on the south coast, but it was quieter, had an air of history and drama (with its rocky shore and cliffs and frequent storms), and attracted fewer summer tourists.

Alexander Comfort—the father—was a slender, "slightly corvine [crow-like] but immensely warm" man, as his grandson described him, who loved learning, which was certainly one of the factors that attracted him to his future wife. He also had a very good baritone voice and good stage presence, which made him a frequent participant in recitals in and around London, the selections ranging from classical to popular fare like Leslie Stuart's grandiose ballad "The Bandolero." An undated but apparently pre–World War I program from the Mount View Literary Society in South London notes a lecture on Handel, followed by Handel performances by four soloists (the last being "Mr. Alexander C. Comfort" offering the aria "Honour and Arms" from *Samson*), followed by selections from the *Messiah* and *Judas Maccabaeus*. An attached photo shows a handsome man with a long neck and firmly set mouth, in white tie, with sandy hair properly brushed back.

Alexander passed his enthusiasm for music to his son, who took up singing in due course. At home, however, Alex's life was shaped primarily by his brilliant and formidable mother. Born in 1883, Elizabeth came from a working-class London family; her father, Joseph, was a baker from the East End who later moved his business to East Dulwich, south of the river.

Recognized early on as a comer, she was sent to Mary Datchelor School, an endowed grammar school for girls in the nearby borough of Camberwell, where a remarkable headmistress named Caroline Rigg groomed her best students for careers as teachers. From there Elizabeth went on to Stockwell College of Education, a teacher-training school also in South London. When she graduated, she joined the staff and taught "everything from commercial studies to physical education" but specialized in French.[6]

In her youth, recalled her grandson Nick, Elizabeth "had striking looks: an elfin face [that she would pass on to her son] topped by a mane of rich red hair."[7] At twenty-three she sharpened her skills in French at a school in Granville on the Norman coast and three years later was awarded a scholarship to Birkbeck, from which she graduated with a First in modern languages in 1912. According to family lore, she was the first woman offered a research position at the University of Oxford, which was still several years away from allowing women to matriculate, but instead returned to Stockwell. Soon after, she met Alexander Comfort and decided to marry him.[8] Alex memorialized the event in a poem many years later:

> My mother in my father's arms—
> a bronze-haired girl, her portraits show,
> so beautiful when she came in
> that all heads turned, and learned too.[9]

Many found Elizabeth "an intellectual bulldozer," her grandson said. It would be easy and at least partially accurate to conclude that she poured her postponed academic ambitions into Alex's education, but it is just as fair to say that she was a born teacher who took a dogmatic and pedagogical approach to everything and everyone. Pronunciation, in her view, had to be just so: "every word in full, every syllable accented." She once told a woman collecting for the poor, who lamented how improvident they were, "Yes, I once heard of a family whose child was born in a manger." Years later, her daughter-in-law—Alex's first wife—would describe Elizabeth Comfort as a "blue-stockinged Lady Bracknell," combining a formidable intellect with the Oscar Wilde character's absolute conviction that she knew the right and proper way to do everything.[10]

Elizabeth carried an important part of her working-class background with her into marriage as well. She was a lifelong member of the Enfield Highway Co-operative Society. Co-operatives (to use the British spelling) were a fixture of working- and lower-middle-class England, Scotland, and Wales from the mid-nineteenth century, although some dated back further: an alternative for low-income families battered by industrial dislocation, rising food prices, and political powerlessness, a way for these households to take some measure of control over their economic future.

Consumer co-ops, especially co-op grocery stores, were by far the largest subgroup. But all co-op societies offered members some form of democratic participation in administration and decision-making.*

Co-ops also had a political dimension. A founder of the movement was Robert Owen, the Welsh manufacturer, reformer, and utopian

* Co-operative societies still have a big profile in the UK in the early twenty-first century. In 2015, nearly fifteen million people were members of one or more UK co-ops. See *The Co-operative Economy 2015: An Ownership Agenda for Britain* (Co-operatives UK, 2015).

socialist, and co-ops' basic principles jibed with mutualism, the version of anarchism associated with Pierre-Joseph Proudhon, which combined a free market with workplace democracy and member-owned banks. Proudhon was well-known in Britain in the mid-nineteenth century, and the Russian anarchist Peter Kropotkin, who lived there for over thirty years, rejected mutualism but praised co-ops as a form of mutual aid and a possible point of departure for an entire society built on the principle. Some members of the movement were also quite interested in anarchism. Kropotkin himself wrote for two leading papers, the *Co-operative News* and the *Scottish Co-operator*, and for the Co-operative Wholesale Society's magazine, the *Wheatsheaf*.[11]

Free-market doctrinaires regarded co-ops as an inferior means of economic growth and possibly a stalking horse for revolutionary Marxism, while Marxists disparaged them as a dead end that distracted the working class from the pursuit of proletarian revolution. Nevertheless, co-ops thrived in industrial Britain, sinking deep roots among the working class who were not so ideologically fixated.

The Enfield Highway Co-operative Society, of which Elizabeth was a member, was a form of credit union, founded in 1872 by workers at the Royal Small Arms factory in the borough adjoining Barnet, which grew by taking over similar co-ops in the vicinity. Such groups offered low-fee savings options to members who in many cases would otherwise have been without a bank.[12] Alexander, despite his more middle-class background, was also a strong supporter of co-ops, his grandson remembered.[13]

Under Elizabeth's tutelage, Alex spoke French almost from birth. He "fell in love with *Cyrano*" at age seven and later said he would have liked to translate Rostand's play, but "because of the French Alexandrines, the rhymes don't work in English.") She had also taught him some Latin by the time he entered school. "My mother brought me up by hand," he said long afterward, referencing the forceful manner with which Mrs. Joe brought up her young brother Pip in Dickens's *Great Expectations*, "and she should have had a large class to teach, because I got it at a very high concentration."[14] She subscribed to *Child Education*, a new magazine for teachers of preschool and primary school children and scoured it for ideas to increase her son's creativity, curiosity, and enthusiasm for reading, numbers, science, and the natural world.

She had a willing pupil. "I really got the treatment," Alex said, "but I'm not knocking it, because it encouraged me."

What Elizabeth's enthusiastic program did not include, at first, was much contact with other children his age, aside from some cousins living nearby. "The doctor thought my mother ought to be relieved of me, because I was becoming an intolerable brat, and that it was better that I was with other children."

Taking that advice to heart, Elizabeth and Alexander sent him away at seven to St. George's, a primary school in Harpenden, not far from Greater London, that advertised "an atmosphere closely related to family life, based on sound Christian principles." While St. George's was one of the Britain's first coeducational boarding schools, offering ballet and musical instruction along with more traditional subjects, Alex found it "pretentious" and quickly came to hate being there. He made an impression anyhow when he, reportedly, greeted a visiting Albert Schweitzer in perfect French, but his time at St. George's ended emphatically when he ran away ("largely out of bravado rather than unhappiness," he later said).

After another spell at home under Elizabeth's direction, his parents sent him as a day student to a preparatory school in Barnet, a "mad" school "run by a chap who had been a policeman in China and who had an extraordinary philosophy of his own; he was inventing a new religion. That lasted one week, and I told him he was reading science fiction," Alex recalled.

Once again his parents sent him away, and this time the result was much happier. Norman Court was situated in and around a handsome Georgian mansion in the town of Potters Bar, not far north of Barnet. Alex's teacher was Henry Walker, "very much the old-style schoolmaster," who encouraged him to push deeper into the classics and prepared him and his schoolmates for the Common Entrance Examination that determined whether students at independent, fee-charging schools qualified for admission to one of the prestigious public schools. Alex had great respect for Walker and would remain at Norman Court for the next four years.

IF THE COMFORTS WERE the picture of a well-established, postwar middle-class family, complete with a precocious son, they were also a little different, starting with the parents' religious background.

Both the Comfort and Fenner tribes were longtime Nonconformists, meaning they were Protestants who didn't "conform" to the teachings of the Church of England. After the Restoration of Charles II in 1660, Presbyterians, Congregationalists, Quakers and later, Unitarians,

Methodists, and others, lived under civil restrictions, although not as harsh as those applied to Roman Catholics. They could not hold public office, join the civil service, or obtain university degrees, yet were required to pay taxes to support the Church of England and could be legally married only by Anglican clergy.

Perhaps in part because they were barred from other traditional paths to advancement in English society, many of them went into commerce and were very successful. Publicly they made much of the values of hard work, temperance, and frugality, by which they projected an image of ultra-respectable Englishness that somewhat balanced out the stigma of their refusal to accept the established church. This quality, along with their frequent economic success, attracted more devotees in the pious mid-Victorian years. The 1851 census of England and Wales found that about half the people who attended Sunday church services were Nonconformists.[15] These people accounted for much of the rising English middle class and a great deal of the energy in Victorian religious life. By then, most of the civil disabilities had been removed, although the great universities of Oxford and Cambridge only started to grant degrees to Nonconformists some years later.

Naturally they became a powerful force in British politics as well, cultivated in particular by the Liberal Party leader William Ewart Gladstone. As expected, Nonconformists supported temperance and sabbath enforcement. Many equated material success with personal virtue, were strongly anti-Catholic, and promoted a "new moral economy" that emphasized sexual restraint, reinforcing the puritanical culture of the Victorian years (although the Unitarians often not so much).[16] But many Nonconformists were politically liberal. Some of the denominations had played a role in the drive to abolish slavery and the slave trade, supported Catholic Emancipation in the 1820s—despite their objection to the Roman church itself—went on to back Gladstone's push for Irish Home Rule later in the century, and generally advocated education for women and women's suffrage. "Old Dissenters" like the extended Comfort family, with their longer history of marginalization, tended to be more liberal than did adherents of the newer sects, who focused more on moral issues.

Like Newtonian science, which encouraged liberal thought over tradition and precedent, and sometimes in alliance with it, Nonconformism was also a fertile ground for English radicalism. William Godwin, the pioneering anarchist thinker, began his career as a Calvinist minister; Thomas Paine's father was a Quaker; and the brilliant eighteenth-century chemist, natural philosopher, and radical pamphleteer Joseph Priestley, whose career Alex would in some respects emulate, was raised a Calvinist before helping to found Unitarianism in England.

Whatever their political stance, Nonconformists were notorious for contentiousness both within and outside their ranks, and the Comforts were no exception. Alex's great-grandfather, Jabez Comfort, was a traveler (salesperson) in gentlemen's walking sticks and a firm Unitarian. Stung by a "violent row" with the local vicar, Alex related years later, "he refused to enter the church thereafter and when his wife died, he lived in sin with his housekeeper for five years and is number one in the registry of civil marriages of 1838 [the first year that civil marriages were legal in England and Wales]."

Jabez's son, Gilbert Humphrey Comfort, was a traveler for the wildly successful Crown Perfumery Company and an extremely devout member of the Plymouth Brethren, a nondenominational movement that arose in the early nineteenth century, emphasized the Bible as supreme authority, and had no clergy, only elders of the congregation. The more extreme of the Brethren didn't vote, and by and large they refused military service as well.[17] One of the founders of the movement, John Nelson Darby, originated the theory of the Rapture: that just before the end of days, Christ will remove his Church from this world and take it to its heavenly destiny. The most famous of the early Brethren, however, was Philip Henry Gosse, a pioneering marine biologist who destroyed his career when he published *Omphalos*, an attempt to prove that the account of the Creation in the Book of Genesis was factual even though geological record showed the earth to be much older. His son, the literary critic Edmund Gosse, went on to write *Father and Son*, a moving account of life with his eccentric and domineering parent.

Father and Son understandably became a favorite book of Alexander Charles Comfort, Gilbert Humphrey's son, who was born in 1882. Gilbert Humphrey was a lonely man whose affection for his children was often stifled by his concern for their souls. Family lore had it that he once got into a furious theological argument on a train, "only to discover that he had consigned a fellow Brother to damnation."[18] Alexander grew up the opposite: a warm and likable man with a fine sense of humor who, his son Alex said, learned from his upbringing "to keep his head down and at the same time to get his own way by manipulating the system according to the rules."[19]

Which did not mean he approved of people who gamed the system to their personal advantage. After finishing secondary school, where he acquired a love of the classics, he went to work at the School Board for London, which in 1904 was merged into the LCC. As he rose through the ranks, he became acquainted with Edward Frank Wise, a brilliant civil servant who, after war broke out, became assistant director of army contracts in the War Office. Wise brought Alexander Comfort along as his personal assistant, among other things putting him in charge of buying wool for soldiers' uniforms.

Alexander got a long and damning look at the methods of British business in a time of national emergency, his son later said. Told to go north and buy the entire crop of wool, of which he had no knowledge, "he read it up from the woolen annual on the train and went up and dealt with these people. They were in a very strong position; the government didn't dictate contracts, they just bought it up."

If the government could get it to begin with, that is. Alexander's first task was to "stop merchants trading with the enemy, who were offering a better price, by diverting cargoes on the high seas," his grandson Nick recalled him saying. "As our casualties grew into the hundreds of thousands, its uniforms were increasingly sourced not from virgin wool but from recycled 'shoddy,' which increasingly meant the uniforms of the dead. Eventually, Grandfather told me with a catch in his voice, one track of the railway from Leeds to Goole was taken up by wagons of bloodied uniforms from the trenches."[20]

Wise did wonders rationalizing the raw materials pipeline and bulldozing bureaucratic resistance, but his aide still had to struggle with numerous bottlenecks, made worse by officials who weren't always impressed by the urgency of the situation.[21] One time, Alexander told his son, all the trams in Bombay were stopped because wartime requisitioning deprived them of the wool used to pack the axle boxes. "He had to explain to a chap they called 'Matthews from Business,' who was very annoyed to find that letters had been answered in his name and said, 'I want to see all my mail.' The next day, they brought him 35 sacks."[22]

Wise was made a Companion of the Order of the Bath for his services during the war, but he came away from the experience radicalized, took a job as economic adviser and London director of the Central Union of Russian Co-operative Societies, and developed a promising career in the left wing of the Labour Party before his death in 1932. Alexander Comfort, who had been a moderate Conservative before the war, came to admire Wise and followed somewhat the same path politically. He voted Labour the rest of his life and, despite his family's commercial origins, passed on to his son a disdain for British capitalists: their practices, their morality, and what he regarded as their personal meanness ("he used to read the [conservative] *Daily Telegraph* to make himself furious," according to his son).[23]

In this, he was in synch with many of the soldiers who served in the Great War, which left behind a long trail of bitterness and disillusion that the British political and economic establishment needed virtually the whole of Alex Comfort's childhood to calm.

"The consoling *après-la-guerre-finie* hopes of the serving soldier included two principal items," Robert Graves and Alan Hodge noted in their firsthand chronicle of the interwar period, *The Long Weekend*: "first a crushing of the German Government, by a defeat of the German Army, and next a clean sweep in Britain of all oppressors, cheats, cowards, skrimshankers, reactionaries and liars who had plagued and betrayed him during his service."[24] In 1919 protests, strikes, and mutinies broke out among troops waiting in France to be shipped home, and a "soviet" was briefly set up among a group of some two thousand infantrymen.[25] Yet thousands more impoverished ex-soldiers were recruited into the Royal Irish Constabulary: the "Black and Tans" who acquired a reputation for savagery in their war against the Irish Republican Army.

The British Empire covered more of the globe than at any time in its history following the postwar carving up of the Ottoman Turkish domains, but people like Alexander Comfort had multiple reasons to persist in their disillusionment. The government was in nearly constant financial trouble and resorted over and over to austerity to solve its problems. When a government subsidy of the coal industry ended in 1925, the mine owners decided to make ends meet by slashing wages and enforcing longer hours, triggering an industry-wide strike that ended in disaster for the mine workers.

Labour hoisted itself to become the second-largest political party in the country, but when it briefly succeeded in forming governments, in 1924 and 1929–31, its leadership was too timid to do much for its working-class constituency, and power soon reverted to the Conservatives. A coalition National Government, dominated by the Tories, was formed in 1931 to address the disaster of the Great Depression, and it held on, ploddingly, for the rest of the decade.

The result was that Alex Comfort grew up in a Britain that presented several contradictory faces at once: dynamic and modernizing; riven by hunger and poverty, social unrest, postwar bitterness, and controversial social and cultural trends; optimistic and proud of its august position in the world; and fearful that that position was slipping away. To the extent that economic prosperity returned, the interwar years saw consumer culture take hold, much of it imported from America, and automobiles became more common. Government subsidies and the rise of building societies sparked a housing boom and a rise in home ownership that reached into the working class.

Personal and family life were changing too. Divorce rates started to increase almost as soon as the war ended, and in 1923 Parliament passed the Matrimonial Causes Act, establishing complete equality between the sexes regarding grounds for divorce and shifting jurisdiction to the Court of Assizes, which made it less costly for poor people.[26]

It is often assumed that in English-speaking countries during the Victorian era and the first decades of the twentieth century, sex was a taboo subject, addressed strictly within the bounds of marriage. Pioneering reformers like Havelock Ellis, Victoria Woodhull, and Margaret Sanger are often portrayed as lonely figures struggling to be heard. In reality, sex was a focus of great, nearly obsessive debate, even if the discourse was filled with anxiety and mostly took place among the educated classes. An extensive literature started to appear in late Victorian days and grew as the new century advanced.[27] Much of it concerned the state of modern marriage and family life, which the Victorians regarded as critical to social stability. Good sex was sometimes regarded as essential to a successful marriage or else as a dangerous wild card that threatened to tear couples and families apart.

On the positive side, reformers and—haltingly—the medical profession began to address sexual problems, of which researchers like Ellis were starting to assemble a more accurate picture.[28] Birth control became more available and acceptable. In 1918 the paleobotanist Marie Stopes published her groundbreaking best seller *Married Love, or Love in Marriage*, which included advice on how to have "great sex." Among other things, it made the audacious claim that women were as capable of powerful sexual response as men, if only couples learned how to achieve it. The book also contained a chapter on birth control. A few years later, Stopes opened the first birth control clinic in the UK. While she initially faced powerful opposition, especially from the Catholic Church, by the end of the '20s Stopes had largely won the war. Doctors began offering information on contraceptives when requested, and the Church of England dropped its opposition.

Acceptance of birth control marked an enormous cultural change, Alex later noted in *The Anxiety Makers*, his short history of medicine's role in the politics of sexual morality. "Why the public dug in its heels at this particular point one can only surmise," he wrote, "but this was the first instance where medical and religious advice, in full chorus, was firmly set aside by the ordinary man."[29]

The birth control campaigns had the greatest material impact of a wider, cross-class movement to loosen conventions in sexual practice that was gaining steam all over the industrialized world. In 1921 the German physician and sexologist Magnus Hirschfeld organized the First Congress for Sex Reform, leading to the foundation of the World League for Sex Reform, which attracted a great deal of British support, including from Stopes, George Bernard Shaw, the writer and pacifist Vera Brittain, and Bertrand Russell and his wife Dora, the latter a social and education reformer. The league held a congress in London in 1929, the same year Russell published his controversial *Marriage and Morals*, which argued that "nastiness" in children was the product of sexual prudery, that married couples should be free to take other partners, and that greater access to information on the subject was critical to addressing sexual unhappiness and abuse. While Russell's book was a bit more than the arbiters of public taste thought proper, sex manuals were becoming popular under the guise of "marriage guidance." In 1926 the Dutch gynecologist Theodoor van de Welde published *Ideal Marriage: Its Physiology and Technique*, the English edition of which sold over half a million copies and remained the most popular such work for decades.

Aside from birth control and divorce, few of these trends made their way into middle- or working-class culture during the years the Comforts were raising their boy, except as subjects of outrage and provocative news headlines. England was still very prudish, *Lady Chatterley's Lover* was still a banned book, and the influence of Mrs. Grundy, the avatar of buttoned-up Britain, was still felt in laws and regulations against pornography, lewdness, adultery, and homosexuality.

Middle-class families could see the world changing around them, however. Religious observance was declining, particularly among Nonconformists, along with their presence as a political force. Lamenting that shift, the Rev. Samuel Chadwick, a preacher in Westminster, declared, "Multitudes have no interest in the things for which the Churches stand. . . . Thousands of young people are being brought up without religious instruction and without religious examples. . . . Woman's rebound from conventional virtue is as daring as her attire."[30]

It was younger people, like the Comfort family, who were not showing up for services. Asked about his parents' religious inclinations years later, Alex said they "weren't anything in particular," in part because his father, growing up under a Plymouth Brother's stern direction, "had had a double dose of it when he was a child."[31] But they did attend New Barnet Congregational Church—a more tolerant denomination—and were friendly with its minister.[32]

Replacing churchgoing among the upper-class youth in the 1920s, the clergy lamented, were restaurants and night clubs, dance crazes, fancy-dress parties, and allegedly, in some cases, dope. The middle class had to make do with more mundane forms of popular entertainment. Alex had a favorite comic strip, J. F. Horrabin's *Japhet and Happy*, published in the daily *News Chronicle*, and both its creator and the strip's huge popularity encapsulate some of the cultural contradictions of the time.[33] Japhet was a boy growing up with his parents, two brothers, and a nearby collection of cousins, in Southwest London. Gradually, Japhet gathered a group of animal friends as well, starting with a small bear named Happy. Besides the daily strip, there were *Japhet and Happy* annual books and a fan club, the Grand United Order of Arkubs, complete with badges, codes, and handshakes, which Alex joined.

The strip about a colorful collection of family and animal companions would appeal to a child brought up in a rather solitary fashion, but Horrabin himself was quite a different character. Somehow this multitalented writer and illustrator managed to make himself a mainstay of family culture in the '20s and '30s while pursuing a parallel and equally public career as a socialist pamphleteer, popular educator, and public speaker. In the later '30s, during the Moscow show trials, he was a member of the British Provisional Committee for the Defence of Leon Trotsky.

How did young Alex Comfort's political consciousness take shape? It started, he later said, when as an early adolescent he read memoirs of soldiers who had served in the Great War.[34] A decade after the conflict ended, memoirs began to spill forth as if a dam had broken, books rivaling each other in their grim accounts of the horrific, traumatizing trench warfare that had left as many as 1.2 million dead and some 1.7 million wounded from the UK and the empire.

First came Edmund Blunden's *Undertones of War* in 1928, followed quickly by Robert Graves's bestselling *Goodbye to All That* and Richard Aldington's fictionalized *Death of a Hero* (both 1929) and Siegfried Sassoon's fictionalized *Sherston* trilogy (1928–30).[35] To these could be added Blunden's acclaimed 1931 edition of *The Poems of Wilfred Owen*, including his memoir of the quintessential Great War poet. In 1933 came another book that had an even stronger impact, Vera Brittain's

Testament of Youth. Also a best seller, it related the author's experience as a wartime nurse; the deaths of her brother, her fiancé, and two of their best friends in the trenches and on the battlefield; and her efforts to rebuild her life and memorialize the dead after the war. *Testament of Youth* seemed to complete the cycle by revisiting the war from a woman's perspective.

These were powerful books that seemed at the time to reopen a national wound that had failed to fully heal. War, they insisted, had changed. World War I had been different from all conflicts before it: more brutal, more hopeless, and, above all, more mechanized. Trench warfare, tanks, aircraft, poison gas, and more powerful artillery had rendered cavalry and gallant infantry charges on the battlefield quaint. The transformation had been an enormous shock to the millions who had to serve, if not to their commanders and political leaders, who instead spent the interwar decades devising further technological advances that were clearly going to make the next war more brutal still: a machine implacably grinding up human beings.

All this suggested that a vast popular movement was required to avert another war. The word "pacifist" described a broad spectrum of activists in '30s Britain, from adherents of pure nonviolence to advocates of "collective peace" enforced by an international body like the League of Nations, and they often had very vague ideas about what they would do if and when the next big conflict broke out. But pacifism, in one form or another, had been a visible and organized tendency in Britain since the late eighteenth century, longer than anywhere else in the world.[36] The UK's first National Peace Congress was held in 1904 in Manchester and was an annual event until the outbreak of World War II. The first Briton to receive the Nobel Peace Prize, in 1903, was Randal Cremer, a trade unionist, member of Parliament, and advocate of arbitration for the settlement of international disputes.

British pacifism had its roots in the middle class, and Nonconformists—especially Quakers and Congregationalists—were always heavily represented among its leaders. As Nonconformists achieved a greater presence in political life, so did the movement against war. Both Arthur Henderson and Ramsey MacDonald, who swapped leadership of the Labour Party for most of the two decades through 1934, identified as some form of pacifist at various points in their careers, and this level of influence translated into British government support for the new League of Nations and for disarmament and collective peace during much of the interwar decades.

By then, antiwar sentiment was strong among a large contingent of people who, for good reasons, dreaded the next war like no other before it and, like Alex's father, were fed up with the political and military elites who appeared to be leading them into it. As the prospect of war again intensified, especially after Hitler's remilitarization of the Rhineland in 1936, pacifists sprang into action.

A year earlier, Dick Sheppard, the retired dean of Canterbury who had been a chaplain at a military hospital in France, had published a letter in the *Manchester Guardian* asking men to send him postcards pledging not to support war. He received 135,000 responses, and from this group the Peace Pledge Union was launched in 1936.[37] Under Sheppard's charismatic leadership, the PPU attracted such luminaries as Brittain, Bertrand Russell, Aldous Huxley, Siegfried Sassoon, and novelists Storm Jameson and Rose Macaulay. In 1936 the PPU launched a widely circulated magazine, *Peace News*.

CHAPTER 2

The Prodigy (1932–1941)

The growing pacifist movement spread to the public schools and universities, where Officers' Training Corps units were long established, serving partly as a means of social elevation. Alex, now at Highgate School, declined to join the Junior Division of the OTC, as many of his classmates did, and instead cast about for ways to demonstrate his opposition to militarism.

He had won a scholarship in classics to Highgate, a four-and-a-half-century-old institution located a short ride on the Underground from his home in Barnet, in 1934. It was another well-considered decision by Alexander and Elizabeth to send him there. Highgate was one of the dozen or so best English public or independent, endowed schools but was distinctly less prestigious than the "posh" institutions, notably Eton and Harrow, that trained well-born boys to be gentlemen.

The class element was less pronounced at Highgate, which recruited talented students, extending scholarships to middle-class and lower-income households, and, since it was located in London, attracted a far more diverse student body, including many Nonconformists, Catholics, and others of less-favored background—although Jews were said to be subject to a quota.[1] The school itself occupied a set of dignified old brick buildings in the Highgate neighborhood of North London, plus a playing field. Instruction was according to the same system as other public schools, but the atmosphere was more cosmopolitan and intellectually sharper.[2] The class system was less oppressive, and the atmosphere more meritocratic. In this it was well suited to receive a boy like Alex, who was focused, unafraid to let on that he had broken a sweat mentally, and happy to celebrate his achievements.

"I think I got it in my head that the way to be loved and make a success was to do well at school," he said years later. "Because I wasn't any good at anything else, sports for instance, I became the typical nerd:

a real swot. And so I dedicated myself to being that, and you really had done it badly if you didn't have a wheelbarrow of books at the end of the term. Prizes."[3] This wasn't quite the whole story. Beyond whatever school happened to require of him, he was constantly looking for new areas to study and understand. To the extent it could, Highgate obliged him, although he could be a bit exhausting. "He is definitely settling down and becoming less excitable," his form master wrote hopefully on his first-term report at his new school.[4]

Alex was the first on either side of his family to be accepted to a public school, an attainment that put him on track for university and a career in law, medicine, the military, high finance, higher academics, or politics: for a middle-class family, a significant move up the ladder of the English class system. Given the manner in which opportunities unfolded for him, he later recalled, he was less conscious of the class system than were a great many English children of his day. "It never occurred to me that there was any such thing as the Establishment," he said.[5] Unlike a child from an upper-class background, however, Alex wouldn't be able to rely on wealth, pedigree, or personal connections to reach the next stage in that pilgrimage. As a scholarship boy, he would have to perform. And even Highgate had its variety of hierarchy: Alex was a day student, not a boarder, and every school day he had to take the train in from Barnet, trudging up the hill to his classes, a forty-five-minute trip door-to-door.

Fortunately for him, instruction at Highgate was excellent.* The headmaster, Dr. John Alexander Hope Johnston, was "a grotesque figure with a red nose," Alex later recalled. "He was enormously fat and he used to appear at Speech Day with a pair of opera glasses and a top hat. But in spite of being such a grotesque figure and abominably pompous and rude to everybody, he was a real genius at choosing staff."[6] Alex spent his first two terms in the Fifth Form and then joined the Classical Sixth. Two of his teachers at that level he later remembered especially fondly. There was Tommy Twidell, the Latin master, an ex-cavalry officer who later taught Alex's son Nick as well. Nick remembered that Twidell would break off from telling the boys they would never pass 'that pappy examination known as the school certificate' to show how to hold your sabre when charging to prevent contact with an opponent wrenching off your arm."[7]

* Highgate also possessed a tangential family connection: the in-laws of Alex's cousin Ken Comfort had sold to Highgate the building that became its new junior school in the '30s.

For Greek, Alex had a parson, Charles Benson, "a long, thin man with very prominent front teeth and an Adam's apple which always got stuck in his clerical collar when he got excited." His first day at Highgate, Benson said to the class, "'You'll have to excuse me boys, I'm a little hoarse,' and from that day on he was known as The Horse, and the boys plagued him unmercifully, but he was a very good guy and he taught very well."[8]

Alex's academic career was a testimony to the continued importance of the classics in British elite schools well into the twentieth century and the boost they could give a student from a non-posh background who embraced them. At Highgate, one of his schoolmates was a boy two years older named Charles Anthony Raven Crosland, whose mother, Jessie Raven, had known Alex's mother at Birkbeck, where both had studied medieval French literature; while Elizabeth graduated with a First in 1912, Jessie finished with a pass.[9] Tony Crosland, who would go on to a prominent career in the Labour Party, was a star: a champion mile runner, an excellent debater, and politically and intellectually precocious, with a subscription to the Left Book Club to prove it. When Alex joined him in the Sixth Form, it was certain they would be rivals. Each year, Highgate awarded the Governor's Prize for Pure Classics, and Tony was considered the pupil most likely to secure it. Instead, Alex took the prize for 1936–37, despite being two years behind Tony, snagging a leather-bound classics library in gold-tooled covers.

Jessie Crosland was furious and never forgot the sight of her son having to settle for second-class honors and a smaller pile of books on Speech Day than Elizabeth Comfort's upstart boy took home. "Everyone believed that his parents helped him with his homework," Jessie would grumble for years whenever a new volume of poetry, fiction, or scientific research appeared with Alex's name on it. Tony must have felt somewhat the same, later noting in his commonplace book that Alex was "unpleasant" at school.[10]

Alex himself admitted that he was "insufferably evangelical" in these years. Unlike his parents—perhaps because he had not had the strict indoctrination his father endured—he was captivated by the religious strain in his family and with them attended New Barnet Congregational Church, then pastored by Norman Goodall, who would later become a leader of the missionary and ecumenical movements in the mainstream Protestant churches.[11] But his interests were widening in other directions too. He took up the piano and then the trumpet, later graduating from the student model to the Vincent Bach D model, on which he performed with the school orchestra. And he began dabbling in chemistry, conducting experiments in the greenhouse behind the family house, where his father was growing grapes.

One day in May 1935, while carrying out one of these trials, he blew himself up.

THAT WAS HOW ALEX described the accident years later. Immersed in the Classical Sixth, he decided to teach himself something of natural science and chemistry at home. "That wasn't exactly science," he later admitted, "that was messing about with chemicals, because I used to pinch chemicals and broken apparatus from the lab. I put a bottle of sulfuric acid in my pocket and it rotted my trousers."[12]

Nevertheless, he saw an opportunity to make something of his attempts when the preparations for King George V's Silver Jubilee—marking the sovereign's twenty-fifth year on the throne—commenced. May 6, the anniversary of the king's coronation, was declared a bank holiday, and church services, parties, pageants, and other celebrations were held across the UK. Fireworks figured prominently. Alex was attempting, with a friend, to make powder for his own fireworks, but their first trial left a crater in the lawn. The two boys had been planning to go to the cinema, but when Elizabeth saw her son's handiwork, she grounded him and sent his friend home. Left alone in the greenhouse, Alex tried again. A spark ignited his concoction, which exploded, shattering the glass-walled greenhouse. His left hand was mangled, and if he had not been wearing his spectacles, he told his son years later, he would have been blinded. Elizabeth called an ambulance, and, while he waited for it in great pain, Alex called to warn his friend against trying the same mixture.[13]

The prospect was that the hand would either be amputated or mended but left completely nonfunctional. One of Alex's aunts gave him £50, concerned that he would never be able to earn his living. But his mother used her savings to secure a top surgeon who could salvage something more usable for Alex. Thomas Twistington Higgins, head surgeon at Great Ormond Street Hospital and a pioneer in pediatric surgery, was the natural candidate. He agreed to take the case and was able to rescue the ball of the hand and reconstruct the thumb as well as leaving a nub of the little finger. The middle three fingers were gone, and the hand looked more like a claw, but Alex had plenty of dexterity with his thumb and could still use it to tie knots, for example. He was given an artificial hand but found it not very workable and learned to make do with what he had.[14]

The accident—sudden, shocking, agonizing—changed Alex's life forever. His absorption in learning and his conspicuous evangelicalism already set him apart from many of the other boys at Highgate. Now, the difference was physical as well.

Adulthood, for others, was often something to be put off, whereas Alex seemed to want to be regarded as an adult as soon as possible. He had never been drawn to sports, but now this was more or less an impossibility—and this at an English public school, where sports were an enormous part of the culture. Why on earth would any woman find him attractive? He had to learn not to draw attention to his hand, lest it be the only thing people noticed about him—for example, by keeping it behind his back while in conversation and in public and generally making sure to be photographed mainly from his good side.

Understandably, Alex's interest in chemistry ebbed, but he only became more curious about natural science. Three specific areas interested him, in roughly the following order of intensity: mollusks, from snails to crabs, limpets, and other creatures found in tidal zones; butterflies; and wild plants. Fields near his home in Barnet gave him the opportunity to look for the latter two, and the Comforts' holidays in Hartland took him to the beaches and coves where he could find mollusks. As he had already established with locomotives, every new interest became a focus of systematic study and classification. His notebooks from his early and mid-teens contain cross-sectional drawings of plants; he kept careful record of the shells he found and collected, some of which he illustrated in pencil and watercolor.

Highgate had only recently started to offer extensive instruction and give out awards in natural sciences.[15] Still, the British Museum's collections helped Alex to identify the specimens he found, widen his knowledge, and plan where his research would take him next. School did offer him another outlet for his creative energies, however.

The Cholmelian was Highgate's student magazine, named for the school's founder, Sir Roger Cholmeley, and its contents ranged from journalism to fiction and poetry. In his third year, around the time he was recovering from his accident, Alex began publishing poems. His early productions were soaked in the lyricism and elevated language of Tennyson and the late Victorian poets, and they drew heavily on his impressions of nature and the places he went on his specimen hunts. But they also show that he was mastering the mechanics of verse and learning to use language colorfully and evocatively. Here is a passage from "Atlantis—a symphonic poem":

Like a bubble through the green
Depth of water upward spinning,
Water-sweet and silver-clean,
So the music faint beginning
Whispers on the dancing waves,
Whispers in the sea-cool caves,
Where the pliant wrack is swinging
With the lapping of the swell,
And the rocks awash are singing:
To the upward leaping bell

Some of Alex's poems in *The Cholmelian* were more personal. From "The Spell":

How can the stars be glad, whose kindly eyes
Gaze through the luminous flocks on tiptoe sailing,
Gaze down, and hearken, hearken to my wailing
Behold my miseries?"[16]

Is he lamenting an absent lover in the solitude of the night, as other lines suggest? Is he simply a self-absorbed adolescent? Or are his "miseries" and aloneness the product of the pain he had endured and that had set him apart physically from other people? No human other than the omniscient narrator appears in these early poems. Arguably, Alex's interest in nature—both in his shell-collecting and butterfly-hunting and in his poetry—owed something to a desire for solitude, where human companionship would not remind him of his injury. Nothing he wrote or said that survives addresses this specifically, however, and, when talking about the accident ("[the time] I blew myself up"), he always did so in a humorously distanced way.

His writing was noticed. Two Comfort poems were selected by poet and classics scholar R. W. Moore for *The Threshold, 1936: An Anthology of Prose and Verse from the Schools of England*. It was the second of a prospective annual series from Blackwell, an academic publisher in Oxford. (The following year, Moore announced in his introduction, girls too would be invited to contribute.) The *Times Literary Supplement*'s reviewer considered the poetry to be "noticeably better" than the prose, singling out "Alexander Comfort, of Highgate School, who shows a remarkable gift for both rhythm and phrase. The poems are no doubt derivative in style, but at least one feels that the poet has made the effects he has tried to make."[17]

In its June 1936 issue, *The Cholmelian* published another Comfort poem, "Birds of Passage," which contained these lines:

> When the last great bale is stowing away, when the heavy
> anchor's weighed
> And the clouds that follow blowing have a voice to be obeyed,
> And back into the distance sinks the haven where we lay,
> The pearly light is calling, and I must be away.

A LITTLE OVER A month later, Alex and his father were in Rotterdam, getting ready to embark on the *Pentridge Hill*, a Dutch tramp steamer ("about 8000 tons burden, old and slow, but a tight ship with a fine crew"), for the first leg of a South Atlantic tour that would last more than two months. Elizabeth and Alexander wanted to him to have a holiday following his recuperation from surgery, and they were able to arrange the trip cheaply. Father and son hired on as extra hands for the voyage, and they aimed to sleep aboard ship while in port rather than taking a hotel. Alex brought with him a letter from the British Museum that would help him take shells, and other specimens he collected along the way, back to Britain when they returned. "I was traveling," he wrote later, "under the guise of an amateur naturalist . . . in the steps of Darwin and Hudson."[18]

The *Pentridge Hill* was bound for Buenos Aires with a cargo of coal, coke, and patent fuel (similar to charcoal briquettes), but first it stopped in Madeira, where Alex and his father went straight to the Lido outside the capital of Funchal to collect shells in the "brown rock spurs" and "intense, dazzling blue water" of the tidal pools: "little speckled pyrenes, marbled in cream and brown, and neat conical yellow and orange top-shells . . . not unlike the ones with which you played in England as a child," whorled shells with their hermit-crab tenants, starfish, urchins, limpets, and many others, which Alex assembled and noted down in his diary. After passing through the Cape Verde islands, the steamer entered the South Atlantic and on August 21 came in sight of land off Brazil.

Alex spent the voyage doing a variety of jobs: chipping paint; preparing crew lists, catalogs of charts, and ship's manifests for the captain; and, of course, taking turns on watch. He loved the life of the ship, the stories the sailors told, and adopted their dress, lingo, and habits whenever it was practical and expected, which was much of the time. He was also keeping a detailed diary, perhaps with a thought to getting it published. "These are the tropics," he recorded.

> I have borrowed a topee [pith helmet] from the first mate; the crew have resorted to the usual expedient of a prison crop, and I have followed their example. One sits on the bitts [metal posts used to secure mooring lines] by the after 'tween-deck bulkhead, while a muscular hand plies scissors and clippers, and removes in a few moments every vestige of a luxurious crop of hair.[19]

In the harbor at Buenos Aires, the Comforts presented their identity certificates, Alex's containing the fingerprints of his right and the thumbprint of his left, "Missing" scrawled over the remaining four boxes. Alex didn't much like the shabby, slightly run-down city he'd arrived in. "Staying in Buenos Aires is like trying to judge France by Marseilles," he commented.[20] "[The day we arrived] we looked in innumerable shops full of lottery tickets and revolvers," Alex wrote. "I was interested in the revolvers."[21]

Soon they were off to San Isidro, outside the city proper, again in search of mollusks and butterflies. They found plenty of fossil and subsoil shells, all marine, left over from the time when the outer lengths of the Rio de la Plata were still filled with seawater, before the land had risen and made the city of Buenos Aires possible.

Alex, sixteen at the time, noted the strong social and economic tensions in the air as well. "There are now two populations in the city," he noted: on one side, the industrialists and old-money families, agents of foreign companies, and then another population, "living in the vilest slums I recollect having seen." "Some, who are employed, and who submit to the conditions of their employers, are graciously permitted to exist . . . [while the rest] make a small living by preying upon society." In the "unequal conflict between the two classes," Alex observed, "it is the unimpassioned, half-amused and half-interested army of emissaries from foreign companies which holds the scales, . . . satisfied in the complete control they exercise over the capital. . . . A derelict remnant of the old democracy, with leanings to Fascism, rules and misrules on a basis of several revolutions a minute."

What would it all come to? Left-wing politicians and activists were calling for nationalization of the railways and industry; right-wing agitators were plastering the walls with large placards, "*Defende su hogar contre el Communismo.*" "The inevitable explosion is on the way," Alex wrote. "When the outburst comes, from whichever side, it will come in an unrestrained *acharnement* unparalleled anywhere else. . . . Such abject poverty and such wasteful and rampant vice have never been permitted throughout history to continue without bringing their due reward to the authors of the condition. That reward is coming in Buenos Aires to a corrupt officialdom and a cynical and inhuman party of speculators."[22]

Rather than returning home on the *Pentridge Hill*, Alex and his father signed onto a Greek ship, the *Demetrios Chandris*, which would take them first to Dakar and then to Liverpool. On board, they were served enormous meals by the captain and his wife, "a German lady, large, anxious and obliging," whom he had married "at a time when he spoke no German and she no Greek—they must have fixed it by signs somehow."

Preparing to disembark in colonial Dakar, Alex wrote, "Our own preparations . . . consisted in the wholesale consumption of quinine." They had been warned that the place was rife with yellow fever, cholera, dysentery, plague "and a particularly mischievous brand of malaria." On September 30, as the ship was preparing to depart, Alex collected all the mud brought up by the anchor and passed it through a fine iron sieve into a tin can. The mud in Dakar Bay was "crammed with shells," he said, and among his findings were a few he later claimed he had added to the standard catalog.[23]

The *Demetrios Chandris* steamed up through the Canary Islands, on October 9 passed Ushant, off the coast of Brittany, and two nights later docked in Liverpool. Would Alex be allowed to bring his specimens into the country? The customs officer left them intact ("being a personal friend of the man who issued my British Museum pass, and knowing a bug-hunter when he saw one"). The Comforts had nothing to declare. "After a journey of thirteen thousand miles we had collected nothing dutiable, not even a specimen of spirit, and true to our ideals we had no hotel labels."[24] Father and son took the train down to London, Alex having missed only a few weeks of Michaelmas term.

UPON HIS RETURN, ALEX wrote a fast-paced, four-part account of his journey for *The Cholmelian*, "Confessions of Odysseus." His experience also inspired several new nature poems and his first published short story, "Cloth of Gold," a South Pacific crime tale that turned on identifying a certain rare mollusk shell and allowed him to show off his knowledge of steamship navigation jargon. Now a sub-editor of the magazine, his most revealing effort, titled "Ode at the Coronation" and dated February 4, 1937, appears to be a parody of the solemn "Coronation Ode" that the poet laureate, John Masefield, was scheduled to read on May 12, the day King George VI and Queen Elizabeth were to be crowned.

> To all that wields the tongue, the sword, the purse—
> To Justices, to Baronets and worse:
> Let Competition, Mother of our Race,
> Smile on the venture with her modest face:
> Nor let our Empire's Dignities abstain,
> But come in force to swell her noble train:
> Vice and Oppression in their coronets,
> And Murder, civilized in Epaulettes,
> Shall walk the streets for all who will to see—
> Instruct the poor, and thrill the bourgeoisie.
> Bring forth the choicest treasures of the Nation,
> Nor spare expense to grace the Celebration—
> Muster thy troops to line the streets, MacDuff,
> And damned be he that dares to say "Hold, enough!"
> So let our soldiers their shoulders brace
> To keep the working classes in their place.

After mocking the supposed accomplishments of the new king, he adds:

> But Kings who err upon the liberal side
> Are straight by Church and State disqualified.

The lines are an obvious reference to Edward VIII, the king's popular older brother, who had abdicated the throne when the Church of England, backed by the government, would not allow him to marry an American divorcée. This topical interjection aside, the poem makes clear that Alex's anger at inequality and exploitation, sharpened in Buenos Aires, had come home to his native land. Not his most artfully constructed work, it nevertheless makes clear what he thought of militarism, empire, the class system, and the sort of spectacle that Britain's upper echelons used to distract hard-pressed working-class and middle-level families like the Comforts. The copy of "Ode at the Coronation" filed among his papers decades later is set up in type, ready to go into *The Cholmelian*. But it was never printed: whether because he got cold feet or because his fellow editors rejected it, is not known.

Asked how his parents reacted to his political and social views, Alex once replied, "Not very strongly."[25] His father was deeply cynical about the system, and it wasn't unusual for people of the Comforts' and Fenners' Nonconformist background to take a moral stance in defiance of the state. Many members of the Plymouth Brethren—the fiercely held faith of Alex's grandfather—had been conscientious objectors during World War I.[26] Quakers and Congregationalists still accounted for much of the pacifist movement during the interwar decades, providing an intellectual foundation as well as some of its most committed members (socialists were conflicted, and the Comintern, under Stalin, still disparaged "bourgeois pacifism").[27] Above all, they sought to bring about a moral awakening through mass organizing that would make it impossible for the authorities not to abandon war. If the churches refused, "in a thoroughgoing and absolute fashion," to accept war, government "would speedily discover other and better ways of dealing with international disputes than by the customary threat of force," Rev. Leyton Richards, a Congregational minister and anti-conscription activist, wrote in 1929: a strategy that would filter into Alex's later thinking.[28]

Antiwar sentiment and suspicion of military preparedness remained strong in the early Depression years. In 1932 an international antiwar congress in The Hague drew over two thousand people from twenty-seven countries. In England, some local councils were moving to abolish OTC units and take down war memorials.[29] Meanwhile, the coalition National Government in Westminster was responding to the economic crisis with austerity measures, including cuts to unemployment benefits. When the Labour leadership more or less went along with most of the government program, the "unofficial Left" turned to other means to express their frustration.

Sit-down strikes, imported from the United States, Poland, and France, broke out for the first time in England in some Monmouthshire mines. A large hunger march to London was organized in January 1934, followed by a still larger one the following year.[30] In October 1936, just as Alex and his father were returning from their tramp steamer tour, a group of two hundred volunteers captured national attention when they marched 291 miles from the economically flattened town of Jarrow, County Durham, to London to demand work. But Parliament did nothing aside from voting the marchers £1 each for train fare back home. They returned amid bitter denunciations of the government's complacency and the "official Left's" lack of fight.[31]

All this was happening as much of Britain was distracted by the tabloid drama of the abdication crisis and arguably helped fuel the anger Alex poured into his unpublished poem. That said, his published schoolboy writing was attracting new friends in more established precincts.

IN NOVEMBER 1937 A semi-retired publishing executive living in Highgate received a copy of the latest *Cholmelian* from Tommy Twidell, Alex's Latin master. It was Alex's last year at Highgate School, and he was preparing to take his scholarship exams. The publisher, Arthur Waugh, was ecstatic over the magazine and especially Alex's verse: "Frankly, and without any reserve I have never read a better piece of work by a schoolboy than your own 'Cloth of Gold.'" Another Comfort contribution, "Trade-Winds," was also "a very good poem," he wrote to Alex. "It is very refreshing to an old Traditionalist like myself to find young poets still standing by the ancient ways of melody and beauty." The gentleman invited Alex to come to tea and have a talk.[32]

Waugh, seventy-one, was the son of a physician and the nephew of Edmund Gosse, the author of Alexander Comfort's favorite book, *Father and Son*. For almost three decades until his retirement in 1930, he was managing director of Chapman & Hall, one of the great names in British publishing, having counted Dickens, Thackeray, Trollope, and Elizabeth Barrett Browning among its authors. After Arthur retired, he remained active with the firm as a reader, consultant, and board chair. Chapman & Hall was already publishing the novels of his son Alec, and in the mid-1930s it added his other son, Evelyn, to the roster. Both sons were board members. Evelyn Waugh once wrote of his father, "I think he can claim to have more books dedicated to him than any living man."[33]

Arthur Waugh had grown up under the thumb of a tyrannical father, and his great-grandson Alexander Waugh has written that such children "often find themselves unable to grow up: they are consumed with a need to relive their childhoods over and over again to get it right." In Arthur's case, that included taking younger writers under his wing and helping them launch their careers. One of these, the novelist Elizabeth Myers, wrote to a friend after meeting him in 1942, "I was taken this afternoon to have tea with Mr and Mrs Arthur Waugh. Mr Waugh is a *glorious* old man. He is just like a character from Dickens, fat, smiling and wise, with a face like a lovely red apple."[34]

Alex paid a call on Waugh during the Christmas holidays.[35] They discussed his career, his plans for university, and the kinds of things he wanted to write. He already aimed to be a novelist as well as a poet, he said, and it's likely that Arthur saw some installments of "Confessions of Odysseus," because the two quickly hatched a plan to get a reworked version of Alex's diary of his travels of the year before published by Chapman & Hall. In March, Arthur sent Alex the terms of a contract for the book, which would be titled *The Silver River*. They would bring it out during the summer, after the author left school. Chapman & Hall would pay him 10 percent royalties, or sixpence, on all copies sold, and also took an option on each of the next five books Alex might write, "whether novels or otherwise (not verse)." He would receive a £25 advance on the next book, plus royalties "rising by stages (described in the contract) to 12 ½% and 15%." For later books under the agreement, the publisher would pay an advance equal to two-thirds of the earnings of the book immediately preceding.[36]

Arthur suggested Alex leave out the diary headings, but Evelyn, who read the manuscript as well and initially suggested holding it back, "did not encourage much alteration," except to subtitle it "'A schoolboy's diary in the Pacific' (or whatever it is)."[37] Alex agreed, and the book appeared with the subtitle, "The Diary of a Schoolboy in the South Atlantic 1936."

As presented to the public on June 16, 1938, *The Silver River* comes across as an advertisement for Alex as much as for itself. The author's photo—a little awkward but also a bit impish, with an eyebrow slightly raised—appears on the front cover, not the back as was customary, and the jacket copy, by Arthur, goes a trifle overboard in announcing Alexander Comfort (his byline here) as a major talent. "Considering the author's age," it reads, "[the book's] charm is the charm of promise, first and foremost, but the publishers believe [it] . . . reveals a talent of which great things may reasonably be expected in the future. They take pleasure in inviting the public to share their confidence, being convinced that all readers of *The Silver River* will keep their eyes upon everything that Mr. Comfort may write in the years to come."

Much later, Alex judged his first book "not very good."[38] While it attracted reviews from the biggest papers, the best were in second-tier publications.

More than one reviewer backhandedly praised the book and the author for being appropriately "unpretentious"—"there is nothing whatever in this volume to lead one to suppose that he has a literary future," one pronounced in friendly vein—and, for the most part, *The Silver River* is just an entertaining diary of an interesting South Atlantic journey. But it also contains hints of the writer and thinker Alex was developing into. The preface lays out—so quickly you could miss it—a rational humanistic philosophy that he would develop for much of the rest of his life. People don't read travel books like his to escape from reality, Alex argued: far from it. "They read to escape *into* it, from a crazy wonderland of armaments, cant, propaganda, and social injustice which the lunacy of humanity has constructed over a period of years. The real world is outside and above all this; it is a world where philosophy and religion are natural, indisputable phenomena, and where all the great discoveries of mankind, from birth to relativity are set in their proper place as manifest appurtenances of a rational, undefiled universe."[39]

Nature is the true order and source of meaning, he says, echoing the Romantic-era spirit he was already trying to cultivate in his poetry. Describing a tropical sunset, he says,

> [It] carries the essence of all human art in itself, [giving] a momentary glimpse of something which I knew once quite well, but have forgotten. I recapture that sunset with its fugitive recollection in music now and then: it is hidden in the "Tragic Overture" of Brahms, and it flashes for a second, now and again, in Mendelssohn and Wagner. There was a full orchestra in the clouds that night, and I have heard the symphony which it played, the bold theme given out on brass and drums echoed round the horizon by all the instruments, but I cannot remember it. I suppose it was the music of the spheres.[40]

Already in *The Silver River*, Alex at seventeen is insisting that the scientific-humanist tradition of the Enlightenment and the Romantic spirit do not conflict with each other in the natural world. And in his assertion about why people read travel books, he's using an argumentative device he would turn to over and over, suggesting to readers that they had been misdirected, that what they had been taught was one thing, but the reality was something quite different.

Alex passed his school and higher certificate exams, with distinctions, in 1937 and was awarded the Robert Styring Scholarship in Classics to Trinity College, Cambridge, on the strength of his performance in the latter. Rather than going up to university, however, he decided to stay an extra year at Highgate. He had never been so busy as a part of the life of the school. He was sub-editor of *The Cholmelian*, joint secretary of the Peace Society, a committee member of the Debating Society and the Christian Union, a member of the 6th Form Society, and a house prefect. But the reason he decided to stay was that he was changing his academic focus. He crammed the additional three terms with science courses to prepare for the first of the national medical examinations, which he passed in Easter term, and in hopes of earning an additional scholarship in natural sciences. He had made a career decision: he was going to become a medical missionary.

How did Alex come by his religious conviction? His parents were barely practicing, but both of their families were intensely involved with their faith. And while Nonconformist Christianity was fading as a cultural and political force in the interwar years in the UK, it was still highly visible and included some of the most famous and respected public figures in the world, many of whom seasoned their beliefs with the kind of humanism that attracted Alex. He later said that in these years he was a "liberal Christian."[41] Liberal Protestant theologians such as Karl Barth, Paul Tillich, and Reinhold Niebuhr were then routinely ranked among the leading intellectuals. The most prominent pacifists in the United States were the Congregationalist A. J. Muste and the Baptist Harry Emerson Fosdick.

Liberal Protestant missionaries of the day were trying, not always successfully, to bring to their work better awareness of the cultures in which they were embedding themselves and a sharper sense that they needed to serve these people, not the other way around. Norman Goodall, whom Alex had known as the pastor of New Barnet Congregational, was now at the London Missionary Society. Sir Wilfred Thomason Grenfell, one of the most famous English missionaries of the era, who had dedicated his life to providing medical care and otherwise assisting the fishing settlements and Indigenous communities on the coast of Labrador, wrote a number of popular books about his experiences. Alex read these and was already thinking about getting his medical training after university at the London Hospital, because that was where Grenfell had trained.[42]

Then there was Albert Schweitzer, the most famous medical missionary of any nationality and one of the most admired human beings of his time after Mohandas Gandhi. Fast on his way to being forgotten now, Schweitzer was a striking Alsatian with a shock of white hair, a walrus moustache, and an air of wisdom and compassion; a Lutheran clergy member and theologian; an organist and musicologist; a physician who founded a famed missionary hospital in Gabon (then a French colony), which he ran until his death in 1965; and, in 1952, winner of the Nobel Peace Prize. He was also an older cousin of another writer who, like Alex, would be profoundly affected by World War II: Jean-Paul Sartre.

Schweitzer periodically visited Europe and the United States to lecture and raise funds. In his talks, he enlarged on an ethical philosophy he called "reverence for life." "Ethics," he said in one of his books, "are responsibility without limit toward all that lives."[43] Elsewhere, he said, "the man who has become a thinking being feels a compulsion to give to every will-to-live the same reverence for life that he gives to his own."[44]

In later years, Schweitzer would be criticized for not maintaining his African hospital up to standards that Europeans would have found acceptable and for his sometimes patronizing attitude toward the people he served. But he was a passionate critic of colonialism and war, and he brought to his work a strong conviction of his responsibility to serve. In a world of Hitlers and Stalins, filled with "armaments, cant, propaganda, and social injustice," Schweitzer seemed to many people a truly heroic figure. He was also a magnetic speaker who attracted overflow crowds on tour and left them with the feeling that his presence had changed them. "Above all, Dr. Schweitzer remains, for me, as a striking manifestation of the life force which he himself respects so profoundly, rather than as a person in the ordinary meaning of the word," one friend and admirer said.[45]

Years later, Kenneth Rexroth, discussing Alex as a poet, would comment, "He has a universality about him in many ways reminiscent of Albert Schweitzer."[46] It may be only family lore that a seven-year-old Alex met Schweitzer on the missionary's visit to the UK in 1928, but he would have been very aware of the doctor's public presence growing up. He would have admired Schweitzer's polymathy and above all the promise the doctor's career seemed to hold that it was possible to combine Christian piety with a strong commitment to social justice and peace along with hands-on work. Even in his early writing, Alex appears to have absorbed the conviction of Schweitzer and other liberal Protestant thinkers that the central ethical issue then, a time when humanity seemed at a moral crossroads, was the individual's relationship with and sense of responsibility toward society, humanity, and the earth.

BESIDES CRAMMING SCIENCE COURSES, Alex found time during his last year at Highgate to put his evolving beliefs into practice. In 1918, peace campaigners in the UK had established the League of Nations Union, which was dedicated to promoting the perceived ideals of the league, including replacement of war with collective security. The idea was that all states should commit to responding collectively to a breach of the peace rather than going to war against each other. In the 1930s the union still had hundreds of thousands of members in Britain and more elsewhere in the Commonwealth. It began to fade with the rise of Hitler, but it briefly got a boost when Mussolini's Italy brazenly invaded Ethiopia without a declaration of war, and the League of Nations imposed economic sanctions on the invader. The sanctions were ineffective, Italy pressed forward, and the impotence of the league and the failure of collective security—not to mention the governments that were supposed to enforce it—were exposed.

Many schools and universities, including Highgate, had chapters of the League of Nations Society supporting its work, but the league's sad response to the Ethiopian debacle did irreparable damage to their morale.[47] Pacifists became convinced that the only way to avoid an even more atrocious war than the last was to build mass opposition to war itself. In the spring of 1937 Alex helped set up a new Peace Society at Highgate, "out of the ashes" of the now-defunct League of Nations Society. *The Cholmelian* announced, "[The Peace Society] welcomes to its meetings all shades of opinion who want to discuss their attitude towards peace, but has rejected in its policy the compromise that crippled the former Society, and devoted itself to purely pacifist activities."

However, the Peace Society wished to "clear up a few common misunderstandings existing about Pacifism in the School." It pointed out, "'Pacifist' is not synonymous with 'doormat,' or 'non-violence' with 'non-resistance.'"[48] Alex, as joint secretary, certainly had a great deal to do with composing these words. The slightly cocky language, as well as the implied demand that passive resistance not subside into merely symbolic resistance, aligned with his later thinking about war and his way of expressing it.**

** The next few years took the Highgate student pacifists of 1937 in many different directions. The Peace Society's other joint secretary, Hilary Charles Morton Jarvis, who would soon join Alex for medical studies at Cambridge, went on to enlist in the Royal Air Force and was shot down over Germany and imprisoned in September 1942. He later wrote a memoir of his early life and his experiences in a German POW camp, Doctor in Chains, under the pseudonym George Morton.

Besides holding discussions and sponsoring visiting speakers, the Peace Society organized first aid classes, "to equip ourselves to be of practical service to others in the accidents which may occur either in time of peace or war." The classes attracted about twenty boys, Alex reported in *The Cholmelian*. While a bit off-topic, they were a clever way of de-demonizing pacifism—the Peace Society's update in the paper came to a few paragraphs, while the OTC's doings took up pages—and to attract boys interested in first aid who might agree to listen to pacifists' perspective as well.

Believing that "an enemy befriended is an enemy disarmed," the Peace Society announced in February 1938 that it was organizing a trip to the areas of Frankfurt and Cologne "to fraternize with a similar party of German schoolboys." Nonmembers were invited to join the trip ("but we warn them that they many come back pacifists!"). Travelers would be staying at youth hostels, and the cost would be £5 13s. for eleven days.[49]

Alex was reasonably aware of the nature of the Nazi regime. He was familiar with *Mein Kampf*, he told his son years later, but he added that it was hard at the time to take reports of German abuses absolutely seriously when so many lies had been spread about them during World War I.[50] In any case, his purpose was to reach out to ordinary Germans, not their government.

Over the Easter holiday, members of the Peace Society made the trip, joining with two groups from the PPU. One, to the Black Forest, appears to have spent most of its time skiing and tobogganing. The other, including Alex, toured the Rhineland, where, he reported, they "were received everywhere with generous hospitality." Nowhere in his brief report does he say whether they gleaned anything of the Nazi leaders' exhortations to war, or how these were absorbed by the public; of the plight of German Jews (Kristallnacht would follow in November); or of Germany's aggressive rearmament and militarization. Nor did he report that the "hospitality" he and his companions received included any discussion of the practical aspects of stopping the German dictatorship from seizing one country after another when it was clearly bent on doing so.[51]

Questions such as these were, of course, on many other people's minds. Alex's mother put away a postcard he sent her from Nuremberg "in case they ever come up the street," he remembered.[52] When Alex left Highgate for Cambridge later that year, the Peace Society fell apart while a new League of Nations Union, ironically, was formed. "The Peace Society has decided to make way for the Union," the new group announced, "since it was due to the desire of many members of the Peace Society that the Union came into being."[53]

If Alex didn't leave a robust pacifist movement behind him at Highgate, he did take away his share of prizes. After placing thirteenth in the Classical Sixth in his first term there, he finished his last two in first place.[54] Upon graduation, he was awarded the John Henry Gregory Prize for the Classical Sixth and two Bodkin Prizes for the Science Sixth, one for biology and the other for science essay.[55]

He entered Cambridge with not only a scholarship in classics but also as senior scholar in natural sciences—with some makeup work to do. "I couldn't get through physics," he admitted of his last year at Highgate. "I loved everything but that."[56] Entering Trinity College, he was required to pass a physics course before he could go on to the heart of the university's curriculum for an MB (Bachelor of Medicine) degree, the UK equivalent of an MD in the United States: anatomy, physiology, oncology, and "gastrology."

ALEX SPENT PART OF his break before entering university in the Orkneys with a Highgate schoolfellow who was carrying out an archaeological dig. Matriculating at Cambridge on November 1, 1938, Michaelmas term, he was assigned a bedroom and study at P3 Great Court, a four-hundred-year-old stone edifice looking onto the main courtyard of Trinity College with a fountain at its center and facing the chapel on the opposite side of the yard. The rooms were spacious, but he had to share a lavatory down the hall and cross the courtyard to take a bath. The college did not provide furniture, Alex recalled, so his father ordered "a bed, table and chairs, sideboard, cupboards, bookcase and more from Greenleaf's, a Jewish carpenter in Shoreditch: total cost £43 5s."[57]

As a proper Cambridge undergraduate, his other capital expense was to purchase a bicycle. This was stolen. When Alex replaced it, he boobytrapped the new vehicle with a hairpin attached to a rat-trap under the seat. "He was its only victim, the pin being removed at Outpatients."[58] The university charged him 7s. 6d. per term to store the bicycle: the same amount he paid to have his shoes cleaned.***

*** He was fined twice for infringement of college regulations, but for what exactly is not known.

At Cambridge he found a far more formal, tradition-bound institution than Highgate, one that took some adjustment for students from a middle-class background. Graduates still comment on the "sheer, ritualized extravagance" of life there, from the dress code around the wearing of academic gowns (dark blue with black facings at Trinity) to the Formal Hall, the Friday-night meal at which grace was said and students and faculty alike were gowned.[59] This was offset by the ramshackle condition of the facility itself, which was prone to leaky roofs, pipes freezing and sometimes bursting during winter, and the heating system failing. It wouldn't have been Cambridge if everyone from undergraduates to fellows hadn't had to anticipate the possibility of several days of deep cold when there was no heat in their quarters.[60]

Alex's tutor was A. S. F. Gow, a legendary Cambridge don who had himself been a student at Trinity and was the son of another. Gow was a Greek scholar and expert on the poet Theocritus, making him an appropriate choice for a young man holding a scholarship in classics. He had also been a close friend of A. E. Housman, Kennedy Professor of Latin at Trinity until his death in 1936 and author of *A Shropshire Lad*, one of the most popular books of poetry in English since its publication in 1896.

Along with King's and St John's, Trinity was one of the three most academically and socially prestigious of the university's twenty-four colleges. Most members of the Cambridge Apostles, the fabled discussion group founded in 1820, were invited to join as undergraduates at one of the three or Jesus or Christ's College. In the decades before Alex went to Cambridge, Apostles from Trinity had included Bertrand Russell, G. E. Moore, Alfred North Whitehead, and Ludwig Wittgenstein.**** As this indicates, the core of the male membership of the Bloomsbury Group, the brilliant circle of British writers, artists, and intellectuals who came together just before World War I, were Trinity undergraduates (along with a few King's College scholars like E. M. Forster and John Maynard Keynes), several of whom later became faculty members.

This cultural outpouring was not a coincidence. Cambridge in the fifty-some years before Alex attended was one of the liveliest and most fertile intellectual and scientific communities in the world. Moore and Russell laid the foundations of twentieth-century analytic philosophy at

**** Another Trinity alumnus whose career, like Alex's, combined literature and natural science—although butterflies, rather than mollusks, were his specialty—was Vladimir Nabokov.

more or less the same time Whitehead and Russell were producing the *Principia Mathematica* (1910–13), their monumental work on the logical foundations of mathematics. Moore's *Principia Ethica* (1903) exerted an enormous influence on British modernism. The book was founded on a philosophy that prized common sense over skepticism. Whether or not you believe it's raining has no effect whatsoever on the fact that it's raining, "Moore's paradox" famously argued. But it delved into more original territory with its distinction between things that are good in themselves—that have intrinsic value—and things that are good as a causal means to other things—that "at any moment, will produce the best total result." Optimistically, Moore held that we can know what is good in itself by intuition—for example, through "the contemplation of beauty, love and truth."[61] This encouraged Virginia Woolf, Forster, and others of the Bloomsbury circle, early in their development, to adopt an outlook that prized art for its own sake and stressed "the importance of personal relationships and the private life" as ethical values.[62]

While some critics found this perspective too self-absorbed and too focused on aesthetics, it also carried an implicit criticism of capitalism. "The modern man thinks that everything ought to be done for the sake of something else, and never for its own sake," Russell wrote. "The notion that the desirable activities are those that bring a profit has made everything topsy-turvy."[63]

Analytic philosophy also stressed common sense but emphasized logical clarity in drawing conclusions about the world. As such, it sought to tie philosophy closer to mathematics and natural science, moving away from metaphysics, which focuses on understanding the fundamental nature of reality. Analytic philosophy had its origins with the eighteenth-century British empiricists, including David Hume and Bishop George Berkeley, and was given the name "positivism" by Auguste Comte, who argued that philosophy must be based only on "positive" facts if humanity is to reach a fully mature understanding of its world. Positivism spread to Germany through the work of Ernst Mach and to the UK through John Stuart Mill.

Building on their work, Russell argued that facts can be independent of one another, not part of any great, unified metaphysical system. He and his student Wittgenstein (in his *Tractatus Logico-Philosophicus*) proposed that an "ideal language" could be found that accurately expresses facts and philosophical propositions using precise, formal logic. Two other groups, the Vienna Circle and the Berlin Circle, calling themselves logical positivists, went beyond Russell's and Wittgenstein's work to argue that the only factual knowledge is scientific knowledge, which can be verified by a physical experiment, and that any philosophical problem is meaningless if it can't be solved by logical analysis.

At this point, analytic philosophy started to splinter. Wittgenstein rejected logical positivism; the *Tractatus* holds that language imposes boundaries on what can be known, and the Austrian philosopher spent much of the rest of his life analyzing how language can be used to achieve philosophical understanding—or its opposite. Other thinkers took analytic philosophy in new directions—including analytic metaphysics!—while developments like the theory of relativity and quantum mechanics called into question both how observable any scientific fact really is and how independent any one object is from another.

The practical impact of positivism and its offspring, analytic philosophy, was that they made analytics the dominant way of "doing" philosophy, especially in the English-speaking world, and forged a closer link between scientific inquiry, pure sciences like physics and mathematics, and philosophy. As such, they provided the substance of scientific humanism, the doctrine that scientific methods can be used to move the development of humankind in rational and beneficial directions, which would color Alex's scientific work as well as his political and social thinking for most of his career.

In 1939, as Alex began his second year at Trinity, Wittgenstein, who had been a lecturer and fellow of the college for ten years, succeeded Moore as Knightbridge Professor of Philosophy. It's doubtful that Alex studied with Wittgenstein or attended his lectures; his program was intensely focused on medicine. But positivism and analytic philosophy were now a strong intellectual tradition at Cambridge, and Alex embraced them. Later he saw the limitations of both. "When I advocated scientific positivism, I think I'm open to the criticism that I ought to have known more about physics as it was understood at the time," he recalled. "I wouldn't have been so positivistic at that time had I been familiar with it."[64]

Because careful scientific study and analysis had been part of his mental makeup from an early age, positivism at this stage simply made sense, however. His meticulous study of locomotives and, later, his research on mollusks show that he was already applying it in earnest by the time he reached Cambridge. He published his first scholarly article, "A New Variety of *Mya Arenaria*," in the *Journal of Conchology* in 1938, the year he joined the Conchological Society of Great Britain and Ireland and just before beginning his first term.[65] He then suspended his work on the creatures until after he completed his medical studies. These absorbed nearly all of his academic work his first two years, which he spent preparing for the Natural Science Tripos at the end of the second.

If Cambridge suited him intellectually, it also made a degree of room for his politics. A few socialists and even Communists made their appearance in the undergraduate ranks in the '20s, at first mostly in the sciences. The brilliant bio-geneticist and evolutionist J. B. S. Haldane, who taught at the university from 1922 to 1933, was a committed socialist and, from 1937, a supporter of the Communist Party. The poet John Cornford, a Communist, helped build Cambridge's Socialist Society and Labour Club into a thousand-strong group by the mid-'30s, a significant presence in an undergraduate student body of about five thousand.[66] Cornford and several undergraduates would die fighting for the Loyalist cause in the Spanish Civil War.

In hindsight, of course, the university's most notorious leftists were the five "Cambridge Spies"—Donald Maclean, Guy Burgess, Kim Philby, Anthony Blunt (who "fathered" Maclean as an Apostle), and John Cairncross—who passed government secrets to the Soviet Union during and immediately after the war. Blunt, at Cambridge, was known mainly as a poet and budding art historian, but Maclean made waves by agitating for the creation of an elected student council as part of a ten-point program that also included "complete freedom of speech and action, . . . the right to use college and university lecture rooms for all political meetings, . . . the abolition of official supervision of Colonial Students, [and] complete equality for women students." By the '70s, most of Maclean's demands had been accepted.[67]

Pacifists had little presence at Cambridge at the time Alex was there, and neither did other non-Marxist opponents of fascism. Nevertheless, early in his residence, Alex demonstrated with other pacifists against the Munich conference at which Prime Minister Neville Chamberlain and French premier Edouard Daladier offered up Czechoslovakia to appease Hitler. He also claimed to have later participated in a rowdier protest when Sir Oswald Mosley, the Hitler manqué of the British Union of Fascists, visited the university—"a bottle of printer's ink with a firecracker in it being dropped into the basement where the Blackshirt leader was speaking," his son wrote—but this story is probably apocryphal.[68] Being of the Left but not a Marxist, Alex had no obvious political home at Cambridge.

Like many if not most people moving away from home for the first time to attend school, he faced the seeming imperative to find his place, to fit in. As institutions geared to produce the future leaders of society, the great universities were about making connections as much as learning, and to be a loner was not encouraged. While Cambridge was more progressive, in many respects, than Oxford or many other British universities, the class system still existed, and there was still the cultural split between scholars and "hearties"—warm, boisterous types—but that was an easy choice so far as Alex was concerned. Fortunately, Cambridge supplied plenty of opportunities to find your set and let it mold you.

Alex joined the Cambridge University Music Society, for which he continued to play the trumpet. Pursuant to his religious faith and with an eye to becoming a medical missionary, he also joined the University Congregational Society, or CongSoc. In that setting he made his first friends at Cambridge, Stephen Harris, a second-year student of serious temperament at Jesus College who was planning to become a minister, and Helen Doyle, a classicist at Newnham, the Cambridge women's college, who would later marry Stephen. That first year, Alex joined them and other friends on an Easter-holiday walking trip that became an annual event.

When he wasn't engrossed in his medical studies, he was writing. Toward the end of Easter term 1939, he sent Arthur Waugh the manuscript of his first extended work of fiction, ominously titled *Send Forth the Sickle*, a historical novel set in Gloucestershire, a place he barely knew. He had doubts about it—"very raw indeed," he said years later.[69] So did Waugh, who sent it on to Evelyn for a reader's report. Evelyn wrote directly to Alex that while he had "a gift for writing," the best course was to put the novel aside for five years, write another book, and then see if the first could be "put to a new use." "At present," he wrote, "I believe the book to have defects which will prove fatal to its success. Too hasty publication would be a discouragement to you and an embarrassment in the future." Graciously, he added, "please don't think that a single moment of the long time you have spent on this book has been wasted. . . . Any good writer has, in his early life, sacrificed at least one book."[70]

Alex sent the letter on to Evelyn's father, who agreed. Alex seems to have taken the rejection with good grace, and he soon began turning over ideas for a second attempt at a novel. Events would quickly give him something closer to home to think about. By the time he returned for his second year in October 1939, Britain was at war with Germany. The university was already holding practice air raids (yellow, purple, and red, in ascending order of urgency), various buildings had been sandbagged, and the cellars of some had been turned into shelters. Over the course of the next three terms, Cambridge became quite a different place. Even before the fall of France in June 1940, rationing had begun, and meat was becoming less available at meals. Air raid practices became more frequent after the French defeat, the Dunkirk evacuation, and the commencement of the Luftwaffe's bombing campaign over Britain. Everyone from undergraduates to fellows was participating as either wardens or in fire or first-aid parties. Typically one spent a week on full duty, a week in reserve, and then an interval with no duties.[71]

One day Alex found himself in London when the air raid sirens went off. He took refuge in a root cellar converted into a bomb shelter in the south London neighborhood of Balham. Afterward he wrote a poem that conveys the macabre, sometimes nightmarish atmosphere of the raids.

These faces—the cold apples in a loft
huddled in rows—each shining green
catching a convex light, under the grey rat's foot
impotent, are not so quiet—

Grey faces, hollow where the wasps
have been at them, after the fungus—turnip lanterns
are not so empty, impartial between self
and the small house under the imminent thunder.

These do not vary as the mind flickers,
blue hollow under jaws, shadows on throat,
not knowing, lying as apples lie
listening to the rat coming through the paper.

Only in this quiet, this hot listening, we hear
the hiss of stars in the river, going out.[72]

Particularly after Britain found itself alone in the war against Hitler, the government became more suspicious of foreigners—notably Germans, of course—and non-mainstream political expression. A large number of refugees from the Nazi regime were already living in Britain before the war began—some 30,000 by 1938.[73] They attracted suspicion, even those who were Jewish. Soon it was decided that all male enemy aliens over sixty were to be arrested and interned in Canada and elsewhere. Popular attitudes sometimes echoed the government's. "There are an awful lot of German refugees in Cambridge and I am constantly overhearing scraps of Hunnish in the streets," Alex's tutor A. S. F. Gow wrote.

In July 1940 Gow reported that three of his own German pupils had been arrested and interned, along with several university lecturers and an examiner in the law. In addition, "the Chairman of Examiners in the Natural Science Tripos was in danger of being jugged owing to some indiscretions of the Peace Pledge Union with which he was connected." The following spring, less than three months before the German invasion of Russia, the Communist *Daily Worker* was suppressed (eliciting "shrill screams from our advanced undergraduate thinkers," Gow wrote).[74]

Alex's course of studies was unaffected by the wartime disruptions; while students in the liberal arts were either volunteering or being called up, undergraduates in medicine and the sciences were left to their work, in anticipation that they would eventually aid the war effort. He himself had no fear of being drafted, since his fingerless left hand made him unfit for service. But the population of the university was changing rapidly. Between his first and second year at Cambridge, the resident student population dropped from 5,491 men and 513 women to 4,353 and 465. By Michaelmas term of his third year, the numbers were 2,756 and 515, and the student body was becoming heavily weighted toward medicine and science. Soon after war was declared, however, students started to arrive from evacuated London institutions. A year later, there were some 1,500 of these academic refugees at Cambridge.[75]

Among them were two young women from London School of Economics. Ruth Harris and Jane Henderson hadn't known each other at LSE but found themselves roommates at Cambridge. Ruth, three years older than Alex, was the older sister of his friend Stephen. She joined CongSoc soon after her arrival and there met Alex. He saw a tall, attractive, blue-eyed, fair-haired young woman from a similar background to his own, if a bit more straitlaced, who shared his love of music. "She recognized a man of excitement and promise," their son recalled. "Before long she was washing his test tubes and making toast on the fire of his draughty rooms. They were an item for the rest of his time at Cambridge."[76]

Alex also got to know Jane—"slight, curly-haired and with glasses"—who attended informal Saturday poetry readings where he and other students would read any selection they happened to like and occasionally some of their own. Afterward the attendees would go to the local health food store for snacks.[77]

Another attendee was Maurice James Craig, an Ulsterman who was "trying to be a mini Oscar Wilde," Alex recalled, "kept black cats and claimed that he was the reincarnation of Akhenaten, king of Egypt," but was "a good poet."[78] Yet another evacuee from LSE who appeared at the readings was Priscilla Craig (unrelated), the niece of Lord Craigavon, the prime minister and hardline Protestant political boss of Northern Ireland, although she herself was leftist-inclined. Priscilla's boyfriend and soon-to-be husband, who wrote and published numerous love poems to her, was Nicholas Moore, who happened to have been the other young contributor, aside from Alex, whom critics had praised when *The Threshold* appeared in 1936. He was also the son of the Cambridge eminence G. E. Moore. Two years older than Alex, Nick had been educated at Leighton Park, a Quaker school in Reading, then at the University of St Andrews before transferring to Cambridge and Trinity in 1938. He had "a large toothy smile like the Great Pumpkin," Alex recalled.[79] "[He] wrote more poetry than anyone I ever met, enormous amounts of it and it was very uneven, but some of it was very good."[80] Nick was also a pacifist and received his exemption from service as a conscientious objector on moral grounds in the fall of 1939.[81]

By their second year at Cambridge they had struck up a friendship, and over the months that followed Nick gradually refocused Alex's attention on poetry, which he had turned away from in favor of his medical studies and his first attempted novel. "Alex, when I first met him, was a born-first-time Christian. He kept white mice in his room, and had cut off the ends of two of his fingers," Nick recalled, not quite accurately. "He was just as voluble then about [poetry] as he later became about the joys of sex."[82]

Nick had begun editing a literary magazine, *Seven*, just before he arrived at Cambridge, which survived for eight issues before folding in 1940. *Seven* published an array of young British poets, some for the first time, who would become prominent in the '40s, including George Barker, G .S. Fraser, Dorian Cooke, J. F. Hendry, and Norman McCaig. Nick also contacted many of the British and American writers living in Paris in the years just before the German invasion and got them to contribute, including Henry Miller, Anaïs Nin, William Saroyan, Lawrence Durrell, and Kay Boyle. The result was a fairly impressive selection of new and avant-garde writing in English at the time.

Alex never contributed to *Seven*, but by his second year he was placing poems in *The Cambridge Review*, the weekly *Observer*, and *The Adelphi*, one of the most important literary magazines of the '20s and '30s, which under its editor, Max Plowman, the first general secretary of the PPU, was moving in a pacifist direction. John Lehmann, a Trinity graduate and influential editor, had published some of Nick's earliest work a couple of years before in his literary magazine, *New Writing*. By 1940 he was managing editor of Virginia and Leonard Woolf's Hogarth Press and was spending part of each week in Cambridge. There he became reacquainted with Nick and also met Alex and several other undergraduate poets. That year Lehmann asked Alex and Nick to edit *Cambridge Poetry 1940*, the second of a projected annual series, Poets of Tomorrow. "I have the impression that Alex did most of the work on the Anthology," Nick later said.[83]

Except for his not-for-publication diatribe against the monarchy and the established order in 1937, Alex's poetry before the war had been unpolitical, drawing on his classical background for its subject matter and some of its effects, especially Greek and Latin pastoral poetry. Now, he began to write about war: its terrors and tragedy and particularly how it could tear human beings apart from each other.

"France" was his most ambitious poem to date. As an undergraduate, he submitted it for the 1941 Chancellor's Medal for English Verse, which ultimately was not awarded that year. It appeared in *The Adelphi*. It sketches out the story of a farm family from the grim years of the Depression to wartime.

> There is neither hand nor ladder
> to thatch our rafters. For the beautiful poplar,
> silk barley flowing, apples and unclipped sheep,
> for the soil there is no victory, Only the earth will pardon.

The son is called up, leaving his young pregnant wife behind, dies on the battlefield and so is unable to return home when the enemy destroy the farm and kill his wife and unborn child. Alex is still looking back to classical poetry, but the effect is more surreal; he mixes in colloquial English and French expressions to make the language more contemporary, similar to what T. S. Eliot had done in *The Waste Land* and other poems.

Another poem from this time, "Letter to a Friend in the Army," is closer to his own experience, which included so many of his fellow undergraduates joining up and leaving Cambridge, and more direct than "France." Here he encounters a classmate, now in uniform and still "talking of girls and music":

You have the harvest,
 you have the power, the licence
 to reap men heedfully.
You are grown terrible. . . .

I am the song you would have sung
 I am your life, your warm
 night in your girl's body,
your child, your music. Whether in sand
or clay you dig your sterner marriage
 we two have known. The flood
 will lie deep, over this city.

By the end, the speaker is no longer a former classmate but the person the newly enlisted soldier might have been, and the life he thinks he can return to, not understanding that war will change him into something "terrible" and destroy the world he is leaving. Both poems appeared along with six others in Alex's first collection, *France and Other Poems*, which was published by Favil Press, a small publisher, in early 1941 as part of its Resurgam younger poets' series (the younger poets themselves paid the cost of printing).[84] The series was edited by Peter Baker, a twenty-year-old second lieutenant in the Royal Artillery with publishing ambitions who would cross Alex's path again. Paul Scott, future author of the *Raj Quartet* series of novels, and Emanuel Litvinoff were among the other poets who got a volume in the series, along with Baker himself—although "volume," due to the wartime paper shortage, meant a single, heavy-stock broadsheet printed on both sides and folded to make six pages total.

"France" especially was a compelling poem, especially for a student who had only visited the country once for two weeks with his mother in the years before the war. "He speaks for the French poor, that is, the bulk of the people, and makes us feel the tragedy of the war, and the grim years before the war, as they knew it," said one critic. "If the promise in Mr. Comfort's poetry is fulfilled, his future writing will be significant for our time."[85]

"France" and "Letter to a Friend in the Army" were also fairly daring material to publish while enrolled at an institution that supported the war effort as a matter of course, especially coming from a student who could count on being spared the sacrifice many of his classmates were bound to make. But Alex was prepared to go further.

On January 23, 1941, he received a letter from Arthur Waugh, to whom he had sent the manuscript of a new novel. "*No Such Liberty* realizes—no, rather: far exceeds my highest expectations," Waugh responded, "and with all my heart I congratulate you upon a really fine piece of work. I have just dispatched it to the office with the suggestion that there is no need of a second opinion: I am so entirely confident of its quality."[86]

The story line of *No Such Liberty* is simple. A young German pathologist, Dr. Helmut Breitz, a Christian pacifist but not a politically active person, and his wife, Anna, an anti-Nazi who helps smuggle conscientious objectors out of Germany, come under suspicion and flee to England as she is about to give birth. As a pacifist, Breitz is classified as a class B alien. He and Anna are placed in internment camps where their child suffers neglect and undernourishment before dying. The novel ends with Breitz and Anna expecting permission to emigrate to the United States, but it's not yet in hand. Much of the action is taken up with the couple's efforts to leave Germany, their struggles in the camps, and Breitz's efforts to secure papers to emigrate. As the novel ends, Breitz stands on the verge of a choice between his old pacifism of conscience and direct action of the type that Anna had embraced. Would he take the next step? We're not told.

Writing during and after the fall of France, the Dunkirk evacuation, the first onslaught of the German Blitzkrieg, and Churchill's stirring May 4 speech to the House of Commons ("We shall fight on the beaches, we shall fight on the landing grounds, we shall fight in the fields and in the streets, we shall fight in the hills; we shall never surrender"), Alex's political objective was clear: to drive home the latent similarities between German and English attitudes and the possibility that the war could turn Britain in the same authoritarian direction as Nazi Germany. Early in the novel, Breitz and Braunstein, his boss at the Central hospital in Cologne, discuss the political situation. Nazism is "a pathological process," Braunstein says, "[and Germany is] a scared, silly nation. We've lost our faith in ourselves ever since we saw those men come home beaten. Now we're scared. We daren't be weak for fear of being imposed on. We daren't be weak for fear of seeming weak. We're scared of the English, of the Jews, of each other."[87]

In England, Breitz thinks he sees something disturbingly similar:

> I realised that the same fear was moving here as in Germany, the fear of being weak, or adhering to right principles lest they should not be

> an expedient, practical policy—to make any concession, for fear of defeat. . . . It's not that you in London are evil; it's not that the infection has gone so far that you beat and jail men, individual men, who tell you that the bacteria of your disease are there. But they are there. And I know that they must and they will grow, till you are as we, and fear has redoubled itself.[88]

What makes *No Such Liberty* a novel rather than a polemic, is the way Alex details Breitz's process toward understanding. Thanks to Braunstein's diagnosis and Anna's political engagement, he changes from a self-satisfied professional leading a relatively insulated life to someone who understands the full implications of his pacifism and the tragedy on all sides that the war is sure to be, much as his creator surely was coming to realize at this time. To make the story concrete, Alex drew on his medical education, details of his trip to the Rhineland before the war (in his foreword, he ironically thanks "the Cologne Hitler-Jugend, who showed me a fair section of Nazi thought and character, explaining its aims and origins"), conversations with some refugees, readings from some recent exposés of their plight, and even his Atlantic shipboard experiences. Alex had taken to heart Evelyn Waugh's implicit suggestion that he should base his first novel on matters he actually knew something about.

Themes appear in *No Such Liberty* that would preoccupy Alex for the next decade and beyond: the State's compulsion to abuse power and its disregard for individual lives, people's vulnerability to forces beyond their control, and, above all, the need for individuals to take a personal, ethical stand against a culture saturated in death and destruction. He had seized on an especially urgent topic to reflect these themes.

Some fifty thousand refugees, a large proportion of them Jews, were in Britain when the war began. The government was slow to define its policy toward them, but it took a hard line once the German invasion of France began. "Collar the lot!" Churchill famously ordered after Mussolini entered the war on Hitler's side, and thousands of Italians resident in the UK were rounded up, regardless of their known political persuasion. Refugees were initially held in a hodgepodge of facilities, including monasteries, but the government quickly began shipping all German, Austrian, and Italian males between sixteen and sixty to internment camps on the Isle of Man and a scattering of other places in Britain itself and in Canada and Australia. The internees included numerous prominent anti-Nazis, including the writer Franz Borkenau, the artist Kurt Schwitters, and the Austrian logical positivist Otto Neurath. Some

Jewish refugees sent to Canada found themselves in the same camps with German prisoners of war. In the scramble to get "enemy aliens" out of Britain, the *Arandora Star*, a passenger ship taking some thirteen hundred German and Italian internees and prisoners of war to Canada, was sailing unaccompanied on July 2, 1940, when it was torpedoed by a German U-boat; 805 people were killed.[89]

Alex's novel was not the first book to call attention to the government's treatment of "aliens." In the summer of 1940, a young Oxford graduate named François Lafitte—the stepson, as it happened, of Havelock Ellis, and a committed radical—was commissioned by Political and Educational Planning, a left-leaning social policy institute, to write a report on the internment issue. He worked fast, and his report, *The Internment of Aliens*, was published in November in a cheap Penguin edition that sold out quickly. Along with the *Arandora Star*, Lafitte's book and another exposé, *Anderson's Prisoners*, by a pseudonymous "Judex" and brought out by the left-wing publisher Victor Gollancz, helped draw attention to the abuse of refugees.[90] By the time *No Such Liberty* appeared, the government was looking for ways to rectify the situation, but it took several years to release even a few thousand of the prisoners and bring them back to Britain, partly owing to the continuing naval war.

"Only the most narrow-minded Jingo would accuse the novelist of 'heartening the enemy' by showing up our callousness to prisoners," Arthur Waugh wrote, adding that Alex's "mastery of material proves you a true artist of wide and human range, to whom all things may become possible." As to the novel's commercial prospects, "I don't see why this book shouldn't sell, if we can catch the market on the crest."[91]

Waugh passed the manuscript to J. G. Gatfield, an editor at Chapman & Hall, who initially "scented pacifist propaganda" but returned with a positive report. Unbeknown to Waugh, however, he had submitted the manuscript to the Censorship Bureau, which objected to chapter 20, in which Breitz survives the sinking of a ship full of refugees, the *Star of Asia*, by the Germans, an incident clearly based on the *Arandora Star*. Gatfield wrote,

> The main objection to this chapter is the picture of panic portrayed, and the statement that the troops were put into the lifeboats before the prisoners. This latter statement, [the censor] says, is untrue and she furthermore pointed out that in such a panic as is depicted it would have been impossible for this to happen. I, personally, resent the fact that the Nazi seamen are highly praised, while not one word

> of credit is given to the British officers and crew, who were, no doubt, performing their duties in the traditional manner of British seamen.[92]

Alex, in reply, argued that his book was fiction. However, he had included a short foreword acknowledging the sources for some of his material along with this statement: "The ghastly thing about this story is that most of it is true. . . . Most of the incidents are real." "Come, come, Mr. Comfort," Gatfield replied, "when faced by such a foreword, we cannot hide behind the word fiction."[93]

Waugh lamented the "tin gods" of publishing and Gatfield's "damn silly" behavior in particular—he didn't think the material would cause a stir if the book was published in its original form—but urged Alex to satisfy the higher authorities as best he could.[94] Alex quickly rewrote chapter 20, taking out the offensive references to the British crew and removing the "ghastly" sentence from the foreword.

This intense back-and-forth over a work of fiction took place at a time when the wartime government was still testing how far it could push censorship and suppression of dissent. Shortly after the fall of France, six members of the PPU were arrested in London and tried for creating and putting up posters that said: "War will cease when men refuse to fight. What are YOU doing about it?"[95]

Publishers found themselves playing a constant guessing game as to how the censors would respond to any new literary work. While there was no legal provision to censor fiction, Gatfield said in a latter to Alex, "The Censorship Bureau has the power to cause the withdrawal from circulation [of] any publication which may be likely to affect the public morale. We cannot afford to take these risks after spending out money on the production of a book."[96]

Alex was not done sparring with his publisher, however. Waugh complained on his behalf to F. W. Walker, Chapman & Hall's production manager, about an illustration proposed for the book jacket, a color drawing of a concentration camp with a German sitting on guard—even though the internment camp in the book was not German. Astonishingly, this "was met by the objection that, for publicity purposes, that didn't matter."[97] Trying a different tack, Alex hinted to Waugh that Penguin had shown some interest in his book, most likely a bluff since Alex had given Chapman & Hall to understand that they had the only manuscript circulating. In any case, Waugh wrote back, "I fancy you would only get a farthing a copy, so it is no real commercial scoop for the author."[98]

Chapman & Hall decided to compromise. Instead of the German internment camp, the wrapper featured a color drawing of a swastika superimposed over a cross, both of them tangled in barbed wire, symbolizing the struggle between Nazism and Christianity. Harmony was restored between author and publisher, but Alex had planted a stake in the ground. Henceforth, publishers would have to contend with a writer who felt it his mission to push boundaries and be provocative. This would not be his last brush with censorship either.

Just before publication, he received a new literary identity when he took Walker's suggestion that he adopt "Alex" rather than "Alexander" as his byline, since it would then be short enough to fit on the spine of the book.[99] In future, he would always be "Alex Comfort" in print.

Reviews of *No Such Liberty* began to appear in June, and responses ranged from moderately high praise to moderate dismissal. The weekly *Spectator* praised it as "a moving book" ("[its] detachment and sober objectivity make its propaganda possible for all but the squeamish") and expressed the hope that it would lead to a "reformation" of Britain's treatment of war refugees.[100] The popular playwright Harold Brighouse, in the *Manchester Guardian*, called Alex's novel a "tour de force," brought off in a "clear, direct style" that "unfailingly suggests that this is a narrative of a personal and a dreadful experience."[101] But the novelist Frank Swinnerton, in the *Observer*, while deeming the novel "clear and sincere," added that it was "highly depressive."[102] And the *Times Literary Supplement* tagged it "a precocious fling of pacifist self-righteousness," the only review—at this stage—that directly attacked its politics.[103]

Arthur Waugh found the reviews underwhelming. He had hoped the *New Statesman and Nation*, which was more sympathetic to pacifists and the Left in general, would review the novel, but it did not. "We have had no commercial luck with the book yet," he reported to Alex on July 4, 1941, although two weeks later it was showing modest but steady sales on the back of the reviews.[104] The book was not making Alex's name as Arthur had hoped it would, thus far—but he remained enthusiastic about his young protégé's future.

ALEX CONTINUED TO WRITE and publish his poetry. He also contributed to theater productions as a deviser of effects ("I had a wonderful witches' cauldron in *Macbeth,* which had a spider and a long elastic stuck in the cauldron, and this thing whizzed over the heads of the audience") and tried his hand at writing plays.[105] He had always had bad teeth, and he had to give up the trumpet when most of them were extracted and replaced with dentures, which gave his smile a slightly leering quality at times.[106] Already in his second year, some of his friends had become concerned that he was too preoccupied with other projects and not giving enough time to reading medicine. As a solution, they persuaded him to join them on walking tours, alongside those he was already taking on Easter holidays, during which they focused on nothing but medicine.[107]

Either his friends needn't have worried or the walking tours worked as intended. Alex sat papers in Physiology, Anatomy, Biochemistry, Pathology, and Zoology for the Part I examinations for the Natural Science Tripos in Easter term 1940 and was awarded a First Class pass, resulting in a senior scholarship that allowed him to stay an extra year. The following year he sat papers in Pathology for the Part II examinations and earned an Upper Second Class pass. Why the falling off?

In that third year at Cambridge, Alex had begun to suffer what were much later found to be severe temporal-lobe migraines. The symptoms included paresthesia—a tickling, prickling sensation and numbness of the skin—and dream scintillations—expanding visual arcs of shining shapes or spots that appeared frequently, often when he was fatigued. He was spared the terrible headaches that usually follow such attacks but couldn't work when they struck—"it was quite disorganizing"—and occasionally, for the first time in his life, fell into episodes of depression. He pushed ahead with preparation for his exams and the writing of *No Such Liberty* with difficulty.

Alex would continue to suffer from the attacks, off and on, for the better part of two decades without a satisfactory diagnosis, along with sporadic depression. In the meanwhile, he gradually became accustomed to them, played them down in front of others, and got on with it, in the English fashion: among other strategies, by working more quickly and intensely in anticipation of an episode that might interrupt him.[108]

What kind of picture did he present to the world on leaving Cambridge to start clinical training? At twenty-one, Alex Comfort was a published novelist, a poet with a small but growing reputation, and an outstanding scholar, and he was preparing for what would certainly be a successful medical career. He continued to collect and study mollusks, although to what end few of his friends knew. His political views were developing in unpredictable directions, and he was growing more determined to incorporate them in his published work.

Physically, he was boyish-looking, slender and about average in height (five feet eight and a half), with brown eyes and a full head of straight brown hair, equipped with a mouthful of dentures and a pair of steel-rimmed glasses that gave him a suitably scholarly look. When he laughed or joked, his eyes twinkled and his mouth assumed a slightly ironic angle, softening the effect created by his damaged left hand. He had already built a reputation as a wit, a bottomless font of interesting if obscure knowledge, and a fine conversationalist. He was developing into a heavy smoker, and within a few years he would be consuming forty cigarettes a day plus smoking a pipe, which only in retrospect seems odd for a physician.[109] While he had few close friends, he could boast a wide circle of acquaintances who valued their connection with him, especially through poetry.

The inner circle of course included Ruth Muriel Harris, to whom *No Such Liberty* was dedicated and to whom he was now tacitly engaged. A note from Arthur Waugh on June 16 mentions, "[A mutual friend] met your lady and she is altogether charming. I was sure of it, without his experienced endorsement, and I wish you both luck with all my heart. I hope before long you will give me the chance of making her acquaintance."

Ruth was born February 1, 1917, in Loughton, a medium-sized community on the edge of Epping Forest and less than ten miles outside London: much like Alex's childhood home of New Barnet, but slightly less suburban. Her family were of somewhat higher social standing than the Comforts and Fenners; they would have abhorred co-operative societies, for example, as breeding grounds of Bolshevism.[110] But they too were essentially middle class and solidly Nonconformist. Ruth long thought, erroneously, that they were descended from French Huguenots, the Protestants who had been forced to leave France by Louis XIV.[111]

Her father, Alfred Harris, was a London printer and a Freemason. As a girl, her mother, Agnes Mabel Stevens, known as May, was said to have been rushed to Paris to be inoculated by Louis Pasteur himself when she was bitten by a possibly rabid dog. May's father, William Edward Stevens, could afford to send her as he was a director of Pickford's, the big moving and storage company. Both sides of Ruth's family were large and very religious. The Harrises were pillars of Loughton Union Church, a joint Congregational and Baptist assembly. William Stevens was a financial supporter of Sir Wilfred Grenfell, the medical missionary whose career had inspired Alex, and May was a hardline opponent of drink and gambling who worked tirelessly to instill her iron morality into her children and grandchildren.

Ruth's parents lived in Ivy Gate, a corner house near Loughton Station and five minutes from the Union Church. When she was four, however, Alfred died at fifty of throat cancer, leaving May with three children under five. Unable to cope with such a household, she decided that Ruth, the eldest, needed her least and sent her to live for a year with a family in Wickford, another Essex town not dissimilar from Loughton. "She was well-treated," her grandson recalled hearing, "but that separation left deep emotional scars."[112]

May moved to another, larger Loughton home, Little Gables, to which Ruth returned after her year away. At eleven she left home again to attend Kent College, a Christian school for girls at Folkstone on the Kentish coast. It was a much happier experience, and she remained there until she was eighteen. What the children were to do next, in the depths of the Depression, was not entirely clear. It was settled that her brother Stephen, who became Alex's friend at Cambridge, would go into the ministry, but Ruth and her sister Alison had no definite careers in front of them after they finished school. Alison went to work at Dr. Barnardo's Homes, a chain of orphanages, as a cook. Later she became a Cordon Bleu chef. Ruth spent a year at an establishment in Vevey, Switzerland, where she too learned to cook as well as speak French, but otherwise remained with her mother in the somewhat narrow confines of Little Gables, finally deciding, at twenty-two, that she wanted to do social work with children. She was accepted at London School of Economics but after war was declared was evacuated to Cambridge along with the rest of the student body.

Introduced to Alex by Stephen, Ruth was immediately attracted. "She recognized a man of excitement and promise who could take her out of the stifling world of Little Gables," their son later said.[113] In some respects they were an odd match—Alex affable and lively, Ruth quieter and more remote—but they came from similar social and religious backgrounds. Both loved music—Ruth had earlier entertained ambitions to become a concert pianist—and they were politically fairly compatible.

Like Alex's family, Ruth's fit the Old Dissenter pattern—"a mix of Labour, the Independent Labour Party, the Fabian Society, democratic socialism, and Nonconformism"—although Ruth herself, like her mother, stuck with the Liberals, the party of Gladstone.[*****] May was a

***** "A mix of Labour": interview with Nicholas Comfort, December 17, 2014; Nicholas Comfort, *Copy!*, 223. The ILP was the Labour Party's more radical rival and sometimes partner and an influential pressure group on the Left until after World War II.

lifelong supporter of Indian home rule; she could not abide Winston Churchill, MP for Epping, which then included Loughton, because of his passionate opposition. Indeed, Ruth was named partly after her mother's friend, neighbor, and fellow Union Church member, Muriel Lester, a well-known missionary, social reformer, and pacifist who, on her missionary travels, had met and worked with Gandhi. In 1931, when Gandhi came to London to attend the Second Roundtable Conference on the future of India, he stayed at Kingsley Hall, the settlement house that Muriel and her sister Doris ran in the East End. One day May was invited to tea with Gandhi and brought Alison with her but not Ruth, who was away at Kent College, for which circumstance she was "deeply envious."[114]

In Ruth, Alex saw an attractive, light-haired young woman with a beautiful profile who was attracted to him and not put off by his damaged hand. Someone whom he could idealize: a few years later he sculpted a plaster relief of Ruth in profile. One of his last contributions to *The Cambridge Review*, a poem titled "For Ruth," includes these lines:

The wind's prints in the corn
  Vary not more than you
As garments queenly worn
  Or subtle sculpture's flow. . . .

Though static beauty die,
  The corn at the wind's kiss
Will blow eternally
  Uncounted loveliness.

They did not have sex, however. Years later, Alex said categorically that he hadn't had any sexual experience before he was married. "A well-spent youth, rather than a more misspent youth," he added wryly, had left him with some "catching up to do."[115] Their son's recollections suggest that Ruth was not eager to get started; her more straitlaced upbringing and the disruption she had experienced after her father's death may have been factors. Under his mother's tutelage, Alex had grown up feeling always apart from other people, especially after his accident and disfigurement. It's possible that he fell in love not just with Ruth but also with the fact that she loved him.[116] For the time being, sex could wait.

CHAPTER 3

Poets and "Conchies" (1941–1942)

"I congratulate you on finding sanctuary at Billericay," Arthur Waugh wrote Alex on July 26, 1941. "I have never been there. I have never heard of anyone going there. I have often wondered why anyone went there." Billericay was (and is) a medium-sized Essex town some twenty miles northeast of London, not unlike the one Alex had grown up in. Local lore had it that the Pilgrims held their last meeting in England there prior to departing for North America in 1620. At the time, one inhabitant later recalled, parts of it still had "the Dickensian feel of a London still half countryfied, but with sordid crime around the corner."[1] It was also the location of St Andrew's Hospital, where Alex would spend his first year of clinical training after receiving his BA from Cambridge in June, at the end of his third year at university.

When Alex arrived at Billericay, armed with his Bachelor of Arts degree, he was embarking on a nomadic four-year stretch that would take him for clinical training to five different hospitals in the UK and Ireland, ending when he received his Bachelor of Medicine and Bachelor of Surgery degrees in 1944 and his Master of Arts from Cambridge the following year along with a license to practice from the Royal College of Physicians, membership in the Royal College of Surgeons, and a Diploma in Child Health from the London Hospital.

While his training kept him mostly in the immediate London area, the worst of the Blitzkrieg was over by the time he began, although German air raids still occurred sporadically. That, and the tremendous death and destruction it wrought—40,000-plus civilians killed and as many as 139,000 injured—meant that much of the training Alex received was on the job. "We were pitched straight into the deep end on our first clinical day," he later said. "At the end of the first month I think I knew more medicine than the people who qualify ordinarily do, because we had to do everything ourselves. So it was hands-on training, the kind you don't usually get in medicine."[2]

He was still getting financial help from his parents to eke out what little support he received through a scholarship from the London Hospital. But he had to use his wits to stay in food at a time when rationing was pinching most British households. Luckily, the countryside near Billericay afforded opportunities for foraging. Years later, Alex liked to tell of the day he went out with an air gun to shoot pigeons and marched down the street afterward with a chicken under one arm, having mistakenly shot a fowl roosting in a tree. And the time he took aim at what he thought was a rabbit, only to find he had nearly shot a napping American flier who had pulled his doubled-peaked cap down over his face. "Hey, bud, don't shoot!" the man pleaded.[3]

At about the same time he was settling in at Billericay—he had rented a room in the home of an elderly vicar and his wife—Alex was meeting in London with Walker and Gatfield at Chapman & Hall about his next projects.[4] He already had a one-act play and a longer collection of poems in hand and was deep into writing his second novel.

In writings he produced in his twenties, Alex would work out many of the ideas and positions—on politics, literature and art, human and sexual behavior—that he would espouse for the rest of his life. Years later, he liked to say that everything he did was part of one large project. He sketched the outline of that project, and quite a bit of the detail, in the decade after he left Cambridge.

ALEX WAS INSULATED FROM wartime service on two counts—his missing fingers and the government's decision not to take scientific and medical students out of school—but he insisted on applying and appearing before a tribunal to put his views as a conscientious objector on record.[5] Cambridge friends who had identified as pacifists had tougher decisions to make. Both Nick Moore and John Bayliss, another aspiring poet who had been at St Catherine's College, had registered as COs and were put to work by the Cambridgeshire War Agricultural Committee, a component of the system established to increase agricultural production, which for them meant hedging, digging ditches, and clearing land for more planting.[6]

All of them, including Alex and Bayliss's friend Derek Stanford, another young writer who soon joined the Non-Combatant Corps, continued to find time to write and contribute poetry to the little magazines that were springing up in the early months and years of the war. What set Alex apart was the volume of writing he produced and got published, the degree to which it expressed—increasingly—his feelings about war, violence, and death, and his willingness to challenge wartime opinion.

A year earlier, still at Cambridge, Alex had written a play in verse and prose, *Cities of the Plain*, subtitled *A Democratic Melodrama*, about a mining community dominated by a business syndicate with the connivance of the municipal government and the local clergy.[7] The miners are sent down into a mountain to dig an ore that destroys their health. Led by a local doctor, the miners go on strike, joined by workers in other trades, and, at just about the same time, the mountain explodes. The combination destroys the town's old social order and places power in the hands of the workers. What will they do with it?

The play provides the first hint that Alex's politics was leaning in the direction of anarchism. The general strike was the central strategy of anarcho-syndicalists, the branch of the movement that concentrated its activism on organized labor. Many of his prospective readers would have had vivid memories of the 1926 miners' strike in Britain and the general strikes that followed in the United States during the Depression. But a play apotheosizing the general strike was not a commercial choice in a country engaged in all-out war with fascism. Alex took *Cities of the Plain* to the Unity Theatre, a company in the East End that specialized in proletarian dramas with a strong agitprop element and that had ties to the Left Book Club and Britain's Communist Party. Just as Alex was settling in at Billericay, Unity agreed to stage it in September 1941 and put it into rehearsal.

Then came the German invasion of Russia in June. Quickly Unity Theatre's policy changed. Now that Stalin's pact with Hitler was no more, Churchill's government quickly formed an alliance with the Soviet dictator, and, from a Communist perspective, capitalist Britain was now necessary to protect the Marxist-Leninist project in Russia. Unity Theatre's management asked Alex to make "certain changes" in his text, and he agreed.

Cities of the Plain certainly qualified as proletarian drama, even if its politics was not specifically Marxist, but in August management changed its mind. They wrote Alex again, informing him that while they still regarded it as "a remarkably good play," they had "taken soundings in the matter" among the people who formed their audiences. "We have been forced to conclude that *Cities*, now, would not have a favourable reception."

> [With the British and Soviet governments collaborating], it has become gradually more obvious that the same collaboration between classes of a specific purpose is necessary within this country, and that the dominant section of our capitalists . . . are fulfilling an objectively progressive role. Consequently, the whole trend of progressive propaganda in this country has been undergoing a change. . . . There is no doubt that however [the audience] may interpret the symbolism of Cities, it will take its message (as related to current events which it will inevitably do) to be not Open up the Western Front, but come back from the front and deal with your capitalists.[8]

Alex had had no idea that he was supposed to be writing "propaganda," and the rejection stung. "They were utterly hopeless at interpreting it in any case," he complained to the poet Henry Treece.[9] He cast about for other ways to get his play produced and published and to draw attention to his poetry, trying to drum up interest in establishing a new "group theater" in London along the lines of the similarly named collective in New York and proposing to the Royal Academy of Dramatic Art that it launch a poetry society that would give public readings.[10] Neither idea caught fire. He was also intent on getting a bigger audience for the poetry that he and his circle were turning out. "I have been putting in some work in the *Horizon* office trying to convert [Cyril] Connolly—who seems quite a decent chap—to your work and mine," he reported to Treece on October 17, "but not very successfully."

Another important figure he appealed to was Herbert Read—poet, art critic and tastemaker, an editor at George Routledge & Sons, and the UK's best-known anarchist at the time—to whom he sent a copy of the play along with a batch of poems in September. Having "no contacts in the theatrical world," Read had to decline to help him with *Cities of the Plain*, and, while he liked the poems, suggested that Alex try to get them published in pamphlet form and inquire again when he had more to offer.[11]

At about the same, however, Alex was getting pushback from another quarter. Chapman & Hall and Arthur Waugh were still keen to publish him, but he was testing their limits with his second novel. With *The Almond Tree: A Legend*, he made another attempt at a historical romance, this time concerning a time and place nearer to his own. The poet Edwin Muir's review of the book said that it attempts to "give a picture of the disintegration of life in Europe between 1910 and 1920," and this is about right. It was also a longer and more ambitious work than *No Such Liberty*. Alex himself said years later that its structure "probably owes more to *Anthony Adverse* than to any more substantial model," and its loose, circular storyline does resemble Hervey Allen's 1933 blockbuster historical novel.[12] He also referred to it as his "Russian novel," and it has something like the dense philosophical underpinning of a novel by Dostoevski.

The protagonists are a Polish family running a farm and vineyard in the Rhineland, headed by a domineering patriarch named Pyotr. The lives of his grandchildren during the upheaval of the First World War provide the substance of the story. The oldest, Yelisaveta, works in the household of a wealthy Paris couple, Monsieur and Madame Roux. Fyodor enrolls in a military academy, becomes a sailor, and finally dies on a lemon plantation in South America. Serge is a philosophy student in Bonn before being drafted into the German Army, and Theresa is married to a German farmer who now runs the vineyard. After the war and Pyotr's death, Serge, badly wounded and now disabled, and Yeli, whose lover has died fighting on the French side, return to the farm and attempt to start new lives there.

Although published during the next global war, *The Almond Tree* carries something of the romantic disillusionment of World War I novels like Hemingway's *A Farewell to Arms*. Serge encounters the horrors of war, and Yeli is preyed on by the sexually ambiguous Madame Roux. When Serge confesses to Yeli that he had deserted the army, he says, "It wasn't running away that spoiled me. It was knowing that you could run away and it didn't matter. I've found what I wanted to know. It doesn't matter what one does. Anything is as good as anything else. I was always afraid I should find that out, but I hoped my mind would not let me believe it." "What is going to happen when other people find out? Yeli asks. "That's why I daren't go on writing," Serge replies. "Everyone will find out. And then hell will break loose."[13]

Earlier, Serge tells the woman he will later marry, "I've only found two certainties—things you can't reach and things you can't avoid. The inevitable and the unattainable." The inevitable is death and the unattainable is "knowing what to do next and why to do it."[14] God is not a real presence in Alex's characters' lives. Between the writing of his first novel, with its Christian-pacifist hero, and his second, he had lost his religious faith. The change was not dramatic, and he never explained what line of reasoning led him to abandon a conviction that had been an important part of his life—and his life planning—during his formative years. Later he would attribute it partly to his "encounter with medicine," and the "death, suffering, and mayhem" he found himself facing for the first time, but he did not elaborate.[15]

In *The Almond Tree* he attempted to work out the questions that followed from a loss of absolute values and the realization of the absoluteness of death, cultural changes he felt had been overtaking European society since 1914. Was this understanding the cause of social disintegration or the outcome? Alex suggested that his characters' troubles, and perhaps by extension society's, stemmed in part from the overly repressive environment in which they grew up. In Fyodor's case, the problem is compounded by time spent in a sadistic military academy. He has sexual feelings for his sister as well as vaguely homosexual longings.

The Almond Tree offers a set of characters who have reached an impasse: a point of absolute defeat. Although Alex never stated this explicitly, the novel can also be read as a thematic prequel to *No Such Liberty*, in which the horrors experienced by the Polish family help to explain Breitz's reluctance to become politically engaged when the Nazis again push Europe toward war. When the family's remaining members gather around the eponymous tree in the last chapter, it doesn't stand as a refuge but rather as "an imminent black cloud. . . . There was never going to be anywhere but this, now. . . . Darkness was a progressive thing."[16] These are almost the last words of a very grim novel.

Alex finished it in October and sent it immediately to Arthur Waugh, who found it "a much more significant work" than *No Such Liberty*. "Indeed, in workmanship, in literary vitality, and (especially) in atmosphere, it is the most impressive thing I have read for a long time." Waugh found the symbolism confusing, however, and feared that one scene, in which Madame Roux attempts to force Yeli into bed with her, could damage the book's commercial prospects. Nothing is described explicitly, and it would probably not create trouble with the censors, Waugh believed. "[But] if the libraries jump to its implication, they will most probably ban the book."[17]

Waugh's colleagues at Chapman & Hall agreed that the scene could hinder the novel's sales, he told Alex, especially "if mischievously quoted by unsympathetic and myopic critics."[18] Ruth too urged him to cut or eliminate it, but, since it was unlikely to encounter trouble with the military censors, Alex stood his ground.[19]

Chapman & Hall conceded the point and remained enthusiastic about the book, but they would indulge their young prodigy only so far. In a December 6 letter, Waugh noted that all publishers were "being seriously mauled about under war-conditions," particularly due to the cost and availability of paper. And he mentioned that *No Such Liberty* had still not sold one thousand copies. Further, "They have taken the book off the weekly returns as being at the end of its tether."

Publication of *The Almond Tree* was scheduled for the following June. But Alex's first novel, despite sluggish sales, was not yet done with him. In the fall, he offered a story to *New Vision*, a little magazine connected to a publishing house of the same name owned and operated by Geoffrey Pittock-Buss, a journalist who was also a supporter of the Indian Freedom Campaign. He received a letter acknowledging his submission from Pittock-Buss's wife, Ilse, a Jewish refugee from Germany. She had read *No Such Liberty*, she wrote, and found it the best account of the plight of refugees who had fled to the UK—better, in some respects, than nonfiction accounts.

George Orwell, who published a late review of the novel in *Adelphi* in October—and who had studied at Eton with A. S. F. Gow, later Alex's tutor at Cambridge—saw the book very differently. Orwell was not yet the towering figure in literature and political thought he would become after the publication of *Animal Farm* and *Nineteen Eighty-Four*. Arguably, he only attained that status in the decade after his death. But for some years he had been a much-published novelist, critic, and commentator, well-connected in the cultural media that Alex was finding his way into. Before the war, he too had been something of a pacifist, despite the danger he knew that fascism represented.

After the German invasion of Poland, however, Orwell changed his mind. He resigned from the Independent Labour Party, which was still advocating resistance to war, and wrote to the authorities offering to serve.[20] In August 1941 he took a job producing cultural talks and news broadcasts for the BBC's Eastern Service.

He was not the only one to abruptly switch positions. Alex remained a pacifist, and an estimated 150,000 to 175,000 Britons were members of one or another absolute pacifist group in 1940, many out of religious conviction. But many of their former comrades began to embrace the war, when it came, as a just struggle in defense of civilization. Longtime and well-known peace campaigners such as the popular philosopher, writer, and lecturer C. E. M. Joad, Labour MP Philip Noel-Baker, Bertrand Russell, Rose Macauley, and Storm Jameson, the novelist and president of English PEN, publicly renounced pacifism in 1940.[21]

Once he had committed himself to the war, Orwell seemed to lose all tolerance for those who didn't share his new position. Everywhere, and not always with a firm basis, he saw defeatism and thinly disguised sympathy with the enemy. His lengthy review of *No Such Liberty* classified Alex's novel as a propaganda tract for this point of view.[22] "It is a good novel as novels go at this moment, but," he argued, "the motive for writing it was not what Trollope or Balzac, or even Tolstoy, would have recognized as a novelist's impulse. It was written in order to put forward the 'message' of pacifism, and it was to fit that 'message' that the main incidents in it were devised." The story Alex tells is a plea for "turn-the-other-cheek pacifism," which "only flourishes among the more prosperous classes, or among workers who have in some way escaped from their own class." Breitz, its protagonist, is able to maintain "his attitude of moral superiority" and contemplate emigrating to the United States only because "people who have money and guns" are protecting him.

Alex was practicing a spurious form of moral equivalency, a "highbrow variant of British hypocrisy," Orwell argued. "The sufferings of his German doctor in a so-called democratic country are so terrible, he implies, as to wipe out every shred of moral justification for the struggle against Fascism." It would be more courageous if the author of *No Such Liberty*, like the collaborationist French leaders Laval and Darlan, simply came out in support of a German victory than to assert that "you can somehow defeat violence by simply submitting to it." Echoing the argument that Stalin had once made about socialists who didn't adhere to the Communist line, Orwell concluded with a chilling logic: "Objectively the pacifist is pro-Nazi."

One of Orwell's many talents as a polemicist was the ability to write seemingly in a white heat while still developing a coherent argument. But in this instance, his zeal to make a case against pacifism seemed to overwhelm his comprehension of the book he was reading. While the main character of *No Such Liberty* is a pacifist, as was the author, the novel itself is not; it ends with no clear path forward for Breitz or for anyone concerned with the impact the war was having on civilized life. And while it spotlights the government's poor treatment of refugees, it does not imply any moral equivalence between Britain and Germany; it only points up abuses that war makes inevitable and warns against the possibility that Britain could resort to conduct like the Nazis'. Nor does it make an argument against resisting Nazism, especially for people living under it.

If this very searching novel had any propagandistic point, it was to refute two other assertions that Orwell happened to make: that "civilization rests ultimately on coercion" and that "we only have the chance of choosing the lesser evil." Preserving civilization depends instead on resisting coercion and rejecting false choices between two evils. Whatever course Breitz takes, implicitly it will be one that follows these principles.[23]

"I'd like to have started an argument over that review of yours," Alex wrote Orwell some months later, "but the Adelphi hadn't room to unleash me." Orwell's attitude toward conscientious objectors was common in the early years of the war. COs suffered much less abuse than they had during World War I, and there were many more of them; some 16,000 people had registered as such in Britain's last big conflict, but almost four times as many—62,301—would register between 1939 and 1945.[24] And while many of the movement's most prominent figures had renounced pacifism, many persevered, including Vera Brittain, the sculptor and printmaker Eric Gill, actress Sybil Thorndike, suffragist Sybil Morrison, and May Harris's old friend Muriel Lester, who made Kingsley Hall a hub for pacifist activity. While the PPU lost members, it survived, and continued to publish *Peace News* straight through the war.[25/*]

"Conchies" and others seen as shirking their duties were stigmatized, however. W. H. Auden and Christopher Isherwood, who opted to spend the war in the United States, came in for bitter criticism. While some pacifists had already set up rural settlements in the '30s, many others, like Alex's friends Nick Moore and John Bayliss, were forced to attempt the country life despite having no knowledge of farming and found themselves working on the land at tasks for which they were lamentably ill-suited amid locals who made them distinctly unwelcome.

When conscientious objectors sought roles in fire brigades and ambulance services, they encountered resentment from—or on behalf of—veterans of the last war. In June 1940, more than fifty local government entities, including the London County Council, banned employment of pacifists in all civil defense positions. Eventually, however, the level of emergency and the shortage of labor was such that the national government forced them to reverse themselves and accept pacifists.[26]

Alex never suffered the extreme hostility that some other pacifists did, and he could be said to have done his part. The PPU approved of pacifists engaging in relief work, and Alex served as a fire watcher at a location between Billericay and Brentwood during his medical training, standing duty to report small fires caused by air raids.[27] Later in the war

* "That ambiguous organization which in the name of peace was performing many actions certain to benefit Hitler," Rebecca West wrote of the PPU in the 1950 first edition of her book *The Meaning of Treason*.

he would treat victims of the German V-1 and V-2 missiles or "buzz bombs," a terrifying early breed of cruise missile. But, like many Britons, seemingly his entire extended family were affected by the war, and in a variety of ways.

His father also fire-watched, from the roof of the LCC headquarters building, and organized protection for London's schools. His cousin Joe Gardiner, Elizabeth's sister Gertrude's son, entered family lore for having killed a German with a spade at the Battle of Arnhem.** Another cousin, John Fenner, died in action with the RAF, while still another, Ken Comfort, commanded a detachment of West African troops in Burma. Ruth, for her part, had a brother-in-law, an army medic, killed at Arnhem, and a cousin, Alfred Sadd, a missionary in the Gilbert & Ellice Islands, who was executed by the Japanese occupiers for refusing to venerate the Japanese flag.[28] On the other hand, her brother Stephen, Alex's friend, was a fellow conchie.***

Critics including Orwell would continue to scrutinize Alex's writing for traces of pacifist sentiment, but that was not the case with *The Almond Tree*, which appeared in June 1942. The novel was widely reviewed—including in the *Manchester Guardian*, the *Spectator*, the *Daily Telegraph*, the *Times Literary Supplement*, and the BBC's weekly magazine, *The Listener*—and the critics' judgments were mostly respectful. The prominent critic—and Dylan Thomas's editor—Richard Church, was one of the most enthusiastic. In the literary magazine *John O'London's Weekly*, he declared Alex "a deliberate and fully conscious artist, who knows exactly what he is doing and why he is doing it." "[*The Almond Tree* is] full of intensely vivid scenes that show the writer's ability to project himself into the observed world. . . . I could say a lot more about this interesting writer. I'll wait for his next book."[29] The *Daily Telegraph* called the book a "sombre novel" of "remarkable power," and the eminent novelist and critic Frank Swinnerton, in the *Observer*, said it held "much promise."

But other critics found *The Almond Tree* too loosely structured; the stories of the grandchildren failed to hang together, and the text was overloaded with "quantities of descriptive details to little apparent

** Decades later, Joe Gardiner told his daughter not to have anything to do with Alex, since Alex had been a "conchie": this when she was attending the University of London and Alex was a fellow at University College London, one of its member institutions. Alex and Joe later reconciled. Nicholas Comfort, email to author, September 27, 2021.

*** Some twenty years later, Stephen would confide in Alex's son Nick that he regretted refusing to serve. Nicholas Comfort, *Copy!*, 453–54.

purpose" (*TLS*). Most praised the writing and the descriptive power of some passages, such as the death of old Pyotr, but few, during wartime, found its underlying theme of impasse and indecision very compelling, and none drew the desired connection with the current political situation. Most disappointing was the prominent poet and translator Edwin Muir's review in *The Listener*. While the novel was "a work of original imagination," he said, he found the story "unconvincing" and showing "signs of immaturity."[30]

Sales were little better than for *No Such Liberty*; only 770 copies of *The Almond Tree* had moved by mid-July. "I suppose it is quite understandable that, at the present time, the reading public should be demanding light, cheerful fiction," Gatfield wrote Alex from Chapman & Hall. "Your novel certainly does not come in that category and that, I think is the reason why the sales are so low."[31] While a darkly serious novel set in the urgent present might arguably have done better, clearly neither the critics nor the reading public were enthusiastic about one that attempted to conjure up a mood that was now two decades in the past.

THE JACKET-FLAP COPY FOR *The Almond Tree* touted it as "the first significant prose production of a young school of Welsh and English poets . . . at once realistic and symbolic." As this suggests, Alex had found a group of writers with whom he shared some common ground aside from university affiliation. As he later told the tale, it began shortly after he moved into his rented quarters in Billericay and was walking to his training at St Andrew's Hospital.

Along the High Street was an old house called Grey Walls, part of a larger structure that also included a Temperance Hotel; in it lived a modestly well-off widow ("formidable, blind," Alex remembered) and her forty-year-old son, Charles Wrey Gardiner, a writer and fledgling publisher.[32] After a couple of very checkered decades that included a great deal of travel, two failed marriages and many casual relationships, a couple of poetry collections, and an autobiography, Gardiner had taken over *Poetry Quarterly*, a magazine originally published by an ex–military officer that accepted virtually anything submitted, mostly stodgily traditional Victorianesque verse. Gardiner wanted to do something more ambitious, but his natural indolence got in the way.

Gardiner's mother had converted a front room of the house into a small antique shop, and her son turned it into a bookshop where he sold his magazine as well as secondhand books, some from his collection.[33] He also published books under the imprint Grey Walls Press. One day in 1940, seventeen-year-old Denise Levertov, who lived in neighboring Ilford and had just begun a job as a nurse at St Andrew's, stopped in and introduced herself. *Poetry Quarterly* soon published Levertov's first poem, "Listening to Distant Guns."[34] Later that year, in the Autumn issue, Gardiner published Alex's appropriately seasonal "Set on the Autumn Head," and the following April Gardiner informed Alex that he had won the magazine's Guinea Award for best poem of the preceding year.[35] Making the actual selection was Samuel Looker, a poet and editor who had been a conscientious objector during World War I and was now publishing with Grey Walls.[36]

When Alex was posted to St Andrew's, Gardiner recalled,

> He at once came to see me at Grey Walls. He said he had always thought of me as a grey bearded old gentleman, probably a vicar. He often looked in during the late afternoons and sat smoking a pipe. He explained that he felt rather sick after dissecting cadavers. One day I talked to him about my editorial policy of printing both the older writers and the young. He was standing behind my editorial chair, a high Jacobean one belonging to my mother. He was picking his nose.
>
> "Can't be done," he said in his laconic manner. "You should back the younger generation."
>
> He had not long been down from Cambridge and he gave me some MSS of his friends there. I realized that he was right. The war between the older generation of poets and the young was almost as bitter as the fighting in the sky above my head.[37]

Alex showed Gardiner a one-act prose drama, *Into Egypt: A Miracle Play*, a wartime variation on the story of the Nativity that he had written for the Adelphi Players, a company associated with both *Adelphi* magazine and the PPU, as well as a collection of poems. Both of these he had offered Chapman & Hall to no interest. The proprietor of Grey Walls agreed to publish the play, and it appeared in January to few and brief but positive reviews. (It also appears to have been produced at least once, in Italy in 1945, by a troupe made up of British soldiers on occupation duty led by Peter Laven, a private from South London who later became a historian of Renaissance Italy.)[38] Meanwhile, Alex was peppering Gardiner with ideas for new books. One was an anthology of mostly younger poets that would stand as a challenge to the school that had dominated the British scene in the '30s and that he quickly set to work on with Robert Greacen, a poet from Northern Ireland the same age as he.

What was so "bitter" about the fighting Gardiner had detected? Poetry during the Depression in the UK was a diverse scene, ranging from William Butler Yeats, the reigning deity, and T. S. Eliot, a powerful figure as an editor at Faber & Faber, to Robert Graves, Dylan Thomas, Lawrence Durrell, and the young Surrealist David Gascoyne. But the most innovative and most widely acclaimed group centered around four poets who had all attended Oxford in the 1920s: W. H. Auden, Stephen Spender, Louis MacNeice, and Cecil Day-Lewis. The "Thirties Poets," or MacSpaunday, as the somewhat older poet Roy Campbell called them, wrote partly in reaction to Eliot and others of the Lost Generation after World War I who seemed to retreat from politics or take a culturally conservative line. The Auden group's writing had a strong personal element and was more accessible stylistically but also exhibited a kind of classical formalism and often reflected their leftist politics. Spender and Auden were vocal supporters of the Spanish Republic against Franco's fascists, and Day-Lewis was briefly a Communist Party member.

The Thirties Poets also engendered a certain amount of resentment, partly because of the degree of critical success they enjoyed, and in part due to anti-gay prejudice against Auden and some other members of his circle, including Christopher Isherwood. The determinedly working-class Orwell fulminated against "nancy poets" from Oxford and Cambridge and "parlour Bolsheviks such as Auden and Spender."[39] Others, younger and less homophobic, were simply looking for a less austere and restricted approach than they perceived in the movement then current. "What we wanted," Nick Moore later said, "was a more adventurous, less exclusive kind of poetry, richer and more varied in language and ideas."[40]

The first poets who made a play to challenge the Auden school were a group calling themselves the New Apocalypse, whose leaders, the Welsh Henry Treece and the Scottish J. F. Hendry, published a manifesto in 1938 and an anthology the following year. Before their movement burned itself out around the end of World War II, the Apocalyptics explained themselves in multiple ways, but their initial impulse was a reaction to modernism: a return to a less cerebral, more emotional approach that jumbled up myth and Surrealism in the service of what Hendry vaguely called "the war for justice to man, to prevent his becoming an object as in abstract art or the Totalitarian State."[41]

Another model was the prophetic poems of William Blake, and the Apocalyptics drew much of their critical inspiration as well as their name from D. H. Lawrence's *Apocalypse*, with its celebration of instinct and the senses over reason and intellect.[42] "The sensibility boys who think with their stomach," was how Frank Thompson, a Communist and army intelligence officer, described these new poets in 1943 to his then-inamorata Iris Murdoch.

Treece campaigned especially loudly for the movement and constantly reached out to poets who might want to jump aboard. In all, three New Apocalypse anthologies were published, and the contributors included Alex, Dylan Thomas, Wrey Gardiner, Nick Moore, Vernon Watkins, and Norman McCaig. Not all of these poets fit easily into Treece's blurry cultural project, but most of them had some sympathy with Treece and Hendry's perception of the zeitgeist at the beginning of a cataclysmic new war: a sense that the world was again going to hell and that the poet's mission was to set about rebuilding it.

Alex's own models in those days, he would recall, were not Treece and his friends but the Cuban Romantic poet José María Heredia and the Greek and Roman classics, whom, he said, he "set about de-classicizing, . . . aiming . . . for a richer timbre and a more luminous effect."[43] In a larger sense, however, most of the younger poets with whom he published—Apocalyptics and others—had a common project, which he described thusly:

> It was a deliberate literary movement, its sources were literary—chiefly the awareness, based on discussion, that the poetic style of the 30's had run out of steam, and we needed to try a different idiom. What we picked was a combination of the individual style of Dylan Thomas, who wrote off the top of his head, with the tradition of [the Elizabethan poet Edmund] Spenser (Treece in particular), and some borrowings from surrealism. The idea was to remagicalize poetry, rather as the 30's had repoliticized it.[44]

Grey Walls provided a nonexclusive focal point for these new poets, presided over by the enigmatic Gardiner, older than most of the people he was publishing, "an essentially introspective being though provided with a rare gargoyle wit," as Derek Stanford recalled. Gardiner looked nothing like the image of an avant-garde poet and publisher. The first time Stanford encountered him, he beheld "a quiet-looking man in a near double-breasted brown suit who carried both those emblems of a

City gent, a small suitcase and an umbrella." In action, however, Alex remembered him as "a natural hippie before his time and in his own way."[45] Once Alex had pushed him beyond the stage of accepting everything submitted, Gardiner envisaged Grey Walls as publishing not for the general public but for an audience of poets. "He tended to divide mankind into two opposing camps between which, he thought, there could be little trafficking," Stanford noted: "the camp of the philistines, vast and vulgar; and the camp of the creators, small but select. This sense of hordes of the artistically indifferent sharpened his fear and contempt at times into misanthropy."[46]

Above all, Gardiner was an aesthete, devoted to literature and art as an escape from the unpleasantness of life. As such, he was given to solipsistic statements like the following: "The group soul is a form of death by spiritual asphyxia. . . . To be alone and to be other than the others with my own reality is all my endeavour." As this suggests, he was not an outstanding businessperson, but he had a collection of poets working for or with Grey Walls at various times who proved surprisingly competent. Besides Alex, who never actually drew a salary, the key players included Frederic Marnau, an anti-Nazi, Czech-born Austro-Hungarian with "dark hair, large sad dark eyes, a dark visage, and a black velour hat," who wrote in German and hung drawings by his friend Oskar Kokoschka in his flat;[47] Sean Jennett, another poet, a "first-rate typographer" and demanding editor;[48] and Alex's Cambridge friend Nick Moore.

"Being out of a job," Moore recalled, "my mother-in-law, an influential person in many ways through her family connections, bought me into [the firm] to learn about publishing."[49] As part of his deal to join Grey Walls, Nick insisted that it move to a less remote location. Gardiner agreed, and they transferred out of his house and into a loft in Vernon Place, near Bloomsbury, although group meetings would often be held at the Olympus, a modest restaurant a short distance away at the corner of Southampton Row.[50]

In the new office, Nick would sit typing out poetry as if it was news copy, Gardiner wrote a few years later. "[He gave] me a poem the length of one of Eliot's Quartets every morning, and each one more curious and eccentric than the last, smoking his pipe of scented tobacco or black gold-tipped Russian cigarettes." Alex, the youngest of the lot, fit in well with this eccentric crew. "His pale face under that appalling beret, his mackintosh, make Alex one of the most curious figures of our time, the heroic toreador of the mad bull of contemporary society," Gardiner described him in a typically purple passage. "It is in him more than in any writer of my time that I have discovered the light of the heart shining and clear like a fisherman's lantern hung over the bows and dipping but steady in the black emptiness of the bay."[51]

As soon as he could persuade Gardiner to let him do so, Alex set about completely redesigning *Poetry Quarterly* to give it a more contemporary look, including switching the typeface to Bodoni, "then becoming fashionable," Gardiner recalled. "The magazine was now full of young poets making a name for themselves. I was printing G. S. Fraser, Norman Nicholson, Alex Comfort, Henry Treece and Nicholas Moore. My early amateur days were over. The circulation had risen from 250 to 500. It was beginning to sell and was now solidly established."[52]

Alex's first job with Grey Walls was to coedit *Lyra: An Anthology of New Lyric* with Robert Greacen. Along with their own verse, it included contributions from Moore, Treece, Watkins, John Bayliss, Roy McFadden (a friend of Greacen's from Belfast), Emanuel Litvinoff (a former conscientious objector then in the service), and Norman Nicholson, an older poet with a more religious bent whom Eliot too was publishing at Faber & Faber.

Alex and Greacen sensed that Herbert Read would be sympathetic to their project and that a preface from Read, an arbiter in both modern art and poetry, would certainly get their anthology noticed. "Alex went to the table, took out a sheet of paper, and just wrote to Read in a few minutes," Greacen recalled. "It would have taken me hours to do that, because I was 22 and writing to a very distinguished man. But Alex just dashed it off, brilliantly."[53]

Read agreed, and his preface to *Lyra* sums up where the Grey Walls poets fit in the British poetry scene of the preceding three decades. Modernists like Eliot and Ezra Pound had responded to "a crumbling civilization" in the wake of World War I with work that "destroyed pretty effectively the prevailing poetic conventions, the Parnassian conventions of the Georgians." They were succeeded by "a younger generation," typified by Auden, "who were also experimentalists, but . . . could concentrate on political and cultural conventions." However, "by the end of the Spanish Civil War, the poetry of action had fought its last ditch." Something new was needed, something "reconstructive." Some of the *Lyra* poets had enlisted, but, Read wrote, "I feel that they are all pacifists in the poetic sense. . . . They have realized that even in the midst of war this reconstructive effort must be made, and their poetry is therefore projected into the new world which has to be created out of the ruins of our civilization."

To illustrate, Read invited the reader to turn to one of Alex's contributions, "The Atoll in the Mind," then and now his most widely admired poem.

> Out of what calm and pools the cool shell grows
> dumb teeth under clear waters, where no currents
> fracture the coral's porous horn
>
> Grows up the mind's stone tree, the honeycomb,
> the plumb brain coral breaking the water's mirror,
> the ebony antler, the cold sugared fan.
>
> All these strange trees stand upward through the water,
> the mind's grey candied points tend to the surface,
> the greater part is out of sight below.
>
> But when on the island's whaleback spring green blades
> new land over water wavers, birds bring seeds
> and tides plant slender trunks by the lagoon
>
> I find the image of the mind's two trees, cast downward,
> one tilting leaves to catch the sun's bright pennies,
> one dark as water, rooted in the bones.

Alex turned to nature, this time to a coral atoll, to express his hope that something strange, new, and fecund could arise from the destruction of war. In this short lyric, Read wrote, "a beautiful metaphor, perfectly controlled and extended, describes with poetic subtlety the essential nature of this recovery."[54] *Lyra* was published in the spring of 1942. Cyril Connolly, reviewing it in the *Observer*, found much of the collection "involved and pretentious" but singled out "The Atoll in the Mind" as "beautiful, subtle, and complete."[55]

Possibly because it had drawn the attention of the editor of *Horizon*, the most influential cultural publication in the UK in the '40s, *Lyra* was also reviewed later in the year in *Partisan Review*, in some ways *Horizon*'s counterpart in the United States. The critic was Clement Greenberg, not yet the art tsar of postwar New York and still writing a great deal about literature, poetry in particular. He found the anthology a mixed bag and even the best of the contributors "very uneven" but singled out "Little Black Box," by Nick Moore, as "one of the most original poems of our age" (although, he added, Moore "is quite bad when he is not good"). About Alex, he wrote, "[Comfort] has the self-confidence and the sense of what he can and cannot do that usually belongs only to older poets. . . . He has a good chance of becoming a major and serious writer."[56]

Despite his reservations, Greenberg saw a lot of promise in these younger British poets, and he understood the characteristics that set them apart from the previous crop, while betraying a degree of homophobia. "Abandoning the positions won by Auden's so-called classicist movement, they are in retreat toward a purer and more personal poetry, are all for neater verse, traditional simplicities, descriptions, emotions in the presence of nature, intimate events and their own love affairs—heterosexual at last." While Greenberg worried that Alex and his comrades might not be ambitious enough, too much inclined to stop short of Auden rather than surpass him, he concluded, "I share the premonitions of a poetic renaissance which Herbert Read gets from the work of these English poets. Much talent is abroad in them, talent enough to defy all remonstrances."

Such words encouraged Alex to try again to get his first full collection published. "It is my ambition," he had told Treece, "to produce a collection representing the revolt of art in this country from war and bloodshed—a kind of prophetic memorial to show that someone at least spoke out."[57] Treece showed Alex's poems to M. J. T. Tambimuttu, the brilliant Sri Lankan editor who in 1938, at age twenty-two, had founded *Poetry London*—allegedly on "a subsidy from an artistic margarine manufacturer"—which quickly became one of the best regarded publications of its type in the UK.[58] Tambi liked Alex's work as well but said that his list was full at present,[59] although he had already published an earlier, longer version of "The Atoll in the Mind," titled "Out of What Calms."[60]

Alex's poetry was appearing more and more often, however, mainly in little magazines but also in anthologies. Kathleen Raine, the poet and Blake scholar, singled him out in her review in the *Manchester Guardian* of another Grey Walls collection, *Three New Poets*.[61] He also contributed a lightly fictionalized prose piece, "Saturday Night," to the summer 1942 edition of John Lehmann's anthology series *New Writing and Daylight*, describing a late-night emergency operation at St Andrew's in which he participated as the "anaesthetics clerk."

The prose in this piece is impeccable and assured, and Alex's account vividly reveals a corner of the world in which he was spending the majority of his time. It is also full of a slightly outrageous humor new to him. The patient, he writes, "might be anything from a J.P. to a retired railwayman, and hanging out of the coat pocket on the locker is the sort of watch chain one associates with a successful trade unionist." The surgical team get their share of deft lightning caricature as well.

> The R.S.O. has got in by the other door, and I can see him, his mask tied over his face, putting on a red rubber apron like a shoemaker. Operating gowns disguise man, like sobriety. Brian, who is short and fat, invariably looks like a cook, not a surgeon, and the aurist, with his little forehead light, like an aseptic Wicked Uncle, who perpetually rubs his gloved hands as if washing them. The R.S.O. has a scowl like a chorister which shows round the ends of the mask, and Catherine has a Ku Klux Klan hood which only shows her eyes and the bulges of her two breasts underneath.

Always in the background is the anxious state of alert pervading every corner of London and its environs. "We cannot hear our local siren because of the wind, and our patients sleep through most alerts, which is as well, seeing that the jet of water from the mains isn't tall enough to reach the incendiaries which fall on the roofs of the [hospital] huts." A final twist punches home the insistent way the grimness of normal life could intrude on the grimness of the war in a hospital setting.

Desmond McCarthy, Britain's leading literary critic, praised "Saturday Night" for its "most remarkable realistic precision." "Realism of such genuine intensity is not attained without something of the poet's gift. . . . If he can tell a story . . . he will go right to the top."[62] Alex's prose was taking other paths too, including art criticism in *Horizon*; a favorable review of a new collection of Joyce's prose, selected by Eliot—perhaps hoping to catch the grandee's attention—in *Tribune*; and a flurry of letters to various publications defending his group of younger poets. He also persuaded Gardiner to let him and another young poet, Peter Wells, launch a new series, *Poetry Folios: A Periodical of Creative Verse*, with Roderic Barrett, a fellow conscientious objector and an aspiring young painter, as art editor. The first installment included poems by Treece, Hendry, Moore, Bayliss, Tambimuttu, and Watkins, along with Alex's first overtly erotic poem, "The Lovers."

His stature, at least for the moment, seemed to be growing more quickly than other young poets', but he was also making an effort to promote them and the loosely defined movement they were beginning to form. He shared their work with both Arthur Waugh at Chapman & Hall and Lehmann at *New Writing*, but neither found it as impressive as his.[63]

He was still a pacifist, but, as his novels suggest, he was searching for the proper stance to take toward the war and Britain's conduct in it. One powerful poem, "Letter from Safety," questions the stoicism of solid citizens who pay for a "necessary" war and send their children off to die in it:

> The upright man who pays for aeroplanes—
> (one son shot down, but still he strikes in tune)
> props up his paper, drinks his tea, canvasses
> the bombs on Lorient, the necessary blockade.[64 / ****]

Just about everybody else in literary and cultural Britain, it appeared, was asking themselves the same questions: how should I address the war in my work, and what role should I myself adopt toward it? Some, like Auden and Isherwood, moved to America, earning the contempt of many suffering through the cataclysm back home. Connolly referred to them as "ambitious young men with a strong instinct of self-preservation, and an eye on the main chance," while Orwell remarked, "Mr. Auden's brand of amoralism is only possible if you are the kind of person who is always somewhere else when the trigger is pulled."[65] The issue was even more unsettling for individuals who opposed war—all war—and didn't want to accept the implied commandment that in exchange for exemption from national service they had to withdraw from the national conversation (in short, that they should shut up and carry on).

Underlying these questions was an even deeper concern, the one that had fueled the growth of the pacifist movement during the '30s: that the new war, given the far greater destructive capabilities of armies twenty years after the last one, could bring the end of civilization. "There is such a doubt about the continuity of civilization as can hardly have existed for hundreds of years," Orwell wrote in January 1941, "and meanwhile there are the air raids, which make continuous intellectual life very difficult."[66] John Lehmann recalled, "[It was] as if our whole civilization was a giant liner that had left its berth and was slowly sailing into unknown waters under a thickening fog."[67] Virginia Woolf's final novel, *Between the Acts*, is often read as an expression of her—and many people's—foreboding that society was about to break apart.[68]

Alex first jumped publicly into this fraught business in early 1942, just after *Lyra* was published and just before *The Almond Tree* appeared.

**** Lorient is a port in Brittany where the Germans had established a u-boat base.

"We were in some ways the 'Enfants Terribles' of our time," Nick Moore later said of himself and Alex. "We were both somewhat pugnacious—at least on paper, and it was perhaps significant that, when *John O'London's Weekly* printed an old-fashioned article headed 'WHERE ARE THE WAR POETS,' its correspondence columns in the next issue were headed by letters about it (by Alex and myself). . . . Neither, of course, knew the other would write."[69]

The article Nick referred to was by Robert Wilson Lynd, a well-known Irish literary essayist. Lynd wanted to know where were the poets writing about Britain's ordeal and the sacrifice of its men-in-arms: the Rupert Brookeses and Wilfred Owenses of the new war?[70] Alex's response, in the March 13 issue, argued that war poetry of the inspirational sort, like Byron's "The Prisoner of Chillon" or Shelley's "Ode to Liberty," was not possible during the conflict then going on, which was "(a) closer and (b) beastlier and as a result one must either treat it in Zolaesque [realistic] prose . . . or in poetry which concentrates on individual tragedy."

"We can either ignore the war," Alex wrote, "in which case we deserve to be ignored, or we can praise it, in which case we shall be phoney, or we can denounce it, in which case we shall be sent to jail by the Government and Coventry by Mr. Lynd. We are too busy in interpreting the truth of the war, the tragedy of everyman—to attempt what I feel Mr. Lynd wants." But there was something different about the poets of the day as well, Alex said, not altogether convincingly. "Where Byron was a Socialist and a militant, most younger writers are Anarchists and near-Pacifists. Mr. Lynd won't therefore agree with their interpretation, but it exists."[71]

Two months later, *Horizon* published "On Interpreting the War," a long letter by Alex that developed these points into a tentative manifesto on the responsibility of the artist. The letter was in response to an essay in which Spender complained that no one had yet produced a poem that addressed the war in any one of what he felt were four key areas: re-creating imaginatively a major event of the war, making a major statement on the nature of the struggle, expressing "positive faith in the democracy for which we are fighting," or making "an effective statement against war."

Alex countered that the first and third were "not artistically feasible": a "Charge of the Light Brigade" about the fall of Singapore to the Japanese Army wouldn't be taken seriously. Good war poetry was being written, but it was "small and personal in scope," focusing on the experience of the average soldier or the civilian victims: the capture of a small village, the lines seen from a night watch post, air raids, a bomb on the hospital down the road. The best poetry—like "Dunkirk," by the Apocalyptic Alan Rook, and even some of Spender's work—viewed the war as a calamity for those engaged in and affected by it, not as a noble struggle: "like an infection, where the patient or the pathogen may win."

If the new writers, like Alex or Rook, were not producing the kind of work Spender seemed to be calling for—commemorating great events, celebrating the cause of British democracy—it was in part because they "didn't see the war as a struggle in the way that Spain was a struggle" but as a vast human tragedy. Modernism, as then understood, could not do this, because it demanded an intellectual precision that the chaos of war didn't allow. Neither could Surrealism, the other popular school of the time, because it was too bound up with neurosis. To capture the true nature of the war would require "a thoroughgoing return to romanticism, and a serious effort to reinstate the idea of the tragic myth," Alex argued. "Its imagery must be imaginative, copious, and in a measure imprecise, or it will fall short of the power which romanticism exercises over the fully-developed mind, the *whole* man."

The difficulty of writing this kind of war poetry stemmed from the fact that modern life was destroying people's sense of community. "We are no longer an integrated body held together by a purpose.... The state has somehow become, for the majority of Englishman, 'They', and no longer 'We.'" One solution to this "ego-isolation" was "the immediate common purpose of an army attacking an objective"; another, "the common purpose of a society for stopping the war." Either way, the greater the adversity, the greater the catharsis that produces great poetry, and Alex ventured to predict that the greatest literature of the war would come from countries like France, Poland, or Czechoslovakia, which had experienced defeat and disaster, rather than from the UK, which had not been defeated or occupied, much as its soldiers and citizens fought and suffered.

There was another path, Alex suggested: fiction, which could capture the "unparalleled violence" of the war and bring it home to the reader. Émile Zola, especially in *La Débâcle*, his novel of the Franco-Prussian War and the Paris Commune, provided a model for this: a novel full of "violent and excessive incident and character" that didn't lapse into sensationalism and "shock effect." But the writer had to also be able to "detach and treat truthfully the persons and events connected with the Nazi conquest of Europe"—including the Germans themselves. "It might almost be wise to take the plunge and write at least partly in the character of a private in the enemy army."[72]

The Apocalyptics had been courting Alex, he was friendly with Treece, and he used some of their language in his letter ("the tragic myth," "the *whole* man"), but he was taking a different road in recommending Zola, the great realistic novelist, as a model. Realism could express tragedy, and so it could contribute to the reinvigoration of romanticism that he was advocating as the right approach to creating a literature of the war then going on. By failing to embrace it—by maintaining a kind of defiant apoliticism and failing to engage with the ordeal that was enveloping their country and the world—many of the Apocalyptics were entering that "sterile vacuum." Poets, and other artists, *had to* speak out about the war, reflect its reality, and expose the absurdity of celebrating it, even when the fight was against a Hitler. Alex was advocating a new movement that recognized this, and it was already being given a name.

A month earlier, Herbert Read gave a talk on the BBC's Indian Service, reprinted in *The Listener*, about what he called the "New Romantic School" that traced the inspiration of poets like Alex, Moore, Treece, Watkins, and Hendry to Dylan Thomas: a movement of younger writers that "threaten[ed] to submerge the realist school" of Auden and Spender.[73] Read picked out a poem by Treece and one by Alex, "The Atoll in the Mind," to quote at length, comparing Alex's work to that of the seventeenth-century English poet George Herbert.

Among the listeners captivated by Alex's poem was the producer of the program on which Read spoke, George Orwell.[74] Not so delighted by Read's presentation was Nick Moore, who later said that he was "horrified" at the designation "New Romantics," since he felt their whole purpose "was to do away with the distinction between classic and romantic and to try to attain the same kind of universality as was achieved by the first Elizabethans and the Metaphysicals" who included, among others, George Herbert.

Alex himself said something similar years later, situating his generation's poetry as part of a rhetorical tradition going back to the Elizabethans, and continuing up through Dryden and Pope and the Romantics, that lent itself to both close observation and grand statements on moral and ethical issues that he felt the modernists had left behind right when it was acutely needed. "I thought language was getting a little impoverished," he said. Much of the political poetry of the '30s was "jejune." Treece was "juicier," although "a bit over the top with it sometimes."[75]

Whether Alex and Moore liked the name or not, Read's decision to tag them as New or Neo-Romantics situated them as part of a larger movement that stretched into the visual arts, including such painters as Cecil Collins, John Craxton, and Graham Sutherland and even the filmmakers Michael Powell and Emeric Pressburger.[76] These artists were reacting against what they felt was the dissociation of modern art—abstraction and surrealism—from representation that spoke to viewers on some primal level. "I am not very interested in what is called pure painting or *objet d'art*," Collins said. "I am concerned with art as a metaphysical experience. . . . Pure art is the prettier side of the utterly empty mechanical desert we call modern civilisation."[77] Whether or not Alex agreed that modern civilization was a "desert," he shared a concern that any kind of art had to function on a moral level and play a positive social role if it was to have meaning.

Read's talk helped draw attention to the quality of the new poets' work, which was already benefiting from the large amounts of down time that many people in the military or government service often found themselves obliged to fill.[78] "The one thing that was booming was poetry," Alex recalled. "A great many soldiers read it, bookshops were full of it, the less brainy critics started asking 'where are the War Poets?' . . . and looking for a new Rupert Brooke."[79] A host of little magazines, including *Poetry Quarterly*, *Poetry London*, and Alex's own *Poetry Folios*, carried poems by young writers, some of them members of His Majesty's forces. These, as well as the many anthologies that appeared during the war, like *Lyra*, Reginald Moore's *Modern Reading*, and an annual series, *New Road*, that Alex and John Bayliss would commence in 1943 ("a sort of English *New Directions*"), were generally short and compact, ideal for soldiers to carry with them since they weighed little and could be read in bite-sized chunks.[80]

Anthologies of poems written by the troops proliferated.[81] One of the more provocative little magazines that appeared after the war began, however, was *NOW*, edited by George Woodcock, a Canadian-born poet, anarchist, and conscientious objector who spent much of the war toiling on a farm in Essex.

NOW was "much the best periodical of the radical kind in England in those years," the poet, critic, and crime novelist Julian Symons later judged, adding, "for anybody wanting to know what non-communist literary radicals thought and hoped during those years, *NOW* must be an indispensable document, as *Horizon*, for example, was not."[82] Alex and Woodcock first met during the Alex's last term at Cambridge. "I would often climb the stone stairs to Alex Comfort's rooms in the Trinity turrets," Woodcock recalled, "admire his collection of cacti, and listen with large pinches of salt to the tall tales he would tell of the faroff voyages to Africa and South America he claimed to have undertaken as a teenager." They would talk as well of the new kind of Romantic-inspired poetry they wanted to write and "elaborate an anarchist-pacifist strategy of victory by evasion and survival."[83]

Woodcock had founded *NOW* in 1940 as an outlet for "good writing": poems and literary prose as well as dissident opinion, particularly on the war. Over the next half-dozen years he attracted a stellar selection of contributors, including Orwell; Julian Huxley; Lawrence Durrell; the poets George Barker, Julian Symons, W. S. Graham, e.e. cummings, and Kenneth Rexroth; André Breton; Henry Miller; Dwight Macdonald; and Victor Serge, not to mention Alex and Herbert Read. But Woodcock courted trouble with his summer 1941 issue, which included pieces by two eccentric antiwar campaigners, Hugh Ross Williamson and the Duke of Bedford, along with an article in which Alex speculated on the future of art forms like dance in a devastated postwar world. ("Artists are being forced to see that their art must pass into some form popular and dispersed enough to survive the utter, and probably forcible, disruption of a national culture."[84])

Williamson was a popular historian who had been connected before the war with a group of radical socialists called the People's Party that had briefly formed an alliance with Oswald Mosley before collapsing. The duke, a wealthy amateur pamphleteer, was "one of those English noblemen who become involved in fringe causes from a sense of duty to the traditional eccentricity of their class," Woodcock later wrote. He was vocally antisemitic, however, and had made headlines in the early months of the war by visiting the German legation in Dublin in an attempt to mediate a truce, a stunt that got him branded as a fascist sympathizer. His only contribution to *NOW* was an innocuous article about the responsibilities of the press.[85] But the presence of the duke and Williamson in the magazine stigmatized it in the eyes of many readers, even on the left. "I was rather shocked to see you in a publication with the D. of Bedford the other day," John Lehmann wrote sharply to Alex in October 1941. "I thought you had more taste and discrimination."

Far more incensed was Orwell, who launched an all-out attack on "defeatism" in his semi-regular "London Letter" to *Partisan Review*.[86] He used selective examples to accuse British pacifists of forming an alliance, whether intentionally or not, with the enemy. Some, like Williamson and the duke, he regarded as eccentric but possibly dangerous. Others he classified as naïve or deluded. Alex he tagged—inaccurately, it would turn out—as "a 'pure' pacifist of the other-cheek school." About Julian Symons, who was Jewish, Orwell said, "[He] writes in a vaguely Fascist strain but is also given to quoting Lenin." More ominously, he wrote, "I do seem to notice a tendency in intellectuals, especially the younger ones, to come to terms with Fascism, and it is a thing to keep one's eye on. . . . If the Germans got to England . . . I think I could make out at least a preliminary list of the people who would go over."

The article provoked a furious response from Alex, Woodcock, and Derek Savage, a Christian pacifist poet Orwell had not mentioned. *Partisan Review* decided to print their letters, along with a response from Orwell, in its September/October issue. Savage's letter defended pacifism. Woodcock defended *NOW* against the suggestion that Williamson and the Duke of Bedford represented his magazine's editorial policy and suggested instead that Orwell, a former officer in Britain's Indian Police and former pacifist now working at the BBC, "conducting British propaganda to fox the Indian masses," himself displayed "the overlapping of left-wing, pacifist and reactionary tendencies of which he accuses others."

Alex's response bit deeper, accusing Orwell, in effect, of the very thing he had dedicated himself to opposing. "Hitler's greatest and irretrievable victory over here was when he persuaded the English people that the only way to lick Fascism was to imitate it," Alex wrote. "Accordingly, we began feverishly jamming into our national life all the minor pieces of Fascist practice which did not include Socialist methods, sitting on the press 'because this is Total War,' making our soldiers jab blood bladders while loud-speakers howl propaganda at them."

While Orwell focused on the catastrophe of a German victory, Alex fixated on the dire impact of the war itself, no matter who won. English writers "are going to be entrusted with the job of saving what remains of the structure of civilized values from Hitler or alternatively from Churchill," he wrote. "The men who, like Orwell, could have helped, are calling us Fascists and presumably dancing around the ruins of Munster Cathedral. We prefer not to join them."[87]

Orwell hit back hard in his response. "Pacifism is objectively pro-Fascist," he wrote, repeating the assertion he had made in his review of *No Such Liberty*. "This is elementary common sense. . . . The idea that you can somehow remain aloof from and superior to the struggle, while living on food which British sailors have to risk their lives to bring you, is a bourgeois illusion bred of money and security." If they were less cowardly, he argued, his antagonists would come out and admit their fascist sympathies rather than hiding behind the notion that pacifism could somehow defeat Hitler. Instead, "they write mentally dishonest propaganda and degrade literary criticism to mutual arse-licking."

Orwell was not interested in pacifism as a moral phenomenon, and he scoffed at Gandhi's example. Arguing that by deflecting Indian activists from more effective paths, the leader of the nonviolent movement for Indian self-rule was being very useful to the British government, Orwell added, "And so he will be to the Japanese if they get there." But he saved his harshest and most personal remarks for Alex, perhaps because he was more familiar with his work, while he didn't know Woodcock or Savage. "Mr Comfort himself wrote one poem I value greatly ('The Atoll in the Mind'), and I wish he would write more of them instead of lifeless propaganda tracts dressed up as novels." "[Comfort's letter] tries to prejudice an [American] audience to whom I am little known by a misrepresentation of my general line," Orwell wrote. He furiously denounced "the sneers, libels, parrot phrases and financially profitable back-scratching which flourish in our English literary world"—to which Alex was presumably a party.

Both Alex and Orwell were concerned about a fascist tendency in the UK, but Alex saw it in the corrupting effects of the war itself, while Orwell found it among pacifists like Alex. In retrospect, Orwell's case against the "Fascifists," as he called them, was a bit hysterical. None of the people he was attacking are known to have secretly helped the Nazis during the war. He did correctly point out that Alex was exaggerating the degree to which Churchill's government was adopting Nazi-like methods—and, he might have added, the degree of pacifism among "younger writers." Certainly, most of his American readers would have agreed with Orwell that the government had no choice but to adopt extreme measures. Americans who paid attention to the news knew that Britain, and especially London, had endured the terror of the Luftwaffe's Blitzkrieg bombing campaign from September 1940 to April 1941, which killed some 41,000, injured 139,000, and dislocated countless others while devastating English cities.

But his complete lack of sympathy with pacifism as such made it impossible for Orwell to understand what its adherents expected to accomplish by speaking against the war. From the start, pacifists including Alex and Vera Brittain had focused on critiquing their government's conduct of the war, including its treatment of refugees and enemy aliens, its abandonment of its prewar commitment to spare civilians in its bombing campaigns, its use of blockades that starved whole populations, and its use of hate speech to turn enemy nations into pariahs. While Whitehall's methods were clearly less murderous than Berlin's, this was no reason not to expose them, and to do so while they were being committed—not out of a misguided sense of loyalty, waiting until afterward to do so. In a pamphlet published about the same time that Alex and Orwell were having their exchange, titled *Humiliation with Honour*, Brittain laid out what she considered to be the duties of pacifists:

> To give whatever assistance we can to those victims of power who endure more than ourselves—prisoners, refugees, the starving, the young, the bereaved. We must keep ourselves imaginatively conscious of the cost of war in human suffering; we must also investigate and expose that cost, and find, if we can, some form of redemptive consolation for those who have to pay it.[88]

Beyond this, she wrote, pacifists must anticipate the world that would follow the war. "We are called upon, humbly and without self-righteousness, to keep alive those civilized values of charity, compassion, and truth to which men return with relief and remorse as soon as the war is over. . . . We must seize upon such evidence of the shape of the future as we are able to acquire." Summing up, she described pacifists' task as "trying to change the course of history by acting as a revolutionary leaven within society." British were dying by the thousands at home as well as on battlefields, subjecting those who took it up to relentless attack even from principled people like Orwell. It was bound to be a dirty job, as the saying goes, but somebody had to do it.

CHAPTER 4

The Neo-Romantic (1941–1943)

Brittain's perspective was already present or at least implicit in much of Alex's writing, including his exchange with Orwell. Later that year, Treece sent him a letter admonishing him not to "advertise" himself as a pacifist. "Somehow, I feel you are going to antagonize the critics by being honest."[1]

Alex's life was racing ahead on other fronts, however, notably his medical training. St Andrew's was functioning as a wartime evacuation center for the London Hospital, which meant it was often flooded with patients from the capital. What with clinical work and lecturing, doctors there were overwhelmed, which forced them to immediately instruct their newly arrived clinical students in history taking and examinations and place them into the wards as student house officers.

Alex, like most of the others, had never before examined a patient, but he was quickly doing procedures, assisting at operations, staffing the emergency room, giving anesthetics under supervision, performing autopsies, and attending lectures. He was assigned three to four patients at a time, owing to which, he later recalled, he acquired relational skills even before he acquired full technical knowledge. His instructors included Clifford Wilson, a leading specialist in nephrology, or the treatment of kidney diseases; Herman Taylor, an innovative surgeon; and Pete Reidy, a onetime rugby footballer and heavyweight boxer, later a renowned plastic surgeon. Another surgeon, G. C. Millis, used to take two students to assist when he made the rounds of smaller hospitals in the area. "He would then make us perform the appendectomies while he assisted," Alex later recalled.[2]

This baptism under fire, which he described in "Saturday Night," was quite different from the hands-off routine of most prewar medical training, and Alex came to value it greatly. "The responsibility was appropriate," he later wrote. "Younger men were commanding troops in action and flying combat aircraft. The atmosphere was not that of a military unit, but esprit de corps was important. Still more important, we were consistently treated as responsible colleagues."

In December, at Billericay, Alex had scarlet fever; Ruth, who had finished her training in social work and was living again with her mother at Little Gables while starting her first job as a child care officer in Bethnal Green, came out to help nurse him through.[3] Shortly before he wrote his reply to Orwell's attack, he transferred from St Andrew's to the London Hospital Annex at Brentwood Community Hospital—closer to London but in a very similar Essex town—for the next stage of his training. He had already started a new novel, an ambitious story set in the French Resistance, that would take him considerably longer to write than his first two.

At some point early in the spring of 1942, he sent a larger collection of poems and an advance copy of *The Almond Tree* to Herbert Read at Routledge. The influential editor was enthusiastic about the novel—"you have the authentic freshness and vividness, something one only finds in the early novels of Lawrence and Joyce"—but felt it lacked structure.[4] He found no such problem with the poems, which Routledge published in October as *A Wreath for the Living*. The *Times Educational Supplement* singled it out in a December 1942 roundup: "With ear to the ground he detects coming events and trends and expresses them in a form sometimes undisciplined, sometimes beautiful, always urgent."[5]

Alex also found time to plead the case of a young painter who had just written an autobiographical first novel: Denton Welch. The talented twenty-six-year-old had endured a brutal education at the Repton School, then suffered a fractured spine in a bicycling accident at age twenty from which he never really recovered. He would die in 1948 of spinal tuberculosis. In between, he produced an accomplished body of art along with two finished novels and an unfinished one, poems, and short stories. Almost everything he wrote came from his life and minute observation of every detail of what went on around him, to the extent that his work has been called Proustian. He was fairly openly homosexual for the time, and quite a bit of his erotic life went into his books as well, making him a forerunner of postwar gay literature. A wide assortment of later writers would name him as an influence, from Barbara Pym and Alan Bennett to William S. Burroughs, who dedicated his 1983 novel, *The Place of Dead Roads*, to Welch.

Before his work reached print, Welch wrote to a multitude of famous figures he thought would be interested in it, hoping they would lend him their support. How he first came into contact with Alex isn't entirely clear, but it appears to have been through Treece, always on the lookout for new Apocalyptics. Treece first contacted Welch to compliment him on some of his poems;[6] the complete absence in Welch's work of any reference to the war or contemporary politics in favor of a private world may have appealed to him. In any event, Welch sent Alex the manuscript of his first novel, *Maiden Voyage*, which the latter passed on to Arthur Waugh, declaring it a work of genius. Waugh was merely puzzled. "For three days I have concentrated on this MS," he wrote back, "hoping that the light was about to break, which would reveal to me the subtlety of the author's interpretation. But the moment never came."[7]

Alex found he got on with the painfully lonely and isolated Welch, who was only a few years older than him, when they met in person. He asked Welch to contribute a piece on contemporary painting to *New Road*, the anthology he was editing, but Welch begged off. Although not a business-minded sort, Alex had learned his way around certain corners of the publishing world quickly, thanks in part to his early connection with Chapman & Hall. Welch was the opposite, almost completely ignorant of the business side of authorship. Alex compared him to Fyodor, the possibly gay character in *The Almond Tree*, who emerges emotionally damaged from a vicious military academy, much as Welch had from the Repton School. "I can see what you mean," Welch responded, although "in real life the adolescent 'me' was, I feel, less direct and much more fuddled."[8]

Alex passed the manuscript on to Read, who read it "with great interest" and recommended to Routledge that they publish it.[9] After a tense encounter with the publisher's libel lawyers, Welch saw *Maiden Voyage* come out early in 1943 with a preface by Edith Sitwell.[10] The book was praised by critics including E. M. Forster and the art curator Kenneth Clark. A successful but tragically short literary career was launched.

Alex's tie with Read was further strengthened by bringing him Welch; it would become one of the most important personal and professional relationships of his life. Once they met in person, "I liked him immensely," Alex later said of Read. "I spent afternoons with him on occasion."[11] While he wasn't one to socialize heavily, there were also less-frequent dinners with Ruth and Read's glamorous wife, Margaret, known to all as Ludo. But he had been aware of Read's work and thought for some time. "I owe a large part of any philosophy I may have to your writings," he wrote back to Read in 1943, when the latter complimented him for articulating what he saw as their shared philosophy in a magazine article.[12]

At the time they met, Read had been a partner at Routledge for three years, but that doesn't begin to describe the unique position he held in British cultural life. A dapper man of middle age, slender and serious, usually sporting a bowtie, Read was a poet, critic, longtime close friend of T. S. Eliot, and a well-known champion of Henry Moore, Barbara Hepworth, Naum Gabo, and other modern British artists. He also advised wealthy patrons like the American art collector Peggy Guggenheim. At the same time, he was an anarchist who had gone public with his beliefs in 1937 after a gestation period that went back decades.

Read was a true tastemaker, grasping the significance of new trends in art and literature—from abstract art and surrealism to the theories of Carl Jung to existentialism—early in their formation and introducing them to the educated British public in elegant, accessible prose. This could work against him with some observers. In a mostly complimentary March 1941 article in *Horizon*, Graham Greene wrote, "[Read is] sometimes at pains to adapt the latest psychological theories before they have proved their validity. . . . Sometimes we suspect that it means little more to him than an attempt to show his Marxist critics that he too is a political animal."[13]

Derek Stanford, in his memoirs, captures what a singular figure Read cut in London during the late '30s, when high culture and political radicalism were converging in the shadow of the fascist threat. In February 1939, the Whitechapel Gallery opened a large Surrealist exhibition sponsored by the Artists International Association as a "demonstration of the Unity of Artists for Peace, Democracy and Cultural Progress." Posters and leaflets declared: "The Exhibition will be opened by THE MAN IN THE STREET." The reference was to a working-class person the organizers would select at random from passersby outside the gallery. Read was advertised as giving the opening speech that Saturday morning. "Clad in a dark double-breasted blue suit with his navy blue polka-dot bow tie, and attended by a highly groomed posse of begowned and bejewelled squaws, he seemed an oddly incongruous presence among so many bohemian uniforms and the sprinkling of rag-tag-and-bobtail from the streets. Elegance of dress is, for some a social gesture; for Read it was more a quiet dandyism—an outward expression of inward and spiritual grace."[14]

But Read was not one of the Oxbridge-educated select. His family were tenant farmers in Yorkshire, which he always regarded as a sort of paradise, and he grew up partly in an orphanage. He attended the

University of Leeds until war broke out in 1914. He was commissioned and finished the war a captain and could have gone on to a military career but gave it up, disillusioned and already moving toward pacifism. Having met Eliot while on leave, he moved to London in 1919 to take a civil service job and begin his literary career. Eliot's magazine *The Criterion* provided the first major platform for his poetry and writings on art and literature, and over the next decade he established himself as an important figure, in part through a popular series of articles collected as *The Meaning of Art* in 1931.

Read was beginning to differentiate himself from the cerebral Eliot and his preferred circle, however. A more intuitive writer and thinker, in books like *Reason and Romanticism* (1926) and *Wordsworth* (1930) he championed the Romantics, including William Blake, and later in the decade he encouraged Treece, persuading Routledge to publish him. But Read's interest in nurturing a new Romanticism was political as well as aesthetic.

Like many other European thinkers, right and left, Read was disgusted by the politics of the interwar years, which veered toward fascist or Bolshevik tyranny or a venal, corrupt form of liberal democracy, dominated by capitalists and with no regard either for workers in the new industrial economy or for traditional communities that were being destroyed or reduced to poverty. That feeling of disgust only grew stronger once the Depression settled in, bolstered by a perception that the masses, rather than revolting, were largely sinking into apathy. World War I, Read wrote in 1930, "was fought for rhetoric—fought for historical phrases and actual misery, fought by politicians and generals with human flesh and blood, fanned by false and artificially created mob passions." "I can conceive of no values . . . for which human life indiscriminately and in the mass should be forcibly sacrificed."[15]

In his 1938 book, *Poetry and Anarchism*, which Eliot persuaded Faber & Faber to publish, Read called for a "politics of the unpolitical." In a society of increasing abundance, he argued, there was no reason human beings should have to continue putting up with the sordid and ruthless politics practiced even by so-called democratic governments. "With modern, mechanical power and modern methods of production, there is or could be a sufficiency of goods to satisfy all reasonable needs," he wrote. "It is only necessary to organize an efficient system of distribution or exchange."

He knew this couldn't simply be wished into being. "The abolition of poverty and the consequent establishment of a classless society is not going to be accomplished without a struggle." The goal was a new society that would balance "reason with romanticism, the understanding with the imagination, function with freedom." "Happiness, peace, contentment," he wrote, "are all one and are due to the perception of this balance."[16] To get there, he advocated a decentralized politics of the kind the nineteenth-century anarchists Proudhon and Kropotkin had described, with power concentrated in small local communities generating their own organic social structure rather than submitting to one imposed by the State. Nor did war or any form of violence have a place in the society Read envisioned. "Anarchism naturally implies pacifism," he declared.[17]

The artist had a role in achieving the kind of balance Read hoped for. He described, in Jungian terms, a "man who mediates between our individual consciousness and the collective unconscious, and thus ensures social reintegration."[18] From this stemmed Read's long-term project of reinfusing modernism with what he saw as the life-affirming, spiritual or transcendental qualities of Romanticism.

By the time he met Alex, most of the elements of Read's political-aesthetic position were in place, expressed in *Poetry and Anarchism* and a subsequent series of pamphlets for Freedom Press, the venerable anarchist publishing house located in Hempstead. He would have more to contribute to anarchist theory in coming years, but he was already influencing the wave of Apocalyptic and Neo-Romantic poets, including Alex. "The figure around whom the greatest part of our new romantic movement revolves is undoubtedly Herbert Read," Alex wrote.[19]

"From the time I read *Poetry and Anarchism*, I called myself an anarchist—something I continued to do for about ten years," Derek Stanford recalled. One thing that attracted Stanford was that Read wasn't advocating a strict ideology along Marxist lines but a more personal struggle for a decentralized society beginning with the practice of mutual aid. "The brand of anarchism I learned from Read was a reflective philosophic attitude as much as any programme for action."[20]

Arguably, Read's disinclination to emphasize class struggle—although he didn't deny its necessity—made it easy for superficially political people to call themselves anarchists without thinking systematically about how to achieve the end of capitalism and the State or working toward that goal. But it also helped people to recognize themselves as anarchists who had previously been hovering on the fringe.

Alex was one such person, it appeared, and, like Read's, his politics arose from the moral and ethical principles he had formed in adopting pacifism, not from top-down political theory or pragmatism. Asked to pinpoint the moment he became an anarchist, he later replied, "Oddly enough, I don't recall, but it clearly occurred or crystallized over time after about 1940."[21]

Two years further on, he still had to work out how to activate his political stance during a war against an unimaginatively brutal regime that had inflicted a reign of terror and genocide in continental Europe. To oppose that regime, was it necessary to enlist under another state opposed to it? How far did one's duty to resist militarism extend? When and to what degree was violence a legitimate response? What should be the objective if one took up arms? Alex answered these questions differently than did Read, who had become an absolute opponent of violence in any form. Only Gandhian passive resistance was acceptable to him, but Alex was unwilling to be so categorical.

ALEX THOUGHT THROUGH HIS position in the course of writing his third novel. He later said that he began *The Power House* in 1941, but the first UK edition of the book dates the writing from February 10, 1942 to July 14, 1943.[22] Certainly the early stages were difficult. "I'm bogged down, after writing 200 pages of bad Zola pastiche," he told Treece.[23] He started the novel while at Brentwood and finished while beginning his final year of medical training at the London Hospital. In the latter stages, he claimed, he composed much of it on a portable typewriter that folded in two, in a community center across the street from the hospital that served as an air raid shelter. There, he said, his attention was occasionally distracted by jazz on the radio and some fellow students who whiled away the time boxing.[24]

The Power House was longer and more intricately plotted than either of his previous novels, and once again his characters were not English. The novel follows two French factory workers and two educated army officers from just before the outbreak of the war through the Fall of France and then to their fates under the Occupation. One of the officers and one of the textile workers join in an attempt by the Maquis—the guerrilla networks who made up the indigenous French resistance to the Occupation—to dynamite a German troop train. Instead, they blow up a passenger train full of women and farmers; one of the protagonists is killed in the action and the other executed. The other two, in the last section of the novel, are prisoners working as slave laborers in the same factory where the story began, now run by the German occupiers. But the prisoners rebel, destroying "La Virginie," the machine that runs the factory's electrical power house, just as the news arrives that Germany has invaded the Soviet Union. The prisoners are to be transported farther east, possibly to camps in Germany or Poland, but their political consciousness has been raised, along with their knowledge that they can act together.

It's not surprising that Alex wrote a novel set in occupied France. He'd been preoccupied with events there for some time. Nancy Cunard, the shipping heir, poet, publisher, and all-around cultural instigator, had thrown herself into assisting the French Resistance, and in 1943 she hatched the idea of putting out a collection of poems about France, written by British poets since the war began, copies of which she would auction to raise funds for the Maquis. She asked Alex for permission to include his long poem "France." He agreed, and *Poems for France* appeared in January 1944. Read, Treece, Vita Sackville-West, Hugh MacDiarmid, and Sylvia Townsend Warner were also among the contributors.[25] Two years later, Cunard translated the book, including Alex's poem, for publication in France ("a most sympathetic and pleasant" translation, he remarked).[26]

The Power House, however, is something else: Alex's effort to write the sort of super-realistic, Zolaesque novel he had argued was one of the only two proper literary responses to the war, along with "poetry which concentrates on individual tragedy." Its story line echoes Hemingway's *For Whom the Bell Tolls* and looks forward to Jean-Paul Sartre's Roads to Freedom trilogy: especially the third novel, *La mort dans l'âme* (1949), which concerns an unsuccessful attempt to defend a French town from the advancing Germans. Like *No Such Liberty*, *The Power House* required research to assemble the details of the textile factory, conditions in occupied France, and the sabotage operation—suggested by a news item he had run across—on which the last half of the book centers. "I am indebted to a great many books, factual and fictional," Alex said in a note to the reader, although his description of a slaughterhouse derived from one he had seen on Moore Street in Dublin. Later, for a newsletter accompanying a book club edition of the novel, he said that he drew his Maquisards from "people I knew who had fought in the IRA" and his Gestapo officers from Black and Tans "and security officials whom I knew," although these claims are difficult to verify and Alex was not always reliable on such matters.[27]

But his descriptions of the region in northeastern France where most of the action takes place came largely from his own observations on vacation with his mother as a child. To his credit, and unlike many postwar writers, he did not romanticize the Maquis, who in reality were riven by factions and competing goals and failed to make much progress at loosening the German grip until the last weeks of the Occupation.[28] Thanks to his excellent knowledge of the language and his wide reading in French, Alex's characters come across as credible and firmly rooted in their specific backgrounds; the two textile workers, Fougueux and Loubain, are "real workmen of northern France," French author André Maurois wrote in the *Chicago Sun Book Week* when *The Power House* was issued in the United States in 1945. "The author knows very well the little world he is writing about."[29]

With *The Power House*, Alex advanced his analysis of humanity's plight during the war and how it could be overcome. His first novel had centered on the dilemma faced by pacifists in flight from the Nazis but unable to engage in the war against them. His second addressed the efforts of a family to navigate the period that had given birth to the current crisis. His third dealt with individuals directly caught up in the bloodshed, devising ways to stay alive and not betray their humanity, at the same time resisting the occupier. Much of the novel's detail derives from reports of the Maquis. By mid-1941, these groups were already operating in northern France and were known to be engaged in sabotage.[30] In a January 29, 1942, radio broadcast, Orwell had called attention to their activities. "Every time a piece of machinery is wrecked or an ammunition dump mysteriously catches fire," he said, "precautions have to be redoubled. . . . When Hitler finally falls, the European workers who idled, shammed sickness, wasted material and damaged machinery in the factories, will have played an important role in his destruction."[31]

There was much more in Alex's novel, however. La Virginie, the machine that runs the power house, an object of fascination to some of the workers, draws on his Neo-Romantic side in suggesting Moloch, the implacable heathen god of the Old Testament who demands child sacrifice. Moloch appears as a warrior of the fallen angels in *Paradise Lost*, in Blake's illustrations of Milton's poem, and as a symbol of everything from money to industrial civilization in general in the work of writers and artists including Karl Marx, Fritz Lang in his visionary 1927 film *Metropolis*, and Allen Ginsberg in his 1956 poem *Howl*.

Like Zola, however, Alex was depicting a set of characters whose actions and ideas were the product of their environment, some of whom would rise above it by reacting against it. What exactly are they rising above? "I rather doubt if at any time in history so many ordinary individuals have realised the personal reality of death as realise it today," Alex wrote in an essay published in late 1943, after he had completed *The Power House*; art that attempted to shield humanity from this realization was no longer viable.[32] Fear of death is closely tied to feelings of personal powerlessness and isolation from which individuals in a deeply alienated modern society all too often seek to escape through violence and sadomasochism: in other words, from any sense of responsibility toward each other.[33]

The resulting plague of violence shows up in war, authoritarianism, and bigotry, but also in people's personal relationships. In *The Almond Tree*, Alex paired graphic scenes of World War I violence with the attempt by Madame Roux to have her way with Yeli, which he insisted on keeping in the novel. In *The Power House*, even before the war commences, there's a sadomasochistic scene between a young woman named Arsule and one of the two textile workers, Lubain. He kills her and has to flee ahead of the police. "I took her but she fought me—she kept yelling, 'Hurt me, hurt me.' I was scared, but she wouldn't let go. She got the cord off her dressing gown and made me tie her with it. She was mad, I tell you. Then I couldn't stop holding her, and suddenly she was dead."[34]

Earlier Alex conveys the dehumanizing effects of capitalism—the environment in which these violent impulses thrive—through a description of the workers in the textile factory that reads more like a herd of animals filing into a slaughterhouse.

> The invisible crowd was closing in, and the patter of their feet on the clinker changed to the sound of sheep trotting and shuffling over cobbles. There were bleating sneezes and words all round. He was surrounded by millions of invisible sheep. . . . The crowd was filing together, queuing like sheep to be dipped, waiting the turn to file over the narrow catwalk of the sluice gates on the middle canal, under the rusty bows and large blind hawse holes of a ship, like a lizard's skull, only the first syllable of her name sticking out of the mist, but her hull shaking with the hammering and beating of the shipwrights inside.[35]

In another essay written later during the war, Alex indicates that he had read *Fear of Freedom*, published in the UK in 1942, in which the German social psychologist Erich Fromm argued that violence and sadism are tied to the retreat into authoritarianism as ways for people to escape the burden that freedom places on them: hence the appeal of fascism.[36] The answer to this dilemma, Alex suggests in his novel, is not armies fighting to impose their will on each other, no matter how right the cause, but a return to individual and collective responsibility through acts of resistance from below, à la the Maquis: sabotage, disobedience, insurrection, a rejection of leaders and prophets.

This is a different kind of pacifism from the "other cheek school" that Orwell had thought he detected in Alex, one that Alex came to refer to as "aggressive pacifism." Violence was permitted, but not in the form of warfare by states or, he suggested, through conspiratorial cells that assumed themselves to be acting on behalf of the people, as in the troop-train disaster he describes in his novel. Instead, it must arise from a genuine social movement and be directed in a responsible way. That social movement is likely to come from the lowest levels of the working class, the ones with the least to lose from the collapse of the state-capitalist system, not from the educated classes that thrive in it. The last word in *The Power House* belongs to an eccentric prisoner, probably an anarchist, named Claus, and it echoes Orwell's 1942 broadcast:

> "We're the weak. We're bombed, starved, taxed, jailed, conscripted, shot or frightened collectively. But at least we aren't broken one by one. We're infinitely pliable, and we've an insuperable resistance in the mass. . . . The weak do a great deal—every woman who hides a deserter, every clerk who doesn't scrutinize a pass, every worker who bungles a fuse, saves somebody's life for a while. Somebody will start, though it needs no starting, an International League of the Weak, . . . a league of all citizens, armies (whether of occupation or liberation), against understrappers, jailers, orators and fools."[37]

FROM BRENTWOOD, ALEX HAD moved to Enfield, near his family home in Barnet, for the next stage of his training, at Chase Farm Hospital. There he worked for the first time with elderly patients. At times, however, his pursuit of so many projects on so many fronts threatened to catch up with him. He appears to have suffered from depression in the months around his move, which kept him from producing any new poems and slowed the writing of *The Power House*.

Renewed migraine attacks may have had something to do with the situation, but nothing in his correspondence refers directly to them. Arthur Waugh, just short of seventy-six and ailing, wrote Alex a concerned letter from his bed on August 27, 1942, entreating him, "[Don't] be discouraged by the check to your own creative impulse, & above all [don't] destroy what you have already written. Put it away in some safe place; go on with the work that lies nearest; and the impulse will return in due season, and with it the flood of ideas. You have been living on your nerves for some time past; attempting much too many activities; we have all been afraid of a breakdown. Relax: slack off: wait."[38]

Nothing calamitous occurred. As usual with Alex, the solution was more work. He kept at his studies along with his novel and some new poems, and on January 16 he moved to another medical setting, this time Dublin's Rotunda Hospital for his midwife training—but not before quarantining for three weeks after a bout of chickenpox.[39] Normally he would have stayed and received his course at the London Hospital, but fewer women were having babies in England due to the war, and expectant mothers largely were being evacuated from London, making Dublin, in neutral Ireland, the closest alternative.

Alex fell in love with Ireland and the Irish almost instantly. "In six months [actually three], Ireland gave me more than any country but my own has ever done," he wrote nearly thirty years later.[40] Shortly after he returned in April, he wrote a travel piece for *Horizon* about his stay, packed with close observations of the ramshackle capital, the hospital, the everyday life and popular culture of the city, and the people themselves. "Much of this letter is a catalogue of incongruities," he apologized. "It sounds too much like an account of holes in the carpet of a hospitable friend."[41] But it is also one of his most warmly affectionate pieces of writing.

Arriving in a country not at war, Alex found it a shock "to be civilly spoken to by an assistant in a grocery store. It was even stranger to meet a chemist who refused payment for pills when he discovered I had a toothache." The Irish didn't mind his English accent, which he nevertheless tried to disguise, and "no patients, except one or two who were better off, would let you leave the house without tea or whiskey." Protestants and Catholics, and their doctors, used separate maternity hospitals—except for the Rotunda, where the legendary master, Bethell Solomons, a Jew, had "reconciled" the tribes more than a dozen years before.[42] Students were on call day or night, requiring them to rush out with their bags in groups of two; somehow, a great many deliveries took place between two and three in the morning.

Alex and his fellow students lived in a hostel. "Every landing smells of turf and Dettol [a disinfectant], which arrives not in bottles but in Rabelaisian churns," he wrote. "[Indeed,] this whole building was designed by Rabelais." Furthermore, the labor ward at the Rotunda, the hospital that figures in Joyce's *Ulysses*, was "also devised by Rabelais"—particularly the gas. The "catalogue of incongruities" that the labor ward left him with was hard to forget.

> The most obvious memories are of blowing up turf fires with an enema syringe, of one or two actual deliveries, of a coloured photograph of St. Bernadette adoring Our Lady of Lourdes, opposite which I sat for nearly twenty-four hours waiting for a case of inertia to be delivered, the peculiar wet warm surface of newborn infants, born covered in grease like a new rifle, the afterbirth putting out the fire, and the voices of children, late on into the night, in the fringe of light from a shaded lamp or pushing little carts to destinations in the darkness. I remember burning round polished logs which are the waste wood from Maguire and Patterson's match-factory, delivering the wife of a long-distance engine driver, and helping a fish porter to smash up boxes for fuel, scaly boxes under a gigantic ribbed market-roof like the sky.

All this activity left Alex very little time to visit art galleries or meet with other writers—the exceptions were Robert Greacen and his old friend from Cambridge, Maurice James Craig, who had largely given up poetry for a career as an architectural historian—although he got in a few daylong excursions in the Dublin area and a one-week trip to the west to visit Yeats's burial place and collect snail specimens for his molluscan research.[*/43] He took the train across the island to Sligo, then caught a bus to Mullaghmore, a village on a like-named peninsula looking out into the North Atlantic and dominated by Benbulbin, a hulking, flat-topped mountain that he scavenged for specimens and inspiration. "There's something about Ben Bulben on the horizon," he said in later years. "It seems to expect one to write."[44] He stayed in rooms above Hannon's, a pub run by a ninety-year-old former Gaiety Girl from

* Years later, Alex claimed that he had gotten into a minor quarrel with one of Ireland's bigger literary celebrities, Flann O'Brien, the novelist and (under the alias Myles na Gopaleen) columnist for the *Irish Times*. Alex called Myles a Surrealist, to which the author replied that he was merely Irish. A nice story but impossible to verify.

Dublin.** Everywhere he heard music and singing, implanting a love for Irish song and poetry that lasted the rest of his life.

Years later, Alex told an interviewer of his search for snail specimens at Benbulbin. He found several but in so doing was confronted by the local constabulary, who, it being wartime, suspected he might be trying to blow up the mountain's bauxite mine. His specimens helped him talk his way out of it.[45]

Just before he returned to England, laden with mollusks, he found time to attend a performance of *Antony and Cleopatra*, allegedly the first in Ireland in one hundred years, at the Gaiety Theatre behind Grafton Street, a creditable production mounted by Micheál Mac Liammóir, cofounder of the Gate Theatre. No sooner had the curtain fallen to conclude Act I, he related, than "a safety-curtain of a brilliant yellow descended with horrible velocity." On it was painted:

ODEAREST SANITIZED INNERSPRING MATTRESS
Actively Antiseptic
Self Sterilizing
Permanently Germproof

"For ten minutes we inspected this without a murmur. At the end of Act II it reappeared. It finally concealed Cleopatra from us when the band played 'God Save Ireland.' The next day I went home."

ON HIS RETURN, ALEX reported to the London Hospital for his final year of training. A few months later, he passed the first of two examinations for his Bachelor of Medicine degree. In April he published possibly the first explicitly political text of his career, a letter to the editor of *Tribune*, the organ of the Labour Party's left wing, which addressed the war directly rather than through writers' and artists' response to it and which reflected some of the positions he had developed in conceiving his first three novels.

> As an Englishman I have a part in the infamy and degradation of our bombing policy, and it is a burden of contempt and hatred which

** Nicholas Comfort, *Copy!*, 119. "Gaiety girl" was a catch-all term for a chorus girl in Edwardian musical comedies.

> no moderate repudiation can lighten. The bombardment of Europe is not the work of soldiers nor of responsible statesmen. It is the work of bloodthirsty fools. . . . No consideration of personal risk run, or personal courage, will be sufficient to solace the conscience of many friends of mine who are pilots [his friend Treece was now serving in the RAF]. . . . Contrast the alacrity and satisfaction which attend each contemptible operation with the subterfuge and sloth which we have displayed in such tasks of constructive policy as the admission to sanctuary of Jewish refugees. . . . There are times when denunciation is both a moral and an aesthetic duty. The present seems to me to be one such, and I invite other writers who share my feelings to say so publicly and as soon as possible.[46]

In February of the preceding year, the Royal Air Force Bomber Command had begun an all-out bombing campaign against German targets. While the government always insisted it never intentionally targeted civilians, very few people were fooled, and plenty of internal memos at the time make clear that this was a lie. As early as 1941, British air officials spoke of the need for "continuous blitz attacks on the densely populated workers and industrial areas," targeting "that section of the population which, in any country, is least mobile and most vulnerable to a general air attack—the working class."[47] Less than four months after Alex's *Tribune* letter appeared, the RAF launched Operation Gomorrah, the eight-day incendiary bombing of Hamburg that killed between thirty-seven thousand and forty thousand people, almost as many as the entire German Blitzkrieg over Britain.

If anything, Alex was late in joining the movement against these atrocities. A Committee for the Abolition of Night Bombing had been agitating since August 1941, changing its name the following year to the Bombing Restriction Committee.[48] Nevertheless, he was quickly attacked in print by none other than Lt. Peter Baker, who just three years earlier had edited the Resurgam series that published Alex's first mini-collection, *France and Other Poems* and was now serving in a reconnaissance unit. Baker denounced Alex as a "humbug" on the grounds that he had no experience of the activities he was criticizing. Alex snapped back, "I want to be able to go about in Europe without having to wear a poster saying: 'I am English, but I didn't do it'. Surely Lieut Baker sees that there are some things that not even a soldier who accepts war should stomach?"[49]

Less than two months later, Alex was back in *Tribune* with "Letter to an American Visitor," a fifteen-stanza poem in *ottava rima*, the Italian form that Byron had perfected as a satiric weapon in the early nineteenth century. Replete with references to Horace's "Ars Poetica" and other classical sources, the poem itself is partly patterned after Byron's "The Vision of Judgment," a satire on the poet laureate Robert Southey's grandiose commemorative poem of the same title, addressed to the late King George III. The model was appropriate, since Byron's annoyance at Southey stemmed from the fact that the laureate was a former radical who had once written a tribute to the fourteenth-century peasant rebel Wat Tyler.

John Atkins, literary editor at the time, recalled that the poem was discussed by *Tribune's* triumvirate: Aneurin Bevan, one of the great figures of the Labour Party left and the paper's titular editor; George Strauss, its publisher and one of its principal backers; and John Kimche, who ran the paper day to day and was a close friend of Orwell. They decided to publish Alex's poem in the interest of democracy and free speech, Atkins said, despite the fact that "it was a full-scale attack on our society and its values and, by extension, the war effort." Additionally, "there was no doubt about its liveliness and, in much of its argument, its accuracy."[50]

Addressed to a fictional "Columbian [American] poet" who had recently returned from Britain, Alex's poem was an uninhibited attack on Churchill and his War Cabinet ("pimps in hardware coronets"), the BBC ("bookie, pimp and vet"), and the artists and writers who had signed on to support and propagandize the war effort.***

> You met them all. You don't require a list
> Of understrapping ghosts who once were writers—
> Who celebrate the size of Britain's fist,
> Write notes for sermons, dish out pep to mitres,
> Fake letters from the Men who Fly our Fighters,
> Cheer when we blast some enemy bungalows—
> Think up atrocities, the artful blighters,
> To keep the grindstone at the public's nose—
> Combining moral uplift and pornography,
> Produced with arty paper and typography.[51]

*** Peter Davison, editor of Orwell's *Complete Works*, noted, "There have been many guesses as to who the visiting American was. In a letter giving the editors permission to reprint the poem, Alex Comfort revealed that 'the visitor was imaginary' (1 August 1995)." George Orwell, *The Complete Works of George Orwell*, vol. 15, *Two Wasted Years, 1943* (London: Secker & Warburg, 1998, 141.

Verse after verse ridiculed Churchill's stirring speeches as "the dim productions of his bulldog brain," reviled the church's willingness to preach "that bombs [were] Christian when the English drop[ped] them," and insinuated that Britain's literary giants were willing to turn out propaganda in exchange for avoiding military service.

Alex aimed an especially mean jab at Louis MacNeice, who was well known in the United States and had joined the BBC about the same time as Orwell to produce cultural programs designed to strengthen American identification with the British cause. One of MacNeice's scripts touched on the Nazis' murderous policies toward people with physical and intellectual disabilities, invoking his younger brother William, who had Down syndrome, for heart-tugging effect. This was too much for Comfort.

> I shan't forgive Macneice *[sic]* his crippled brother
> Whom just a year ago on New Year's Day
> The Germans murdered in a radio play.

By contrast, Alex paused briefly to defend MacNeice's friend Auden, who had been reviled for moving to the United States after the war began:

> Out of the looney-bin, they say,
> A quiet place where men with minds could write.

What Alex left out bears mentioning. He could have attacked Orwell for enlisting with the BBC to propagandize India in the face of the British overlords' wartime repression of the Congress Party and imprisonment of its leaders. Neither did he attack his friends Herbert Read and George Woodcock, who by now were participating in Orwell's radio programs. This may simply reflect the fact that the BBC's Indian broadcasts were difficult to hear in Britain, leaving Alex unaware who was featured on them. Since Orwell sometimes included poetry by Alex and the other Neo-Romantics, it's also possible that Alex regarded him as too valuable a literary ally to abuse directly in print.

Alex was careful about such things. He had originally composed his poem the previous fall, as "Address to a Distinguished Visitor," addressed to Archibald MacLeish, the American poet and Librarian of Congress. Why MacLeish? Possibly because the verse drama Alex had written a couple of years earlier, *Cities of the Plain*, had been influenced by *Panic*, a similar work by MacLeish set during the bank panic of 1933, as the critic H. Peschmann speculated after Alex's play was published.****

Alex sent his poem first to Clement Greenberg at *Partisan Review*, who liked it and agreed with some of its sentiments.[52] The editors turned the poem down, however, on account of MacLeish, who in 1940 had given a speech to the American Association for Adult Education in which he asserted, preposterously, that Ernest Hemingway, John Dos Passos, and other American writers of the disillusioned Lost Generation had to "face the fact that the books they wrote in the years just after the War have done more to disarm democracy in the face of fascism than any other single influence."[53]

"Far from being the sane, principled artist you appeal to against your own betrayers of culture," Greenberg's colleague Dwight Macdonald wrote Alex, "[MacLeish is] actually the leading American prototype of the tendency you satirize! That so basic an error in evaluation is even possible shows the great chasm in wartime between this country and your own. (A chasm of non-information, I mean, of course)."[54] By the time the poem appeared in *Tribune*, Alex had scrubbed all references to MacLeish.

When he submitted the poem to *Tribune*, Alex took the precaution of using an assumed name, "Obadiah Hornbooke," and the editors were good enough to supply the following footnote: "In fairness to 'Mr. Hornbooke,' it should be stated that he was willing to sign his name if we insisted, but preferred a pseudonym."

Alex had landed a few justified blows, but he had come disturbingly close to dismissing the unprecedented atrocities Germany was committing and impugning the motives of many artists and writers who were working hard and without much reward to defeat fascism. According to Atkins, *Tribune* literary editor John Bevan later said that one reason he agreed to publish "Hornbooke" was that it provoked Orwell to write what he knew would be a strong, clear-headed response.[55] The gambit worked. Two weeks later, on June 18, Orwell—under his own name—responded in *Tribune* with his own Byronic satire, "As One Non-Combatant to Another (A Letter to 'Obadiah Hornbooke')." Orwell decried a poet—unmistakably Alex—

Where slogans serve for thought and sneers for answers—

**** H. Peschmann, "Earth Takes Vengeance," *New English Weekly*, October 21, 1943. Alex may also have had in mind the two poetic dramas that Auden and Isherwood created in the '30s, *The Dog Beneath the Skin* (1935) and *The Ascent of F6* (1937).

You've chosen well your moment to appear
And hold your nose amid a world of horror
Like Dr. Bowdler walking through Gomorrah.

"Your hands are clean, and so were Pontius Pilate's," Orwell went on, before accusing Alex of enjoying life on the sidelines without "even a libel action" while benefiting from the sacrifice of others in the war against Hitler.

After this outburst, the poem ends on a friendly note. Orwell was always suspicious of saintly figures, although he would be elevated into one after his death, and he urged Alex not to set himself apart from principled antifascists who would welcome his help in the fight against Hitler.

For the half-way saint and cautious hero,
Whose head's unbloody even if "unbowed,"
My admiration's near to zero;
So my last words would be: Come off that cloud,
Unship those wings that hardly dared to flitter,
And spout your halo for a pint of bitter.

As this suggests, behind the scenes, Alex and Orwell were cautiously friendly. In July 1942, following Orwell's *Partisan Review* diatribe against defeatists, when Alex, George Woodcock, and Julian Symons were writing in protest, Alex had asked what Orwell meant by saying that the *Adelphi*, in which they had both been published, had "once or twice engaged in Jew-baiting of a mild kind." Orwell wrote him back, explaining that he had been referring principally to some incidents before the war, not anything more recent.[56]

Alex thanked him for the clarification. More importantly, he conceded Orwell's point that some pacifists, including *Adelphi* founder John Middleton Murry, who was now editing *Peace News* for the PPU, tried to argue against the war on grounds that were ethically incompatible: that violence is wrong and immoral and that the conflict with Germany would destabilize the British Empire.***** Alex, who was now composing his first straightforwardly anarchist novel, had no trouble rejecting

***** Alex had no use for Middleton Murry, whom he later remembered as "a most unpleasant pseud who made his living by peddling his wife Katherine Mansfield's bones from a handcart, metaphorically, of course," an accusation Alex claimed to have made to his face. AC, letter to Arthur E. Salmon, August 28, 1980.

pacifist arguments that bolstered the right. "I have written a commination to J. M. Murry but he did not print it," he added.[57] The following month, Alex queried Orwell about submitting something to *New Road*, Grey Walls's annual anthology, and Orwell agreed.[58] A cut-down version of his short memoir, "Looking Back at the Spanish Civil War," would appear in the first, 1943 edition of the series.

Somehow the antagonists seemed to realize they had a lot in common, and the same pattern of mutual attack and reconciliation followed the publication of the *Tribune* poems. "As a piece of verse your contribution was immensely better, a thing most of the people who spoke to me about it hadn't noticed," Orwell wrote Alex soon after. "I think no one noticed that your stanzas had the same rhyme going right the way through. There is no respect for virtuosity nowadays."

New Road 1943 had by then been published. "So New one hardly dares say anything about it," Connelly wrote in the *Observer*. "In Alexander Comfort the writers of the 'forties have found their John Lehmann."[59] Orwell was impressed by the quality of the poetry—and the newness: "I should think half the writers were not known to me before." He promised to get E. M. Forster to discuss *New Road* on the BBC's India service and suggested Alex try to get copies of it to people in India—"there is a small public for such things . . . and they are starved for books at present"—and recruit some to write for him.[60]

A leftist like Orwell was one thing, but what would Arthur Waugh, Alex's kindly, cricket-loving publisher, the old-school Tory who had promoted his career from such an early age, have thought of his protégé's pseudonymous attacks on the war and the State in a socialist newspaper? We don't know, and it's likely he never knew about them. Waugh had a stroke on April 3, 1943, and died on June 25, less than two weeks after his last board meeting at Chapman & Hall.[61] His last surviving letter to Alex, sent October 27, had included some comments by his son Alec on *The Almond Tree*, plus news that sales of the novel had come to 1,106 copies, concluding, "Every best wish to yourself, & kind remembrances to Ruth."

Following Arthur's death, Alex wrote his widow, Catherine, "It isn't only that I owed to him personally any success I may have had as a writer—I counted him as one of my best friends."[62] This was deserved. At an extremely young age, Alex had found a powerful and devoted literary champion and a deeply sympathetic ear. But he was finding another one in Herbert Read.

Alex had almost finished writing *The Power House* by the time

Waugh passed on, but the unavoidable fact was that his first two novels had not achieved the popular success Chapman & Hall had hoped for, and, without his friend involved, the publisher might not take up the new one. Once the manuscript was complete, Alex sent it to Read along with a new collection of poems, a series of eight elegies.

About the latter, Read was encouraging but stern. "You are at a critical stage in your poetical development," he wrote Alex in July, "and your next volume should be one which does not leave any doubt about your progress. Although I find a good deal to admire in all these elegies, and like some of them without reservation, . . . I feel that as a collection they are a little forced, and give the impression that you have compelled yourself to strike a major attitude." Read advised him to take some more time over the poems and show them to "one or two other competent critics."[63]

Three weeks later, nevertheless, Read was satisfied enough to announce that he would be showing the poems to Eliot and felt certain his friend would give them a look. That he did, and in September Read sent the poems back to Alex with only minor criticisms, mostly from Eliot, "which seem to point to blemishes that could be removed by a more careful consideration of your technique. Apart from these sorts of faults I can say that my liking for the poems has only increased with my repeated reading of them."[64]

About *The Power House*, Read was encouraging as well. "If Chapman & Hall refuse to publish your novel we shall be very glad to see it," he told Alex in July, "although I must say that the length will be a formidable handicap."[65]

Chapman & Hall still had an option on Alex's next two books but declined to pick it up, and, in October, T. Murray Ragg, Routledge's fiction and poetry editor, sent him an agreement to publish the new novel. Like Read, however, he was concerned about its length. They pressed Alex to cut it, even offering to take the highly unusual step of setting it up in galleys at his expense to make the job easier. He agreed, and they supplied him the galley, billing him £50. In the end, however, he cut the text very little.[66]

With Alex's third novel in production and his final year of medical training nearing completion, Alex and Ruth decided it was time to marry. They had been engaged, effectively, for nearly three years. Ruth's rock-ribbed mother May naturally had had qualms early on about her daughter marrying a man who had journeyed from enthusiastic Christianity to frank nonbelief, but she liked Alex personally and was mollified by his enduring love of church music. He was now training in London, and Ruth was working in the city, which at last made setting up housekeeping practical. In October they were married at the Union Church in Loughton, with Jack Newport, a friend from Cambridge CongSoc, serving as Alex's best man.[67] Wed, they at last consummated their bond. Later, devoted as always to imagery from nature, Alex wrote the following short poem to his new wife:

> There is a white mare that my love keeps
> unridden in a hillside meadow—white
> as a white pebble, veined like a stone
> a white horse, whiter than a girl.
>
> And now for three nights sleeping I have seen
> her body naked as a tree for marriage
> pale as a stone that the net of water covers
>
> and her veined breasts like hills—the swallow islands
> still on the corn's green water: and I know
> her dark hairs gathered round an open rose
>
> her pebbles lying under the dappled sea.
> And I will ride her thighs' white horses.[68]

CHAPTER 5

Blacklisted (1943–1945)

The same month he was married, Alex published a short essay in the poet Robert Herring's literary magazine, *Life and Letters To-day.*[1] Titled "An Exposition of Irresponsibility," it begins: "To the Editor of *Partisan Review.*" Was it submitted and rejected, perhaps for coming too close to advocating the end of the State? Possibly, but there is no record that he ever actually sent it to the American magazine. The essay marks his first step in taking the elements of the political development he traced in his first three novels and weaving them together into a systematic political, social, and aesthetic philosophy. That process would continue for the remainder of the decade, even as he continued to publish new poetry, fiction, and scientific research.

Alex tried to explain what drove writers like himself to pursue a line of thought founded on Romanticism. He laid out three points:

- "History is not a process amenable to reason"; in other words, human history is not the story of steady progress we've been taught it is, morally or politically.
- Since human beings aren't immortal, life has no inherent significance; neither a Christian nor a Marxist perspective is valid. But some valid set of principles for human conduct can be found in myth.
- Human beings have "a congenital inability not to abuse power." Democracy must be rejected "because the majority is consistently wrong, a priori." So must fascism, because it is "nothing more nor less than the attempt to use the negative in man as a cohering force." The State, through which these systems express themselves, "having consistently shown itself to be evil, in so far as we understand at all what 'evil' means, has absolved us by its idiocy."

That left anarchism as the remaining valid form of human organization. But what responsibility does that place on humans, either as individuals or as a community? "We now bear and accept no responsibility to any group, to any body for its own sake, not even to ourselves, but only as individuals," Alex argued. "Those who join voluntarily or by compulsion in them have constructed worlds for themselves in which we have no part at all. . . . Accordingly we now are our own worlds and our own governments—our politics have been thoroughly atomized." If all bonds to states or corporate entities, with their various "idiocies," are dissolved, then those who refuse to make allegiance are "at continual variance" with "the corporate, and with all who are prepared to delegate their minds, whether to a single ruler or to a committee of rulers." Alex added, "It looks as though the sole remaining factor standing between the possibility of living a sane life and its destruction by lunatics is the disobedience of the individual."

At a time when governments—even democratic governments—were commanding their subjects in uniform to commit unspeakable acts, Alex was arguing for both a radical individualism and a radical commitment to collective responsibility through disobedience. The artist has a special obligation, he added: "Most human beings are robbed of their voices either by force or by fraud." It is the artist's duty to speak for them. "The weak of this world, the raw material from which both the hostages and the firing squad, the airman and his civilian victims, the Indian and the fellow who flogs him, are recruited, are the people to whom I personally feel a responsibility. And when the sufferings of one or another are held up as a bait to induce me to inflict further suffering on others, all I can reasonably do is disobey and lend the victims my voice."

"An Exposition of Irresponsibility" is partly a proto-anarchist manifesto, but it also sought to move the British pacifist movement out of the impasse in which it had been stuck since failing to keep Europe from going to war. The PPU had flourished in the late '30s for two reasons: first, the government didn't consider it a serious threat (it could never claim more than 136,000 members, and the number of conscientious objectors after war broke out was relatively small); and, second, it had deliberately avoided creating an ideology of its own, in the interests of drawing in as many people as possible.

Especially after the fall of France, this was no longer tenable.

Alex was taking what Read had asserted in *Poetry and Anarchism*—"Anarchism naturally implies pacifism"—and turning it on its head. "There remains to us only anarchism," he wrote, because it stood squarely against the institutions and habits of obedience that produced war to begin with and because it valued every individual's responsibility to every other. To be viable, pacifism had to oppose not just war but also the State.

Historian Martin Ceadel has noted that pacifism and anarchism are similar in that both are built on the hope "that what has come to be regarded as normal human behavior can be changed for the better," and that this change would be "fundamental."[2] It's not too surprising, then, that other pacifists came to conclusions bearing some resemblance to Alex's by the end of the war, at least in private. Vera Brittain wrote in an unpublished manuscript that her wartime pamphlets represented "a small part of democracy's universal resistance-movement against the all-powerful State, and a characteristic reaction of the individual and independent mind against the totalitarianism of our time."[3] But in 1943 Alex was introducing a new, anarcho-humanist element into the discussion of why and how to resist war.

The following January he put his commitments into practice, sending a letter to the subscribers of *Poetry Folios*, plus other luminaries of the British artistic and literary worlds, with the following appeal: "Many people who have an interest as artists in cultural and human values are disquieted at our present bombing policy. I have drawn up a declaration and protest in the hope that a larger number of people in the categories of writers, artists and musicians, all specially concerned with the values of cultural life and civilisation, may be willing to add their signatures and so increase the effectiveness of the memorial. I enclose a copy of the proposed wording herewith, and beg you to unite with other signatories."

The declaration itself was extremely blunt:

> We the undersigned regard with growing disquietude the wanton destruction of civilian life and national culture by the Government's policy of aerial bombardment, which seems to us to imitate in an aggravated form the example of the Germans. We do not accept the denials issued by the Government of the charge that such bombardment is indiscriminate; and we feel it to be our duty as writers, artists and musicians to protest against it in the strongest possible terms, as an offence against humanity.

The declaration endorsed a recent appeal by the International Red Cross Committee to all belligerent powers to halt "methods of warfare that affect civilian lives" and protested that "the principles of international law for the protection of lives and property are being relegated more and more to the background in favor of the unreserved pursuit of total warfare."

The response to Alex's solicitation was enthusiastic. While a few friends, such as Stephen Spender, declined to endorse it ("I am a coward, obviously, in this choice," he wrote back), the names he gathered and released in support of the declaration included Vera Brittain and Denton Welch; musicians Benjamin Britten, Peter Pears, and Clifford Curzon; playwright Laurence Housman and poet James Kirkup; and such friends and allies as Herbert Read, Derek Savage, and George Woodcock.[4]

Despite the caliber of the signatories, the declaration failed to attract much attention, and what there was tended to be unsympathetic. "To the piffling minority of Britons who object to Allied bombings as 'an offence against humanity' were added 26 names last week," the weekly *News Review* reported sneeringly on March 23. But the magazine then listed all the names, along with a description of each, suggesting that it didn't consider their protest such a minor affair after all.

As this indicates, attacks on writers who did not stand squarely behind the war effort were still common in the last full year of the conflict. In another article in *Partisan Review*, Alex reported to his American readers that Alfred Noyes, the popular poet, had published a book, *The Edge of the Abyss*, that was drawing quite a bit of attention. It argued that society was suffering from a collapse in the belief in absolute good and evil, and it blamed especially Marcel Proust, James Joyce, and D. H. Lawrence, branding their works as "a root-cause of fascism." [5] Shortly thereafter, a group of twelve painters had published an open letter to the Council for the Encouragement of Music and the Arts, a four-year-old government-funded organization, complaining that it was giving money to organize a tour of what they termed "decadent" artists, whose work, presumably, was too modern and not patriotic enough.

Institutions in the UK were responding to these pressures. In an article in *Partisan Review*, Alex related how he had gone to the BBC to discuss giving a talk on recent British writing aimed partly at newly liberated France. (He had earlier been included on a panel discussion with Desmond MacCarthy, Spender, and Day Lewis about writing for broadcast—many of the younger poets, he said, would not care to write verse commissioned by the BBC—and had just published a short story in *The Listener*.)[6] But he had been told, jokingly, not to be too highbrow. "Of course, if you were talking to India it would be different, but we have no intelligent public here." He named some books he might discuss, and his interviewer remarked that he hadn't mentioned any war books. That's because he was a pacifist, Alex replied.

> The interviewer's jaw dropped. "This is terrible—we probably can't use you at all—there's a directive against people-not-wholly-in-sympathy being allowed to broadcast on any subject. . . . But if we can't ask you to broadcast I must have your word that you will treat the matter in strict confidence." I told him that he could blacklist me, but I was damned if I'd hush up for him. . . . The way youngsters straight from college are impounded to write scripts . . . makes me think that I am not the first person to get what I believe you call the bum's rush.

What the BBC wanted during wartime, as did Britain's cultural establishment in general, was propaganda, not critical thinking. Alex responded by hatching a plan to bring a group of younger British writers to recently liberated Paris to read from their work, and he appealed to Nancy Cunard, asking whether she knew anyone who could get permission—it still being wartime—to take books over for potential sponsors and perhaps bring back some new French works. "For our part, we could arrange return readings of new French poetry, if only we could get the stuff," he wrote.[7] He asked the poet and critic Alec Craig—a scholar of banned books in England—to set up an event in London along these lines, and he also contacted Herbert Read and T. S. Eliot, as well as the actor and Free French broadcaster Jacques Brunius about participating, but the project appears to have gone no further.[8]

Orwell, meanwhile, gave Alex an opportunity to drive home the point about the corruption of literature by propaganda. A few months after their exchange in *Tribune*, Orwell had left the BBC to become the paper's literary editor. Aiming to widen its array of voices, he wrote letters of invitation on his first day at the desk to Eliot, Treece, and Comfort. "Of course I can't undertake in advance to print anything but would always read anything of yours with interest," he wrote Alex, "[although] we can't undertake to print direct pacifist propaganda." He added, "I should like very much if you could do another satirical poem."[9]

Alex accordingly submitted a second anonymous poem to Orwell, and it was published on June 30. Titled, with a slight change in the spelling of the alleged author's last name, "The Little Apocalypse of Obadiah Hornbrook," it satirized wartime propagandists:

"Where are the writers?" "All around you, look—
Peddling democracy like pigs in clover."

The poem imagines Wordsworth summoned from heaven by Noyes to churn out "slime" for the cause of war. "We need some pens to help us peddle fetters," Hornbrook tells Wordsworth. "Cheer like a sport when Hamburg slums get pasted."

Writers on both sides of the Atlantic knew perfectly well what they were endorsing when they championed the war, Alex charged, while the dissidents—like the American pacifist poet Kenneth Patchen, who Alex was recommending to Grey Walls—saw their work ignored.

"America?" "MacLeish is going strong,
Teaching the others how to like the stink
Of putrefaction, mixing Right and Wrong
Like apple pie and cream, or turd and ink,
Helping the bloodstained caravan along,
Teaching the cannon-fodder what to think
(I ought to warn you, though, not to hobnob
With Kenneth Patchen, or you'll lose your job.)"

Should Alex's friends at *Partisan Review* have seen the poem, they surely would have been pleased that he had taken their criticisms of MacLeish to heart. At home it elicited some furious letters, most of them castigating *Tribune* for publishing such an attack. Orwell responded, first reassuring the paper's readers that he did not agree with "Hornbrook," then adding that there were lines the editors would not cross: "We wouldn't print an article in praise of antisemitism, for instance. But granted the necessary minimum of agreement, literary merit is the only thing that matters."

Orwell went a bit further in defending Comfort. "I should be the last to claim that we are morally superior to our enemies," he wrote, "and there is quite a strong case for saying that British imperialism is actually worse than Nazism." Certainly, there was more freedom of expression in "the blackest patches of the British Empire" than in the totalitarian countries, he said. "[But] I want that to remain true. And by sometimes giving a hearing to unpopular opinions, I think we help it to do so."[10]

"Unpopular" was putting it mildly. In April, Vera Brittain had published *Seeds of Chaos: What Mass Bombing Really Means*, a pamphlet revealing the brutality and human cost of the government's strategic bombing campaign. A shorter version, "Massacre by Bombing," had appeared a month earlier in the United States. President Franklin Delano Roosevelt attacked it, saying that one could either be for the Germans and the Japanese or support the "maintenance of civilization" but not both.[11] American journalist and broadcaster William L. Shirer accused Brittain of using Nazi propaganda to make her case.[12] When Shirer's article was reprinted in the *British Weekly* in May, the publication refused to allow Brittain space to reply.[13]

Alex found a place for his next major statement at about the same time in George Woodcock's *NOW*, the same magazine Orwell had earlier condemned for publishing an article by the Duke of Bedford. "Art and Social Responsibility" recast and expanded the analysis he had begun in "An Exposition of Irresponsibility" a few months earlier, drawing a clearer connection between Romanticism as an aesthetic and as opposition to war and the State, and what set it apart from the "classicism" he attributed to poets of the Auden school.[14]

"The classic sees man as master and the romantic as victim of his environment," he wrote. "The essence of Romanticism is the acceptance of a sense tragedy." And this was derived from the knowledge of death, Alex wrote. Art is the ultimate protest against death, the only way that humans can achieve a form of permanence. All too often, however, they attempt to deny or negate death by subsuming themselves in society or the State, which compel them either through subtlety or violence to do their will. Fascism is an example of this. "[Fascism is] the attempt to summate the destructive impulses and to use them as a basis for society. It teaches, logically, contempt for death and suffering in oneself and in others. It teaches that the individual is unreal, and therefore death, the termination of the individual, is unreal also."

Therein lies the "genuine satisfaction" that people often find in authoritarian societies: a sense of belonging, a kind of immortality. Orwell, in *Nineteen Eighty-Four*, would memorably define the vision of his dystopia as "a boot stamping on a human face—forever." For Alex, fascism was more complex and more seductive. "Society is not only a form of abrogating moral responsibility, it is a womb into which one can crawl back and become immortal because unborn." Thereby, however, our own personalities are lost.

Alex, like Read, was searching in psychoanalysis for the neurotic symptoms—a kind of insanity—he saw in humanity's acceptance of war. "Men who participate in corporate action which involves the abrogation of personality—who are members of any society to which they attribute quasi-human properties and admit obligations, are[,] while so participating, madmen. Madmen are at present murdering Jews. Madmen are bombarding the cities of Europe." Very few of these "madmen" were outlandish monsters, Hitlers or Himmlers, Alex said. Rather, they are all around us: our neighbors, colleagues, friends. In a passage paraphrased from the manuscript of *The Power House*, he wrote,

> The man whom one knows—a good fellow, able to live as an individual a life which is free from any conscious assaults on the rights of others, who does not make a practice of beating his own head or the heads of others against walls, who is sane, with whom one eats or drinks—this same man can very well return one evening to talk or drink with you again and catalogue the most grotesque and contemptible actions which he has performed, or which he supports, with full approval and a fixed delusion of their rightness, solely because he is now acting as a member of some organized group. It is this frantic prostration before society, this masochistic attitude . . . which explains the obedience of so many populations to rogues and brutes who pull the strings and make Leviathan walk.

What could we do to avoid following this treacherous path? Three things, Alex advised:

- Recognize the seeds of madness in ourselves.
- Avoid "all bodies, groups, teams, gangs, organised squads, whether they are directed at killing Jews, flogging Indians, or bombing Berlin"—but "not hate or distrust any . . . singly."
- Fight back from concealment, being prepared to "humour, to cajole, to deceive, to appease, to compromise, to run at the right moments."

While Alex didn't deny the existence of class war—"nobody in his senses could deny" it—at present, he urged, "The war is not between classes. The war is at root between individuals and society." The goal must be to secede from society and the State and in their place form communities of free individuals practicing mutual aid. The earth will be inherited by the weak, Alex wrote, optimistically, "though they are forced to fight, plot, deceive for every inch of the legacy, . . . taxed, killed, frightened, conscripted, deceived, interned collectively." Echoing Schweitzer's definition of ethics as "responsibility without limit toward all that lives," he called upon artists to help by recognizing "boundless responsibility to men, especially to all those who are deprived of their voices." He added, "We must demand the right to secession as the one square foot of ground which is solid and from which we can look at and interpret the gigantic chaos of human existence."

"Art and Social Responsibility" is not one of Alex's most elegant texts. The writing is often clumsy, his terms are not always well defined, and he repeats himself and bludgeons home point after point. He declares victory, in cultural terms, where he has no business doing so: "History has driven us from classicism to romanticism, and the migration has been almost universal among sensitive writers." Really?

Trying to point out where one could find the sort of "free communities" he was urging humans to create, Alex directed his reader to air raid shelters during bombing raids, "Dachau or Huyton," and the Russian collective farms. "These are the largest communities in which anarchism is real." There, "standing aside preliminary to creation is not resented to the same degree as in the societies . . . whose sole virtue is their unanimity in error." Comparing conditions among Dachau inmates to anarchism and ascribing to the prisoners the power to create in the face of oncoming starvation and murder was about as unthinking, not to mention insensitive, a statement as a writer could make who argued for "boundless responsibility" for the voiceless.

But the essay is genuinely urgent, and much of its argument is prescient. "The man one knows" is precisely the person Orwell, just a few years later, would describe as the model citizen of Oceania in *Nineteen Eighty-Four*. "I rather doubt," Alex wrote, "if ever in history there have been so many who realized the emotional fact of death." In this, he was referring to people like himself who had grown up during the increasingly ominous years leading up to the war, but it would apply even more starkly little more than a year after he wrote these words, once the atomic bomb had changed the world, and he it would return to it throughout his career.

Alex's essay attracted both sympathetic and very unsympathetic criticism. In *The Freethinker*, a secular humanist magazine, the journalist and detective novelist John Rowland praised it as an exciting, challenging piece of argument and Alex as possibly "one of the really important writers of the next 20 or 30 years" but feared—inaccurately—that he was urging writers to "retire into ineffective isolation" at a time of crisis. He also accused Alex of glossing over centuries of human progress and obsessing too much on recent dire developments like fascism.[15]

Writing in *Tribune*, Julian Symons, a Trotskyist who had been Alex's ally in the quarrel with Orwell, was far harsher and for better reason. He zeroed in on Alex's dislike of "groups": "Did I not receive a few weeks ago a communication from Mr. Comfort asking me to sign a manifesto against indiscriminate Allied bombing of Germany? And was not Mr. Comfort sponsoring there a bit of group activity? It is true that he says 'I recognise the seeds of madness in myself,' so that manifesto must have suggested itself on one of his bad days."[16] There must be something wrong with a definition of "groups," according to Symons, that lumped in Nazi murderers of Jews with British bomber pilots, very much including an enormous "inflation of the individual ego."

What neither Rowland nor Symons seemed to register, in part because Alex did not define his terms carefully, was that he was arguing specifically against groups that served the established order—the one that had brought about the present war on either side—and in favor of a new kind of human community outside the State. Other, more powerful people appear to have understood how subversive his message was, however.

Still smarting from his treatment by the BBC earlier in the year, Alex wrote a letter to Rhys J. Davies, Labour MP for Westhoughton in Lancashire and a pacifist, about the incident. Davies wrote back to him on October 6, saying, "I am not a bit surprised at your experience with the B.B.C. I know of two experiences too which show that the Corporation are not by any means tolerant to those who hold views opposed to Government policy." He asked Alex to read a question he had prepared for debate in the Commons and for permission to show his letter to the minister of information as an instance in which the BBC "has been grossly unfair to minority opinion."[17]

By coincidence, the same day, the network's head of European productions, W. P. Rilla, wrote to Alex asking to discuss with him a series of broadcasts to the continent, much of which was in the process of being liberated from the Nazis, about "the current English literary scene." Rilla wanted to know whether Alex would make a recording to be used in the series and asked for his views on a list of additional proposed contributors that was attached to the letter.[18]

Alex informed Davies about the BBC's offer, and the MP again volunteered to "use the information we have about the Black List of the Corporation" when the House debated issues related to the ministry of information. "I wish all the citizens of our country had a tithe of your courage," he declared, but he suggested that Alex leave the matter to him for the time being.[19]

Alex did not. He wrote back to Rilla, noting that the proposed discussion seemed to be confined to "acquiescent writers" and asking if his name had been included on a "black list" within the organization. Rilla replied immediately, assuring him, "I was completely unaware that any discrimination against your broadcasting, and, indeed, any 'black list' to which you refer, existed anywhere in the Corporation." The literary broadcasts to Europe would not be limited to writers who toed the government line—"any such idea would destroy the very nature of the programme." He added, "Nobody has so far raised any query against your name." Rilla invited Alex to discuss "the whole matter" with him over lunch.[20]

The invitation was accepted. Following their meeting, Alex sent Rilla notes for a talk, which Rilla proceeded to turn into a rough script for a dialogue between them. This he sent to Alex on October 18. Alex's reply concluded bluntly, speaking for himself and other war resisters and touching on his arguments in "Art and Social Responsibility": "We set ourselves a task in 1940—we tried to keep sane, to remember we were human beings, not to be taken in by hate-propaganda from either side. We've tried to stick to the ideal of personal responsibility and artistic freedom. I don't think we've done too badly. At any rate, we've kept on writing."

Cryptically, Rilla wrote that he still had to get in touch with Hilton Brown, the novelist and poet who was head of talks at the BBC, to "clear up your position" before the program could go forward, noting that Brown had been hard to reach. He reminded Alex that the recording date was set for Wednesday, October 25, from 2:00 to 2:30 p.m.[21]

On October 23, Comfort received a letter from the actor and writer Robert Speaight, then working for the network, informing him that his contribution to the program on "the present situation and prospects for English literature" would not be used. By way of explanation, Speaight wrote:

> You will, I think, realise that the European Service is bound by rather strict political considerations and we have to be very careful about letting anything on the air which might be liable to misinterpretation by our listeners. I wholly respect the sincerity and frankness of your views, but I do feel that they might very easily be misunderstood and lead people to think that they are more generally shared in this country than in fact I believe they are. I should not wish to constrain you to any false modification of what you evidently feel very strongly and

> so I hope we may allow the matter to rest where it stands with no ill will on either side.[22]

Alex was sufficiently upset by this ever-so-considerate rejection that he cast about for some way to put pressure on the network. After some weeks, he wrote a letter summarizing the incident to the *New Statesman and Nation*, which it printed in full, but if he expected it to ignite a storm of protest on his behalf—from Davies, for example—he was disappointed. Seeing it, Read wrote him that it was "a good letter," and he was glad the paper gave it prominence. "I do not think I or anyone can usefully intervene, but I hold myself in readiness. I have no prospective engagements with the BBC, but I propose in all communications in the future to sign myself 'Anarchist & Pacifist', just so that they cannot plead ignorance." Encouragingly, he added, "I had lunch with Eliot on Thursday and he seemed to regard your action as fully justified."[23]

We know today that the BBC indeed made a policy of not allowing anyone on the air who held pacifist or Communist beliefs.[24] Alex's voice would not be heard on the BBC airwaves again until two years after the war. He couldn't complain, however, that his words were being censored in print. His second collection with Routledge, *Elegies*—the poems he had shown to Read the previous summer, with some additions—was published in July. The additions included two poems that drew on his time in Ireland, another to Ruth, and one written in the character of the exiled Athenian orator (and Demosthenes's rival) Aeschines. On the back of these new efforts, his reputation was continuing to grow.

"Mr Comfort's best poems show a mastery of movement in confident paragraphs of verse," the Cambridge scholar S. Gorley Putt wrote in the political and literary weekly *Time and Tide*. "There is sound poetic skill in this little book, and we can expect good things from Mr Comfort."[25] Peschmann, in the *New English Weekly*, came close to capturing the effect Alex was striving for, noting a "pervading sentiment of deep pessimism," that "in all ways man had gone astray or perverted the right and natural life-giving order of existence."[26]

The poems are gloomy—one is about the accidental drowning of a student off the beach of Bettystown, near Dublin—but the point is not to enable a wallow in despair but to engender an acceptance of the presence of death, to reveal how essential it is to savoring the beauty of life. Observing some old men sitting on park benches, he writes:

Their knowledge reads the leaves: the dead and the children
Speak to them voice and voice beside the lawns.
Under their waiting feet the old lovers lie
In a bridal sleep below the pools of leaves
While on their eyes fall spinning the winged seeds.[27]

Philippa Bosanquet, later the Oxford don Philippa Foot, noted for her explorations of rationality and moral judgment, gave a copy of *Elegies* as a birthday present in 1944 to her friend and flatmate Iris Murdoch.[28]

SHORTLY AFTER *ELEGIES* APPEARED, Routledge brought out *The Power House*, paving the way with a good deal of promotion. An excerpt had appeared in the latest edition of John Lehmann's annual anthology, *New Writing and Daylight*, and Routledge's advertising blurb promised the reader, "Out of it all emerges a social philosophy as unconventional as it is profound."[29] V. S. Pritchett devoted almost all of his June 26 "Book Talk" on the BBC to the novel.[30] It became Alex's most widely reviewed book yet, receiving more coverage than any of his books until *The Joy of Sex* nearly thirty years later, and it drew enthusiastic reviews from some leading critics and novelists.

Kate O'Brien led the way, in the *Spectator*: "Here is a bitter, relentless talent. Here is someone who will have no easy talk, who knows the sickness, the sterility which man has wrought on man. . . . The greatness of Mr. Comfort's book is that in it he has truly exposed the bleak and broken hearts of millions of his fellowmen; if he and a few others of his generation can see so unblinkingly the pass to which humanity has brought itself, perhaps there is hope."[31] Richard Church, who had found *The Almond Tree* so promising, declared that *The Power House* confirmed Alex as a novelist "so emotionally and intellectually disciplined as to be able at will to present his interpretation of life, not by argument, but by direct image and incident."[32]

Another leading novelist, L. P. Hartley, called *The Power House* "nobly conceived and executed with unfailing mastery, [making] much contemporary fiction seem feeble and insincere." Like some other critics, Hartley praised Alex's attention to detail in a landscape he'd had to pull together from other people's accounts; but, he added, "absorption in detail tends to depersonalize a book."

For other critics, that was the trouble: the book was drowning in detail, and the characters failed to come alive. Perhaps to firm up a setting he hadn't experienced firsthand, the *New Statesman and Nation's* critic complained, "he particularizes everything that appears, whether it is necessary or not" or else resorts to similes. "If people emerge from the darkness, they must emerge like rabbits from a hole. If ivy hangs from a building, it has to look like tar falling from a pot."[33] Zola achieved realism in his fiction by personally investigating the places and people he wrote about; lacking the opportunity to do so, Alex had to strain at it.

Some of the reaction to *The Power House* depended on whether certain critics approved of Zola-esque realism at all, or of the author's politics. The *New Statesman*, under Kingsley Martin, the editor who had refused to print Orwell's dispatches from Spain because they were critical of the Soviet Union, couldn't be expected to like a pacifist novel published while Stalin's Russia was fighting for its life, and it didn't.

What is remarkable, however, is how few critics were offended by Alex's plea for an uprising against both sides of the war. This may have been a result of the book's timing. The defeat of Germany and the end of the war in Europe were less than a year away, and the British public was becoming more responsive to criticism of the war's conduct. Churchill's government was just months from being turned out of office. In an undated private letter, Richard Aldington, whose World War I novel *Death of a Hero* Alex had likely read as a boy, commented, "Of course I agree very much with Comfort's point of view. He is trying to keep some humanity, instead of being the dupe of the innumerable party lice and the journalist pimps and all those who outrage civiliszation [*sic*] by putting party above humanity and politics above morality."[34]

Sales were lively if not on the best seller level.[35] In December *John O' London's Weekly* named *The Power House* one of the best books of the year, tied for fifth place behind G. M. Trevelyan's *English Social History*.[36]

By then Alex himself was looking ahead to the end of the war and asking what the prospects would be for people's recovery of the sense of responsibility that the State, in his view, had worked to suppress. Europe and the world were entering into another period like the decades between the world wars, with another and even greater cataclysm possibly waiting at the other end. But he was optimistic. "I believe that in the interval of exhaustion which elapses between this war and the next," he wrote in "October 1944," published that fall in *NOW*, "we can so undermine the calf-like obedience which made possible 1914 and 1939 that when the next irresponsibles try to make it bear their weight, it will precipitate them into the filth where they deserve to be."[37]

He had lost none of his contempt for writers and artists turned war propagandist or who had practiced self-censorship to stay out of trouble. *Horizon*, which studiously stayed above politics, "is full of gratitude that through four full years of war not one word has been censored," he wrote. "Who the mischief wants to censor it? . . . It has busily maintained intellectual morale and quieted the intellectual conscience, and its service to the war has been very nearly the equal to its service to literature." ("I don't trust *Horizon* or its works, but have no objection if they like to print me," he told Treece.)[38]

The Maquis offered inspiration, however. While the French Resistance fighters might have been reabsorbed into their own country's politics, they had shown the way to "keep the shell of society while devouring its heart and undermining its tyranny." Resistance to conscription—which would continue to be in force in the UK until 1960—was one obvious place to begin, underscoring Alex's point that "the choice is not between socialism and fascism but between life and obedience."

THE POWER HOUSE MAY not have been the literary breakthrough that his publisher had hoped, but it raised Alex's public profile considerably: enough to be noticeable to his literary comrades at Grey Walls Press.

He was now launched on his medical career, installed in his first real job as house physician at the London Hospital, and had set up housekeeping with Ruth in a flat in Brunswick Square, near Bloomsbury and not too far from the new Grey Walls offices at Vernon Place. Wrey Gardiner couldn't help but note that Alex's student attire of mackintosh and "appalling" beret were gone, and that he was looking very smart in new suits and overcoats. He was also full of the success of his new novel and at the same time suffering another bout of depression. "How to be successful though depressed?" the perpetually impecunious Gardiner wondered.[39]

Alex had been a fixture of Grey Walls for over three years. Although never an employee, he was a font of book ideas and sometimes helped Gardiner sift through the mounting number of submissions received as the publisher's profile grew. Quality varied greatly. Once Alex suggested they set up a subsidiary company producing a line of lavatory paper on the floor below, with a chute connecting the offices.

But he had never been part of the highly social, pub-crawling literary scene that burgeoned during the war in Fitzrovia, the district overlapping

Camden and Westminster, and of which Tambimuttu as well as Gardiner and some of his writers were very much a part. Too busy with his studies and the rapid pace of his writing—always in an attempt to keep two steps ahead of migraine—he now had not only a wife but a best friend in Ruth, and his marriage provided most of the practical and emotional support and comradeship he needed. He never had any other friend with whom he could share his innermost thoughts, and didn't seem to need one, his son later said.[40] The heavy drinking and predatory atmosphere of the Wheatsheaf and the other fabled Fitzrovia pubs would not have appealed to him in any case. Iris Murdoch commented on the "brutish and emotional opaqueness" of Tambi and his circle—a euphemism for crude sexist behavior?—and Alex undoubtedly would not have felt at home in it either.[41]

"This may surprise you," he had informed Treece during his first year at London Hospital, "but I have extremely few social contacts myself, I never go to literary functions, and I mix far more with scientists than with writers."[42]

He could be very critical, in fact, of writers who spent too much time socializing in drinking establishments. In Dublin during Alex's midwife training, Robert Greacan recalled, "I took him to meet some friends of mine at a pub and he drank only half a pint. Later he said, 'Look Bob, you shouldn't hang around at pubs with these people. You'll get no work done.' I always had the impression he felt I was lazy."[43]

He still dropped by Grey Walls, however, met Gardiner, Marnau, and Nick Moore for lunch semi-regularly to discuss their respective projects, and joined them for book launches and poetry events. Gardiner remembered one such occasion, in 1944, the day the English-language version of Marnau's collection, *The Wounds of the Apostles*, appeared. Alex, Gardiner, Marnau, and Marnau's translator met for lunch, then coffee and trifle and cream at a café, the Florida, and then on to a poetry reading. At the latter, Gardner wrote, "I take a back seat with Ruth, Alex's wife. We always seem to meet on these occasions. Alex, I think, is nervous." After several readings, Eliot arises and "steals the thunder from the younger men, making thunder sound like thunder and drops of water like drops of water." Eliot accepts a copy of Marnau's book from Gardiner. "Fred is terribly pleased. We all go out into the London rain, people giving each other quick glances wondering who you are, and the famous being careful not to look at anybody, not to be buttonholed, not to seem to notice their enemies."[44]

If these occasions were not frequent, Alex had nevertheless established himself as "the Voltaire of Neo-Romanticism," as the critic Charles Hamblett—who was not a great fan—called him in 1945. "Comfort is a phenomenon, an embryonic *Zeitgeist* sired by germinal acid and of the times. . . . An incredibly prolific genius, Comfort absorbed the anarchic principles [of Read] and transformed them into powerful works of art, notably his *Elegies* and the novels. . . . He has rejected the shams of civilisation, but has, in pique, as it seems to me, rejected humanity by refusing to join in the struggle."[45]

Neo-Romanticism was becoming inconceivable without him, at least to its devotees. "After Herbert Read," said Derek Stanford, "nobody did so much to provide the movement as a whole with a political and social theory. . . . His opinions, taken as a whole, possessed an imposing consistency, and one gained the impression (by no means wholly true) that Neo-Romanticism was not just a matter of so many individual poems, stories and paintings, but a body of work produced beneath the umbrella of a clear cohesive theory."[46]

Alex cut a noticeable figure in London's youngish literary circles, at least when he found himself among them. "There was not a small amount of the schoolboy in him—the boy prodigy in the school laboratory conducting precocious experiments with 'stinks,'" Stanford recalled, "but what struck me most about him was his amazing conversation. Indeed, he talked like an angel who has swallowed an entire set of the *Encyclopaedia Britannica*, digested it and made it his own."

Once, Stanford said, Alex and Ruth encountered him sitting on the white stone seat opposite New Square in Lincoln's Inn, reading a book. Eager to show Alex a passage—it was the French anarchist Georges Sorel's *Reflections on Violence*—he cut himself on a razor blade he used as a pencil sharpener and bookmark. While Ruth bandaged his bleeding finger, Alex delivered a jokingly Freudian analysis of what had just happened. "The blade, he said, was clearly the knife of a masochist who was secretly hoping to hurt himself. Who else, he asked, could I possibly name who carried round a naked razor blade in this fashion?"[47]

If there was any swagger in Alex, it showed itself when he offered advice to other writers. One of these was Martin Seymour-Smith, then still a student at Highgate, who in 1944 sent him some poems and asked him what to do next. Alex was greatly impressed by the poems and supplied Seymour-Smith with a long list of publications and editors to approach, without failing to mention his name. Alongside, he offered a few dos and don'ts, including:

- "Don't go to literary parties, and be a total abstainer—the reverse has dried up more promising poets than I could name.
- "Treat all approaches by the MoI [Ministry of Information] as if they came from the Devil, which, from your point of view, they do. Only negotiate with the BBC on the understanding that you are doing them a favour!
- "Never pay any money to anybody for publishing anything. If you are approached by publishers, . . . go and see the proprietor and demand payment.
- "Write in season & out of season."[48]

It wasn't just his erudition but the impression of intellectual wholeness he projected that struck Stanford and others of Alex's literary contemporaries. While many of them were still unsure of their philosophical and political postures, Alex always seemed to have the problem—whatever it was—decoded, to have weighed the facts, incorporated them into a solid and consistent worldview, and arrived at a reasoned course of action, not just a superficial opinion. Where they were emotional and instinctual, he projected an air of method and finality, no doubt an inheritance from his mother and his habit of scientific research. "I think that the difference between us in the matter of the climate in which we feel our isolation is due in some degree to the fact that you possess much more detachment than I," his friend, the poet Emanuel Litvinoff, wrote him in 1946. "One feels from you that your crisis is in the past. You have a maturity that I shall never have and that has nothing to do with years."[49]

Others took Alex's "detachment" a bit more sourly. John Atkins, poet and literary editor of *Tribune* when Alex published his first Byronic satire, recalled, "On the occasions when I met him he appeared to be so single-minded as to lack the normal graces of human intercourse. He was like a machine which had been set for a certain, definable end. I never heard him say anything interesting because (I felt) it would be wasteful to utter opinions which did not find expression in print."

From Atkins's perspective, Alex was a talented writer whose name had got ahead of his accomplishments to date. "Slight in build and given to quick nervous gestures, he had built up an enviable reputation as a poet on a very slender basis. . . . Of all the writers of my time he was the one who was most successful in becoming the Fashion with the coteries, which of course is quite different from being popular or a best-seller." Once, Atkins said, he sent Alex a poem, noting that he certainly wouldn't want to publish it since its author didn't belong to "the charmed circle." Alex published the poem. "[This] confirmed my suspicion," Atkins wrote, "that quality didn't come into it and that pinpricks could do the trick."[50]

Whether it's fair to call it a "charmed circle" or even a "coterie," Alex was tireless on behalf of the artists with whom he identified. Along with crafting a unifying theory of Neo-Romantic thought and writing, he was calling attention to the movement's visual artists. He started writing reviews of art exhibitions soon after he left Cambridge, just a few years after a new circle of painters and sculptors arose whose work drew on myth, the British landscape, and their own notions of an ancient and enduring British folk culture. As such, they rejected abstraction in favor of overtly symbolic representations, filling their canvases with stark scenery, phantasmagoric creatures, and brightly colored imaginary landscapes that were quirky but often visually lush. While writers like Alex, Henry Treece, and Nick Moore found some of their inspiration in Blake's poems, artists like Cecil Collins, Graham Sutherland, John Craxton, and Gerald Wilde absorbed his pastoral and apocalyptic imagery. The writers at Grey Walls Press were drawn to these contemporary artists powerfully, and in a very personal way.

In February 1944 Alex and Wrey Gardiner attended the first solo show by Collins, at the Lefevre Galleries on King Street. Gardiner was impressed enough to buy one of Collins's paintings, *Three Fools in a Storm*: "three clown-like figures, one holding an oil lamp, another a dog on a lead, all skating over surrealist waves." He found it "truly representative of the three people who first created the Grey Walls Press, Alex Comfort, Nicholas Moore and myself." When he went back the next day to pick up his purchase, he found that the gallery had been bombed but the exhibit removed to a safe place.[51]

Alex, meanwhile, was at work on a review of the Collins show, which appeared in March in the *New English Weekly*. The painting that Gardiner bought was part of a series featuring characters dressed like fools from a medieval court, and Alex saw in them a close representation of his own thoughts about the attitude artists needed to adopt in a world that seemed to be destroying itself. "Collins' . . . Fools," he wrote, "are obviously conceived both as a creation and as a statement of his own relation to society—they are not just reiterations of Picasso's harlequins, but a picture of the new attitude of dissociation from the products of organised Reason which is being forced upon artists today, and I feel that what Collins is asserting is the obligation upon the possessors of minds to set up in business as Fools forthwith."[52]

Alex was certainly reading some of his own political concerns into what he saw, but Collins's outlook did have a lot in common with his. Two of his works had been exhibited at the 1936 International Surrealist Exhibition in London, which Read had helped organize, and in 1940 he became an instructor at Dartington Hall School, part of the experimental artistic community that a wealthy couple, Dorothy and Leonard Elmhirst, had established in 1925. There he moved away from Surrealism and allied himself with the Neo-Romantics. Even before his review appeared, Alex wrote to Collins, asking him to sign on to his protest against the Allies' aerial bombing campaign and complimenting his work. Collins wrote back, thanking Alex, mentioning that he was very interested in Alex's poetry, and suggesting they meet.

Alex and Gardiner ushered Collins into the Grey Walls circle, for whom he began contributing book jacket designs and other illustrations.

What Alex liked in Collins's work was its sense of organic development and its occasional satire. In an introduction to a monograph on Collins in 1946, he wrote that the artist's pictures "suggest something that has grown or has been made . . . much as the individual leaves make up the pattern of a tree."[53] The satire shows through in *Fool Picking His Nose in front of a Bishop* and *Procession of Fools*, which poke fun at the pretensions of the wealthy and powerful, both from 1940.[54]

Alex kept up his friendship with Collins for many years, reviewing another solo show in 1948 and delivering a lecture on his work—at Collins's request—in 1951 at the Institute of Contemporary Arts in London. To the end of his active life, Alex would keep at least one Collins painting in his home.

There's no doubt that Alex had a profound feeling for Collins's work and that of some of the other Neo-Romantic artists. Could he have helped but think, like his friend Gardiner, that the Fool somehow stood for himself: a figure apart from other people, benign and wishing them good but determinedly, perhaps helplessly, unique? In his case, it was a hand with no fingers rather than a peaked cap and motley costume that made the visual difference, but the attitude that grew out of that difference—that was forced on him, to some extent—was similar.

Alex was looking for a moral awakening in the visual arts, just as he sought in poetry and the novel, and it was for this reason that he had little patience for most surrealist and abstract art. Surrealism, in its obsession with dreams and madness, was "a communication of a neurosis," while the abstractionists' preoccupation with form was a flight from the collapse of civilization, an "exit via childhood." When Alex signed on as one of the sponsors of the new Institute of Contemporary Arts, which Herbert Read, Roland Penrose, and Geoffrey Grigson, along with a selection of wealthy benefactors, set up in 1946 to showcase radical and avant-garde art and host related lectures and discussions, culture, and politics, he doubtless saw it as an opportunity to put his own ideas and hopes across.

IN MUCH OF HIS artistic and literary criticism, Alex felt he was speaking for the Neo-Romantics as a movement if not individually, as their "Voltaire." But there had always been a tension between the Neo-Romantic school and the more myth-obsessed poets of the New Apocalypse, especially for Alex, whose poetry still showed some of Eliot's influence, who modeled his fiction on Zola's realism, and who couldn't cut himself off from politics as many of the Apocalyptics committed themselves to do. Gardiner felt he was losing the person who had helped him turn his small publishing enterprise into a literary presence.

"At one time my liking for him was almost physical," he wrote in 1946. "[Now] as his reputation increases I feel he will some day pass into another world which is not my world." Reading a proof of *The Power House*, Gardiner admitted, "he shows the insanity of society. He says what should have been said long ago and has not been said by the timid and the suckers." But this wasn't the sort of writing that appealed to the proprietor of Grey Walls. "He is a genius, though suffering from a powerful indigestion of long catalogues of the appearances of reality. . . . He is potted Zola watered down for the British nine-and-sixpenny novel-reading bourgeoisie."[55]

But Alex was also attracting attention outside the UK with his work. Probably the first of his poems to be published in the United States was "The Lovers," which had appeared in *A Wreath for the Living* and which *Poetry* magazine selected for its June 1942 issue. A year later he appeared again in *Poetry* with a new poem, "A Vision of Venus." Oscar Williams, an American poet and editor of a popular line of anthologies, included three of Alex's works in his collection *New Poems 1943*.[56]

Alex's *Partisan Review* connection, Dwight Macdonald, to whom he had sent a short story, "The Martyrdom of the House," passed it along to Holley Cantine, a writer, anarchist, and war resister who was editing a radical political-cultural magazine, *Retort*, in Woodstock, New York, which had been the home to a colony of artists, radicals, and assorted vegetarians and mystics since the early years of the century.[57] This forged a link between Alex and American left-wing poets and anarchists that would tighten throughout the decade. Cantine took the story for *Retort* and sent Alex back issues of the magazine—it had also featured early work by Kenneth Patchen, Robert Duncan, and Saul Bellow and had a large readership among conscientious objectors—asking him to show them to Read, Savage, and Woodcock. "We feel we have a great deal in common with all of you, and would like to get better acquainted." He also asked Alex to send him copies of Freedom Press's publications, some of which Macdonald had showed him.[58]

In September 1944 Alex heard from Woodcock that Henry Miller, the author of *Tropic of Cancer,* the most celebrated banned writer in the United States and a pacifist, had read "October 1944"—"with delight and amazement"—in the latest issue of *NOW* and wanted to get in touch with its author. "Amazed that in England you have this much freedom of expression," Miller marveled. "One would be lynched here for such utterances."[59]

Miller, living in semi-isolation in Big Sur, on the California coast, followed up with a letter to Alex in January, offering to try to get "October 1944" published in the States, although admitting that the prospects were slim.[60] But he also suggested that Alex contact George Leite, a poet and bookseller who lived near Miller's cabin in Big Sur and published *Circle* magazine in Berkeley. Alex would publish three poems and stories in *Circle* over the next several years. Miller also sent a new antiwar essay by Alex to Caresse Crosby, the avant-garde publisher and Lost Generation fixture, who was starting a literary journal, *Portfolio*, from her wartime home in Washington, DC. Crosby was becoming an antiwar activist herself. She published Alex's piece in the summer of 1945 as "Somnambulists in Freedom: The War as Seen by an English Anarchist."[61]

The traffic was flowing in both directions. Alex had already included two poems by Kenneth Patchen in the fifth issue of *Poetry Folios*, published in 1943, having received them from Cantine at *Retort*, and promised more of the American writer's work in future issues.[62] He was also discussing with Gardiner the publication of a collection of Patchen's poems, and perhaps one of Kenneth Rexroth's, in the UK.[*/63] Alex and

* Alex also urged Gardiner to publish Patchen's surrealist novel, *The Journal of Albion Moonlight*, but Gardiner refused, partly because of its length and partly because he didn't think its pacifism would attract a readership. Wrey Gardiner, letter to Arthur Salmon, February 12, 1981.

John Bayliss's 1944 edition of *New Road* contained a poem by Jean Giono that had originally appeared in English in *The Phoenix*, a pacifist publication run out of Woodstock in the late '30s by James Cooney, a former Communist who was expelled from the party for anarchist tendencies, and his wife, Blanche, a poet.[64]

It's not surprising that Macdonald helped guide Alex into this new circle of correspondents and contributors. In 1943 the mercurial Dwight had resigned from *Partisan Review*'s editorial board and launched a new bimonthly, *Politics*. Macdonald had moved toward a pacifist position, which his former colleagues considered but rejected, and was much more strongly critical of the US conduct of the war than they were. This put him and Alex in roughly the same camp, and when *Partisan Review* editor Philip Rahv wrote to Orwell about the split, asking if he would continue to contribute to the magazine, he mentioned, "The Alex Comfort gang keeps sending stuff, but we're pretty tired of their shenanigans . . . and politically they are beyond the pale."[65]

The deepest relationship Alex formed within the American scene at this time, however, was with Rexroth. The two grew close enough that Rexroth took the trouble of connecting Alex with the head of the Conchology Club of Southern California, from whom he wanted to request study materials and specimens for his research on mollusks.[66] A mostly self-educated poet, scholar, and critic, Rexroth had been the central figure since the early 1930s in the Bay Area cultural scene that gave birth to the postwar San Francisco Renaissance. He was also an anarchist and pacifist who, with his wife Marie Kass, helped Japanese Americans seeking to avoid internment during the war. Aside from his own work, he translated poetry from Chinese, French, Spanish, and Japanese, and he followed developments in British poetry keenly.

During the '30s, Rexroth had been less than enthusiastic about the Auden school and what he called its "rigorous rationalism, this suppression of all acknowledgement of personality, feeling, intuition, the denial of communication and of the existence of emotion," and he sought out work that brought reason and emotion back together.[67] In the work of the Neo-Romantics, he felt he had found the British counterpart to his own project.

In 1945 he read some of Alex's poems to the University of California English Club and reported that they were well received.[68] By then he was preparing an anthology of new British poets that his publisher, New Directions, would issue in 1947 with a long, well-informed introduction by Rexroth himself. While he was assembling it, he relied heavily on the

Grey Walls group for help, and he and Alex—whose letters at this time were otherwise usually brief and to the point—shared a long, gossipy correspondence about sources, poets they liked and disliked, and literary politics in general.

What was bringing together Apocalyptics and Neo-Romantics in the UK and radical bohemians in the United States? All these groups were reacting to some extent against the high modernists and the Auden group; all came of age in the run-up to World War II; all were centered around a slew of little magazines with little capital and relatively modest readerships; some were more sexually explicit in their writing; and all were influenced, culturally if not politically, by anarchism and pacifism rather than Marxism. Advocating neither violent revolution nor liberal democracy, many of them would have subscribed to Holly Cantine's argument, in *Retort*, that the realistic radical alternative should concern itself with "building up a nucleus of the new society 'within the shell of the old.'"[69]

Along with Rexroth and Patchen, the American writers who were drawn into this transatlantic nexus included Robert Duncan and Anaïs Nin. Lawrence Durrell and the poet David Gascoyne participated from the UK as well. Each group included an esteemed older writer—Read in Britain, Miller in America—who had a great influence on the participants in both countries. D. H. Lawrence was another frequent reference point for both.**

Some of these writers were more or less apolitical; others were beginning to stake out a new kind of politics that would blossom in the late '50s and '60s and was different from the class-struggle politics of the prewar decades. The scholar James Tracy calls it "radical pacifism" and has described it this way:

> A tactical commitment to direct action; an agenda that posited race and militarism (instead of labor) as the central social issues in the United States; an experimental protest style that emphasized media-savvy, symbolic confrontation with institutions deemed oppressive; an ethos that privileged action over analysis and extolled nonviolent individual resistance, especially when it involved "putting one's body on the line"; and an organization structure that was

** Cooney had aspired to found a "Lawrentian colony" in the Woodstock area. Alf Evers, *Woodstock: History of an American Town* (Woodstock, NY: Overlook Press, 1987), 600–602.

nonhierarchical, decentralized, and oriented toward concensus [*sic*] decision making.[70]

Tracy is describing the gestation of the New Left in the United States, but British writer-activists were undergoing a similar line of development. A form of militant pacifism began in both countries before the war. Afterward, it would have to address the decision by both governments to retain the draft, to build nuclear arsenals, and to engage in a Cold War with the Soviet Bloc. While the PPU and its supporters were keeping an antiwar movement alive in Britain during the war, the War Resisters League and the new Congress for Racial Equality (CORE) in the United States were pushing nonviolent disobedience into the struggles against war and racism. Dwight Macdonald, meanwhile, was writing essays in *Politics* emphasizing the centrality of individual moral choice that resembled those Alex was writing.[71]

At the same time he was establishing contacts in America, Alex was coming into closer touch with the anarchist movement in the UK, thanks in part to Woodcock, who in 1942 had become a regular contributor to *War Commentary*, the biweekly dissident publication that Freedom Press was putting out. The following year, tired of producing *NOW* essentially on his own and losing money on it, he agreed to let the Freedom collective take it over while he remained its editor.[72] By the time Alex contributed "Art and Social Responsibility" and "October 1944" to *NOW*, therefore, he was writing for a publication that identified clearly as anarchist. Soon he was attending and delivering talks at Freedom's Friday evening lecture series, in its offices in the top floors of a house in Hampstead, near the Finchley Road tube station. The talks "would vary in quality," Woodcock recalled, "from brilliant (if it happened to be someone like Comfort or the Belgian Surrealist E. L. T. Mesens) to excruciatingly boring (if it happened to be one of the rare proletarians who had been enticed into the movement)."[73]

WHAT KIND OF A movement—and tradition—was Alex embracing? Anarchism coalesced as an ideology in the mid-nineteenth century in the writings of the French philosopher and activist Pierre-Joseph Proudhon and two Russians, Peter Kropotkin and Mikhail Bakunin. All identified as socialists, but what set them apart from Marx and his followers was their insistence that a revolution against capitalism that secured true economic and social freedom and equality couldn't succeed unless it overthrew the State as well. Hence, they often described themselves as libertarian socialists as well as anarchists.[***]

Anarchism from the beginning was an international movement, and while it had its greatest organizing successes in continental Europe, three important precursors were English: William Blake, the political theorist and novelist William Godwin, and Godwin's son-in-law, the poet Percy Bysshe Shelley. As the nineteenth century wore on, other prominent British thinkers, writers, and artists espoused some elements of anarchism at various times, including William Morris, Oscar Wilde, Bertrand Russell, and Edward Carpenter.

A popular movement that could credibly be described as anarchist started to form in the 1880s, by which time a critical mass of foreign workers and political refugees had established themselves in London and other large cities, some of whom began forming clubs that declared themselves against government and the State. Important anarchist figures like the Germans Johann Most, Max Nettlau, and Rudolf Rocker lived in London for short periods, and Kropotkin made his home in the UK for more than thirty years starting in 1886. These figures made London one of the leading intellectual centers of European anarchism, with its largest following in the Yiddish-speaking Jewish community of the East End.

But efforts to generate a mass anarchist movement among British workers in the 1890s and early 1900s largely failed, hampered in part by the image that congealed around the movement as a coterie of bomb-throwing fanatics, especially from 1894, when a French anarchist accidentally detonated a pocketful of explosives outside the Royal Observatory in Greenwich Park, killing only himself.[****]

Despite these setbacks, aspects of anarchism were working their way into British culture, finding points of commonality with the island's folk traditions. From the time of the True Levellers or Diggers during the seventeenth-century English Civil War, the idea that the people had a natural right to pull down enclosures, take and live off the land as a propertyless "common treasury, as it was first made for all," had maintained a tenuous hold on the popular imagination.[74]

*** Alex once referred to Kropotkin as "the founder of ethology"—the scientific study of animal behavior—due to his emphasis, in his landmark book *Mutual Aid: A Factor of Evolution* (1899), "on the deepseatedness of the human and primate need for relationship." AC, "Out of Touch," *Guardian*, February 18, 1972.

**** This sensational incident was fodder for two famous novels: Joseph Conrad's *The Secret Agent* (1907) and G.K. Chesterton's *The Man Who Was Thursday* (1908).

Kropotkin's writings advocating small-scale farming and decentralized industrial production jibed with this line of thought. Once anarchism acquired a following in the UK, cooperative agrarian experiments started to pop up, including Millthorpe, near Sheffield, which Edward Carpenter established and where he lived for almost forty years. During both the First and Second World Wars, groups of pacifists banded together to work the land.

By the time war broke out again in 1939, hundreds of such communities existed in Britain, some anarchist, some Christian, some a bit of both, some neither.[75] They helped keep together a small but close-knit anarchist community in Britain through decades of ups and downs.

The through line from the early decades of British anarchism to Alex's time was Freedom Press, which Kropotkin and Nettlau had cofounded in 1886 and which began publishing the monthly newspaper *Freedom* the same year. Often surviving through the generosity of a small group of activists and supporters, Freedom Press published a stream of pamphlets aimed at working-class audiences and vocally opposed both the Boer War and Britain's entry into World War I.[76]

British anarchism reached a low point after the war, as many radicals embraced Marxist-Leninism following the October Revolution in Russia, and much of the working class embraced the Labour Party, which had close ties to the union movement. Additionally, the Jewish working-class community in the East End, which had supplied much of the movement's popular following, was beginning to age and disperse. Freedom Press limped along with greater and greater difficulty, and by the mid-1930s its newspaper had effectively ceased publication.

Two events revived the Freedom collective and, by extension, the British anarchist movement: the Spanish Civil War and the arrival of two Italian anarchists with sharp minds and strong personalities, Marie-Louise Berneri and her husband, Vero Recchioni, who Anglicized his name to Vernon Richards. Both were second-generation antifascists. Berneri's father, Camillo, had organized the first brigade of Italian volunteers to fight against Franco's insurrection in Spain. There he was murdered by members of the Communist Party. Joining Freedom Press, Richards and Berneri launched a new biweekly paper, *Spain and the World*, in part to offer the anarchist position on the civil war, countering the pro-Soviet *New Statesman and Nation*.[77]

The new paper was timely and well-edited, and it attracted a talented new coterie of members and fellow travelers to the Freedom collective. After the fall of the Spanish Republic in 1939, the paper changed its name to *Revolt!* for a short time before becoming *War Commentary*. After the war, Richards and Berneri would retitle it *Freedom*, echoing the name of the earlier publication.

In his autobiography, *Letter to the Past*, Woodcock says that the Freedom collective at the time Alex joined was still divided between "syndicalists" and "intellectuals." The first group hoped to revive British anarchism through labor organizing while the second took a two-track approach of developing it as a political and social theory while attaching it to causes like ending war and militarism that they felt could attract a broad base across class lines.[78] Despite having been raised by Italian working-class revolutionaries, Richards and Berneri were more of the intellectual inclination, as were some of the newer members of the collective, including Woodcock, John Hewetson (a physician), Philip Sansom (an artist), and Colin Ward, a soldier and architect who learned about anarchism through *War Commentary* and would become one of the most important British anarchist social thinkers of the postwar decades.

The intellectual tendency gradually gained the upper hand in the movement, in part because the working-class, syndicalist contingent was aging and in part because the intellectuals had better luck attracting younger members, such as Alex, who were not as enamored of violent revolution. They had paid attention to what happened in the aftermath in Russia and instead sought a path through anarchism to overthrow the State by undermining it and building new social formations outside it.

Alex, then, was entering the movement just as it was redefining itself not only in opposition to the war but also in anticipation of the world that would follow the war. The battle of wills between the two tendencies was bitter and sometimes verged on violence.[*****]

In September, just before "October 1944" appeared in *NOW*, he wrote to Read, asking if Routledge would object to his publishing a pamphlet through Freedom Press. Read said there would be no objection but added that a tug-of-war was still roiling the collective. "It is the same old story," he complained, "the proletarian distrust of anything they don't understand and can't appreciate: their hatred of the artist."[79] Alex worried at times that, in turning away from mass organizing,

***** Woodcock told of an occasion when a group of syndicalists sent a pair of Spanish anarchist refugee "*pistoleros*" and two ex-IRA operatives to invade Berneri's and Richards's flat and extract money from them, allegedly to be distributed to other comrades. When the Freedom Press group complained, the perpetrators returned and smashed their printing equipment. Colin Ward, "Obituary: Vernon Richards," *Guardian*, February 4, 2002.

anarchism—the British variety, at least—might be shrinking into a middle-class intellectual-bohemian clique and that his friend Read might be pulling it too far in that direction.

For the time being, however, the intellectuals and the syndicalists were united by a more immediate threat to the movement. On December 12, a squad from Special Branch raided the Freedom Press offices on a warrant issued under Defence Regulation 39A, which made it an offense to "endeavour to cause disaffection amongst persons engaged . . . in his Majesty's Service." At the same time, Special Branch raided the homes of at least five members of the collective, including Richards and Berneri. According to Woodcock, the raid was in response to a manifesto published in *War Commentary* that the editors intended to circulate to members of the armed forces, calling upon them to practice mass disobedience as soon as the war was over, if not before.[80]

Shortly thereafter, soldiers and sailors who had been in correspondence with Freedom Press or had subscriptions to its publications had their kits searched, and copies of *War Commentary*, *Peace News*, and *NOW* were seized.[81]

Why was the government so concerned about the agitations of a small group of London anarchists? Many people in power, doubtless including Churchill, remembered the tense months just after World War I ended, when some ten thousand soldiers at Folkestone had refused to board ship to return to France, military personnel in Calais went on strike, and HMS *Kilbride*, a patrol vessel at Milford Haven, raised the red flag.[82] "That winter of 1918–1919 was the nearest Britain ever came to social revolution," historian David Lamb later wrote.[83] Political and social tensions in Britain during World War II were more severe than is often recalled, and the government, which was already looking ahead apprehensively to the end of the conflict, were well aware of the history of political unrest in conscript armies throughout Europe following demobilization, often spreading into the labor force.[84]

Special Branch, the unit of the police that worked with the intelligence and security services (MI5), had been surveilling the Freedom group for several years, intercepted its publications in the mail on occasion, and was very concerned about the message the group was sending. A report on a meeting held July 7, 1942, noted that over four hundred people attended—possibly an exaggeration—including service members and three American soldiers, and that "loud applause" greeted one speaker who said there was no enthusiasm for the war within the service and another who claimed there were "thousands of deserters."[85]

"Mutiny in the British Army," an article published in *War Commentary* in May 1944, argued that the "discussion of post war demobilization should naturally recall the discussion of the subject in 1918." *Common Wealth*, a syndicalist publication, noted, "There is every sign of terror at the prospect of a political awakening in the Services."[86]

As soon as they got word of the raids, Read and Woodcock met and decided to petition a wide list of writers, artists, and other public personalities to sign a letter of protest. Two letters were eventually published, in *Tribune* and the *New Statesman and Nation*. With the war winding toward its end, public figures were less concerned about appearing to be less than 100 percent behind the government, and the letters were signed by a wide range of luminaries, including Alex, Orwell, T. S. Eliot, E. M. Forster, Stephen Spender, Osbert Sitwell, Bertrand Russell, Julian Symons, and Dylan Thomas.[87] "We submit that such actions [as the Freedom raid] are prejudicial to the liberty of speech and writing," the *New Statesman* letter warned. "If they are allowed to pass without protest, they may become precedents for future prosecutions of individuals or of organizations devoted to the spreading of opinions disliked by the authorities. Once started, a process of this nature may well result in an intellectual tyranny of an extreme kind."[88]

None of this stopped the authorities from arresting the four core members of the Freedom collective—Berneri, Richards, John Hewetson, and Philip Sansom—on charges of conspiring "to undermine the affections of members of His Majesty's Forces." Shortly before their case came up at Marylebone Police Station on March 1, the Freedom Press Defence Committee was got up with Read as chair, Orwell as vice-chair, Woodcock as secretary, and Alex among the members.

Evidence introduced in the trial included copies of *War Commentary* that referenced the setting up of soviets and workers' councils in Germany and Russia following World War I, the British rail strike of 1919, and bad conditions in training camps during the recent war. Prosecutors made much of a Freedom Press flyer dated October 25, 1944, asking readers to introduce "new comrades" to the publication.[89] The results, however, were less dramatic than the Crown would have liked. Berneri was acquitted, since under English law a wife couldn't conspire with her husband. She "looked so much the part of a tragedy queen that the all-male jurors sought and found a technicality on which to release her," is how Woodcock put it. The three, presumably less-appealing male editors received comparatively light sentences of nine months' imprisonment in Wormwood Scrubs.[90]

Helping in this respect was the publicity the case received and the support of prominent people, who by then also included Harold Laski, Augustus John, Sybil Thorndike, and Henry Moore. The trial itself helped to spread the very ideas the government had attempted to suppress, Woodcock remembered: "All the so-called seditious writings—poetry and prose—on which the prosecution based its case were read in court, and the daily papers reported them almost verbatim, so that ideas that had previously reached only a few thousand people through *War Commentary* now reached several millions, courtesy of Lord Beaverbrook and Lord Rothermere."[91]

Afterward the support group was reorganized as the Freedom Defence Committee, a civil liberties watchdog, which met in the back room of the Freedom Press bookshop and typed its letters and appeals on a typewriter donated by Orwell.[92] Alex remained a sponsor, and Orwell continued to serve as vice-chair until the committee dissolved in 1949.

This suggests how the political atmosphere had changed by the end of the war. Earlier, when Alex asked Stephen Spender to sign his declaration against civilian bombing, the poet had declined. When the Freedom Press case materialized, Spender was willing to say yes, although he dragged his feet. "Characteristically," he then kept away from civil liberties issues after being reprimanded by his boss at the Foreign Office, Woodcock recalled.[93]

Alex played a cautious role behind the scenes. When Read first asked him to join the Freedom Defence Committee, although he accepted, his reply betrayed a good deal of anxiety about what measures a too-militant protest could bring down on the committee members, including himself. "The Defence Committee had better restrain itself at the moment to raising cash, protesting against the Sedition Act in general, and preparing a public agitation in the event of the accused being sentenced," he said in a letter to Read. "Get the defending barrister to advice *[sic]* the [committee], if you can, to avoid any legal impropriety. By the way, if the case comes under the Act, the action of the police, though odious, was legally proper if they had a warrant from a Judge in chambers."[94]

Alex was as concerned about how the defendants and the committee would be received by the public as he was about "legal impropriety." In this he had a lot in common with Orwell. Neither placed any faith in violent revolution, and they shared a perception that England was essentially a middle-class nation. Radicals and socialists would have to convince a large section of this rather inward-looking population—roughly, the one they themselves came from—if society was to be transformed. Orwell had already expressed this position in his notorious diatribe against left-wing eccentrics in *The Road to Wigan Pier* in 1937.****** Alex, not for the last time, was privately more concerned during the Freedom trial about creating the wrong impression with respectable society than he let on in public.

On the other hand, he wrote a letter to *The Listener* about the arrests that was far less circumspect than the one placed by the Freedom Defence Committee. "If anyone of your readers feels that the suppression of this minority is unimportant to English political liberty, I can only say that the bombing of Guernica was unimportant to European political liberty, except in so far as it was the testing ground for the weapons of Fascism," he wrote. Should anyone place their hope in the Labour government that was expected to take office after the upcoming general election, he reminded them that Churchill's coalition government was already putting peacetime conscription into effect. "The Minister at present responsible for the abuse of the regulations is a Labour Minister," he noted.[95]

Alex also supplied one of the scattered moments of comedy at the Freedom trial itself. "One day I spotted Alex Comfort in the audience," Woodcock recalled. Minus the other digits, the thumb of his left hand "seemed to have elongated with use." Woodcock noted further that, while "listening intently to an obscure passage in the evidence, he began to pick his nose meditatively with that long talon of a thumb. I looked across the court and saw Mr. Justice Birkett in his scarlet robes, equally absorbed in the evidence; he glanced in Comfort's direction and then, equally abstractedly, began to pick his nose with a long and bony forefinger."[96]

****** "We have reached a stage when the very word 'Socialism' calls up, on the one hand, a picture of aeroplanes, tractors, and huge glittering factories of glass and concrete; on the other, a picture of vegetarians with wilting beards, of Bolshevik commissars (half gangster, half gramophone), of earnest ladies in sandals, shock-headed Marxists chewing polysyllables, escaped Quakers, birth-control fanatics, and Labour Party backstairs-crawlers." George Orwell, *The Road to Wigan Pier* (New York: Houghton Mifflin Harcourt, 1972), 216.

CHAPTER 6

Against the Cold War (1945–1949)

Alex Comfort and George Orwell met in person for the first and only time in 1945, just after the Freedom Press trial and the publication of *Animal Farm:* as Alex remembered, at a pub in Bermondsey. He was getting over another of his depressions.[1] On a positive note, he had moved on to become resident medical officer at the Royal Waterloo Hospital for Children and Women, and Orwell had left *Tribune*, although he was still contributing his "As I Please" column for the paper. "I was shocked to see how ill he looked," Alex recalled in a remembrance and reassessment he wrote almost forty years later.

They had already found common ground in the rally to defend Freedom Press, and soon a much more cataclysmic event would bring them closer together politically. The war had ended in Europe with Germany's surrender on May 8, but war continued in the Pacific. On August 6, American bombers detonated an atomic weapon over the Japanese city of Hiroshima; three days later, they dropped another on Nagasaki. The exact number of casualties from the only military use of nuclear weapons to date may never be known, but totals are estimated from 129,000 to 226,000, while many more were affected by radiation (subsequent cancer, birth defects, and other conditions). US officials tried to hide some of the worst effects of their act and argued that the bombing of largely civilian targets was necessary to compel Japan to surrender: a claim that has been strongly disputed ever since.

Unarguable, however, was the change in millions of people's consciousness that the first use of nuclear weapons brought about. Everyone who could read and pay attention seemed to grasp that the world had changed profoundly. Two days later, the front page of just one London newspaper, the *Evening Standard*, was crowded with headlines including "The World Waits: Dust Still Hides Hiroshima," "So Opens a New Era for Man," "A Greater Thing than Discovery of Electricity," "Uranium Is in This Village," and "Vatican View: 'Absolutely Opposed.'"

The American atrocity in Japan, following the March fire-bombing of Tokyo that left over one hundred thousand dead, seemed to confirm everything that Alex had been writing for the past couple of years about the psychopathy of the State and the habits of individual compliance and irresponsibility it inculcates in its subjects. His first thought was about the ominous lack of outrage he sensed among the intelligentsia of his own country. "Even if we allow for the exaggeration of early reports," he wrote in a letter to the *New Statesman and Nation*, published just five days after Hiroshima, "the failure of English liberal thought to dissociate itself immediately from such actions, and to demand their immediate end, is likely to cover us with merited disgrace in the eyes of history and of every sane contemporary."

In an article for *War Commentary* less than two weeks after the Hiroshima bombing, he employed some of the strongest language he would ever commit to print: "We have just witnessed an act of criminal lunacy which must be without parallel in recorded history. A city of 300,000 people [Hiroshima] has been suddenly and deliberately obliterated and its inhabitants murdered by the English and American governments. . . . We have dissented and protested in the past, but the time for dissent and protest are over. The men who did this are criminal lunatics. Unless this final atrocity is irrevocably and unquestionably brought home to them by public opinion, we have no claim to be human beings."[2]

Ascribing the bombing to the English as well as the American government was erroneous. But Alex was not wrong in arguing that the nuclear attacks were a logical extension of the Allied bombing campaign and more than two decades of State infatuation with aerial warfare, which, he contended, had conditioned the public to accept atrocities as just another element of modern war. "The sickening cant about indiscriminate bombardment, the lies about liberty and justice, have appeared for what they are," he wrote. "One need only consider how last Monday's announcement would have affected the nation if it had been made in 1937 to realise how profoundly our responsibility has degenerated, and how much the practice of fascism has been sold to us since then. An endless iteration of enemy brutality has been used to acclimatise us to crimes which have now reached the magnitude of this massacre."*

* Dwight Macdonald, in the August 1945 issue of *Politics*, was just as emphatic, declaring that "atomic bombs are the natural product of the kind of society we have created" and that "we must 'get' the modern state before it 'gets' us."

Orwell, writing in *Tribune* in October and with the benefit of a couple of months' distance from the actual events, was less focused on the bomb's impact on mass psychology than its effect on the State itself, and this left him gravely pessimistic. "The discovery of the atomic bomb, so far from reversing history, will simply intensify the trends which have been apparent for a dozen years at least," he wrote. Chiefly he was thinking of the rise of a very few superpowers that he feared would dominate the world, forging "an epoch as horribly stable as the slave empires of antiquity." Without quite saying so, he indicated that three empires would dominate this new "permanent state of 'cold war,'" most likely some combination of Western Europe and the United States, the Soviet Union, and "East Asia, dominated by China."[3]

The bomb, because of the industrial resources needed to produce it, would reinforce and speed up this grim trend, which foreshadowed the dystopia he was already turning into compelling fiction in the manuscript of *Nineteen Eighty-Four*. Alex read Orwell's piece with great interest and shot off a letter to *Tribune's* editors in response. Acknowledging that "Orwell puts his finger, as usual, on the wider analytical point" (that different types of weapons tend to produce particular types of societies), he nevertheless argued, "Another conclusion is possible besides mere resignation to the omnipotence of tyrants equipped with nuclear energy. Not only are social institutions dictated by weapon-power: so are revolutionary tactics, and it seems to me that Orwell has made the case for the tactical use of disobedience, which he has tended to condemn in the past as pacifism."[4]

"Few if any new techniques have been devised or can be devised to counter disobedience," he argued. The very size of the State and the complexity of its new weapons systems would work against it, while its opponents' smallness and agility would help them—but only if they chose withdrawal of support over compromise. Which they should: "We have seen the collapse of the moral pretensions of this country, in the massacre of Europe's civilians, of America and the pronouncements of its tycoon-politicians and in the atom bomb, of Russia in the betrayal of libertarian socialism." Pacifists had to therefore become anarcho-pacifists. "The liberal tradition of Europe rests without exaggeration in the hands of those who are ready to resist war and conscription, and every invasion of the rights and responsibilities of men. We are the sole revolutionary movement which does not carry within it the seeds of post-revolutionary tyranny."[5]

Both Alex and Orwell were right, in their particular ways. Orwell was right that a global political stalemate had begun and that the bomb and the technological arms race accompanying it would take the power and pervasiveness of the State to new levels. And Alex was right that there were effective ways for rebels and dissidents to bring about social and political change in the teeth of State domination: namely, a new politics of mass disobedience.

ALEX'S WRITINGS AGAINST WAR and the State were appearing in the United States as well as the UK, thanks to a connection he had established with the *Conscientious Objector*, a monthly newspaper for pacifists edited by Jay Nelson Tuck, a New York City journalist. Sometimes, however, he found that the pacifist community was more committed than he to absolute nonviolence. When the newsletter reprinted his *War Commentary* piece on Hiroshima, for example, it preceded the article with a note saying that, while the editors agreed that the bombing was an act of "criminal lunacy," they couldn't endorse the "condign punishment" of the perpetrators. "In the first place, we don't know what punishment fits the crime in this case, and in the second place, if we did we would not inflict it." Better to "encourage a rebirth of spiritual values and individual conscience."[6]

More important for Alex's career in a popular and commercial sense, however, was his mainstream American debut with the US publication of *The Power House*. In October 1944 Viking Press had agreed to publish the novel, and it duly appeared the following March. Viking was headed by Ben Huebsch, one of the more daring American publishers of the time. He had been the first in the country to bring out books by Joyce and Lawrence, not to mention the French syndicalist Georges Sorel, through his previous company, B. W. Huebsch, and later published other foreign authors including Franz Werfel, Lion Feuchtwanger, and Rumer Godden. A forthright leftist, he would come under suspicion later in the decade as being a closet Communist.

Ben Huebsch offered a $500 advance for *The Power House* plus royalties of 10 percent on the first five thousand copies sold, 12.5 percent on the next five thousand, and 15 percent on any sales above ten thousand. He was "dubious" that *The Power House* would have much popular appeal and expected it would be expensive to produce, but Huebsch was sufficiently impressed that he asked for an option on Alex's next novel. Routledge accepted for Alex, who only asked to withhold rights to film sales, concerned that the industry might distort his work.[7]

The Power House quickly earned a positive review in the commercially powerful *Book-of-the-Month Club News* from the popular novelist and critic Dorothy Canfield Fisher: "A mighty book. . . . In every line it gives us implicitly that unspoken comment on human life that we get only from valid works of art."[8] But it also drew one of the most peculiar reviews of Alex's career from the formidable New York intellectual Diana Trilling. Writing in *The Nation*, Trilling confessed, "Because of its author's place among the younger British intellectuals, 'The Power House' claimed my attention. I was not able to engage it. I read the first two dozen pages three times without having any notion of what I was reading; then I made several firm attempts to break into the story at a later point of its development, each time without success. This report must therefore stand for the whole of my review."[9]

Alex had better luck with the *New York Times*, which assigned the Irish novelist and critic Francis Hackett to review his novel. Hackett found it stunning. "'The Power House' howls to Heaven, and you have to listen to its howling," he declared in the sometimes breathless manner of American book reviews at the time. It is a painful novel, Hackett said, but it "affirms agony in a manner so cool and dry that it has kinship with the poetry of Rimbaud."[10] John Chamberlain, in *Life*, complained that Alex's technique "has just about as much finesse as the hulking Lenny in *Of Mice and Men*" but added, "[He] has a powerful and bitter feeling about the plight of the individual in a day of universally conscripted men, and his feeling triumphs over his gaucherie."[11]

The most perceptive review, however, came from Harry Hansen, the book critic of the *New York World-Telegram*, who had reported from the trenches during World War I. Commentators who disliked *The Power House* "would have been better pleased if Mr. Comfort . . . had specifically declared that he was speaking only of Nazis," Hansen wrote in a piece titled "War as Madness." "But he didn't. He had human beings in mind, and he thought about individuals as sane men who had become cells in an insane organism, and took orders from that organism." The book held out little hope, Hansen concluded. "It is a terrible thing to believe, but the chances are it is true."[12]

The Power House was extensively reviewed, down to regional newspapers like the *Akron Beacon Journal* and the *San Diego Union*. Collectively, the American critics pointed out plenty of flaws—the novel was too long, too mired in detail, the characters too thin—but overall it was well received.** In part this was because it was the first lengthy fictional treatment most of them had read of the fall of France, the Occupation, and the Resistance. Partly for that reason, publishers on the continent were taking a bet on the book as well. Besides the United States, 1945 and 1946 saw Ljus Forlag, a Swedish house, agree to publish a translation, and a Dutch publisher, Republiek Der Letteren, express interest, while the French house Louis Nagel requested rights to translate and publish *No Such Liberty*.[13]

Curiously, though, very few of the critics made a comment on the author's very clear political stance—or indeed seemed fully aware of it. Possibly because it appeared in the United States when the war in Europe was ending, no one seemed to think that a howl of protest against war in general was still in poor taste.

"Perhaps, at the time of its publication, there was the fear that the book encouraged the position of the conscientious objector," the poet Marguerite Young wrote mordantly in the newspaper of the same name. "Now that, since the atomic bomb, every man is a conscientious objector—or almost every man—that fear should certainly have dissolved like the doomed cities of Japan."[14]

Young was reviewing a second Comfort book that Viking brought out later that year in the United States, *The Song of Lazarus*, a collection that brought together the poems in *A Wreath for the Living* and *Elegies*, plus some new work, including the long title poem, a shorter French translation of which was already going to press in Pierre Seghers's influential anthology *Poésie 45*. Young, who had just won a poetry prize from the National Academy of Arts and Letters for her second collection—and would go on to write the massive cult novel *Miss Mackintosh, My Darling*—declared Alex "one of the most striking of our modern poets," and *The Song of Lazarus* received several other positive reviews. But two of America's more promising younger poets, William Jay Smith, the future poet laureate, and Randall Jarrell, were not impressed.

"The poems, if they ever existed in the mind of the author, have been killed in the cooking," Smith concluded of *The Death of Lazarus* in *Poetry* magazine. Jarrell had read *The Power House* and at least one of Alex's political essays, and he attacked his subject's politics scathingly.

** On June 27, Alex's editor at Routledge, Tom Ragg, wrote to Huebsch at Viking, "[Alex is] very worried at the complete absence of any bad reviews of THE POWER HOUSE. Is it possible, I wonder[,] that you have only sent the good reviews? If so, he would very much like you to send over a batch of bad reviews so that he may consider whether there is any constructive criticism in them."

"Mr. Comfort believes in conscientious disobedience: if no one obeys the government there will be no war. There can be war only because people are dupes. . . . And he never wonders: how does it feel to be a dupe?" That placed a barrier between him and the millions serving in the current war. "He is right and they are wrong; and he cannot share the sympathetic, unwilling identity in which all their differences are buried."[15]

Neither Smith nor Jarrell could see anything but cliché in the more emotional poetry that people like Alex were producing, especially when they attempted to introduce traditional Romantic metaphors with nature, love and sex, and death. It is true that the Neo-Romantics' poetry frequently dissolved into vague, unoriginal symbolism. Smith dismissed Alex's politics entirely as "nihilism." Jarrell came close to denying that it was possible for a pacifist to express any credible feeling about war. Yet, nowhere in the poems they were reviewing did Alex sound a condescending note toward people who died for their government, only sorrow, pity, and outrage.

But if Alex was reading his American critics dispassionately he would have taken away a warning: his anger at the war was in danger of turning his poetry into a series of ad hominem attacks lacking the finesse of his best work. Less than two years after *The Song of Lazarus* appeared in the States, he published another collection with Routledge, *The Signal to Engage*, in which his rage seemed to boil over. The title referenced the message to board an enemy ship in an old British sea shanty ("the signal to engage will be a whistle and a holler").[16] In "Song for the Heroes," he told future conscripts,

> But know you are choosing. When they begin to appeal
> to your better nature, your righteous indignation,
> your pity for men like yourselves, stand still.
>
> Look down and see the lice upon your hide.[17]

The new collection also contained "The Song of Lazarus," one section of which, "Notes for My Son," included the following:

> Remember when you hear them beginning to say Freedom
> Look carefully—see who it is that they want you to butcher. . . .
>
> Beware. The blood of a child does not smell so bitter
> If you have to shed it with a high moral purpose. . . .

So that when they come to sell you their bloody corruption
you will gather the spit of your chest
and plant it in their faces.[18]

It's possible to turn this kind of anger into good poetry. Paul Éluard, the ex-Surrealist and committed Communist who became the most celebrated poet of the French Resistance, did so, as did Kenneth Patchen, the American poet whose Romantic sensibility most resembled Alex's. Alex admired both of these writers greatly. He dedicated "The Song of Lazarus" to Éluard and supplied a preface to a Grey Walls selection of Patchen's verse at about the same time.[19] But his poems of political outrage are less disciplined and precise in their language than Éluard's, and as a result they fulminate rather than convey. They are far less vigorous than Patchen's proto-Beat verse and use language less imaginatively, and, whereas Patchen adds a touch of satire to make his poems hit home more forcefully, Alex's are too often stuck in deadening earnest.

He was still capable of some fine verse, especially when he focused on nature and ideas, moving away from war itself to contemplate his and humanity's place in the universe. In "None but My Foe to Be My Guide," he wrote,

For Freedom and Beauty are not fixed stars,
but cut by man only from his own flesh,
but lit by man, only for his sojourn

because our shot into the cup of sky
brings back no echo, brings back no echo ever:
because man's mind lives at his stature's length

because the stars have for us no earnest of winning
because there is no resurrection
because all things are against us, we are ourselves.[20]

The Signal to Engage did receive some positive reviews, including from Julian Symons, but more than a few critics noticed that his style was no longer developing but becoming monotonous. Richard Church, who had been so enthusiastic about his work a few years before, complained that Alex was "still too much concerned with vengeance against 'them'"—whoever "they" were—and that this was becoming an idée fixe. "We are still waiting [for him] to fulfill the great promise of his early prose and verse," Church concluded.[21]

Years later, *The Signal to Engage* comes across as Alex's attempt to say in verse what he had already said better in prose. In the spring of 1945, he revised some of his recent essays and pulled them together in a book that summed up his ethical and philosophical perspective, including his thinking about war, the State, and the moral duty of the artist in society. Routledge turned it down for unspecified "legal reasons," and Alex brought it instead to Falcon Press, where he once again crossed paths with Peter Baker.[22]

The same man who had earlier published *France and Other Poems* under another imprint and then denounced Alex as a "humbug" for criticizing Britain's war, Baker was a brash, ambitious, but unreliable schemer who had compiled a record for recklessness and insubordination during the war but somehow managed to come out of it with a captaincy in intelligence and a Military Cross. With money from his father, a film producer at Ealing Studios, he set up Falcon Press, hoping to take advantage of the boom in publishing that had begun during the war.[23] Lacking any substantial track record in the business, he persuaded Wrey Gardiner to join forces with him. Each became a director of the other's firm, and the two publishers moved into only slightly classier premises at 7 Crown Passage ("a warren of small rooms with trampoline flooring and a snakepit of plumbing," the poet Roland Gant remembered).[24] Here, off Pall Mall, they shared production, marketing, and administrative staff. Muriel Spark, who worked there in the late '40s, would fictionalize Grey Walls/Falcon years later as Ullswater Press in her novel *A Far Cry from Kensington*. In the book, one of the firm's creditors, "a small printer, had taken the difficulties of Ullswater Press so personally as to employ a man with a raincoat to stand in the lane outside our office windows all morning and afternoon, staring up. That's all he did: stare up. This was supposed to put us to shame."[25]

But the new arrangement provided enough new capital that Grey Walls was able to at last pay its printers and issue many more titles—Gardiner had never produced more than five in a year—while Baker leveraged the additional revenue to expand into other businesses: aircraft parts, wine sales, realty, and more.[26]

One of the first products of the new partnership was Alex's book of essays, now titled *Art and Social Responsibility: Lectures on the Ideology of Romanticism*, which Falcon Press brought out in the fall of 1946.[27] It included the title essay and "October 1944," both of which he had published in *NOW* two years before, plus essays on "The Critical Significance of Romanticism" and "Romanticism, Primitivism and Kitsch-Culture." Some of the material Alex had delivered as lectures to the Oxford University English Association, but it had all gone through an extensive rewriting and expansion. In an introductory note he thanked Julian Symons for his criticisms of the title essay in its *NOW* incarnation: "[Symons] convinced me where I was wrong and pointed out to me where I had made myself misunderstood."

Now that the war was over, Alex was able to turn "Art and Social Responsibility" into a comprehensive, incisive piece of writing. He started from the perception that the same forces that were supposed to be forging human society—human beings—into something greater, more rational and civilized, something that could transcend mortality, were instead producing war, oppression, and the loss of our humanity. The result was a new kind of barbarism in which society was "allowed to become personalized and regarded as a super-individual."[28]

The history of Western society is the progress of a shifting of the functions of "justice, mutual aid and creative work out of the hands of individuals and into the hands of professional exponents." All too often, the individual takes refuge in the new "super-individual," which Alex called "society": the State, with its ruthless capitalist economy, reliance on force and violence, and assumption that its way was the only way. The individual surrenders all responsibility for society's actions in order to escape death, "to rid himself of the selfhood which, subconsciously, he knows must die. . . . By participating in a human society, he had bought the abrogation of the fear of death at the price of his personality."

Society becomes "a womb into which one can crawl back and become immortal because unborn."

"The consciousness of personal responsibility," Alex argued, "is the factor which differentiates human relationships from superficially similar animal societies," and Romanticism—"the belief in the human conflict against the Universe and against power"—is the only ideology that insists on the primacy of individuals and their obligation to accept responsibility for each other. Along with personal responsibility, anarchism, Romanticism's political "offspring," finds mutual aid, direct action, and community (not society) to be "the three criteria of a civilised community." For anyone who accepts this view of reality, Alex wrote, "all wars are irrelevant unless they destroy the mechanism of delegation and leave him a human being again, faced with the necessity of mutual aid."

Artists have a special responsibility in this struggle: to "stand aside from society." Since society often grants them a privileged position, they must embrace the duty to speak for the voiceless. But the artist "has absolutely no right to claim exemptions or privileges except in his capacity as a human being. The artist employs his form as the voice of a great multitude. . . . The artist in barbarian society is the only true representative of the people," and art "is the sole way open to man of protesting against his destiny."

Where was the class struggle in the midst of this war of the individual against "barbarian" society? Class warfare was certainly real, but Alex argued that the experience of Stalinism had shown that "classless" societies were just as capable of creating a state as "super-individual" ones, and could be just as heavily impregnated with barbarism. This being the case, class war is still a "truth," but it is "a partial truth only."

Given the escalating violence of the "Megalopolitan civilisation" that society—class-based or otherwise—was creating, it was likely to collapse or immolate itself, Alex believed. "The whole doctrine of romanticism is a doctrine of preparation to survive the decay stage of civilisation, with its attendant conscription, repression and terrorism." Alex's hope was that the weak would then inherit the earth: "their clinging among the wreckage to mutual aid perpetuates civilisation." "Then in a decade or two," he predicted in a passage that echoes his language in "The Atoll in the Mind," "they begin like coral insects to construct a new load for their backs . . . the community of the weak, the greatest conspiracy in history, which is ceaseless." The tools would be the same ones he recommended in *The Power House*: refusal and disobedience, sabotage, insurrection.

How these methods could be scaled up to the point where they challenged the State, he did not say. But Alex was arguing that this rebellion would only occur if humanity underwent a revolution in consciousness: an awakening wrought by education, psychology and other aspects of science, and new attempts at building community through mutual aid. *Art and Social Responsibility* was a manifesto as much as a philosophical-social analysis; it looks back to the writings of the previous generation of English social reformers and visionaries, including Gerald Heard and Aldous Huxley, and forward to the New Left of the 1960s.

Now that the war was over, it was easier for some critics to at least consider the dilemma Alex was proposing, without accusing him of defeatism or puerility. Julian Symons, who had attacked "Art and Social Responsibility" in its earlier form, acknowledged that the new book forced home "the immense dangers of the complete abrogation of personal responsibility. . . . Both for artists and politicians, this is one of the central problems of our time: the forms of our lives, and of our art, depend upon the way in which it is solved."[29]

The poet and critic Margaret Willy praised Alex's "astringent pen" and "merciless clarity of vision," declaring him "among the most challenging, formidable and fully adult young thinkers of our day." "How terribly true it is," she wrote, "that, in a state of war, 'each sincere citizen feels responsibility to society in the abstract, and none to the people he kills.'"[30]

Not everyone was able to forgive Alex his wartime pacifism. An unsigned review in the *Birmingham Post* expressed outrage that "with clever sophistry" he would attempt to trace a line of descent from his philosophy to Milton, Shelley, and Zola.[31] An even more vituperative piece in *The Listener* tagged his writing as "aggressive, polemical . . . , and an undistinguished plea for anarchy": a set of "intemperate hectorings."[32] Reading it decades later, however, *Art and Social Responsibility* stands as one of Alex's most important and prescient works, signaling a new turn in radical thinking at the beginning of the postwar years. At least a few people thought so at the time. The poet Adrian Mitchell, later a leading figure in the British antiwar movement, called it "one of my bibles" and recalled carrying Alex and Kenneth Patchen's works with him in his pack during his national service in the RAF.[33]

Echoes of Alex's perspective would appear in what would become two of the key texts of the postwar period: Orwell's *Nineteen Eighty-Four*, in which the individual is taught to find personal peace, order, and fulfillment under the heel of Big Brother, and Ginsberg's *Howl*, with its poets and artists driven mad under the looming presence of Moloch.

Above all, Alex's book was a call for the Left to place the individual back at the center of its political and social analysis, because, in his view, without the individual's will to resist—to disobey—no revolution could succeed. The "responsible" artist's task was to reveal the reality of oppression, violence, and war, and to help forge the necessary culture of disobedience. On the other side, Alex argued, were arrayed the thousand temptations of popular culture or "kitsch-culture" which appeal to the individual's desire for security, for vicarious participation in life, and for the exorcism of death, through "motor races, gladiatorial shows, circuses—or by its denial in some form, Revivalist meetings, elaborate public funerals." "What Roman society provided in its circuses, or Germany in its military displays, contemporary Anglo-American society provides in its pseudo-popular art."[34] The only way to overcome these cultural currents, nurtured by the State, was to build a new consciousness and a new culture of disobedience.

IN THE EARLY POSTWAR years, Alex's standing as a writer was curious. None of his books—poetry, fiction, polemic—had been an out-and-out success with critics, and, with the qualified exception of *The Power House*, sales had been no more than modest. But he was consistently described as a comer: a potentially great talent who was expected soon to produce something great. He was still in his mid-twenties, and there was plenty of time, but new literary reputations were being forged constantly. How much longer would it be before others would come along with just as much talent and, perhaps, a greater knack for pleasing the critics and the public?

Alex was keenly aware of the problem, especially when it was articulated by people he respected. In his BBC radio talk on *The Power House*, V. S. Pritchett had praised the novel as "an immensely exciting narrative—the description of the meeting against the Germans at the end is almost unbearably, insidiously vivid. It burns you like acid." But "the sheer weight of trivial daily life blows down like crowds of autumn leaves on the characters and submerges them."

In a letter to Alex in which he enclosed a draft of his talk, Pritchett went a bit farther. "[*The Power House* is] an enormously impressive novel with serious faults—and serious writing!" he said. "I shall look forward with great eagerness to your next book."[35] He would be especially enthusiastic, he added, if it was about England rather than a half-imagined foreign setting with characters of whom Alex had no daily experience.***

Part of the problem was that, in a time when many moral decisions—notably, whether to fight or at least resist the fascists—appeared clear and urgent, Alex insisted on problematizing them. His characters never start the story committed to a specific cause, like Robert Jordan in *For Whom the Bell Tolls*, nor do they end by signing on to one. He was interested instead in how they maintained their individuality and integrity in a world of clashing ideologies, and how they sought to forge something revolutionary out of that individuality.

There always seemed to be something lacking, however: Alex himself. Whereas some novelists were only able to write fictional autobiography, he was uninterested in doing so (or perhaps unable). His life was work,

*** Pritchett liked Alex's poetry well enough, however, to include "A Legend of Uno"—a 1946 satirical rhyming verse tale in which the British establishment elect Satan as their presiding officer—in *Turnstile One*, his 1948 anthology of writings from the *New Statesman and Nation*.

and while he succeeded at creating rounded characters to inhabit the often terrible, vividly described landscapes in which they found themselves, they lacked the extra spark that might have come from injecting something of himself into one or more of them.

This is one way of looking at Alex's fictional work but not the only one. Why did he persist in writing novels and stories set anywhere but where he himself lived? Was there really so little of Alex in his books? The literary scholar Arthur E. Salmon later observed that many of Alex's protagonists are, like him, intellectuals, and, more specifically, they are individuals consumed with making sense of a world that seemed to have gone lunatic: Breitz in *No Such Liberty*, Serge in *The Almond Tree*, even the German soldier Claus in *The Power House*. "All are persecuted, harried and locked up, imprisoned, by persons who symbolize or represent irrational forms of authority. . . . A sense of exile, victimization, entrapment, powerlessness, isolation, alienation, anxiety, and unending frustration characterize much of Comfort's art."[36]

Occasionally in his poetry, such as "Letter to a Friend in the Army," alienation takes the form of a rift between the poet and his fellow students who had committed themselves to the war. Alex had a strong empathy with this condition, despite his engaging presence, owing in part to his rather solitary upbringing, in part to his rare precociousness, and in part to his physical infirmity. It's not surprising, then, that so many of his fictional characters also feel fundamentally alone.

As an anarcho-pacifist, the longer the war continued, the longer he felt himself at odds with the society in which he lived. At the same time, his determined focus on the suffering the war inflicted on the continent—far worse than what Britain endured during the Blitz, bad as that was—revealed a sense that the real struggle of life against death was happening elsewhere than among the people of his own country. How could he write about life in Britain during wartime when the suffering in Lidice, Belsen, and Hamburg was so much more terrible?

Years later, he offered a brief description of the fiction he had been writing that resembles the sinister visions in Kafka. There is a kind of novel, somewhere between the picaresque and the realistic novel, "which it is hard at times to avoid writing," he said. "That is the novel that is realistic, but the reality it depicts is fantasy come to life and enacted in history. In our time a writer possessed by a fantasy . . . does not need to invent a situation in which it can be expressed; other similarly preoccupied people in positions of authority are already expressing these fantasies in current affairs."[37] Through his characters,

Alex projected himself into that dire "fantasy"—of exile, homelessness, violence, and atrocity—and he urgently wanted his readers to feel it as he did.

He didn't apologize for writing novels of ideas. In a statement for the biographical dictionary *Twentieth Century Authors* in 1955, he said: "While the suspicion of propagandist art is sound, it obscures the fact that all writing has content. The content of mine is what I think and believe about human responsibility, and accordingly everything I write is didactic, since I have tried to express my preoccupations both in action and in print."[38] While writers in English do produce novels of ideas that win acclaim—Orwell's *Animal Farm* and *Nineteen Eighty-Four* are prime examples—they are often more accepted on the continent, where Voltaire's *Candide*, Sartre's *La Nausée*, and Mann's *The Magic Mountain* are among the masterpieces. Alex was widely read in French literature, and his immersion in that tradition may have made it more natural for him than for other English writers to use the novel as a vehicle for his social and political thought.

He kept at it in a volume of short stories, *Letters from an Outpost*, which Routledge published in 1947. Only two of the twelve stories took place anywhere that was recognizably British. Others were set in Greece, France, Germany, and Palestine, and the rest in unidentified foreign, faintly Eastern European–sounding places. Once again, the common theme was an individual's alienation from the demands and assumptions of a tyrannical society.

In one chilling story, "The Martyrdom of the House," a group of retreating French soldiers stay overnight in an untouched country house—and trash it just before the Germans arrive and take them prisoner. Another, more fanciful story struck closer to home. "A Citizen with Thirty-Nine Vertebrae" may have been Alex's first effort at satire. The story concerns an anarchist couple in Berlin who desperately want to make sure their newborn son—they've named him Maxim Wilkes Bakunin Pacek—never has to serve in the army. To prevent this, Pacek, the father, takes his son to a surgeon who operates on Maxim to give him a tail.

> "You can only conscript men [he tells the narrator], not monkeys. Monkeys have no stake in society, and the lunatics let them alone. There are no civil penalties attached to being a monkey—except that you can't vote, and who wants to? The University. . ."

> "Doesn't give diplomas to monkeys."
>
> "How do you know? There weren't any monkeys in our year. I'll bet my boots nobody with a tail ever sat."

The boy grows up with the tail but otherwise thrives—until he turns eighteen, when his fellows start to be called up, and the newspapers mount a campaign against Maxim's unfair "immunity." He is seized by soldiers who cut off his tail, and he is sentenced to a long term of imprisonment. Afterward he is converted. "After all," he says, "one must not withstand the Cause of Humanity." Later he is killed fighting in a war.

Maxim bears a resemblance to his creator, whose injured hand had helped keep him out of the war, but Maxim's fate suggests a more pessimistic conclusion: that no amount of disability will keep the State from getting what it wants, most of all the soul of the individual. The story isn't entirely successful, but it reflects Alex's reading of Kafka and carries hints of Winston Smith, whose story Orwell was busy writing in *Nineteen Eighty-Four*.

As usual, *Letters from an Outpost* got a mixed reception. "There is not one story in this book that does not strike home," the poet Stevie Smith declared in *John O'London's Weekly*, but the novelist Olivia Manning, in the *Spectator*, found in the less realistic stories "a sad collapse into the maudlin."[39] By now, however, Alex was established as a figure in the literary world.

In June 1947, Rexroth's *New British Poets: An Anthology* appeared in the United States. "I would be inclined to say that [Comfort], Woodcock, and Savage are the most remarkable of the young men who came first to prominence during the War," Rexroth wrote in his introduction, "and it is significant that they are all anarchists, 'personalists,' and pacifists."[40] The same year, the first lengthy critical work on Alex's poetry appeared: a chapter in Derek Stanford's book, *The Freedom of Poetry: Studies in Contemporary Verse*, which also discussed David Gascoyne, Herbert Read, and Kathleen Raine, among others. Stanford singled Alex out as "a sort of pocket Voltaire, and still under thirty years of age."[41] But since the book was published by Grey Walls, he could be accused of bias.

In May 1945 the literary agent David Higham, of Pearn, Pollinger & Higham, had written to Herbert Read at Routledge, asking if Alex was represented. Read said he was not, adding that the time had come when he needed to be. Higham's firm had an impressive roster of well-known authors, including Read, Edith and Osbert Sitwell, Christopher Isherwood, John Buchan, Dorothy L. Sayers, Vita Sackville-West, John Cowper Powys, T. H. White, Dylan Thomas, and, before his death, Dick Sheppard.[42] Higham himself was one of the most amusing and personable characters on the London literary and publishing scene, and Alex signed on. Their professional relationship would last more than twenty years.[43]

Alex's home life was solidifying too. By the end of the war, Ruth's job as a child care officer had shifted to Rotherhithe. The office in Bethnal Green out of which she had previously worked had been hit by a V-1 bomb while she was eating her lunch in the park nearby. She and Alex had had to vacate their Brunswick Square flat in a rush in early 1945 and move in with Ruth's mother, when the owners, who had been interned in a Japanese prison camp, suddenly returned.[44]

Luckily Alex and Ruth had already engaged to buy their first house, a smallish, semi-detached brick residence built during the 1930s at 20 Honor Oak Road in Forest Hill, a quiet, aptly named district in the borough of Lewisham, south of the Thames, and by November they were moved in. Damaged slightly by German bombing, the house was nevertheless in move-in condition, although they would have to make some repairs and repaint once ensconced.[45] The following summer, their first and only child, Nicholas Alfred Fenner Comfort (the middle names were, respectively, his maternal grandfather's first and his paternal grandmother's last), was born on August 4 at Guy's Hospital in nearby Southwark. Since the hospital lies within the sound of Bow Bells, Nick qualified as a Cockney.[46]

After her son's birth, Ruth quit her job to focus on home life. Alex helped out, sometimes bathing Nick and singing to him popular and music hall songs he had learned as a medical student: "Riding Down from Bangor," "She Was Only a Bird in a Gilded Cage," "Don't Steal My Prayer Book, Mr. Burgular," and "Tit-Willow" from Gilbert and Sullivan's *The Mikado*.[47] Settling in, Alex made friends with the curator of the Horniman Museum, the great anthropological collection, which was located just four hundred yards from the house and linked up nicely with his growing interest in the development of human societies and cultures.

He had left his post at the Royal Waterloo Hospital, and—armed with his diploma in child health, which included psychological training—was working as medical officer at the Toddlers' Clinics, Borough of Camberwell, which had just reopened following the war, and as a hospital research assistant.[48] The latter was an unpaid position, and he eked it out with work as a locum, filling in for general practitioners who were absent. The arrangement gave him more time to write.

In September 1946 Alex was one of a group of writers who answered a series of questions in *Horizon* on "the cost of letters": how much money a writer needed to get by, whether it was possible to earn that sum by writing, whether literature suffered when writers had to make their living in some other way, and whether the State should subsidize writers. Alex responded that he lived on a combined income of £500 per annum, with his wife and child. That contrasted with Elizabeth Bowen's statement that she would require £3,500, and Cyril Connolly's that a writer must have "upwards of five pounds a day net," or £1,825 per year, unless "he is prepared to die young of syphilis."

"I would not try to live entirely upon literary work myself," Alex wrote, "even though at the moment I probably could get paid for everything I write without being obliged to alter it." Aside from the fact that he was not earning a princely living either from his day job or his writing, Alex differed from some of the others who answered the *Horizon* questionnaire in how little he regarded writers as being owed anything special. "The State," Connolly wrote, "*must* supplant private patronage," and Bowen too thought that writers who showed distinction should receive some support. Alex, by contrast, argued that the artist should not "touch the State or its money with a barge-pole," because the artist's job was to "be human, fight death and obedience, work like anyone else, since that is part of humanness, . . . and produce the work which you feel compatible with these ideas."[49]

Nonliterary work could enrich creation, as Alex believed his medical and scientific work did. In fact, it reinforced his view that artists and writers had the same responsibilities as everyone else, if not more so. This stark declaration was a bit disingenuous. Alex and Ruth were getting some help from his parents. But aside from his drive to write, to agitate, and to express his beliefs in several literary modes, he was living the quiet life of a young doctor with a wife and son in a tranquil, middle-class neighborhood of London.

He even acquired his first car. Alex had learned to drive before the war on his father's little Morris. At the time, Morris made nearly one out of every four automobiles in Britain.[50] But he had failed his driving test. (His father felt the examiner had flunked Alex because of his disability and angrily extracted a letter of apology from the Ministry of Transport.) When the war came and transportation became scarce, holders of provisional licenses (learners' permits) were allowed to drive, and the issue became moot, but Alex waited to buy a car until two years after Nick was born. The chosen vehicle was a prewar used Morris with a crank handle, and he kept it in an alley garage across from the house in Forest Hill. On weekends he would work under the chassis wearing a soldier's tin hat for protection. As a doctor, he kept a medical kit with him when on the road, in case he encountered an accident; it included morphine and then-legal heroin, Nick remembered.[51]

The literary pub scene in Fitzrovia was still flourishing after the war, but Alex had no more to do with it than he had earlier. He still saw his friends at Grey Walls semi-regularly; he was advising Gardiner on an impressionistic memoir the publisher was writing of his life during the war years. But he published the last issue of *Poetry Folios* in 1947. "I felt we'd had enough of the New Romantic thing," he later said, "and the next lot of poets were writing differently."[52] Instead, he was concentrating on polemical writing for the PPU and Freedom Press.

Britain did not end conscription after the war ended. Instead, the Allied occupation of Germany and Austria; the civil war in Greece, in which the British army intervened on the side of the monarchy; and the crises in India and Palestine that led to independence for both in 1947, kept British troops engaged abroad—as would the Korean War and the independence struggle in Kenya a few years later. As a result, the new Labour government kept conscription in place, then pushed through the National Service Act of 1948, which remained in force until 1960. In the run-up to the act's passage, the PPU launched a campaign against conscription, for which Alex wrote a pamphlet, *Peace and Disobedience*. In it he denounced not just the draft but also those pacifists who availed themselves of the right to register as conscientious objectors but did nothing to resist the war itself.

Choosing "licensed objection" over "total resistance," he wrote, "is morally comparable with membership of the Gestapo as a potato-peeler, on condition that one is not asked to murder anyone." The case for pacifism, Alex asserted, "rests solely upon the historic theory of anarchism, and it is because the PPU takes its stand upon a pledge of disobedience that I believe it to be a relevant organisation." The job of the pacifist movement therefore was not to salve its members' consciences but to support and encourage resistance to the forces that made conscription necessary in the first place: implicitly, the State.[53]

Whether all members of the PPU agreed with him was doubtful. But Alex took his call for disobedience into another realm the same year, in a June 1946 article for *Common Wealth*, "Science Must Disobey." The article was occasioned by two events: the arrest and confession of Alan Nunn May, a British physicist, for supplying atomic research (including small samples of the isotopes Uranium-233 and 235) to the Soviet GRU or military intelligence; and the passage of the Atomic Energy Act, the counterpart of a similar law in the United States, which promoted the development of nuclear energy and gave the minister of supply nearly total control over nuclear research conducted in the UK.[54] "It will become a penal offence in this country, for the first time since the Middle Ages, to conduct scientific investigation into an entire field of natural phenomena or to publish observations concerning them," Alex wrote.

At a time when tensions were rising between the Western and Eastern Blocs, he was one of the few people to question the rationality of government—and, presumably, its favored private contractors—monopolizing knowledge about nuclear weapons and energy development, especially when one government had recently used an atomic weapon to kill hundreds of thousands of people. Nunn May was sentenced to ten years' hard labor, even though he protested that in passing on research to the Soviet Union he was only trying to help secure victory over Germany and Japan and further "the development of the peaceful uses of atomic energy."[55] Alex condemned the sentence as "vindictive and disgraceful" and accused the government of trying to "intimidate research workers who [had] shown themselves increasingly unwilling to submit their judgment to that of policyless and irresponsible nationalists."

This practice should be unacceptable to any responsible scientist with a conscience, he believed. "The time has come when scientific workers should seriously consider withdrawing their co-operation from all states and governments that threaten the general welfare of humanity," Alex wrote. "It is becoming the duty of science to disobey."

IN THE EARLY SUMMER of 1948, Daisy Elizabeth Fenner Comfort died suddenly. She had gone into hospital for a hysterectomy and died there owing to a problem with the anaesthetic. She was only sixty-three but had been the center of her husband's life for the thirty-three years of their marriage and had lived to see her son married, with a family of his own, and launched on a career that appeared to make use of all the education and erudition she had trained him to assimilate and build upon. She remained a part of Alexander's life after her death: he continued to live at Havengore, continued her practice of canning fruit, and did not fail to say good-bye to her familiar presence each morning when he went to work.[56]

Elizabeth's personality was stamped deeply on her son's. He was astonishingly versatile intellectually, a lightning-quick study, and unafraid to make controversial assertions, but he could also be dogmatic, settled in his views once he established them, and unforgiving of human frailties or personal plights when making judgments. Both the positive and the negative aspects of his manner of thought trace to his family background as well. Both his grandfather and great-grandfather were the kind of Nonconformists who loved to pick a point of theology or religious practice and defy the world to challenge them. Elizabeth did much the same with grammar and every aspect of child upbringing. This intellectual bullheadedness—or bloody-mindedness, as he liked to call it, approvingly—shows up again in Alex's strong criticism of registered conscientious objectors and his command that scientists disobey.

It's no wonder, then, that some critics found Alex abrasive and, for a twentysomething, presumptuous. But another, more analytical side to his mind was developing at the same time.

Alex had resumed his study of mollusks while still completing his medical training, and, as the decade wore on, he published more and more papers on the subject: two in 1946, three in 1947, two in 1948, eight in 1949, and five in 1950. Aside from the *Journal of Conchology*, his findings were appearing in leading publications including *The Lancet*, *Nature*, *Science*, and *Biochemical Journal*. His subjects included everything from snails—land and water—to limpets, abalone, and oysters. In 1949 he received his PhD from the University of London for a dissertation titled "The Acid-Soluble Pigments of Molluscan Shells (with Special Reference to Porphyrins)." It summed up much of his work, especially on shell pigments as a marker of aging in mollusks.

At the same time, his medical practice was inducing him to take a more analytic approach to his study of humanity. In May 1945, while still at the Royal Waterloo Hospital, he had helped direct the treatment of an infant who had acquired severe congenital syphilis from her father. The child had a high fever, a rash covering much of her body, enlarged tibiae, a high white blood cell count, and bloody nasal discharge. She was treated with a total of 702,000 units of penicillin in short courses, combined with more traditional drugs, and within two months, the symptoms were gone. Alex wrote the results up in *The Lancet*, concluding that penicillin had proved itself useful in treating "exceptionally severe infantile syphilis," contributing in a small way to scientists' understanding of the new miracle drug.[57]

A year later, at the Camberwell Toddlers' Clinics, he oversaw the postwar restoration of a public health program for children aged two to five, his first venture into public health. Camberwell had been one of the London neighborhoods hardest hit both during the Blitz and the Germans' V-1 and V-2 bombing later in the war.[58] Alex held a series of five infant welfare clinics, or weekly advisory meetings, with parents and children. "Health visitors" canvassed the neighborhood, issuing invitations and scheduling meetings at which Alex and staff took the children's histories, gave physical examinations, advised on treatments, and made referrals where needed. Among other items, he asked all mothers of circumcised children why the operation had been undertaken and reported the results of the survey in the *British Medical Journal*.[59] The clinics also served as distribution centers for food supplements and "dietetic extras" from the Ministry of Health.

The project gave Alex a close-up look at how the war, which he had so strongly opposed, had affected families in a district where households ranged from relatively affluent to working class. His findings, published in *The Lancet*, offer a snapshot of doctors' struggle to modernize pediatrics in the face of wartime trauma and traditional beliefs, but he also couldn't resist adding some of his pet concerns to his evaluation.

"Higher wages, evacuation and the bombing of slums, Government supplements to diet, and improved health education have borne remarkable fruit in the physical state of London children," he wrote. "At the same time conscription, the universal cheapening of human responsibility, the small family, gross housing deficiencies (especially the attempt to rear children in flats), and the fraying of parental nerves through shortages and enforced sexual deprivation have contributed a psychological debit balance."[60]

Wartime disorganization had left the population less than 50 percent vaccinated. Military service and migration had disrupted family-practice medicine, which meant that parents and children were receiving care willy-nilly from multiple providers. "One child was receiving three separate supplies of phenobarbital for her non-epileptic seizures," Alex reported.

Parents were bedeviling children with their own stresses and obsessional habits over matters like dirt, bowel movements, and anorexia. "'I've kept him on the pot for two hours, he's that stubborn,' is a landmark in the deformation of a personality, though in our cases the child generally won." While parents often blamed their children's problems on "prenatal trouble by bombs," according to Alex, "parental neurosis proved to be our most contagious disease, and one to which children possessed no resistance whatever. . . . The clinics spent as much time on minor psychiatry as on all the other activities combined."

To address these problems, Alex recommended the clinics take two nonclinical steps: better liaison with local practitioners and closer cooperation with marriage guidance counselors and psychiatric clinics. Physical health was not as serious a problem for postwar England as mental health and the stresses of war and an industrial urban society with its inherent precariousness.

Influenced, perhaps, by his medical and scientific work—nurtured, in turn, by his childhood habit of collecting specimens, compiling and classifying data from railroad engines to seashells—a more dispassionate tone was creeping into Alex's writing. "Mr. Comfort's critical style is more suited to the pamphlet than to the serious essay," the *Times Literary Supplement*'s critic wrote of *The Novel and Our Time*, a book-length essay that Alex published in 1948 on how contemporary fiction reflected changes in society and was being changed by them.[61] But increasingly his goal was to analyze and understand the causes of the violence and injustice he saw around him, and the social structures that perpetuated them, rather than simply to expose and denounce these evils in moral terms, and his prose reflected this.

He was becoming more concerned with the problem of power in society and how it manifested itself in popular culture. In 1947 he published two essays in *NOW*, one on censorship and pornography, the other on sadistic and violent imagery in modern literature. The first made the argument that some form of literary censorship has always existed in societies where power is wielded in a top-down manner, originally out of fear of "primitive animism," later stemming from fear that literature might contain hidden criticisms of power or religion or illicit references to sexual matters. "Rulers have always had a hardly-conscious conviction that sexual freedom was in some way related to political liberty [and a related need] to appear as the upholders of a morality increasingly based upon fear."[62]

The other *NOW* piece was prompted by the popularity of violent crime novels. It reads like an expansion on "Raffles and Miss Blandish," a piece that Orwell had published in *Horizon* in 1944 about the devolution of crime fiction from the days of Raffles, the gentleman burglar who E. W. Hornung (brother-in-law of A. Conan Doyle) had created in 1898, to James Hadley Chase's 1939 bestseller, *No Orchids for Miss Blandish*. The latter—"The toughest novel you ever read," the original jacket boasted—concerned the kidnapping of a society heiress by a sadistic gang who rape her and hold her for ransom. Orwell ascribed the popularity of writers like Chase to "the mingled boredom and brutality of war."[63]

Alex detected something more ominous. "The substratum of social and sexual frustration, the natural idealization of the criminal who is in revolt against society which allows the irresponsibles to forget his viciousness," these "have gone into the ancestry of Miss Blandish, of Hitler, of the War for Democracy," Alex wrote. "Sadism is notorious as a refuge for the impotent and physically frustrated," he warned. "[While it is] latent in all societies, as it is in individuals, its invasion of literature and public life marks the termination of a society."[64]

Strongly reflected in these essays is Alex's absorption of Freud as well as the writings of the American architectural critic and urban historian Lewis Mumford. In two important books, *Technics and Civilization* (1934) and *The Culture of Cities* (1938), Mumford had traced the role of technology in Western society and the shift of human populations and cultures into large urban conglomerations or megalopolises. Mumford, whose thought bore some similarities to Read's, warned that Western civilization was becoming too dependent on technology and that cities built to serve an industrial-capitalist model were breeding deep social injustices and imbalances.

A proponent of the so-called garden city movement, Mumford argued for decongesting cities, intermingling residential neighborhoods and industrial areas with greenbelts and agriculture. The grim alternative, he prophesied, could be the totalitarian brutality and destruction that would occur during World War II. In a 1944 book, *The Condition of Man*, Mumford called himself an "organic humanist," which meant that he viewed humans as part of the natural world, beings who needed a healthy environment, space to breathe and not to feel too oppressed to thrive. The future of humanity, Mumford believed, would depend to a great extent on whether organic humanism could assert control over the rise of technology and the industrial economic order that facilitated it. Alex found himself agreeing with Mumford's analysis of the social transformations taking place in the urban industrial world, since it suggested an explanation for the kind of society that could acquiesce in the terrible slaughter of World War II.

A third writer in whom Alex took a keen interest in the postwar years was Albert Camus. The Algerian-French philosopher and novelist had been editor of *Combat*, a Resistance newssheet, during the last years of the war and continued as editor when it transformed into a full-fledged daily paper afterward. As such, he moved its slant from communism to a morally based independent leftism that stood aside from party politics. Alex was deeply impressed by Camus's sensational first novel, *L'Étranger*, published in the UK as *The Outsider* in 1946, whose antihero, Mersault, kills an Arab man who quarreled with one of Mersault's neighbors. On trial for his life, the murderer doesn't deny he committed the act but refuses to show any remorse, explaining that he always lives only in the moment, and he is condemned to die. To Alex, *L'Étranger* was "one of the most remarkable psychological studies I remember reading—remarkable as a novel and even more remarkable in its interpretation of an affectless, delinquent individual. . . . Mersault comments on the whole pattern of modern life."

Camus's second novel, *La Peste*, was published in the UK as *The Plague* two years later. Like the first, it was acclaimed. Reviewing it in *Tribune*, Alex called the philosophy expressed in the novel "the conviction of a sane human being." "[It] made me want to stand up and cheer."[65]

L'Étranger struck Alex as a fictional portrait of the sort of irresponsible individual he seemed to find on all sides during the war. *La Peste* he saw as Camus's effort to come to grips with the societal conditions that produced such a person. The novel tells the story of a fictional plague in the Algerian port of Oran, its progress, the response of the townspeople under quarantine, and their efforts to adjust once the plague runs its course.

Critics often interpret the plague itself—the infection that the characters in the novel pass to one another—as a metaphor for the deeply compromised moral condition of French society under Nazi and Vichy rule: it was "*the* novel of the occupation and the Resistance," one wrote, fairly typically.[66] Alex didn't take issue with this but thought Camus was making a broader point, one akin to his own argument in *Art and Social Responsibility*. "We know the germ of Camus's plague," he wrote. "I've been writing about it for some time under the name of Irresponsible Obedience."

Camus was careful not to blame the plague on any particular person or group, but he did describe its effects in words that could easily have come from Alex's pen (at least in English translation): "that foul procedure whereby filthy mouths stinking of plague told a fettered man that he was going to die, and scientifically arranged things so that he should die." In another article about the novel two years later, Alex concluded, "Power itself is the Plague, with which we, through acquiescence, are infected. . . . The individual is responsible, and the remedy lies in his responsibility."[67]

At the time of his encounter with Camus's work, Alex was writing a new novel, and something of the French author's prose—terse, almost hardboiled in *L'Étranger*, coolly analytical in *La Peste*—was rubbing off on him. The new book took place in a North African city; its protagonist was Shmul Weinstock, a young poet who returns to the Jewish ghetto where he was born just before it is sealed off by the German and Italian occupiers and is bombed by the British. The survivors are herded into a British internment camp—exchanging one set of captors for another—where Shmul becomes involved tangentially in a plot to murder Gellert, a German soldier whose life he had saved earlier. He's imprisoned but at the end of the novel manages to escape the city.

Alex later said that he had planned to title the new book *In Dubious Battle*, the phrase Milton used, in *Paradise Lost*, to describe Satan's struggle with God, but changed his mind when he learned that John Steinbeck had given the same title to a 1936 novel.[68] Instead he called it *On This Side Nothing*, emphasizing the powerlessness that his main character feels. It was Alex's best novel to date, a briskly told yarn of capture and escape, almost a thriller, with a protagonist who's more assertive and less a passive victim than those in his earlier books.

Once again, Alex chose to tell the story of a man whose background was very different from his own, in a setting he didn't know firsthand ("you mustn't underrate the importance of fake actuality," he later joked).[69] And once again he created a character infused with his own stance—half chosen, half inescapable—as a social outsider. Shmul never fully commits to the assassination of Gellert and breaks out of the city partly so he won't have to participate in the trial of the German's killers. Nor can he commit, either sexually or ideologically, to a young woman, Rachel, a Zionist who wants to escape to Palestine with him.

In these respects, Shmul resembles Mersault, who can't experience what Alex called "normal emotion."[70] But as a Jew, he is even more of an outsider. While he was writing his novel, Alex discussed it with Emanuel Litvinoff, who had joined the British Army after a period as a conscientious objector, specifically to fight the Nazis. He had also written a notable poem, "Struma," about the explosion in the Eastern Mediterranean of a ship carrying nearly eight hundred Jewish refugees hoping to go to Palestine after the British had rejected their request and

Turkey had refused them permission to travel there by land. All but one passenger died.

Litvinoff was unable to tell him anything about North African Jews. He had grown up in Whitechapel, and his people were Eastern European. But he did speak, in a letter, about the circumstances of a family displaced and torn away from its roots, and some of these details and impressions made their way into Alex's book. Shmul comes from a community that is in the process of being violently broken up, leaving him feeling doubly exiled, and, even though his family is—or was—more prosperous, he identifies with the poorest Jewish refugees, not to mention others living outside the law. "If you have a culture which is a non-culture, you can't keep it going even if you want to," Alex has him tell us, "and the Jews and the bums and the jailbirds and the deserters start a new one under your feet that cracks your whole edifice like mushrooms cracking a pavement."[71]

A new world would be born amid the very exile and despair that had been imposed on its people, Shmul asserts hopefully, and not out of nationalistic and state-building enterprises like the one Rachel urges him to join in Israel. "If I went, I would be backing the notion that freedom is something national," he says.

Ben Huebsch, who read the manuscript while aboard ship on a trip to Sweden, was enthusiastic. It was "astounding" how Alex identified himself with his narrator "and how [he] portray[ed] the other types of Jew in their thought and action." "One can only hope that the book may cause a few more people to become suspicious of a social system which accepts or resigns itself to force and violence as a means of settling international disputes. You can count on our promoting the book sympathetically in the States, and successfully, too, I hope."[72]

On This Side Nothing received some excellent reviews when it appeared in early 1949. "Mr. Comfort writes with a brilliantly bitter clarity," Charles Poore said in the *New York Times*.[73] Richard McLaughlin in the *Saturday Review of Literature* praised the novel's "rare insights into human character."[74] But much of the response to the novel depended on whether the main character rubbed the reviewer the right way or the wrong way. Poore called Shmul "a Hamlet," but others found him too negative, a nihilist who glorifies the criminal and can't muster any collective loyalty even when the world is going to hell. "Alex Comfort, a young English intellectual who appears to have belief in nothing save the worth of the individual, has selected as protagonist of his novel an individual unlikely to arouse sympathy for his belief," the *Sunday New York Times Book Review's* critic, Mary Sutphen Hurst, concluded.[75]

Another source of disquiet was the novel's attitude toward Jews and Zionism. A review in *Commentary*, the monthly that the American Jewish Committee had launched just after the war, found *On This Side Nothing* a powerful novel but that once again the Jew had been made into a "symbol of human striving," "a stereotype just as unreal and just as disturbing as the one the anti-Semite has created."[76]

Months before his novel appeared in print, Alex had published an article in *New Israel* arguing against the establishment of a Jewish state. While acknowledging the unparalleled suffering that made the case for the new country, he urged Jews to resist the impulse. "The Jews are the sole civilized group who have learned through a long history of dispossession to retain the basic human pattern of mutual aid," he wrote. "The future orientation of all anti-totalitarian planning" would be determined by the fate of the kibbutzim," the Jewish settlers' experiments in communal living. "The infection of Israel with orthodox power institutions, under pressure of danger, would be a disaster." He added, "A State of Israel modelled upon orthodox power institutions will be drawn inevitably into the pattern of Great Power intrigue."[77]

From a later vantage point, that conclusion appears prophetic, but at the time the stance of a character like Shmul seemed to be fading into irrelevance.

CHAPTER 7

The Anarchist (1947–1951)

Alex had been absent from radio since his dustup with the BBC in 1944 over its proposed broadcasts on the English literary scene. That changed three years later, after the corporation inaugurated the Third Programme, its arts-and-culture network. Suddenly Alex was just the sort of contributor the BBC wanted more of, and it brought him a much wider audience in turn.

When it launched on September 29, 1946, the Third Programme became the third major leg in the BBC's offering to British listeners, along with the established Home Service and a newly formed Light Programme, which took over the popular entertainment side. It broadcast from 6:00 p.m. to midnight every evening, and its audience would remain quite small. But the Third carved out a uniquely important place in British life, building a devoted audience among the intelligentsia. By the mid-'50s, *The Listener*, which leaned heavily on the network's intellectual content to fill its pages, had a circulation of over fifty thousand, more than any serious periodical except the *New Statesman and Nation.*[1]

To be featured regularly on the Third Programme, as Alex would soon be, was a portal into wider public prominence. Leading newspapers and other print publications promoted and reviewed its musical and theater offerings and discussed the lectures and debates it hosted.

Religious programming had become a major part of the BBC's menu during the war and continued to be for a long time afterward, and the Church of England, plus the Roman Catholic Church and some major Protestant denominations, exercised a good deal of influence on the network's other offerings. The Third Programme was the exception. It made room for a crop of liberal humanist scientists, philosophers, writers, and critics who had been coming of age intellectually at the great universities during the interwar years and beyond, as well as some of their elders.

"Humanist" was already on the way to becoming an all-inclusive epithet hurled by morally conservative and religious public figures anxious to reverse the secularization of society, but in the postwar years British humanists were a fairly distinct group, including such household names as Bertrand Russell, Julian Huxley, philosopher A. J. Ayer, psychologist Margaret Knight, mathematician and scientist Jacob Bronowski, and increasingly Alex Comfort. Most were atheists or agnostics who believed it was possible to build a moral society without religion, anchored in science and rational discourse.[2] Politically, they tended to support decolonization, an easing of east-west hostilities, abortion on demand, free access to contraception and artificial insemination, an end to literary censorship, decriminalization of homosexuality, and availability of voluntary euthanasia, among other causes that irritated the traditionally-minded.

Mary Webb, the democratic socialist and cofounder of the Fabian Society who was one of the humanists' intellectual parents, wrote in 1926, "The religion of science [is] destined to submerge all religion based on tradition and revelation."[3] Within a few decades, her prophecy seemed to be coming true, at least for a certain segment of the population. By the early '60s, Alex could write, "At the present time, the public turns increasingly to science for the solution to its problems."[4] The Third Programme could take some credit for this development.

Poetry and other readings, lectures and discussions of literature, and big- idea talks and symposia were staples of the Third. Alex proved himself adept at several formats. On July 26, 1947, he read "The Lemmings," one of the stories from *Letters from an Outpost*. On August 13, 1948, he delivered a lecture on "Criticism and Tradition in Contemporary Poetry." On December 9, 1948, he delivered a talk on humanity and ethics, part of a series titled "The Right Thing to Do," which the PPU then published as a pamphlet. And a week later he participated in a discussion of the myth of Prometheus. The latter two were just the kind of topics the BBC had approached him about during the war, before it pulled the rug out from under him on political grounds. The fact that he combined the roles of scientist, doctor, poet, and novelist made him an all-around intellectual of the sort the BBC liked to feature.

It helped also that he developed a cordial relationship with P. H. Newby, one of the programmers in the Third's Talks Department, who in 1958 would become controller or head of the Third. Described in a *New Yorker* profile as "a quiet, unworldly, rather sphinx-like man, whose large head and tightly drawn mouth gave him a cerebral look,"

Newby had a personal and social background—that of an erudite person who had not been raised in what was considered polite society—that would have made him simpatico with Alex.*

By early 1949, Alex's profile had grown sufficiently that he made his first appearance as a guest on *The Brains Trust*, the Home Service's panel show in which a group of experts answered questions sent in by the audience. The show had been enormously popular during the war but was winding down and would soon go off the air. Alex would return frequently as a panelist when BBC Television began carrying it in the 1950s.

That summer he was back on the Home Service with a four-part series of fifteen-minute lectures collectively titled "The Pattern of the Future." Routledge then published them, verbatim, in book form. The jacket copy said that they were the first to be delivered "under the new policy of the B.B.C., by which religious controversy is to take an increasing place in broadcasting," reflecting criticism that the network was not giving enough airtime to nonbelievers and non-Christians.[5] They would also be Alex's first brush with wide public controversy.

His lectures laid out the philosophy of scientific humanism that had been developing in his mind and along the edges of his writing ever since his years at Cambridge. He started with the assertion that there is no sign of positive moral purpose in the universe, except in humans themselves, that what we attribute to the voice of God is the echo of our own voice. Humanity in Western cultures, he said, was undergoing an "adolescence" in which it needed to move on from its earlier beliefs, much as the scaffolding is taken away from a building. A new tradition needed to be developed while retaining the best of the values those earlier beliefs inculcated in us. "We can begin to steer the universe, and we can begin to steer ourselves," he declared."[6]

The essence of this new tradition would be the maintenance of responsibility between humans as a critical tool in their struggle with a morally neutral universe. Responsibility in turn leans on our commitment to truth: that is, our refusal to allow our wishes to overshoot our assessment of reality.[7] The greatest obstacle we face is the desire for power, for two reasons: first, because it claims an allegiance that interferes with our responsibility to each other, and, second, because it attracts individuals

* Ved Mehta, "Onward and Upward with the Arts," *New Yorker*, May 18, 1963. In 1968 Newby would win the first Booker Prize for Something to Answer For, a novel set during the Suez Crisis of 1956 and with a theme—an individual's responsibility for their own actions versus those of their government—that would have been at home in one of Alex's novels.

who seek to assert control over others for its own sake. Disobedience must be our response to this threat. We must assert the right to say no.

"We keep hearing that there were not enough of these [disobedient] men in Germany lately," Alex said. "[But] there are not enough in our own society." The proof: "the permanent war-economy, with its secrecy, witch-hunts, and its hysterical and destructive attitudes." Neither communism nor liberal democracy are capable of freeing us from these evils or encouraging a greater sense of responsibility between humans, since "both assume that institutions are the main means of altering conduct, and both regard power as a necessary element in maintaining society."[8]

Fortunately, we now have the means, Alex argued, through disciplines like sociology and psychiatry, to analyze and expose the factors that make for a society centered on power rather than life. These include the connection between "mental abnormality and the desire for power" and our inclination to delegate power to politicians, police, and cultural icons like athletes and film stars. Changing course starts with changing our minds. "Whatever you may have been told to the contrary, I ask you to believe that there is no tyranny which is independent of its public. . . . And while we must hold that the nineteenth-century idea of revolution is not an answer to our problems, . . . there is one revolution we can all produce at once, in the privacy of our homes. We may not be able to prevent atrocities by other people, but we can at least decline to commit them ourselves."[9]

What prevented people from achieving the "private" revolution Alex was calling for? Upbringing and education, followed by the "centralisation of life at the expense of balance and sociality" and "the belief that coercion is capable of producing social attitudes." In the era of ever-growing stockpiles of weapons of mass destruction, "either we have got to get rid of the coercive conception of government, or it will get rid of us."[10]

The first step would be to understand that human nature does not have to remain as it is; we can change it. Centralized power is less supple and more vulnerable to individual disobedience than a small village tyranny. It is also less capable of harnessing science than a free society, because it discourages independent judgment. Our hope is in the creation of small experimental societies, "ranging from the Jewish kibbutzim to schools, colonies for delinquents, groups of neighbours: through public education, prosaic-looking activities such as child guidance: through the growth of ideas and attitudes."[11] Alex called this the "revolution towards sociality," and his final message was optimistic: that "history runs one way only," and that we can bring about that revolution ourselves, starting today.

While Alex's text was being approved by the BBC, the network's head of religious broadcasting was notified and asked to announce prior to the broadcast that a Christian speaker would present a lecture on the same topic two months later.[12] The producers were right to take notice. By the time Alex was delivering the second lecture of the series, mail was pouring in. Some congratulated the network for airing the series ("if the B.B.C. passed this with their eyes open I congratulate them"), and some found it historic ("I cannot say more than that I felt your series was perhaps the most significant piece of broadcasting there has yet been"). One writer ("Mrs. L. Crabtree" of Liverpool) commented, however, that it "only got by the Programme Director by assuring him that all the Devout would be in bed by 10.30 p.m."

Not all of them. "The B.B.C. sometimes forgets that it isn't a theatre with a Bloomsbury-only audience," the radio critic Adrian Paul admonished. "It forgets that it comes right into every family circle. . . . I was shocked. Not so much by Dr. Alex, but by the B.B.C. taking the risk of offending a few million listeners."

One long, ranting letter, also from Liverpool and laced with antisemitic buzzwords, ended with the writer declaring, "I would rather be a wild man from Boneo [*sic*] with no knowledge of Christianity and as a result of which have eaten a dozen missionaries than the likes of you." Fr. Cyril Martindale, a distinguished Jesuit scholar, demanded the BBC "discontinue" the talks "at once." A third letter was from a writer who described herself as "a very ordinary woman with two lovely children and good husband." "Incidentally," she added, "I have not long to live, owing to a leaking heart valve." Alex's first lecture—provocatively titled "Is Christianity True?"—had dealt her "a devastating blow," she said, robbing her "of comfort and much happiness." "I am very bewildered and hope you or someone can help," she pleaded.

With such correspondence in mind, Alex concluded his final lecture in his best bedside manner, reassuring those Christians who had written him letters "stressing the need for personal salvation." "I'm entirely with them," he said. "Personal salvation, a change of personal attitude, is precisely what we do need . . . if by religion we mean the deeper moral levels of human awareness." In a seemingly deliberate full-circle gesture reaching back to his own religious heritage, he ended by quoting *The Pilgrim's Progress*, the seventeenth-century Nonconformist preacher John Bunyan's Christian allegory, urging his listeners to push forward into the new tradition he envisioned: "I must venture. To go back is nothing but death."[13]

Like Orwell's political essays, "The Pattern of the Future" was grounded, to a fault, in a moral understanding of the choices facing humanity. Alex said nothing about the class system or class struggle, racism, or any other factor that could thwart a "revolution toward sociality." His understanding of power, at least as he expressed it in his lectures, was thin, and his hope that authoritarian governments would fail to harness science to their cause was being dashed even as he spoke. But his argument could be expected to appeal to many middle- and working-class people who felt excluded or incapable of supporting a proletarian revolution, didn't see one on the horizon anyway, but had lost faith in the State, capitalism, and other institutions of Western society.

Alex was proving himself an elegant and able communicator. "The Pattern of the Future" was one of his best prose productions thus far and an exemplary piece of intelligent, thought-provoking broadcasting for a popular audience, although the fifteen-minute slot prompted one listener to complain that he spoke too fast.[14] The BBC was pleased with the attention it received, and in the coming year he developed a new program (*Control of Old Age*) and served as script consultant for an episode of a medical program, *Matters of Life and Death*, the latter for a fee of ten guineas (£10 10s.).[15]

His books were still not selling in quantity. On August 11, 1948, he had received a statement from Paul Scott, now secretary of Falcon Press, informing him that *Art and Social Responsibility* had earned him exactly £39 6s. 3d. The following November, Routledge said they still had 1,385 copies of *Letters from an Outpost* left unsold and had received an offer of 5d. apiece for the lot from a remainder dealer.[16] But his broadcasting was bringing him wider visibility, which made it easier for him to pick up occasional paying assignments as a book critic for *Tribune*, reviewing mostly scientific and medical texts but also such items as Éluard's *Poésie ininterrompue*, Joyce Cary's *The Horse's Mouth*, the Kinsey report, and the second volume of the United Nations War Crimes Commission report on the trials of Nazi war criminals.

And he still had a day job. In 1948 Alex left the Toddlers' Clinics to join the London Hospital Medical College in Whitechapel as demonstrator in physiology—essentially a tutor who worked with students to master laboratory technique. In August of the following year, after he had received his PhD, the medical college hired him as a pre-clinical lecturer in physiology, at the modest salary of £700 per annum, to be increased to £900 in October, along with participation in a contributory retirement plan.[17] The new position still left him time for writing and his molluscan research, not to mention radio appearances and lectures. And that fall he distilled his experience as a demonstrator into a short textbook, *First-Year Physiological Technique*, that provided tips for students on how to handle apparatus and conduct basic experiments.

The point of this practical and potentially very dry text, he wrote, was that one could not always "receive verbal coaching before the class," and "short hours with long syllabuses leave little enough time for the actual experiment." But to lighten the text, he couldn't resist commencing each chapter with an appropriate passage from *Alice's Adventures in Wonderland*. Chapter 3, "Stimulators and Stimulation," begins with the Mad Hatter's tea party: "'The Dormouse is asleep again,' said the Hatter, and he poured a little hot tea on its nose."[18] A reviewer in *The Lancet* noted the entertainment value that set Alex's book apart from similar instructional pieces. "This excellent booklet is written in so light a vein that it is tempting to make a laudatory pun on Dr. Alex Comfort's surname," the anonymous writer said. "There is a full pennyworth on every page and no student should be without it."[19]

Stimulating readers or an audience—waking them up to what he felt was a moral or ethical wrong, a lapse in human responsibility, or an abuse of power—was becoming Alex's stock in trade. Increasingly, however, he was couching his arguments in the form of social criticism rather than polemic. One subject that afforded him more and more opportunity to do so was sex.

ON MAY 31, 1947, the *Oxford Mail* reported on a talk that Alex had given the night before to the University Socialist Club. The topic: "Sexual Ethics in a Free Society."[20] The newspaper's brief summary reads like a trial run of the core argument the twenty-seven-year-old lecturer would make continually over the next three decades about the connection between sex and sociality and the harmful effects that life under capitalism was having on both. "Not moral decay, but the barbarism of urban life accounts for the breakdown of marriage and family," he declared. Capitalism not only condemns people to lives of constant economic precarity but also induces them to live the more creative side of their lives vicariously, through films and books, he argued. "Endemic anxiety which this kind of life breeds destroys the possibility of the physiological conditions of sexual stability," he said, and military conscription aggravates the problem. Real marriage in a militarized society is impossible if a healthy marriage is defined as "a voluntary and permanent relationship for mutual sexual enjoyment and the founding of a family," and promiscuity was inevitable.

Several months later, at a time when a criminal justice reform bill was being debated, *The Lancet* published a letter from Alex protesting the "irrational treatment" meted out to "sexual delinquents" under current laws. "Homosexuality by consent between adults and in private is punishable on very nearly the same basis as homosexual rape," he wrote. This made it morally impossible for any psychiatrist to cooperate with the courts in such matters. Alex suggested reducing the number of punishable categories to three: conduct offensive to public decency, sexual assault, and sexual assault or seduction of minors of either sex. The change would recognize the right to privacy in sexual matters and end the blackmailing of "respectable homosexuals." "The constitutional invert who conducts himself decently is no more a suitable subject for prolonged treatment than he is for permanent segregation."[21]

The implicit message was that the whole category of sexual delinquent was useless and damaging, and that assault or behavior likely to alarm others did not have to be dealt with as "sexual" crimes—and shouldn't. On the other hand, in his lecture Alex was still assuming that "sexual ethics" were important mainly insofar as they affected the institution of marriage, and his letter still assumed there was something abnormal about homosexuality. But these were only his first publicly expressed opinions on sex. At about the same time, a book appeared in the United States that would move his thinking further in the direction it was already headed.

Sexual Behavior in the Human Male, by the zoologist Alfred C. Kinsey and two colleagues at Indiana University, grew out of research the team had conducted starting nearly ten years earlier and that grew to include one-on-one interviews with some twelve thousand white American males. The book was a sensation, thanks in part to a cleverly executed prerelease campaign by which Kinsey introduced its findings to journalists, scholars, and potential reviewers. In little more than two months, the six-hundred-page book was reviewed and otherwise covered—positively—in virtually every major American publication and had sold more than two hundred thousand copies in hardback.[22] Copies were being eagerly obtained in the UK as well, largely through bookshops like HK Lewis in Bloomsbury, which specialized in medical publications. In the case of Kinsey's book, these shops would almost certainly have made sure to sell only to doctors or other appropriate professionals, to avoid running afoul of the obscenity laws.[23]

The headline findings were hard to ignore, among them that more than a third of males had engaged in a homosexual experience to the point of orgasm, that sex with animals occurred in as much as 17 percent of the survey sample in some rural areas, and that premarital and extramarital intercourse, including with prostitutes, was far higher than had been assumed. Most dramatically, at least eight out of ten American males in Kinsey's sample had at some time engaged in some form of sexual behavior that would lay them open to criminal prosecution.[24]

The Kinsey report was big news in the UK as well as the United States. Its research methods and the assumptions behind the findings would come under attack as anthropologists, religious figures, and even literary critics began to pore over them, but this was still in the future when Alex became one of the first British critics to review the book, first for *Freedom* and then for the *New Statesman and Nation*. "The report is hard to obtain in England, but any intelligent reader who can obtain a copy should do so," he advised. "Its effect upon the reform of our attitude to sexuality, in medicine, in society, and in personal life, is bound to be far-reaching."[25]

Alex teased out three key implications from Kinsey's research. First and most obviously, laws relating to sexual offenses were wildly out of step with actual patterns of behavior. Second, the most dramatic group differences were not between religious communities but between levels of education: a proxy, to some extent, for social class. These "differed as widely as those of separate nations," Alex observed. "The lowest groups regarded all forms of pre-coital play, as well as masturbation, as abnormal or immoral, but indulged widely in premarital intercourse (over ninety percent) while the college levels reject premarital and extramarital intercourse but accept masturbation and 'petting' as normal and desirable."[26] Perhaps because he lived in a society where educational and class lines were more firmly drawn, Alex emphasized this aspect of Kinsey's research more than most American critics did.

The third key implication, Alex wrote in *Freedom*, was the most radical: "the overthrow of the entire statistical conception of 'normality' on which many ideas in social morality have been based." Since Kinsey had demonstrated that human behavior showed an "imperceptible gradation from the wholly heterosexual to the wholly homosexual, . . . "homosexuality as a clinical entity cannot be seriously upheld," Alex argued.

Reform of sex laws would have to shift focus. Whereas reformers had previously campaigned to keep "abnormal" subjects from being punished for their "illness," it was now clear that they weren't abnormal at all, merely expressing types of sexuality that were "general if not normal."

Anarchists needed to pay especially close attention to research like Kinsey's, Alex argued, because they would need to rely more on social psychology and anthropology to bolster their case against capitalism, the State, and the society they nurtured. Kinsey was demonstrating what should be a general assumption for anarchists: "the rationalist view that no form of behaviour is unacceptable unless it has demonstrable ill effects on the individual or others."

The idea that sexual freedom, or a restructuring of sexual relations, was closely related to the achievement of political freedom and economic justice had been around for a long time, and by the end of the nineteenth century it was common in Britain's radical communities, especially the anarchists.[27] In 1896 Edward Carpenter, the utopian socialist writer and thinker who was friendly with both anarchists and Labour Party politicians, published *Love's Coming of Age*, a widely read book that advocated companionate marriage and both hetero- and homosexual relations outside of marriage. (Carpenter was also a vegetarian before it was fashionable and is said to have introduced sandals to England.)[28] Oscar Wilde was not only the author of "De Profundis," the narrative and philosophical testament of his ordeal as England's most famous prosecuted homosexual, but also of the 1891 essay "The Soul of Man under Socialism," a personal argument for anarchism influenced by his friendship with Kropotkin.

After World War II, British anarchists faced another challenge: how to relaunch their movement after a conflict from which the State had emerged stronger than ever. If Stalinism suggested that political revolution might be a dead end, and much of the working class was being co-opted by the new social democratic system that the Labour Government was instituting, then how was a social revolution to be brought about? The Freedom Press group, with which Alex and Read were still closely associated, was especially caught up with this question. Sexual liberation suggested itself strongly as one area to address.

In 1945 Marie Louise Berneri published an essay in *NOW* on the Austrian renegade psychoanalyst Wilhelm Reich, whose *The Function of the Orgasm* had been published in English for the first time a couple of years prior and whose brother-in-law practiced medicine with John Hewetson, another member of the Freedom collective.[29] Reich, by this time, was living in the United States, where his critique of sexual repression would have a deep influence on intellectuals including Allen Ginsberg, Norman Mailer, Saul Bellow, and William S. Burroughs, but he was not yet peddling "orgone accumulators," alleged to capture a species of life force, to these cognoscenti.

Reich was in the middle of a long journey from communism to quasi-conservatism and from influential theorist to crackpot visionary, but at this stage Berneri saw him as an anarchist fellow traveler who usefully traced authoritarianism to sexual repression in childhood and beyond. Freud held that inhibitions were an essential part of individual development. Reich considered them simply a negation of life. Berneri quoted Reich approvingly: "Sexual suppression is an essential instrument in the production of economic enslavement. Thus, sexual suppression in the infant and the adolescent is not . . . the prerequisite of cultural development, sociality, diligence and cleanliness; it is the exact opposite."

After Alex's death in 2000, his son would receive a letter from a nurse who had worked with him at the Royal Waterloo Hospital at about the time Berneri was writing about Reich. Alex had once said, according to the nurse, that he wanted to write two books: one on Ireland and the other "the ultimate book about sex."[30]

But his thinking was running in the opposite direction from Berneri's. While he agreed that there was a connection between sexual and political repression, he turned the dynamic around, making economic enslavement and related forms of oppression the cause and sexual problems the effect. He also was English. The historian Lesley A. Hall observes that on the whole, the character of the "British school of sexology . . . has been pragmatic and empirical, lacking the theoretical constructs emanating from the continent, as one might expect, given the British empirical intellectual tradition."[31] Going forward, Alex would always approach sex as a scientist and physician in the empirical tradition, emphasizing evidence and sensory perception over theory.

In the months after his reviews of the Kinsey report appeared, Alex delivered a series of lectures that detailed his thinking about sex and its place in society. In October 1948 Freedom Press published them as a short book, *Barbarism and Sexual Freedom*. Alex himself called the book "a political tract," although its real objective was to fit sex into the critique of modern society and the State that he had summed up in *Art and Social Responsibility*. But what did he mean by "barbarism"? "The name of a society which is orientated towards death rather than life is barbarism," he wrote. "Barbarism is the world of the concentration camp, the conscript, and the atom bomb; and in step with the suppression of life and of personal freedom which barbarism entails goes the deformation of normal sexuality."[32]

The "barbaric" world that capitalism and the State were molding—one of economic precarity, militarism, individual irresponsibility in the face of power, and the uprooting of older, communal patterns of living—was "deforming" sexual relations as well, Alex argued, yielding "the increasing instability of the family, the falling birth rate, venereal disease, prostitution, and overtly sexual crime." This in turn was damaging human relations in general by diminishing our capacity for sociality. "The prime social importance of sexuality lies in the fact that it is the driving-force behind personal relationships of a non-sexual type, and that it dictates, through the form of the family, the whole basis of institutional and non-institutional society and the final and critical stages of personality-growth."[33]

Modern society's perspective on sexual behavior was fatally skewed, Alex contended. Teenage sexuality was forbidden, even though the teen years were the pivotal time when individuals develop their sociality, their ability to form groups, empathize, and cooperate with each other. Sex was a vital part of this process because it was one of the most basic ways that humans learned to express their desires and accommodate each other's, rather than regarding relationships as power games or outlets for violent impulses. "We cannot inhibit or suppress the desire of the adolescent for a sexual gratification to which he is entitled without compelling him to enter permanent marriage unprepared and uninstructed," Alex argued, "and much so-called delinquency depends on the failure of society to admit this."[34]

While adolescent sexuality was forbidden and "inversion" criminalized, he noted, a great deal of sexual violence was tolerated or even celebrated. "One may get seven years for homosexuality by consent—[while] for savagely beating a child, the sadist might possibly get six months." Yet, the "sexual athlete," by which he meant the man who forces himself on women, was "not guilty of any punishable offence" and instead was "the leading figure of many films."[35]

Alex was not necessarily arguing in favor of teenage sexual intercourse, but—he was perhaps deliberately vague on this point—he called for tolerance of teens indulging in "sexual equivalents" or "petting." A reasonable rule of thumb, he advised, was "that no sexual activity is undesirable in itself unless it involves harm to the participants or to others, or is repugnant to one of them." But separating social policy on sex from every other area of social policy was impossible. "There is no defining-line between erotic and non-erotic personal relationships. Defects in one produce defects in the other."[36] Alex was not just calling for reform of public attitudes and policies regarding sex, but for a social revolution. "A general outbreak of public resistance to militarism would contribute more to the removal of sexual imbalance than any action through the channels which we have come to regard as political," he commented.

Anarchism promised the most "scientifically legitimate" approach to sexual ethics, he argued, because it emphasized "the removal of power and the refusal to employ power-institutions as a vehicle for reformist measures." That didn't mean he wouldn't support some reforms as a stopgap. Research on more reliable contraceptives, reform of penal laws concerning sex offenders, nudity and "indecent" literature, and the extension of child—and adult—sex education, including "a wider and more courageous encouragement and toleration of pre-adult sexual play" and "the teaching of erotics to adults" would all help remove the neurosis and violence from sexual relations and make them a better channel for promoting sociality, what Alex called "the forgotten art of being human."[37]

Alex didn't waste much space on complications stemming from class tensions, other than to note that the less educated were not as advanced toward his goal as were more-educated people. "At present there is evidence that the most educated groups, by long study and struggle, are regaining the kind of normality which is general in the behaviour of lower animals," he said tersely. Did this mean that the ignorant masses had to be made to follow the example of their betters? And who were these "most educated groups": the ultra-sophisticated staff of Connolly's *Horizon*, for example, with their merry-go-round of relationships?[38] He did not say.

Barbarism and Sexual Freedom received excellent reviews in *Freedom* and, some months later, *Retort*—two anarchist publications—but none in the mainstream media, and Vernon Richards at Freedom Press reported that the book sold poorly and lost money. However, it did earn a surprisingly sympathetic and astute review in *The Medical Officer*, a journal largely for physicians working in public health. "It is a stimulating book," the anonymous reviewer concluded, "well put together[,] and its argument well worth considering."[39] Word of Alex's book reached Alfred Kinsey, who contacted Freedom Press to obtain a copy and asked the publisher to pass on his contact information to the author, whom he said he would like to meet.[40]

ALEX'S SHORT BOOK ALSO attracted the attention of Mervyn Horder, managing director of Gerald Duckworth & Company, a mainly literary publisher that was planning a new series of books on the social sciences. Horder wrote to Alex in February, proposing that he write a volume on "the sociology of sex": "We have been greatly impressed by the good sense in that book of yours published by Freedom Press, and would be willing to accept an extended version of the same."[41] Horder's father, a doctor to the royal family, was active in the birth control movement, but once his colleagues got a look at *Barbarism*, they found they wanted something a bit less polemical. "Are countries with long-standing conscription like France less sexually 'healthy' than the English were before conscription?" one reader wondered. "(He seems to have military service in the brain.) . . . [But] he is eminently sensible when it gets down to brass tacks."[42]

A little over a year later, Alex's new book, *Sexual Behaviour in Society*, appeared both from Duckworth and, in the United States, from Viking. Why were these publishers keen to bring out such a book? One reason, almost certainly, is that a market for informative books on sex was growing. The success of Kinsey's book was extraordinary, considering the multitude of scandalous areas it covered. But it wasn't the first to explore this ground.

In the UK, Eustace Chesser, a psychologist and gynecologist with a Harley Street practice, had published a book in 1940 entitled *Love without Fear: A Plain Guide to Sex Technique for Every Married Adult*, that discussed frankly such subjects as sexual stimulation, sadomasochism, contraception, androgyny, sexual neuroses, and how to prolong intercourse, capped off with a plea for the removal of prohibitions on abortion. Two years later, Chesser was prosecuted under the Obscenity Act. Rather than plead guilty and pay a fine, he and his publisher let the case go to a jury trial. Surprisingly, he was found not guilty, on the argument that his book was intended only to promote good marital relations, was sold only through reputable bookshops, and was priced too high to be purchased by under-age individuals.[43] The case was a limited though significant landmark in freeing straightforward discussion of sex from the stigma of obscenity. More to the point for publishers like Duckworth and Viking, Chesser's book went on to sell in the hundreds of thousands of copies, including in the United States.

Another, related reason Alex caught publishers' attention was that in *Barbarism and Sexual Freedom* he had hit on an original angle: to discuss sex as a sociological issue rather than a medical, psychological, or moral matter. Something was beginning to change, if not in public attitudes about sex then at least in private behavior, and Alex's lectures had captured some of this social tension. The frequency of single motherhood among women of childbearing age in the United States nearly tripled between 1940 and 1960, rising from 7.1 newborns per 1,000 to 21.6, according to a 2004 study—suggesting a sharp rise in sex outside of marriage. The increase was smaller in the UK—from 5 percent to 8 percent of all births between 1955 and 1967—but still noticeable.[44] There's no single explanation for the shift, but the US researcher, Alan Petigny, noted that "after 15 years of Depression and war, there was also a desire on the part of Americans to live in the moment and enjoy life, and they were accordingly less likely to defer to traditional restraints on their behavior."[45]

Also contributing was the fact that the war had created a huge disruption in millions of people's lives, delaying marriage and childbearing and pulling them away from their stable communities to other parts of the country where new opportunities beckoned. Between 1948 and 1971, the annual relocation rate in the United States held at about 19–20 percent, according to the Census Bureau, meaning that every year, one-fifth of the population moved. It was the longest and largest period of peacetime mobility in American history.[46] Not so coincidentally, use of contraceptives was rising fast, even in decades before the Pill was introduced. In 1939, when Planned Parenthood contacted 1,400 doctors to supply contraceptive assistance in underserviced communities, 210 responded, and the organization considered the campaign a success. In 1955 Planned Parenthood had more than 2,200 doctors and medical students and some 6,000 nurses in training.[47]

Britain too had gone through the Depression and the war, when service in the armed forces created opportunities for both straight and gay men and women to form attachments outside marriage, while women who stayed at home alone often produced illegitimate children.[48] In the aftermath, more people were leaving rural areas for the cities, especially London, while city dwellers were moving into new commuter estates. Additionally, as rationing and other grim features of wartime austerity lingered, some two million Britons emigrated, mostly to Canada and elsewhere in the Commonwealth.[49] The British, like the Americans, were becoming more mobile, and individuals were more likely to find themselves in new and unfamiliar places where social patterns were in flux.

It's not surprising, then, that people living vastly different lives than they had expected—in many cases, these were the parents of the more famously liberated '60s Generation—would experiment in their personal behavior and want information and perspective about it from experts. Books like Kinsey's and Chesser's were not causing people to have more sex in more different ways and settings, as traditionalists worried. They were popular because people were having more sex.

Not that public attitudes, or norms, were catching up with private behavior, at least not yet. With *Sexual Behaviour in Society*, Alex was wading into the discussion reluctantly, he wrote, because of the high "emotive temperature" of the subject, and he aimed his book not at the general public but at various types of social worker who felt called upon—increasingly—to address public misconceptions and distortions about sex. His approach remained sober and scientific. "Much medical writing on marriage guidance and sexual hygiene is severely handicapped by its attempts to provide scientific grounds for traditional patterns of behavior," he argued, "rather than to assess behavior and its consequences as a basis for ethics."[50]

He disapproved also of what would later be described as New Age types—"zealots who put forward theories about sex as a mystique or a transcendent human activity"—because they obscured its place among "human social activities."[51] This, along with the lack of hard data about sexual behavior and response, was accountable for a great deal of misleading, fearful, and plain wrong information masquerading as sensible advice.

Much of the content of the new book reiterated or expanded on *Barbarism and Sexual Freedom*, but its objectives were more specific. First, Alex wanted to push physicians to become better educated and provide better information about sex. In a 1949 letter to *The Lancet*, he complained that the newly qualified doctor of that year was no better equipped to counsel his or her patients about sexual matters than in 1914 ("indeed, he often shares all the prejudices of his time"). As a result, he charged in an article in the *International Journal of Sexology*, the patient was "very often willing to discuss it with anyone except his own medical adviser."[52] One of the greatest obstacles to reducing the volume of anxiety and misinformation about sex was the lack of knowledge and training of doctors themselves, Alex would argue for many years to come.

He also wanted to convince members of the humanistic professions—social workers and counselors, physicians, scientists, educators, psychologists, and sociologists—that they should join in the kind of social revolution he was advocating, because it was the highest objective of their calling. "In attacking the traditional ethics of political power, as well as those of sexual conduct," he wrote, "[sociology] is comparable with the position of public health in attacking smallpox." The study of human behavior, including sex, was giving experts the data and tools to analyze it much more accurately, which in turn would enable humanity to determine a social and sexual ethics based on information rather than outdated beliefs and the demands of power elites.[53]

An unparalleled demand for practical information about sex was already making these developments more urgent, Alex argued, and Kinsey's research was demonstrating the possibility of understanding real human sexual behavior much better. What are we trying to achieve? Alex's answer was a kind of future primitivism that would reconcile humanity's technological achievements with the more harmonious social patterns of so-called primitive cultures that got lost in their march toward a more complex industrial civilization. "[Society] must be based on the exchange of personal responsibility which goes by the name of mutual aid, and its cohesion and order maintained by the attitudes of its individual members, and not by any system of institutional power as we now know it. [Such a society] abandons the view of human misconduct as the product of something immutable in the individual which requires to be suppressed by force from without as a condition of public order."[54]

Alongside instructing social workers about sex counseling, Alex was proposing that they join in a project to achieve a nonauthoritarian, anarchist society. "The present age is an age, in England, of very depressed revolutionaries," he noted.[55] He referred to people who had been inspired by the Russian Revolution and then by antifascism but then been disillusioned or simply bewildered by what followed those struggles. The "application of sociology to life" that he was proposing would be at least as difficult and require just as much sacrifice to achieve, but, he argued, it would stand a better chance of success because it attacked the dysfunction in human relations at a human level rather than by taking over institutions that were set up to maintain the status quo. Developing and encouraging the practice of a new sexual ethics built on personal responsibility and grounded in real knowledge of human behavior would be one important step in this direction.

Alex was hoping to inspire a humanistic revolt of the professionals against the folly and destructiveness of the State, religion, capitalism, and the family, but in spite of his idealism he displayed some of the faults of the professional classes himself. Calling for better and more available contraceptives, he bemoaned that low birth rates had become "a threat to the persistence of the intelligent classes of the community" and suggested, chillingly, that the balance could be redressed "by making contraception possible and available for the least intelligent families, whose higher fertility is not a matter of choice."[56]

Alex made the same male-centered assumptions as other writers on sex in the mid-twentieth century. The sections of his book that discuss childhood sexuality focused almost entirely on boys, not girls. Arguing that social anxiety over adultery is misplaced, he counseled that unfaithfulness was an "escape behavior in men" and that wives should simply understand and forgive it. "The duality of ethical standards is clearly indefensible," he allowed, but he had nothing to add to this very important point.

Worse, and in spite of his own argument that sexual ethics needed to be based on real data on sexual behavior, Alex accepted other male sexologists' nasty tendency to turn women's sexuality into a problem. "Every woman who fails to finds a permanent sexual and social partner is likely to present, in any society, a psychiatric problem of varying complexity, and modern knowledge does not suggest that her difficulties can be resolved at a cheap rate by any change in accepted patterns of conduct," he said flatly.[57] In the end, male-female monogamy was still the best form of family structure, even if one of the parties—most likely the woman—had to make some allowances.

The sexism lurking behind some of Alex's analysis was typical of a time when even writers who thought themselves progressive in sexual matters took phallocentrism as natural, assumed heterosexuality as the norm, and still considered boys' emerging sexuality more important than girls'.[58] Not surprisingly, those feelings eluded most critics who reviewed *Sexual Behaviour in Society*, almost all of whom were men. *Sexual Behaviour* was widely reviewed, and most of the notices were at least as positive as these.

The *New York Times* critic Frank G. Slaughter praised it as "a sane, humanistic evaluation of the place of sex in all phases of human living" and wrote approvingly of Alex's argument relating sexual "maladjustments" to a state-dominated society in which "the dignity of the individual seems largely ignored."[59] "Every parent, every teacher and every social worker should set himself to think as clearly and coolly as he can about the fundamental issues raised in this provocative little book," the *Times Educational Supplement* advised.[60] Dannie Abse, a Welsh physician who was also beginning to make a name for himself as a poet, noted positively in *Public Opinion*, "Dr. Comfort writes as an informed scientist, but the spirit of protest inherent in his poetry has gently overflowed into this more objective and scholastic thesis."[61]

Dachine Rainer, the young American poet and anarchist who had worked for Dwight Macdonald's magazine *Politics* before becoming Holley Cantine's partner at *Retort*, was the only woman to review the book, and she was just as happy that Alex avoided the romantic and spiritual. "Despite the lucidity of anarchist thinking in sociology," she wrote, "anarchists are notorious cranks in many departments, like dietetics and sexology. When we consider the quaintly morbid guilt-inspired theories and practices of Thoreau, Gandhi, Tolstoi in these matters, and the hysterical anti-puritan reaction of Reich, it is good to find someone as nearly balanced as Alex Comfort."[62]

The British popular press understood Alex's book as a much more radical document. The conservative *Daily Telegraph* ran a headline on May 14, 1950, "Doctor's Sex Proposals Jolt British Conventions," under which it noted that Alex was pushing for "more sex-freedom for adolescents" and quoted the following passage prominently: "Young people claim access to sexuality as a right and are justified in doing so."

This was still not what the general British public or its appointed protectors wanted to hear. The *Telegraph* noted that the appearance of Alex's book coincided with "a fresh wave of moral censorship in the art and cinema worlds"; the London County Council had recently forced an open-air art show on the Thames Embankment to remove two nude oil paintings the LCC deemed "undesirable" for public exhibition.[63] This new postwar wave of censorship and sexual repression would last clear into the early '60s, even as underlying social change threatened to boil over. Prosecutions for indecency—mostly related to homosexuality—peaked in England between 1953 and 1957.[64]

It didn't escape a couple of the critics that there was actually next to no new data or firsthand observation in *Sexual Behaviour*. Most of the content was derived from earlier studies—from Freud to Kinsey, Krafft-Ebing, and Margaret Mead—all annotated and put through Alex's analytic wringer. "Dr Comfort writes with excellent sense," Paul Bloomfield said in *Time and Tide*, "though this time he says nothing that many educated people have not taken for granted for a long time now."[65]

While Alex was a biologist and physician with a formidable collection of degrees following his name, he had himself done no original research on sexual practices, aside from the observations he had made of families at the Royal Waterloo Hospital and as medical officer at the

Toddlers' Clinics. Of course, sexology in the immediate postwar years was still just beginning to establish itself as a legitimate area of study. It could be said to date only from 1938, when Havelock Ellis, the year before he died, was awarded the fellowship of the Royal Society of Physicians. Kinsey had no professional background in it when he began his research, and William Masters and Virginia Johnson, a few years later, had no more qualifications than Alex.

The most original elements of his book, already present in *Barbarism and Sexual Freedom*, were its joining of a critique of sexual attitudes and mores with a critique of capitalist society and the State and its insistence that sex be treated as a factor of sociality, not just a personal or medical matter. But this was enough to attract the attention of a small collection of sexual researchers and theorists, a network that Alex would keep in close touch with for the next two decades.

Kinsey, having received a copy of *Barbarism and Sexual Freedom* from Freedom Press in 1949, wrote back endorsing the generalizations Alex had made from his data.[66] Alex was now issuing a steady stream of articles and letters on sex. In late 1949 in a letter in *The Lancet*, he objecting to proposals to disallow contraceptive sales through vending machines, arguing that if rubbers were less available, then teens in particular would be at greater risk of pregnancy.[67] Shortly thereafter, in February 1950, he published an article in the *International Journal of Sexology*, "Sex Education in the Medical Curriculum," that attracted a good deal of attention.

Here he was on firmer ground, drawing on his experience as a lecturer in physiology to highlight a very real problem. The medical curriculum in UK hospital and university medical schools then contained nothing on "sexual hygiene or on marriage guidance," he reported. As a result, "sex education of the public in England has almost certainly outstripped sex education of doctors," even though one's family doctor ought to be the first person one consulted on sexual issues.

Physicians could educate themselves on the subject by reading current literature. "[But] much that is written is highly speculative, insufficiently accurate or explicit, or even, in a few cases, manifestly paranoid," Alex warned, "and the whole subject has a fatal fascination for psychopaths and fanatics." As an example, he noted that a surprising number of medical students regarded homosexuality "as a predominantly endocrine problem," and gay patients who tried to consult a physician ran the risk of getting a "good talking to" rather than an adequate investigation.

To alleviate the problem, Alex proposed a "syllabus on sexual hygiene" for medical students, covering such topics as coitus and orgasm, elementary psychology, sexual psychopathology, economic and legal problems of marriage, contraceptives, infertility, venereal disease, and the psychology of marriage. Luckily, he said, he had detected "a fairly widespread desire for information among students and junior clinicians generally." The article put him in close touch with Cyril Bibby, editor of the *International Journal of Sexology*, who in April asked him to join the editorial board as its resident physiologist.[68]

MOST DISCUSSION ABOUT REFORMING sex laws and rationalizing sex education took a top-down approach, at least in the English-speaking countries, and Alex's writings reflected this. Was there really a need for violent, class-based revolution, he asked rhetorically in a 1949 book review, when, on so many matters, scientific humanism was the answer? Revolution could be most easily effected "not by agitators waving posters but by the application of the normal methods of research to society." The review, in *Freedom*, was of two new books on crime and delinquency, one of which, *Society and Its Criminals*, was by Paul Reiwald, a German-born lawyer and criminologist living in Switzerland. Reiwald took a psychological approach to understanding crime. Despite the fact that criminal law was built on a rationalist intellectual structure, its application was highly emotional. Society seemed to need its sociopaths and psychopaths, who gave it the opportunity for an emotional discharge by administering punishment.

Certain offenses—murder most of all—Reiwald labeled "satisfactory" crimes, since they tend to generate the most emotional excitement. "Unsatisfactory" ones, like embezzlement, generate very little. The most fortunate offender is the white-collar criminal, "in that his crime gives rise to less emotional reactions." Hence, white-collar crime is punished less frequently and less harshly. "Criminal psychology for me begins not with the criminal, but with the society which inflicts the punishment," Reiwald wrote.[69]

As long as this pattern continued, he concluded, society would continue to produce criminals. He tentatively suggested that an "autocratic" criminal law was bound to produce an autocratic system of government. "This is particularly true in our time, when power is represented by a peculiarly unpleasant type of person, the sado-masochist, who has ruined entire countries, for example, Germany." The answer, Reiwald argued, was to replace the aggression of criminal law with "non-violence and self-government as a means of education."[70]

Reiwald's book was one of many that grappled, from various angles, with the hard look that the Nazi era had afforded at the depths to which human society could sink—and to find its causes. Alex had reviewed several in the years after the war, but *Society and Its Criminals* carried wider implications, he concluded. "It automatically commits science to further and further study, not only of delinquents in court or in prison, but [also] of delinquents in society and in office."[71]

Alex was already working on just such an analysis. In the fall of 1950, Routledge issued his short treatise *Authority and Delinquency in the Modern State: A Criminological Approach to the Problem of Power*, which scholars including David Goodway and Peter Marshall are certainly right to call his outstanding contribution to anarchist thought.[72]

The book quotes Reiwald several times, but it also elaborates on the assertion Alex had made repeatedly in his wartime writings: that the individuals in positions of leadership who had ordered the invasion of countries, the bombing of civilians, the building of the death-camp system, and finally the creation and use of the atomic bomb were criminal psychopaths. The nature of the modern State, he argued, is to select such people for positions of power and then to encourage their "delinquent" behavior.

Alex's argument was timely. The leadership of at least one great power in the recent war was undoubtedly made up of psychopaths, and there was a great hunger to understand the psychological underpinnings of this development and the likelihood of it happening again.

Alex agreed with such thinkers as Theodor Adorno, Hannah Arendt, and Abraham Maslow that authoritarianism—or delinquency—had origins in individual and group psychology. But he went a step further, arguing that the institution of the State was needed to give it full expression. In his introduction to a slightly revised edition of *Authority and Delinquency* twenty years later, he wrote of "the growing awareness that, great as is the nuisance-value of the criminal in urban society, the centralized pattern of government is to-day dependent for its continued function upon a supply of individuals whose personalities and attitudes in no way differ from those of admitted psychopathic delinquents. . . . The egocentric psychopath who swindles in the financial field is punishable—if his activities are political, he enjoys immunity and esteem, and may take part in the determination of laws."[73]

Alex was taking a familiar idea and turning it on its head. The British historian Lord Acton famously stated that "absolute power corrupts absolutely." The Russian anarchist Mikhail Bakunin put it this way: "Nothing is more dangerous for man's private morality than the habit of command. The best man, the most intelligent, disinterested, generous, pure, will infallibly and always be spoiled at this trade."[74] Alex argued the opposite: that individuals who find themselves in positions of power come pre-spoiled, because the State deliberately selects "delinquents" for positions of power.

What makes a person a "delinquent"? "The chief factor is the assertion . . . of the right of the actor to behave without regard of others. . . . The opportunities for this kind of accepted and acceptable delinquency lie almost entirely within the pattern of power."[75] The growing size, reach, and complexity of the State were making it more rather than less likely that it would attract people with a "delinquent" frame of mind.

Nor were strong convictions or idealism a safeguard against criminality. "Few leaders have surpassed Adolf Hitler in their sense of mission," Alex observed. Governments in the modern era had become more rather than less preoccupied with foreign policy and war, he argued, because they give the sorts of people who occupy positions of power the biggest arena in which to posture and self-dramatize: "The insistence of such leaders on the possession of nuclear weapons is an integral part of the use to which they put the opportunities of foreign policy—they make their exits and entrances more sensational, they heighten the dramatic tension of the performance—like the street urchin's knife, they carry a pleasing ability to frighten the owner and everyone else."[76]

The difference between the "urchin" and the nuclear-enabled world leader was the State. Molded to some extent by delinquent personalities, it encouraged them to seek positions of leadership, providing them with a platform from which to act out their fantasies and aggressions. What about the vast majority of people who are not decision-makers in their societies? "Fear"—of crime, of terrorism, of communism, of unfamiliar others—"maintained by legislative and commercial groups as a main technique of persuasion, has already become our most important means of government," Alex argued.[77] With elite groups of leaders and legislators increasingly in charge of complex state-capitalist systems, more or less free to make decisions they do not themselves have to enforce, the hard work falls to agents who then rationalize their actions by placing responsibility on their bosses or simply argue that they are doing the will of the nation: another form of fantasy encouraged by the State.

Alex's description of this pattern, with its mounting viciousness, showed up clearly in the murderous dynamic of Nazi Germany. The society it creates, he argued, emphasizes punishment and retribution over education as a way to modify behavior among the masses, encourages aggression over cooperation, pathologizes the working class when it resists its treatment under the capitalist system, and discourages the development of sociality as a counterweight or alternative to the State and capitalism.[78]

All of this applied just as well to the Marxist conception of revolution, Alex added, with "its failure to come to terms with the psychopathology of office, which has distorted its constructive intentions exactly as in other societies, if not more so. . . . No real revolution can be brought about through the interplay of aggressions and projections which makes up almost the whole of traditional political thought, both governmental and revolutionary."[79]

Authority and Delinquency covers a range of subtopics, from penal systems and world government to revolution, the development of human character, and the formation of political elites. But Alex was really making a sociological, not a political argument, since the nature and shaping of society is where he believed the heart of the matter lay. Both democratic and authoritarian governments have in common the "belief that the state is a mechanism whereby human conduct can be modified," he wrote. "The shifts in political thought," from Hobbes to Locke to Rousseau to Marx, "are all shifts in our assumptions about the nature and impulses of individuals." He rejected world government, because it would still depend on coercion rather than education and the practice of mutual aid to maintain sociality, and by further centralizing government it would provide even greater opportunities for delinquents in power. Resistance to authority would still be the greatest weapon against tyranny, and a world government would be no more inclined than the current assortment to tolerate it.[80]

Aside from Reiwald, *Authority and Delinquency* may have been influenced by *Nineteen Eighty-Four*, which had appeared the previous June. Alex later recalled that the one time he and Orwell met in person, Orwell "told me about the new novel he was working on, *Nineteen Eighty-Four*, which I took to be a political statement against dictatorship. His reply was astonishing—that it was, but that the model in his mind was also that of the neurotic's internal 'thought police,' with Big Brother as the superego."[81] *Authority and Delinquency* was a critique of society at the time and the way it molded individuals, and, despite its setting in the future, so may Orwell's novel have been. His and Alex's mutual friend Julian Symons, with whom Orwell discussed the novel, later wrote that *Nineteen Eighty-Four* "was intended only as an extrapolation of possibilities in the nature of society inherent at the time it was written."[82]

Neither book locates tyranny in a single supervillain. Orwell's Big Brother is a shadowy figure, despite the cult of personality constructed around him, and Alex stressed that the characteristics of psychopaths-in-power are not unusual. Every day we encounter people who could be just as abusive and murderous given the right circumstances. There are differences, however. Orwell's novel describes comprehensively the ways in which the Inner Party induces loyalty and even love in its subjects. Alex's treatise is mainly concerned with how the State reproduces itself by modeling the personalities it needs to lead it, creating a psychological profile of Big Brother, in effect.

Another difference is that Alex volunteered a six-part recipe for ending the regime of delinquents in authority:

- *Education*, to promote public awareness of specific problems like war and social neuroses.
- *Experiments in communal living and control of resources*, to instill a daily practice of living and functioning outside the State.
- *Pressure*—exactly what kind he did not specify—*to break up larger components of government and business* and to increase workers' control of production.
- *"Propaganda" and "instruction"*—of both children and adults—to make sociality a more prominent part of character formation within the family.
- *Psychiatry*, which could help to "adjust" the individual in the direction of rejecting and resisting "bad institutions."
- *Public resistance* and the willingness to disobey.[83]

Some of these changes could be achieved through reform of existing institutions, but most would have to take place outside of the State. Just as he had in his books and lectures on sex, Alex was emphasizing sociality and personal responsibility as the primary goals. The social revolution must start from the level of the household and the local community, bypassing the State. When the political revolution arrived, it would be "experimental and tentative, rather than dogmatic and Messianic."

Alex got a chance to flesh out his argument—and his attitude toward Marxism—in an exchange in *The Listener* with Hyman Levy, a mathematician at Imperial College London and member of the British Communist Party, who gave a talk on the Third Programme on "The Marxist View of Liberty." Levy argued that liberty is not a birthright but something that humans acquire by recognizing the necessities of life, then imposing discipline on themselves—"by all on all alike"—that in turns frees them from the "bonds of the primitive."[84]

In a letter to the editor after Levy's talk was published, Alex agreed with this, but he added that the kind of self-discipline Levy was arguing for was a function of cultural upbringing. Therefore, the problem of human liberty in a given society was "predominantly a mental health problem," centered on which personality type expressed itself in that society's institutions. While Marxism emphasized responsibility to others, it also accepted "power as a technique (the dictatorship of the proletariat)," "external father figures (the Party, the Leader)," "the coercion of dissidents," and "compulsory patterns of thought." Therefore, the "psychiatric problem" faced by Marxist societies was not very different from the one that bourgeois societies faced. "All societies in which power-centred forces and individuals exist are sick," he concluded, and the solution is "educational, sexual and psychiatric reorientation" rather than reforms in a political structure that remains power-centered.[85]

Levy, in a reply, dismissed Alex's analysis as too vague and his prescriptions as wishful thinking. Precisely what parts of the political structure are "sick"? Alex didn't say. Would problems like corruption, vested interests, and the wage structure disappear if a "mentally healthy" system was substituted? "I have heard this kind of view expressed by evangelists but not so far by psychiatrists," Levy observed.[86] But the problem with Marxism, Alex responded in a second letter, was that it aimed to attack these problems "by strictly political and economic paths, and by means which give scope for the continuance of aggressive behaviour-patterns." There was no obvious reason to believe that a proletarian revolution and takeover of the State apparatus would solve this problem or relieve us of the need to consider our responsibility to each other and humanity as a whole.

It was not frivolous, at a time when states were rapidly arming themselves with nuclear weapons, to say that the choice between peace and war depended on "the personality and the fears and suspicions which a particular general or foreign minister derived from his childhood." Concentration camps and atomic bombs were the products of existing cultures and their leaders' pathologies, at least in part, and abolishing them would depend on their subjects' ability to stimulate "responsible disobedience."[87]

Arriving amidst the aftershocks of a world war and its unparalleled atrocities—undoubtedly committed by the State—and what appeared to be a chronically violent postwar period, Alex's anarchist treatise enjoyed a surprisingly positive reception from mainstream reviewers. One of his comrades in the PPU, the prison reformer and anti–death penalty activist Margery Fry, in *Tribune*, called *Authority and Delinquency* "fascinating, disturbing, [and] courageous."[88] *The Listener* found it "a brilliant analysis of large-scale centralised communities," and the *Liverpool Post* praised "this important and compelling book."[89] It even received positive notices from two religious publications, *Blackfriars*—a Catholic journal—and the *Baptist Times*, and prompted an invitation for Alex to address the National Association of Probation Officers ("to develop further some of the arguments set out in your recently published book").[90] Several critics recognized it correctly as an argument for a society guided by scientific humanism, and several noted—with an occasional whiff of sarcasm—that it leaned very heavily on categories of Freudian psychology.

Alex seemed to be arguing that "changes in character structure are more important than changes in economic or political power," said a US academic publication, the *Journal of Criminal Law, Criminology, and Police Science*.[91] Another academic reviewer, B. R. Hinchliff, in the *British Journal of Sociology*, took the point further. Psychiatry could doubtless throw light on some political problems, but wasn't it going a bit far to argue that adjustment and neurosis, the same analytic categories that were used to understand groups like families and coworkers, could be applied to complex social organizations of hundreds of millions of humans? People always want seemingly contradictory things, Hinchliff noted: world peace but also national independence, for example. That didn't arise from "unconscious and unresolved mental conflicts." Alex's psychological analysis worked much better in *Sexual Behaviour in Society*, which Hinchliff also reviewed, since it applied to husbands, wives, and parents, not millions of their fellow citizens.[92]

Other critics too pointed out that *Authority and Delinquency* covered a great deal of ground without providing a lot of evidence: for instance, that changes in social structure depend on changes in methods of bringing up children.[93] Alex admitted that much of what he said could not be tested without a firsthand psychological study of "psychopaths in power," and the only group on whom anything like such a study had ever been done was the captured Nazi leaders. But he was not pretending to have the last word on the psychology of leadership. He was trying to persuade his readers that it was no longer possible to reform the State. It would have to be shaken off and replaced with a decentralized system based on mutual aid if the problem of abuse of power was to be solved.

AUTHORITY AND DELINQUENCY WAS the fullest expression of his political and social philosophy that Alex had yet made. It shortly became a primary influence on a leading figure in the relatively new field of social psychology, one of the disciplines Alex felt would be crucial to the development of an anarchist critique of the State.[94]

The American researcher Stanley Milgram cited the book as one of three primary influences on his work, including his famous 1960–63 experiment in obedience, in which he tested volunteers' willingness to inflict pain on other individuals when an authority figure told them it was imperative they do so.[**] Like Alex, Milgram was affected deeply by World War II and the Holocaust, even at a distance. Also like Alex—and another important postwar intellectual figure, Hannah Arendt—he placed great importance on humans' ability to behave responsibly toward each other, and wanted to understand how they could be brought to disregard it. What his experiment revealed, Milgram wrote, was "the capacity for man to abandon his humanity, indeed, the inevitability that he does so, as he merges his unique personality into larger institutional structures. This is a fatal flaw nature has designed into us, and which in the long run gives our species only a modest chance of survival."[95] In his more pessimistic moments, Alex would likely have agreed.

One person who regrettably did not live to read *Authority and Delinquency* was George Orwell, who died in January 1950. In the preceding several years, the two had communicated very little, and Orwell maintained his earlier suspicions of anarchists and pacifists, despite the common ground he and Alex occupied on the Freedom Defence Committee and the issue of nuclear armaments. Around the same time he met Alex for drinks, he was still able to write, in a 1945 essay, "There is a minority of intellectual pacifists, whose real though unacknowledged motive appears to be hatred of western democracy and admiration of

** Other influences on Milgram's research were *The Ghost in the Machine* (1967), by Orwell's friend Arthur Koestler, and a conceptual analysis of authority by Robert Bierstedt. Stanley Milgram, *Obedience to Authority: An Experimental View* (New York: Harper Perennial, 1975), https://archive.org/stream/ObedienceToAuthority_368/milgram_djvu.txt.

totalitarianism."[96] These feelings deepened in his last years, as the Cold War set in and the Communist East and the capitalist West appeared to him increasingly an either-or choice, whereas Alex, at about the same time, was hopefully searching for ways to bring about a social revolution without violence—or at least, too much violence.

In August 1951, Alex delivered a lecture to the Freedom collective's Anarchist Summer School, later reprinted in a pamphlet, that expanded on the arguments he had made in *Authority and Delinquency*.[97] "A scientific attempt to ferret out the actual, concrete factors in society, the family, and the individual which lead to 'crime' of the delinquent type is in itself a revolutionary activity," he declared.

Revolutionaries would have to train themselves differently than they had in the days of the Bolshevik Revolution or the Spanish Civil War, and disseminate a very different sort of message to the working class and middle class.

> Personally, I would like to see more of us, those who can, taking training in social sciences or engaging in research in this field. . . . I want to see something done which has not been done before—a concerted, unbiased, and properly documented attempt to disseminate accurate teaching of the results of modern child psychiatry, social psychology and political psychology to the general public on the same scale as we have in the past tried to disseminate revolutionary propaganda.

An obvious objection was that this would place a coterie of intellectuals in the position of lecturing working-class families on what make them tick. Alex didn't see why this had to be a problem. "The worker wants the information, and wants it now, exactly as he wants the doctor, or as the intellectual wants food and coal, and in terms of mutual aid each relies on the other to deliver the goods. I think this is the complement of what other comrades are doing in industry by pressing for such things as workers' control and local autonomy—the two go together."

In letters to Herbert Read, Alex argued that the anarchist community, for the time being in the UK, would have to accept the role of an "idea factory" rather than a "mass movement," and he made some specific proposals for putting this scheme into practice. These included creating a syllabus for an anarchist encyclopedia ("a book of the general stature of *Das Kapital*") that would incorporate practical matters like town planning, psychology, education, and communal living experiments. He also wanted to see a "small anarchist exhibition" as part of the Festival of

Britain, a program of local and touring exhibitions that the Labour government staged in 1951 to celebrate the nation's recovery from the war.

"What an optimist you are!" Read wrote back to his friend.[98] And it is difficult not to be incredulous at the notion that disseminating psychological and sociological research to the masses could spark a revolution. But Alex was quite serious that his course was the only way forward for the anarchist movement. Science was proving to him that power, delinquency, and other maladjustments could be "attacked by the methods which got rid of epidemic disease," he said in his lecture. "[But] as a minority movement, our best chance lies in our power of forming opinion. By learning how free men are made, and why they are in short supply to-day, psychiatry seems to be filling a role which is not less revolutionary for being unspectacular."[99]

"I agree I'm an optimist," he wrote back to Read in a fever of excitement. But he reported that Vernon Richards and John Hewetson at Freedom Press were both keen on the idea of an encyclopedia, "with psychology replacing Engels and economics." He asked if it was possible to "convoke a group of men we know to be sympathetic to the broad principle (not necessarily 'anarchism' with a slogan on a pole) who could write a manifesto of this kind in detail? I think at the present time it could have real historical importance." Failing that, Alex said, "[I will] do the requisite reading and concoct the whole thing myself."

Alexander, Elizabeth, young Alex Comfort.
Family collection

Postcard. Barnet, England

Young Alex Comfort on ship. Family collection

Arthur Waugh photo. Evelyn Waugh Archives, Somerset UK

Alex Comfort at Cambridge with sandbags. Family collection

Alex Comfort photo portrait. Courtesy of Howard Coster

Alex and Ruth's wedding. Family collection

Wrey Gardiner

Herbert Read.
Vernon Richards, Archive Berneri

CHAPTER 8

The Public Intellectual (1949–1956)

Alex feared that if he was to pull together a comprehensive, practical anarchist encyclopedia, he would "need to be exiled to find time to write it."[1] As it happened, the encyclopedia was never written, nor did Alex or anyone mount an anarchist exhibition at the Festival of Britain. His life was taking a different turn, one that veered away from anarchist theory, poetry, and medicine as he plunged deeper into scientific research and political activism.

By the time he received his PhD in 1949, Alex had published nearly twenty papers on mollusks, either alone or in collaboration. He was soliciting and exchanging specimens with researchers in the United States and Latin America and regularly joining field expeditions organized by the Conchological Society. On one, in April 1950 to Paignton, Devon, he discovered the first definite specimens in the UK of a small, brownish snail, *Hygromia cinctella*, that had originated in the Mediterranean countries.[2] To avoid disturbing his companions at such times, he typically wore a glove on his damaged left hand.[3] (Later, he came to joke about it, once telling a scientific colleague that the accident occurred when he was in the IRA.)[4]

Increasingly, however, he wanted to transfer his work from aging in mollusks to aging in other creatures, including humans. And he wanted to be paid for his work, which thus far he had done entirely on his own time and at his own expense. Soon after his thirtieth birthday, he applied to the British Empire Cancer Campaign for a fellowship but was turned down.[5] At about the same time, he contacted Peter Medawar, professor of zoology and dean of sciences at the University of Birmingham, who was doing groundbreaking work in immunology that would later make organ transplants possible (he would share the 1960 Nobel Prize in Physiology or Medicine for his discoveries). Medawar, who was five years older than Alex, was also keenly interested in the aging process and was already planning to start a new program in the field in the following academic year. "There is a most urgent need for simple fundamental work on aging," he said, and Alex he found to be "a man very well worth having," but he had no room for a new researcher at present and was uncertain of his own plans at the university.[6]

There was also the problem of funding. Medawar suggested Alex approach the Nuffield Foundation, which William Morris, Viscount Nuffield—the creator of Alex's old Morris motorcar—had set up seven years earlier to fund research in science and social science. In November, at Medawar's urging, the foundation offered Alex a personal grant of £1,000 a year for two years to work under him at Birmingham, with further funding for research materials and travel to conferences.[7] Plans changed when Medawar agreed to take a post as professor of zoology and comparative anatomy at University College London (UCL). Alex would come with him, and in July 1951 he was confirmed as honorary research assistant in the biology of old age in the Department of Zoology, supported by his grant from the Nuffield. He started work on September 1.[8]

In a sense, Alex was sticking close to home institutionally. He had carried out his medical studies and received his PhD from the University of London, of which the London Hospital Medical College, where he had been teaching for three years, was a unit, as was his new base, University College. But the relationship between these institutions was looser than this implies. Each college functioned largely independently, and the administrative structure and procedures the university imposed, rather than pulling them closer together, made it "the most tiresome academic institution in the Western world," Medawar later commented.[9] But Alex had landed in a place that was ideally suited to both his personality and the work he wanted to do. UCL itself was one of the UK's most important research and teaching institutions outside Cambridge and Oxford, and it boasted a dazzling group of researchers at the time he arrived.

Besides Medawar, Alex's colleagues in the Department of Zoology included G. P. "Gip" Wells, son of the novelist H. G. Wells and a leading comparative physiologist; biologist Anne McLaren, the first woman elected to the Royal Society; biologist and geneticist John Maynard Smith; and, down the corridor and most prominently, J. B. S. Haldane, the brilliant geneticist and one of the greatest popularizers (and biggest personalities) in British science in the mid-twentieth century. Jack Haldane, like a number of Alex's workmates, had been a Communist—and a passionate defender of Stalin's regime—although he left the

Communist Party of Great Britain in 1950. There is some irony in this. UCL had been badly damaged by bombing during the war, and it struggled financially in the aftermath. Haldane himself had once donated £300 of his salary to his department's kitty.[10] But by the time Medawar and Alex arrived, it was getting back on its feet thanks in large part to funding from the Nuffield Foundation but also from the US Public Health Service. That fact sometimes made the department's "Communist sympathizers" a bit grumpy, Medawar recalled.[11]

As an institution, UCL "had a cosy, friendly atmosphere" and it was "easy to begin to develop feelings of loyalty towards it," Medawar said. The Zoology Department was housed in a "rambling barn of a building" that had once been a warehouse for J. Shoolbred & Company, London's first large department store, on nearby Tottenham Court Road. The entrance, in a fairly gloomy courtyard, boasted, inexplicably, a pair of large door handles in the shape of a naked woman and man, with a large pool of axolotls (Mexican salamanders) just inside. The entire ground floor was taken up, newcomers were told, by "suites of sumptuous lavatories." The eccentric layout extended to the department itself, "a rambling gormenghastly structure with many rooms in unexpected places."[12]

ALEX HAD BEGUN A new phase of his life and career. After authoring seventeen books in the '40s—eighteen, if *France and Other Poems* is counted as a full-length book—along with others he either edited or translated, he would publish only three in the decade that had just begun. His poetry and fiction slowed to a trickle, and he produced no further political theory to build on *Authority and Delinquency*, although he found many new occasions to apply the framework he had already developed. Instead, he would author or coauthor some forty more scientific papers and in his spare time would publish seemingly countless book reviews for *Tribune* and other publications along with a great deal of journalism and commentary for antiwar and antinuclear publications. He threw himself into lecturing and organizing for these causes as well. The BBC was warming to him, and his appearances on both the Third Programme and the Home Service were becoming more frequent. "The post brought half a dozen requests every day," his son remembers.[13]

Alex's life was also changing in other respects. The circle of writers and activists who had populated his personal and creative world during the war years and immediately thereafter was breaking up (along with their audience, it seemed). Adrian Mitchell, then eighteen, later recalled seeing Alex and Dylan Thomas read at the National Book League in 1950. "There can't have been more than three or four people under forty in the audience," he wrote. "Most of them were ladies with the sort of hats worn at church weddings. Certainly poets should be interested in communicating with the middle-aged middle-class, but equally certainly if everybody else stays away from the sexual heavenfire of Dylan Thomas and the tough, witty, healing poems of Alex Comfort, something's wrong."[14]

"What has happened to the war poets?" an anonymous writer in the *Daily Herald* asked in 1953. "Some who were beginning to make names in the early 'forties have found more practical ways of making a living. Alex Comfort is a doctor. Roy Fuller and Roy MacFadden are solicitors. Howard Sergeant is an accountant. Jon Silkin is a skilled plumber."[15]

As noted, Orwell had died in 1950. Marie Louise Berneri had died of pneumonia in April 1949, shortly after completing *Journey through Utopia*, her historical survey of ideal communities. Alex and her comrades from Freedom Press scattered her ashes on the grounds of Kenwood House, at the northern edge of Hampstead Heath.[16] Vernon Richards kept the publishing house, bookshop, and newspaper going ably, but George Woodcock had stopped publishing *NOW* in 1947 and moved back to Canada permanently two years later. Connolly shut down *Horizon* in 1950. Denise Levertov moved to the United States in 1947, where she established herself as a major poet. The Surrealist poet David Gascoyne moved to France after the war, suffered a nervous breakdown, and published little after the mid-'50s. Julian Symons largely abandoned poetry, becoming a successful crime novelist and all-around man of letters, while Nick Moore, Alex's Cambridge comrade, quit Grey Walls, published a well-received collection, *The Glass Tower*, in 1944, and then gradually gave up poetry to concentrate on organic gardening. Henry Treece, the proselytizer for the New Apocalypse, stopped writing poetry as well and began turning out historical romances for young readers (specializing in the Viking period). Dylan Thomas, one of the group's principal inspirations, died in 1953. Tambimuttu had temporarily shut down *Poetry London* and moved back to Sri Lanka in 1949. Fred Marnau largely abandoned his writing career, leaving Grey Walls to work as a travel agent.

Grey Walls itself, and *Poetry Quarterly*, which had been the center of so much of Alex's literary activity, were fading away, then flamed out rather spectacularly. Thanks to Peter Baker's money, Wrey Gardiner had greatly expanded Grey Walls book publishing in the late '40s just as the wartime popularity of small volumes of poetry was losing momentum. But Baker was determined to build his holdings into an empire of unrelated businesses, and, by 1949, Falcon Press—the imprint he had brought together with Grey Walls—was £49,000 in debt.[17] The following year, Baker was elected as a Conservative to the House of Commons—the youngest member, at twenty-nine. He continued to expand his non-publishing businesses.

Gardiner was getting uneasy with the "lunatic atmosphere" of Crown Passage and took a side job as literary editor of *Public Opinion* to compensate for his reduced salary at his own firm. Then, one day in 1954, he returned from a holiday to find that he was the only director of the combined firms who had not resigned. Baker's empire, now seventeen companies, was £650,000 in debt, and Baker had forged signatures on papers "guaranteeing" the funds. He was arrested, brought to trial, convicted, and in a flurry of dire headlines, sentenced to seven years imprisonment. Gardiner tried to save Grey Walls from the smashup but was unsuccessful, and the firm was dissolved along with the rest of the interlocked businesses.

The feckless Baker was not much mourned by his authors, who had often had trouble getting promised money out of him. ("I told you he was a case when I first saw him," Alex reminded Gardiner in a letter once the dust had settled.)[18] Gardiner was another matter. He had sold the house in Billericay, bought some other properties, and was trying, unsuccessfully, to make a living as a landlord and by selling his antiques. He would eke out a lonely, threadbare existence until his death in 1981. (The last of his four autobiographies is titled *The Answer to Life Is No.*) Despite his eccentricities, impracticality, philandering, and failed marriages, authors like Alex, Derek Stanford, and Muriel Spark loved him for his devotion to poetry.[19] Spark had worked for Gardiner briefly and published one of her early books, a selection of Emily Bronte's poems, with Grey Walls in 1952.

The last edition of *Poetry Quarterly* had appeared in 1953. Stanford later wrote that its passing was "like the loss of a friend." "It was an indication that the sands of Neo-Romanticism were now running feebly through the glass."[20] Gardiner no longer liked the submissions he was receiving. "Much of what is written today would qualify for a quick shot at the waste paper basket," he declared in an editorial in the Autumn 1953 issue. Styles and fashion were changing, and he found he could no longer "go with the young moderns," the new crop of poets who were superseding the Neo-Romantics and seeking emphatically to bury them.[21]

Even when they were attracting peak attention during the war years, the Neo-Romantics had absorbed some harsh criticism, in part because critics tended to lump them in with the blearier Apocalyptics. After the war, the attacks only got worse. The new poets who rose to prominence in those years looked back to Auden and his circle for inspiration but rejected his politics. And they firmly rejected the emotionalism they saw in the intervening generation of poets. Instead, they prized skepticism, irony, classicism, and a very conscious cultural Englishness; one of their number, Donald Davie, published a critical work in 1952 titled *Purity of Diction in English Verse*. Other poets who followed the new trend included Philip Larkin, Kingsley Amis, Robert Conquest, John Wain, and Elizabeth Jennings. In a 1954 article, Davie gave them a collective name: the Movement. Conquest, in a 1956 collection titled *New Lines*, took pains to set the Movement apart from the '40s crowd, with their "diffuse and sentimental verbiage," "hollow technical pirouettes," and "surrender to subjectivity."[22]

Not everybody liked the outcome. Ted Hughes, who rose to prominence soon after, called Movement poetry "crabbed and moribund" and complained that it had abandoned "the whole historical exploration into spirit life," replacing it with "pedantic, frivolous, tea-and-biscuits Oxford High Anglicanism."[23] But for some years the Movement would represent the dominant aesthetic in English poetry, pushing into the shadows the stream that Alex and his companions had attempted to launch.

Alex certainly had a hunch that the tide was against him when he titled his new collection, published just a few months before he began work at UCL, *And All but He Departed*. The reference is to a stanza in the Irish poet Thomas Moore's 1815 poem "Oft in the Stilly Night":

> I feel like one,
> Who treads alone
> Some banquet-hall deserted,
> Whose lights are fled,
> Whose garlands dead,
> And all but he departed!

The new book was Alex's first collection in five years. In it he included memories of the time he had spent in Sligo during his midwife training, of a trip to Paris in 1949, and, as always, carefully observed images of the natural world: birds, fish, mountains, rivers, seashore, and clouds ("Grazing in numberless herds / White cattle on a far slope of space"). It contained only one poem referencing the war: "A Virtual Image," a moving meditation on his cousin John Fenner, killed serving in the RAF. But the new collection was just as informed as ever by his political concerns. The Korean War was raging, and more than one poem satirized the use of words like "freedom" and "democracy" to justify mass slaughter. But some of the new poems also reflected his thinking about death and the danger of not recognizing it as an "emotional fact." In "Concerning the Nature of Things," a response to Lucretius's "De Rerum Natura," he suggested that all life finds its center in the inevitable physical dissolution:

> In the fulness of time: all things
> move to a centre, travel
>
> by mile or inch, to reach
> the effortless still Sargasso Sea—
>
> the smooth shot of water, the sharp
> anchors of metal, the soft
>
> globes of oil, the dull
> burrs of earth move
>
> unbreakable ductile dusts
> the motes in the knothole beam
>
> being what they are, travel
> like bees at sundown back.[24]

The last, most powerful poem in the collection, "Seeing the War Films," added a new idea: that documentary film and photography have changed consciousness by capturing life in a way that prevents us from dismissing or forgetting what we've done or has been done in our name. The victims are granted a kind of enteral life.

> One turned her back. A child carried a child.
> A child ran searching, will always run. No sound
> out of his desperate oval mouth—what we have written

we have written: nothing will change it. If
we shout *Look, she is there* he will not hear. . .

You stay with us
an after-image of the colder light
on a white ground, dark—on the white ground
dark, beside the path, a liberated child.

And I the child will run always, but never knowing
a senile general and two frightened men
for whose prestige I, suddenly lost,
being four years old, and seeming
after long searching to have fallen asleep
am here, cannot be buried. In this immutable dream.
Once we could kill people and they would die.[25]

Together the poems in *And All but He Departed* put into verse the concerns Alex had addressed in *Art and Social Responsibility*, including, of course, the critical importance of disobedience to preserving any kind of civilization. "This is the work I do," he wrote in one of the longer poems, "The Sleeping Princess":

I gather your scattered No
your inarticulate salvage
of bloodymindedness
drive your doubts in a row
as a fence between you and the eyeless, voiceless, press

of those who were Citizens,
who waited another week,
whose poor disguises failed,
who did not speak soon enough,
who thought it useless to speak,
whose No was killed by custom, and they by custom killed.[26]

In all of the verse he had produced since his first published work while at university, Alex explained years later, his project had been to "bring the rhetorical tradition back into poetry to see what could be done with it in modern English."[27] This was poetry of eloquence and grand pronouncements, which had essentially been abandoned by the modernists. For over a decade, the reception of his poetry and the other Neo-Romantics' had depended on the critics' willingness to take this project seriously. Judging from the reviews of *And All but He Departed*, the final answer was no.

Several praised his detailed observation and vivid expression. But one wrote, "I wish he would restrain his propagandist zeal, which often intervenes to spoil a good poem." Another said, "His impatience with society is impressive, it is informed by both intelligence and emotion, but he seems to be too impatient about the business of writing poetry. It is not enough to raise the voice and assume a minatory rhythm and tone and trust to an important-sounding but static rhetoric. Rhetoric may be a neglected element in poetry, but [Comfort is a] rhetoritician rather than a poet." This time around, his new book was not published in the United States. Despite Ben Huebsch's enthusiasm for Alex, Viking Press appeared to have lost interest.

ALEX WOULD NOT COMPLETE a new collection for almost a decade, and the amount of verse he published in between—for poetry magazines, primarily—was sparse. He was appearing before the public as much as ever, both in print and as a public speaker, but mainly in two guises: as an agitator, campaigner, and polemicist for nuclear disarmament, and as a scientific researcher and popularizer, in fields ranging from old age to physiology and sexology. Since he had no new idea for a novel, he said, he could not force himself to write one.[28] He still wrote occasionally for Freedom Press, including for *Freedom*, the magazine that had succeeded *War Commentary*, but when the collective attempted to reconcile its intellectual and syndicalist factions after the war under the umbrella of a new Federation of Anarchist Groups, both Alex and Herbert Read stayed aloof, not wishing to risk butting heads with the syndicalists once more.[29]

Besides the time consumed by his new course of research on aging, what drove Alex—like many others—was a deep sense of emergency. During the war, the focal point was aerial bombardment of civilians. Now it was the escalation of tensions between the superpowers and the growing role of nuclear weapons in their rivalry. The Soviet Union detonated its first atomic device in 1949, the United States tested the first thermonuclear or hydrogen bomb in 1952, and the Soviets followed suit the year after that. The previous half-decade had seen the Soviet occupation of Eastern Europe, the hiving off of the Russian postwar occupation zone as East Germany, the creation of West Berlin as an island of noncommunist rule within the new state, and finally the Maoist victory in the Chinese Revolution. The two hydrogen bomb tests came in the middle of the Korean War, a slaughter that resulted in more than three million civilian deaths and created what seemed like an irresistible temptation for one or the other side to use the new weapon. All through the period, a number of countries, with the United States conspicuously in the lead, were constructing networks of fallout shelters in case of such an event, further raising the level of nuclear paranoia.

Gradually, the US-Soviet nuclear rivalry would devolve into a quasi-institutionalized status quo, punctuated by occasional flare-ups like the Berlin crisis of 1961 (when the Soviet-backed government of East Germany hastily constructed a wall dividing the city) and the standoff over Russian placement of nuclear missiles in Cuba in 1962. But in the early '50s, and for many years thereafter, the rapid growth of nuclear arsenals seemed to place the world on a hair-trigger. Britain would explode a plutonium bomb in 1952, France would conduct its first test in 1960, and all the nuclear powers conducted frequent live weapons tests.

Governments' efforts to downplay the risks and normalize the existence of these weapons tended to have the opposite effect. A UK government pamphlet on the hydrogen bomb—what it was, what a nuclear explosion would be like, and what dangers radiation posed—was less than reassuring when it offered safety advice such as this: "Window panes should be white-washed and anything inflammable removed from doorways and windows; otherwise the heat flash will have its best chance to start fires."

Humanity and the earth could be just one reckless, irrational move away from destruction, and Westminster's decision to tighten its alliance with the United States as a member of the new North Atlantic Treaty Organization (NATO) while creating its own independent nuclear deterrent only ratcheted up the risk.

This understanding saturates nearly everything Alex wrote and said on behalf of disarmament and geopolitics in these years, and it often struck a sympathetic nerve. In February 1951, as the butchery in Korea escalated and talk of a wider conflict between the Soviets and the United States grew louder, Alex and Herbert Read sent a letter to the *New Statesman and Nation* advocating replacement of "the present national policy" with "complete and unilateral disarmament" or else "an agreed upon policy of disarmament between the Western Powers and the U.S.S.R."

Their argument, in essence, was simple: Should Stalin decide to overrun Europe, there was little that a group of nations still recovering from the last war could do to stop him. Furthermore, with the United States and Russia nuclear-armed, war would mean the destruction of Europe, with neither side winning. "We do not believe that [domination by an imperialist Soviet Union] approaches in gravity the threat, not merely of atomic war, but [also] of the consequences of mass rearmament and of prolonged artificial war-hysteria." A Soviet occupation of Europe, on the other hand, would at least enable Britons to save "the largest part of the intellectual and moral tradition" of their country and exert some influence over events going forward.

"We are not simpletons, sentimentalists, or fellow-travellers," Alex and Read insisted. They understood the history and current practices of the Soviet Union but had to conclude that unilateral disarmament was the sole rational policy for the UK on "moral, psychological and practical grounds." They therefore stated their intention to "refuse any participation, moral or physical, in war between East and West."[30]

With government policy moving in the opposite direction, they complained, "a virtual censorship" of their position was in place, "such as has never existed in the past." The letter prompted a flood of personal letters—"we undoubtedly touched off a minor explosion," Read wrote to Alex.[31] Much if not most was in their favor, and many thanked the authors for helping them to feel less isolated. "A few of my friends and I feel that the least we can do is to let you know that your views have our support and you have our thanks for expressing them so clearly," one Londoner wrote Alex. "I can promise you that you will not be without friends when the going gets difficult." A woman from Surrey wrote, "I think the general public are uneasy at the weakness of the government in resisting American pressure and it might be possible to crystallize the general feeling if people whose names were known would speak out as you have done."

An organized movement for unilateral disarmament was still several years in the future in Britain, but the early postwar period was a heyday for public intellectuals worried about the prospect of another, even worse war and anxious to do something about it. From Albert Einstein, Thomas Mann, and Bertrand Russell to Vera Brittain, Jean-Paul Sartre, and Richard Wright, prominent writers and thinkers seemed constantly to be writing letters to the press like the one Alex and Read had crafted—if less blunt in their proposals—or else adding their names to joint statements calling for a de-escalation of the mounting Cold War rhetoric.

Alex's name frequently appeared on such statements. In April 1951, as a follow-on to their *New Statesman* letter, he and Read pulled together ten other British writers to launch the Authors World Peace Appeal, a rather nonspecific statement that pledged them to "encourage an international settlement through peaceful negotiation" while condemning "writing liable to sharpen existing dangers and hatred."[32] Other signatories included Siegfried Sassoon, the playwrights Christopher Fry and Sean O'Casey, short story writer and poet A. E. Coppard, and novelist and critic Compton Mackenzie. Over the next several years the roster would grow to more than seven hundred. In July 1952, Alex and many of the other writers who signed the appeal published a letter in the *Times* of London calling for a protest to the secretary general of the UN against the use of napalm by UN forces in Korea, allegedly in civilian areas.[33]

Most of Alex's public presence, however, was in connection with PPU-sponsored events and in the pages of its newspaper, *Peace News*. At the end of the war, the PPU had been at low ebb, but its core membership rededicated themselves as the Cold War set in. A meeting at London's Central Hall in 1948 that featured Alex, Vera Brittain, Sybil Thorndyke, Laurence Housman, and Michael Tippett drew a full house, and Tippett, Benjamin Britten, and Alex became its most visible sponsors in the months that followed.[34] What made Alex an especially valuable voice for the pacifist movement, in comparison with other activists, was his rhetoric, which was humorous, blunt, and highly provocative. His moral indignation had always carried a hint of the thunderous Protestant sermons that were part of his family history, and he was ready at any time to declare his beliefs. This made him very quotable.

At a conference to introduce the Authors World Peace Appeal, at the Cinematograph Exhibitors' Association hall, he declared right away that he was a pacifist. "And as those who have read my writings may know, [I'm] practically the opponent of every Government in existence." Nuclear arms control talks that the UN was conducting at Lake Success, New York, he dismissed as "buffoonery."[35] At a demonstration organized by the PPU in Trafalgar Square on July 22, he claimed, "If Hitler wasn't dead, he would now be holding a commission under General Eisenhower." (Eisenhower had recently taken office as NATO's supreme allied commander, Europe.) "The one thing this country cannot afford is to be 'defended' by the American Army."[36]

The year before, Alex had provoked outrage in the House of Commons when the PPU published his coyly titled pamphlet, "Civil Defence: What YOU Should Do Now!" The point of this satirical piece was that in an atomic war, the very idea of civil defense, as it had been practiced during the last war, was absurd, and any pretense otherwise by the government a sham. Designed to look like a government-issue precautionary leaflet, the publication warned, "If our cities should ever again be the object of attack, it will be the duty of every citizen to take what steps he can to protect himself and help his neighbors." What steps would those be?

1. He can clear out of the country now, while the going is good.
2. He can wrap himself in brown paper . . . get under the kitchen table, and hope for the best.
3. He can stand in the next General Election, get into the Cabinet, and issue inspiring appeals for endurance from the deep shelters under Whitehall.

Should the reader not find these alternatives appealing, there was "only one course open": "To see that war does not break out, demand that we stop threatening the Russians with atomic bombs [and] force the authorities to make reasonable proposals on disarmament."

The PPU distributed one hundred thousand copies of "Civil Defence," flooding the South London boroughs of Bermondsey and Camberwell, and printed the text on the front page of the September 22 issue of *Peace News*. In response, Harmar Nicholls, Conservative member for Peterborough, entered a question in the House of Commons demanding that Home Secretary James Chuter Ede explain what steps he was taking to prevent the PPU from circulating this "defeatist pamphlet," hindering recruitment to Civil Defence, and "undermining the morale of those who have already been recruited."

Ede joined in denouncing the publication as baseless and wrong in its assertions, but there was little he could do, as it didn't resemble a government bulletin closely enough to prompt legal action (the color schemes were different, the PPU hastened to point out). Alex had signed the piece, and he then wrote the Home Office asking the secretary to point out any inaccuracies in the pamphlet.[37] A Civil Defence Department staffer wrote back acknowledging that there were none per se but that having a trained Civil Defence force would certainly reduce the number of casualties from a nuclear attack, in contrast to "the experience of unprepared Japanese cities."[38]

Alex then issued his own statement, "as author of the 'subversive pamphlet.'" "My intention was to advocate not the passive acceptance of slavery," he declared, "but an independent foreign policy for a country which, compared with Russia and America, would be irreparably damaged by atomic attack."[39]

Another pamphlet, "How to Read the Newspapers (and Listen to the News Bulletins)," undated but from the same period, Alex wrote for the Medical Association for the Prevention of War, a group of prominent doctors working for disarmament that he had joined soon after it was formed in 1951. An amusing but careful dissection of government propaganda as served up in the mainstream media, the piece looks ahead to the kind of textual analysis that figures like Noam Chomsky would practice decades later. "The art of propagandamanship is threefold," Alex informed his readers: "say it loud, say it often, and attach it to something people care about—preferably something they are scared of." What distinguishes "Our Side" from "Their Side"? "If Our Side are displaying firmness somewhere, what would Their Side do in the same circumstances? 'Campaign of Terrorism Against the Local Population,' of course." Do "we" ever kill people? "We kill only bandits, fanatical Reds, diehard Nazis." Alex included a glossary aimed at helping readers play the "News Game": "interrogation, firmness, screening" on Our Side, "torture, repression, purge" on Their Side.

The pamphlet ended with an admonition: "Learn to play the News Game. It may save your life and the lives of others. To ensure your success in this task is a medical necessity."

Sometimes he could go a bit too far for some of his collaborators. A leaflet he wrote for the PPU in 1951, stating the case for British neutrality in the Cold War, was rejected and instead turned into a by-lined article for *Peace News* because some of the organizers were "[not] completely happy at the rather strong anti-American bias" of the piece and felt it was the PPU's business "to mediate rather than to irritate."[40]

Alongside his pamphleteering, however, Alex maintained a heavy schedule of both public speaking and writing of the op-ed variety. He fielded requests from the London Anarchist Group (to address an "agitational" antiwar meeting), the Marriage Law Reform Society (for his endorsement of a bill sanctioning divorce after seven years' separation), the Manchester University Rationalist Society, the Cambridge Scientists' Anti-War Group, the London Fabian Society (to address a conference on "science and belief"), the National Peace Council (for another conference address), the Political Science Society of the London School of Economics (for a lecture on "the contemporary anarchist approach to authority"), and the Council of Christians and Jews (for a contribution to its magazine on "The Influence of the Cinema in the Shaping of Patterns of Thought and Feeling").

One of the more curious invitations Alex accepted came from the Braziers Park School of Integrative Social Research, a combination intentional community and institute for the study of various types of progressive, communitarian, and vaguely spiritual thought. Dorothy Glaister, a progressive educator who had founded the school in 1950 with her husband, psychiatrist J. Norman Glaister, had met Alex at a PPU meeting in Trafalgar Square and subsequently asked him to read and comment on a lecture she had written and hoped to persuade the BBC to let her deliver, on "the positive implications of non-violence." He did so, and several months later he accepted the Glaisters' invitation to attend and speak at their August summer school, held at a country house and estate in Oxfordshire, bringing Ruth and Nick with him.

No doubt the intention was to cultivate Alex as a member or supporter of the newborn community. Shortly before they traveled, however, Norman Glaister contacted Alex again on behalf of Glynn Faithfull, an academic and former wartime spy who was a trustee of the school. Faithfull's Austrian-born wife, Eva, was looking for a playmate for their five-year-old daughter and hoped that five-year-old Nick might fit the bill. Nick's companion, as it happened, was Marianne Faithfull, the future British Invasion chanteuse.[41]

Aside from his sometimes provocative style, what was it that put Alex in such high demand? While not everyone agreed with his point of view, his politics at least seemed worth exploring, and his scientific and literary credentials marked him out as a serious person rather than a crackpot. This shift in consciousness might not have led so many different organizations to Alex's door, however, if not for his growing presence on the BBC, which made him one of Britain's better-known public intellectuals even though he was still in his early thirties. That, in turn, made him a popular source of comment on political and cultural issues of all sorts—and especially valuable to politically unconventional pressure groups like the PPU.

BBC listeners encountered Comfort no matter their area of interest, it seemed. In April 1951 he reviewed the *Oxford Book of American Verse* on the Third Programme. In June the BBC English Service to Asia included excerpts from a *Tribune* article by Alex, "Gandhi's Greatness," in its *Asian Digest* broadcast. August brought a talk on "Research in Aging" for the Far Eastern Service, and in November he joined a panel for *Question Time*, a new program similar to *The Brains Trust*, in which experts gave impromptu answers to questions send in by listeners.

Occasionally the network let Alex take his broadcasts in a more personal direction. In January 1952 he worked with a BBC sound engineer to produce "Trains with Faces," a revisitation of his childhood hobby of trainspotting. He was taking Nick, now five years old, back to his old haunts in Barnet to watch the trains going through the Hadley Tunnel and found that many of the old steam engines he had loved were still running. Accordingly, Alex and the engineer scoured the lines coming into London to record the whistles of the locomotives he wanted to highlight. One class, the Robinson Director, gave them particular trouble, almost necessitating a trip to Birmingham to run them down.[42]

As this suggests, the network was finding Alex a useful source of programming ideas, and at irregular intervals he was invited by the corporation higher-ups—such as Lord Simon of Wythenshawe, BBC chair; Mary Somerville, controller of the Talks Division; and his friend P. H. Newby, Somerville's second in command—to throw around ideas. "I wonder whether you would be free to come and have dinner at my flat on Wednesday, May 16th with Professor [Barbara] Wooton [sociologist and governor of the BBC] and one or two of the Talks producers?" Somerville wrote Alex on April 27, 1951. "We plan to have an argy bargy [vigourous discussion] on broadcasting and the Social Sciences." The result was that Alex began to be heard more frequently on the Home Service, with its much larger audience, as well as the Third Programme.

WHAT WAS ALEX USING the BBC platform to say? When the occasion or the topic allowed, he was putting into popular form the arguments he had made earlier about war, the power structure, and the centrality of personal responsibility at a time when the opportunities for governments to perpetrate mass destruction and death were growing. In a November 1951 Third Programme talk, "Social Responsibility in Science and Art," he argued that artists could no longer think of their sole duty as aesthetic, and scientists could no longer reject any direct concern for the application of their results.

Those positions had broken down, he said, "in the face of the experience we have had with Nazism, in the face of the atom bomb, and the advent of policy-determination by mass hysteria." Scientists, in the postwar reality, had to resist the pull of "co-optation with anti-human and destructive policies"; otherwise, they had to take responsibility for the production and eventual use of nuclear weapons, not to mention "the destruction of all scientific liberty by one or another totalitarianism." Artists—and especially novelists, who had the largest mass audience and whose work embraced the largest portion of their culture—needed to treat the content of their work as an ethically serious matter, much as Alex saw Camus doing in *The Plague*.[43]

Listeners from as far away as Alberta wrote in to agree with Alex's stand, and, when his talk appeared in *The Listener*, the magazine received requests from the United States and the UK to republish it. The BBC was giving humanists like him more leeway to spread their message. In 1956–57 he broadcast a series of talks on the North of England Home Service titled "The Case for Humanism, or Can Science Make Us Good?"[44] When he got down to discussing current political developments, however, Alex was more often in *Peace News, Freedom*, other activist publications, and some of the daily press, and less frequently on the BBC. Usually he wanted to talk about the United States, the Soviet Union, the possibility of a nonaligned policy that steered clear of both superpowers, and the need for anarchists and pacifists to harness education and social psychology to build resistance to war and the State.

As early as 1948—before Britain had conducted its first atomic test—Alex was urging fellow Brits to stay out of the Cold War, in part to avoid contributing to the increase of tensions and partly to avoid the authoritarian tendencies he saw developing in the nuclear-armed states.[45] The leaders of the United States and the Soviet Union were both sociopathic, he argued in article after article over the next decade, as evidenced by the "politico-sexual delusions of Senator McCarthy and the vast increase of sadism and projected aggression in literature" in the one and the "tyrannical and paranoid elements in Communist philosophy" in the other. "Bourgeois scientists are not afraid of unorthodox ideas," he wrote in *Tribune* in 1954, "provided these do not lead to effective political or social action. Marxist thinkers are not afraid of political action, but they are afraid of unorthodox ideas which might lead to a revision of their philosophy."[46]

But Washington was more frightening, on the whole, than Moscow, Alex concluded. Despite its secret police, deportations, detentions, and squashing of dissent—much of which the West too practiced during wartime—the Soviet ideology included a number of "life-centred standards, such as sociality, co-operation, and control of environment by man, which makes it quite impossible to treat it as a negative or a wholly pathological force."[47]

Much of this assertion, needless to say, was made on faith. But in the many articles and opinion pieces he wrote in the '50s, and in the talks and speeches he delivered, Alex was quite likely one of the harshest British voices on US conduct around the world at the time. Washington's rejection of a UN commission's recommendation for mediation of the conflict between North and South Korea had killed the idea of collective security that was supposed to ensure peace in the postwar period, he charged.[48] "It has been argued that this is a police action," he wrote once the war was in its third year. "In what civilised country would the police massacre the population of a city to reassert law and order?"[49]

He could go much farther. "What is coming to the top in America today," he wrote in a letter to the *New Statesman and Nation*, "is not the need for self-defence, or even the need for imperialist expansion, but the need for an enemy, a need arising from psychopathology, not politics. If there were no Soviet Union, no Communism, it would have been necessary to invent them. . . . The last time a great nation became the prey of forces of this kind, the outcome was written in Belsen."[50] By joining the American war in Korea, Alex told a PPU meeting in Trafalgar Square in July 1952, his own country was left "without any moral authority to criticize the Russians, the Chinese, or, for that matter, the Nazis themselves."[51]

Not surprisingly, his arguments provoked a good deal of outrage. One "W. Smith," London, wrote him at home with a set of lyrics set to the Irish drinking song, "Mush Mush": "THERE'S ANOTHER ONE BORN EVERY MINUTE / OVER FOURTEEN HUNDRED A DAY, / PEOPLE WHO SIGN 'PEACE-PETITIONS', / WHO WILL OUR FREEDOMS BETRAY."

In a more serious vein was a letter to the editor of the *New Statesman* in response to Alex's own, from his erstwhile friend Stephen Spender. Spender had made his break with Communism in the late '40s, when he contributed an essay to the much-discussed collection *The God That Failed* along with other ex-Leninists including Arthur Koestler, Ignazio Silone, and Richard Wright, and had just published an autobiography, *World within World*, that described his political pilgrimage more fully. He then commenced doing speaking tours for the Congress for Cultural Freedom, a liberal anti-Communist group.[52] Soon he would take over editing *Encounter* magazine, which like the Congress for Cultural Freedom was later revealed to be secretly funded by the US Central Intelligence Agency.

In his *New Statesman* letter, Spender came close to tagging Alex as a Soviet fellow traveler. "At the back of Dr. Comfort's psychiatric mumbo-jumbo there is just an ordinary Communist interpretation of American policy," he wrote. "It is surely still possible to analyse the situation in sane language without accusing the framers of the Marshall Plan of being 'mental patients.'"[53]

Alex replied, pointing out that he hadn't accused the architects of the Marshall Plan of being mental patients—only leaders like Eisenhower, who had recently made statements strongly suggesting he was prepared to use nuclear weapons—and that American scholars and intellectuals like Lewis Mumford had themselves expressed concerns that possession of the atom and hydrogen bombs was turning Washington's defense policy pathological.[54] But it wasn't only reborn anticommunists like Spender who disagreed with Alex's geopolitical analysis or his program for undermining the State. Some of his fellow anarchists also had their objections. S. E. Parker, a British anarchist, asked how an enemy of the State could imagine that Britain could or would use its leverage to moderate the conflict between Washington and Moscow—in other words, solve the problem of war within the existing social and political framework. "The only way to achieve the pacifist society in which war would be abolished is to work for a social revolution fundamentally to change the structure of society and, consequently, the relationship of man to man."[55]

The point of Alex's sometimes overheated rhetoric, however, was not to provoke fights with the likes of Spender or flog hopeless mediation schemes. It was to urge the British people not to take sides in the Cold War and, just as importantly, to persuade Britons in science and the arts to help build bridges with their counterparts on the other side of the Iron Curtain. This was urgent not just if tensions that could lead to nuclear war were to be tamped down but to preserve a common civilization in a world the Cold War was tearing apart.

In July 1951, when the Soviet government launched an English-language publication, *News: A Fortnightly Searchlight on World Events*, Alex suggested to the executive committee of the PPU that he contribute an article explaining its position and urging friendship between the Russian and British peoples, even if their governments remained hostile. The Moscow-based paper published a cut-down version of his piece, and the PPU then reprinted it as a pamphlet, "Through the Iron Curtain." Years later, it can read as a hopelessly naïve appeal to people living under a dictatorship that left them no power to express themselves, indicating that Alex had learned nothing from his quixotic schoolboy tour of

Germany in 1938. But it was also a reasonable if longshot attempt to persuade people on both sides of the divide not to give in to the fear their governments wanted to instill in them. "From our knowledge of the British public," he wrote, "we assure you that every free and unsponsored visit by a private individual to your country, or by a Soviet subject to Britain, could do more to allay suspicion and reduce the risk of war than could be undone by ten determined spies."

To put his appeal in more concrete terms, he decided to write a novel dramatizing the argument behind it. *A Giant's Strength* contains some familiar elements: a hero who has been rendered stateless, and a chaotic, destabilizing social setting that calls familiar values into question. At least one of the characters exhibits some of the affectlessness and lack of normal emotion of Camus's Mersault. But Alex was frank about his intention in writing the novel. "Certainly it is propaganda, but not for either of the present combatants," he wrote for the book jacket. "Once we see the world in terms of real people, we cease to be hysterical about it."

Alex still wasn't taking V. S. Pritchett's advice that he write a story drawn from his own experience. The main character is Julius Hedler, a German mathematician with a talent for building "calculating machines"—early computers. During the war, the German military has him working on rocket technology. Afterward the American occupiers keep him at his work, but he escapes to the eastern zone of Berlin, where the Soviets send him to a facility in Tashkent to work on similar projects. Fed up, he tries to escape by plane to Persia "or any other country where he would be indispensable to nobody." But after the pilot refuses to take him, he kills the pilot and finds himself stranded in the Turkestan desert, where a fortnight later he is captured by Afghan bandits. Major Serkin, a Soviet intelligence officer, sets out to find the missing Hedler, but the trail quickly goes cold. Unbeknown to Serkin, however, a scientific expedition led by Shemirin, a hydrologist who had known Hedler in Tashkent, stumbles on the bandits who captured Hedler, and, in the skirmish that follows, Hedler saves Shemirin's life.

What should Shemirin, an idealistic young Communist, do? His expedition a failure, he will have to go back to Moscow and accept whatever punishment will be handed out. Should he bring Hedler back and hope it redounds in his favor? His guide, Anosov, an old anarchist, persuades him to let Hedler escape across the frontier but extracts a promise that Hedler will never again work for imperialists, warmongers, or enemies of Russia. He agrees. "Remember your promise," Shemirin says as Anosov conducts Hedler over the border.

The story is trimmer and moves faster than Alex's previous novels, but it still benefits from his adeptness at physical description. He makes Hedler's struggle to stay alive in the desert gripping, even if there's more of it than the story really needs. But Alex's real purpose is to bring a together a group of characters with various ideological affiliations—to communism (Shemirin), to anarchy (Anosov), to order and process (Serkin), and apparently to nothing (Hedler)—and find out whether they can discover common ground in their humanity. The answer is yes. But toward the end of the book, Alex slips in a deeply disturbing thought experiment.

Serkin finds a letter in Tashkent, written to Shemirin by Hedler before his attempted escape by plane but never delivered. In it Hedler speculates on whether "the machine itself is not the ultimate solution" to the problem of human organization. "As you know," he writes, "it is theoretically possible to construct a machine capable of arriving at judgments. If we can provide such a machine with the factual material, it is both logical and inerrant. . . . It could represent a complete disembodiment of the integrative power of the State . . . capable of its own wisdom, incorruptible, unambitious . . . able to exercise mercy and judgment."

How could such a machine be programmed? Very simply, Hedler explains. Humanity has done so—"frequently and amply—in the Constitution of the United States, in your own constitution."

> When such a machine exists, I will accept it. A State with pentodes for deputies, integrators for government, the supremacy in the hands of a crystal clock or the inexorable disintegration of radium, and hang it over the worktable, as you hang the portrait of a political leader. Could we define its terms? Our punch cards could amplify the terms, amplify freedom, democracy, responsibility into intelligible symbols. . . . Let us punch the cards at one of the periods when the Revolution is actually with us, and let us devise means to electrocute anyone who attempts to change them, other than in accord with the principles we then embody in them.

"If I had the courage of my convictions," Hedler declares, "I'd stay and develop such a machine." But who would punch the cards? "They would be punched in secret . . . by those who have nothing in them but the determination that the machine shall survive, and they in it. A machine dedicated to the principle that all men are created equal, possessing certain inalienable rights, incapable of riding any man down."[56]

Alex puts these words in the mouth of a character whose grip on human values is uncertain, who killed a person who had done him no harm, and who, as the book ends, is slipping out of Russia with a bare promise not to serve the delinquents of society. One who imagines building a machine that could never serve the delinquents and would kill anyone who tried to program it otherwise. Would Shemerin have let him go if he had seen Hedler's letter?

A Giant's Strength, in this passage, is the closest Alex ever came to writing a fictional answer to *Nineteen Eighty-Four*, one that goes beyond Orwell's nightmare. The ultimate solution to tyranny—to Big Brother—could itself be an even greater tyranny, one that could appeal persuasively to the very humanistic values that are supposed to keep us from accepting oppression. The Nazi state had demonstrated the extent to which technology could be harnessed to serve a homicidal regime, but couldn't the machine still become a monster, even when programmed with the most liberal of ideologies? Alex never expanded on Hedler's speculation outside the novel, but he appeared to be commenting principally on the State: that the only logical way for it to avoid becoming a despotism would be to eliminate any human direction whatsoever, but that this too would result in tyranny.

The possibility of putting such a scheme into operation was certainly a long way off, but plenty of people were speculating on the extent to which machines could be made to carry out some aspects of human thought and decision-making, and not only in the realm of science fiction. Two years earlier, the English mathematician, pioneering computer scientist, and World War II codebreaker Alan Turing had published a seminal paper, "Computing Machinery and Intelligence," in which he proposed that a machine—given the right amount of memory and computing capacity—could act in ways that closely resemble the cognitive behavior of a human being.[57] The term "artificial intelligence" was coined just a few years later, in 1956, by a group of American scientists.

While Alex never mentioned Turing's paper, it attracted attention when it was published, and he was likely to have been aware of it. *A Giant's Strength* itself took more time to get right than his previous novels, however. When he submitted it to Routledge in early 1951, Herbert Read told him the ending was too ambiguous. "You don't resolve anything by escorting a man to a frontier," he complained. "Can't we follow him eastward? And having created the Shemirin-Anosov-Hedler triangle can't you do something with it? Erect a square on its hypotenuse (I've never written that word since I was at school!)?"[58]

Read admitted he was old-fashioned in preferring his drama to resolve neatly, and Alex kept the ending as it was. But then Read informed him that Routledge's other readers felt the text was too short for a novel, although the writing was "just as imaginative as ever."[59] Could he either add it to a volume with another story or stories, or else expand it into a full-length novel? Alex chose the latter course and by late June had beefed up his typescript by some 25 percent.[60]

Even so, *A Giant's Strength* was not published until the fall of the following year, and, if Routledge had misgivings, so did Viking, which did not bring the book out in the United States, ending Alex's relationship with his American publisher. Alex later claimed that Viking turned down the novel because they thought it was too sympathetic to its Russian characters.[61] (The book was published in France, however, by Olivet.) Once again his novel attracted mixed reviews: a few seeing it as excellent, some respectful but not enthusiastic, all of them noting, somewhat regretfully, that it was a "novel of ideas." Almost all the British critics praised his powers of description and scene-setting, especially the plane crash and the bandit attack, and some singled out his ability to turn characters of whom he had no personal understanding—Russian security officers, a German mathematician—into three-dimensional personalities. But only one reviewer, the novelist Arthur Calder-Marshall in *The Listener*, seemed to be in sympathy with the kind of work Alex had tried to create.

"*A Giant's Strength* is a carefully constructed conversation piece, which makes one feel how easy such things were in the time of Voltaire," Calder-Marshall wrote. "[Alex's plea for people to see beyond ideologies] is wise, mature and undogmatic. He writes as an artist, with a deep moral purpose which adds to rather than distracts from his judgment of human beings. As a doctor, he regards hysteria as the principal enemy of civilization, whether it is manifested as love or hatred."[62] On the other hand, the eminent critic Philip Toynbee, in the *Observer*, dismissed the message of Alex's "well-intentioned but grossly confused political tract" as "silly and naïve." In nearly all human conflicts, Toynbee argued, one side is more right than the other, and, in the Cold War, Alex was shirking his duty to decide which one was which.[63]

Both Calder-Marshall and Toynbee were disaffected former members of the Communist Party. Neither they nor any of the other reviewers appeared to grasp the larger questions about technology, the scientist, and the State that the novel attempted to raise. Alex noted this wryly in a reply to a review in the *New Statesman and Nation* by George D. Painter (later celebrated for his two-volume biography of Proust), who complained that Hedler, a murderer, "makes a deplorable representative of pacifist and neutral man." "Can you, I wonder, spare me the space to say how much I agree with him?" Alex wrote in a letter to the editor.[64]

TOYNBEE CRITICIZED HIS REFUSAL to take sides between East and West as "easy" and "indulgent," but in real life Alex had to tread carefully to avoid being labeled a communist sympathizer. In his "Through the Iron Curtain" pamphlet, he took care to inform his Russian (and British) readers that the PPU had "not associated itself with the appeal launched by the World Peace Council," the Soviet-sponsored counterpart of the Congress for Cultural Freedom, although he noted that members were free to associate with the council and that the PPU had protested efforts to suppress the council's activities. Even in an article for *The Nation* (which called him "one of Britain's foremost political pamphleteers"), explaining the impact of McCarthyism on European opinion of the United States, he allowed, "On the issue of justice and civil liberties the Communists are demonstrably and insupportably the worse."[65]

He also avoided associating himself with organizations and events that carried any tinge of red. In July 1951 he turned down an invitation from the Yugoslav National Committee for the Defence of Peace to attend a peace conference in Zagreb that fall. The agenda was hard to object to—condemnation of aggression, arms reduction, aid to underdeveloped countries—and even Eleanor Roosevelt had encouraged Americans to attend, but Alex nevertheless rejected the offer.[66]

Earlier that year, he found himself in an awkward position regarding a campaign he had helped found: the Authors World Peace Appeal. On May 30, Sybil Morrison, the chairman of the PPU, wrote him that Vera Brittain had agreed to join the executive committee and give it six months of active work. Two weeks later Brittain wrote to Alex in confidence, informing him, "[I have been warned,] by a literary organisation which I respect, to have nothing to do with the Authors' Committee, as it is merely another attempt by the Communists to use pacifists as stooges!" Since she had already agreed to serve, she felt she should at least attend one or two meetings but asked Alex to first let her know who else had signed up and how the project originated.[67]

Alex answered that the campaign included individual writers who were pro-Soviet and that he had wanted "a fighting pacifist" ("who doesn't mind a political rough house and isn't afraid of the CP"), but he offered to extricate her from her commitment.[68] On reflection, Brittain decided to participate after all, with some conditions. "I don't want to offend people who have doubtless swallowed many of their own prejudices in order to accept me on the Committee," she wrote him on June 20. "[However,] I could not put my name to any public appeal which included the names of prominent Communists without adversely affecting my husband's political work—and this has already suffered enough from my pacifism."* She would nevertheless attempt to be useful "in the background."[69]

Sometime later, Alex himself resigned from the executive committee of the Authors World Peace Appeal when it appeared that it was being captured by a communist faction, although he remained a signatory.[70] And he was still intent on developing links between Russia and the UK outside official circles.

In 1954 the Society for Cultural Relations with the USSR, a thirty-year-old group aimed at promoting understanding between the UK and the Soviet Union—of which Jack Haldane had been a prominent member—sponsored a fact-finding delegation of nineteen British doctors on a three-week visit to Russia. T. F. Fox, editor of *The Lancet*, and Lord Amulree, a pioneer in geriatric medicine and head of the Medical Society for the Care of the Elderly, were among the principal organizers.

Alex was acquainted with Fox, who sometimes let him publish articles and letters in the journal classifying war as a medical and health problem, and he eagerly joined the expedition.[71] His job in part was to collect and assess estimates of life expectancy. Stalin had died the year before, the Thaw was just beginning, and Moscow was allowing visits back and forth between Soviet and non-Soviet doctors for the first time in many years. Eager to demonstrate that their medical practice was on a par with the West, his guides showed Alex such wonders as a dog with a transplanted lung, he told young Nick.[72] He also picked up a reading knowledge of Russian and a smattering of conversational ability in the language.[73]

Upon the team's return, Fox pulled together a two-part report covering their findings and observations, ranging from child health, hospital care, and pensions to the caliber of doctors, their training, and their pay in specific fields like internal medicine, oncology, and neurology. Speaking for the entire team, Fox's report was generally very positive. He seemed in awe of the progress that Soviet health care had made since

* Brittain's husband, George Catlin, was an academic political scientist.

he had last visited Russia, in 1936. But he couldn't believe Soviet doctors would be able to "play their full part in the development of medicine until their research-workers [were] able to work without looking over their shoulders" and no longer had to fear being tagged as "lackeys of bourgeois science" and the like for accepting Western discoveries.[74]

Alex, by contrast, was determined not to leave a sour note in the wake of the expedition. In a letter to *The Lancet* expanding on life expectancy data Fox had summarized, he noted that the Soviets were sensitive to comparisons between their vital statistics and those of noncommunist countries. "We might ourselves be less inclined to such comparisons," he said, in a dig at his country's status as a colonial overlord, "if we were obliged to average the actuarial data for all the territories in which we are the responsible health authority." He hoped the "very real friendships and the normality of relations" established during the visit would lead to fewer "invidious comparisons" and more cooperation on "promoting longer life and better health."[75]

Later that year Alex wrote an article for *The Lancet* noting hopefully that the *Bulletin of the Academy of Sciences of the U.S.S.R.* had just published a series of reviews on biological theory in the West. Biology was the subject that had most divided Western and Soviet scientists during the Stalin decades, and Alex took it to be a significant step that Soviet scientists could once again write fairly dispassionately about it. If this development spread to other areas of research, "a damaging fissure in scientific goodwill" would close."[76]

Alex was getting quite a bit ahead of himself, because still hovering over the effort to build bridges between Western and Soviet scientists was a single name: Lysenko.

A favorite of Stalin's, Trofim Lysenko was a Soviet agronomist and biologist who in 1940 became director of the Institute of Genetics in the Soviet Academy of Sciences. He dismissed standard Mendelian genetics—which held that the evolution of new genetic traits in animals and plants takes place entirely within cells—as racist and fascist and a Western bourgeois error. Instead, he endorsed the discredited Lamarckian theory that characteristics acquired by one generation in response to environment would be inherited by its descendants. In the '30s, agricultural practices based on Lamarckism had contributed to the famine that killed millions in the Soviet Union (they would wreak havoc on Chinese farmers as well in the '50s). But Lysenko amassed such power that Nikolai Vavilov, an internationally renowned Russian geneticist who disagreed with him, was demoted, arrested, and died in prison in 1943.

Lysenkoism grew to become a kind of religion in Soviet science, alienating many Western geneticists. Julian Huxley, after a visit to Russia in 1945 with a party of UK and other European scientists (during which he was subjected to an appallingly uninformed conversation with the man himself), wrote a book, *Soviet Genetics and World Science*, in which he denounced Lysenko's theories as "largely based on ancient superstitions."[77] When Stalin put his protégé in charge of Soviet biology in 1948, opinion among Western scientists turned sharply against any form of cooperation with their Russian counterparts.[78]

Lysenko still held all his posts at the time Alex and his colleagues visited Russia in 1954, and while his reputation was starting to fade now that his mentor was dead, the damage to relations between the scientific communities was deep. A few Communist Party members—including Haldane, whose most important work was founded on Mendelian genetics and who had been a friend of Vavilov—had dodged around the issues and for a long time refused to denounce Stalin's science tsar, doing harm to their own reputations, but eventually had to move on. Haldane left the party in 1950, although he never explicitly denounced Lysenkoism.[**]

In this, he had a fairly congenial home at UCL, where even Medawar admitted that his staff included several members with "strongly Communist sympathies," making "the Zoology Department of the College, and perhaps even the College as a whole, an object of suspicion by Intelligence."[79] Alex, of course, was another member of Medawar's department. Coupled with the fact that some US and UK scientists who went only so far as suggesting that Lysenko's theories should be tested like any other were blackballed and fell under suspicion of treason, this suggests the danger of the minefield he stepped into with his 1954 article in *The Lancet*.[***]

** Medawar later wrote that the inimitable Haldane "was a complete innocent politically and believed everything he was told. . . . His liking and admiration for the working class was purely notional and his colleagues soon formed the opinion that he couldn't bear the sight of them." Peter Medawar, *Memoir of a Thinking Radish* (Oxford: Oxford University Press, 1986), 128.

*** For example, Ralph Spitzer, a chemist at Oregon State University, was forced out of his position in 1949 for arguing in a journal article that Lysenko's work shouldn't be dismissed simply because it had the Soviet government's backing. Thereafter he was unable to get a permanent job in the United States and moved to Canada for the rest of his career. A decade later, Bernard Malamud based his novel, *A New Life*, in part on the Spitzer case. See William DeJong-Lambert, *The Cold War Politics of Research: An Introduction to the Lysenko Affair* (New York: Springer, 2012).

Alex took the *Bulletin* article he had read as evidence that Soviet biologists and geneticists were ready to meet their Western counterparts halfway on such topics as inherited traits. But what he went on to describe suggested otherwise. "The general drift of this analysis," he wrote, "is to emphasise first that Western genetics is not static, and second that it is coming closer to the position adopted by Soviet genetics. This second conclusion may displease those who rejected Lysenko root and branch, . . . but there is little doubt that . . . if Soviet scientists construe the growing Western interest in extranuclear inheritance [i.e., outside the cell nucleus] as evidence of a change of heart[,] nobody will wish to quarrel with that view."[80]

Alex was suggesting, first, that any reconciliation would have to include Western scientists accepting some elements of a genetic theory that was discredited everywhere but the Soviet Union, and, second, that some of them were ready to do just that. He went on to recommend to his scientific colleagues that they ought to be more polite in commenting on their Soviet counterparts' work. "[If they] do not cease to be critical, they will at least display the same controversial good manners."

He completely misread the inclinations of the vast majority of Western scientists. He was also displaying a troubling tendency to put his hopes for a post-Stalin reconciliation of East and West ahead of his responsibility as a scientific researcher and to speak up against the persecution of dissenters like Vavilov.

Why he took this route is not entirely clear. Alex was not a geneticist, and he was emphatically not a Communist. He was aware too of whom he was dealing. In 1956, in a reciprocal effort, he offered to write the introduction to a book on medicine in the Soviet Union that the pro-Soviet Society for Cultural Relations (SCR) with the USSR—his sponsor on his trip to Russia—was shopping to publishers. However, after Pergamon Press, an academic house, agreed to bring the book out, he begged off, citing a full schedule.[81] He may have decided not to associate his name too closely with the SCR. In a personal letter a short time later he acknowledged, "It is and was a stooge organisation acting as a mouthpiece for the Soviet Government." Still, it was useful "as a source of information and a means of getting contacts in Russia." He added that "as an anarchist" he didn't cherish illusions about "the morality of the Soviet government."[82] But he also felt that Western science could be just as misdirected, in its own way.

In a February 18, 1955 article in *Tribune*, he denounced a "Science and Freedom" conference that the CIA-funded Congress for Cultural

Freedom—"an anti-Communist propaganda body whose sponsorship and finances are not specified"—had held in Hamburg. The conference report said not a word about the problems of hunger, infant mortality, or the misuse of atomic power, Alex complained, or "any of the aspects of that application of science to human welfare on which all future history depends." Five years later, he still had no use for the congress. When the French poet Pierre Emmanuel, whose work he respected, invited him to attend a conference it was sponsoring in Copenhagen on "The Writer and the Welfare State," he declined, calling the organization "anti-communist stooges on the best Communist model." "I have never written for *Encounter* magazine [sponsored by the congress] for the same reason."[83]

By contrast, Alex was genuinely impressed, during his visit to Russia, with the practical achievements of Soviet science in the decades since the revolution, often under crisis conditions. In an unpublished draft of a lecture written in late 1955 or early 1956, he conceded,

> Russians have been their own worst enemies in damaging [their standing with] Western scientists by invariably publicizing their least reliable, most ideologically contentious and most grandiose work. Whether their experimental conclusions are right or wrong, the real measure of Russian biological science is not Lysenko and Lepeschinskaya, but a solid body of quite uncontroversial but often brilliant research which might have been produced under any ideology, in fields like climatology, desert ecology and soil conservation, geology, biochemistry, and surveying.****

While Soviet science could "become stuck" if Communist political orthodoxy kept it tied down, Alex believed this was a greater danger in the West, where science was "becoming increasingly stuck through the combined effects of fear of Communism and inability to apply itself to large-scale useful work"—to which he might have added its increasingly compromised involvement with nuclear and other weapons research. He saw signs of all this in the Western scientific establishment's eagerness to use Lysenkoism as a political punching bag, at the expense of any serious effort to understand and engage with the totality of Soviet science.

**** AC, unpublished manuscript, 1955 or 1956. Olga Lepeshinskaya (1871–1963) was a Soviet biologist and a favorite of Stalin who believed, among other things, in spontaneous generation: that living organisms could arise from nonliving matter.

Haldane's biographer, Samanth Subramanian, found the Lysenko affair "a perfect encapsulation of the ways in which science is not siloed, the ways in which it is affected by politics, and the human fallibility of scientists."[84] In Alex's case, his predilection for bloody-mindedness—for being deliberately stubborn or uncooperative, sometimes for its own sake—may have kept him from loudly denouncing Stalin's geneticist. He simply wasn't going to do or say anything that could create the appearance that he was taking a side in the Cold War, however much of an annoyance he created. But he also believed deeply in the need to keep theoretical and practical, humane science closely bound together: for all science to have a humanistic direction. He felt this connection was weakening in the West, particularly with the advent of the Bomb, but was staying relatively strong in the East. Accordingly, keeping lines of communication open was the overriding concern in much of what he wrote about the Iron Curtain divide in the '50s and into the '60s.

"Unless Britain does in fact withdraw from the Cold War," he warned, "she will very soon risk the loss of large sections of her academic personnel to India and other neutral countries where the application of science to serious matters is still possible. . . . Should this withdrawal take place, the possibility of safeguarding the objective tradition in science and combining it with social effectiveness will return in force."[85]

ANOTHER REASON ALEX SEEMED to cut the Eastern Bloc more slack than the Western, may have been that, living in the West, he simply had a greater likelihood of influencing the conduct of his government than the one the other side of the Iron Curtain. But this sometimes tied him in knots.

On October 23, 1956, a student protest ignited the Hungarian Revolution against the Communist regime. Workers' councils assumed power in some parts of the country, general strikes were called, and militias formed to resist the Soviet occupation. On October 24, a new government under Prime Minister Imre Nagy took over. Soon after, Nagy announced that Hungary was withdrawing from the Warsaw Pact to become a nonaligned country, released political prisoners, and pledged to hold free and fair elections. While Washington hinted vaguely that outside help was coming—a pledge it could not keep without sparking war with Russia—a brief period of indecision in Moscow ended when Khrushchev sent twelve fresh divisions into Hungary to crush the revolt.

Tens of thousands of rebels were arrested and imprisoned and more than two hundred executed. Nagy and members of his government were tried and executed for treason.

On November 10, just as the Red Army was completing its work, Alex and Herbert Read each received a postal telegram asking them to respond to an SOS message from the Hungarian Writers Association. The message asked them to apply immediately to the Hungarian embassy in London for visas, giving as their reason that they wanted to investigate "deeply disturbing reports" of the events in the country. "Unlikely visa request will be granted now," the message said, "but more visa applications the greater the moral pressure on Russian for restraint."

The telegram, which was going to "one hundred prominent British writers," was signed by Stephen Spender; Arthur Koestler, the Hungarian-British ex-Communist and author of *Darkness at Noon*, who was now active in the Congress for Cultural Freedom; and George Mikes, a Hungarian-born British journalist and humorist. The recipients were to let a "Mrs. Walmsley," 21 Earls Terrace, Kensington, know if they would apply for visas and, if so, whether this could be revealed publicly.

Alex shot off a letter the same day to Mrs. Walmsley, asking for the actual text of the appeal from the Hungarian writers. Spender's and Koestler's names had set off alarm bells. "I am not prepared to join in anything got up by the signatories of this telegram," he wrote. "I suspect them of political motives, and I am sure that their activities and those of their associates have played a part in bringing about the present tragedy." The same day, Read sent him a note asking his views and suggesting they write a letter to the *New Statesman and Nation*. They had been out of touch, and Read still thought that Alex had joined Medawar at Birmingham rather than UCL.

Alex agreed, adding that applying for visas would merely make them "look like idiots" when they got the visas and couldn't go. But he said, "[I am ready] to go beyond calling for mere political moves like disarmament, and call for all-out individual resistance to government here and now. If the wording were sensible the audience wouldn't be confined to people who wear sandals and read *Freedom*."

What made him think such an appeal, in the face of Soviet tanks, would work? It was the Suez Crisis, which occurred almost simultaneously with the Hungarian uprising and directly involved the British government.

Nasser's Egyptian government had seized control of the Suez Canal in July 1956. When Israel invaded Egypt in late October, and the UK and France subsequently issued a ceasefire ultimatum and then began to bomb Cairo, it quickly became clear that the chain of events had been planned beforehand and that the French and British governments had lied to the public about their intentions. When Khrushchev made veiled threats to respond with Soviet nuclear weapons if Egypt was not evacuated, and Washington decided not to support its allies in London and Paris—and threatened to withdraw financial support—Prime Minister Anthony Eden was forced to call a ceasefire on November 7. Suddenly the notion of a permanent nuclear stalemate between the superpowers felt less than convincing.

To activists like Alex, the Suez Crisis also revealed just how dishonest and reckless nuclear-armed governments could be. Conservative Party leaders and even much of the Labour opposition were blindsided by how quickly and loudly members of the public expressed their outrage, often in hastily called neighborhood assemblies and demonstrations. Alex was early in the streets. When the news came round of the attack on Egypt, Nick remembered him jumping in his car and driving down Loughton High Road with the driver's-side window open, yelling, "Kick the bastards out!"[86]

He may have had some impact. In his letter to Read shortly after the ceasefire, Alex was elated: "The spirit of this highly proper suburb was nearer Kropotkin last week than ever I saw it, at least so far as the spontaneous rise of direct action and mutual aid was concerned."[87] At a Labour-organized meeting in Loughton two weeks later, he attacked the government for alienating Britain's friends abroad. "I think the time has come to consider not how the Government can be influenced but how it can be removed," he said.[88]

Anything he and Read wrote would have to address the Suez and Hungarian crises together. Over the next month they worked on a letter to the *New Statesman* but couldn't get it right. Should they ridicule Eden and Khrushchev? Read thought not, that the real enemy was public apathy. Should they tone down their appeal for disobedience, for fear of editors' rejection? They sent the final draft to the *New Statesman* on December 10, but by that time both crises had abated and the press and politicians had moved on. Their letter was never published, in part because the moment had passed and in part because they were addressing a spirit of opposition that was still trying to define itself—and seemed not to have anything much to contribute in the present circumstances.

"We do not need world government; we need world resistance to government," they wrote. "If the government will not disarm—and who imagines they will?—the people can and must disarm them. . . . We believe that in these weeks a crack has opened that will spread eventually through the whole construction of power in modern societies."[89] They were correct that the Suez and Hungarian crises were giving birth to something new in the UK: something that would expand into a mass movement over the next decade. But what did this all mean in the present to the hundreds of thousands of Hungarians in prison or forced flee their country, or to Egyptians trying to rebuild portions of their capital city, or to the Jews whose property was seized by Nasser's government and who also had to leave their country? To them, Alex and Read had nothing to say beyond vaguely exhorting "massive resistance."

Alex did make one small gesture with regard to Hungary. He wrote the Society for Cultural Relations with the USSR—which he knew to be a Soviet mouthpiece—asking it to "convey something of members' views on Hungary to the Russians." Predictably, the society declined, on grounds that the message was "political."[90]

CHAPTER 9

Science and Sex (1952–1958)

As his work on the 1954 Soviet expedition suggests, after joining Medawar's research staff at UCL three years earlier, Alex had quickly established himself as a researcher on human aging. Prior to this he had already settled into a home life that would remain stable, in appearance if not always in fact, for the next two decades. Nick was now six and had started school the year before. Some days Alex dropped his son off at Frearn Road Infants' School, opposite Peckham Rye Park, on his way to his job at the medical college. Other days Nick walked with a classmate.[1]

Robert Greacen, now working at the United Nations Association of Great Britain and Northern Ireland, still saw the family occasionally and was surprised to find that Alex was a rather strict parent. Once Robert and his wife and daughter went to the theater with the three Comforts, and Nick misbehaved. Alex clapped the boy's cap back on his head and loudly told him to correct himself.[2] Nick didn't remember his father being especially tough, however—"he might have told me he'd give me a thick ear, but he never did." Once Nick lost his father's watch and was quickly forgiven. On Sundays, when Ruth went to church services, father and son would go to nearby Sydenham Hill Station to watch the steam engines of the Continental Express line pass through. Nick readily took up his Alex's intense interest in trains.[3]

Homelife was calm, but never entirely, Nick remembered. At breakfast, Alex read the relatively left-leaning *News Chronicle* and liked to listen to the news on the radio, carrying on a running commentary about the folly, fear, and disaster relayed. Ruth listened patiently but switched to more tranquil piano music on the Third Programme once her husband was out of the house or busy with something. In her spare moments she turned to her hobby of needlework. ("He wasn't restful to be with," his friend Greacen recalled. "When I spent two or three hours with him,

I'd go away absolutely tired; my head would be filled with all he'd said about literature and politics.")

When Alex was not lecturing at the medical college or attending to his research on mollusks, he worked at home, writing, maintaining his correspondence, or else, when a migraine hit, attempting to sleep through it. He was also adjusting to another change in his life, this one self-enforced. Until 1950 he had been a heavy smoker, but when Richard Doll and Austin Hill released their report in the *British Medical Journal* linking smoking to cancer, he abruptly quit.[4]

Otherwise, every minute was filled, it seemed. While the family lived at Forest Hill, Alex started keeping a commonplace book: a binder in which he noted down quotations from French and English poets, song lyrics, epigrams by the likes of Addison, excerpts from Hindu texts, and other bits of text he might want to cite in his own writings, as well as pasting in clippings that struck his sense of the culturally irrational. One item, from the *News of the World*, March 20, 1960, is typical:

> "Although she put up quite a good fight she ended with her clothing practically in ribbons.
> "When she got home she had lost her upper denture, one of her gloves and her handbag.
> "Happily she had retained her virginity."

Alex took after his father, developing a passion for do-it-yourself electronics. At the medical college, he got to know a technical instructor named Leon Bernstein, who guided him on how to build various types of apparatus. The armed forces were putting a great deal of gear, especially communications equipment, on the market after the war, and what he couldn't get directly from this trove, he could find at Imhof's, the big electronics store in Tottenham Court Road. "We bought up all the old RAF surplus and we turned all their old oscilloscopes into cardioscopes and all their radio equipment into medical equipment," Alex recalled. "I was building stuff all the time."[5] That included a ham radio outfit that Alex set up in the Forest Hill house; the family's first television set, which he cobbled together from RAF surplus using glued-together Weetabix breakfast cereal for sound insulation[6] and installed in an old green-and-yellow cupboard; and a burglar alarm for his mother-in-law, May, at Little Gables. His maimed left hand never seemed to pose a problem, even when he had to use a soldering iron.[7]

With Nick growing and the family acquiring more possessions—including an upright piano on which Alex would pick out Bach—Alex and Ruth sold the Forest Hill house a couple of months after he took up his Nuffield grant at UCL, buying a larger one in Loughton, the suburb just north of London where Ruth had grown up. She had never accustomed herself to South London and wanted to live nearer her mother and other family members. Their new home, at 44 The Avenue, was just half a mile from Little Gables and also an easier commute to Alex's new job. It had a name, Tavycombe, but, as Alex preferred "The Hornet's Nest," Ruth settled for no name at all.

Built in the '30s, the house had four bedrooms and a spacious rear yard, but like Barnet, where Alex had spent his childhood, Loughton was still a mix of old and new. Close to the center of London via the tube, it was nevertheless still fairly self-contained, with a cinema (the Majestic) and a plethora of shops including a clothing store and a butcher shop that delivered orders by bicycle. Loughton bordered on Epping Forest, where Nick and his friends could play, sail toy boats, or ride their bicycles, and where in winter Alex let Nick use the steerable sled his parents had bought for him at the 1924 British Empire Exhibition.

The only times the Comforts absolutely had to leave, Nick remembered, were to go to the dentist and to take his grandmother's—and, eventually, his mother's—furs to storage in the nearby suburb of Leytonstone.[8] Alex, then, found himself situated on Ruth's turf, living in somewhat the manner in which she had been brought up.

Was he restive? "I don't think you would have inferred my political opinions from my lifestyle," he said years later.[9] But he had some like-minded neighbors, including friends from his Cambridge days, and the area was culturally lively. Peter Abrahams, the South African "Coloured" journalist, novelist, and memoirist, lived with his wife Daphne in a council flat on Jessel Road. He and Alex were friends until the Abrahamses moved to Jamaica in 1956.[10] Alex and Ruth supported the State Cinema, an art house theater on Leytonstone High Road, and, farther afield, the Theatre Workshop, led by Joan Littlewood, the radical theater pioneer and provocateur. Alex maintained his connection with the Institute of Contemporary Arts, now in Piccadilly, and he and Ruth often attended events there with Herbert and Ludo Read. While the talk was often over Ruth's head ("she didn't share Alex's intellectual interests," Robert Greacen remembered), she enjoyed the company and the social occasions that went with being the wife of a noted author and scientist.[11]

Alex's new, £1,000 annual grant—plus expenses—was twice the

amount he had reported earning in his 1946 article in *Horizon*, but it was considerably short of the £1,825 that Connolly had said was necessary for a writer to subsist. He was still turning out book reviews and occasionally took editorial assignments, such as when he revised and translated a book on Louis Pasteur from French (agreed-upon fee: £40 to £50, depending on the amount of alteration necessary).[12] Sometimes, when he accepted paid speaking engagements, he had to compromise his publicly professed principles. In August 1958, for example, he made his first trip to the United States to conduct a seminar for the Division of Biological and Medical Research at the Argonne National Laboratory in Chicago, a government-funded developer of nuclear technology that had designed the first nuclear-powered submarine for the US Navy.

Nevertheless, the Comforts were able to afford annual family vacations: to Cornwall (1954), North Wales (1955), France, and Ireland, returning to Mullaghmore, the tiny village in Sligo that Alex had visited while doing his midwife training (1956, 1957, and 1961). During a trip to the Lake District in 1960, when they competed at catching trout, Alex impressed Nick with his method of tying flies, making creative use of his injured left hand.[13]

On a trip without Nick to Yugoslavia in 1954, Alex and Ruth were accompanied by Ruth's old roommate from Cambridge, Jane Henderson, who had kept in touch with the family after taking her degree in social science from the University of London following the war. Born in 1921, the only daughter of an engineer, Jane had spent three years in Toronto as a family caseworker, returning back to England to teach at the University of Leicester. She had an adventurous and inquiring mind and was fond of young Nick, and, as she maintained a London flat in Lady Margaret Road, Kentish Town, near her parents, the Comforts saw her often.

ALEX KEPT A CABINET of his mollusks at The Avenue, and a human skull on a bookcase—he liked to say it was from a nineteenth-century Patagonian, and Nick's young friends found it thrilling—but otherwise he confined his scientific projects to his new office on the second floor of the building at UCL that housed the Department of Zoology. And while he kept a chromatograph in his office to continue his work on mollusk shell pigments, he was now embarked on a very different course of research, one with as complex and controversial a track record, in its own way, as sexual behavior.

Humans had been anguishing for millennia over the facts of aging and death, what caused them, and how, possibly, they could be prevented. But this was especially so in the modern era, when science seemed to offer better ways to understand physical causes and effects. Francis Bacon, René Descartes, Benjamin Franklin, and the marquis de Condorcet were a few of the philosopher-scientists who speculated on the possibility of radical life extension or even the abolition of death.* Interest sharpened as the twentieth century began and noticeable increases in life expectancy suggested that aging and death were actually giving way as humans' control of their bodies and their environment grew. But what was the best, most scientifically robust way to move ahead?

"Science continues to be a channel for magic," the British political philosopher Paul Gray has written.[14] Over the two centuries since the Enlightenment, gerontology, the study of aging, had been plagued by loony theories and crackpot treatments, from cryonics to fresh cell therapy. The Swiss surgeon Paul Niehans liked to harvest cells from New Zealand black sheep; Serge Voronoff, a French surgeon, favored chimpanzee testicles. Such treatments had often enjoyed the support of fabulously rich patrons looking to cheat death.** As a result, a patina of quackery had persistently hung about the field.

Gerontology had also suffered from a surfeit of explanations: a blizzard of widely differing theories of how aging works. As late as 1990, the Russian biologist Zhores Medvedev, Alex's friend, itemized over two hundred theories of aging, which he also classified into sub-theories.[15] The cranks and crackpots contributed their share, but the problem is more fundamental, because aging is so hard to pin down. As a field of biomedicine, it overlaps physiology, biology, genetics, statistics (measuring patterns of aging across populations), epidemiology, and more. That being the case, could it even be described as a discrete field?

Scientists have always disagreed profoundly as to whether a common biological mechanism exists to regulate the aging process, and whether it can be measured: for instance, as Alex later suggested, whether biomarkers—molecules indicating the presence of normal or abnormal patterns—could be identified for aging. And what, after all, was the

* "A period must one day arrive," Condorcet (1743–94) wrote, "when death will be nothing more than the effect of extraordinary accidents [and] the duration between the birth of man and his decay will have no assignable limit." Cited in Jonathan Weiner, *Long for This World: The Strange Science of Immortality* (New York: Ecco, 2011), 37.

** Aldous Huxley satirized quack anti-aging therapies and therapists and their patrons in his 1939 novel *After Many a Summer*.

objective of gerontological research? Was it to find ways to extend life to hitherto outlandish lengths, producing, say, the first 150-year-old? Or was it to extend the likelihood of healthy, vigorous life: to make 80 the new 50? And what was the best way to proceed: to look for a common mechanism controlling loss of vigor, or to target individual ailments that tend to accompany aging, like cancer, dementia, and cardiovascular disease?

All of this suggests Peter Medawar's audacity when he announced he was initiating a new research program on aging at UCL and bringing aboard Alex, a researcher who as yet had no expertise in human or even in mammalian aging. But they did have some fairly recent discoveries and theories to work with.

Serious study of aging began in the wake of Charles Darwin's writings. Since then, evolution had always played some role in scientists' understanding of it. The first major contribution was by the German biologist August Weismann, who in 1883 theorized that life may once have been unlimited in duration but that death appeared as a way to weed out those who became sick, crippled, or infirm along the way, otherwise they would hold back the progress of the species.[16] Another popular theory was proposed by the Russian biologist Elie Metchnikoff in the early years of the twentieth century: that aging was caused by toxic activity of bacteria in the intestines and that consuming lactic acid—for example, in yogurt—could lengthen the lifespan. (He himself drank sour milk every day to treat the problem.)[17]

Jack Haldane suggested a more refined version of Metchnikoff's theory in 1941, ten years before Alex joined him at UCL. In his book *New Paths in Genetics*, he examined Huntington's disease, a condition that causes a progressive breakdown of nerve cells in the brain, leading to life-threatening complications. Haldane noted that Huntington's generally doesn't strike until age thirty and has few effects until we're past forty, by which point, for most of human history, individual humans were done with reproduction and nurturing of offspring. Therefore, Haldane theorized, the gene coded with the disease was effectively harmless, since Huntington's didn't keep humans from fulfilling their essential biological function of perpetuating the species and there was no reason for natural selection to weed it out.[18]

In the fall of 1951, when Medawar assumed his post in zoology at UCL, the topic of his inaugural lecture was aging. Titled "An Unsolved Problem of Biology," it extended Haldane's theory to all causes of the condition.[19] Even if our bodies—and those of other animals—never aged, Medawar proposed, a large percentage of early humans died early thanks to predators, environmental factors, intraspecies conflict, or sheer accidents, and very old individuals would still be very rare, even if they remained vigorous. Therefore, few of us would ever experience Huntington's, colon cancer, or the other threats that accumulate after we reach a certain age, and nature would have few opportunities to work its brutal worst. While many of us today live relatively sheltered lives that keep us around to experience these maladies, this was not the case for the vast majority of human history.

Natural selection, then, has nothing to do with aging itself and can be of no help in understanding its effects. The Darwinian process just doesn't care about us after a certain stage.*** But Medawar was optimistic that science could do more. In fact, he said, it should be possible to extend "the whole life span symmetrically, as if the seven ages of man were marked out on a piece of rubber and then stretched."[20] There was no single mechanism that controlled aging; instead, it was the result of an accumulation of genetic characteristics that turned against the body as it aged, producing everything from cancers to osteoporosis. There are also basic processes like cellular and hormonal decline, in one combination or another. Some of these diseases and conditions might have overlapping effects on other ailments. Attacking them separately and together could produce improvements in the quality of later life and in mortality rates.

For UK researchers, at least, Medawar's lecture was a watershed event. It seemed to open up a new way to think about and organize research on aging, and along with an earlier essay, "Old Age and Natural Death," it attracted a great deal of attention after it was published as a short book the following year.[21] It also supplied the theoretical frame for the work Alex would be doing in gerontology over the next two decades.**** "Gerontology in its modern sense dates from about 1950," he later declared. "Before that, the idea of controlling human ageing remained the preserve of quacks and optimists."[22]

*** Later research has found otherwise. The human lifespan is significantly longer than that of chimpanzees, a close relative, in part because humans have more evolved immune functions and partly due to stronger nurturing behaviors. See Benjamin C. Trumble and Caleb E. Finch, "The Exposome in Human Evolution: From Dust to Diesel," *The Quarterly Review of Biology*, December 2019.

**** Alex disliked the term "gerontology," which in Greek refers strictly to the study of old men (γέροντες). He preferred geratology, which meant the study of old age (γῆρας) in general, but conceded that the former was "probably too well grown for eradication." AC, *The Biology of Senescence* (New York: Rinehart, 1956), 3n.

The logical next step, he and Medawar agreed, was to collect data on aging—or "senescence," then the scientific term for the process of deterioration with age—for multiple populations and species. This would allow them to formulate hypotheses about how evolution had affected genetic differences between those groups, in hopes of finding a common biological basis for the diseases that tend to hit the elderly.[23] The first subtopic Alex chose to focus on was the growth cycle of long-lived humans. But first he had to find the data. The December 1, 1951, issues of both *The Lancet* and the *British Medical Journal* ran letters from Alex announcing that he was seeking help from anyone who had records or who was willing to assemble them. In particular, he wanted data that "could determine the mean age at menarche [the first occurrence of menstruation] and menopause of women who have reached the age of 80 or more."

In 1954 he and Medawar brought a host of statistical data on survival rates that Alex had assembled to the first CIBA Foundation Colloquium on Aging, in London. It was the first truly international scientific conference on aging and, some hoped, a golden opportunity to establish a common global approach to research on the subject.[24] Instead, the opposite happened when Alex argued for the assembled scientists to accept Medawar's simple working definition of senescence as "the increase in liability to die at advanced age." Following Medawar's theory, he also urged that there was no "underlying unity" to the aging process, that it had diverse causes. Two eminent American cellular biologists, Edmund Cowdry and Albert Lansing, rejected both statements.

The New York-based Josiah Macy Foundation had been funding surveys on aging since the '30s and had convened a major conference on the biology of aging in 1937. Programs the Macy Foundation funded had nurtured experimental biologists like Cowdry and Lansing, who believed that the cell was the arena in which aging took place and that it occurred in more or less the same way across all animal species. The British researchers, as Darwinian evolutionists, emphasized the differences between species and argued that any treatments for aging should be across populations with similar life cycles and other characteristics. Another American gerontologist, Nathan Shock, took a position somewhere in between. He argued for identifying patterns of "normal" and "abnormal" aging in individuals and integrating gerontology with medical research on cancer, heart disease, and other diseases of the elderly.

The CIBA conference set up a tension in gerontological research that would last for decades. One group focused on cellular biology, another group on species differences—because cells might behave differently depending on the creature they were attached to—and yet another on specific medical problems. The divergence reflected cultural and institutional differences as well. Cowdry and Lansing were funded by foundations set up to pursue basic biological research; Alex and Medawar by the Nuffield Foundation, which linked gerontological research with the social and economic issues facing the aged, a combination known as social medicine; and Shock by the US National Institutes of Health, whose programs were disease-focused "biomedicine."

These differences weren't very precise at first, only becoming more so later on, and Alex's own research in the '50s didn't neatly separate into one or another category. In the first years of his Nuffield fellowship, aside from collecting data on species survival rates, he wrote or cowrote several papers on porphyrins—chemicals involved in production of hemoglobin—and on the effect of heparin, a blood thinner, on lipoproteins, the substances that carry cholesterol through the bloodstream. The overall aim was to understand how these processes might be affected by aging, or vice versa, and determine whether treatments could be devised for conditions that tend to develop with old age.

All of this he pursued in cramped quarters and with modest resources. "I live in a lab with 200 fish all opening and shutting their mouths like the citizens of Billericay looking in through your bookshop window way back," he wrote in 1955 in a letter to Wrey Gardiner.[25] The fish—*Lebistes reticulatus*, better known as guppies—were the subject of a long-range investigation into the relationship of physical growth to aging in animals. To help him maintain his specimens and track their progress, he had an assistant who doubled as a secretary as well as a junior researcher.[*****]

Mary Sydenham, secretary to Haldane, who had his own office down the corridor from Alex, wrote Alex years later, remembering him inhabiting "a very small, rather grotty room with lots of microscopes."[26] Despite the close quarters, he needed help, in part because of the injury to his left hand and partly because he was—by common agreement and his own admission—never a great laboratory scientist. ("It's not my real forte; I'm a chair-borne investigator," he later said.)[27] His colleague John Maynard Smith remembered that when Alex was conducting

***** For several years, this was Fanny Doljanski, an Israeli cellular biologist who later, at Hebrew University-Hadassah Medical School, did important work related to the behavior of cancers. Fanny Doljanski, letter to AC, October 6, 1958.

experiments involving fruit flies in the early '50s, Jean Clarke, the technician in the Zoology Department labs, "was very quickly convinced that no fly looked after by Alex would live for more than one week. So we more or less took over because we felt sorry for him." But these experiments got Clarke and Maynard Smith interested in aging in fruit flies, and they went on to produce important work on the subject over the next decade.[28]

Alex seldom complained about his quarters or the sometimes questionable conditions in the zoology building. "Cockroaches in the soup—how horrible!" the UCL secretary once wrote Alex in response to a complaint. "I shall send a copy of your letter to the Chairman of the Refectory Committee."[29] He nevertheless enjoyed conversations over lunch with his colleagues in the common room, where he occasionally brought Nick as his guest.[30]

Alex might have made more of his laboratory work if he had always felt physically up to it. His migraine attacks—still not diagnosed as such—were more frequent in the mid-'50s, and early in 1954 he was hospitalized with an ulcer.[31] As always, his attacks were—or seemed to be—accompanied by periods of depression.[32] Why he became depressed is not clear, but it's worth remembering that Alex needed to work, and to be kept from the tasks he set for himself was difficult to tolerate; he once referred to his attacks as "quite disorganizing."[33] It is reasonable to suppose that this would have dampened his normally high spirits. But he could always find a way to get on with it, and it was during this difficult period that he wrote his first major scientific work, *The Biology of Senescence*.

In this relatively short book, Alex reviewed practically the entire research literature to date on aging—the bibliography includes some 750 books and papers, in German, French, Russian, and Italian as well as English—and attempted to separate what was really known by the '50s from the misguided theories and speculation still crowding the terrain. In doing so, he created the first comprehensive assessment of the field of gerontology.

This was needed for two reasons. First, he said, most existing general theories of senescence, which often guided research, were deeply penetrated by distracting ideas from metaphysics and popular belief, even if the researchers didn't realize it, owing "much to folk-lore on one hand and to the emotional make-up of the authors on the other." The number and range of theories was staggering: from seemingly plausible suggestions like cellular wear and tear, Metchnikoff's intestinal bacteria, and changes in specific tissues to such dubious notions as the accumulation of heavy water, the effects of cosmic rays, and the action of gravity. Many theories were very recent, and all had been taken quite seriously at one time or another. Collectively, Alex found, they were more like a catalog than a process of discovery, and most showed little sign of historical development after they were first proposed. In other words, no one had produced any solid proof by way of experiment.

Alex's self-appointed role was to rationalize this mass of material, enabling other researchers to take their work in directions that were most likely to yield useful results: something he did through the book as well as his own unique system of organizing facts and findings. "Alex was an encyclopaedist who would have relished the modern computer data base," his friend, the biologist Robin Holliday, later said. "As it was, he put together an impressive and very comprehensive card index system documenting all research on gerontology."[34]

Another reason Alex's book was needed was that doctors were increasingly demanding something like it. Since advances in public health were stretching the human lifespan, mainly through improvements in childhood mortality, people were surviving longer, and physicians were confronted more frequently with diseases related to old age. "Age-linked diseases are coming to account for well over half the major clinical material in any Western medical practice," Alex wrote. "The physician is constantly referring to the biologist for a scientific basis for geriatrics, and finding that it is not there."[35] And while the amount of material available to researchers was growing, it wasn't increasing rapidly enough to address the medical need.

The most recent general theory was proposed by George Parker Bidder, a British marine biologist, who held in a 1932 paper that aging began once growth stopped. To prove it, he pointed to what he claimed were differences between two types of vertebrates: fish and land mammals. To get about on their feet, Bidder reasoned, land mammals had evolved to stop growing at a certain point, after which aging would set in. This was not necessary for fish and amphibians, which did not need to walk; their growth rates merely slowed, and they didn't exhibit aging.[36] But in the two decades following Bidder's paper, no further sweeping explanations appeared.

"The decline in abstract speculation about old age is probably in itself a very good augury for research," Alex said drily, and he began his discussion of what was truly known with a more elaborate version of the definition he and Medawar had offered at the CIBA conference.

Senescence, he wrote, is "a general title for the group of effects which, in various phyla, lead to a decreasing expectation of life with increasing age." What it was not, he argued, was a single "fundamental," "inherent," identifiable thing or process, "and attempts to find one underlying cellular property which explains all instances of such a change are probably misplaced."[37]

From there he reviewed the types of senescence thought to occur in different species: mechanical senescence, caused by the deterioration of specific body parts; accumulation and depletion, when the body acquires too much of a substance, such as calcium, or is exhausted by spawning; and morphogenetic senescence, when bodily processes break down. He also surveyed the statistics on longevity for every species that had been studied, from protozoa to mollusks, amphibians, birds, fish, and mammals. Alex then assessed what was known about the influence of factors including inherited genetic traits, differences in longevity between the sexes in different species, the relationship of growth to aging, and the effects of diet and of hormonal behavior. There could be other factors, of course. He grouped these together as "senescence" because they cause deterioration ("in other words, because humans dislike them").

But was it possible to construct a working hypothesis about the nature of senescence from all this data—not a new general theory but a summation that could provide biologists with an agenda for the next stages in experimentation? Alex offered one, derived from Haldane and Medawar's proposals. The functioning of the human body, he argued, is a homeostatic mechanism, a self-regulating set of many processes that together keep the body functioning and adjusting to new conditions. Once past child-bearing age, the efficiency of the mechanism starts to break down. It "ultimately dies of old age because it is now an unstable system which is provided with no further sequence of operational instructions, and in which divergent processes are no longer co-ordinated to maintain function." Senescence is therefore "typically an undirected process—not a part of the programme, but a weakening of the directive force of the programme." It has no biological function but is "the subversion of function."[38]

The gerontologist's task was to devise means of keeping human beings alive longer. Could this be done? Yes, Alex argued. Alleviating the wear and tear on specific body parts probably wouldn't have much effect on aging, and reversing a complex set of processes like morphogenesis was probably not possible, but reversing aspects of that process probably was, given a great deal of future exploration and experimentation. Alex laid out six key questions that gerontology would have to answer as part of that project:

- Does senescence occur in all vertebrates? If not, what can be learned from those that do not experience it?
- Among vertebrates, does senescence coexist with some aspects of bodily growth?
- Can senescence be slowed down in mammals after puberty?
- Can further bodily growth be induced artificially in mature vertebrates?
- What are the limits of self-maintenance for the process by which cells divide and reproduce?
- Do some individual tissues in mammals—for instance, of the heart or the ovaries—age at a different rate from those in the rest of the host's body?[39]

He then took a step further, with a plea for gerontology not to wall itself off in laboratories and hospitals but instead to define itself as an aspect of social medicine. The biology of humans—or any animal—can't be discussed without relation to their ecology, he argued. Remaining socially engaged "almost certainly" leads to longer life, he argued, but while premodern societies valued the elderly and gave them an active place in the community, modern society increasingly consigned them to nursing homes and other isolated facilities. The exception, Alex said, are "those who retain, perhaps, some of the magico-social functions of the primitive elder (politicians, judges and clergy)." How much of "senile 'involution,'" he wrote,

> Is the effect of the compulsory psychological and social "winding-up" imposed on the human individual by our form of society and our norms for the behaviour of old people we do not yet know, but it is certainly a very considerable part, and the most important measures for the prolonging of useful individual life which come within the range of the immediately practicable are all concerned with social adjustment.[40]

As an approach to aging, social medicine would have appealed to Alex more than to many other gerontologists, his friend and colleague in the field, Caleb Finch, later observed. Unlike many of them, he was a medical doctor, trained as a physiologist, which inclined him to see aging as "an integrated, systemic process," rather than a set of unrelated conditions, Finch thought.[41] It wouldn't be until the following decade, however, that social activists and some researchers in the United States and the UK started calling attention to the damage done by forced retirement and the warehousing of the elderly in hospitals and nursing homes. When *The Biology of Senescence* appeared in April 1956, none of the critics noted this aspect of the book, but they grasped the significance of the investigation Alex had made. In fact, the book attracted some of the best notices of his overall writing career, critics calling it "the most important review to date on the biology of aging" (*Journal of Gerontology*), "a must for any investigator in the field of biologic aging" (*Science*), and "a turning point in contemporary ideas about aging" (*Isis*).

Even some scientists who were critical of his approach had good words for Alex's book. Albert Lansing, with whom he had tangled at the 1954 CIBA conference, congratulated him on producing "the first thoughtful volume on the biology of aging" in forty years. Lansing still completely disagreed with Alex and Medawar's definition of senescence, but he allowed, "It is almost as unsupported by fact as my often repeated view to the opposite. Onus need not be reflected in either of these two diametrically opposed working hypotheses at least until final solution of the problem relegates one or the other to limbo."******

Alex attracted praise for producing an unusually readable scientific text. "Not the least of his services to gerontology is the attractive liveliness of his writing, which makes a work of scientific importance a pleasure to read," the *British Medical Journal* declared.[42] Although the book included its share of graphs and tables, Alex had pulled off the trick of writing an in-depth scientific survey, the vast majority of which could still be easily read by the average literate person with the very occasional help of a dictionary, which suggests why two mainstream publishers, Routledge in the UK and Rinehart in the United States, brought it out, rather than an academic or technical house.

All of this was, no doubt, intentional. Thanks in part to his broadcast work, Alex was by now a veteran popularizer as well as a respected scientist, and his goal in part, which comes through in the conclusion

****** Albert I. Lansing, "The Biology of Senescence," *American Scientist* 45, no. 2 (March 1957). Alex had crossed swords with Lansing in 1953, when he published a paper that stuck a pin into a famous finding of his older rival: that the offspring of older fruit flies have shorter lifespans than those of younger parents. The "Lansing Effect" generalized this finding to other species, but Alex found no Lansing Effect in one type of fruit fly. AC, "The Absence of a Lansing Effect in *Drosophila Subobscura*," *Nature*, July 11, 1953.

to the book, was to build popular support for the field in which he was now working and encourage other biologists to participate. The American historian of science Gerald Gruman, who would later write an important monograph on the history of ideas for the prolongation of human life, noted that the crucial experiments Alex suggested were "kept within the financial and organizational bounds of gerontology as it actually is rather than as it might be."[43] In the months after *The Biology of Senescence* appeared, Alex published short articles based on it in *The Lancet*, *Nature*, and even in *The Listener*.

YEARS LATER, THE BRITISH gerontologist Robin Holliday wrote, "Alex Comfort has done more than anyone else to be the 'propagandist' for gerontology. . . . He was one of the few writers . . . able to communicate effectively to a wide spectrum of persons, including those who do not have an academic background."[44] Since *The Biology of Senescence* was designed as an up-to-date review of the entire field, it set up Alex as a one-stop source of information and opinion on the state of aging studies. The gossip column for the *Daily Sketch*, a London tabloid, for May 7, 1952, notes a party for Belgian novelist Georges Simenon at Brown's Hotel, the guests including Rose Macaulay, Angus Wilson, Stevie Smith, and Alex, who was buttonholed by the *Sketch's* correspondent about his research.

"A most entertaining talker," Alex spoke enthusiastically about his work on old age and noted the efficacy of using fruit flies—drosophila—to study aging, since they live four days if they're lucky. How important was the study of aging? Alex described "the sad tradition of false teeth and spectacles being handed down and around in the less privileged families as if they were jewelry." Wouldn't it be beneficial if science could alleviate the infirmities of old age for poor people as well as the better off?

Once *The Biology of Senescence* appeared, his profile and public presence as a scientist expanded, even more so after the CIBA Foundation, funded by the Swiss pharmaceutical company, gave him its 1958 award for research on aging (including a check for £200).[45] The following year he served as one of the two representatives of the British Society for Research on Aging on the organizing committee for the CIBA Foundation's 1959 Symposium on Aging.[46]He carried on an enthusiastic correspondence with L. V. Komarov, a biologist at the Institute of

Higher Nervous Activity in Moscow. Alex had not met any gerontologists during his visit to the Soviet Union in 1954, but Komarov was interested in establishing an international study group on life span, and Alex volunteered to help him in any way he could: by translating and circulating his appeal, referring him to other leading researchers, and sending him some of the latest papers from the United States and the UK.[47] Nothing substantial came of the project, but Western and Soviet researchers began to meet and mix more freely at international conferences on aging.

By then, he was speaking and lecturing frequently on the topic, and invariably press coverage focused on the extension of life. Since mortality rates are a special interest of life insurance actuaries, in 1958 he was even invited to deliver the Institute of Actuaries' annual Alfred Watson Memorial Lecture, on "Mortality and the Nature of the Aging Process."[48]

One lay reader who took in his book's message deeply was Alex's old acquaintance from the Grey Walls Press days, Muriel Spark. After her stint working for Wrey Gardiner and Peter Baker in Crown Passage, she had become general secretary of the Poetry Society and editor of its magazine, *Poetry Review*. The society—staid, traditional, and conservative—represented the exact opposite of the sensibility that Gardiner, Alex, and their friends had cultivated at Grey Walls. Spark tried to bring *Poetry Review* into the twentieth century and managed to get some of the Grey Walls poets published between its covers. But the older members of the society were against her, particularly Marie Stopes, the pioneering sex counselor and birth control advocate. In less than two years, Spark was out of the job. In response, Alex, G. S. Fraser, Robert Greacen, and several other of the poets she had tried to promote wrote the society a letter of protest dissociating themselves from *Poetry Review*.[49]

A decade later the situation was quite different. Spark was no longer living with Alex's old friend Derek Stanford, and she had just published her first two novels to great acclaim. For her third, she was planning a story about a circle of elderly Londoners who all receive a mysterious phone call telling them "Remember you must die." One character is a retired sociologist doing gerontological research who investigates the phone calls and the effect they have on his friends. For the scientific underpinning to this part of the story, which was published as *Memento Mori* in 1959, and even some of its phrasing, Spark relied on *The Biology of Senescence* as well as *Old Age: Its Compensation and Rewards*, a 1947 book by the Swiss physician Adolf Vischer. This became known some sixty years later, when her working notes for the novel became available.[50]

Most immediately, however, Alex was less interested in the theory of aging than in making his own contribution to the field. *The Biology of Senescence* was written as an aid to his own research, he explained, "in a subject where it is difficult to know where to begin."[51] Almost from the time he took up the Nuffield fellowship, he wanted to know how life span was affected by the age of the individual's parents at the time of conception. He pursued this line of investigation across species—from invertebrates to dogs, cats, horses, and humans—which meant gathering often hard-to-find statistics.

As he had with his political thought in the '40s, whenever possible he followed up a scholarly treatment with a popularized presentation of his findings in print, a broadcast, or both. In 1958 he published a paper in the *Journal of Gerontology*, "The Longevity and Mortality of Thoroughbred Mares," following it up the next year with a similar paper on thoroughbred stallions. Why horses? In the UK, at least, they were the mammals for whom data on life span were most easily collected. "It took several years' hard work, even in this dog-loving country, to muster enough accurate dog records to plot three quite inadequate survival curves," he explained. "Millions of pups are registered at birth with the Kennel Club, but unfortunately, they are not de-registered when they die." (He did, however, publish several papers on the subject.) Farm animals were often culled, eaten, or put down. For thoroughbred horses, on the other hand, a large number of complete lives were traceable through the *General Stud Book*.[52]

Alex later told a friend, the Russian biologist and dissident Zhores Medvedev, that he got the idea for his study when V. O. Vitt, a Soviet expert in animal husbandry, sent him copies of his research papers on Russian thoroughbreds following Alex's visit to the Soviet Union.[53] He eventually extracted more than 10,000 life histories from data that appeared in the *Stud Book* in 1860–64 and 1875–80. It was not easy. Many horses had the same name, and some would disappear from the record when they were not out to stud, then reappear several years later. But the study produced results. In an early data run of 1,272 lives, Alex found that the median age of death for gray thoroughbred mares was shorter than for those of other colors: twenty years versus twenty-two.[54] But he found no difference based on age of parents: "the progeny of old stallions live just as long as the progeny of young stallions." And in contrast to human males, whose lives tend to be shorter than females, stallions "seem to live rather longer than mares."[55]

These facts amounted to just a couple of entries in the vast number of species comparisons that gerontologists were making, but they also gave Alex, who had never been to a racetrack, the material for an entertaining December 1960 broadcast on the Home Service, afterward published in *The Listener*, on the curious lore he found in the *Stud Book*. Many of the Derby winners—St. Simon, Flying Fox, Solario—seemed like old friends, since they later lent their names to engines on the London and North Eastern Railway that he had observed. The names could be topical; the year of the Paris Commune, 1871, saw mares named Communiste, Anarchiste, and Pétroleuse. Much of his work scoring horses' lives Alex did while commuting on the tube.

> [One day I saw a jockey]—he couldn't [have been] anything else—staring hard at the back of the *Stud Book* and at my slide-rule. He probably thought I had a system. He did not say anything; in fact the only racing man to whom I mentioned my research on the Stud Book said "How long they live? They don't bet on that, you know." But I got the better of him, because the work was lucky enough to win a scientific prize, the only money I ever won on horses and the only time I ever heard of a horse being backed for length of life.[56]

In a BBC audience survey, 44 percent of the sample gave Alex ether an A or an A+ for his talk on thoroughbreds, which the research department chalked up partly to his way of making the subject matter interesting and amusing and in part to his easy style as a broadcaster. "He had a manner which suggested that he was speaking to one listener alone, both being seated in a very comfortable room," the listener said.[57]

Alex's office full of guppies started to yield more significant results not long after his research on thoroughbred mares appeared. He had been pondering George Parker Bidder's popular theory about vertebrates—that fish and aquatic amphibians don't experience senescence, while land mammals do—almost from the time he began his aging studies. He aimed to test it by tracking his specimens of *Lebistes*.

In 1960 he published the first of three papers in the journal *Gerontologia* that demonstrated this was not the case. After observing his guppies in different aquatic cultures and on different diets, he found that all had survival curves similar to those of small mammals. All vertebrates, then, age. Alex's experiments also made a strong case that growth and senescence are not mutually exclusive. A body can continue to grow even as parts wear out, even in fish.[58]

Every time a generalization seemed to apply across species, he found, it slipped away. In 1961, in an article for *Scientific American* reviewing the known data on animal life spans and the factors thought to affect them, he noted that longevity in mammals is roughly correlated with size but that large and small tortoises alike can live to a great age. Cold-blooded animals generally live longer at colder temperatures, Alex observed, but fruit flies exposed to higher temperatures didn't have shorter lives than those that were not. And while he stood by Medawar's theory of the declining effect of natural selection after fertility ends, he noted that small birds can live for many years even after they are done reproducing. But he felt confident enough to isolate three environmental factors that consistently had an effect on the life spans of laboratory animals and therefore might affect human aging as well: body temperature, rate of food intake, and ionizing radiation.[59]

In 1960 Alex joined the New York Academy of Sciences.[60] In 1962 he received a Doctor of Science degree in the field of gerontology from the University of London, in part for his research on the lifespan of fish.[61] This work has held up well over the years; scientists have since shown that aging occurs in the presence of growth in several other species of fish. Later, studies of tissue Alex collected revealed "senile changes" in his specimens' gonads, liver, kidneys, and brain comparable to those in aging mammals.[62]

THE BIOLOGY OF SENESCENCE, along with his research work, placed Alex in the upper stratum of a field that was finally starting to attract real scientific talent, along with the money needed to support it. He looked every inch the scientist too, complete with horn-rimmed glasses, a neat moustache, and a wardrobe of tailored suits. He was no longer the boyish wunderkind of the previous decade, but in his thirties he still had a trim figure and was still, of course, an engaging talker. And he continued to be careful, when delivering a paper, addressing a PPU meeting, or otherwise speaking in public, to keep his left hand tucked behind his back.

Alex still had a good deal of time for matters unrelated to his day job. "The lucky thing," he said years later, "is that I've always been able to do exactly what I like." Aging—and guppies—were his stated research focus at UCL. But, he later recalled, "I could do it in my own time. Provided I produced results, nobody was going to complain about what else I did. I didn't have any obligations other than looking after my animals and seeing the experiments went on."[63]

He needed the remaining hours to eke out his family's living as a book reviewer, to write and campaign for nuclear disarmament with the PPU, and to pursue another line of research he had not completely dropped.

Ever since the publication of *Sexual Behaviour in Society*, organizations pushing for reform of laws relating to marriage and sex had been asking for Alex's support, or at least his endorsement, including the Abortion Law Reform Association and the Marriage Law Reform Society, which lobbied for looser restrictions on divorce. His position as an anarchist, at least with these left-leaning organizations, didn't seem to stand in the way. In 1951, the Marriage Law Reform Society wrote asking him to submit proposals to a commission that Clement Attlee's Labour Government, then in its final months, had set up to address the topic. "Although your views may be regarded as heretical and you may wish to express condemnation of the existing institution as such altogether," the chair of the society assured him, "I cannot help feel that it would be good for the Royal Commission to be faced with anarchist views on marriage, although it may not consider them to be practicable."[64]

If he submitted anything to the commission, it hasn't survived. But Alex was still concerned about the effects a violent, authoritarian society had on personal responsibility, including in sexual relations, and he had mixed feelings as to how the tension between the two would resolve itself.

Alex got his chance to speak out a year later, when the psychiatrist and criminologist D. J. West published his landmark study, *Homosexuality*. The book, by a closeted gay man, was the first highlight in a flurry of activity around the subject. Postwar Britain had seen a crackdown on male homosexual acts. The home secretary in Churchill's last cabinet, Sir David Maxwell Fyfe, proclaimed a crusade against "this plague," and by the end of 1954 the number of men who were in prison for "unnatural offenses" had ballooned to 1,043 from just 62 on average in the early '30s.[65] The press carried reports of the trial and possible suicide of the codebreaker Alan Turing as well as a series of high-profile trials for solicitation, "gross indecency," and related charges enmeshing the actor John Gielgud, the Conservative politician Lord Montague of Beaulieu, and other prominent people. At the time West's book was published, a special Home Office committee was already studying the subject, and a panel organized by the British Medical Association was preparing a report to submit to the committee.

West's book was a milestone for dispassionate, professional discussion of homosexuality in Britain. It trashed the beliefs that it was "unnatural" and that gay men preyed on children, and it gave critics of the UK's anti-sodomy laws an opening to speak up on the subject without being branded as immoral for doing so. It was hardly a model by later standards, however, in part because it worked so hard to be dispassionate."

The closest West came to normalizing homosexuality was to place it at one end of a continuum. "Children are not born with the sex instinct specifically directed to one sex or the other," he wrote. "Exclusive preference for the opposite sex is an acquired trait, and involves the repression of a certain amount of homosexual feeling which is natural to the human being."[66]

Alex accepted this assertion, adding in his review of West's book for *The Lancet* that "upbringing in the widest sense" is what determines a same-sex orientation. He also praised it for providing information not grounded in anger, fear, and ignorance. But his real aim in reviewing the book was to draw attention to the people who insisted on punishing gay people. "The attitude which a person will adopt to the question of punishing homosexual behavior, like his attitude toward capital punishment, is so predictable in terms of his personality that it can be used as a marker for test purposes," he wrote. "In fact for some the psychology of anti-homosexualism bears some resemblance to the psychology of anti-semitism." In any case, he argued, there was no justification from any point of view for the laws against sodomy; if homosexual behavior really was a threat to the community, then clearly the laws had failed to rein it in, and if it was not, "then we have a good deal to answer for."[67]

While West's book may not have been fully enlightened by later standards, it was starkly better than the British Medical Association report, which came out a few months later and makes for chilling reading. Although cloaked in clinical language, the underlying assumption of the report was that gay men were "offenders" in need of "treatment"; the kindest terminology it offered was that they were "disabled." Although it criticized then-current laws for creating "a background of excessive fear," the report praised them for creating "a public opinion against" homosexual behavior. Amazingly, it spoke favorably of stilboestrol, a drug used to dampen libido, as a treatment for "highly sexed" patients; this was the drug that Alan Turing had agreed to take in lieu of going to prison after his conviction for indecency, and he was taking it prior to his suicide. Most troublingly, however, the report recommended isolating homosexuals in "small experimental treatment centres" where they could work, exercise, and study under strict discipline and supervision, with an aim to renouncing their behavior.[68]

The Lancet gave Alex a good deal of space to comment on the report, since the very conservative BMA's recommendations were likely to have a strong influence on the special Home Office committee. He found it a huge disappointment: a document that contained some solid medical research, though not enough, accompanying a set of conclusions and recommendations that seemed to have arisen from the more bigoted corners of the Sunday press. It offered no evidence about the one matter that medicine might be expected to address—whether homosexual behavior actually had ill effects on the individual or society, apart from the suffering that social rejection caused—and it failed to note that every human society contained gay people, their treatment ranging from complete toleration to deep aversion.

The language of the report was what most disturbed him, however. It was riddled with scare words like "insidious," "perverted," "indulgence," and even the vaguely McCarthyesque "homosexuals and their sympathizers." "The general tendency of this diction," he wrote, "is to reverse the sense of the scientific evidence, and to counter any emotional disinflation of the subject. That a predominantly psychiatric and scientific committee should let itself be reported in such language is frightening."

The report betrayed itself by blaming homosexual practices on a "weakening sense of personal responsibility with regard to social and national welfare in a significant proportion of the population," implying that any loosening of sexual restrictions, either for gay or straight people, was somehow an act of subversion. It was quite the opposite, Alex concluded. New knowledge about society was "leading to a rejection of pontifical and magical regulations upon conduct." If a teenage boy or man was not disturbed by the memory of a "homosexual experiment," that could only be "a gain rather than a loss to the mental health and morale of the future."[69]

The BMA report was issued in December 1955. The report of the Departmental Committee on Homosexual Offences and Prostitution—known as the Wolfenden report, after its chair, the educator Sir John Wolfenden—was published almost two years later, in September 1957. In between, a great deal of public discussion and informal education took place, thanks in part to the stories of some previously closeted gay men who decided to come forward, along with commentaries like Alex's. When the Wolfenden report appeared, it inclined toward his viewpoint.

Outlawing homosexuality was an impingement on civil rights, and private morality or immorality was "not the law's business."[70] The committee recommended that homosexual behavior be decriminalized. "It is not, in our view, the function of the law to intervene in the private life of citizens, or to seek to enforce any particular pattern of behaviour."

The report made numerous concessions to Mrs. Grundy, at least one of them laughable. At the outset of its meetings, Wolfenden himself, ostensibly so as not to offend the four women on the fifteen-member panel, decided that the words "Huntley" and "Palmers" would be used during the proceedings instead of "homosexual" and "prostitute" (after Huntley & Palmers, the biscuit maker). More importantly, the recommendations included retaining the penalties against offenses to "public decency" and setting the age of consent for homosexual acts at twenty-one, despite the fact that the age of consent for heterosexual acts was sixteen.

The report raised discussion in the press to a high pitch, however. Some minds were certainly changed, and the BMA was among the first organizations to endorse the report's conclusions.[71] The following March, Alex was a signatory to a letter to the editor of the *Times*, supporting the Wolfenden report's recommendation that homosexual acts be decriminalized. Other signers included J. B. Priestley and his wife, the archaeologist Jacquetta Hawkes; Julian Huxley; Stephen Spender; C. Day Lewis; Angus Wilson; Barbara Wooton; and Isaiah Berlin. A week later Alex published a long opinion piece in *Tribune* hailing the report as "the first clear recognition of the difference between public law and private morals," opening the way to more rational attitudes about sex in general.[72] Two months after, the *Times* letter signatories formed the core of the Homosexual Law Reform Society, founded by the academic and literary critic A. E. Dyson.[73]

A large chunk of the British intelligentsia, it appeared, including the archbishops of Canterbury and York, had united behind the Wolfenden report. and there's little doubt that sexual attitudes were loosening in '50s Britain. Seemingly everyone knew someone who was out of the closet, at least to them, and even counted among their friends gay and lesbian couples who lived together more or less openly. In Alex's case, these included his fellow PPU campaigners, Michael Tippett, Benjamin Britten, and Sybil Morrison, whose partner was Myrtle Solomon, another PPU activist. It's not clear that the educated class's embrace of Wolfenden was altogether helpful in getting the panel's recommendations accepted, however.

Members of the Homosexual Law Reform Society met with Home Secretary Rab Butler about the report in June and created a draft bill embodying the recommendations. After numerous delays, the Commons held a typically long, rambling discussion of the report on November 26, 1958, over a year after it was published. During that time, opposition had congealed, and the debate was replete with the kind of terminology Alex had deplored in the BMA report: "sin," "perversion," "unnatural," "corruption," and so on. The House never exhibited any strong support for any of the recommendations, and at around eleven in the evening it resolved merely to "take note" of the report. It would be another nine years before Parliament again considered decriminalizing homosexual behavior.

There was still much educating and agitation to be done, and the Homosexual Law Reform Society dug in for a long campaign, even establishing a charity, the Albany Trust, to fund its work. The struggle to put gay rights on the public agenda had unstuck something in Alex as well; he was now writing more, and more forcefully, about the legal and cultural barriers to sensible policies regarding sex. He kept writing about sexual liberation over the next several years, but his focus differed from that of Dyson and the other campaigners. The danger to society was not from homosexuals, fetishists, pornographers, sexually active teens, or other "perverts" but from those people who disliked their behavior yet were inordinately obsessed with them.

What concerned Alex most was that willful withholding of information about sex from the young would lead to unwanted pregnancies, children born to unwilling and incapable parents, and destroyed lives, all in the name of upholding an abstract moral principle. In a May 1957 letter to *The Lancet*, he observed that social agencies would enjoy more practical success preventing unwanted pregnancies by promoting access to and better use of contraceptives than by discouraging young people from having sex. He was promptly attacked by a member of the Church of England Moral Welfare Council who insisted that the cause of underage pregnancy was not lack of access to contraceptives but rather "carelessness, laziness, and lack of self-control and moral fibre."[74]

Two years later, the Obscene Publications Act was up for debate in Parliament. It would pass in July, for the first time allowing publications with sexual content to be sold if they were "in the interests of science, literature, art or learning, or of other objects of general concern." "'Sex and violence' literature is attacked in proportion to its content, not of violence, but of sex," Alex observed. "The drive behind the prohibition [of sexual literature] carries a strong wish to impose itself on others," he argued in a letter to the *Manchester Guardian.* "Not all demands for censorship are made by disturbed people, but their terms of reference in our culture have been." Since it's always possible for the individual to close a book he or she dislikes, the proper thing was to abolish censorship of literature "in every context involving free adult choice."[75]

What was really needed, Alex argued, echoing Kinsey, was better information and a better comprehension of the varieties of human sexual practice, something like an anthropological approach to the subject. The more we understood who does what, and why, he thought, the less anxiety and fear these practices would provoke and the better able professionals would be to address anything harmful in them.

In a review of two new biographies of Havelock Ellis in February 1959 in the *Observer*, Alex argued that Ellis's seven-volume series, *Studies in the Psychology of Sex,* was "the first attempt to study the natural history of human sexual behavior, rather than its pathology."[76] By gathering facts and case studies "without the value-judgment implicit in Freud's idea of maturity," Ellis had started a project that extended through Kinsey and now had the benefit of post-Freudian work plus a wider range of anthropological studies, but it still had a long way to go. Even the Wolfenden committee, Alex observed, was never able to obtain any reliable estimate of the incidence of homosexuality in England, the alleged problem it was set up to study.

Sometime in the mid-'50s, Alex decided to tackle the project himself, becoming something of a folklorist of underground sexual practices. He collected materials of all sorts, much as he was pulling together data and research on aging. He assembled a card file with notes scrawled and references pasted in about everything from puberty, psychoanalysis, venereal disease, and sex among primates to bondage, sadomasochism and other fetishes, sex in various religious traditions and tribal societies, female circumcision, homosexuality, transvestitism, sexual behavior of politicians, aphrodisiacs, yogic body postures, spousal exchange, oral sex, and even such sinister topics as infanticide, punishment, and deliberate and accidental killings.

Alex also collected sex surveys and questionnaires from magazines and journals, mail-order catalogs from suppliers of sex toys and paraphernalia ("rubber goods"), and clippings from sex magazines and throwaway tabloids distributed in the Soho red-light district featuring voyeuristic, pseudo-factual accounts of sex cults and other "unnatural practices." His files eventually extended to thousands of card entries.

He was also collecting or consulting more formal sex guides, some dating back to the Renaissance, in the restricted collections of libraries in the UK and on the continent. As a bonus, he gathered and committed to memory a vast number of limericks, bawdy and otherwise. In this he likely received a head start from an American friend, the self-taught erotic folklorist and bibliophile Gershon Legman, whose formidable collection, *The Limerick: 1700 Examples with Notes, Variants and Index*, had first appeared anonymously in France in 1953.[77] Friends and acquaintances became used to Alex's knack for producing the apt limerick for whatever topic they might be discussing.

Alex was tapping into a small group of researchers with whom he could share material and ideas. These included two members of Kinsey's inner circle, Wardell Pomeroy and Cornelia Christenson, who were carrying on their mentor's work at Indiana University's Kinsey Institute following his death in 1956. Early in 1958, during his first trip to the United States, Alex visited the institute and discussed how they could help each other find items they were looking for. Since American law at the time prohibited the importation of "obscene" or "immoral" matter, Alex did Pomeroy the favor of summarizing the contents of a UK publication in which he was interested: *London Life*, a "naughty" men's magazine featuring photos of women in provocative poses and articles and letters with an accent on footwear and other fetishes. Once the Kinsey Institute won a landmark case determining that such materials were not, by definition, obscene if they were in the hands of scientific researchers, Alex was free to send more artifacts directly.[78]

What he intended to do with this accumulated data, lore, and sometimes seamy material was unclear at the time. He appears not to have discussed this research with anyone outside the field.

CHAPTER 10

Make Love, Not War (1956–1962)

Alex's scientific work never slowed his stream of polemics against the Cold War and nuclear arms, but at times he felt as though he was writing mainly for himself and a small group of political sympathizers. It was clear to him that the "psychopaths in office" were creating a "culture of militarism and fear" on both sides of the Atlantic.[1] Where was the event, or series of events, that would spark a mass movement against the Bomb? The turning point finally came in the second half of the '50s.

Britain stepped up its commitment to nuclear arms with a series of hydrogen bomb tests between 1956 and 1958. But the catalyst for the new mass opposition was an event that involved the Bomb itself only marginally: the Suez Crisis. After Britain's humiliating ceasefire in November 1956, Alex and Sir Herbert Read (he had accepted a knighthood in 1953, to the dismay of his friends in the anarchist community) noted in their letter to the *New Statesman and Nation*, "There is an entirely new spirit abroad—from London to Budapest. It is a spirit of passive, but determined and constructive, insurrection. If it holds, we can transform human society."[2]

If that was really what was happening, Alex was determined to encourage it. In the two months between the invasion and the withdrawal of British and French troops from Egypt at the end of the year, he built a crude transmitter that he used to launch his own pirate radio station. Working almost entirely in secret, with no collaborators, he broadcast a nightly radio message calling on listeners to protest the invasion and demand that Britain unilaterally scrap its nuclear arsenal. His broadcasts reached very few people, but as the crisis ended he was committed to action and ready to expand his antinuclear work.

For the next half-dozen years, Alex believed he was helping to bring about the kind of mass refusal of authority he had longed for as a pacifist during World War II—and that success was imminent. The intimations of failure were present from the start of the new movement, however.

AFTER THE SUEZ CRISIS wound down, Alex joined two new disarmament groups with drastically different styles. The Emergency Committee for Direct Action against Nuclear War, later known simply as the Direct Action Committee (DAC), was formed in April 1957 after Harold Steele, an activist, was prevented from sailing into the H-bomb testing area around Christmas Island. In response, supporters formed a committee to organize a fifty-two-mile march from London to the government's nuclear weapons research facility at Aldermaston. Alex was asked to become a sponsor the following spring.[3] Principal members also included his two editors at *Peace News*, Hugh Brock and J. Allen Skinner, who had reoriented the newspaper to focus more on the antinuclear struggle, as well as Bertrand Russell and *Goon Show* comedian Spike Milligan. The DAC's ideological slant was distinctly leftist, and strategically the members favored nonviolent direct action.

The Campaign for Nuclear Disarmament (CND), a more mainstream group, was launched a short time after the DAC. In the months following Suez, many activists had expected they could work through the left wing of the Labour Party to bring unilateral nuclear disarmament into the political mainstream. Most of those hopes were dashed when party treasurer Aneurin Bevan, long considered the leader of the Labour Left, came out against it at the annual party conference in October 1957, saying, "It would send a British Foreign Secretary naked into the conference-chamber."

The DAC and the CND came together in the wake of an outpouring of antinuclear protest from a host of leading scientists and humanitarians. In 1955 Russell, Albert Einstein, and Linus Pauling—all Nobel laureates—issued a manifesto calling for the abolition of thermonuclear weapons and war itself. In 1957 Pauling took the lead on a petition, signed by some two thousand American scientists, appealing for an end to nuclear weapons testing. Alex signed in November, when the petition campaign was extended outside the United States.[4] The same year, another Nobel laureate, Albert Schweitzer—the fifth-most-admired man in the world, according to a poll—broadcast a "Declaration of Conscience" demanding that world leaders act on their stated principles and end the development and testing of nuclear weapons. In response, US intelligence agencies investigated Schweitzer and his charity organization for communist ties, and he was blacklisted for several years in America. But his declaration met with expressions of support from around the world.[5]

The *New Statesman and Nation* received an enormous response to an article by J. B. Priestley published on November 12, "Russia, the Atom Bomb and the West," espousing unilateral disarmament. *New Statesman* editor Kingsley Martin then called a meeting at which the CND was born. Bertrand Russell was president of the new group, and Canon John Collins, an Anglican priest and longtime peace activist, was chair. The initial organizing meeting attracted so much attendance—and attention—that a follow-up was quickly organized for February at Central Hall Westminster. There a policy statement confirmed the goal of unilateral disarmament. After the meeting, some one thousand of the attendees staged a spontaneous march to Downing Street, where several were arrested.

Alex joined a host of prominent figures signing on as members of the CND's Honorary Committee, including Priestley, Vera Brittain, Cyril Connolly, E. P. Thompson, Ralph Milliband, Herbert Read, Julian Huxley, Edith Evans, Benjamin Britten, Doris Lessing, E. M. Forster, and Jacob Bronowski. Alex had been associated with many of these on previous campaigns. This star-studded cast ensured high visibility for the CND but also a moderate political strategy. This was centered at first on a renewed effort to influence Labour to adopt unilateralism as a party pledge, supported by rank-and-file members organized in local branches.

The DAC, by contrast, took a more confrontational stance intended to build irresistible pressure through marches, rallies, and civil disobedience. Alex found this "outside" approach far more appealing than attempting to work within the system. Since government tends to attract individuals who covet instruments of coercion like the Bomb, organizing against it through existing political channels made no sense. "What is needed in modern societies is not increased government but the growth of rational and responsible disobedience," he said, echoing his pronouncements during the war.[6]

The CND, after some hesitation, decided to support the DAC's four-day march from Trafalgar Square to Aldermaston. Four thousand marchers swelled to some ten thousand for the final rally on Easter Day 1958, at which Alex was a principal speaker. He had already addressed an open-air evening rally on Good Friday, the first day, in Treaty Road, Hounslow, at which he ignited the assembly by declaring "Civil disobedience is necessary!" "Strike now!" the crowd responded. In a speech he had worked on carefully with April Carter, secretary of the DAC, and Gene Sharp, the American theorist of nonviolent resistance who was then an assistant editor of *Peace News*, he noted that the march would be taking place on the twenty-first anniversary of the bombing of Guernica by Hitler's air forces during the Spanish Civil War. What was then called fascism, politicians now regarded as "praiseworthy realism," he said, charging that the major parties of all the great powers were following the principles of Guernica: that a massacre of civilians was an acceptable military action.[7]

The painter, poster designer, and longtime pacifist Walter E. Spradbery wrote Alex following the march: "Just a line to say how excellent, courageous, and inspiring your splendidly-delivered speech was at Hounslow on Good Friday evening. My fatigue disappeared before the intensity and spirit you put into it."[8]

The march was a cultural as well as political coup. Thousands in the UK and elsewhere would see Lindsey Anderson and Karel Reisz's Free Cinema documentary of the event, *March to Aldermaston*, and the place name quickly became synonymous with the campaign against H-bomb production. The film, some of it shot from above, captures something of the spirit of the event, with swarms of people filling the roads and spilling onto sidewalks, fields, and other adjacent spaces, less like a march than a curiously ebullient procession of pilgrims or a community on the move.

The next year the CND took over organizing the event and decided to reverse course, sending the participants from Aldermaston to Trafalgar Square, ending it nearly in the seat of government. The 1959 march engaged as many as twenty thousand people, and the following year, by which time it had become accepted as an annual event, somewhere between thirty thousand and one hundred thousand participated, according to various estimates. CND membership also grew quickly, to 500 adult groups around the country, 100 college groups, and 160 youth groups by 1960, organized into seven regional circles.[9]

Alex, Ruth, and young Nick participated every year in the Aldermaston convergences, usually joining the march itself for one long stretch—their record was two days—and then attending the closing rally. Occasionally on the march they would encounter their neighbor, Jack Straw, the future Labour foreign secretary and lord chancellor, who was about Nick's age and whose father had been a conscientious objector during the war.[10]

Alex called the awakening in the aftermath of the Suez Crisis and the formation of the DAC "the greatest movement in this island since the days of the Chartists."* It was the germination of a "maquis of peace" willing to face police violence and even prison for their cause.[11] While this was probably an exaggeration, the movement for nuclear disarmament appeared very much like a fulfillment of the politics that Alex and other anarchists and pacifists had practiced during the war since, as George Woodcock pointed out, the DAC did not aim to create a new political party or practice mainstream electoral politics, but to directly bring about concrete change from outside the system.[12] Alex threw himself into work for both the CND and the DAC. In his professional life, including at UCL, he had almost always shied away from positions that involved management or administration, and while he had served for a time on the PPU National Council, he never took major leadership or deliberative positions in the CND or the DAC, despite being asked to from time to time. He saw himself, instead, as an educator, an inspirer, and occasionally a spokesperson.

The momentum behind the Ban the Bomb movement was sufficiently intense that the BBC couldn't ignore it, and the network occasionally turned to Alex. On March 31, 1958, a week before the first Aldermaston march, he appeared on the popular news magazine program *Panorama* along with John Collins, Doris Lessing, and Michael Foot, the Labour parliamentarian, *Tribune* editor, and CND founding member.[13] Not a consistently good platform speaker—Nicolas Walter, a journalist, anarchist, and fellow anti-nuclear campaigner, said that he mumbled, and another activist who saw him address a crowd in these years later said that he was barely audible—he was nevertheless excellent at addressing smaller, indoor audiences, where he could use the skills he had honed over a decade and a half of lecturing and radio broadcasting.[14]

For the CND, he traveled England addressing informational meetings, often with other scientists who could speak authoritatively about the effects of a nuclear explosion or accident to audiences still acquainting themselves with the terminology of nuclear weapons. Hornsey Town Hall; Watford Town Hall; St Albans; Stewart Hall, Norwich; Putney and Roehampton; Coleman's Institute, Redhill; Congregational Hall, Blackheath Village; St Pancras Town Hall; and Enfield City School are some of the locations on flyers that carry his name.

* Cited in Christopher Driver, *The Disarmers: A Study in Protest* (London: Hodder and Stoughton, 1964), 59. The Chartists were a political reform movement in early Victorian England that campaigned for passage of a charter extending voting rights for the working class.

Photographs from the period provide a precise sense of what these meetings were like. The setting was generally a public hall or church meeting room. A cloth-covered table with microphone, lectern, and a pitcher of water looked out over rows of chairs filled with polite, neatly dressed citizens, of a variety of ages but concentrated in the early middle years. The speakers looked very much like their audience. People to whom the CND appealed tended to be educated, politically aware, but not necessarily radical or culturally outside the mainstream. The CND liked to pose the issue of the Bomb in as apolitical a way as possible. Nuclear weapons were a menace to health and public safety. They were also a provocation to war, the kind of devastating conflict Britain had just lived through and which its people had no desire to experience again.

Alex looked just the part to deliver this message. His glasses and neat mustache gave him a properly expert, academic air, and his calm demeanor reassured his audience that they could rely on whatever information he imparted. Invariably he wore a well-fitting tailored suit and a tie—darker colors for indoors and colder weather, white for the summer months—adding to his air of professional respectability.

Setting him apart from other CND speakers, however, was the humor he injected into an intensely serious subject, always heavily laced with scorn for the political leaders of the nuclear powers, and a strong suggestion that the key to stopping the Bomb's proliferation was individuals' willingness to disobey government. In his garage, he constructed an oversized cardboard dinosaur costume with a long tail—barely recognizable as such—for a marcher to wear with an accompanying sign reading, "TOO LITTLE BRAIN / TOO MUCH ARMOUR / DO YOU WANT TO BE EXTINCT?" A photo from a London march shows Alex, in the beret and raincoat that were his typical garb on such occasions, looking back at an elderly marcher who attempts to explain to a bewildered-looking police officer what the dinosaur was about. The dinosaur proved popular, however, and local CND affiliates sometimes asked to borrow it for their own marches and demonstrations.[15]

Less amusingly, shortly after the first Aldermaston march and a television appearance with Collins in which they grilled the home secretary about the H-bomb, Alex addressed an audience in Norwich in near-apocalyptic terms. Nuclear weapons were a symptom of "moral bankruptcy," he said, and a form of "ceremonial suicide." The installations about to be situated in Britain were "not a precaution against war but part of . . .' [U.S. Secretary of State] John Foster Dulles's precaution against peace." Further: "Our survival depends from minute to minute on the judgment of two men—Mr. Khrushchev, who seems to me to drink a great deal more than is good for him, and President Eisenhower, who has just recovered from a disease of the brain.** He is a sick man and I am sorry that he is in that position. But we do not let a sick man drive a train."[16]

Alex's intense focus on civil disobedience kept him somewhat at odds with his comrades, even among the sponsors of the more militant DAC. When the DAC's executive committee planned a nine-week picket at Aldermaston beginning in September 1958, and the suggestion was made for a sit-down protest to cap it off, he was initially one of the few sponsors who supported the idea (the sit-down was ultimately approved and took place).[17]

In May, in the flush of success after the first march, he had helped April Carter and Gene Sharp draft a "Charter of Rights in the Nuclear Age" for the DAC, declaring that if the government should continue to violate these rights by testing and building nuclear weapons, the signatories' answer would be direct action and possibly a civil disobedience campaign. Carter and Sharp suggested pulling together the DAC's sponsors for a public signing ceremony at Runnymede, the meadow in Surrey, twenty miles from London, where King John had signed the Magna Carta and the Charter of the Forest in 1215, figuring the location would tie their efforts to the tradition of English political and civil liberties. Alex, characteristically, objected to the "Runnymede project" on the grounds that a signing ceremony without a direct action component, in a not very accessible location, would have little impact and be out of keeping with the DAC's mission.[18]

The disarmament campaign, however, showed signs of turning into a genuine mass movement. What Alex encountered at the marches and his speaking engagements, and was helping to propagate, was something new in Britain, something nearly unthinkable in the decades before the war: a grassroots political upswelling that cut across class lines. Out of this, the seeds of a new counterculture were becoming visible, represented by the circular logo that artist Gerald Holtom designed for the CND, which included a modified cross forming a composite of the semaphore signals for N and D (for nuclear disarmament), and which would become an icon of the '60s New Left. Speaking at the first Aldermaston march, Michael Foot called the Ban the Bomb movement a "crusade,"

** Eisenhower suffered several publicized health scares during his presidency, including a stroke in November 1957.

but the march itself had an air of celebration: "an Easter carnival," as the *Daily Telegraph* described it.

> Marchers were supposed to remain silent. But they laughed, talked, and "skiffled" their way along. . . . [They were] a fantastically varied lot, in fantastically varied garb. Bearded old men; girls in slacks, high heels, and red, white and blue stockings; children in prams and push-chairs; and a boy of 17 in bare feet. . . . [The boy] refused to give his name, saying that he had had several arguments with his headmaster about the H-bomb. "I am strongly against it," he informed me. . . . [A] band from a Highgate school, carried a poster, "Sixth-formers for peace."[19]

Prior to the war it hadn't been uncommon for politically conscious people of the upper echelons, like Alex's colleague Haldane, to support and even organize strikes and left-wing political actions. Lengthy marches weren't a new tactic, either. In the spring and summer of 1958, many still had memories of the 1936 Jarrow March. But, unlike the marchers of two decades earlier, many if not most of the Aldermaston campaigners were young and, like Alex, middle-class in background. The cause itself held no direct economic appeal to the working class; most of the largest labor unions opposed unilateralism, in fact. Politically the marchers ranged from moderates who were active in the Labour Party to anarchists, Communists, and assorted other leftists, including the unaffiliated young who sympathized with the disarmament movement and found it a convenient vehicle to express their dissatisfaction with what they saw as the materialistic postwar society their elders were building.

These tensions were embodied in the uneasy alliance between the CND and the DAC. The CND leaders were torn between their desire to build a popular movement and the perceived need to preserve some shred of support from Labour. The DAC and its supporters were less sanguine about working through the traditional political process. Following the success of the first Aldermaston march, the DAC leadership seemed to agree with Alex that the next logical step was civil disobedience. In December 1958 it organized sit-down protests at a rocket base under construction near the East Anglian village of North Pickenham, with the aim of winning over workers employed on nuclear projects. The following March, Alex joined a two-week campaign of picketing, leafleting, and open-air meetings in Stevenage, just north of London, where Britain's new intermediate-range ballistic missile, the Blue Streak, was being built. The campaign was rewarded by an hour-long strike by

Stevenage building crews, although the armaments workers remained on the job.

The trades union organizers of decades past had readymade communities to draw from: towns and neighborhoods where families often went back generations and solidarity was built not just in factories, dockyards, and construction sites but also in parlors, kitchens, churches, and public halls. The Ban the Bomb movement—culturally diverse, geographically dispersed—lacked this naturally occurring support network. Yet the marches and sit-down demonstrations that drew supporters together (sometimes for days) required a strong sense of community to succeed. Notwithstanding the CND's desire to present a solemnly moving spectacle, its more militant supporters, not to mention the DAC, insisted that something was needed to create a sense of camaraderie and shared experience.

The first year, a six-piece jazz band, playing "When the Saints Go Marching In," had accompanied the marchers from London to Aldermaston, it was reported, and a folk-dance troupe performed at stopping places along the route.[20] But something more besides chanted slogans was needed to keep the marchers engaged. Stepping up were a small coterie of folk singers and songwriters, including Arlo Tatum, Matt McGinn, and Ewan MacColl and his American partner, Peggy Seeger. Together they assembled lyrics to be sung to familiar tunes, printed them, and handed them to the marchers from a van.

With his musical training, facility with words and verse, and long attachment to Irish poetry and rebel songs, Alex quickly joined them. He showed a sketch for a song titled "First Things First" to John Hasted, a physicist and politically like-minded colleague at UCL who was also a singer and leader in the burgeoning folk music revival. With Hasted supplying the melody, Alex concocted a lyric cheerfully connecting football with the antinuclear struggle:

On the night of the Wembley Cup Final,
  I had a most horrible dream.
I'd just been invited to play for United
  and Matt put me into the team.
Like a regular hero I charged down the field,
  the goal lay wide open ahead.
The crowd bellowed shoot,
  I'd the ball on me boot,
When the ref blew his whistle and said:

"Ban the Bomb! It's the highest priority.
    Don't stand there kicking that ball.
If some bloody mutton should sit on the button
    There'll be no more soccer at all.
O you who think nothing of scragging the ref
    Just get this idea in your head.
The crowd that turns up when we play for the cup
    Could scrag old Macmillstone instead."[21]

For the first Aldermaston march, Alex produced a singalong set to the tune of "John Brown's Body," titled "Ban, Ban, Ban the Bloody H-Bomb." It proved popular enough to elicit requests for more impromptu verses, and Alex obliged with such titles as "The Young CND," "Sit, Brother, Sit," and "The Nuclear Springclean," all written in a quasi-working-class lingo and usually ridiculing establishment politicians like De Gaulle, Khrushchev, Prime Minister Harold Macmillan ("Macmillstone"), and Labour opposition leader Hugh Gaitskell.

Musically not very imaginative, miles below the caliber of his serious verse, but engaging nonetheless, Alex's songs posed nuclear disarmament as the commonsense conclusion of practical working people trying to get on with their lives in the face of their comically megalomaniacal betters. They received numerous workouts as the disarmament campaign gathered momentum. Topic Records, the pioneering British folk label that had begun life in 1939 as an offshoot of the Communist-led Workers' Music Association and had since provided a home for performers like MacColl and Pete Seeger, licensed "First Things First," which it released in 1958 as "Peculiar Dream."[22]

For a time, Alex maintained correspondence with members of the left-wing folk song community in the United States as well. He met Pete Seeger (Peggy Seeger's half-brother), visiting the UK, who was taken with "First Things First" and wrote a tune for another of Alex's songs, "One Man's Hands." "I wish to God that we had more songwriters here in the States that could measure up to the standards of excellence which you all have set in Britain," he wrote Alex on his return.[23]

Several of Alex's other songs were first published in Hasted's *SING* magazine, a UK counterpart to *Sing Out!*, the magazine of the American folk revival, and Seeger asked him for songs to publish in *Broadside*, a smaller counterpart of *Sing Out!*, but cautioned him against sending pieces aimed too specifically at British audiences—or, it seemed, that were too racy. When Seeger wanted to print Alex's song "The Young

CND," in *Sing Out!*, he insisted on swapping out the phrase "pinch your cherry" for "steal your nuclear secrets," since Alex's words would be considered sufficiently "vulgar" in the United States to "prevent wide singing of the song."[24] The complete, uncensored lyrics appeared in September 1962 in *YEAH 4*, the fourth issue of the underground magazine published in mimeograph form by Tuli Kupferberg, the poet, activist, and future vocalist for the Fugs.[25]

For a time, Alex was enthusiastic enough about his modest part in the folk song movement to acquire some long-playing records of American and British musicians to go along with his records of Irish songs and even built several Appalachian-style dulcimers, which he learned to play at home after a fashion, despite his maimed left hand.[26]

EVEN AS THE BAN the Bomb campaign grew and started to send down deeper cultural roots, quarrels within the movement worsened. The CND was torn between moderates, like Canon Collins, and its more militant members, most prominently Bertrand Russell, who preferred the DAC's confrontational tactics. Alex clearly fell into the latter group. As an anarchist, he used the platform the movement gave him to press his listeners not just to oppose nuclear weapons but to see the coming of the Bomb as a turning point in history, to which the only logical response was to disobey and rebel against the entire order that had created them. Appearing with the anti-Nazi German pastor and theologian Martin Niemöller at the annual general meeting of the PPU on April 20, 1958, he declared, "The rebellion against nuclear suicide is part of a far wider struggle, of men against inhumanity, not war only. . . . It is anger against the whole ill-conditioned growth of cant, inhumanity and double-talk in office, against collusion between party leaderships, against leaders with a vested interest in international strife because they cannot think of a policy to put in its place."[27] This was a call for an end to politics as it was currently practiced, and Niemöller responded, saying, "What we all need is an active pacifism which will not be satisfied with just rejecting and outlawing war, but which will put all its emphasis on establishing, improving and consolidating peace."

The movement, with the heightened visibility the Ban the Bomb campaign was giving it, had to guard against being co-opted by the people in power, Alex warned.

> The pacifist movement is an established feature of English society. It receives, on occasion, acknowledgments of respect from the Establishment. . . . The trouble is that to some extent we have become part of the Establishment. We have become an insurance policy against an effective public resistance to war. The only thing which is of greater political value to a government than absence of opposition is the existence of an opposition it knows it can control, a bag into which dangerous public tendencies can be diverted, and within which they can expend their energies in ways which endanger nobody.[28]

Although he was speaking at a PPU meeting, Alex's address was at least partially aimed at the CND leadership, who were now openly opposing more direct confrontation as well as efforts to widen the scope of the antinuclear campaign.

Relations grew frostier just before Christmas, when the DAC organized a weekend occupation of a site at Swaffham, Norfolk, where a US base for nuclear-armed Thor intermediate-range ballistic missiles was being constructed. Forty-five activists were arrested, some of whom were jailed over the holiday when they refused to give police an assurance they would not return to the site. After the CND objected vocally to the arrests, Alex, with *Peace News* editor Hugh Brock's cooperation, authored an editorial defending the DAC and criticizing the CND for taking a stand against another organization engaged in peace work.

That provoked an angry letter to Alex from Sybil Morrison, who objected to the use of *Peace News*—the PPU's "organ"—to support one side of the controversy. She also objected to Alex's peremptory tone, which sounded to her "like an edict from the prefects' room, or, by gad sir, perhaps from the officer's mess!" After a conciliatory letter from Alex, Morrison wrote back to say she had not taken his comments personally, adding that she hoped she would be ready to go to prison herself "if it seemed to me that I could do no other" although "my one experience doesn't exactly endear me to the idea!"[29]

The differences were too deep to paper over, however. In September 1960, Russell resigned as president of the CND and, with members of the DAC, launched a new organization headed by a committee of prominent individuals and dedicated to civil disobedience against nuclear weapons, to be called the Committee of 100.[30]

Alex had developed a good rapport with Russell since the CND's founding. Accordingly, his was one of the initial one hundred signatures solicited by the gray eminence of the movement.[31] The others included

Herbert Read, poet Hugh MacDiarmid, painter Augustus John, actor John Neville, and playwrights John Arden, John Osborne, and Shelagh Delaney. Russell's prestige guaranteed a diverse group, though Alex regretted that more scientists didn't sign on.[32] Compared with the CND, a higher proportion of the organizers who did much of the day-to-day work were, like Alex, pacifists or anarchists or both, and the committee's tactics were accordingly confrontational. The committee proposed to carry out actions only if two thousand or more agreed to take part, however, and activists pledged themselves to nonviolence. Their exceedingly ambitious aim was to confront the government with a campaign of civil disobedience large enough to force it to disarm. How would that happen? In the text of a speech he gave numerous times in the first year of the committee's existence, Alex urged,

> You can take direct action. You can insist that this country become morally clean by immediately withdrawing from this criminal conspiracy to destroy mankind. Renounce all the nuclear weapons in your possession, abolish all missile bases in this country, and then with clean hands and with moral authority, invite all other nations to form a third force, a disarmed force, that will confront the American and Russian giants with the weapons of sanity, human faith, and mutual love. This may be a desperate form of idealism, but it offers more hope for mankind than the so-called realism of atomic deterrence.[33]

Given the size of nuclear stockpiles decades later, and the failure of the superpowers to stop other nations from acquiring them, a program such as the Committee of 100 was proposing sounds fantastic. But in 1960 it was backed by a growing popular movement, it had many prominent supporters and a high public profile, and it appeared to be developing a robust culture of resistance. If it could continue to build its hard-core membership by staging attention-getting direct actions close to the centers of power, perhaps it had a chance to succeed.

The committee's determination to win immediately, rather than settle into a process of working patiently for a long-term scaling back and phasing out of nuclear weapons, reflected the position Alex had been taking for some time. It also set the committee outside of mainstream political discussion. "Politicians, who do not hesitate to join the C.N.D., shy away from the Committee of 100," the *Observer* reported. "With its Aldermaston Marches and its abortive bid to take over the Labour Party, [the CND] has become a familiar sight, almost an object of affection. But the Committee of 100, with its strange name and its emphasis on civil disobedience, is a comparatively new, unknown, body."[34]

It still had in common with the CND a commitment to nonviolence, however. Following the practice of the American civil rights movement, activists were expected to go limp when arrested and remain so until they were taken to a police station. That prompted another occasional song from Alex, titled "Go Limp," soon heard at civil rights rallies in the United States as well. Jazz-soul singer and activist Nina Simone began featuring it in performance, and it would turn up on her 1964 album, *Nina Simone in Concert*.[35]

The Committee of 100's first action, a sit-down demonstration in front of the Ministry of Defence on February 18, 1961, drew some forty-two hundred participants, twelve hundred of whom risked arrest by refusing an order to disperse, though the police made none. That year's Aldermaston march was the biggest yet, and five hundred marchers affiliated with the committee peeled off to demonstrate in front of the American Embassy in Grosvenor Square. This time arrests were made. When activists gathered outside Savile Row police station to demand their release, a scuffle broke out, and another twenty-five wound up in police custody.[36]

The new campaign was now launching one action after another. Soon after the Easter march, thirty-five veterans of the DAC mounted a seven-week trek to the new American submarine base at Holy Loch in Argyll. "Flapless Mac[millan] will get a shock if the Yankees switch that blast on. / His balls'll be in the Holy Loch and his clubs in Aldermaston," went a new song by Alex, "The Writing on the Wall," set appropriately to the tune of "Yankee Doodle Dandy." Some two thousand people took part in the final march to the base, where seventy tried to board a submarine tender and another two hundred sat down on the pier. Scottish police and US sailors attacked and dispersed the demonstrators.

The movement was drawing the anger of the rowdy Right, which was stirring to life in Britain in the early '60s. Soon after the Committee of 100 announced a march to Whitehall for April 29, 1961, someone threw a brick through the window of its office in Finsbury Park. The next time Alex came to the office, recalled Michael Randle, the secretary of the committee, he had a shillelagh in one hand and declared, "If those fascists want to come up here, they can deal with me!"[37] The march nevertheless drew 10,000 demonstrators; over 2,000 sat down and blocked the road, and 862 were arrested. The bigger the participation, and the more arrests the police made, the more visible the campaign grew.

As one of the more recognized members of the committee, Alex was by now not only a calling card for the organizers but a target for opponents who were beginning to resent—or worse—the constant presence of disarmament in the news. "Dear Doctor, I consider that the actions taken by you and your co-criminals of the 'Committee of 100' are those of traitors," began a particularly vitriolic letter he received following the Whitehall action. "Your correct home should be a cell in Wormwood Scrubs or Pentonville . . . for your seditious activities. Let's hope that it is not long before you are on your way there."[38]

But the committee was already planning what would become its most celebrated—and deplored—action, a mass sit-down demonstration in Trafalgar Square scheduled for September 17, to be followed by a march the short distance to Parliament Square.

Both the activists and the government had a strong sense that the nuclear controversy was coming to a head. It was the year of the Berlin Crisis; East Germany had erected the Berlin Wall in August to prevent defectors fleeing to the West, Washington had responded by reinforcing its troops in Germany, and Khrushchev was dropping hints that the Soviet Union was getting ready to test the most powerful nuclear bomb yet. "When statesmen think that ending all human life is a method of policy, they need to be brought back to reality," stated a leaflet from the committee announcing the sit-down demo.

The government was growing concerned about the size of the crowds the anti-Bomb campaign was attracting, including for acts of civil disobedience. Anxious to stall the momentum of the campaign, it banned access to Trafalgar Square under the Public Order Act. The authorities also ratcheted up their surveillance of the organizers. Several members at a press conference alleged that they had been followed for days by plainclothes officers and that the police had planted spies at their meetings.

Alex worried that his phone was tapped. Nick remembered him listening for a loud click when he picked up the receiver; if he heard this—or thought so—he would first say "Good evening, inspector, and I hope your piles go down" before contacting the operator.[39] On a similar suspicion, one committee member arranged to make a "plant" call to a friend, telling him about a sit-down that was supposed to take place at a certain time at Watford Town Hall. No demonstration was planned, but when the stated time arrived, the police were there waiting. Scotland Yard denied it had engaged in wiretapping, but allowed that some members could have been under "observation."[40]

Neither the CND nor the Committee of 100 were Soviet front

organizations, as the Right sometimes claimed, but that didn't mean Russian intelligence operatives weren't interested in them and their more conspicuous members. In 1961 a "beaten-down little attaché" calling himself "Smith," "with 'spook' written all over him," approached Alex, saying he was an admirer of the Brontës and wanted someone to collect information for him about the readership of English-language Soviet publications. "We met twice (I think)," Alex recalled, at a Hungarian restaurant on Lower Regent Street, "paying alternate bills." Alex was curious what Smith was really up to, but then things started to happen. Someone burgled his house without taking anything, he recalled, and an old schoolfriend, Norman Hutchinson, who was in the Cabinet Office, was advised to stay away from him. Alex then broke off relations with Smith by calling him at the Soviet embassy on an open line; that ended their meetings.[41]

Less than a week before the Trafalgar Square sit-down, thirty-six committee members, Alex and Russell among them, were summoned to Bow Street Magistrates' Court: the same place where Oscar Wilde and the suffragists Emmeline and Cristabel Pankhurst had been charged decades earlier. Under the six-hundred-year-old Justices of the Peace Act, the court accused the organizers of having "incited members of the public to commit breaches of the peace." More specifically, the charge stated, the organizers had "incited divers persons unknown unlawfully to obstruct the highway at or in the vicinity of Parliament Square, Westminster, S.W.1. on 17th September, 1961, and [were] likely to persevere in such unlawful conduct."

Some fifty supporters gathered outside the court at 9:30 a.m. on September 12, when Russell, his wife Edith, and the other committee members arrived. At eighty-nine, the tall, gaunt, white-haired peer was still a charismatic figure, and his presence guaranteed the court date heavy media coverage. About twenty supporters were able to enter the courtroom, and they applauded for half a minute when Russell protested the court's refusal to let him or his comrades make political statements.[42]

The committee members were presented with a stark choice: agree to be "bound over," meaning to pledge good behavior for the next twelve months, which in turn meant avoiding the Trafalgar Square event and staying away from any other such occasions—or be imprisoned. Thirty-two of the thirty-six members, including Alex, Michael Randle, the Russells, playwright Arnold Wesker, and playwright and screenwriter Robert Bolt, refused to be bound over and were incarcerated just before the sit-down was to take place. The Russells received sentences of two months in Brixton Prison—quickly reduced to one week each—while the rest were sentenced to one month each in Drake Hall, a minimum-security, open-air prison in Staffordshire. Alex would later joke that he had enjoyed his time in Bow Street, "teaching *Finnegan's Wake* . . . to Earl Russell" while they awaited their hearing (later he would say he had taught the peer "several Irish rebel songs"[43]).

The September 17 sit-down went ahead without them. The committee members were well aware that their imprisonment created excellent publicity; "if you condemn us you will be helping our cause and helping humanity," Russell told the court.[44] Nearly 12,000 activists gathered, prepared to be arrested, while a smaller contingent gathered at Holy Loch. Determined to stop the crowd at Trafalgar Square from advancing to the vicinity of Parliament, the authorities issued an order banning processions and assemblies, effective well into the night, and deployed more than fifteen hundred police and eight hundred special constables, along with two troops of mounted police ("one of the strongest cordons ever seen at a London demonstration," according to the *Daily Mail*).[45] The police arrested 1,314 persons, of whom 658 were released on bail while the rest spent the night in jail.[46] The arrestees included such people of note as Herbert and Ludo Read, Doris Lessing, and John Osborne, but, just as importantly, the paper noted that the average age of the demonstrators "appeared to be little over 21," underscoring the impact the Ban the Bomb movement was having among young people.

The Trafalgar Square action enjoyed heavy media exposure, although most press accounts played it as a victory for the police, since they kept the activists away from Parliament. The stage seemed to be set for a further ramping-up once the Committee of 100 members regrouped following their prison sentences.

ALEX—AND RUTH—ENJOYED plenty of support from family and friends during his imprisonment and afterward. "Bully for you!" his comrades at the Loughton CND branch wrote him in prison on September 23, ahead of the Trafalgar Square action. "Sunday's going to be terrific, so make room for more." The playwright Ann Jellicoe, who would enjoy a great West End success the following year with the sex comedy *The Knack*, wrote Ruth offering help, adding, "We all feel we must support our friends who have made this sacrifice and taken this stand."[47]Alex's friend Fred Marnau, from Grey Walls days, called to express his solidarity, and Ruth's redoubtable mother May, in a humorous mood, wrote Alex directly, to ask what he was doing—"not tying up chrysanthemums, taking clippings etc. I suppose!"—and assure him that Ruth was being well looked after by her friends.[48]

On September 19, a week after his sentencing at Bow Street, he paid a fine of £25, promised to keep the peace and be "of good behavior toward Her Majesty and all her liege people, and especially toward the Commissioner of Police of the metropolis for the term of 12 months"—essentially the promise he had refused to make before the Trafalgar Square sit-down—and walked free. Others took similar deals to shorten their terms. Alex promptly wrote a squib for *Peace News* about his prison stay:

> Greetings from all the members of the Committee of 100 in Drake Hall prison. We have been able to follow the report of Sunday's demonstration. As the reports came in on television and by word of mouth the effect on the entire prison as electric. Anonymous shouts of "ban the bomb" were heard on parade, and whenever two or three people were gathered together, whether warders, prisoners or both, there was a member of the Committee in the midst of them engaged in heated argument, explanation or discussion.
>
> A strong detachment, led by Michael Scott [an Anglican clergy-member and well-known activist], has occupied the Current Affairs class. The prison authorities whilst sticking to their duty treated us with courtesy and consideration.
>
> As I have had to get back to work, my own and the Committee's, I duly admitted that I owed Her Majesty £25 and was discharged this morning. That must be a great load off Her Majesty's mind, and I am delighted to think that the next time I protest against nuclear war I shall not only be helping to save our homes from the activities of mental patients but also to preserve the monarchy from bankruptcy.[49]

The jaunty tone of his note belied the fact that Alex was beginning to change focus after several years of intense activism on top of his scientific work. He had always sought visibility for his ideas, his writing, and his causes, but the attention that the civil disobedience campaign attracted was more personally directed and perhaps a bit frightening for a man with responsibilities who was leading a full life in other arenas. For the first time, his notoriety was affecting his family.

"I think I hoped he would simply pay up and come home, but he refused to be bound over," Nick recalled of his father's imprisonment.

By then attending Highgate School, he endured mocking from schoolmates (concerning "my father the jailbird").[50] It was all of a piece with his upbringing, however. Alex had never allowed Nick, as a younger boy, to play with toy guns or to see war movies at the Majestic, although the rules were not strictly enforced.[51]

Despite his experience as a conscientious objector and the risks he had run with his campaign against indiscriminate bombing during the war, Alex had never before been arrested or imprisoned. His long career in hospitals and research and educational institutions may also have made him more willing to follow orders than some of his comrades. Some of them were quite surprised, given that Alex's rhetoric had marked him as one of the most confrontational members of the CND and then the Committee of 100. In Drake Hall, recalled Michael Randle, who was imprisoned with him, Alex "certainly behaved differently than I had expected—a bit less anarchist-style than most of us in there." The prisoners were subjected to a military-style routine, including marches and drills—"quick march, left-right, left-right. We didn't do all of that, of course, but Alex was clicking his heels, doing the left-right, and that rather shocked me."[52]

Neither was he immune to concerns about the impact of his activism on his career. Early in 1962, Alex, Randle, and several coconspirators, including the poet Christopher Logue and the journalist Murray Sayle, calling themselves the Voice of Nuclear Disarmament, launched their own radio station, initially from a transmitter hidden at UCL.[53] The broadcasts they put out over a fifty-watt set (price: £7) had a range of only five miles, but within that area they came through fairly clearly. Alex occasionally contributed talks, and the station also played recordings of Russell, Vanessa Redgrave, and speeches from the most recent Aldermaston march.[54]

Whether Alex had anything directly to do with launching other such radio projects is unclear, but among his papers is a March 2, 1961, letter from a person in Newcastle-upon-Tyne, addressed to "George," asking for technical advice on setting up "Voice for Nuclear Disarmament" for Tyneside. While no reply survives, it's possible that the letter was really directed to Alex, who often took requests for advice on where to get recording or transmission equipment. But when Randle and his friends set up their transmitter at UCL, where Alex had his office and laboratory, he warned them that "tracking devices" could discover the transmitter's whereabouts and strongly urged that it be moved.[55] Later they broadcast from two locations: a house in Hampstead and another in South London.[56]

Alex never suggested that his time in Drake Hall changed his mind about the rightness of the Committee of 100's tactics, but he had become reluctant to engage in civil disobedience again. In a 1963 interview, he simply said, "I don't sit down in the street now because I have so many things to do."[57]

"It was obviously worth it" to go to prison, he said years later. "We turned a local demonstration into an international incident, and prison is one of the most effective rostra there is if you want to attract media attention."[58] After the Trafalgar Square sit-down, he contributed to the Defence Committee fund set up to help the arrestees.[59] He would continue to write and speak against nuclear arms until the end of his active life and helped support the Committee of 100 financially for the remainder of its existence.[60] But he never took part in planning another action like the Trafalgar Square sit-down, only wrote occasionally for *Peace News*, and stopped producing pamphlets and statements and delivering speeches for the cause. Although his position remained the same, he was no longer a regularly-seen public presence in the pacifist and antinuclear movements.

WITH OR WITHOUT ALEX, the disarmament campaign found itself at a crossroads following the Trafalgar Square sit-down. The momentum of the campaign—the frequency of new actions, the intense media attention they attracted, and the increasingly aggressive government response—seemed to overwhelm its organizers, even some of the veterans. Almost half the original members of the Committee of 100 quit and were replaced after Trafalgar Square, mostly by younger organizers determined to be even more confrontational.

The committee's efforts to build on the splashy coverage of the sit-down fell flat. A nationwide demonstration and series of civil disobedience actions called for December 9 drew twenty-two hundred people—but the boldest, a march onto an unfenced NATO base near the Essex village of Wethersfield, attracted only six hundred, whereas the committee had called for fifty thousand. Herbert Read, objecting to the implicit threat that the marchers might use force to take the airbase, resigned from the Committee of 100 rather than endorse the action. "We provide entertainment and not enlightenment to the man in the street," he complained.[61] It marked the first and last time that Alex found himself on the opposite side politically from his old friend.

The 1962 Aldermaston march was as large as the previous year's, but the dissension within the committee was palpable. One faction wanted to widen its mandate from nuclear disarmament to promoting pacifism in general. It carried the day, but the change of focus cost the committee much of its popular base. The 1963 march—including an anarchist contingent hoisting a banner reading "Ban the Lot!"—was, for the first time, smaller than the preceding year's, the committee was having financial difficulties, and supporters were beginning to question what exactly the disarmament campaign had accomplished.[62]

Arguably, the direct-action wing of the Ban the Bomb movement was becoming the victim of its own conviction—which Alex himself had promoted—that mass civil disobedience could win a quick and decisive victory by exposing the inhumanity of people in office and sparking popular revulsion at their behavior.

What prevented it from doing so, above all, was its failure to generate mass antinuclear sentiment in the union movement, something it had attempted unsuccessfully among the armaments workers at Stevenage. If it had succeeded, it might have forced the Labour leadership to get in line. In 1963 the UK's signature to the Nuclear Test Ban Treaty would tamp down much of the popular alarm over atomic weapons—despite the fact that nuclear bases remained on British soil. Having failed to broaden the antinuclear movement into other areas of politics, the committee and the CND had nowhere further to go.

They still had the people with them. A 1963 poll found that a clear majority of Britons supported unilateral nuclear disarmament.[63] But the media had judged it was safe to move on, and politicians approached such inconvenient signs as a matter to be finessed rather than clear messages from the people who put them in office.

Uneasy about what the movement might do to further ratchet up the pressure, the government was taking sterner measures with activists. Two months after Trafalgar Square, Special Branch raided the offices of the Committee of 100 and the homes of six members, arresting them on charges under the Official Secrets Act. Convicted, the men received sentences of eighteen months imprisonment, while the women were given twelve months.[64]

The 1965 Aldermaston march would be the last of the annual events, although it would be revived in 1972 and 2004.

The Committee of 100's more immediate problems had already begun in the weeks and months after the Trafalgar Square sit-down, however, when legal and other costs were soaring in the wake of a series of actions that had resulted in thousands of arrests.[65] In addition, the time absorbed by their cases made many activists less available. Alex helped with fund-raising by packaging several of his more popular songs into a collection in pamphlet form that *SING* brought out under the punning title *Are You Sitting Comfortably?* It was priced at sixpence. "At Dr Comfort's request the profits from this publication will be donated to the Committee of 100," a note read.

IN THE FALL OF 1961, just after his release from prison, Alex published a new novel, his first in nine years. In the interim, he had been busy, but his last fictional works hadn't encouraged him to keep at it. Routledge had remaindered *On This Side Nothing* (at 9d. a copy for 624 remaining copies) two years after it appeared,[66] and *A Giant's Strength* was remaindered less than a year after publication (at the slightly more remunerative rate of a shilling apiece for 124 copies).[67] *Come Out to Play* couldn't have been more different from these earlier, relentlessly serious novels. He later called it the first of his "laughing novels."[68] Zola was no longer his model.

"If I write about England, I intend to write a political satire," Alex later recalled saying to people who asked why his earlier fiction was nearly all situated in other places.[69] The new book was a satire of the British political establishment, with strong echoes of *Scoop*, Evelyn Waugh's prewar poke at the Beaverbrook newspapers. The framework of the novel is a comic caper: a financially pinched biologist, Dr. George Goggins, and his Argentine-Irish-Hungarian girlfriend, Dulcinea Fuentes y McGredy, open a sex clinic, discover the world's "first effective general aphrodisiac," and precipitate a sexual and perhaps political revolution as the masters of the universe learn to enjoy good intercourse.

As a prescription for revolution, *Come Out to Play* was quite different from the speeches and articles Alex had been turning out for the better part of a decade, advocating mass civil disobedience. It displayed a different side of his personality from those earlier books too, one that had previously emerged mainly in conversation and in some of his radio broadcasts: the skilled and slightly irreverent interviewee and occasional presenter, the dinner-table raconteur who knew how to bring his points home with a humorous twist. His politics had not changed, but in his new novel he aimed to encourage a cultural uprising, spiked with satire, against the enemies of a sane society rather than a direct political assault, and this would remain his objective in nearly all his subsequent fiction. "I would rather read *Candide* than almost any other novel," he said years later. "One of the troubles with writing something in the style of *The Power House* was that it didn't give any scope for Voltairean mockery, which was Voltaire's most devastating move."[70]

The satiric targets of *Come Out to Play* are dated, and the notion of drugs and better sex turning the powerful into puppy dogs even more so, but the novel remains entertaining because the spectacle of buffoonish bigwigs taken down to a human level always amuses, and because Alex's voice—in the mouth of Goggins, his first-person narrator—is fresh and appealing. "Goggins is Alex to a T," a later acquaintance said.[71] The author's distinctive brand of humor comes through in touches such as the name he gives to his aphrodisiac—"3-blindmycin"—and "the Friworld," a bit of invented jargon he used to describe the social agglomeration of English and American diplomats and functionaries, NATO brass, and bureaucrats crowded into Paris at the time.

Goggins suggests something else about his creator. For all that he could be a righteous scourge of hypocrites and war criminals, Alex also liked the image of himself as a rascally figure, subverting the authorities through knowing humor and a refusal to be killed by their kindnesses, then ducking back into anonymity rather than letting the mantle of power fall onto his shoulders. In *The Power House*, he had invoked Til Eulenspiegel, the trickster of German folklore, and Simplicissimus, the eponymous picaresque survivor hero of Grimmelhausen's novel of the Thirty Years' War, as representing the part of humanity that would eventually end the "rule of the strong."[72] That persona suggested his new novel would have popular appeal, but first Alex had to find a publisher.

Tom Ragg, his fiction editor at Routledge, had died in 1953.[73] Alex's previous novels were out of print, and the firm had ceased publishing fiction.[74] Accordingly, his agent, David Higham, tried *Come Out to Play* first with Secker and Warburg—"I'm sure we should offer this to publishers of intelligence (none of the others would want it!)," Higham wrote him.[75] After Secker turned it down, they tried Eyre & Spottiswode, who said yes and also accepted a new volume of poetry. "For the most part the [novel] seems to me entirely delightful and I think that the only people who will get cross with it are the sort of people we shall be delighted to disagree with," Eyre's talented publisher, Maurice Temple Smith, wrote Higham.

Temple Smith was a good match for Alex. A Cambridge graduate five years younger than his new author, he had scored a great success in 1957 with *Room at the Top*, John Braine's novel of regional career ladder-climbing.[***] He was also a friend of the artist and fantasy novelist Mervyn Peake, whose last completed novel of the *Gormenghast* series, *Titus Alone*, he edited and published. He lived the very social life of an English publishing executive, but his tastes in writing were more serious and offbeat, and he lived in Hampstead, an artistic neighborhood where Freedom Press once had its office, rather than one of the posher areas. He was also one of the few people in London who could rival Alex's knowledge of limericks and knack for making them up on the spot.[76]

Some of Alex's satire placed Temple Smith in a slightly uncomfortable position, however. Alongside its publishing arm, Eyre & Spottiswode were Her Majesty's printers, supplying stationery and other items to the queen, which obliged the firm to maintain a polite relationship with the royal family. "Mr. and Mrs. Jones," a couple who figure toward the end of *Come Out to Play* as "patients" of Goggins and Dulcinea, were transparently based on the queen's sister, Princess Margaret, and her husband, photographer Anthony Armstrong-Jones, earl of Snowden, who were rumored to be having marital difficulties ranging from infidelity to homosexuality. Temple Smith wanted these passages changed. "All we ask is that Comfort should be calculatedly vague about the couple concerned so that no direct reference is made, or seems to be made, to the Queen's family," he wrote. He also asked that Alex change the name of one character, Jebb Jollyboy, a careerist civil servant, because it sounded too much like that of Gladwyn Jebb, a prominent British diplomat.[77]

Alex and Ruth's friend Jane Henderson had raised the same concern about "Mr. and Mrs. Jones" after he sent her a copy of the manuscript a few months earlier. "It's one of the very few books that made me laugh out loud—not just inside," she wrote him. "[But] at present there just aren't that many other royal couples [besides the Snowdens]." Singling them out might attract the wrong kind of attention, she advised, "if the gutter press is short on news." That in turn, she warned, could affect Alex's career prospects, especially since Goggins was clearly Alex's stand-in. "What do you mean you don't care [whether you are identified with the character]? Do you mean it's water off a duck's back—which is one thing—or you don't care whether or not you get a chair in human biology in this country?" The academic higher-ups would "talk about

*** Providing Braine with advice, encouragement, and representation was Paul Scott, Alex's old friend from Falcon Press, now a literary agent. Hilary Spurling, *Paul Scott: A Life of the Author of* The Raj Quartet (New York: W. W. Norton, 1990), 182.

intellectual freedom—and bringing science into disrepute—in the same breath."[78]

Such was the degree of deference the monarchy continued to command in Britain. Alex compromised by changing the Joneses to the "Johnsons," although most au courant readers would have known at once to whom he was referring. Jebb Jollyboy kept his name. All of this becomes slightly ironic in context. The book was published at approximately the same time that War Minister John Profumo was embarking on his ill-fated affair with the nineteen-year-old model Christine Keeler. Two years later, the revelation of the Profumo affair in the press, raising the possibility that a Soviet agent might have used Keeler to obtain military secrets from her paramour, embarrassed the Conservative Party and helped end Macmillan's premiership. With the Profumo scandal, sex shook the established order, as Alex had suggested it might. Indeed, it invaded Britons' daily news as it had on no occasion since the abdication crisis, though this time it was a politician, not a member of the royal family, who was the catalyst.

There were no professional repercussions for Alex after the fall 1961 publication of *Come Out to Play*, however, and the reviewers concentrated on the book's literary merits and good humor rather than any latent scandal. Some found the satire heavy-handed ("roughly speaking, about as funny and delicate as two elephants dancing the samba," said the *Times* review), and even the positive notices acknowledged that the names he gave some of his characters were a bit much (the foreign secretary's name is "Fossil-Fundament").

Others, doubtless in part because they were inclined to agree politically with the author, were highly amused. "Mr. Comfort offers the refreshingly heretical notion that Sex is Fun," the *Spectator* concluded, "and [he] makes it very funny indeed—Goggins, in more ways than one, takes all the sacred cows by the horns and twists them sharply." The *Guardian* critic wrote, "Everybody, when they look at the horrors of the world, thinks 'if only,' and fills in the rest of the sentence according to their own recipe. This is the sexologist's completion of the sentence." A gratifying personal note came from Julian Huxley: "I have just been reading your 'Come out to play,' to console me while convalescing from a nasty attack of tropical malaria—it is extremely entertaining!"[79]

Come Out to Play was no best-seller, but it sold moderately well and even attracted some interest in a possible movie adaptation. Donald MacLean, a writer-producer and production executive at the BBC with aspirations to be a feature film director, contacted Alex about this.

MacLean would write a treatment and submit it to a producer he knew was looking for properties. Alex was interested and suggested Peter Sellers and Sophia Loren, who had just costarred in a film of Bernard Shaw's *The Millionairess*, as Goggins and Dulcinea. His novel fit in well with the new, politically and socially daring British satire of the period, which was making successes of *The Goon Show* (Sellers's introduction to fame and the brainchild of Alex's CND comrade, Spike Milligan), the comedy revue *Beyond the Fringe*, the satirical TV variety show *That Was the Week That Was* (an "explosion onto the screen," Nick Comfort recalled), and the scandal sheet *Private Eye*.[80] MacLean agreed that Sellers would be well cast, although, having worked with him on *The Goon Show* some years before, he warned, "[Sellers] improvises his dialogue and situations, and generally makes life bloody difficult." In February 1962, MacLean promised to drop by a treatment for Alex to critique, but nothing further appears to have come of the project.[81]

As always with his fiction, Alex wasn't just story-telling when he wrote *Come Out to Play*. He was speculating: testing out ideas, theories, and ideological stances, putting them in the minds and mouths of his characters to see how they played in a fictional simulation. This time, his what-ifs were the possibility of olfactory aphrodisiacs and the concept of a sex clinic. He was himself reviewing research on pheromones: chemicals produced by the body that act as signals to other individuals.****

This was still largely speculation, but Alex's other big idea—the sex clinic—was shortly to become a reality. In 1964, when William Masters and Virginia Johnson opened their Reproductive Biology Research Foundation, its mission included training sex therapists, and they soon developed a two-week psychotherapy program for couples. Earlier, Masters and Johnson were the first sex researchers to actually observe couples having intercourse. Referring to *Come Out to Play*, Bill Masters later said that Alex "wrote a parody on the type of thing we're doing—before he knew about us. It was a delightful little farce, but it happened to have a helluva lot of clinical application. But he didn't know it at the time."[82]

Masters and Johnson themselves suggested a more sober-minded version of Goggins and Dulcinea, despite the fact that Alex was not yet acquainted with the St. Louis clinicians. "*Come Out to Play* started [out] to be simply a comic novel," Alex wrote in 1975, in a publisher's note to

**** He would not publish on the subject until a decade later. AC, "Likelihood of Human Pheromones," *Nature* 230 (1971).

an first American edition of the book. "Now I think it was the manifesto of which *The Joy of Sex* commences the implementation."

HOW MIGHT ONE RECONCILE the righteous activism of the Committee of 100 with the more humorous, culturally subversive approach to effecting change that *Come Out to Play* suggested? Alex never addressed the question, but at the time it may not have seemed such an abrupt shift.

Mass protest was a fundamentally different kind of political practice from the workplace- and community-centered organizing of previous decades, which fit in much better with electoral campaigning. Lacking a grassroots base, the antinuclear movement worked in a more oblique way to change public opinion—"politics carried out by other means," Woodcock called it—which could be through spectacle, direct action, or media outreach but had the objective, in every case, of capturing public attention. Humor, culture jamming (as it would later be known), and other means of exposing the emperor's lack of clothes were as much a part of the arsenal as solemn declarations, marches, and petitions.

Much as the civil rights marches of the early 1960s helped give birth to the counterculture of the latter part of the decade in the United States, the nuclear disarmament movement was a seedbed of the liberated, less class-bound society that appeared to be burgeoning in the UK. Participation was a social and cultural as well as a political statement. Within a couple of years, the Beatles would explode onto the scene, and an irreverent, cross-class youth culture in Britain became more prominent.

The Aldermaston marchers—trudging for days, camping, enduring hours of tense standoff with the authorities, only their group solidarity giving them a chance of success—seemed to embody the new society in a nutshell. Many were attracted to the disarmament campaign by the presence of Bertrand Russell, an antiauthoritarian whom many of them—including Alex—had read at university and someone who had made his own notorious experiments in free love in the '20s.[83]

Charles Radcliffe, the future Situationist and anthropologist of youth subcultures who was also active in the campaign, called the young people who joined the nuclear disarmament movement "the largest and most influential youth movement in British history." Anyone who doubts that the CND was primarily a youth organization, he wrote, "should read contemporary reports of Aldermaston marches."[84] The marchers' political commitment ranged from very deep to nearly nonexistent, but they had in common a feeling that the movement would provide a place and a group of people with whom they felt at home. For young people looking for a cause or even just vaguely rebellious, Aldermaston was one of the things one *did*, and social, cultural, and sexual liberation were as much a draw as political engagement.

With *Come Out to Play*, then, Alex was appealing to approximately the same audience he had worked to recruit for the marches and sit-downs of the CND, the DAC, and the Committee of 100. This young audience shared not only a dread of nuclear annihilation but also the intuition that the victory of "life-affirming values," such as sexual liberation, was bound up with the achievement of disarmament and an end to war. Responding to this audience, other British artists were following somewhat the same trajectory as Alex. Karel Reisz, for instance, who codirected *March to Aldermaston*, made his name in 1960 with the gritty working-class drama *Saturday Night and Sunday Morning*, but followed it with *Morgan!*, a wacky, fantasy-filled comedy, and an extravagant film about the life of Isadora Duncan, both starring onetime disarmament campaigner Vanessa Redgrave. Other filmmakers of the realist, Kitchen Sink school took similar routes.

The year after Alex's new novel appeared, Eyre & Spottiswoode brought out a new collection of his poetry, the first in more than a decade, which Routledge had earlier rejected (saying it wasn't long enough).[85] *Haste to the Wedding* consists partly of stray poems Alex had written in the preceding decade and partly of newer ones that represented a departure from the "more Rilkean" verse he had written in the '40s, he said in a recorded interview for the British Council a few years later. These newer poems drew on the tradition of "gallant compliment" of the seventeenth- and eighteenth-century English poets. Almost all were short, pithy, and rhymed, unlike much of his earlier work.

One of the best of the first group was "Dylan Thomas on a Gramophone Record," an elegy that Alex had written after the poet's death and that had appeared in John Lehmann's *London Magazine* the year before.[86] Instead of his usual classical imagery and references, Alex used the Christian ceremony of the Eucharist to capture what was lost and what remained with Thomas's passing. He imagines the poet cut down by the "mortal moon" and baked into a "communion-thin" wafer.

> It waits for neither wine nor priest
>
> but set on its side—

holding the thorn against its breast
the wafer turns to word.
The "sapphire nail" falls, and
up stands his voice like a harvest ghost
out of the hungry dish.
But the word that lies in that black host
can never again be flesh.

Of the newer poems, the critic, educator, anarchist, and noted rock climber Harold Drasdo singled out "In the Museum," in which a moment of understanding passes between a poet and a young woman sketching a ruin from the graves of Ur. Drasdo deemed it one of the most remarkable poems of the past decade and compared it favorably with Philip Larkin's "Churchgoing."[87] It was a well-observed comparison. Alex's new poems were more in line with the very controlled writing of Larkin and the other Movement poets than with the Neo-Romantics with whom he had earlier identified so strongly. The grand rhetoric still cropped up here and there, but most of his new work was characterized by "lucidity, accessibility, rhyme, and structured form," the scholar Arthur Salmon later noted.[88] It would continue to do so in his later collections.

Haste to the Wedding also contained another tribute to a deceased poet, Emily Dickinson; "Medieval," in which the poet contemplates his age ("Forty's the roof of age, they say"); and a couple of poems of protest—against sell-out politicians and idealists who've lost their ideals. The rest celebrate physical love and the free exercise thereof.

Lady, the whimsical restraints
imposed by inexperienced saints
on modes of procreation
have little interest for us.
We share the honours without fuss
by frequent alternation.[89]

Despite Alex's claim to be reviving a poetic genre that dated back two centuries, some critics were outraged by his mildly suggestive poems (one, "The Charmer," starts out in limerick form). Others, at a time when the Beats were arriving in the hands of British readers, found them too mild. For the eminent critic A. Alvarez, Alex's writing was "too crude and aggressive for his frankness to seem any less obsessive than the more conventional English reticence."[90]

But some greeted the new collection admiringly. The critic and broadcaster Derek Parker, in *Poetry Review*, called *Haste to the Wedding* "witty, unaffected and intensely readable." "The technical proficiency of these verses (five-finger exercises in almost every meaning of the phrase) is very considerable, and one or two poems are as good as anything Dr. Comfort has yet done." Above all, Alex's new poems lacked "the stifling sense of respectability and sensitivity surrounding almost all contemporary poets like a shroud."[91] The poet Richard Kell, in a roundup of British poetry for 1962, couldn't see why anyone would object to the kind of verse Alex was putting out, if it was well done. "If a poet is exuberantly interested in the varieties of sexual behavior," he wrote, "and feels like celebrating them in light verse that is both humorous and clever, I am prepared to be entertained: as I was in this case."[92]

As the jacket copy announced, Alex's poems were "in celebration of the pleasure which men and women can have in each other—of love as play—and up in arms against that ponderous, public, destructive world which threatens the private delight."[93] This was a logical extension of the public positions he had taken on sex since delivering the talks that were published as *Barbarism and Sexual Freedom* more than a dozen years earlier. "The basic problem of war prevention lies, perhaps, in bringing these life-centered values into education and the home—a problem wrapped up with the whole structure of the family, sexual and personal attitude," he had written in 1954.[94] The difference in the early '60s was that Alex's personal life was starting to reflect his ideas.

Both *Come Out to Play* and *Haste to the Wedding*, like most of his previous books, were dedicated to his wife. "For Ruth, who put ideas in my head," was the inscription for the first; for the second, he chose a line from Catullus: "For Ruth: *ne diu taceat procax fescennina iocatio*" ("Nor longer silent is lewd Fescinnine jest"). But the references would have puzzled just about anyone who knew the couple. Ruth was not the sort either to give her husband "ideas" or to appreciate "lewd" humor in general. The covert dedicatee may have been Jane Henderson, with whom Alex had begun an affair.

Alex and Ruth's marriage had not been in crisis, but their circumstances were changing as they entered middle age. Nick started at Highgate, his father's old public school, in 1959, and for the first five terms he was a full boarder, thereafter coming home only on the weekends. They were only able to afford the tuition because Nick had won a scholarship, and Ruth went back to work as a child care officer for the Essex County Council to help defray the expense, the first time she had held a job since Nick was born. The job was demanding and necessitated her relearning to drive and buying a car—an Austin A40 Farina.[95] But it also gave her more time away from Alex, whose relentless activity could at times be too much for her.[96]

Ruth and Alex's inclinations were changing as well. Goggins wasn't just a fictional alter ego but a reflection of the way Alex was beginning to see himself. Always entertaining when he presided at the dinner table—he didn't converse, he discoursed, Ruth used to say—he now took to making the occasional, mildly racy joke in mixed company, which always provoked Ruth to stiffen and look away. Earlier, when Nick's school circulated a letter to parents asking them to give their sons a talk on sex ("personal hygiene"), Alex's chat with his twelve-year-old quickly descended into paternal embarrassment, and Nick had to fill in the gaps by consulting his father's medical texts. Looking back, "I probably heard less talk about sex than the average child," Nick said.[97]

Now Alex enjoyed pushing his wife to relax some of her Nonconformist modesty. More than once, Nick recalled, Alex asked her to wear her bikini while gardening so that he could better enjoy watching her from the window. One morning, after the milkman in his horse-drawn cart had passed down their street, he asked her to take a shovel, collect the manure left behind, and use it to fertilize the flowerbeds—again, in her bikini. Ruth obliged.

Suburban life still suited her, but her own marriage and family life no longer quite fit the model. Alex was traveling more, and, with Nick boarding at Highgate, she was more often alone. She had been close friends with a neighbor family, Jack and Vi Hollingsworth, and their three children. When Vi died, Ruth and Jack grew close, but then he remarried, and the family grew more distant.[98] By 1960 she had grown depressed, and Alex arranged for her to see Desmond Pond, an eminent British psychiatrist who had been at Clare College, Cambridge, at the same time he was at Trinity. Ruth had "a desperate loneliness inside her," Pond told Alex. She was unable to help herself, he said. [99] He suggested inpatient treatment, but Ruth was only willing to commit to outpatient sessions, and she began these soon afterward. It was about this time too that she returned to work, perhaps as much to fight the loneliness as to help cover Nick's schooling.

She kept trying to make their life together accommodate Alex's sharper interest in the physical—they briefly took up ballroom dancing, for instance—but Alex didn't really want Ruth to change. He needed a woman who, like his mother, would put him at the center of her world and provide a substitute for the fuller social life he never felt the need or the desire to pursue. In this respect, his marriage was successful and suited him well on its own terms. He wanted something else besides.

So too, apparently, did Jane Henderson. If Jane had taken a different route in life from that of her former roommate, she was also quite a different personality. Ruth was dark blonde, attractive, friendly, but somewhat formal, not given to physical displays—Nick recalled that she only hugged him once in her life, when he was accepted to Cambridge—and not one to broadcast her views or preferences. As to the latter, she tended to defer to her more outspoken husband. Their son speculates that she retained some of her religious faith after Alex abandoned his in the '40s, but it was hard to know for sure, because she generally left this topic to her husband as well. Ruth inspired a great deal of affection from her family and friends—she was "admired," her son recalled—but not passion.

Shorter, with dark, wavy hair, Jane was not conventionally attractive, but she could be striking in her own, more bohemian way, and she projected a stronger physical presence than her friend, her hair brushed back casually rather than tamed into a more conventional coiffure and her lipstick often not applied precisely according to code. Unlike Ruth, Jane was more apt to display her emotions; she was opinionated and spoke her mind, and when she wanted something, made it plain.[100]

At the dinner table, Jane enjoyed sparring with Alex in a way that Ruth preferred not to, and, as the '50s wore on, she had more opportunities to do so. Jane sometimes came along on weekend trips with them and Nick, and mid-decade she accompanied Alex and Ruth on a holiday to Yugoslavia. When away, Jane wrote letters to both, as well as to Nick, who regarded her as an unofficial aunt. Returning from a family vacation, the Comforts would often stay at Jane's flat in London before heading home to Loughton. Jane came more and more to think of herself as part of the household. Their concerns—especially Alex's—were hers—for instance, the risks he ran in basing some of the characters in *Come Out to Play* on prominent people.

She said later that she had always been a little bit in love with Alex going back to Cambridge.[101] Nick, though, located the beginning of the affair in 1960, about the time his father was writing *Come Out to Play*. The turning point was perhaps been an evening when Alex told Nick he had taken Jane out to dinner "to discuss some problems she was having."[102] That may have been more than an excuse: while she projected a good deal of self-assurance in company, Jane was not living the life she had foreseen for herself. Her career, after a fellowship at the prestigious Tavistock Institute in social science, had stagnated. By the end of the decade, rather than moving up the ladder in teaching, social work, child psychology, or academics, she was working as a librarian at the London School of Economics. She had never married, nor had she enjoyed much sexual experience.

Jane needed someone in her life, but so did Alex, although he may not have realized it at first. Nick later recalled that Jane was more apt to praise Alex's accomplishments, to the point of a fierce loyalty, whereas Ruth was always more measured.[103] They began having sex at Jane's flat on Lady Margaret Road, in the manner of many such involvements, but Alex, who Nick, looking back, believed had never looked at another woman previously, found himself in an unexpectedly intense situation. Jane was a more passionate person than his wife. She could be emotionally demanding. Rather than bringing him up short, Alex found this exciting, if a little frightening. Emotionally as well as physically, and in a remarkably short time, he felt closer—more intimate—with Jane than he ever had with anyone. Sex with her wasn't merely dutiful or simply desire acted on but something more consuming. It was as if he was finally experiencing, in full color, something he had only known in black and white.

Together, in the privacy of a London flat, these two middle-class, middle-aged people set off on a sexual voyage of discovery. There was something almost child-like in good sex, they found, to their delight. "Bed is the place to play all the games you have ever wanted to play, at the play-level," Alex would write years later in *The Joy of Sex*.[104] Or, as he expressed it in one of the poems in *Haste to the Wedding*,

> Babies' and lovers' toes express
> ecstacies of wantonness.
> That's a language which we lose
> with the trick of wearing shoes[105]

Alex and Jane tried different positions and techniques and began documenting the results in drawings, Polaroids, and a notebook. When they seemed to run out of ideas, Alex could access his growing pile of research on sexual practices. For the most part, Alex and Jane's preferred recreations were fairly conventional—bondage and role-playing he found more interesting to read about than to indulge in—but because they were making up for lost time, they wanted to know everything about their new obsession, and as quickly as possible. The affair had turned an interest in sex, which for Alex had been a quasi-academic side interest, into a genuine physical experience. But he couldn't stop being a scientist and social thinker. As such, the next step was to know more about the experience. The step after that would be to reveal his findings and conclusions to the world.

This was still some ways off, however. Most immediately, Alex had to tell Ruth about Jane, because it became clear the affair was not going to quietly play itself out. Despite his unconventional views on sex, Alex took his responsibility to Ruth and Nick seriously. But he lacked close friends to whom he could turn for advice aside from his wife—"there was never a person he could share his innermost thoughts with," Nick would recall.[106] Like many in such a position, he took the path of least resistance.

"When I was small, we didn't have arguments in our home; I didn't hear a raised voice until around 1960," Nick remembered. "My father was an extremely polite and considerate person, and my mother was brought up not to argue with people. It was really a placid home." There was no need for this to change, it seemed, when Alex gave Ruth to understand, after less than a year of morning and evening trysts with Jane, that he wanted an open marriage.

Alex didn't want to give up a relationship that worked well for him just because he had started a second. Ruth was a familiar and popular figure with his family and professional colleagues, he was part of her family scene in Loughton, and in the comparatively straitlaced world of British scientific academia, he had reason to be concerned about the impact of a divorce on his career. Ruth, as it happened, didn't want to abandon an agreeable life as the wife of an eminent biologist and literary figure who was, moreover, a conscientious if not abundant provider, however painful the new reality was. For perhaps the first time, they had genuine arguments.

But for the time being, she also wanted the affair to remain a secret outside the family. Ruth would continue to be Alex's only partner so far as their friends and professional acquaintances knew. Working out the details of the new arrangement would take time, but Ruth insisted early on that Alex save the weekends for her, while Jane, for her part, was willing to accept an imperfect arrangement to be with a man she by now deeply loved. Nick didn't need to know anything had changed, the adults thought, because he was at school most of the time. In the meantime, his parents did their best to maintain a semblance of normality.

The family continued to take vacations together, and in 1961, when the affair was as much as a year old, Jane accompanied the three of them on their Irish holiday in Mullaghmore.

Despite Alex's political nonconformity, it was really a fairly ordinary affair, confined to a London flat and clearly destined to make all three participants unhappy. Ironically, what gave it a chance of continuing—at least for a time—was not any commitment to some radical ideal of open relationship but instead their Englishness, their impulse to carry on and make the best of it. Ruth, the stoic, still loved Alex, and the new arrangement represented the only way to retain the stability she cherished. Alex, even amid the excitement of his adventure with Jane, wanted to preserve something of that stability too. Jane had Alex, part-time—and perhaps eventually, all the time. At least for the time being, he rationalized, sharing himself between these two women was the best way to do the right thing for everyone.

CHAPTER 11

The Controversialist (1962–1965)

"*Come Out to Play* makes Dr. Comfort's brand image even more baffling than before," *Punch*'s reviewer R. G. G. Price wrote when the novel appeared. "Poet, essayist, philosophic anarchist and specialist in the biology of ageing, sometimes he bursts out all over the place, reviewing, publishing books, fighting in the correspondence columns of the weeklies, and sometimes he disappears completely from view."[1]

The last was seldom the case in '60s, when every facet of politics, culture, and science seemed to be reshaping itself with bewildering speed. Alex's media profile expanded accordingly. Between 1961 and the end of 1970 he published eight new books, mostly nonfiction, plus a translation and a revision of a previous translation; twenty-six scientific papers, mostly on aging; more than eighty book reviews; dozens of other articles; and too many letters to the editor to count. Starting in 1964, he edited a new scientific journal, *Experimental Gerontology*, through Robert Maxwell's Pergamon Press, and he edited a series of books on aspects of human nature for the publisher Thomas Nelson and Sons.* He wrote and narrated two television documentaries for the BBC, supplied the story line for a drama on BBC TV, and wrote two unproduced scripts, while continuing to appear steadily as a guest on network programs. As his profile in the field of aging grew, he was traveling and addressing scientific conferences and colloquia more and more often and was quoted as an expert in articles and features.

Alex was once again writing about sex, but after his imprisonment he published much less about day-to-day politics, and after *Haste to the Wedding* and *Come Out to Play* he again lapsed into silence as a novelist

* Later the despoiler of Mirror Group Newspapers' pension fund, "Captain Bob" Maxwell sent Alex a Christmas card every year. Nicholas Comfort, *Copy!*, 362.

and poet. Instead, he was emerging as one of Britain's better-known all-around public intellectuals. A sense of the figure he cut comes through in a 1966 book review by Anthony Burgess. "To adherents of unreason," Burgess wrote, "Dr Comfort has become one of the rational (meaning anarchic or permissive) devils, joining the distinguished company of monsters like Machiavelli, Voltaire, and Bernard Shaw. On television he has the unnerving predatory look of a cant-hunter, and his name suggests something apotropaic conferred by the superstitious, as Central European peasants called the weasel 'pretty kindly one.'"

He was no longer as trim as he had been in his thirties, and a 1963 profile piece in the *Observer* described him thus: "Rounded, compact, and apparently stable, he looked, especially in long shot, curiously like the late Harold Laski."** After having renounced smoking for a number of years, he was back to cigars—cheap ones, "made of lettuce and kleenex," he once said—and from this time on was rarely seen without one in hand and several more in his pocket.[2]

Many of his writings from the '60s deal with science and its conjunction with culture and human behavior in general. Together, his book reviews—always concise, witty, and attuned to the bigger picture—form a close commentary on many of the currents running through European and American thought during the decade. Authors he wrote about included colleagues like Medawar, Haldane, Julian Huxley, Zhores Medvedev, and James Watson, as well as Masters and Johnson, Herbert Marcuse, Michel Foucault, Arthur Koestler, Konrad Lorenz, William S. Burroughs (*Nova Express* he considered "bilge"), Rachel Carson, Benjamin Spock, Lewis Mumford, Thomas Szasz, and Michael Crichton.

Anarchism and scientific humanism were still the main pillars of Alex's philosophical position, along with a dose of Freudian psychology. In the '40s, in books like *Art and Social Responsibility* and *Authority and Delinquency*, he had analyzed the State, its penchant for violence and psychopathic behavior, and the importance of individual resistance to its commands. But he also emphasized the need for education and experiments in cooperative and communal living as means to develop a public geared to resist the State.[3] This, almost as much as his opposition to nuclear weapons, was what had made him such a passionate participant in the nuclear disarmament campaigns.

Other anarchists were trying to bring their intellectual tradition into

** Harold Laski (1893–1950), political philosopher and economist, was a leading spokesperson for British Marxism in the '30s and '40s.

line with scientific humanism. When *Reconstruir*, an Argentine anarchist journal, invited Alex to contribute, the editors noted that one of their purposes was "to put Anarchism 'in tune' (up-to-date) with the modern developments of sociology and social psychology, anthropology and economics."[4] Alex sought to create an intellectual and programmatic underpinning for this part of his thinking: the role that science and medicine would need to play to help achieve a just society without capitalism and the State. Between *Come Out to Play* and *Haste to the Wedding*, he published another book that pulled together some of his thoughts on these issues.

The project started with a lecture he delivered at UCL in January 1960, that was then published as "Darwin and Freud" in the July 16, 1960, issue of *The Lancet*. Alex's lecture is essentially an argument for greater collaboration between biologists and psychoanalysts. Darwin's and Freud's theories complement and complete each other, he said, yet the two fields rarely come into contact. "They are the godparents of man's objectivity toward Man," he wrote, Darwin demonstrating that humans aren't unique, and Freud that "we have no insight into our own motives." Many people still did not accept Darwin's findings, and, Alex wrote, "general scientists have treated Freud rather as the Americans have treated the Communist Chinese—by mixing a morose hostility with the public pretence that he is not there."

Darwin could have learned from Freud to factor the development of human consciousness into his theory of natural selection. Freud had trouble explaining what role infantile sexuality, the Oedipal complex, fear of castration, and sexual "deviations" like homosexuality played in human evolution. They were there—or so he thought—but what purpose did they serve? Darwin, Alex suggested, could have helped out by noting that they might have functioned in early human societies to keep children from fighting with their parents—and, more intriguingly, that sexual repression contributed to the mind's division into conscious and unconscious levels, which in turn could have produced "the most significant adaptation in mammalian history, the emergence of conceptual thought."

These what-ifs served to reinforce Alex's point that there was a nongenetic side to human evolution. A year later he revised his talk for inclusion in a new book, *Darwin and the Naked Lady: Discursive Essays on Biology and Art*. The essays included a piece on Indian erotic art and another on the origins of sex-and-violence literature, by the likes of Mickey Spillane and Ian Fleming ("non-pictorial comic books written for the literate"), in third-century Alexandrine Greek novels like *Daphnis and Chloe*.[5]

HERBERT READ FOUND ALEX'S argument in *Darwin and the Naked Lady* a bit obscure and asked him to write a preface to clarify it (he didn't), but one old friend and colleague, Jack Haldane, was greatly interested, even if he wasn't sure he agreed with all of it.

In November 1956, just as the Suez Crisis was reaching its peak, Haldane had announced he was leaving UCL to take a position at the Indian Statistical Institute (ISI) in Calcutta (Kolkata). Asked if the invasion of Egypt by Britain and its allies was a reason, he said yes, and added a second: the US military bases in the UK. "I want to live in a free country where there are no foreign troops all over the place," he said. "Yes, I do mean Americans."[6]

The ISI was keen to build up India into a scientific power, and Haldane was the foremost geneticist of his time. It made sense for its director, P. C. Mahalanobis, a brilliant statistician and scientific polymath who was arguably as much a creator of modern India as Gandhi or Nehru, to recruit him to direct a program on animal and plant genetics. The sixty-five-year-old Haldane fell in love with India instantly, taught himself Sanskrit and Bengali, gave up eating meat, and adopted the Indian dhoti and kurta as his habitual dress, even on trips back to Europe, the United States, and the UK ("60 years in socks is enough").[7]

Haldane quickly relaunched his research at the ICI, assisted by an able Indian staff, and he was soon urging old friends, from Isaiah Berlin to Aldous Huxley, to visit him in his new home.[8] But he was the same obstreperous character he had always been. In February 1961 he quarreled, predictably, with the autocratic Mahalanobis and set up his own institute in Bubhaneswar, the capital of Odisha state. In November, after reading *Darwin and the Naked Lady*, Haldane wrote Alex a long letter brimming with observations and suggestions for further research. Then he shifted to his other reason for writing. "Seriously, why don't you come here?" he asked. "Given your political views, I can't see why you don't come visit India with a view to considering residence here. We have politicians quite as psychopathic as any Europeans or Americans, but they are fortunately almost powerless. There is much to be said for insufficient government, though it is very irritating. You would find it hard to get your children a decent education, but they would probably not be bombed. And they could wander about naked in their early years."[9]

Sparked by his continuing study of different forms of sexual experience and perhaps by Haldane's emigration four years earlier, Alex was already quite interested in India. In 1959 he wrote an article on the function of erotic art for his old publisher John Lehmann, now running the *London Magazine*, which he later reworked for *Darwin and the Naked Lady*. Starting with a discussion of some recently published books on Hindu erotic sculpture, Alex asked why Westerners were shocked by the explicit representations of sex in the temples of Khajuraho and Konarak, and whether Indian artists who idealized genital pleasure might not be shocked by the sadistic iconography in the Christian tradition.

His real purpose, however, was argue for the West to encourage art explicitly intended to stimulate desire rather than suppress it. "Incitement is inherent in all art that 'celebrates' human pleasures," Alex argued, "and a wholly worthy artistic aim." Doing so might even help break down the wall going up between high art and the general public. "Creative artists are the professional makers of amulets—of objects wanted for the Wrong Reasons." Turning their attention to the erotic, "they just might find an audience among live people, who want art for the wrong reasons." They might form a counterbalance to what he saw as Western society's celebration of death.[10]

Alex was far from the only Westerner who detected solutions to his culture's neuroses in an Asian society. What set him apart was that he wasn't interested in Indian religion so much as its philosophical tradition and culture, and the impact they could have on the social: on attitudes toward pleasure and pain, on habits of thought, and how these might dovetail with liberatory trends in Europe and America. He was therefore decidedly averse to Western mystics who pretended to interpret Indian spirituality for their home audiences. "The people in our culture who are most receptive to Asian philosophies tend precisely and fatally to be those incapable by nature of critical re-presentation," he complained in a scathing review of a book by the expatriate English popularizer Alan W. Watts. The best go-betweens, instead, were "scientific sceptics" like Haldane.[11]

Alex got his chance to experience India firsthand in 1962, when Mahalanobis invited him to spend two months at the ISI lecturing on gerontology and recent breakthroughs in medical science. He contributed several articles to the *Calcutta Statesman* suggesting directions that Indian research on aging could take and continued a study of Sanskrit language and literature, with help from Mahalanobis, that he had already begun in England. "P.C.M. introduced me to India," he wrote in a tribute after Mahalanobis's death in 1972. "What I got [was] the equivalent of a second education which will remain with me for life [from] someone to whom I owe as much as to anyone I ever met."[12]

Whether Alex took Haldane's advice and visited Khajuraho and Konarak is not known, but he saw a good deal of his old colleague as well and thought him a *sadhu* (holy man or sage).[13] "He said he was the only Hindu atheist," Alex recalled of Haldane, with obvious admiration, "but when one saw him *in situ* it was obvious that he was a natural Kshatriya, a philosopher of the warrior caste. He belonged."[14]

After Ireland, India's culture, people, and thought had a more powerful impact on Alex than any other outside England. He maintained contact with several scientists he met there, and in later years India would influence his philosophical and even his scientific work. Like many visitors, once he left, he was perpetually on the lookout for an excuse to go back. When he returned home, he came laden with Indian fabrics, artifacts, a notebook full of recipes, and even, for Nick, an LP by the sitar virtuoso Ravi Shankar, telling his son this was going to be the next big thing, information the fifteen-year-old received somewhat quizzically at the time. Indian food was now Alex's culinary passion. "I could subsist exclusively on curry," he said a few years later, "and I like it hotter than the holes in hell."[15] That Christmas, he curried the family's traditional midday meal, and, when Nick visited him at UCL, which he did regularly, they would lunch at one of the nearby curry palaces: the Agra, the Shahi, the Noor Jahan.[16]

Armed with a fair knowledge of Sanskrit, Alex was eager to get back to a project he had started the previous year: a translation of a classic twelfth-century Indian erotic text that went by several titles: the *Ratirahasya* ("Secrets of Rati'), the *Koka Shastra* ("Scripture of Koka"), and *The Secret of the Game of Love*. Later he said that his initial work on the text gave him the idea for *Come Out to Play*.[17] Higham circulated it to most of the prominent UK publishing houses in fall of 1961, but they all turned it down, with some regrets. Maurice Temple Smith at Eyre & Spottiswode would have "liked very much" to publish it, but as Her Majesty's printers, the firm had even more trepidations than it had expressed about *Come Out to Play*.[18]

The project lay dormant for over a year, until Alex returned from India, but then Mervyn Horder at Gerald Duckworth, which had brought out *Sexual Behavior in Society*, volunteered a suggestion. "It is one of the rare cases," he advised, "where a rather sober little preface by someone professionally concerned like the Chairman of the Marriage Guidance Council, or some friendly O.M. or similar who could hardly be gainsaid, would do a good job of work."[19] In February 1963 Alex showed his translation to W. G. Archer, a former Indian civil servant and keeper of the Indian Section at the Victoria and Albert Museum, who was now retired.[20] Archer was a leading scholar of Indian art and literature, as was his wife, Mildred. Both were socialists and had been supporters of the independence movement. Most important, Archer had brought out several books with the publisher George Allen and Unwin and was about to issue another, a new edition of the *Kama Sutra*, which Alex was reviewing.[21] Once this was launched, Archer thought the *Ratirahasya*, which he considered the most important Indian treatise on love after the *Kama Sutra,* would be an excellent follow-up.[22]

Alex had written an introduction giving an interpretation of the text and an overview of the tradition of Indian erotic literature. Archer, writing to publisher Rayner Unwin, called it a "quite exceptionally brilliant piece of work which makes a very real contribution to Indian studies and at the same time places the text in a modern context." The translation itself was "admirably put."[23] Unwin was reluctant—his firm was taking a chance with the *Kama Sutra* and was "leaning over backwards" not to be seen as one of "'those publishers.'"[24] But Archer pressed him, arguing that if he turned Comfort down, Alex was bound to go elsewhere. "You then get not a welcome successor but a very definite rival. Does this really make sense?"[25] After some vetting to assure himself that the new book would not create legal problems, Unwin agreed.[26] His provisos were that Alex expand his introduction to include a more detailed survey of the major Indian erotic texts and leave out a set of illustrations and diagrams he had found of various bandhas, or coital postures, described in the book. In other words, Unwin wanted the whole presentation to be as scholarly and tasteful as possible.

Alex agreed to revise the introduction, while the matter of the illustrations was left up in the air. He had wanted to use *The Secret of the Game of Love* as the title of the book, but Archer and Unwin persuaded him to accept a more circumspect title: *The Koka Shastra and Other Medieval Indian Writings on Love*. With that, it seemed, the deal was done.

But then the trouble began. Transliterated into English, Sanskrit has a wealth of diacritical marks indicating how the letters are to be pronounced. Alex had pitched his translation to Archer partly as a means of bringing to a popular audience a text that had never before appeared in English, yet now he wanted to use a maximum of diacritics, since "it looks better that way to the pandits [the learned]." Archer, who was impressed by Alex's knowledge but had a great deal more background as a Sanskrit scholar, preferred to keep diacritics, footnotes, and other scholarly apparatus to a minimum, lest the general reader be put off. After Archer marked up Alex's manuscript to eliminate any that were not absolutely necessary, Alex spent a morning "with an india-rubber," reversing the changes.[27]

Archer would not be the last to discover just how difficult Alex could be. "He is a creature of sudden whims, impulses, moods, etc etc, inconsistencies, contradictions that one just can't predict," a frustrated Archer complained to Unwin. "In spite of all his protestations that he is writing for the 'general public,' what he really has in mind is a tiny group of Sanskritists whom he wants to impress. He is therefore irremediably wedded to a great deal of almost unintelligible detail that a 'Kama Sutra reader' would just make nothing of. So there we are!" Caustically, Alex told Archer he had no use for an editor, only a publisher, and suggested that Unwin himself would have to mediate their relationship from then on.[28]

Alex agreed to minimize the diacriticals—Krishna would do rather than Kṛṣṇa—but next he quarreled over Archer's preface, which he thought too long, "parasitic"—presumably stealing some of Alex's own content—and therefore a bid to "take over" the book. Unwin stood by the preface, which had nothing but good to say about Alex's translation and scholarship, but then Archer complained that his collaborator had let a host of spelling errors and inconsistencies creep into the page proofs—and had inserted diacritics into his preface without consulting him.[29] These were removed, Unwin keeping Alex in the dark as much as possible, but more delays resulted when Alex, through his agent, insisted that the translation be copyrighted to him rather than to the press.[30]

As Christmas approached, further disagreements arose. The publisher was getting cold feet about some of the less conventional matter the book covered. Alex wrote directly to Sir Stanley Unwin, chairman of the firm and Rayner's father, informing him, "I cannot remove the reference to plural intercourse without falsifying the text." The point was taken. But then the illustrations became a sticking point. Alex had reluctantly agreed to let Unwin omit the illustrated bandhas, which no one but he seemed to like, but now Archer was upset that the publisher wanted to omit a set of diagrams as well. "It is the first time that any scholar has attempted to show what these ancient Indian texts are describing and the diagrams are a very real aid to understanding them," he pleaded. "If we abandon the diagrams, we are losing the chance to make a real scholarly advance."[31]

The diagrams themselves were fairly innocuous, the long-suffering Unwin agreed, but he had other concerns. In 1959, the Obscene Publications Act had narrowed the grounds for ordering erotic publications banned. It still defined obscenity as "depraved and corrupt" language but added that a few naughty words here and there were not enough to make the case and that publication could take place if the work was shown to be in "the public good"—that is, "in the interests of science, literature, art or learning, or of other objects of general concern." That opened the way for *Regina v. Penguin*, the historic decision at the Old Bailey that finally allowed the UK publication the following year of *Lady Chatterley's Lover*, D. H. Lawrence's long-banned, sexually frank novel about an affair between a gamekeeper and his aristocratic employer's wife.[32] That decision inspired Philip Larkin's famous quip, in his poem "Annus Mirabilis":

> Sexual intercourse began
> In nineteen sixty-three
> (which was rather late for me)—
> Between the end of the "Chatterley" ban
> And the Beatles' first LP.

Matters weren't so settled as that would suggest, however, and in December 1963, when Unwin was preparing to publish Alex's *Koka Shastra*, another obscenity case was brewing, this one involving John Cleland's bawdy 1748 novel, *Memoirs of a Woman of Pleasure*, better known as *Fanny Hill*. A small publisher, Mayflower Books, had brought out an unexpurgated paperback edition of the novel. When the Bow Street magistrate Sir Robert Blundell got word, he had copies seized from Mayflower and from a bookshop on Tottenham Court Road and proceeded to prosecute the bookseller.

Headlines about the *Fanny Hill* case prompted Rayner Unwin to hold up publication of *The Koka Shastra* until a decision came down. If the Director of Public Prosecutions won the case, he told Alex, "then almost certainly he will attempt to broaden the area of definition that he has established, and *The Koka Shastra* might give him an opening [to] jump on retailers in magistrates courts." That would make it extremely difficult if not impossible for Unwin to get the book into bookshops. If

Alex wanted his book out without further delay, Unwin concluded, he would have to agree to do so without the diagrams.[33] Alex capitulated. (The Crown won its case over *Fanny Hill* but lost on appeal.)

The long-suffering Unwin was proved right on another point he had raised with Archer before agreeing to take on the book, however: that it may have been beaten to the punch. The *Kama Sutra* had been a publishing success—it couldn't fail to be, having previously been ranked as one of the most-pirated books in the English language—but it left only crumbs in its wake, and Unwin failed to sell many copies of *The Koka Shastra*.[34] "Even the diagrams would not have made much difference at this stage," Unwin wrote Archer when the latter inquired about sales. "The fact is that the revolution has occurred and this is no longer so sensational or extraordinary as it would have been say a couple of years ago."[35]

All was not lost. The book found a British paperback publisher, Tandem Books, in 1965, and an American publisher, Stein and Day, the same year.[36] Ballantine Books signed on as the US paperback publisher of *The Koka Shastra* shortly thereafter. Even Spain, still under the dour heel of Generalissimo Franco, was interested. Sagitario, a Barcelona publisher, agreed to put out a Spanish translation of Alex's text, also in 1965.[37]

At a time when sexual frankness seemed to be breaking out all over, even a determinedly scholarly production was bound to excite comment if not huge sales, and, as usual, Alex's introduction and notes were witty and lucid. ("Avoidance of the index finger as too heavy is a piece of advice which no Western text on marriage counselling seems to have discovered. The Indian lover normally uses more than one finger at a time, keeping the tips together"[38]). His love of and immersion in Indian culture too came through engagingly. A reviewer for the *Sunday Telegraph* helpfully characterized *The Koka Shastra* as not strictly a sex guide but rather a marriage manual, a book of advice to husbands on how to understand and satisfy a wife in order to maintain a successful marriage: a distinction that would have reassured the censors.[39]

IN APRIL 1963, JUST as relations were turning frosty with Archer and just as Higham was stepping in to keep matters civil with Unwin, Alex wrote his literary representative of eighteen years with some bad news. After a session with his accountant over taxes, he had decided he could no longer afford the services of an agent. Higham could continue to represent him on any overseas sales or translations of *The Koka Shastra*. "[But as for future books,] I am afraid the inexorable logic of economics etc. etc. means that I shall have to revert to handling my own literary business." None of this, of course, reflected on Higham himself, whom Alex regarded as a diligent agent and a "personal friend."

Money matters were pressing, however. In March 1964, he contacted Higham again about selling the manuscripts and typescripts of his novels as well as his recent poetry notebooks, "containing a mixture of science, limericks, notes and work-in-progress." "I am only prepared to part with these if the prices were substantial (not necessarily 'sensational')," he stipulated.[40] Nothing came of the effort, and the material would remain in his possession for many years to come. At about the same time, Alex and Ruth appear to have talked with their neighbors about selling some land they owned in common but were turned down.[41]

Alex's annual fellowships from the Nuffield Foundation were coming to an end, and he was attempting—with the support of Medawar, who had left UCL to become director of the National Institute for Medical Research in 1962—to secure a new grant from the UK Medical Research Council to continue his work on aging. Nick was finishing up at Highgate and preparing for his exams, aiming to follow his father to Cambridge and Trinity College. Also like his father, he would need a scholarship to make ends meet. Ruth continued with her job at the Essex County Council, and Alex could still be relied on to fill out the household budget by way of his writing, but with his only steady source of income in doubt, the family cast about for ways to raise money.

Three months later, the air began to clear. Alex received his grant from the Medical Research Council—for seven years rather than one. Nick took his exams in December and was admitted to Trinity, with a scholarship in history. He took one more term at Highgate, then got a summer job at the *Guardian*—formerly the *Manchester Guardian*, now moved to London, but still publishing his father's book reviews regularly—as a messenger and occasional cub reporter. He would start at Trinity in September 1964.[42]

Something else cleared up around this time as well: Alex's migraines. Nearly twenty years after the attacks had first hit, no one had yet properly diagnosed them; his doctors thought the bouts of depression they occasionally brought on were the chief matter. The mystery finally cleared up when he was asked to refer an acquaintance to a psychotherapist, and recommended someone he had heard of: Denis Hill, who chaired the Institute of Psychiatry at the University of London. He decided to see Hill himself, and when he described his symptoms, "Hill's grin got broader and broader and he said, 'That's not a neurotic condition you have, that's an aura. You're having a temporal lobe migraine.'"[43] It was the first time Alex had heard the word "migraine" used to describe his condition.

Treating it was a trial-and-error affair. Hill, one of the first doctors in Britain to use an electroencephalograph and a leader in neuropsychiatry, first tried Alex on tricyclic antidepressants, which manipulate the reabsorption of some neurotransmitters, but they didn't entirely eliminate the attacks. Then he tried phenelzine, or Nardil, a monoamine oxidase inhibitor (MAOI) used to treat varieties of anxiety, trauma, and stress. It worked, and, except for a few minor episodes in later years, Alex was finally free of the mysterious attacks. Nick recalled, however, that his father once attended a party where he ate cheese—off-limits to persons taking Nardil—and came home behaving as if drunk. It may well have been the first and only time Ruth saw him in such a state.

IN MAY 1962, SOON after Alex returned from India, Penguin Books, which had issued *Sexual Behaviour in Society* in paperback after its initial publication a dozen years before, contacted Mervyn Horder at Duckworth to inquire about reissuing it.[44] The book had sold well and been translated into several other languages, and, if anything, the market seemed to be more welcoming to books on the topic. Alex let Horder know that he was already working on a revised edition of the book. They settled on *Sex in Society* as the title, and Higham—not yet let go as Alex's agent—quickly negotiated a US paperback deal with New American Library, which already had a deal to publish a popular book on aging that Alex was working on simultaneously.[45] When Horder received the new manuscript from Alex in August, he was pleased. "The book has grown up in a gratifying manner," he wrote back, "and I hope we shall give it the good show it deserves."[46]

Behind this eager correspondence was all parties' strong feeling that something big—a sexual revolution—was at hand, the latest one, anyway. The term "sexual revolution" had appeared as early as 1929, shortly after Margaret Mead published *Coming of Age in Samoa* in the United States, and in 1945 a book by Wilhelm Reich was published under that title in the UK. Copies of that volume were among the six tons of Reich's books, journals, and papers that were burned by order of the US Food and Drug Administration in New York City in August 1956, barely a year before Reich's tragic death in a federal prison.

Times really were changing, however. In previous decades a figure like Reich would have been persecuted, ostracized, and died in complete obscurity. In 1957 Reich's prosecution and death made him a very public martyr, and, in both the UK and the United States, what seemed like an endless series of legal challenges to the increasingly outmoded Victorian social code were grabbing headlines. Some succeeded, and some failed, but even the latter added to the pressure for reform. And while progress appeared to be faster in America, the process was oddly parallel: *Lady Chatterley's Lover* and *Fanny Hill* were the subject of groundbreaking court cases in both countries.

In the UK, scandal, and the hypocrisies it inevitably revealed, played a role in forcing the public to face the fact that official morality had little to do with private sexual practice. At the end of the year, while *Sex in Society* was under preparation at Duckworth, the Profumo case broke in the media. In fairly rapid succession the war minister denied having been involved with Christine Keeler, then was forced to admit he had lied, step down from his post, and leave Parliament. The tabloids went into a frenzy, feeding on a story that included seedy Soho nightlife, gunplay, vengeful West Indian boyfriends, and rumors of a naked masked man who served as a waiter at sex parties. The scandal helped to destabilize the Conservative government, which would be voted out the following year. John Profumo would go on to recover his good name working for the Toynbee Hall settlement in the East End, and would be named a Commander of the British Empire in 1975. Stephen Ward, a fashionable osteopath—the queen's husband and consort, Prince Philip, had been a patient—who had introduced Profumo to Keeler but later revealed the war minister's lies to the press, was made the sacrificial lamb.

In what looked like an act of political revenge, Ward, facing ruin, was charged with procuring and living off immoral earnings. Although the case was flimsy, he was convicted. He died of an overdose of barbiturates before he could be sentenced. At his funeral, one of the wreaths was dedicated "To Stephen Ward—A victim of British hypocrisy" and signed by a who's who of British artists and writers, including Alex, Penelope Gilliatt, Doris Lessing, Joan Littlewood, John Osborne, Alan Sillitoe, and Kenneth Tynan. Six weeks later, Alex received a near-hysterical anonymous letter addressing him as "Ring-leader of 20 Hypocritical Authors, Self-righteous Pacifist & Free-Lover, Champion of Vice, Ponces

& Prostitutes" and accusing him of giving "the name of Fool to every man who loves his wife and honours noble womanhood."

Historians have argued that the Profumo affair administered a death blow to the old, upper-class leadership of the Conservative Party, paving the way for the supposed meritocrats who eventually triumphed under Margaret Thatcher. This was suspected at the time as well. The pundit Malcolm Muggeridge's piece on the scandal in the *Sunday Mirror* was headlined "The Slow, Sure Death of the Upper Classes."[47] But the scandal fueled very different responses from different parts of the public. To the cultural and political Left, it demonstrated that changing attitudes about sex were part and parcel of the struggle against a rotten British establishment. The Right viewed the affair as another sign of widespread moral decay, and as such it became a rallying point for a new puritanical movement was just getting off the ground under the leadership of conservative Catholic and Protestant clergy and laypeople.[48]

Behind the headlines and denunciations, however, the sexual revolution in the early '60s was a stealthier and not altogether political affair, driven by demographic changes that had been percolating since the war, in such disparate settings as suburban bedrooms, flats and bedsits where younger people were enjoying a newfound freedom from their families, strip clubs, and bars and other safe spaces where queer people increasingly recognized themselves as a distinct community. The fashion for Wilhelm Reich's theories—and his orgone boxes—among the intelligentsia, and his persecution and death, may provide the dramatic peaks of the story, but the real changes in society were better reflected in the unpretentious popular writing of the postwar decades: the avalanche of cheap paperback novels that catered to public curiosity about lives more daring and dangerous than their own, with stories about lesbian and gay people, nudists, sadomasochists, interracial sex, and, not incidentally, cheating wives and husbands.[49]

What Kinsey had discovered and made known, Alex wrote a few years later, "was not the 'fantasies of the deranged' but the real lives of domestic squares."[50] A more representative figure of the period than Profumo, Stephen Ward, or Reich was Edna O'Brien, who in 1959 left an Ireland seemingly obsessed with female chastity, almost literally escaping with her fiancé to England with her father and brother in hot pursuit.[51] She then had two children, divorced, and wrote the *Country Girls* trilogy (1960–64), which broke numerous taboos on sexual and social matters in Ireland. Her novels were denounced as "filth" by Irish officials and burned in her hometown, but O'Brien went on to make a life for herself in London as a single mother and increasingly acclaimed author. "How do you describe a taste?" she wrote in a story in which the main character tastes her first fig and then takes a new lover into her bed. "They were a new food and he was a new man and that night in my bed he was both stranger and lover, which I used to think was the ideal bed partner."[52]

Changes that had been under way for some time suddenly accelerated. One survey estimated that 64 percent of married women in the UK had had premarital sex with their husbands between 1961 and 1965, up from 52 percent in 1956–60.[53] One innovation made an even more stark difference. The oral contraceptive pill was okayed by the US Food and Drug Administration in 1960 and approved in the UK for use by married women the following year, although not for other women until 1974.[54] While the Pill probably didn't convince more people to have more sex, its rapid adoption highlights how quickly behavior was changing in both countries.[55] Already by the '40s, some 80 percent of women in the UK were using some form of birth control. But the Pill was the first truly reliable method, and it caught on fast; by 1964, an estimated 480,000 women in the UK had used it, and by 1969, 48 percent of all women then aged twenty-three had done so. In 1964 as well, Britain's first birth control clinic specifically for unmarried women opened in London.[56] These developments inspired Alex to write a piece of comic verse attacking the Catholic Church's dogged insistence on the rhythm method as the only acceptable method of birth control, which the *New Statesman* published as "Vatican Roulette" on April 2, 1965:

> In nineteen hundred and sixty-two
> One afternoon we'd nothing to do—
> I don't know how but a stork got through;
> First blood to Father Squeezum! . . .

Alex had already argued in 1950 that the public wanted reliable, non-moralistic information about sex and that doctors and counselors were not satisfying the demand, often because they didn't have the information themselves. With *Sex in Society*, he linked the demand for reform of attitudes and policies on sex to the need for broader social change. About half the material hadn't appeared in *Sexual Behaviour in Society*, and the new book was addressed not to physicians and social workers specifically but rather to the general reader. It was also more radical in its advocacy of sexual freedom than the earlier book.

"The first lesson we need to learn in reading any literature which purports to advise on, or describe, sexual behaviour (this present book included) is that it is probably for the most part a statement of preference, prejudice and opinion," he wrote early in the text, "and only a statement of fact where it presents cast-iron evidence based on critical observation." *Sex in Society* was the most comprehensive expression of Alex's views on sex as a social phenomenon, but it was not an authoritative study. Above all, it was an optimist's plea for a relaxation of anxiety and fear around sex, a turn away from treating it as a problem and toward "sociality, permissivity, and a lowering of tension." The big question, he wrote, "is whether this can happen in time to prevent a breakdown of civilization. My personal belief is that it can and will."[57]

The basis of his confidence was threefold: changing attitudes among the young, "the growth of rational knowledge and its application to sexual ethics," and the availability of reliable contraceptives and artificial insemination. Kinsey had at last opened the way for serious study of sex as an aspect of social behavior. In time this would chase away the myths surrounding sexual activities and preferences. Contraception, especially with the appearance of the Pill, Alex noted, was playing "a role in extending freedom of choice and deepening human relationships" by removing a major source of anxiety from sexual relations. As such, it was developing into "a human right and a human freedom."[58]

These developments Alex saw as part of a larger process by which humanity arrived "at the point of reconciling its technological achievement with the type of social living that is sometimes approached by primitive societies, . . . [of] getting both 'togetherness' and technology, both mutual aid and modern medicine." As always, Alex was eager to emphasize that science, technology, and objective study were not enemies but indispensable allies in the struggle for human freedom. If this trend—a broad bringing-together of physical science and social science—should continue, then "man [would be] presented with the opportunity of attaining his adulthood." Humankind would be more relaxed, less driven and competitive, and more able to enjoy living for its own sake. Sex, or "erotic interests," would assume a new role. "[It would replace] not only the adventitious excitements we now pursue, but a fair part of individualistic art and the whole of residual religion."[59]

Sexual reform should focus on four areas: the treatment of so-called sexual deviants, the treatment of adolescents just entering their sexually mature years, the problem of gender identity, and the pattern of married and family life. Most problems related to the place of homosexuals and prostitutes in society had to do with the way they were regarded by the society, not with their specific behavior, Alex argued. While homosexuality might or might not be evidence of a neurosis, society's attitude toward it most definitely was. If that attitude changed, then social problems attributed to homosexuality would largely cease.[60]

Similarly, problems related to teen sexuality were largely a product of adults' anxious attempts to suppress it. Adolescents were becoming sexually mature earlier; teenage boys, especially since they tended to be more sexually aggressive, needed "some rudimentary insight into the ways in which girls' responses differed from their own." Instead, British schoolboys were, at best, getting literature on "hygiene" and "clean living" that was liable to do as much damage as pornography.[61]

Adults should encourage at least some degree of exploration with "sexual equivalents" such as "petting" (Alex didn't specify exactly what practices he had in mind), since they accustom boys and girls to "the need for mutual accommodation and respect." They also tend to increase the chances that boys' and girls' first experience with actual intercourse would be a good one. "Coitus *will* probably follow within a few years, and the fact should be accepted and allowed for." Accordingly, "it seems an important aim of sex education to see . . . that the boy's or the girl's first encounter with sex . . . shall be frankly pleasurable, not merely tolerated."[62]

Alex proposed two rules for sex at any age: "Thou shalt not exploit another person's feelings and wantonly expose them to an experience of rejection," and "Thou shalt not under any circumstances negligently risk producing an unwanted child." Contraceptives would solve much of the problem, Alex predicted, allowing adolescents to progress from play to earnest "in easy stages." Much of the rest would be solved by parents themselves showing their children a less-anxious, more-relaxed attitude toward sex.[63]

What about men and women who don't feel at home with the sex they were born into? Following the lead of John Money, a sexologist at Johns Hopkins University, Alex made a distinction between "sex" and "gender."[64] Gender roles are almost entirely learned, he wrote, "acquired by a complicated process of unconscious imitation and acquisition from both parents." Most people, as a result, "harbour some attributes normally referred to the other sex, which may become manifest in special situations, or remain as a shadowy second-self." There was nothing outlandish about this, he argued, since different societies had different standards as to what was expected of each sex; "beards are alternately manly and effeminate, women may be expected to faint away or to drive tractors and land with airborne troops."[65]

When dealing with "children of doubtful sex," surgical reassignment may be justified, Alex said, beginning around the time of puberty. What's not justified is to force the individual to give up the gender role he or she is comfortable with.[66]

As this suggests, *Sex and Society* was a remarkably progressive book for the time. But it's impossible to read the pages on marriage and adultery without Alex's relationships with Jane and Ruth coming to mind. While they contain some good sense, they read like an apologia for his behavior toward his wife and his girlfriend.

Some readers noticed that while much of Alex's thesis dovetailed with *Marriage and Morals*, Bertrand Russell's once-scandalous 1929 book had argued that married couples should be able to take other partners, Russell had also insisted that sex and love must go together.[67] Alex was asserting that impersonal sex could also be healthy. The monogamous marriage is still the best situation for raising children, he wrote, provided it is stable and happy. But society was experiencing a change in attitude toward middle age in which men and women who had already raised one family were "still free to make a second attempt," bolstered by the awareness that sexual desire doesn't have an endpoint. "A form of sexual polyamory has become a serious competitor to monogamy as a pattern of material conduct," he declared, citing no evidence.[68]

The belief that one cannot sincerely love two people at once is "culture-manufactured"—the French had long known better, Alex informed the reader—and adultery could help to maintain marriages rather than destroy them by providing an "adulterous prop" that keeps the partners "on their feet." Instead of encouraging one party to feel wronged and the other guilty, marriage counselors and concerned relatives should try to tone down "the operatic aspects of marriage" and "reduce the emotional difficulties of this kind to the level of other personal problems." This, Alex said, is part of "the humanistic interpretation of sexual ethics." Insisting on complete monogamy, like complete abstinence before marriage, "is "biologically speaking quite unrealistic."[69]

Nowhere in this section of the book does Alex address the many complications his analysis ignored: to start with, the double standard that society applied to wives as opposed to husbands who commit adultery, the uneven power dynamic within the traditional marriage, and the economic precarity that wives feared when their marriage felt threatened. The ethic he was describing would have fit well in the pretend world of sexual relations that *Playboy* was selling in America, or possibly in some quite different future society, but not in the world as it was.

Sex in Society reflected the ways in which Alex was still a product of his time, however radical much of his thinking, but also some of the limitations of scientific humanism, with its deep faith in education based on fact and objective study to solve the problems of a humanity that was not—and didn't always want to be—entirely rational. While he strongly defended gay rights, he clung to some outworn beliefs about homosexuality derived from Freud: that it was the result of "persistent Oedipal anxieties" or "failure to establish a proper relationship with the other sex." He still wasn't fully prepared, in other words, to treat gay people as normal. And he spoke of agitation for gay rights "based on their separateness, and even an assertion of superiority of feeling or aesthetic sense" as creating difficulties "in trying to modify homosexuality by treatment"—as if that were either necessary or feasible.[70]

While he opposed criminalization of prostitution, he pathologized it, blaming "emotional problems, low intelligence, frigidity, unconscious homosexuality, and regression" over simple economic necessity for producing "the fully developed psychopathic prostitute." As for women as a group, Alex was not one of the many male sexologists who still questioned the existence of female orgasm, but he suggested that women, biologically, may be less sexually "aggressive" than males. "Every woman who fails to find a permanent sexual and social partner is likely to present, in any society, a psychiatric problem of varying complexity," he wrote, pathologizing female sexuality and framing it as a problem for society—presumably men—to address.[71]

The frequent cultural arrogance of scientific humanism comes through in Alex's discussion of contraception. While the "intelligent classes" were adopting it fairly readily, he argued, it was urgent to make contraceptives more easily available "for less intelligent families, whose high fertility is not a matter of choice."[72] Often, although by no means always, when he stepped into his role of scientific pundit, Alex's anarchist politics seemed to take a back seat.

Critics praised the book. "Out of the incessant flow of books on sex there are very few which can be recommended as unequivocally as this one," the *Sunday Times* declared. "In a world where . . . magical remedies are held out as serious guides, Comfort's book shines like the good deed it is," the social anthropologist Peter Worsley concluded in the *Guardian*.[73]

SO SAID SOME ELEMENTS of the British intelligentsia. Those reviews appeared in May 1963, soon after the book came out. Some weeks later, BBC TV decided to devote an episode of its Sunday evening program *This Nation Tomorrow* to "Sex and Family Life." Alex would get about ten minutes to deliver a summary of the ideas in his book, after which he would discuss them with a panel. The documentary programs producer, who worked closely with him on the script, wanted him to focus especially on sexual behavior of "youngsters under the age of twenty" and married life for people over forty.[74]

The broadcast took place on Sunday, July 14. Alex was introduced as "a writer, medical biologist, and anarchist." He lifted the language of his presentation directly from his book, including "I think we have come to the view that chastity is no more a virtue than malnutrition" and his dual commandments against exploiting another person's feelings and negligently risking the production of an unwanted baby. He also noted that "many marriages need an adulterous prop to keep them on their feet." The conversation that followed was more than civil. Alex's argument won a measure of respect from Ruth Robinson, wife of the bishop of Woolwich, representing a liberal Christian point of view.[75]

Among the BBC's mass audience, the reaction was quite different. Within twenty-four hours, forty-four viewers called in to complain, many directing their comments to "the upper echelons of the BBC," producer Derek Holroyde wrote Alex, along with just four calls praising the program.[76] Both Alex and the network were flooded with mail. One missive consisted only of a torn-out newspaper squib about the broadcast and the scribbled note, "YOU FILTHY HYPOCRITICAL SWINE – GET OUT!" Another, addressed jointly to Alex and the bishop of Woolwich (rather than his wife), charged, "Our young people are sinking into a slough of filth. Each one of you is guilty of accelerating the pace of descent." In a somewhat more compassionate vein, one viewer wrote: "[May] the Blessed Virgin . . . pray for you that you may change your views and humble yourself to accept the teachings of Her Divine Son."

Some writers took a different view, agreeing with Alex's commandments and thanking him for taking "a serious approach to a difficult problem." But the matter hit the newspapers almost overnight. "Frank Sex Talk Jolts the BBC," said one headline." Another, longer piece by the *Daily Mirror*'s widely read agony aunt (advice columnist) Marjorie Proops, was headlined "TV Talk on Sex Starts Storm." Proops applauded Alex and the BBC for speaking "wisdom" about teen sex where it was likely to be condemned—"it made a refreshing change to listen to a man who faces facts" about teenage sexuality—but Barbara Cartland, the romance novelist, complained in a column ("Dangerous Rubbish, Doctor") in the gossipy tabloid *News of the World* that Alex and the network were peddling "insidious propaganda for selfish sexuality."

The powerful, faith-based Public Morality Council complained that the "Sex and Family Life" broadcast itself "was weighted against an adequate expression of the viewpoint of the churches"—even though Alex, as a nonreligious person, was a minority among the participants.[77] The argument extended into the House of Lords, where a television bill laying down a code for the showing of violence to younger viewers was being debated. A Tory member, Lord Conesford, called attention to Alex's appearance on *This Nation Tomorrow* to argue that the bill should be broadened to include sexual content. "I should have thought the possibility of harm from what Dr. Comfort said was at least as great as any harm from the portrayal of violence," he declared. When another peer noted that the program had been broadcast after 10:00 p.m., when few children were viewing, Conesford stuck to his guns.[78]

None of this chatter, symptomatic of a rising moral panic over teenage misbehavior, was exactly unwelcome at the BBC itself. The "upper echelons" to whom complaints had been directed were "perfectly happy" with the program, Holroyde told Alex, and were ordering more copies of the transcript than he could quickly produce. The director of television briefly considered broadcasting a follow-up discussion with Alex the following Sunday on *Meeting-Point*, the BBC's religious discussion program, then put it off indefinitely.[79] When the press got wind of the idea, however, the network stated that it had asked Alex to appear but that he had declined. "We regard Mr. Comfort as an apostle of the New Morality," said producer Oliver Hunkin. "I want to stage this programme in the future."[80]

"I think the religious boys got the fire-brigade out," Alex told the *Sunday Telegraph*, explaining why he was declining the opportunity to answer back. "I am quite happy that they should answer me if they want to but, for myself, I am against come-backs." Besides which, the gulf between his critics and himself was too wide to bridge. "They believe in the Law of God. I am an atheist. I believe in responsibility, and one way of achieving this is by greater tolerance. But I don't see why I should say this on one of *their* programmes."

Later that week, the *Daily Herald* visited Alex in his UCL office to discuss the controversy. "It is hard to reconcile the tousled, mild-looking bespectacled man in the cluttered study with fierce sex controversy," reporter Tom Baistow wrote. Explaining his statements on the BBC, Alex said, "I wasn't trying to start a barny [fight]. What I was advocating was honest recognition of what *happens*.. . . . I believe we must treat people as whole person and not try to control them so that they have to do what we want them to do."[81]

The article noted that Alex had a son of sixteen in school and that his wife Ruth, an LCC children's officer, had her own views on the subject. "She would have given a very different talk," was all Alex would say about that, "with a sly smile."

In November Alex kicked up another fuss on another BBC program, *Man Tomorrow*. Again taking off from his book, he argued that contraceptives represented "a new human freedom in itself" by enabling humans to "enjoy sex as play, which is one of the most important biological functions."[82] After Malcolm Muggeridge, in the *Evening Standard*, declared that the argument for removing "restraints" on sexual behavior ignored how "prone are mortal men to bury their heads in the trough of their own appetites," one reader responded that Alex's views should have gone "out with the fall of the Roman Empire."[83] Several months later, Mary Whitehouse, a teacher and sex counselor who had just begun her puritanical Clean Up TV campaign, suggested that another TV talk by Alex, on portrayals of violence in art, was responsible for the headline-making "invasion" of the seaside resort of Clacton by teenage Mods and Rockers over Easter weekend and the fights that broke out between them.[84]

THE SEETHING OVERREACTION TO Alex's television appearances suggests a sometimes overlooked truth about Britain in the '60s. While youth culture, rock and roll, and a new sexual openness—in some circles, at least—were changing the country, they were locked in a tug-of-war with reactionaries and moral vigilantes who were simultaneously establishing themselves as a conspicuous pressure group.*** Mrs. Grundy was more than capable, on occasion, of drowning out the cultural revolution. Figures like Muggeridge and Whitehouse were mouthpieces for a great fear that the perceived other side, from Alex, Bertrand Russell, and Eustace Chesser to the Beatles, Vanessa Redgrave, and Mick Jagger, were

*** Bernard Levin aptly titled his 1970 history of Britain during the '60s *The Pendulum Years*.

part of a humanist conspiracy to destroy Christianity that was gradually extending its tentacles into media, government, schools, and even the more liberal branches of organized religion. Pressure groups—including the Public Morality Council, Moral Rearmament, and the National Viewers and Listeners Association—pushed the police, local licensing authorities, and the lord chamberlain (who had the power to censor theatrical productions) to mount "the most organized and effective moral vigilantism witnessed in late modern Britain" during the twenty years following the war, the historian Callum G. Brown writes.[85]

Following his appearance on *This Nation Tomorrow*, the humanist side rallied around Alex. The Ethical Union, an umbrella group of ethical and humanist societies whose president was Julian Huxley, asked permission to publish his statement at the beginning of the program in its *News and Notes*.[86] The Cambridge Humanists invited him to expand on his remarks at their next convocation.[87] And the debates society at Goldsmiths College, University of London, invited him to propose a formal debate on the motion "Contraception and free love are not detrimental to society."[88]

THE YEARS-LONG BAN the Bomb campaign and the new politics of direct action that it fostered had given a boost to UK anarchism since a number of anarchists were prominent in the struggle. Alex's conspicuous work in all three of the campaign's main channels—the CND, the DAC, and the Committee of 100—increased his stature in the movement as well. Nicolas Walter, now a fellow member of the committee, published an article in the April 1962 issue of Freedom Press's monthly magazine *Anarchy* in which he called Alex "the true voice of nuclear disarmament, much more than that of Bertrand Russell or anyone else." Alex's wartime and postwar writings had prefigured the essentially moral stand of the Ban the Bomb movement, Walter said, especially with his assertion in "Art and Social Responsibility" that "every government that intends war is as much our enemy as ever the Germans were" and that "the safeguard of peace is not a vast army but an unreliable public."[89] "What he said is as valid and valuable today as it was then, when he was a very young man who kept his head when all about were losing theirs," wrote Walter.

Anarchists were attracted to Alex's views on sex as well. *Anarchy*, edited by his comrade Colin Ward, devoted its November 1963 issue almost entirely to an analysis of his political thought, an article on his fiction and poetry, a review of *Sex in Society*, and a bibliography of his major written works. "Certainly if every teacher, social worker or psychiatrist who reads *Authority and Delinquency* and *Sex in Society* were to apply these two books' implications in daily practice, a revolutionary social change would be set in motion," John Ellerby wrote in "The Anarchism of Alex Comfort." In "Sex, Kicks and Comfort," Charles Radcliffe noted that when he was reading *Sex in Society* on the bus one day—its dust jacket featured a reproduction of Rodin's sculpture *Le Baiser*, which depicts a naked couple embracing—the "middle-aged, flower-pot hatted woman" sitting next to him exclaimed, "How dare you read that filthy book!" He concluded, "[*Sex in Society* is] an important, interesting, and often brilliant piece of scientific writing, . . . as witty as it is serious."

Radcliffe, twenty-one at the time, and his then-partner, Diana Shelley, were active in the Ban the Bomb movement. Earlier in 1963 they had written Alex, asking if *Art and Social Responsibility* was likely to be reissued in the near future. "It was through reading this book that we became anarchists," they said, "and yet it is now almost unavailable, at a time when more and more young people, like us, are becoming sympathetic to anarchism as a result of the Committee of 100 activities." Alex was receiving other inquiries about his books from the '40s, and he invariably replied that he would only reissue them if he could first revise them, and he was too busy to do that. Radcliffe went on to found *Heatwave*, a short-lived but influential libertarian socialist journal that published "The Seeds of Social Destruction," his pioneering account of English youth subcultures, and that connected him with the English section of the Situationist International.****

Alex received a different sort of request two years later when Albert Meltzer contacted him about "Maturity," one of the poems in *Haste to the Wedding*. Alex's contemporary and an activist seemingly with a finger in every aspect of British anarchism, Meltzer had recently founded

**** After the Situationists expelled Radcliffe and several other English members "for maniacal excesses," they started a new group, King Mob, one of whose occasional participants was Malcolm McLaren, soon to become a London fashion provocateur and later manager of the Sex Pistols. "Charles Radcliffe" was listed as "political adviser" on the sleeve of the 1969 Jefferson Airplane album, *Volunteers*. Jon Savage, *England's Dreaming: Anarchy, Sex Pistols, Punk Rock and Beyond* (New York: St. Martin's Press, 1991), 32–35; see also Charles Radcliffe, *Don't Start Me Talking: Subculture, Situationism and the Sixties* (Bread and Circuses Publishing, 2018).

Wooden Shoe Press, a rival to Freedom Press, which he considered not radical enough. Now he wanted permission to reprint "Maturity" in *Cuddon's Cosmopolitan Review*, his satirical anarchist journal, and as an epigraph to a book he was writing, a history of anarchist organizing in London from 1935 to 1955. "Maturity," a warning to revolutionaries who grow up and sell out, would regrettably have made a fine choice for many a book following the careers of a generation of activists:

Let them turn to the bottle
the Yogi and the rope,
some of them to Uncle Joe,
some of them to the Pope—

One by one grown prosperous
of excellent intent
they set their names on the payroll
of God and Government; . . .

All fierce beasts grow corpulent,
mature and come to hand.
Lions lie down with sheepskin wolves—
we will see them damned.

Alex's angle on anarchism was finding a receptive audience outside the UK as well. When a new anarchist archive and library, the Centre International de Recherches sur l'Anarchisme, was set up in Geneva, Switzerland, in the late '50s, Alex accepted a seat on its honorary committee.[90] In Argentina, *Reconstruir*, the libertarian newspaper that had earlier asked him to contribute and was now converting itself into a monthly review, and Américalee, an anarchist publisher, both located in Buenos Aires, were enjoying the period of relative freedom that followed the overthrow of the Peron dictatorship in 1955. Both were keen to translate and publish Alex's writings. César Milstein, an Argentine biochemist doing research at Cambridge—he would win the Nobel Prize in Physiology or Medicine in 1984—was a member of both collectives. He met Alex through Colin Ward in 1959, and Alex readily agreed to help.[91] At Ward's suggestion, Américalee, which had already published works by Camus and Herbert Read, asked for and received permission from Routledge to publish a Spanish edition of *Authority and Delinquency* for Argentine readers, which appeared in 1960.

The attention that his earlier work was receiving in the early to mid-'60s from the likes of Meltzer, Walter, and Radcliffe and from Colin Ward and others at Freedom Press, was no coincidence.

Personal responsibility, disobedience to irresponsible authority, and a new focus on the politics of the personal—the central points of Alex's activist philosophy in the '40s—were much the same ones that preoccupied many of the younger activists who emerged from the Aldermaston marches in the UK and the Civil Rights movement in the US, When a group calling itself the New Island Community set about raising funds in 1963 to establish "an international co-operative settlement" on an island off the coast of Queensland, Australia, modeled on the Israeli kibbutzim, it must have seemed only natural for them to ask permission to give Alex's name as a sponsor (Herbert Read, they informed him, had already agreed to do so).[92]

CHAPTER 12

"Emotional Technology" (1965–1971)

In January 1965 Alex replied to a letter in response to one of his articles, "[It may be] the problem of our age . . . [to] stop worrying that the irrational is 'daft, useless and sex-inspired' and learn to use and live with it without being either controlled by or scared of it. We're programmed biologically for this, and this is what art does."[1]

As a scientific humanist, Alex believed deeply in the power of science, observation, and experiment to better human life—almost any aspect of it. But he was also aware that since irrationality was human, it too must have some origin or purpose, stemming from human evolution, that the biologist could tease out. Ever since his days as a Neo-Romantic poet, Alex had been an admirer of Blake, whose work, he later said, constituted "the only religion based on experimental introspection" and "the only sort of mysticism that fits a post-scientific age in pursuit of an emotional technology."[2]

What did he mean by an "emotional technology"? As the '60s wore on, Alex turned back to his analysis in *Authority and Delinquency* of sociopaths in charge of the State and considered whether it wasn't the State but rather Western culture itself that was putting humanity at risk.

In a 1960 talk on the BBC Third Programme about the prospects for science in the coming decade, referring to the stockpiling and testing of nuclear weapons, he had noted "the astounding sight of the whole vast technical and intellectual effort of man being diverted down the drain of a few individuals' imaginations—pyramid-building, but in a form which endangers the actual survival of the species." Eliminating protein deficiencies in Africa, leprosy, hookworm, and traffic accidents was entirely possible in this technologically and scientifically sophisticated world—but only if they constituted a threat to these individuals' power or piqued their aggressive or destructive fantasies.[3] Politics itself had become a kind of "play therapy for psychopaths."[4]

The question was whether these unhappy realities were related in some way to human biology. Alex first grappled with this possibility in a course he devised at UCL in the early '60s and repeated several times. "I used to start by giving a lecture on the difference between man and other animals," he remembered, "then lectures on the differences between human individuals which covered immunology, sex, race, all these other things. Then I questioned the criteria of normality in medicine and what is normal and what is abnormal, and got them thinking about that."[5]

Out of these lectures came a book, published in 1966 as *Nature and Human Nature*, that explored in a little more than two hundred lucidly written pages the biological history of modern humanity and its likely future. ("One thinks of [H. G.] Wells, urgent populariser," Anthony Burgess said in his review, "except that Comfort's prose-style is better."[6]) It is one of Alex's best books and still a fine example of clearly communicated scientific exposition and argument for a general audience, despite some outdated information and findings (and his use of "man" for "human," with the accompanying pronouns).

"Man is the only animal . . . inherently able, corporately and individually, to be his own worst enemy," he found. Not only do humans not behave as a single species, instead preying on each other, but "the human individual" is also often "in deadly conflict with himself."[7] The suicide rate was the most obvious example; others were diseases of stress, such as hypertension and gastric ulcers.

Alex was talking primarily about Western society, which was rapidly exporting its way of life to every corner of the earth. How did this begin? Evolution, he argued, required humans to be able to control processes external to ourselves, which in turn required developing the brain's capacity to function as a logical system. But that meant leaving behind the "emotional technology" that regulates our relationships and generates our sense of ourselves as creatures in a social and natural world. The result was loss of empathy and sociality and the proliferation of sociopaths and psychopaths. Fortunately, humans still had rationalism and the scientific method, which, if used correctly, could help them detect and admit their need for an emotional technology—that is, to "feel and accept our emotions."

The good news was that the rationality humans had developed over millennia could help them reconstitute that emotional technology, if they would only apply it to the task." Having attained the level of abstract thinking necessary to achieve the scientific revolution, we can go back to universalism and to a sense of identity with, and 'non-violence' towards nature without being hamstrung by it or getting sentimental about it."[8]

Far from being purely rational creatures, humans were wired for some forms of broadly spiritual experience: for ritual and ceremony, for games, for drama and dance, and for sexuality, Alex argued, the kinds of ecstatic experiences that earlier and many contemporary non-Western cultures found in their religions. "We have seen how often and assiduously human beings try to produce 'oceanic' feelings of well-being by means extending from dancing and heroin to yoga, sex and meditation on the Passion. I suspect that these sexually tinged and euphoric sensations . . . evolved at earlier stages on the way up; I further suspect that their original function is social and tranquillizing, and that some of our psychological problems, as well, no doubt, as some of our intellectual achievements, arise from their non-use—from having at some stage in evolution 'switched them off' as spontaneous and continual experiences."[9]

Scientists, whether they admitted it or not, owed their discoveries and breakthroughs as much to inspiration as writers and painters did their artistic achievements, Alex said. He credited Peter Medawar with the insight that "scientific originality is a preconscious and inspirational activity: reality-centred hard work comes later."[10]

Oddly for a book that took some fairly audacious intellectual leaps and painted a dim picture of organized religion, *Nature and Human Nature* earned some deeply appreciative reviews. "Dr Comfort gives us, with admirable succinctness, the human situation as it stands at present and how it came about," Anthony Burgess said in the *Guardian*. "Our immediate priority is to survive: this book shows us how we may do it."[11] Even a critic for the *Catholic Times*, after giving Alex a poke for his lack of Christianity ("something must have happened to him to prejudice him violently"), went on to recommend the book. The need for a technology of the emotions "is so obviously true once the facts are all marshalled before one," reviewer David L. Edwards wrote, "and is so learnedly, reasonably and humanely expressed here, that a Christian who is prepared to work at these questions must suppress the occasional irritation and react mainly with gratitude for the guidance afforded by a brilliant humanist."[12]

Alex continued to develop the ideas in *Nature and Human Nature* in articles and lectures over the next several years, especially about the social importance of play. In a 1967 paper delivered at the new University of Bath as part of a conference on technology and society, he defined play as "a non-serious activity which we allow to children and young animals, and occasionally to adults, in which literalism is suspended, mermaids can be assumed to be 'real' for the purposes of the game, and children be allowed (though not actively 'encouraged') to 'believe' in them." "Play" is also the field in which an emotional technology is created. What adults in Western society, with its impressive physical and intellectual technologies, all too often lacked was "a repertoire of non-reality-bound 'games' which will involve release, controlled acting out, and a measure of consequent self-adjustment."[13]

When we do allow these games in, the results can be negative—for example, the acting-out by sociopaths in positions of power. But Alex was not pleading for the abandonment of scientific objectivity or a return to God. Rather, he was saying that humans needed to rediscover "the simple sensory and emotional enjoyment of our skins." One already available tool was psychotherapy, but he also suggested that scientists look at customs from other cultures, such as the Hindu *sādhanā*: practices for attaining dispassion and detachment from worldly things.[14]

Alex's prescriptions for modern humanity were essentially the same ones he had advocated in his lecture almost a decade and a half earlier at Freedom Press's Anarchist Summer School. "If it sounds square, to the involved, to say that the answer lies in intellectual disciplines like ethology, psychoanalysis, primatology, anthropology, and the general study of Man—at a time when scientists are being written off as being as antihuman as politicians—one can only point out that for better or worse we *are* discursive beings, and in this culture we feel more easily and more soundly when we also make the effort to understand," he wrote in 1968.[15]

But he was arguing, in a decade when many younger people appeared to be rejecting science, that science must be accompanied by a technology of the emotions. In a review of *The Double Helix*, James Watson's account of how he and his colleagues identified the structure of DNA, Alex praised Watson's willingness to expose the drama behind the discovery, to expose biology as a practice that must engage both the emotional and the intellectual technology of the researcher.[16] Elsewhere he described hard science as a "protective suit we put on for certain important intellectual and practical operations." "[But] even then the suit leaks," he added, which is why we also need a technology of the emotions.[17]

Elements of the argument Alex put forth in *Nature and Human Nature* and his University of Bath lecture, which was published as "A Technology of the Emotions?," found their way—along with some striking location shots—into the first television documentary he wrote and presented for BBC television, "A Traveller in the Dream Time." It appeared Saturday, June 3, 1967, on BBC2 as the second episode of a new series titled *One Pair of Eyes*, in each of which a notable figure discussed an issue close to their heart. Later presenters would include Margaret Drabble, Dudley Moore, Peter Sellers, and Tom Stoppard. Against a tracking shot of Stonehenge, Alex told viewers,

> Science and magic have never really parted company. Our ancestors built Stonehenge to make contact through ceremony with the sun, the moon, the seasons. But what they built was an observatory. . . . Science is likely to be our best way of regaining contact with our world, and with our needs, if only we're good at it. But magical and unconscious motives will keep upsetting our plans, unless we relearn some of the older human techniques of feeling—or at least rethink them.[18]

Later in the program Alex shows footage of a group of Indigenous Australians dancing and informs viewers, "These men are dancing as part of a ceremony which expresses their feelings about death. . . . They paint their bodies to identify themselves with ancestors and figures out of the Dream Time." Then he shows the interior of a discotheque in London where people are dancing to a song by Pink Floyd. "Dancing is just beginning to get back some of its old power for us," Alex says. Next comes a "West Indian religious service."

Art is another way to get back that old power. Alex takes us into the studio of his friend, the sculptor Reg Butler, who had been a conscientious objector during World War II and who talks about his work as "a kind of being." Outside a mental hospital, Alex informs us that "psychotherapy is the ritual par excellence which we've designed to fit our culture because it uses understanding to enable us to feel." He closes with a short interview with Nicolas Walter at a demonstration outside the Houses of Parliament where some activists are being hauled off by police. "Bloody-mindedness is one of man's most important evolutionary achievements," Alex says. "One political name for it is direct action." Asking Walter what the term means to him, Walter replies, "If it's illegal to publish something, it's direct action to publish it. That's action. If it's illegal to say something, it's direct action to say it. . . . Your pamphlets were direct action in their own way; this is direct action in another way."

It was a neat trick to introduce direct action and a facet of anarchism to Saturday-evening TV audiences, but the program was a bit of a muddle as a précis of Alex's argument about the need for a technology of the emotions, and it got a mixed critical response. A reviewer for the *Morning Star* (the renamed *Daily Worker*) called it "a disappointment from someone whose contribution to television discussions is usually clear-cut and stimulating." The *Times* critic Michael Billington liked the program and acknowledged that it forced him to think, but he questioned whether modern life could be so starved for spontaneous physical self-expression when "Dr. Comfort never seemed to run out of examples of the sort of thing he meant."[19]

The same thing could have been said of the entire argument he'd been developing in *Nature and Human Nature*. From a later vantage point, it's clear that Alex was piling more consequence onto his theoretical structure than it could support. Both in the book and the BBC program, he patronizingly lumped together a diversity of Indigenous cultures to fit a neat distinction between Western and "primitive" habits of mind. He didn't bother to explain what material forces—or others—prompted certain humans to develop a technology for using the brain as a logical system and others not so much, if indeed the divide was really that stark. And his suggested solution—"the simple sensory and emotional enjoyment of our skins"—was fuzzy enough to be right at home in the budding human potential movement.

As a scientist, however, Alex was right to follow a chain of logic in seeking a physical origin for the problems that concerned him, and he was right as a biologist to focus on the human mind. Power, greed, class conflict, and material desire could certainly explain why people in authority would want to develop the human mind in a particular direction, but from Alex's point of view it also made sense to ask why humans were susceptible to these impulses.

ALEX'S DEVOTION TO BIOLOGY, and his ambitions for it as a framework for understanding human behavior, placed him in a direct line from British evolutionists like T. H. Huxley, H. G. Wells, and Haldane, but with some of their weaknesses and blind spots as well.

In 1929–30, Wells, his son G. P. Wells, and T. H. Huxley's grandson Julian, published one of the biggest best sellers in popular science, *The Science of Life: A Summary of Contemporary Knowledge about Life and Its Possibilities*. The three-volume work summed up for popular audiences most of what scientists knew about the body, patterns of life, reproduction, the human mind, and human evolution. In the '30s and for a long time thereafter, everybody who was interested in the subject and spoke English—as well as a few other languages—either read it or was assumed to have done. Alex was certainly one of these. One of the more disturbing passages in *The Science of Life* reads as follows: "Perhaps in years to come our descendants will look with intelligence over their pedigree, and if there is a probability of recessive genius in a family and no reason to suspect a grave recessive taint they will deliberately encourage inbreeding. A rather grim Utopia might be devised in which for some generations . . . inbreeding would be made compulsory, with a prompt resort to the lethal chamber for any undesirable results. A grim Utopia, no doubt, but in that manner our race might be purged of its evil recessives forever."[20]

Eugenics, the pseudoscientific study of how to breed human beings for optimum mental and physical characteristics, was regarded as anything but pseudo in the decades leading up to World War II. Eugenics was an outgrowth of genetics—still a relatively young branch of science—and most geneticists treated it at least as a respectable matter for discussion, even if they didn't themselves believe in it. On the Right it was a near obsession, but aspects of eugenics claimed adherents and inquiring minds in the Left as well, including Havelock Ellis and the American birth-control pioneer Margaret Sanger. Some feminists took it up as a talking point in securing greater control of reproduction for women.[21] The Soviet Union hosted an influential Russian Eugenics Society in the 1920s. And not everyone who invoked the term was a scientifically minded racist; some were geneticists who wanted to understand how certain traits or conditions were passed along.

Even after the fall of Nazi Germany, which had applied eugenics and "racial hygiene" more murderously than any state in history, the idea of harnessing biological knowledge to guide human development in presumably positive directions never really died, although the focus shifted from weeding out "defective" persons to encouraging the "best" to reproduce. In November 1962, the CIBA Foundation held a "Man and His Future" conference in London. The participants included Medawar, Haldane, Julian Huxley, mathematician Jacob Bronowski, and molecular biologist Francis Crick. Alex reported on the most recent lines of research on human aging; Haldane, in his now-customary Indian garb, delivered a long, provocative paper, "Biological Possibilities for the Human Species in the Next Ten Thousand Years"; and American molecular biologist Joshua Lederberg spoke on "The Biological Future of Man," focusing on genetics and eugenics.

Haldane argued that while it wasn't possible to train most people to equal the achievements of Beethoven, Einstein, or Gandhi, it was "desirable that the fraction of persons with such capacity should be increased." He offered as a suggestion the production of clones from cells of persons "of attested ability." Another possibility for improving the race might be the deliberate provocation of genetic mutations or hybridization with animals to incorporate "valuable capacities" from these other species.[22]

Lederberg argued that genetic research had to focus on ways to increase human intelligence: "The present population of the world is not intelligent enough to keep itself from being blown up." Given the possibility of artificial insemination, reproduction probably should not be left up to individual choice, he argued, since if people could "choose the father of their children, will they not choose just the more notorious projections of their own images, exaggerated by the publicity given to the advertised donors?" Alex responded that it wasn't low IQ but "personality problems and emotional disturbances" in its leaders that placed humanity in danger of blowing itself up, to which Lederberg replied, "These are just as likely to be under genetic control." Alex countered that they could probably be reined in more simply by upbringing than by trying to "alter the genetic constitution."[23]

The discussion then moved on to other matters, suggesting that no one especially wanted to pursue Alex's objections to the path Lederberg and Haldane seemed to be taking. But Alex too was inclined to treat notions that could be grouped broadly under the eugenics banner as issues to discuss rather than dangerous ideas to be shot down. In 1969 he reviewed a new book by the geneticist C. D. Darlington, a student of Haldane's who had broken with his mentor over the Lysenko affair. Darlington held strong views on the alleged intellectual differences between races. He had opposed the 1950 UNESCO Statement of Race, which condemned racism in the wake of the Nazis. His new book, *The Evolution of Man and Society*, argued that genetic transmission played a much larger role in human social development than most scientists were prepared to admit.

Behind this was a sly argument about interracial coupling. Inbreeding was not a good thing for any population, Darlington conceded, but successful hybridization of the races depended on the preservation of the "tribes" that made it possible. Was this his way of standing up for Indigenous communities, under threat from the bulldozer of capitalist overdevelopment? Or was Darlington just smuggling his disapproval of race mixing back into the scientific discourse?

In his review, Alex couldn't bring himself to think the worst of Darlington. The book was "a thought-provocation," "wrongheaded at times but impressive in sum," he found, infuriating but not fascist ("not as Darlington sees it"). Instead, it was "an extreme statement of what could be called the genetic view of man," a "reminder that man has genes as well as customs."[24] Darlington's ideas had a long and disturbing pedigree that Alex surely was aware of, yet he was either too polite to say so or too uneasy about taking a firm position on the limits of genetic determinism.

Either way, why? The answer may go back to *The Science of Life*. The Wells-Huxley book had inspired a generation of biologists with the thought that their field held the key to improving human life. In a 1971 review of *An Introduction to the Study of Man* by the zoologist J. Z. Young, Alex said that a new book along the lines of *The Science of Life* was "badly needed," but the task was now much more difficult. It would have to cover the spread of biology into the study of human behavior, including anthropology, religion, politics, depth psychology ("the rationalistic exploration of feeling"), cytogenetics (the study of chromosomes), and information theory "to form an overall biology of Man."[25]

Biology, in other words, must take in everything related to humankind. Since genetics was part of biology, how could geneticists be barred from probing into every aspect of human behavior and development, including areas for which culture and upbringing were assumed to be responsible? Whatever else he felt personally, Alex's belief in the need for biology to inform other fields inclined him against placing restrictions on other scientists carrying this work forward, even if they were sometimes disturbingly wrongheaded.

ALEX WAS CARRYING FORWARD his own work on aging: particularly the effect of changes of diet, using his guppies as test subjects. While he was now connected with the Medical Research Council rather than the Nuffield Foundation, his place at UCL and his research routine remained the same through the '60s. UCL and the Zoology Department had changed, however. Medawar, his closest intellectual collaborator on aging, was now at the National Institute for Medical Research; Haldane, in India, died of cancer in 1964; and John Maynard Smith, Haldane's student and an important biologist and geneticist, had left UCL to help found the University of Sussex.

Alex was on good terms with his younger colleagues, although his work was less intimately connected with theirs. One of these was Krishna Dronamraju, an Indian geneticist and student of Haldane's who later wrote several books about Haldane's work. He got to know Alex slightly while at UCL's Galton Laboratory in 1961–62 and later remembered him as "a highly nervous, chain-smoking individual who spoke very fast," informal and friendly, who liked to cite Indian philosophy in conversation. Alex struck Dronamraju, who tended to rate everyone against his mentor's lofty standard, as someone who tried to emulate Haldane but was a "dilettante" in science compared to the eminent geneticist.[26]

Dronamraju remembered Alex as "not shy about admitting when he didn't know about something." He was, however, instantly conversant in all the latest developments in his field.[27] In the '60s, there was a lot to keep up with. In 1964 he brought out a new edition of his book on gerontology, this time titled *Ageing: The Biology of Senescence*. Enough new findings had surfaced in the preceding eight years that it was effectively a new book, more than one hundred pages longer. The bibliography alone had added another twenty pages.

Alex divided the work in the field into two lines of research. Somatic mutation—mutative changes in certain of the body's cell types—had excited a lot of interest from biologists. Could these changes explain aging and differences in the rate of aging between individuals? There was a great deal of research by dozens of scientists to back up some kind of relationship, but Alex found none of it conclusive. For one thing, his colleague Maynard Smith had pointed out that the amount of mutation would have to be huge to account for the observed rate of aging.[28]

Another possibility with which Alex associated himself at this time had to do with damage to cells, particularly those that do not divide, such as brain and muscle cells. Since they survive in the same form for very long periods, he suggested, they could accumulate damage before dying altogether, which could make them less vigorous as well as affect other parts of the bodily system.[29] In this, Alex was at least partially coming around to the thinking of his former rivals, Cowdry and Lansing, who had long argued that the cell was the proper place to look for a fundamental aging process.

The second new area of research was on the effects of ionizing radiation, such as nuclear radiation but also exposure to gamma rays and X-rays in medicine and industry. There is "no other immediately obvious line of attack on age problems which seems to hold out better prospects for fundamental advance," Alex said. Since Hiroshima, scientists had conducted a great many experiments, mostly exposing mice and other small animals to radiation, with a great many interesting results: more tumors in exposed subjects and all-around premature aging, although this couldn't be firmly ascribed to the radiation. One study found that radiologists themselves suffered a significant increase in early death from leukemia and other diseases. But all of this work was still in an early stage.[30]

The same year, Alex published a version of *Aging: The Biology of Senescence* for popular audiences, *The Process of Aging*, in the United States. In the new book he covered the history of efforts to understand and arrest aging, the longevity ranges for animals and humans, and the then-current theories about factors affecting loss of physical and mental vigor. He also took time to discuss the "social medicine" aspect of old-age studies: society's treatment of the aged and especially "the wastage and personal frustration caused by the . . . convention" of forced retirement, which he branded "a serious social ill."[31] As was his habit, he peppered the book with some of his large supply of amusing stories about aging, such as one from Giovanni Pietro Maffei's sixteenth-century *History of the Indies* in which an elderly Bengali wheedled a generous pension out of a Portuguese general by persuading the colonialist that he was 335 years old.[32]

Where should gerontology go next? Should it focus on specific diseases associated with old age, for example, or on searching for more fundamental causes of aging? Alex cautioned that there was "no known rejuvenatory nostrum that could prolong life."[33] Rather than waste time searching for one, what was needed was "properly designed critical tests to clear up the fundamentals of the nature of the ageing process." He cited three key questions those tests could address: why non-dividing cells die, how the cell population in humans declines with age, and how newly produced cells in older bodies differ from those in younger ones.

This line of inquiry, which he called experimental gerontology, made more sense than disease-specific research, Alex argued. At least in the most privileged countries, people were living longer than ever before. But the way people thought about this change was upside down. While plenty of medicines and treatments had been developed that helped the elderly live longer, the most important changes had happened on the other end: lower infant mortality (meaning more children growing up to reach old age) and fewer women dying in childbirth. But those gains were largely accomplished, and while focusing on specific diseases might extend life by a few years, it would not necessarily enable people to live more vigorous, happier lives in their eighties or nineties. Understanding the more fundamental causes of aging—at the cellular or chromosomal level, perhaps—could make this possible. "Stopping or slowing the clock at a later age," Alex wrote, "would be a much more useful achievement," and it could be realized much more rapidly.

Years could be added to human life, but the more profound change would be to render the prospect of individual survival "open-ended." "The knowledge of our fixed life span—an idea we verbalize quite freely but do not admit fully to consciousness—may well play a much bigger part in our emotional life than we realize," Alex suggested. "It is one of the most unpleasant intellectual discoveries we make in childhood. If we lost it, it would alter both us and our culture."[34] Since he first started writing poetry, fiction, and political analysis, Alex had been preoccupied with death, the greater consciousness of the immediacy of death he perceived in the modern age, and the culture of death he found in the State. (Awareness of death "is a good deal more important than the awareness of sexual problems which Freud put forward," he said some years later. "This has played a very, very large part in human thinking and the formation of human society."[35]) In biology and gerontology, he had found another front on which to fight it. Fight it we will, he argued, because humans had always wanted to.

The Process of Ageing got terrific reviews—novelist William Trevor "unreservedly recommended" it to BBC audiences, and the eminent pediatrician Douglas Hubble, in the *British Medical Journal*, praised it as "an admirable little book, well written, easily read, and packed with interesting information." But did Alex's message get across? Several of the critics understood him to be saying that gerontologists should focus on extending life and vigor, not life alone, which was correct. Several, however, zeroed in on one particular finding Alex referenced in the book—that in rats deprived of food, the aging process slowed down, then speeded up when their rations were restored—even though he was a long way from suggesting austerity diets for humans. Even thoughtful lay readers, it seemed, found themselves drawn to the quick fix.

The Process of Ageing was published in the UK in March 1966. It launched Alex on a multiyear series of tours, lectures, and scholarly conferences during which he urged his listeners to talk up the need for fundamental research and press the government to fund a crash program to get it done. For the first time, a clear path forward seemed to reveal itself. But first the public had to support it. "Over the last ten years research on ageing has shed its association with monkey glands and become respectable, but not imaginatively popular," he said in a widely reported lecture at the Royal Society of Arts on March 30, portions of which were transcribed in the *Guardian*.

But what if Britain made it a priority? he asked, appealing to his listeners' patriotic side. "If we could recruit three people of potential Nobel quality, it seems likely that we could corner this field for Britain and speed up its development, exactly as was done by Crick and Kendrew's work on D.N.A. The position is much like that of atomic energy before the Manhattan Project."

Ignoring the irony of an activist against nuclear weapons appealing to the example of the research project that begat them, Alex called for the setting up of "an ad hoc institute within a university, which would make it clear to young and coming biologists that this is a subject which society takes seriously and which deserves their consideration." His supporters could count on the funds from government, he predicted. "From my contacts with local authorities, the Ministry of Health, the geriatricians and the scientists, I think we can."[36] The whole thing could be launched for £500,000 a year at the start, Alex estimated, and he raised the stakes in a November 1967 cover story for the *Sunday Times Magazine*: "Unless we encourage more scientific investment here, the first breakthrough will see us brain-drained." Further, laurels would be earned by other countries. Already, he noted, the United States was boosting its budget for research on aging, and the Soviet Union was starting to follow suit.[37]

Alex wasn't proselytizing only in the UK, however. Over the next two years he addressed audiences in Saskatoon (at the University of Saskatchewan) and in Indianapolis, Louisville, San Diego (at an American Cancer Society seminar), and other US cities, some of these part of a tour sponsored by the three-year-old Glenn Foundation for Medical Research, which was set up to fund research and education on aging.[38] He gave much the same talk in each place, emphasizing the need for a crash program—in particular to develop a "clock" that could time the start of decline—and always making the distinction between life extension and the extension of vigorous life. Offering an illustration Americans would find compelling, he described vigor as the ability to get out of the way of an oncoming car by means of sight, hearing, and reflex—and, if one was hit, the ability to recover.[39] "I think this will be an area of American interest because this is where it's happening. Most of the work is American at the moment," he told a reporter in Santa Barbara, by way of encouragement.[40]

He took his crusade to television as well. On Wednesday, September 25, 1968, BBC2 audiences could tune in "Comfort on Ageing," an episode of the network's science and philosophy series *Horizon*, that Alex wrote and narrated. By this time he had honed his presentation for popular audiences, and the one-hour documentary was lucid, assured, authoritative, and engrossing. Alex surveyed the stages of aging and posed two of the principal sets of theories: that aging amounted to either a "programmed switching-off of cells" or random damage at the molecular level. Along the way, he invoked the life of Bach and quoted Yeats, Rabelais, and Wei Po Yung, the mysterious Chinese alchemist, said to have been the first to describe the chemical composition of gunpowder: "shrewd quotations which really made sense and told one something about the subject," the *Catholic Herald's* critic said.[41] He tied it all up with his plea for funding of aging research.

Alex threw all his skills as a communicator into his push for funding, but he was working against four difficult obstacles: promoters of quack rejuvenation treatments that still sopped up a great deal of money and public interest; persistently negative public attitudes about old age; a weakening of government commitment to aging research; and his own lack of progress at hard research.

He took every opportunity to denounce physicians pushing hormone or cellular treatments meant to reverse aging. In the mid-'60s, Pat McGrady, an American magazine journalist, was researching a book, *The Youth Doctors*, about these dubious purveyors and their rich and glamorous customers. He consulted Alex steadily, and the picture McGrady painted was "both embarrassing and extremely funny," as Alex said in a review once the book was published in 1968.[42] If the rejuvenators "can produce a decent experiment, even a single one, which suggests that their remedy produces objective effects other than by suggestion, I shall be happy to start talking about how it does so," he told McGrady, noting that some had made a great deal of money without ever having been published in a peer-reviewed scientific journal. "The air of hanky-panky, instant cookery, and big money . . . strikes me as pathognomonic."*

More seriously, the quacks were making work difficult for biologists

* "Pathognomonic": characteristic of a disease. Patrick M. McGrady Jr., *The Youth Doctors* (New York: Coward-McCann, 1968), 97.

performing real gerontological research. Testosterone, despite its dubious use as a male sex aid, had possibilities for combating muscular weakness, one of the afflictions of old age, Alex noted. But it was difficult to get serious biologists to reassess its clinical uses "because of the raised eyebrows of their colleagues . . . after years of monkey glands and potency-pills."[43]

Public interest in rejuvenation was understandable, and all that Alex could offer instead was an expensive public research program pursuing arcane alleyways of knowledge, with incremental improvements at the end. He was always honest about this, but, without a glitzy reward in the near term, most people seemed unwilling to think about such an unpleasant subject as old age and death. And the media seemed happy to perpetuate stereotypes of aging for the sake of a catchy intro, even when they covered Alex's talks, lectures, and books. "It is one of the most unpleasant discoveries that we all grow old," the *Oxford Mail* said in its piece "Comfort on Ageing."[44] Malcolm Muggeridge, in his review of *The Process of Ageing* in the *Observer*, said that since he opposed any undue prolongation of a painful part of life, "I must hate Dr Alex Comfort, whose exuberant, and, one supposes, expert scientific effort is bent to this end."[45]

A change of public attitude was needed, Alex pressed at every opportunity. He put the point as strongly as he could in his *Sunday Times* feature, which was illustrated with drawings that aged celebrities ranging from Jackie Kennedy to Mick Jagger, promoting the realization, hopefully, that old age happens to everyone.

> We neglect and dislike old people, we store them in chronic wards where they will not hamper the life of their children. In this we are less humane than the Eskimos, who allow the incurably sick to die with dignity by exposing them on an icefloe—and far less humane than peasant communities which allow them dignity and employment in the homes of their family. . .. In addition to investment in fundamental research and in the medicine of old age, we need a new attitude, as a culture, towards the worth of old people. Self interest, if we care to think for a moment, demands that we take this matter seriously.[46]

After the social anthropologist Edmund Leach delivered the BBC's annual Reith Lecture in 1967 and remarked that no one in their late fifties could be expected to produce creative work in the sciences, Alex, appearing on a follow-up broadcast, responded with one of his patented political digs: "Scientifically speaking, it's codswollop. . . . An unselective age of compulsory retirement is, to my mind, quite one of the silliest ideas that I think I've yet heard of. . . . The problem is to get rid of inflexibles and ineducables of all ages, particularly in the places they congregate, like university committees and political office."**

Alongside these ingrained habits of thought, the '60s were punctuated by a great fear, mostly in higher circles, of overpopulation. Wouldn't an increase in the length of human life simply yield more elderly and increase the burden on their families and communities? Alex had a simple, twofold answer to such concerns: first, that they partook of the same prejudices about the aged that society needed to lose; second, that overdependence was exactly what gerontology was trying to reduce by increasing the number of years of vigorous life. If it succeeded, then "every day of productive life gained should be a gain to humanity."[47] But his point was lost in the tumult.*** In 1968 Paul and Anne Ehrlich produced a best seller, *The Population Bomb*, which foresaw worldwide famine and social upheaval within a decade if the birthrate couldn't be reduced, and in 1972 the elite Club of Rome sold some twelve million copies of *The Limits to Growth*, a slightly less pessimistic report that nevertheless shocked governments by predicting that if the world population kept growing and consumption patterns remained the same, the human race would be unable to support itself within a century.

Overpopulation fears could dampen enthusiasm for aging research but were still mainly theoretical. What especially concerned Alex was the dislike that doctors often displayed toward the elderly, something he labeled "gerontophobia." "Our manner may be that which the anti-Semite, ashamed of his prejudice, adopts toward his Jewish friends," Alex remarked. "I recognized it in myself, and it took no special insight to detect it in the literature."

While he hadn't practiced medicine since joining UCL fifteen years earlier, the problem of how to get the medical profession to overcome

** "Out of the Air," *The Listener*, December 28, 1967. Afterward, Mick Rhodes, producer of BBC Radio's Science Unit, complimented Alex for "coming in and saying rude things to Edmund Leach ("we thought it was a very good bit of rudery." Mick Rhodes, letter to AC, December 18, 1967.

*** Alex had a sharp exchange over the possibly malign consequences of life extension on a BBC Radio 3 program in July 1971 with Shirley Williams, a high-ranking Labour MP and the daughter of his old PPU comrade Vera Brittain. P. B. Medawar et al., "Aging," *The Listener*, July 18, 1971.

its prejudices and focus more on elder care was becoming a bigger preoccupation for Alex, partly because he was fielding personal appeals for his involvement. In the fall of 1966, Bertrand Russell, ninety-four years old, asked Alex to help him find a physician. Alex promised to ask Lord Amulree, who was by then the UK's leading geriatrician and had helped organize the 1954 visit by British doctors to the Soviet Union that Alex had joined, to see Russell. Amulree, who had just retired from practice, declined, and Alex referred Russell instead to Norman Exton-Smith, another outstanding geriatrician who had been at Cambridge at the same time as Alex and had later worked with Amulree at University College Hospital.[48]

Doctors on their level who specialized in elder care were few, however. A year later, in an article for the journal *Medical Opinion and Review*, Alex speculated that doctors, with their commitment to treat and cure, were uncomfortable working with people they knew they could not cure in the usual way—"denying our self-image as dragon slayers"—and with the constant reminder that they themselves would age. As a student, he had noticed how teachers counseled that one therapy or operation after another was "unnecessary" because the patient was old. The image imparted to students was of "the well-behaved, asexual, uncomplaining subject, patiently awaiting the next world, to be kept as a pet if cheeringly vigorous, if not, to be jollied and avoided."[49]

A "huge submerged element of magic and counter-transference" was still embedded in "the iceberg of modern medicine," Alex argued in his Freudian manner, and part of the tension concerned doctors' unstated preference for "satisfactory" patients: the ones who could get well and thus make the physician feel good. A technology of the emotions was needed to be a doctor rather than just a medical technologist, but too many preferred to take refuge in the latter role. Alex proposed a program of group sessions, starting at the beginning of medical education, to teach "the biology of human relations and simultaneously, to give the student supportive insight into his own experience of becoming a physician." If control of human aging processes was really feasible, the need for doctors who were more emotionally accustomed to working with the elderly would only grow.

The larger issue Alex raised was not new. In the United States, the Age Discrimination in Employment Act, outlawing mandatory retirement, was passed in 1967, the same year his article appeared, and some important research programs on age-based inequality dated back to the '50s.[50] However, very few individuals in the UK with access to major media were trying to turn it into a headline issue in the following decade. Alex may have hoped that "gerontophobia" would catch on and give a name to a new popular cause, but a more readily understandable term prevailed instead.

While at the National Institute of Mental Health, Robert N. Butler, an American psychiatrist and gerontologist, had coauthored the landmark 1963 report *Human Aging: A Biological and Behavioral Study*, which showed that many of the psychiatric states associated with old age—"senility"—resulted more from disease, depression, and personality traits than from aging. For a 1969 story in the *Washington Post* by a young reporter named Carl Bernstein, Butler coined the term "ageism," and he analogized it closely to racism and sexism.[51] "Ageism is the great sleeper in American life," Butler predicted later that year, in the *Gerontologist*, and the term became a focal point of a new movement for the rights of the elderly in America.[52]

The third great barrier to support for fundamental research on aging that Alex encountered concerned scientific and institutional attitudes toward gerontology as a project. The trend in aging research was shifting. Alex's research since he joined UCL in 1952 had mostly followed two paths: statistical studies of lifespan in animals and humans, and observation of aging patterns in guppies and other creatures under different conditions. But in America, where gerontology was starting to attract more attention, research was concentrating at the cellular and molecular level, where the sort of "clock" Alex was looking for was assumed to be located, if anywhere.

Politics was the other area of change. In Britain, research on old age had been viewed as a facet of social medicine, a uniquely British approach to medical science that took hold after World War II. It was founded on a humanistic belief that medical problems needed to be addressed in combination with social and psychological problems, along with a positivistic emphasis on statistics and statistical research as the best route to establishing connections and finding solutions. Amulree had defined gerontology as the study "of those elderly sick with social and economic problems."[53] Alex's *Authority and Delinquency*, with its argument about the social selection of psychopaths for public office, had taken a similar approach and prompted a complimentary letter from James Lorimer Halliday, the Scottish physician who pioneered a more holistic approach to understanding and treating illness.[54]

In the second half of the '60s, however, as public policy started shifting rightward, social medicine lost government and institutional backing.

Community doctors directly involved in service provision managed to maintain their support, but the kind of holistic approach that combined medical care with research and public policy advocacy did not.[55] At the same time, funding for aging research shifted from biology to pharmacology. Instead of the kind of academically linked institution Alex was campaigning for—with "three persons of potential Nobel quality," that would take a holistic approach to improving the later years of life—the favored approach centered on large hospitals and focused on specific diseases. In that setting, the work had a greater chance to produce quick results for patients—but also for drug manufacturers and providers.

By the late '60s, the shift was becoming clear to researchers like Alex. In a lecture at the University of Saskatchewan, he complained, "The whole tendency of medicine, of public health—whether social or political—and of all the social progress which has been made in most countries is to produce a squarer and squarer curve." But the job of gerontology, as he saw it, should be to induce the whole curve "to move to the right": toward longer vigorous life.[56]

The fourth barrier Alex encountered was related to his own work in the field. While he pushed for a major financial commitment to basic research, he himself had produced scarcely any since the early '60s. He was continuing his experiments and observations of fish, but at a time when the focus of gerontological research was shifting directly to humans—a change he was himself promoting—his work with *Lebistes* seemed less and less important. By 1969 he had not published a paper based on laboratory observation or experimentation—the chief intellectual product of any scientist—in five years, despite the fact that he had been director of the Medical Research Council's Group on Aging that whole time. He spent a great chunk of his professional time traveling and lecturing, and he admitted privately that this was beginning to be very apparent.****

In January 1969, Sir Peter Medawar (he had been knighted in 1965) wrote a stern letter, in confidence, to the council in answer to an inquiry about a report that Alex had just submitted on his group's work.[57] "I don't think anyone on the Biology Board will need to be told that the experimental work described in the Report doesn't amount to very much," he said. "Comfort's lengthy philosophical preamble combines a

**** "Trying to write a report for the MRC explaining why I've spent 5 years travelling around rather than getting on with research." AC, letter to Marilyn Yalom, December 17, 1968.

general case for the Groups apostolic mission with a number of special reasons why he seems unable to fulfil it." The only interesting results reported, Medawar said, were by a member of Alex's team who had started her work under the guidance of John Maynard Smith; about the rest, there was "nothing distinctive." Clearly, said Medawar, Alex had "neither the drive nor the organizational ability to run a Research Group in the conventional sense of this term."

That didn't mean Alex himself wasn't worth supporting. "The fact remains that Comfort is a most unusual and gifted person who does indirectly promote medically significant research, so I am, and have always been, in favour of his being supported as a man." In what way, Medawar did not specify, however, nor did he directly recommend that the council itself provide that support. As to why not, the answer, at least partially, was that Medawar himself was souring on gerontological research generally. "Senescence," he wrote several years later, "is part of the natural order of things. It is not one that should be interfered with without the utmost care and circumspection." The time span required for experimentation on humans was too long and too costly, and many people were right to worry that the outcome could be some nightmare out of science fiction.[58] This suggests it would have taken quite a remarkable proposal to persuade Medawar to back any further research on aging.

But much of what he said about Alex rang true. Until the council appointed him to the directorship of the Group on Aging, Alex had always avoided managerial work, knowing, perhaps, that he wasn't suited to it. But he had taken the job anyway. Nor was he a natural laboratory scientist, and neither disease-related nor cellular research—the two directions that gerontology was likely to take going forward—were areas where he could expect to make an important contribution.

Perhaps he wouldn't have been surprised by the opinion Medawar had passed on to the council about his work. A few months earlier, following the 1968 presidential election, he had written to a friend that he was "seriously thinking of touting for a U.S. job—if I can find a board of academic suckers to finance it. Wish I knew if the Nixon admin was going to go for gerontology as a vote-getter—have a good mind to call the president-elect with a line of sales talk!"[59] He may have had a feeling that his grant from the Medical Research Council would not be renewed when it ended in 1971.

It's also possible that Alex never knew about Medawar's confidential note. They continued to exchange cordial letters from time to time, occasionally did favors for one another, and Alex always spoke of Medawar with great respect. The same year he wrote the letter, Medawar had a crippling stroke. He continued his work on immunology but was no longer as influential a figure in biomedical research as he had been. Whatever his feelings about Alex's work, Medawar's stroke was bad for anyone hoping to see a revival of fundamental research on aging in the UK.

Alex wasn't done promoting his vision for gerontology, however. In 1965 an American biologist, Leonard Hayflick, had published a study refuting the widely held theory that normal vertebrate cells were essentially immortal, that they could keep dividing and replicating forever if they were kept in stable laboratory conditions. Working at the Wistar Institute in Philadelphia, Hayflick found that normal human fetal cells could only divide some forty to fifty times before they stopped, and only cancer cells could do so indefinitely.*****

The "Hayflick limit," as it came to be known, took some time to penetrate the world of research on aging, since Hayflick himself was relatively new to biogerontology, but Alex quickly realized that it bolstered his argument for fundamental research on cells. If cells were where aging took place—not at organ level, in the muscles or tissues, or across human populations—then there was no point in taking a piecemeal, disease-specific approach to the problem. Anything that called itself research on aging would have to explore the processes that caused the building blocks of the human body to fail.

Focusing on the biology of the cell also fit with Alex's desire to push biology into more channels of life study. He and Medawar often spoke of aging in cells as a "loss of program": the playing out of a process, implanted in a snippet of genetic code, that might date to the fertilization of the egg and that had now reached its end.[60] That being the case, gerontology wasn't only the study of aging, it was also the study of processes extending throughout life, and that could help unravel mysteries and address ailments that occurred much earlier, not just at the end of life.[61]

The other nagging problem: how to study aging in humans. Since humans live so much longer than most other animals—including other mammals—studying human life span had always been difficult. In 1958 Alex's friend Nathan Shock, head of the Gerontology Research Center at the National Institutes of Health, launched the Baltimore Longitudinal Study of Aging, which over the next fifty-plus years would include more

***** Stem cells and cancer cells, however, did appear to divide indefinitely. Leonard Hayflick, "The Limited In Vitro Lifetime of Human Diploid Cell Strains," *Experimental Cell Research*, March 1965.

than three thousand participants (it was ongoing in 2022). It gradually yielded important findings about the role of genetics in aging, how aging affects personality and memory, and some of the factors that can slow it down or speed it up (diet, weight, degree of involvement in society).[62]

Alex felt that faster progress was possible. As early as 1963 he was characterizing gerontology as the search for a "clock" or "time-keeping mechanism" of the human body.[63] Three years later, he thought he had found a way around the difficulty, one that had already met with some success. In 1965 a group of researchers with the Atomic Bomb Casualty Commission that Washington had set up to investigate the effects of radiation on survivors of the Hiroshima and Nagasaki blasts published a report on a study they had made of 437 survivors. The study aimed to determine whether the rate of aging had increased for these survivors, using a battery of nine tests, including skin elasticity, hand-grip strength, visual acuity, and systolic blood pressure. The subjects were retested periodically to find out how rapidly each of these factors changed.[64]

Alex proposed a similar study of one hundred to five hundred subjects, aged fifty, from a fairly closed group, such as prisoners, retirees, a religious order, or people working for the same employer. They would be all male or all female, to screen out any variations due to menopause, and Alex proposed expanding the number of tests to as many as sixty, including height standing, height when seated, healing after a biopsy, heart size, and diastolic blood pressure. There would be two objectives: first, to find out which of the variables were the "real" biomarkers, or signs of aging and which could be dismissed; second, to systematically test substances that were thought to affect the rate of aging: food additives—for example, antioxidants like vitamins C and E—or anticaloric drugs.

The project was attractively simple and inexpensive to conduct, Alex argued, and the Japanese study had started to yield findings within about five years. If this held true for his group of subjects, within a comparatively short period of time, gerontologists would have a much better idea where to focus their cellular research and what sort of interventions would have a genuine impact on the rate of aging.

Alex's proposal first appeared formally in an article in *The Lancet* of December 1969, which he forwarded to the Medical Research Council along with a memo asking them to consider the project. "The prime objective," he wrote, would be "the comparison of apparent aging of different measurables in the same individual, the attempt to infer the number and jurisdiction of possible 'aging clocks,' and, eventually, the assessment of treatments designed to affect the rate of aging." He asked the council to convene a group, before deciding to fund the study, to explore what the test components would be, the frequency of retests, and whether it could be combined with other screening programs.

His enthusiasm came through in his *Lancet* article. "Experimental gerontology may well prove the medical growth stock of the next decade," he declared. "The tool we have in mind is as necessary to a fundamental advance in public health as is a radiotelescope to advance in cosmology—and much cheaper."[65] In an address to the Faculty of Actuaries the following February, he said that using his "test-battery," as he called it, "direct experiment on the delaying of aging in man is virtually certain to be in hand somewhere by 1975." An "agent" that reduced the rate of aging would be available within fifteen years, he predicted (he sometimes said twenty), and the increase in healthy life span could be as much as 20 percent.[66] A year later, Alex won the Dr. Heinz Karger Memorial Prize for another paper on his idea, "Basic Research in Gerontology."[67]

He made his prediction of fast results often enough, in talks, interviews (from the *Torquay Herald Express* to *Modern Nursing Home*), and articles, that *Time* magazine featured him prominently in an August 1972 piece on the prospects for living longer. As if to nudge prospective sponsors of his test battery, he and his colleagues in the Group on Aging performed an experiment in which they put mice on a diet heavier in antioxidants than the standard and found they lived longer.[68] He also presented on the test-battery idea at a major conference, the International Forum on the Control of Human Aging, in September 1971.[69] Early in 1972 he did the same at the Huxley Foundation's conference on aging in New York.[70]

The test-battery approach appealed to Alex's holistic conception of aging research, but a degree of self-interest lurked behind his efforts as well. His grant from the Medical Research Council was winding down, and he wanted to know if there was a future for him as a gerontologist in the UK. Additionally, the test-battery project played to his strengths as a researcher, which were observation and statistical evaluation rather than molecular- or cellular-level study. But no one was biting. Neither the council nor any other institution, British or American, appears to have responded to his proposal. While it's impossible to say why exactly, it's likely that, with the budget crises and economic shocks that hit the UK especially at the end of the '60s and the beginning of the '70s, there wasn't much appetite for spending on basic research projects that didn't promise an immediate payoff.

In a 1971 BBC Radio 3 symposium on aging that included Alex, Medawar, and several other scientists and politicians, Medawar put the situation bluntly when discussing the challenge of getting from the experimental stage to the point where an "elixir" against aging was actually available to the public. "It's enormous in terms of man hours, tens of thousands of man hours—hundreds of thousands of pounds," he said flatly. "The money certainly won't be forthcoming from the Medical Research Council."[71]

CHAPTER 13

Traveling Friar (1964–1971)

Jack Haldane, who died in 1964, had not only provided the tentative hypothesis behind Alex's work on aging but also a kind of template for the life he was attempting, with some success, to lead. In 1924 Haldane had published a book—originally a lecture—*Daedalus; or, Science and the Future*, in which he argued that humans were at last in a position, through their knowledge of genetics and with the help of in vitro fertilization, to design their own future evolution. To handle this terrible responsibility without stumbling into disaster, humans would have to build a new ethics, informed by science and different from the ethics of Christianity and the other monotheistic religions. *Daedalus* became essential reading for scores of prominent British and European scientists and intellectuals: Bertrand Russell, Albert Einstein, Aldous Huxley (whose dystopian classic *Brave New World* was partially inspired by it), and many others.[1] Alex never referred to Haldane's work as a factor in his intellectual development, but the problem he laid out in *Daedalus* is clearly reflected in Alex's thinking.

What Alex liked about him above all was, naturally, his bloody-mindedness: his seeming compulsion to be uncooperative, rightly or wrongly. He regaled Nick with stories about Haldane and especially liked one dating to 1913, when the drivers of the city of Oxford's horse-drawn trams went on strike and the city sent in strikebreakers to keep the trams running. One evening, Haldane, then an undergraduate, stepped into the middle of a much-trafficked street and bellowed the Athanasian Creed, in Latin, attracting a large enough crowd to block the trams.

In November 1967, four years after Haldane died, Alex joined a group of scientists for a discussion on BBC radio of his old colleague's legacy. He singled out the openness to unfamiliar ideas and modes of thinking that Haldane showed when he moved to India. "Faced with students clamouring for computers and electron microscopes," Alex remembered, "he made them buy notebooks and sit down to count the petals on the flowers which fell off the bushes. And after a year's counting the Guru's disciples found they had upset the classification of the whole genus of plants."[2]

The same year, Alex reviewed Haldane's last book, a collection of essays titled *Science and Life* that he said exemplified scientific rationalism. The scientist's greatest task, he wrote, was to "learn to think and to feel with equal relevance and contextual appropriateness," something Haldane accomplished through a combination of "judgment with eclecticism, and total openness with a ready perception of nonsense in all its forms."

Who was Haldane? "Hindu? Rationalist? Irrationalist? Chiefly, so far as these essays are concerned, a complete human being," Alex wrote. "The task of becoming such is what Haldane's kind of rationalism is basically about."[3]

That was the task Alex had set himself, and over the years, it had changed him. Several months earlier, Dan Callahan, an academic at Simon Fraser University in Vancouver, who had written a dissertation on Alex's work and was venturing to assemble a bibliography of his writings, asked where he could find some of his early manuscripts.[4] "I can't really remember most of what was in the early books," Alex replied. "I thought I was creating it consciously as 'strong' stuff, but a lot of it came back during a recent analysis. I have a feeling that I have only recently become a person and can now go back to some of the self which, as an undergraduate, lived only on paper."[5] A few years later, he looked back again on his previous self in a poem:

> I wonder where the man I was is gone—
> not here, not dead, not sleeping; somewhere else.
> I've shed his fears and many of his talents
> also his inexperience;
> I could not write poems like his today.[6]

Despite the frustration he was starting to feel in his scientific career, the '60s may have been one of the happiest periods in Alex's life, even if the two women to whom he had committed himself might not have experienced it that way. His son Nick has guessed that he may have been in psychoanalysis at this time, although most likely informally, with a colleague. If so, it may have helped him to see his life whole, rather as a succession of project, as had been his mode.

His research and teaching left him time for writing and broadcasting, and as a sought-after speaker at scientific conferences, he traveled to the United States, throughout Europe, and even behind the Iron Curtain to Czechoslovakia and Russia. "Alex is delightful," one scientist who attended gerontological conferences with him said. "Put him in a seminar, and when things get deadly dull, he will suddenly sum up the proceedings in a limerick."[7]

Alex enjoyed the travel and companionship his schedule brought him. "Like the rabbit I need to keep on the run," he told a friend.[8] While he was officially the director of a research group on aging, in reality his job was "that of being a missionary friar" he told an American reporter in 1969. "I travel from country to country rather than doing much research myself, and I talk to people and try to put the results together."[9]

He enjoyed both a well-ordered home life with Ruth—Nick was now at Cambridge, where he joined CongSoc, just as his father had some twenty-five years earlier—and a more intense emotional and sexual experience with Jane.[10] Prompted in part by the Indian, Chinese, and Italian Renaissance manuals and "posture books" he was researching and collecting, Alex and Jane experimented with different positions and occasional fantasies, recording them in a notebook they entitled "Our ABC, by John and Jane Thomas" and taking Polaroids of themselves in action. Jane "coaxed me to jot down my observations, so I made a practice of it," Alex later recalled.[11]

There were other women in his life as well: up to a point. In his letter to Callahan, Alex mentioned that his recent nonscientific writing included thirteen poems—his first in several years—"for a girl in Vienna." This was Madeleine Jenewein, a secretary or conference organizer at the Vienna Academy of Medicine, whom he had met in 1967 and had subsequently corresponded with, sending her letters, poems, pictures of himself, and a copy of *Come Out to Play* ("while reading it I got more often the feeling that Goggins is you," she wrote back). Madeleine was twenty years younger than Alex, and her letters back to him suggest that she found him a charming presence in her life at a time when she was deciding what to do next professionally. He bought her a necklace and saw her again at a conference in Vienna in November, during which they strolled about the city together. "You live here, I live—nowhere," he wrote in one of his poems to her.[12] If another of the poems is to be believed, they had sex during his first visit but not the second.[13] The

"Vienna Poems," one of which is addressed directly to Madeleine, would wait eleven years before they were published.

In December 1968 Alex met Marilyn Yalom, an American academic at California State University, Hayward, specializing in French literature, who was in London with her husband Irvin, a psychiatrist, on his sabbatical from Stanford. Marilyn had proposed an article for *ADAM International Review*, a literary magazine edited by the Romanian-born Miron Grindea, on C. F. Ramuz, a Swiss novelist whose *Présence de la mort* Alex had revised in translation more than twenty years earlier. That prompted Grindea, who knew Alex, to bring the three of them together for lunch.

After the holidays, Marilyn contacted Alex, asking him to look over two or three pages of a translation she was making of Ramuz's early novel *Aline*.[14] The two met for tea, after which he gave her a quick tour of UCL, including the school's oddest attraction: the cabinet in the South Cloisters displaying the preserved body of Jeremy Bentham. Having paid their respects to the Utilitarian philosopher, they had lunch at one of the nearby Indian restaurants that Alex favored. It was the first time she had dined on Indian food with someone who had a real knowledge of it, Marilyn much later recalled.[15]

They hit it off right away, talking first about medieval and Renaissance French poetry and then about anything and everything. The man sitting opposite Marilyn was forty-seven, "with green/blue eyes, a little pudgy, and he did have that amazing hand." What she noticed first, however, was his "endless vocabulary. He spoke fast, but in complete sentences, as though he was composing an essay as he went on." At some point, the conversation became more personal, and Alex told Marilyn, possibly a little proudly, that he had two households, with a wife and a mistress, and that the arrangement could be stressful. They then went to the British Museum, where Alex showed her around the section of Indian sculpture. Afterward, she told Irv he had to meet "this remarkable man," and soon the three had dinner together.

They would remain close friends most of the rest of Alex's life. "What we were in love with was his mind," Marilyn said, "such an original, unusual, poetic mind. I never felt that he was tendentious or preaching at us, or at me. He was extremely sensitive to other people, kind and thoughtful." Although their friendship never threatened either relationship—Alex and Irv developed a good rapport, and Jane and Marilyn became friendly; the Yaloms never met Ruth—it was always understood that Alex was a bit in love with Marilyn, and she a bit with him, if less so.

They wrote long letters back and forth, Alex helped ship some antiques she had bought in London to her home in Palo Alto when Marilyn and Irv returned from his sabbatical, and he even helped her with travel arrangements on at least one occasion when she came to London alone.

That fall, Alex was in Palo Alto for a short visit.; In June 1969 he traveled to California to deliver a lecture in San Francisco and then attend a conference in San Diego. Afterward, he spent a long holiday with the Yaloms at their house on Robles Ridge Road in Palo Alto. He left an impression of the place in a poem he wrote soon after, and of the other life it suggested he might have had:

By the gate of the garden are two pepper trees
and coral-pink beads and green skeleton fish
swing from their fingers and swim in the breeze:
an alternative life rushes by in a flash.[16]

Marilyn and Irv gave him the bedroom next to theirs, and he got to know their three older children as well as Ben, a newborn, to whom Alex had already written some lines: more about the boy's mother, actually.

Your mother's bonny, whom you'll shortly see—
I envy you the spot that you are in.
You'll find her gentle, as she was to me,
suckle with pleasure where my hand has been.[17]

In the evenings, he cooked Tandoori meals for the family. During the day, he could work in the garden for hours, helping Marilyn and the children plant trees; her daughter Eve remembered him once wearing a Speedo bathing suit as he dug. He always sang as he worked, often Henry Purcell or another sixteenth- or seventeenth-century English composer.[18] He had a "sweet voice," Marilyn remembered, in spite of his dentures. As many others noted, he had a dry wit, and a quick one. When the subject came up of a friend of the Yaloms who had had a mastectomy, and Marilyn asked Alex what he would do if he was making love to such a woman, he replied, "I'd be particularly nice to the one."[19]

His nearly photographic memory constantly astonished the family. Once he went with Marilyn and Irv to a performance of a play by Racine in a new translation. The next morning he recited chunks of the text while working outside. Another time, they had dinner at the home of a Palo Alto neighbor, Russel Lee, who had founded one of first group medical practices in the country and was known for his trove of limericks; Alex and their host traded selections back and forth for what seemed like hours, Marilyn recalled.[20]

The Yaloms were something new in Alex's life, and from then on he would see them—especially Marilyn—whenever he could: at their home, in London, or when they happened to be in the same city together. Partly, it was their way of living and the community they belonged to. Both were nearing forty, but their major work was still ahead of them. Irv, already a tenured professor at Stanford, would publish *The Theory and Practice of Group Psychotherapy* in 1970 and ten years later, with Alex's encouragement, would write another influential book, *Existential Psychotherapy* (which Alex would blurb as "an irreducible classic" in the field).[21] In 1976 Marilyn would join the Clayman Institute for Gender Research at Stanford, after which she became an important feminist scholar, writing a series of important books starting with *Maternity, Mortality, and the Literature of Madness* (1985), which traced a link between maternity and mental breakdown in some women writers.

Alex made other friends in the Stanford community when he stayed with the Yaloms. One was Leonard Hayflick, the discoverer of the Hayflick Limit on cellular aging, who was now a professor there. A brilliant, forty-five-year-old biologist, Hayflick met Alex in 1970, at a summer class he directed on aging. Two years later, he invited Alex to be a guest lecturer for one of a series of classes on aging at his Stanford home. The students were excited to meet the author of *The Joy of Sex*; one of them brought her copy of the book to class, which Alex signed, in characteristic style, "To one of my best students. Alex Comfort." He and Hayflick remained in close contact thereafter.[22]

Despite his wide net of contacts and acquaintances in science, Alex had never had a circle of really close friends in the academic community, and his home life with Ruth in Loughton, which continued despite his attachment to Jane, was rather ordinary. "Do have a good Christmas," he wrote Marilyn around holiday time in 1971, when he was going through a bout of depression. "I always want to hire a man to have these holidays en famille for me, like Bob Hope—they tend to bring one down, I find, compared with work."[23]

The Yaloms and their friends in and around Stanford were something different: a family outside of his own with whom he enjoyed spending personal time, friends other than Ruth and Jane who could get him to talk about himself rather than about practical matters, politics, or the arts. Marilyn drew him out about his childhood, including his having never felt attractive growing up and having married Ruth partly as a response to her loving him.

Middle-aged men are sometimes attracted to much younger women who presumably make them feel young again. Others are attracted to women much closer in age or the same age as themselves, whom they see as their ideal partner, the person they would have spent all those years with if they had only known. Marilyn was twelve years younger than Alex, a petite woman with a glowing smile and bright eyes; she was also accomplished and erudite, someone he could talk with about some of his favorite subjects as an equal. She also clearly admired his intellect; he was, she later said, one of only two geniuses she had met in her life. Up to now he had seldom been one to write long personal letters, but to Marilyn, he did, often decorated with comic drawings of his guppies. An unmistakable ache comes through in one that he sent soon after she and Irv moved back to the States in 1968.

> I paid a little visit to the Portobello Road [where they had shopped for antiques and books], pretending you were with me. In fact you're seldom away from me when I walk about London and see things I'd like to be able to show you or enjoy with you. There will be nothing so nice in my life to look forward to as the prospect of seeing you again; one day, it's my fantasy, in a place where we are both footloose strangers who can be kids and not responsible upholders of academic dignity (we didn't do badly but could do better).[24]

On occasion, the relationship went deeper. Sometime in the early '70s, Marilyn needed to stay overnight in London on her way back to the United States. She spent the night with Alex and Jane in Jane's flat. When she was back at home, she wrote both of them. "In every way it was what I needed," she said. She had had "a very happy reunion with Irv": "Amongst other things, I told him of the night we three spent together and even something of the sexual relationship between Alex and me, putting it all in the pre-Benjy past as something that is over (and I do think that is for the best, all around)." She hoped that the four of them could continue with a friendship "which means more and more to me."[25] Most likely she was referring to an episode she and Alex had enjoyed when she and Irv were living in London, before Ben was born; clearly, Jane knew about it.

For the time being, Marilyn had her wish, and all proceeded smoothly. Years later, and long after the publication of *The Joy of*

Sex, she insisted that Alex had always been a gentleman. "He was very romantic," she said. "The picture of him as lecherous doesn't get it. He was the last person to thrust himself on someone."

AS AN ADULT, ALEX always included in his personal presentation some small emblem of rebellion, even when his professional position required him to outfit himself in respectable suit and tie. In the '40s and '50s it was the beret that embarrassed Wrey Gardiner and then Ruth and Nick. In the mid-'60s it was the small van he drove when he needed to use an auto (he generally took the train to UCL from Loughton, or the tube from Jane's apartment), on the dashboard of which he had taped a condom. A cheeky acknowledgment, perhaps, of the way the world so often saw him.

Later, in the United States, it was seemingly taken for granted that the success of *The Joy of Sex* hurtled Alex into a new role as sex guru that he'd never really wanted. The truth is that he had been living with that tag in the UK at least since his discussion of teenage sex on the BBC in 1963. After that, he seemed to have a place on everybody's mental list as a go-to defender of sexual license.

In fall 1964, Bob Guccione, an expatriate American who had been attempting to launch himself as a painter in the UK, announced a new magazine called *Penthouse*. In a targeted mailing to prospective subscribers, Guccione boasted that the first "Collectors' Copy" would contain "THE LARGEST COLLECTION OF WORLD FAMOUS AUTHORS EVER ASSEMBLED IN *ANY* SINGLE ISSUE OF *ANY* BRITISH MAGAZINE AT *ANY* TIME IN HISTORY!!!" Among the contributors would be Alex (with a satirical piece, "On Subliminal Self-Advertising"), Julian Huxley (with "an analytic piece on race hatred"), Alan Sillitoe, Colin Wilson, and the Situationist provocateur Alex Trocchi.

Penthouse was to be more than a magazine, Guccione asserted. It was "a cause, a revolution which will stimulate every intelligent man and woman in Britain today," the standard-bearer of an "unprecedented and monumental struggle for moral and intellectual freedom." In its pages, readers would find out "the truth about aphrodisiacs," learn "how to meet girls" and "why beautiful women make lousy lovers," and hear "the case for polygamy." A "GIANT NUDE PULLOUT" would also be included—for free.

In December—two months before the first issue of *Penthouse* was set to appear—three MPs (two Labour and one Tory) denounced the magazine as "morally corrupting" and asked the postmaster general to stop Guccione's brochures, which included some revealing photos of models, from being circulated. John Cordle, Tory MP for Bournemouth East, asked the attorney general to refer the matter to the director of prosecutions.[26] Alex had already heard personally from his CND acquaintance Sir Richard Acland, complaining that he and his wife had received a *Penthouse* brochure—a copy of which he enclosed with his letter—and asking whether the inclusion of Alex's name had been a "misrepresentation."[27]

Shortly afterward, a letter from Alex was published in the *Guardian* in which he said he had heard from "certain gentlemen," urging him to withdraw his contribution from the magazine. "Since I like their tone even less than that of the handout to which they object, I shall give them no joy," Alex wrote. He also ventured to say that it was unfair to judge the magazine before it appeared, and that in any case, it could "hardly be more immature or mischievous than much of what we read in sermons, or in the publications of the BMA [British Medical Association]."[28]

But he continued to hear from people who had received brochures with his name on them, including many of his colleagues at UCL. On February 9, less than two weeks before the first issue was due to hit the mails and a few bookstalls—many bookshops and chains were refusing to carry it after the dust-up in Parliament—he wrote to Guccione about the brochures, which he called "embarrassing tripe. I was willing to wear this as a practical joke on the prudes, but the joke is now wearing thin to the point of becoming academically expensive; as a contributor I can, and if necessary will, repudiate any share in the circular; I hope the magazine won't require apology." As it was, he turned down Guccione's invitation to serve as *Penthouse's* science editor, adding that if the magazine's promotions didn't shape up, he would not contribute again. He then sent a letter to the editor of the *Guardian*, stating his hope that the magazine's publicity would be in better taste in the future.[29]

Predictably, the hullabaloo only helped Guccione to cash in. The first issue sold 150,000 copies, which, the publisher claimed, made *Penthouse* the biggest-selling monthly magazine in Britain. "Have you come across a thing called *Penthouse*?" Iris Murdoch wrote her friend, the novelist and critic Brigid Brophy, that fall. "It's a new pornographic glossy magazine given over mainly to pictures of naked and semi-naked girls. . . . The thing masquerades as a 'progressive form of opinon [*sic*]' etc. etc. and is contributed to by Colin Wilson and Alex Comfort. I think it's extremely disgraceful!"[30]

Four years later, Guccione would launch *Penthouse* in the United States as well and reap a fortune. In the meantime, he invited Alex to lunch to "discuss a few ideas."[31] That appears not to have come about, and Alex never again contributed to the magazine, although his lone appearance in *Penthouse* led to at least one solicitation to publish in another, less pretentious British men's magazine, *King*, which he also turned down.[32] In the future he would be more careful.

Penthouse, however, in its hopelessly cheesy and exploitative way, was an indicator of the change that was gaining speed in British culture, whether in public or still under cover. In June 1967, with a Labour government in power, Parliament approved the Family Planning Act, which made contraception readily available through the National Health Service. Barely two weeks later, Parliament passed (by a one-vote margin) the Sexual Offences Act, which decriminalized homosexual activity between consenting adults in private, although not in Scotland or Northern Ireland. In October, abortion was legalized in the UK, although not in all circumstances. In a matter of months, many of the reforms that Alex and others had been calling for since the Wolfenden report appeared, a decade earlier, had become law.

The previous year, William Masters and Virginia Johnson had published their groundbreaking *Human Sexual Response* in the United States and the UK, a book written as drily as possible and replete with aggravating physiological jargon. ("The authors have no valid defence [for] the English style in which their results are phrased," Alex said in his review.)[33] The book for the first time presented the results of actual laboratory observation of sex acts and the subjects' response to them. It was a best-selling sensation, was translated into over thirty languages, and boosted the sex therapy practice that Masters and Johnson had launched in 1964 while inspiring a host of imitators.

Alex reviewed *Human Sexual Response* twice, for the *New Statesman* and *The Lancet*, the latter article published one day after the former. He was especially impressed by their findings that "senile impotence" in males was a "sexual fable"—in reality, sexual response just slowed down, something Alex had surmised—and about the functioning of the clitoris that also dispelled a number of myths.[34]

Alex wrote to Masters, congratulating both researchers on their book and letting them know that the UK medical press had generally greeted it positively ("the ineducables among us having kept quiet").[35] Masters and Johnson had already seen his reviews, which they had "enjoyed thoroughly," and they promised to meet the next time Alex was in the States.[36]

What most delighted Alex about *Human Sexual Response* was that it put facts about sex before the public, in what he considered the best scientific tradition. Surely information was the strongest weapon in the fight against sexual anxieties. A further sign of change, however, put him back in hot water without his writing a word to provoke the attacks.

The Protestant religious establishment had come a fair distance since the mid-'50s, when the Church of England hierarchy had successfully opposed the queen's sister, Princess Margaret, marrying a divorced commoner. The same year *Human Sexual Response* was published, the archbishop of Canterbury acknowledged that the church should not interfere in the making of laws for secular society and recommended the breakdown of marriage as grounds for divorce, a much more flexible standard than previously.[37] In October 1966—some eight months before Parliament enacted its series of reforms—a working party of the British Council of Churches, which included the Church of England and the major Nonconformist denominations, issued a report titled *Sex and Morality*. Rather than making a case that sex outside marriage was wrong, the report concluded that it was impossible to create one set of rules on the matter and that Christians "should instead be led to an understanding of sex which would enable them to make up their own minds."

The report quoted approvingly the two "unbreakable rules" that Alex, who it described as a "radical sex pundit," had laid out in *Sex in Society* and his subsequent 1963 BBC broadcast: "Thou shalt not exploit another person's feelings and wantonly expose them to an experience of rejection," and "Thou shalt not under any circumstances negligently risk producing an unwanted child." The text went on to assert—going a bit too far—that if those two rules were honored, it would "rule out most of the extramarital intercourse that actually occurs."[38]

That additional point wasn't enough to shield the council from attacks by conservative moralists. "What on earth are the Churches doing signing a concordat with Dr Comfort anyhow?" an October 21 letter to the editor of the *Spectator* asked. A more comprehensive attack appeared the following month in the *Catholic Herald*, written by David Holbrook, a fellow of King's College, Cambridge, and literary scholar who had once been a vocal member of the Communist Party. Holbrook grouped Alex with the Marquis de Sade and Wilhelm Reich as advocates of a dehumanized form of sexuality that divorced it from human emotional needs and "substituted an intellectual scheme for man."[39] The *Herald* gave Alex space to respond, and in his letter he complained that Holbrook had "closely implied" that he advocated bringing up children in common and wanted all restraints on sexual behavior removed. He referred Holbrook to *Sex and Society* for a full refutation of the charges.[40]

Holbrook wrote back, branding Alex for his "willingness to write for 'girlie' magazines," presumably having *Penthouse* in mind.[41] What he never addressed in his attacks—nor did many of the legion who disparaged Alex's views in these and later years—was the fundamental point that sex in a morally repressive society was deeply anxiety-ridden, and that this was responsible for a great deal of the unhappiness, oppression, and violence that occurred in sexual relationships, married or otherwise. Alex was determined to press the argument. In a brief interview in the *Observer* in December, he mentioned he was writing a new book to be titled *The Anxiety Makers*. The subject would be the role of medical science in the manufacturing of public anxiety in the name of morality and health. "As recently as 1930," Alex told the *Observer*, "they were selling chastity belts for children. In the late nineteenth century people were practicing circumcision as a cure for epilepsy. . . . Tonsils were thought to be responsible for suicide, Englishmen's horse faces and pretty well any disease which flesh is heir to." The neurosis ran deep still, Alex said; even today. "we are anxious about being anxious."[42]

The Anxiety Makers was conceived in March 1966 as the first volume of a series that Alex was to edit for John Constable & Company, onetime publisher of Sir Walter Scott and Bram Stoker, to be collectively titled The Natural History of Society.[43] It would include volumes on "under-the-counter literature," fashion and fetishism, "hooliganism," prostitution, and, curiously, nuns. A volume on jealousy (never published) was to be written by Phyllis and Eberhard Kronhausen, San Diego-based psychotherapists who had written a number of books on sex and who in 1968 would organize the First International Exhibition of Erotic Art in Lund, Sweden, including some items contributed by Alex.[44] The deal was arranged with James Mitchell, a hyper-driven, twenty-seven-year-old editor at Constable who was keen to launch ambitious, attention-getting projects with name writers and who had a seemingly limitless file-drawer of ideas in his head.

As far back as *Sexual Behavior in Society* in 1950, Alex had held doctors and the medical establishment responsible for propagating or at least tolerating much of the longstanding cautionary nonsense about sex acts. His new book analyzed the development of this tendency in a more systematic way, highlighting the degree to which physicians had let their judgment be conditioned by dogma and popular prejudices. He drew on his research in hundreds of years of Western writing on sex and sexual morality, including decades of articles and letters in British and European medical journals.

Alex had favorably reviewed Michel Foucault's *Madness and Civilization*, and the argument he presented in *The Anxiety Makers* anticipates some aspects of the one that Foucault would make in his History of Sexuality series, minus the explicit political and economic elements and written in a more accessible and entertaining style. Alex defined anxiety as fear "with a large psychosymbolic load."[45] Western culture creates and fosters anxiety as a means of social control, he said. Anxiety about sex is one of the most important varieties, "the main driving-power behind its religious and ethical life." In the centuries before the Enlightenment, sex was regulated through religion. Since then, the physician had increasingly taken the place of the priest in such matters. The physician, in other words, had become the central maintainer of anxiety.

Pre- and extramarital sex, masturbation, promiscuity, female sexuality in general, and interracial sex were still condemned as immoral and degrading—maybe even more so—but less on spiritual grounds than for reasons of health ("hygiene") and social cohesion: the maintenance of the family, a steady flow of well-adjusted children, and increasingly the preservation of supposedly superior races. The rise of the middle classes in the nineteenth century saw the production of anxiety around these matters reach a "flood tide," and medical science took the lead in supplying the rationales.

Alex tells four related stories in *The Anxiety Makers*. First is the conversion of cultural norms and folk beliefs about sex into alleged medical knowledge, often involving the need to keep women subordinate. Next came the great hysteria over masturbation, which began in earnest with a 1710 pamphlet by "an anonymous clergyman turned quack," written to promote a bogus remedy, and which then raged for two centuries and sometimes included shockingly cruel treatments for curing both boys and girls of the habit. At about the same time, medicine was promoting the need for "inner cleanliness"—that is, anxiety over bowel functions—which was held to be the key to curing everything from lassitude to epilepsy. The fourth story Alex tells is about the ills that medicine didn't address while it focused on these other supposed curses: venereal diseases, unwanted pregnancies, and inability to conceive. The spirochete and the spermatozoan were the "two major physical allies of conventional sexual anxiety," Alex wrote, and it took the great outbreaks of venereal disease among the armed forces during World War I to compel the British and American governments to do anything about them. Separating coitus from the risk of fertility, either through contraception or artificial insemination, was of course too socially destabilizing to contemplate.

The age of anxiety hadn't ended in the postwar era, Alex argued. Sexual puritans, decades before the so-called right to life movement began, had already learned to couch their propaganda in gentler, less overtly moralistic language, even if they were peddling the same old anxieties.[46] The panic over drug abuse—by the young and people of color, while the behavior of adult white people was passed over—suggested that moral outrage could always find new targets to replace the old. But four changes offered hope: better contraceptives, artificial insemination, the gradual erosion in the scientific community of the idea of "normality," and, most important, ordinary people's own contrariness.

Alex ended the book on an ambiguous note. Cultural conservatives weren't the only anxiety makers. People like himself were increasingly worried about the Bomb, genetic modification, and the general misuse of science for profit or political domination by government and the private sector. Ordinary people had voted with their feet against the church, the State, the medical establishment, and in many cases their own upbringing, to obtain greater sexual freedom. The challenge was to persuade them to take seriously these other, very urgent anxieties. As an anarchist, Alex felt that it was ordinary people who would uproot them as well.

The Anxiety Makers received generous publicity thanks to Nelson, which announced the Natural History of Society series to every press contact it could muster. It was reviewed widely and excerpted in the *Daily Mail* and the *Observer*, and Alex was interviewed about the book several times. By now, critics all seemed to have a reasonable idea what to expect from a new Comfort book. "Whether he likes it or not," said the *Birmingham Post*, "Dr. Comfort has become regarded as a spokesman for the liberal, humanist view of contemporary moral problems, and it is impossible to consider this book apart from the permissive-moralistic, humanist-Christian controversy."[47]

Only a very few failed to be shocked by the examples of ignorant, misguided, cruel, and dogmatic treatment he dug out of the depths of eighteenth-, nineteenth-, and even many twentieth-century medical texts. And many reviewers accepted, for the most part, his judgment that doctors had caused as much havoc in the service of sexual repression and anxiety formation as priests or preachers. But the worst abuses dated from the nineteenth century and seemed to be on the decline. Some of the examples he gave were rehearsed in a book that came out a short time earlier, *The Other Victorians: A Study of Sexuality and Pornography in Mid-nineteenth Century England*, by the American scholar Steven Marcus.

Medicine and medical science didn't exist in a vacuum, Michael Rapoport said in the *Morning Star*. They were always informed by the culture of a specific time and place, and *The Anxiety Makers* never addressed how cultural forces act on them.[48] Might sexual liberation create its own distinctive set of anxieties? An otherwise very positive review in the *Sunday Times* by Alex's friend Anthony Storr, a prominent psychiatrist, noted that he was "largely content to catalogue the absurdities of past and present rather than attempt to explain them."[49] The novelist and critic Malcolm Bradbury, in *The Listener*, complained that Alex's seeming assertion that "rationalistic medicine and the capacity of people to vote with their genitalia is the way to progress" may limit our ability to understand the complexities of the modern world; there's just more to it than that.[50]

But the biggest problem with the book was the flimsiness of an argument centered on the idea of "anxiety." It was all very well to condemn the manufacturing of anxiety in regard to sex, an area in which there was clearly much too much of it. But when Alex noted how liberals attempt to leverage anxiety about the Bomb or the dehumanizing effects of rapid technological change, the psychiatrist Charles Rycroft complained in the *Observer*, he failed to develop the theme.[51] Is it ever all right to foster anxiety, especially if "one's daily occupation is to inculcate and foster realism," as it is for a doctor? What if science itself is being used for bad ends? Alex raised the question but did not answer it.

The Anxiety Makers was the kind of highly readable book that Alex had learned to write quickly and easily: stuffed with learning but with a glibness about it that anyone solidly acquainted with the subject matter would instantly sense. It ended right where a deeper social analysis ought to begin. It also betrayed an unspoken foreboding, which some critics caught in their comments. Alex believed deeply in science and its capacity to facilitate human liberation, at least when coupled with an understanding of the irrational. But what if science had gone too far in letting itself be exploited and misused?

He did address this point in the later pages of the book. "None of the consequences of science are alarming *per se*," he wrote. What was alarming was its "paranoid use." "This applies to psychotropic drugs, atomic explosives, birth control, brain surgery, artificial pregnancy, genetic modification—the lot." Alex often criticized people who were too ready to throw science overboard rather than trust that its discoveries would not be misused, but he wasn't sure himself that these people weren't at least partially right. "One can end up wondering if one is anxiety-making over the dangers of expressing sane anxiety. It is an unenviable position."[52] He saw no easy out.

THE COPYRIGHT ON *THE Anxiety Makers* didn't belong to Alex personally but rather to an entity called Books and Broadcasts Ltd. Alex ("Dr. A. Comfort, director and secretary") and Jane ("Miss J. T. Henderson, director and chairman") had set it up as a private company in 1964, about the time that Alex had chipped in £2,700 toward the £4,000 purchase price of a leasehold flat for Jane at 10 Fisher House on Ward Road, a new development in Tufnell Park, North London. Alex's contribution was structured as a loan to the company, and the rest was financed "from current funds," according to the minutes of a meeting of the two directors on August 27. At another meeting on December 10, Alex made a formal agreement for Books and Broadcasts to act as his literary agent with respect to radio and television appearances in the UK, for a 10 percent commission. Alex agreed to sell the rights to *Nature and Human Nature*, which he had just finished writing, to the company for a lump sum "to be negotiated in the light of offers received from publishers." And he informed David Higham that Books and Broadcasts was the new owner of his edition of the *Koka Shastra*, over which the agent was then negotiating with the Dutch publisher Nieuwe Wieken.[53]

Besides gaining some tax advantages, the point of setting up Books and Broadcasts appears to have been to give Jane a share of the money Alex made from his literary work. Some four years into their relationship, Alex was assuming more responsibility for Jane, in a somewhat oblique manner, and setting up a full-fledged second household for the two of them. The company would be based at the Fisher House flat, and Jane was to receive ten shillings per week as rent for the office space. Remuneration for the two directors was set at £1,360 for the first year of operation, 1964–65. Board meetings were duly recorded—the minutes rarely took up more than a single typed page—and an auditor was hired to prepare the accounts.

Initially, business consisted entirely of Alex's books and various broadcast ideas he concocted for the BBC. The first of these was a satirical thriller eventually titled *The Devil's Eggshell*, which he sold to the network, where the writer David Weir developed it in into a teleplay. The story is reminiscent of *Come Out to Play*, except that everything goes wrong in the end. A group of scientists, tired of being used by power-hungry politicians, plant strange cylindrical objects at sites of train wrecks, famines, and other disasters around the world. The idea is for these hints of an alien invasion to rally people to demand that their leaders behave responsibly and implement social reforms. Instead, the plot backfires, and a hard-right dictator takes over in the UK, guillotining the would-be reformers; eventually, the old crowd of politicians come back, only with new repressive powers.

The Devil's Eggshell was broadcast on June 28, 1966, as part of the BBC's *Play of the Month* series, but it wasn't well received except for an amusing performance by Leonard Rossiter as the prime minister. "Occasionally a serious political thought protruded awkwardly amid the schoolboyish Whitehall hokum," the *Daily Telegraph* said next morning.

Alex submitted two more story ideas to the BBC, one of them about the sixteenth-century German occultist and proto-modern scientific thinker Heinrich Cornelius Agrippa von Nettesheim: a "Brechtian" piece "without the didacticism," is how he described it.[54] Not surprisingly, the network turned it down.

Aside from his sense of responsibility to Jane, Alex set up Books and Broadcasts out of a desire to take a more businesslike, profit-driven approach to his writing. He was looking for opportunities to expand his reach from books, articles, and TV production into editorial services and even author representation. His most immediate publishing project, however, was the Natural History of Society series, of which *The Anxiety Makers* was supposed to be the first entry. Alex and James Mitchell quickly got tentative authors' agreements for eleven books in the series, with another fifteen under negotiation by August 1966 and "a similar number likely to materialize over the next 12 months," Alex reported to Books and Broadcasts. Furthermore, Mitchell arranged for Panther, an upstart paperback imprint that was attempting to give Penguin a run for its money, to bring out the first six titles in softcover and help sell the continental rights at the upcoming Frankfurt Book Fair.[55]

It was not always clear, however, in dealing with publishers, what position Books and Broadcasts actually held in the transaction. In October 1966, Weidenfeld & Nicholson approached Alex about editing another series, an International Library of Sexology, and a meeting was set up in Hamburg to discuss the project. According to the minutes of their next board meeting, Alex and Jane determined that they would draft a contract, either between Books and Broadcasts and Wiedenfeld or between Alex and Weidenfeld with Books and Broadcasts acting as agents, "whichever might appear the more advantageous."[56] How they would have assessed one as more advantageous than the other is not clear, and in any case the project went no further.

Alex's efforts to turn Books and Broadcasts into a literary agent were not successful either. In 1968 the firm represented two aspiring novelists he had met through the Yaloms and who wanted to sell their books in the UK. Morton Grosser, a design engineer, had published his first novel, *The Hobby Shop*, with Houghton Mifflin the previous year. Alex found it "delightful" and thought it had "a very good chance" in the UK, but after he showed copies to a small London publisher, Elek Books, and several of the larger houses, no bids emerged.[57] The result was no happier for Irving Sarnoff, a New York University psychology professor who was also trying his hand at a novel.[58]

ALEX HIMSELF WAS IN demand, however. He was still corresponding with a handful of Russian gerontologists and sending them copies of his books when requested.[59] In 1967 he attended a conference on aging at the Institute of Experimental Biology and Pathology in Kiev (Kyiv). One of the scientists he met was Zhores Medvedev, the biologist and identical twin of the teacher and historian Roy Medvedev. Zhores had circulated a draft of his critical history of Soviet genetics, *The Rise and Fall of T. D. Lysenko*, in 1962, but the brothers were just beginning to come to the authorities' attention as dissidents.* Zhores was doing important work on aging at the cellular level and he and Alex quickly formed a fast friendship, touring the city and taking a close look at the institute, which greatly impressed Alex.[60] Years later, Medvedev recalled that Alex spoke "extremely rapid English" and asked him questions about sex life in Russia ("which I, unfortunately, was not able to answer," he said).[61]

* Medvedev would come under serious attack in 1969, when a microfilm of the book was smuggled out of the country, translated and published in the West. Francisco J. Ayala, "The Rise and Fall of T. D. Lysenko," *American Journal of Human Genetics*, November 1969.

Basic research on aging dated from the early '30s in Russia, thanks in part to Stalin's interest in the field, and the Institute of Experimental Biology and Pathology was a leading center for gerontological work. ("In the USSR, when the government made an institute, it made it big," Medvedev recalled.)[62] Medvedev had read *The Biology of Senescence* in a Moscow library after it came out. "It was, at the time, quite a unique book," he recalled. "In the '50s, nobody wrote a book like that, with such a wide perspective." When the second edition was published in the Soviet Union in the mid-'60s, Medvedev himself wrote the preface. By then, some of his papers had been published in the West, and he was a known name to researchers like Alex.

Russian gerontological research focused on aging as a fundamental process, rather than a collection of unrelated ailments, which meant that Medvedev and Alex were on the same page from a scientific perspective. Politically, it's fair to say they were not that far apart either. While Medvedev and his brother were growing more harshly critical of their government they retained some measure of faith in the Bolshevik experiment. Alex was a confirmed anti–Cold Warrior who believed in building bridges between the scientific communities on either side of the Iron Curtain. Before he left, Medvedev gave him a copy of the statement that Aleksandr Solzhenitsyn had circulated at the May meeting of the Soviet Writers Congress, in which the novelist demanded an end to censorship and that the Soviet Writers Union protect the rights, freedoms, and lives of the country's writers, to be passed on to the *Times* of London for publication. Alex took the document with him, but, by the time he returned home, so many other visitors had circulated it in the West that it was already well known.[63]

Alex and Zhores kept in touch as best they could in the years that followed, exchanging letters and papers, as the Medvedev brothers came under increased scrutiny. Zhores helped set up a bank account in Kiev to receive the royalties from sales of Alex's book, which Alex intended to donate to a philanthropy.[64] But as Zhores found himself taking a stronger stand against the Soviet government, so did his friend.

It was a gradual process, since his own government and its superpower ally were still giving Alex plenty to complain about. In 1962 Robert Soblen, a Russian-born psychiatrist who was alleged to have committed espionage for the Soviets after coming to the United States in 1941, jumped bail before a sentence of life imprisonment was to begin. He escaped to Israel but was caught and flown to London and then back to the United States. There he filed a claim for political asylum. That sparked a campaign in the United States and the UK against his deportation. Ruth Prothero, a German-born doctor in Middlesex who had been active in the underground anarchist movement in Germany during the early Nazi years and had known Soblen then, appealed to Alex for his support. They had known each other through Freedom Press.[65] Alex added his name to the appeal, but Soblen's petition was denied, and he died on September 11 of an overdose of barbiturates.

As American intervention escalated the Vietnam War in 1964 and 1965, Alex, like Russell and others in the disarmament movement, shifted much of his criticism from nuclear weapons to the Labour government's continued support—short of sending British troops—for Washington's policy in Southeast Asia. "The Prime Minister's wish to be left to pursue 'delicate and private diplomatic negotiations' is comprehensible, and the negotiations, if real, are laudable," Alex wrote in the *New Statesman*. "But a great many people, not only in Britain nor in the Labour Party, think that there would be a very much better chance of avoiding a catastrophe for the Vietnamese (to say nothing of the rest of us) if someone at this stage was prepared to be both publicly and deliberately undiplomatic."[66]

He was decidedly undiplomatic in 1967 when *Encounter*'s secret funding by the CIA and MI6 was finally exposed. In a little more than a dozen years, *Encounter* had built itself into one of the more prestigious intellectual journals in the Anglo-American world, a flagship of anticommunist liberalism, even though rumors had circulated constantly about who was backing it. The editors, including Stephen Spender and the Americans Irving Kristol and Melvin Lasky, skillfully built a roster of eminent contributors, many of whom had earlier been Trotskyists or other varieties of leftist but who had cured themselves of that inclination and now rarely if ever criticized US foreign policy. Alex had consistently avoided *Encounter* and its sponsor, the Congress for Cultural Freedom (CCF), for this reason and said so on occasion.

When the left-wing American Catholic magazine *Ramparts* produced concrete evidence of the CIA connection, the CCF at last stopped dispensing false denials. Spender resigned, but Lasky secured private foundation money to replace the CIA's bankroll, and *Encounter* limped along until 1991, although it never regained its earlier prominence.

Lasky protested that the magazine's funding didn't matter: "Nobody ever interfered in the editorial workings, no outsider hired or fired, and no outside 'suggestion' or 'guidance' was acceptable."[67] But this missed the point. The CCF and its backers had carefully selected an editorial team who in turn constructed an echo chamber in which anticommunist intellectuals who did not come off as too conservative collectively promoted a view of the Soviet Union as purely evil and the West as largely benign, placing the struggle for "cultural freedom" entirely on the eastern side of the Iron Curtain. "The sad thing about *Encounter*," Alex wrote in a letter to the *Guardian*, "is that the editors weren't under CIA pressure." Citing an article by Kingsley Amis defending the US war in Vietnam, he went on to say, "The fact that . . . such things should be written in cold blood by the unbribed and unsubsidized is what shakes me. Professionals would be bad enough, without unpaid volunteers."[68] Predictably, the novelist and poet John Wain, a strong supporter of *Encounter*, replied by accusing Alex and other critics of joining in a "smear campaign" aimed at destroying "our best magazine."[69]

There was only so far Alex would go in working against the Cold War, however. He reached his limit with the George Blake affair. Blake, who had served in the Dutch resistance during World War II before escaping to Britain and joining MI6, became a double agent when he was captured following the outbreak of the Korean War and held in the North, where he embraced communism. After his release and return to the UK, he passed on copies of thousands of MI6 documents to the KGB. After he was apprehended in 1962, he was tried and sentenced to forty-two years in prison.

Two of Alex's colleagues on the Committee of 100, Michael Randle and Pat Pottle, met Blake while both were serving time in Wormwood Scrubs for their role in organizing the committee's nonviolent direct action at Wethersfield air base in 1962, and his case stirred their rage at Britain's conduct in the Cold War. The length of Blake's sentence was "vicious and indefensible," they felt, and he had been blamed to an exaggerated extent for the deaths of other agents he had allegedly betrayed. In their view, Blake's activities were no worse than what UK and US agents were doing behind the Iron Curtain and throughout the developing world during the same period. Why was Blake not being exchanged for one or more captured British agents imprisoned in Russia, as was the usual practice? Was it because he was foreign-born and partly Jewish, unlike the posh Cambridge spies, Philby, Maclean, and Burgess? Finally, Randle and Pottle objected to the way Blake's trial was held: in secret and under an extensive press blackout, leaving the public with no way to know whether justice was being done. (Years later, Pottle learned that the court records had been destroyed).[70]

After their release, along with another ex-prisoner, Seán Bourke, they hatched a plan to help Blake escape from prison.[71] Early in 1966, Randle began contacting former comrades from the Committee of 100 to ask for their help. Alex and Randle had been imprisoned together when they refused to be bound over during the Trafalgar Square sit-down demo five years earlier, and Alex had helped him launch the Voice of Disarmament radio station. Randle asked Alex for funds and a safe house to help smuggle Blake out of the country once he'd been sprung from Wormwood Scrubs.[72]

After hearing Randle's case for the operation, Alex declined to get involved. "They were very well-intentioned, upright and honest people," he said years later of Randle and Pottle, "but I said it was no part of CND or the Committee of 100 to get involved with dubious agents, and the authorities would have been watching the operation in the hope of discrediting CND." Blake was not opposed to nuclear weapons, so his case had nothing directly to do with the antinuclear movement's work. And what if the whole thing was a ruse, and MI6 had hoodwinked them into participating in a scheme to re-embed Blake as a double agent with the KGB? "At that point I said it sounds like a damn silly idea to me because you have no idea which side Blake is on or who he's been talking to, or even whether this is being planted on you."[73]

Randle approached a mutual friend and fellow antinuclear organizer, April Carter, and she too turned him down, for similar reasons.[74] Nevertheless, he, Pottle, and Bourke found other supporters and got to work planning Blake's escape, which went off in good Hollywood fashion in October 1966. (Alfred Hitchcock tried for several years to make a movie of it.)[75] Randle and his wife Anne took Blake across the Channel from Dover in a secret compartment of the family van and deposited him in East Berlin on December 19.[76] After the news hit of the prison break, and despite his misgivings about the affair, Alex said nothing to the authorities.

He got the opportunity to extend a hand to his comrades the following year, when a group of forty-two activists broke in and briefly occupied the Greek embassy in London, one week after a military junta, with Washington's encouragement, had seized power in Athens. Randle and Terry Chandler, another comrade from the Committee of 100, were brought to trial for leading the action and sentenced to twelve and fifteen months' imprisonment, respectively. Alex wrote a furious letter to the *Guardian* after the verdict against his friends: "Dangerous men who have incurred the wrath of every stuffed shirt in the country; when they see injustice in office, here or abroad, they have risked their necks to stop it and to persuade others to do likewise. Of course they must rot in gaol (how else can the trade unionism of bastards in office be preserved?)."[77]

He then sent a large check to Anne Randle and cosponsored a fund for political prisoners to benefit Michael, Terry Chandler, and a third imprisoned activist, Derek Foley. "Those who demonstrate in the name of Liberty and for Causes which most of us support are entitled to our aid," the sponsors declared in an ad in the *Guardian*.[78] Alex and Ruth kept up a supportive correspondence with Chandler for several months as he appealed his case.[79]

Many of the controversies Alex weighed in on during the second half of the '60s were less overtly political and more concerned with freedom of expression, however. In February and March 1967, he answered an appeal from the publisher Neville Spearman Ltd, which had put out *Sam, the Ceiling Needs Painting* and *Sam around the World*, two books of sex-related cartoons. When a London bookseller, Ashcroft & Daw, faced a destruction order against its stock of the books, Neville Armstrong, the publisher's founder, recruited a team of prominent witnesses, including Alex, to appear at a hearing on the case.[80]

At just about the same time came an appeal in a more significant prosecution. The publisher John Calder, of Calder and Boyars, had brought out *Last Exit to Brooklyn*, a brutal, sexually explicit American novel by Hubert Selby Jr., populated by laborers, prostitutes, and gang members. The book was well received in the UK and sold moderately well until Tory MP Sir Cyril Black filed a private prosecution against it in Marlborough Street Magistrates' Court. The chief metropolitan magistrate scoured the district for copies of the book and seized three from the offices of Calder and Boyars. Rather than accept the seizures, Calder elected to face a trial for obscenity in the Old Bailey.

The publisher lined up some sixty witnesses to testify to the novel's artistic merit, including Alex—who had been suggested to him by James Mitchell—and the scholars Frank Kermode and A. Alvarez.[81] Alex was reluctant at first to get involved in the most significant legal case of literary censorship in Britain since *Lady Chatterley*, not because he agreed with the charges but because he was against the banning of any book on any grounds. That wouldn't make him very helpful at picking out why an exception should be made for Selby's novel in particular, he explained in a letter to Calder.[82] The publisher replied that Alex wouldn't have to testify about the novel's decency but only "to explain the motivation of the author . . . and what you believe about the connection between reading and behavior." Moreover, it behooved Alex to stand up for the novel, because, Calder warned, "booksellers are already timid and would become much more so, and every local crank will be taking out his own prosecution against Darwin, Freud, and yourself."[83]

That appears to have clinched the deal. In April the *Daily Mirror* reported that the *Last Exit to Brooklyn* case was "snowballing to historic proportions" as "some of Britain's most eloquent free thinkers have leaped to its aid." Sponsors of a Free Art Legal Fund to cover the costs of the defense included Alex, Samuel Beckett, Anthony Burgess, Edna O'Brien, and Kenneth Tynan.[84] At the nine-day trial, defense counsel called some thirty witnesses—"as many as the jury could take," Calder said—before getting to Alex, who did not end up testifying. There was a reason. "You are known for your controversial views," Calder told him later, "and having seen the kind of jury we had, Counsel was afraid of having these brought against you by the prosecution. This may well have been a mistake, but there it is."[85]

In November, the verdict came down against the publishers, who were fined £100 and ordered to pay £500 toward prosecution costs along with some £1,500 in their own costs of counsel. Calder and Boyars appealed and in the interim announced that the Free Art Legal Fund was being converted into a permanent Defense of Literature and the Arts Society that members of the public could join to help fight censorship. The intention, Calder said, was "to rouse parliamentary and public opinion and fight back against Moral Rearmament, the Billy Graham Crusade, and Mary Whitehouse, all of whom have put pressure, for instance, on the BBC."[86] The verdict was reversed on appeal in 1968, another blow in a war against literary censorship that was still some distance from victory.

Less than a year later, a massive invasion of Czechoslovakia by Soviet and other Warsaw Pact armies put an end to the period of liberalization known as the Prague Spring, igniting a campaign of nonviolent civil disobedience in Czechoslovakia as well as protests around the world, including in other Soviet Bloc nations. War Resisters International (WRI), the umbrella group that included the PPU, coordinated protests in Moscow, Budapest, Warsaw, and Sofia, with Michael Randle, now chair of WRI, and April Carter as chief organizers.

Alex was in a somewhat awkward position. He was just as critical of Washington's domineering geopolitics as ever, besides which he was still pursuing his dream of chipping away at the Cold War through scientific cooperation. He had always included contributions from Soviet and other Warsaw Pact scientists in the pages of *Experimental Gerontology*, for example, and would continue to do so. After a conference in Prague the previous fall, he had corresponded enthusiastically with a colleague at the Institute for Experimental Gerontology in Basel about the possibility of setting up an "international laboratory" that could bring together the efforts of scientists on both sides of the Iron Curtain.[87] How would he square such a project with the blatant repression occurring in Soviet-occupied Eastern Europe?

He supported the WRI protests and wrote a short piece in *New Society* praising *Support Czechoslovakia*, a pamphlet that Randle and Carter had rushed out to tell the story of the actions just after they were deported for their role. "Recommended reading," he said, "for those who pretend that the opponents of psychopaths in the Friworld [NATO] governments never speak out against pig-politicians in the communist countries." In reality, he asserted, Randle and Carter were part of an "anti-Pig movement" that now extended "from Prague to the Catholic church and from Tokyo to the American campuses." The "pigs," as he defined them, were "crass bureaucratic bosses, policemen, and thick-headed officials, who object to free exchange of human thought and would stop it if they could."[88] His angle was to support the growing dissident movement in the Soviet bloc, without allowing himself to be reflexively tagged as a supporter of his own government.

There was nothing evasive about this position, since autocrats under the patronage of Washington—from South Vietnam to Greece to Brazil—were committing plenty of crimes in the name of anticommunism in these years. In 1967 Alex signed on to an appeal organized by PEN International for the release of the Russian writers Andrei Sinyavsky and Yuri Daniel, who had been convicted of anti-Soviet agitation and propaganda and sent to forced labor camps, and the Greek composer Mikis Theodorakis, who had been jailed by the military government following the April coup. (This appeal, dated December 5, 1967, was also one of the last political statements that Herbert Read signed before his death the following June, and thus his and Alex's last collaboration.) Both cases received enormous attention worldwide. Theodorakis was the first person of note to fall victim to the new regime in Athens, while Sinyavsky and Daniel were well known in the West through their smuggled-out writings, and their trial triggered protests in the Soviet Union and abroad. Their sentencing also marked the end of the Khrushchev Thaw.

Alex's distress at the turn of events comes through in his letter to PEN International joining its appeal for Sinyavsky and Daniel. "This would have been a deplorable case in any country," he wrote, but particularly "at a time when we are getting an increasing opening-up of scientific and literary exchange with Russia." In an additional note sent the same day, he couldn't help but suggest that he still held out more hope for freedom in the Soviet Bloc than in the West. "Most Russians I have met seem to agree that the sentences were a last-ditch reprisal by Blimps left over from Stalinism," he said.[89]

This was several months before the Czech invasion, and he was, of course, quite wrong. But when he had to write in response to the Russian government's treatment of Zhores Medvedev, he was still determined not to denounce the Soviet Union. After years of KGB harassment and the repeated denial of his requests to attend international scientific conferences outside the Iron Curtain, Medvedev was arrested in 1970 and placed in a mental hospital where he was pronounced acutely ill with "incipient schizophrenia" and "paranoid delusions of reforming society." After a storm of protest at home and abroad, including a letter to the Ministry of Health from physicist Andrei Sakharov and two Soviet Nobel laureates in physics, he was released, nineteen days after his committal to the asylum.

The following year, he published *The Medvedev Papers*, an often grimly funny tour of the world of Soviet science. It was quickly followed by a second book, cowritten with his brother, *A Question of Madness* (a direct translation of the Russian title: *Who's Crazy Now?*), which not only detailed his ordeal but also exposed the use of psychiatric hospitals to imprison hundreds of other Soviet dissidents. Both had to be smuggled out of Russia to see the light of day. Alex reviewed both books in the *Guardian*. In both articles he paid tribute to his friend's courage and devotion to science but warned his readers not to get the wrong idea of the author. Medvedev "is not against communism or against the Soviet Union," he wrote, regarding *The Medvedev Papers*. "He is as transparently patriotic a scientist as any country would hope to produce. . . . Embittered enemies of the Soviet Union, of whom I am not one, might have the decency to keep quiet about this book; it is the friends, not the enemies, of that country who should applaud it—and particularly those who have the privilege of working with Russian biologists and know their quality and their difficulties."[90]

If they "want their science to play the part Lenin, for one, intended," the authorities in Moscow needed to support Medvedev, rather than "let their mental eunuchs call the tune," Alex declared. Rather than being locked up, Medvedev should get the Lenin Prize.

Dealing directly with his friend's consignment to a "Kafkaesque" mental institution, Alex warned his readers that before they become "too smug about democracy," they should consider that "we might easily find ourselves in the same boat." "There are enough conformist psychiatric writings in the West (about the 'immaturity' of the young, of revolutionaries, of pot-smokers, of avant-garde artists) to make us watch our step. The fuel is there if someone should want to make use of it."[91]

What Alex found heartening in Medvedev's case was the fact that some Soviet scientists—and perhaps some sympathetic people in Soviet officialdom—had thrown in their lot with him, risking career ruination but moving the government to back down. Alex may not have had a clear picture of the differences between a full-fledged police state and one that still included significant checks on the people in power. But his comments on the Medvedev and Sinyavsky-Daniel cases and on the repression of the Prague Spring make clear that as a Briton and a denizen of the noncommunist West, he considered it his first task to warn his country against moving further in an authoritarian direction, and only then to protest the regime in place on the other side.

CONSIDERING HIS STRONG—almost reflexive—criticism of US foreign policy, it would seem unlikely that Alex would warm up to America itself and to Americans, but that was exactly what happened in the late '60s and early '70s. He was traveling and speaking in the United States more frequently, had struck up several good friendships, including with the Yaloms and Nathan Shock, the American gerontologist who was now head of the Gerontology Research Center at the National Institutes of Health, and was beginning to develop institutional ties as well. He was also keeping in frequent contact with Pat McGrady, the journalist who had written *The Youth Doctors* and was now at work on a follow-up, *The Love Doctors*, about American sex therapists, liberationists, and advice columnists.

When Michael Murphy, president of the Esalen Institute, West Coast hub of the human potential movement, traveled to the UK in 1970, he contacted Alex in hopes of meeting with him to discuss work being done in "Group Therapy, the Behavioral Sciences, and the Therapeutic Community" in Britain, aiming to establish a continuing interchange of ideas.[92] Alex was recommended to Murphy by Theodore Roszak, an academic colleague of Marilyn Yalom at California State University,

Hayward (he had also briefly edited *Peace News* in London in the mid-'60s), who had just published *The Making of a Counter-Culture*, a much-discussed book that found a common thread connecting hippies, antiwar activists, dropouts, and other young nonconformists in their rejection of the technocracy at the apex of modern industrial society. Alex had written to Roszak praising his book, and Roszak in turn asked Alex for permission to republish his lecture, "A Technology of the Emotions?" in a collection of recent cultural and social thought.[93] When it appeared in 1972 under the audacious title *Sources: An Anthology of Contemporary Materials Useful for Preserving Sanity while Braving the Great Technological Wilderness*, the book did not include Alex's essay.[94] Nevertheless, Alex backed Roszak's successful application for a Guggenheim fellowship.[95]

American publishers were finding Alex's work attractive again. Ballantine brought out a cheap paperback edition of the *Koka Shastra* in 1966. Harper & Row published *Nature and Human Nature* in America the same year, retitled—to Alex's consternation—*The Nature of Human Nature*, and it sold well. Three years later, Harper went back for a fifteen-hundred-copy reprint of the hardcover edition, even though a mass-market paperback was available, and editor Nahum Waxman asked him what he was working on, hoping they could get together on a new project soon.[96]

As Alex got to know the States better, particularly California, he was beginning to feel more at home there. "San Francisco is the only American city I know with this European kind of night life," he wrote Marilyn Yalom after a conference in Italy, "meaning not honkytonk but walking about the streets, sitting in cafes, and meeting people. Maybe New Orleans as well."[97] Increasingly, he could see a place for himself on the other side of the Atlantic. For one thing, there was less to keep him at home. Ruth's days were filled by her job as a child care officer, and Nick, having completed his education at Trinity College, Cambridge, was launched on his journalistic career with the *Morning Telegraph* in Sheffield. Jane, it seemed, was ready for any change Alex wanted to make, provided she didn't lose him. Preparing for an aging conference in Washington in August 1971, Alex notified Marilyn that he had "written a suitable mixture of pep, science and Billy Graham exortation [*sic*] to get the press campaigning for a Great Leap Forward—if Nixon will play I shall have a private aeroplane before you can say Methuselah."[98]

His American acquaintances were directing him down other paths as well. Hearing that Alex would be in Los Angeles in April 1968, Roy

Walford, a researcher in aging at University of California, Los Angeles, Medical School, suggested he contact John Thomas Idlet, better known simply as John Thomas, a poet and living legend in Venice Beach's dropout community who had read and admired *Darwin and the Naked Lady*. "Go to his place after telephoning him," Walford advised, "rather than suggesting that he meet you elsewhere, because he has quite a fantastic pad completely papered with pornographic and other pictures, which you will dig."[99]

It's not known whether Alex met John Thomas. In March 1970, however, Pat McGrady wrote him from New York to report on an interview he had conducted with Masters and Johnson for *The Love Doctors*. Alex, by this time, had visited them at least once. "They were, to put it mildly, overwhelmed by you," McGrady reported. "In a good way, that is."[100] ("Comfort is so much fun," Johnson said. "If we could learn to produce on a twenty-four-hour level the way he does, I think we'd probably have it made. I just get so exhausted." "Five or six hours is all I can stand," said Masters. "I end up out of breath while he's talking.")[101]

In the same letter, McGrady recommended that Alex meet two other sex therapists the next time he was on the West Coast, William Hartman and Marilyn Fithian, whose Center for Marital and Sexual Studies located in Long Beach, was generically similar to Masters and Johnson's clinic. They had also coauthored *Nudist Society*, a recently published study of nudism in America. But McGrady waxed rhapsodic about a year-old retreat in Topanga Canyon, some twenty minutes north of Santa Monica by car, called Sandstone.

Established by John and Barbara Williamson, a successful aerospace engineer and inventor and a successful insurance salesperson, respectively, the retreat was not, strictly speaking, a nudist colony but rather a quasi-intentional community that aimed rather vaguely to encourage "the free expression of total relationships." The fourteen-acre property was perched up a narrow, slightly scarifying road, to one side of a canyon overlooking the Pacific Ocean and with views of Santa Monica and Malibu. It was laid out like a weekend home for a well-to-do family, with a sprawling main house, volleyball court, swimming pool, garden, and hiking trails.

The Williamsons had purchased the house and property in 1968 and opened it the following year as the Sandstone Foundation for Community Systems Research, Inc. Along with a core, full-time community of up to ten people, Sandstone hosted regular Wednesday-night and weekend members-and-guests-only parties, which included hundreds of couples, ranging from bankers and entertainment industry figures to writers, psychiatrists, and academics to carpenters and plumbers who were all free to pair up for sex with whomsoever they shared an attraction, in a large "ballroom," fitted out with mattresses, in the main house. One Sandstone member described descending into the dimly lit room and noticing the "smells of sticky bodies getting it on" and the up-and-down motion of bodies on the floor, rather like the pumpjacks on the oil derricks offshore from Long Beach.[102] The comfortable, plushly furnished house also had an upstairs living room with a look that one regular described as "middle-class ostentatious," where couples could meet and mingle with the permanent residents and enjoy a potluck dinner before going downstairs.[103]

As McGrady described it to Alex, "[Sandstone is] a very hip, refreshing swingers' home of which the focus is a seven-unit extended marriage dictated over by the owners, who have heard of you and would welcome you if you popped by." When McGrady and his wife, Colleen, visited in the course of his research for *The Love Doctors*, he said, "[We] went down to the room with the 60 foot red shag rug for a drink with the proprietors, and were amused to find a couple doing 69 with various wallpaper patterns being projected onto them by a slide projector from the bar. . . . You find everything in California, everything."

He was wrong on one count; Sandstone admitted only couples, either married or not, with very few exceptions. So-called swingers were frowned upon. But Alex was more than intrigued, and over the next two years, he came to the retreat whenever his travel itinerary permitted, striking up a friendly acquaintance with John Williamson and several of the other core members.[104] He even briefly toyed with the idea of organizing a group of like-minded people to create a similar experimental community in the UK.[105]

Alex had been interested in nudism—or naturism or just sunbathing, as its practitioners often called it—for some time; in November 1965 he and Jane had made a day visit to Diogenes Sun Club, a member-owned naturist club in Buckinghamshire, but they appear not to have joined. Later he published an article, "Nudes—who's eccentric?," that surveyed the naturist scene in the UK, taking pains to emphasize how normal—for lack of a better word—the habitués of clubs and retreats that offered group nudity really were. Most were middle- or working-class, he noted, and a very high proportion were married couples accompanied by children.

"Were intelligence ever to become allied with moral hygiene," he wrote, "I can imagine the Churches and the British Medical Association collecting money to finance [nudist clubs] in the interests of public health, and the positive improvement of our attitudes to sex through a gentle and enjoyable type of group therapy."[106]

Sex was rarely an element at most nudist camps, however. Sandstone was something more: "an extended experiment in open sexuality," as Alex later described it.[107] The Williamsons' objective was to find out how a community would structure itself if all elements of possessiveness or ownership were removed from relations between couples. Open sexuality was the "flypaper" that attracted potential participants but not the end point, John Williamson said.[108] Heavy drinking was discouraged, drugs generally were not allowed—the Williamsons wanted to stay on good terms with the police—and abusive behavior was grounds for quick ejection. The "club"—the dues-paying membership that Sandstone set up for its visitors—covered the bills and helped spread the word about the Williamsons' and their friends' experiment, but they never thought of themselves as running either a sex club or nudist getaway.[109] Prospective members were interviewed and screened for any indication they might violate the rules.

Residents and visitors typically went without clothes but weren't required to, although Alex quickly noticed another similarity with the folks at English naturist retreats: they were not, for the most part, either college-age or what could be described as hippies. Sandstone appealed to a generally well-off and well-educated membership, and the Williamsons were eager to attract well-known people who were interesting, charismatic, or likely to attracted funding and bring more paying members in their wake, even relaxing the couples-only rule in such cases.[110] Members and frequent guests during its close to four years in operation included the columnist and cultural historian Max Lerner; entertainers Bobby Darin and Sammy Davis Jr.; Daniel Ellsberg, the ex-military analyst who exposed the Pentagon Papers; football player and actor Bernie Casey; psychotherapists Ralph and Lucy Yaney; archaeologist Sally Binford; Motown Records mogul Berry Gordy Jr.; Jean-Philippe Rigaud, a prominent French anthropologist; and best-selling author Gay Talese, who was researching a book about the sexual revolution in America.

For the Sandstone community, Alex was one of the more cherished of these big names, in part because of the warm, amusing presence he brought to the retreat. "He was there quite often on the weekends," Barbara Williamson recalled, usually by himself but occasionally with Jane, "and was very happy and at home."[111] Jonathan Dana, who was directing a documentary about Sandstone along with his wife, Anne

"Bunny" Dana, and a small crew in 1971 and 1972, remembered him sitting on the back lawn, writing on a yellow legal pad, or by the fireplace in the main house, in extended conversations with John Williamson. He was almost never not talking, in fact. Alex was "impish, funny, smart, totally egalitarian, loved to hang out, and was lovely to be with," Dana recalled. "He was interested in people, especially women, was jocular, always in a good mood. Everybody was extremely proud to have him there."[112]

In the book he eventually published, *Thy Neighbor's Wife*, Talese painted a picture of Alex in the ballroom that the subject came to dislike intensely.

> Often the nude biologist Dr. Alex Comfort, brandishing a cigar, traipsed through the room between the prone bodies with the professional air of a lepidopterist strolling through the fields waving a butterfly net, or an ornithologist tracking along the surf a rare breed of tern. A gray-haired bespectacled man with a well-preserved body, Dr. Comfort was unabashedly drawn to the sight of sexually engaged couples and their concomitant cooing, considering such to be enchanting and endlessly instructive, and with the least bit of encouragement—after he had deposited his cigar in a safe place—he would join a friendly clutch of bodies and contribute to the merriment. . . . He was a rarity in the medical profession, one who brought a bedside manner to an orgy.[113]

When the erotic painter Betty Dodson, who would soon be leading sex workshops for women, made a visit to Sandstone from New York ("she freaked all the guys out because she got her hair cut in a crewcut," Barbara Williamson recalled), she noticed Alex watching her in the ballroom one night.[114] She motioned for him to join her party, then asked him to "do my clitoris while I fondled this younger guy." Finding that he had only a thumb on his left hand, she licked it and applied it to the appropriate spot.[115]

SANDSTONE SEEMED TO REPRESENT, for Alex, the mainstreaming of a less anxious and possessive sexual culture in the modern world, not one that was confined to an in-group or subculture. That said, he also perceived the politicized youth movements of the late '60s, which he had seen stirring to life in the Aldermaston marches, as a tremendously hopeful development. When the PPU held its annual conference in Liverpool in April 1969, he published a letter in its journal, *The Pacifist,* calling on the membership to widen their advocacy beyond disarmament and an end to war to encompass mass disobedience to authority: something he took to be the essential next step in a transformation of society.

"The fact of the new Revolution is this," he wrote: "that free, concerned and educated people are basically and rightly ungovernable, and that refusal to obey gratuitous orders is the stamp of this state of mind. This is an anti-pig revolution—against those who, having allowed themselves to be non-people, want us to be the same."[116]

In a May 1969 review of Herbert Marcuse's *An Essay on Liberation,* he predicted that this revolution would be "as great as that of the Romantic movement": "It involves a wholly new view of life—conservation in place of 'enterprise,' inner space replacing outer space, old values suddenly seen as repellent."[117] In an article two years later for the Center for the Study of Democratic Institutions, a Santa Barbara–based think tank that was courting him, Alex laid out four facets of the "new sensibility" he hoped would power the next wave of change: personal, not institutional, and therefore antipolitical; biological, not technological; spiritually empirical, cultivating the technology of the emotions; and ungovernable, resisting the brainwashing of "modern assembly-line education."[118]

What he had in mind was quite different from the more traditional revolutions that were roiling the developing world. Castro and Ho Chi Minh had their constructive but also their "frankly terrorist" sides; like all previous revolutionary leaders, they would eventually put to their own uses the "tide of popular courage" that had carried them to power. In October 1969, in a review of another Marcuse text, the counterculture bible *Eros and Civilization*—"compulsory reading"—he contrasted the Ho-Castro brand of social and political transformation with that of the "Marcusian premature antifascists" of the "hippie generation," whom he saw heralding "a radical shift towards the sensory, the imaginative and the quietist as against the hellbent and the exploitative modes."[119] Along with a more relaxed, socially open approach to sex, something of this sensibility was what he saw percolating in places like Sandstone and possibly spreading into the broader community.

How would such a transformation come about? Not through a single event, replacing one authoritarian or performatively democratic regime with another, he wrote in 1971, in a review of *The Pentagon of*

Power, Lewis Mumford's interpretation of technocracy, but by moving toward "militancy and protest as constant civic activities."[120] The goal was the "passive, but determined and constructive, insurrection" that he and Herbert Read had called for during the 1956 Hungarian uprising.

Alex was in Vancouver in March and April 1971 to deliver a series of talks at Simon Fraser University and the University of British Columbia. He had acquired an academic following in the Pacific Northwest over the preceding two decades, including Dan Callahan and Jerry Zaslove, an English professor, at Simon Fraser; Wayne Burns, a professor of English at the University of Washington; and John Doheny, English professor at the University of British Columbia. He had visited and spoken at their invitation several times already. In one of his talks on this occasion, at Simon Fraser, he tried to sum up his latest political thinking. He titled it "What Rough Beast?" after the famous lines from Yeats's foreboding poem, "The Second Coming": "And what rough beast, its hour come round at last, / Slouches towards Bethlehem to be born?"

What he produced was very like the political analysis he had constructed in the first years after the war, updated for a time when the West's political consensus was disintegrating. France was convulsed with protests, occupation of major universities, and the largest general strike in the country's history. The Prague Spring seemed briefly to crack open the Soviet bloc, until it was put down. Soon, armed underground groups would be fomenting insurrection in Germany, Italy, and a dozen countries in Latin America. In the United States, anti–Vietnam War protests were swelling, and the 1968 election, beginning with the violent repression of demonstrators against the party hierarchy at the Chicago Democratic Convention and followed by the backlash of Richard Nixon's victory, revealed a possibly unbridgeable political divide. Vietnam was inspiring larger and larger protests in the UK too. The Weather Underground began a campaign of violent direct action in the United States in 1969, and the Angry Brigade emerged as a UK counterpart of sorts the following year, just months before Alex would have been formulating "What Rough Beast?"

Was there a common denominator to all this rage, and what chance did it have to pull humanity out of the corner into which it seemed to have been confined by irrational authority armed with hyper-destructive weapons and a vast ability to manipulate its subjects? Alex maintained that before political revolution, there had to be a cultural transformation, which he hoped he was witnessing. "We don't need a revolt against reason," he told his listeners in Vancouver, "a return to God, a revival of magic, or any brand of right- or left-wing Jungian populism. We need a return to reason in emotionally literate terms." "Old style liberals," the kind who backed the New Deal in the United States and the Labour government's reforms in the UK after the war—and supported civil rights and an end to the Vietnam War but nothing that would fundamentally alter the economic structure—were unlikely to bring about this change because they didn't fully understand the stakes.

Anarchism, instead, was the necessary path, he argued, precisely because of its minimally prescriptive nature. "If you commit yourself to non-paternalistic, non-directive solutions, in the way the modern psychiatrist commits himself to non-directive counselling, you commit yourself to a very total empiricism, almost a non-ideology," he told his listeners. The "essence of anarchism" was

> in recognizing that not even the anarchist's preferences may be imposed. . . . Anarchism in this sense is the only ideology which has room for the type of change which we are likely to observe in human history, whatever our wishes may be, and that is the illogical mixture of old and new. . . . We may well end with a mixture of anarchism and democracy or something of the sort which is very ill-pleasing for neatness and very offensive to ideologists but which is empirically justified because it has grown that way in response to reasonable needs and, above all, the overriding need to make power subject to protest.

One could call the new culture he was describing "adhocracy," but, however it was arrived at, "the proper modality of change was protest and personal resistance, rather than coercive revolution."[121]

Alex had an idea where such a change might happen first. In his review of *The Pentagon of Power*, he guessed, "It takes an American, a citizen of an anti-imperialist tradition gone imperialist, and an inheritor of the American mixture of optimism, techniques, populism, and public violence, to see this trend in full. Probably it will take America to enact the change."[122]

He was already considering how he might nudge America in that direction.

CHAPTER 14

Sex for Pleasure (1963–1971)

The historian Hera Cook later described *The Joy of Sex* as the last major text in a line of discourse that began with Marie Stopes's *Married Love* in 1918, making it the endpoint of a half-century in which reformers had focused on demystifying sex, clearing away thickets of misinformation, and enabling couples—heterosexuals, mainly—to have sex safely and without fear, aided by better and more available birth control. When Alex decided, in the early '70s, to write his own sex manual, it was to encourage readers to change their attitude toward sexual behavior: to banish guilt and anxiety in favor of pleasure and human understanding.

With that presumably accomplished, sex could start to play the role it should naturally assume between individuals: promoting sociality and mutual satisfaction as well as procreation. Achieving this wouldn't be simple in a world riddled with violence, economic exploitation, and fear, of which sexual repression was one element. But the effort to get there was part of what Alex understood as the humanist project: as Julian Huxley had expressed it, to realize "possibilities of knowing, feeling, and willing to the fullest extent."[1]

As far back as the mid-'40s, Alex had told a nurse at Royal Waterloo Hospital that he wanted to write "the ultimate book about sex."[2] In 1964, in the introduction to his translation of the *Koka Shastra*, he said that what was "profitable" to modern English readers in classic Hindu erotic literature was its attitude of "acceptance and pleasure where we have for generations been taught to look for danger and guilt."[3] Not long afterward, in *Sex and Society*, he made a case for a new literature of sexual enjoyment that "treated it at the level of ballroom dancing"; this would "heighten the element of play which . . . is perhaps the marker of good sexual adjustment, if not the cause of it."[4]

One genre of erotic literature—in India especially—was the catalog of postures: a book detailing the many hundreds of positions and techniques that two people could use when giving each other pleasure. Every sexually articulate culture was preoccupied to some extent with postures, Alex asserted, likening them to "the elaboration of dance figures."[5] This perhaps helps explain the craze for ballroom dancing he had pursued with Ruth a few years earlier. He was already compiling some elements of a modern posture book in the notebook he kept with June, and around the time he was working on the *Koka Shastra* he happened upon a treasure trove.

Das Goldene Buch der Liebe oder die Renaissance im Geschlechtsleben: Ein Eros-Kodex fur Beide Geschlechter—in English, *The Golden Book of Love, or the Renaissance in Sexual Life: An Eros-Code for Both Sexes*—was one of the most astonishing productions in the history of sex literature. Written by a Viennese teacher—it's not clear of what—named Josef Weckerle and published privately in Vienna in two hefty volumes in 1907 under the pseudonym "L. van der Weck-Erlen," the book contained 531 numbered and classified sexual positions, with names like "Cuissade," "Croupade," "Flanquette," "In-the-Saddle," and "Cantilever," along with some conventional male and female anatomy and a description of a kind of lottery system by which couples were supposed to decide which positions to assume.

Alex first read about Weckerle's book in Kinsey's *Sexual Behavior in the Human Male*—Kinsey had a copy—and later obtained a microfilm from the Vienna State Library, plus a copy of a series of illustrations made for the book by the American erotic illustrator Mahlon Blaine that were in the Kinsey collection.[6] He thought it "quite the best European treatise on coital postures, and the only one to approach the Indian spirit." In both the *Koka Shastra* and *Sex in Society*, he quoted Weckerle's dictum that "too much sex never wore out anyone, except a weakling who is out of training."[7] Hoping possibly to get *The Golden Book of Love* published in the UK or the United States, he translated it—but only the "atlas" of positions, since he didn't consider the other material of enough interest to modern readers—and wrote an introduction, sharing copies of the manuscript with his Vancouver friends, John Doheny and Wayne Burns.[8]

But the project lay fallow until 1966, when Alex heard, for the first time in years, from his American pen pal Gershon Legman. Legman had first contacted Alex in the late '40s, after reading several of Alex's pieces in *NOW*. In 1949, after *Barbarism and Sexual Freedom* came out, he sent Alex a copy of a short book he had just self-published, *Love*

& Death: A Study in Censorship, which argued, echoing Reich, that American society's fear of sex had spawned a sadistic, dehumanizing culture of violence, expressed through comic books, pulp fiction, and even the work of relatively high-brow writers like Ernest Hemingway that led directly to violent crime. Why, he asked in a text full of skillfully rendered but hyperbolic prose, was it possible to sell exhaustingly blood-drenched crime stories to the public, yet displaying a single act of affectionate intercourse could earn one a prison term? A year later, and despite positive reviews in publications like *Harper's*, *The New Republic*, and the *New York Times*—additionally, Sartre excerpted it in his journal, *Les temps modern*—*Love & Death* was barred from the U.S. mails on grounds of obscenity.[9]

Alex wrote back, calling Legman's analysis "extraordinarily sound" and *Love & Death* "one of the nicest Swiftian pieces of the age," adding that while his own analysis was different, he might quote Legman on this point.[10] Legman replied with a forward look at his latest, very Freudian cogitations, on "homosexuality as the result of the castration complex and the connection with science-fiction and fascism," along with a query whether *Love & Death* might be publishable in the UK.[11] No reply from Alex survives, but Legman was also pressing him to contribute to a literary magazine he co-edited, *Neurotica*, which had published several of the Beat writers as well as the Canadian media theorist, Marshall McLuhan. That project fell through when *Neurotica* folded, and by the early '60s, Legman was living in self-imposed exile on a rural property in Provence and on his way to becoming a legend among rare book and manuscript collectors and dealers.

In 1964 Alex had written a review for *Folklore* magazine of *The Horn Book*, Legman's deeply researched study of underground erotic publishing, bawdy songs, the limerick, and a few of his pet peeves. Alex praised the book's scholarship but even more its "hard-working, pugnacious, and likeable author."[12] Legman in turn had been impressed by Alex's *Koka Shastra* translation, and two years later, John Lyle, an Exeter bookseller specializing in Surrealist books, suggested to him that Alex might be able to help track down a work he was looking for on naturism.

Legman wrote Alex a letter on May 16, 1966, reintroducing himself, and, in his reply, Alex mentioned that he had sent a copy of *Love and Death* to James Mitchell at Constable, for possible inclusion in their Natural History of Society series. "I stole practically every meaningful insight [in *Love and Death*] from your *Barbarism and Sexual Freedom*,"

Legman confessed.[13] "Constable liked *Love and Death*," Alex reported. But the publisher wanted it updated, a task Legman did not take up.[14] Meanwhile, Legman offered to help Alex with suggested sources for illustrations to a projected series of volumes on the history of erotic art that Alex had undertaken to edit for G. P. Putnam's.[15]

Alex also mentioned that he was translating Weckerle. Legman turned out to be another fan of the mysterious Viennese, having written a preface on the broader history of "technique manuals" for a translation by an American publisher.[16] Alex suggested they combine Legman's preface with his own translation and introduction and publish the book pseudonymously. That way, Alex's standing in the medical profession wouldn't be threatened by "Weckerle's very definite eccentricities."[17]

"D'accord," Legman replied. Weckerle's "deepest idea," he suggested, was that an "atlas" of postures could be just the thing to save marriage by keeping the man from seeking variety elsewhere: "monogamy by means of technique experimentation, vs. don juanism as 'personal' experimentation."[18] This would also be a good hook for a publisher looking for a respectable reason to put money into an explicit sex guide. But on June 9, he informed Alex that the American publisher had decided not to go ahead with the book, and that he was pitching it to Mitchell instead. Once Mitchell "fully understood" what Legman was proposing, however, he was "a bit taken aback."[19] The project seems to have died with that, and Alex's translation and introduction to Weckerle went back on the shelf.

The Golden Book of Love was an odd, underground work intended for an exclusive subset of connoisseurs. Even if they had found a publisher, Alex and Legman would have had difficulty making it acceptable to a mainstream audience. With his next venture into the field of sex manuals, Alex's task was easier.

In 1964 publisher Neville Spearman struck a deal with New English Library, a mass-market paperback publisher, to bring out a new UK edition of the Scandinavian best seller, *An ABZ of Love*. Alex was engaged to revise the existing translation for an English audience.[20] *An ABZ of Love* had sold more than one million copies when it was published in Denmark, Norway, and Sweden in 1961. Two years later, it was translated and published in the United States, where it sold modestly. (Kurt Vonnegut Jr. owned a copy, which he advised his wife to consult on the subject of sex.)[21] Neville Spearman was betting that Alex's editorial touch—and perhaps his name—could help it to connect more successfully with readers in the UK.

A book-length glossary of terms related to sex and different types of sexual behavior, with illustrative sketches, *An ABZ of Love* was different from just about any other sex guide available in English at the time: in presentation, in voice, and in attitude. The authors were a Danish couple, Inge and Sten Hegeler, psychologists who had a long-running sex advice column in the Danish newspaper *Ekstra-bladet*. This was nothing new in Scandinavia, where sex advice columns had been around since the pre-war years and the culture already accommodated some popularizing of sexual knowledge. Like Alex, the Hegelers were thus part of a positivist tradition that emphasized the need to reveal the scientific truth to the people, about sex as much as anything else.[22]

Their column and their book made "Inge & Sten" celebrities in Scandinavia. One very important factor in their success was the distinctive voice they adopted: wry, playful, friendly, frank, nonacademic, never cheesy or salacious, treating sex as much as possible like any other ordinary activity, meaning there was nothing about it that anyone couldn't or shouldn't openly discuss. The Hegelers' first book, in fact, had been a children's book on sex published in 1948, titled *Peter and Caroline*. And their principal audience was quite different from what Weckerle might have envisioned: from thirty to sixty years old, experienced but keen to improve their sex lives, and interested to know more about the variety of sexual experience in the world.

The authors presented themselves skillfully in interviews and profiles as utterly normal, bourgeois Danes whose personal lives were of a piece with the advice they offered. In photos of the couple, they were always affectionate, rubbing their noses together, for instance. Sten Hegeler later lamented that they didn't fit easily into any one camp: not radical enough for most feminists, too popular and superficial for the academics, and "too far out" for many others.[23] But that betwixt-and-between position also meant, as they surely knew, that they were at least a little bit acceptable to all of these groups and to the public at large.

By the early '70s, the Hegelers were getting from five hundred to one thousand letters a week asking their advice and opinions, and not only from Scandinavia. They used their perch to dispel anxiety and stereotypes, attack the culture of phallocentricity and male privilege, and encourage acceptance of homosexuality, single motherhood, a less-macho upbringing for boys, and more attention to female orgasm.[24] All of this was of a piece with the approach Alex had been advocating for years but with a little more humor thrown in. Here is his barely edited version of their "Submission" entry in *An ABZ of Love*:

> When Elvis Presley sings to the girl: "Be mine tonight!" the idea is that she should submit to him, give herself to him, become his. He never becomes hers.
>
> To submit to or give oneself to a man, is somehow reminiscent of a cow piously allowing itself to be led to the slaughterhouse. This is not in the interests of either party.[25]

Alex's edition of the book didn't come out until 1969 and wasn't a huge seller, but it attracted effusive reviews from some of Britain's bigger cultural names. Brigid Brophy in the *New Statesman* called it "the best book ever published on the subject," and Marjorie Proops in the *Daily Mirror* rightly described it as "an O-level book for adults." *An ABZ of Love*, along with Weckerle's creation, gave Alex the template for what would become *The Joy of Sex*: the structure (a posture book), the purported authorship (by an ordinary couple), the voice (frank, good-humored, never salacious), the presentation (tasteful, with drawings rather than photos), and the intended audience (experienced heterosexual couples).

But he needed something more—a provocation—to finally take on writing a popular sex manual for moderns, a successor to the Sanskrit and Renaissance Italian texts he had been searching out and studying for the better part of two decades. He got it from David Reuben, a California medical doctor and psychiatrist who in 1969 published a guidebook in question-and-answer format, *Everything You Always Wanted to Know about Sex but Were Afraid to Ask*, that spent fifty-five weeks in first place on the *New York Times* bestseller list and was a top seller in fifty-one other countries as well. With its cheeky title and perky style ("Mr. Sperm" and "Miss Egg" get together), it may have demystified sex for many people and contributed to more frank discussion, abetted by Reuben's appearances on *The Tonight Show* and an extensive book tour.

Well-informed parties, however, were taken aback by some of his alleged information. According to Reuben, "blind girls" were adept at "secret masturbation"—whatever that was—"orgasm usually brings on a lapse of consciousness," and a woman without a clitoris could have an orgasm. His opinions, stated as fact, included that all prostitutes hate men, that lesbianism is "immature," that "some of the fattest people are homosexuals," and that Coca-Cola is "the best douche available." In 1972 *Playboy* ran a feature identifying one hundred factual errors in his book: more than one for every four pages of the 368-page tome.

More seriously, in a book that claimed to liberate readers from the puritanism of the past, Reuben reinforced some of the worst cultural assumptions about sex, and even added a few curious ones of his own. Implicitly, sex is overwhelmingly about satisfying men's desire for pleasure and women's yearning to procreate. "Once the ovaries stop," he declared, "the very essence of being a woman stops." "Perversions" included anything other than "the penis-vagina version of sex." Homosexuals were naturally more promiscuous than other people, yet they merely perform a sad imitation of straight sex; fortunately, psychiatry could turn them into "happy, well-adjusted" heterosexuals. Lesbianism he dealt with under the general heading "Prostitution."

Alex dismissed Reuben's writing as "eccentric porn." Addressing an audience of Temple University medical students a few years later, he charged, "Reuben not only sounds as if he never had any sex himself, but [also] as if he never talked to anyone who has."[26] Besides being full of misinformation, *Everything You Always Wanted to Know about Sex* perversely contributed to worsening their anxieties—about whether they had the right anatomy, were gay or straight, or were having sex the wrong way—in the name of liberating them, Alex charged. Other books coming out at roughly the same time had some of the same problems. Another number-one bestseller, *The Sensuous Woman*, written pseudonymously (as "J"), by a woman named Terry Garrity, put much greater emphasis on women's pleasure but still assumed the basic objective of sex to be securing a relationship with a man. "I don't care if you are built like a truck driver or Twiggy," wrote Garrity. "No excuses. You can attract a man worth your attention, drive him wild with pleasure and keep him coming back eagerly for more."[27]

Alex told more than one version of the origin story of *The Joy of Sex* in later years—sometimes, it took him just two weeks to write, sometimes, two months—but it's clear from his preface to the book that he intended it as a corrective to a sexual revolution that seemed to be veering in the wrong direction.[28] "The permissive society has permitted everything from worried and po-faced admonition to eccentric porn," he wrote. "Most bookstalls carry a rash of 'straight' books which stop short of answers, and 'counseling' magazines based on unpractical, if not pathological, fantasy. It is high time adult readers were treated to some humane and experienced sense."[29] Books like Reuben's might encourage more people to have more sex but wouldn't relieve them of their anxieties about it. That's what Alex intended to correct.

UNDERSTANDING FROM A LATER vantage point what Alex was trying to create with *The Joy of Sex* takes some study, since the physical appearance of the final product—cover, layout, illustrations—would account for so much of its impact. Even the title has to be temporarily forgotten, since it wasn't concocted until months after the text was finalized and shortly before publication. The text was the starting point, the source of its appeal, and the key reference point for the designers. "I've always said Alex's voice, his input and textual style, were vitally important," recalled Max Monsarrat, who became the book's principal editor. "Without his tone and style, the book wouldn't have had any success at all. It would have come across as a straight textbook."[30]

Over the years, Alex had developed a communicative voice well suited to the fluid and engaging but authoritative style favored by the BBC and the great British dailies, which helped make him a constant presence on the airwaves and in their pages. For his new book, however, he aimed for a much wider audience. To engage it, experience was at least as important as credentials. The Hegelers presented themselves to their audience as a couple much like those who would be reading their books and columns. If he wanted to achieve something similar, Alex too would have to adopt a more popular voice.

His new book would have no quotes from the Latin or from Elizabethan poets. It would not reference scientific or behavioral texts, expecting the reader to be familiar with the source; it would contain no footnotes; and there would be no introductory discourse on human biology or psychology. Neither would Alex, the rational humanist and anarchist, load down the subject with mystical-spiritual New Ageism or atavistic notions of the Male and the Female. In this respect, his book fit fairly snugly within the British intellectual tradition of empiricism in which he had been educated, which sought knowledge in sensory experience rather than by constructing theoretical frameworks, the practice favored by continental European thinkers of the time.[31]

He also tried to keep his language au courant. Rather than anxieties and fears, his book would address the reader's "hangups"; peak sexual experiences would not be "extraordinary" but instead "mind-blowing." And wherever possible, the text would use a pithy (if sometimes mixed) metaphor to drive its point home: "Most wives who don't like Chinese food will eat it occasionally for the pleasure of seeing a Sinophile husband enjoy it, and vice versa."[32] The whole book would function largely as an invitation to couples who were no longer beginners to have more and better sex, including experimenting with variations that would keep it fresh and perhaps even help keep their relationship strong.

The tone would be reassuringly familiar and down-to-earth: "A well-designed bedroom can be a sexual gymnasium without it being embarrassing to let elderly relatives leave their coats there."[33] The text would have a sense of humor (while it is okay to make love in a shower stall, "don't pull down the fixture, however—it isn't weightbearing"). But Alex kept it free of four-letter words, leering descriptions, and cheap double-entendres. His intention was "to cure the notion, born of non-discussion, that common sex needs are odd or weird."[34] A cheesy tone would defeat the purpose and, not incidentally, mark his book as pornographic.

What immediately set his text apart from previous big-selling guides, including Marie Stopes's *Married Love*, van de Welde's *Ideal Marriage*, and even *The Sensuous Woman*, was that it did not assume the couple reading it were married. While it contained a "Problems" section, the only assumption was that its readers were healthy, untroubled, and simply wanted to have better sex. Most fundamentally, as the scholar Amy DeRogatis later pointed out, it decentered the orgasm as the be-all and end-all of sexual activity, encouraging readers to treat every part of the body as a potential zone of pleasure.[35]

Very little of this would have surprised anyone who had followed Alex's writings over the preceding decade and already knew him as an advocate of what one religious publication called "sex as a thrilling form of 'indoor sport.'"[36] At every turn, he emphasized the reader's freedom to choose. Nothing was mandatory, everything was subject to discussion and negotiation, every individual's fantasies and preferences were distinct, and there was nothing to be ashamed of, if honestly revealed. Not everyone had the same needs and preferences, but "since sex is cooperative, you can cater to one another alternately to bridge gaps."[37]

As always, Alex placed a great deal of emphasis on sex as play. "Bed is the place to play all the games you have ever wanted to play, at the play-level," he wrote. "If we are able to transmit the sense of play which is essential to a full, enterprising and healthily immature view of sex between committed people, we would be performing a mitzvah." He also found space to touch on the connection of sex and sociality, without belaboring the point. "The starting point of all lovemaking is close bodily contact. Love has been defined as the harmony of two souls and the contact of two epidermes. It is also, from our infancy, the starting point of human relationships and needs."[38]

That's as close to a philosophic statement as Alex would make in the book, although he would later declare, "*The Joy of Sex* is an expression of my anarchism."[39] The point, this time, was more limited: to help people express all of themselves—"our whole skin surface, our feelings of identity, aggression and so on, and all of our fantasy needs"—in the one setting where it's not forbidden to do so. Alex had been talking and writing about play and mutuality in physical relationships for years; his new book would offer some tips on how to practice these arts. One's whole skin "is a genital organ," he declared ("firm pressure on the sole at the instep, however administered, is erogenic to most people"). So the range of techniques and variations was just about unlimited; sex didn't have to be confined to "the good old face-to-face matrimonial" or even penetration. Lest his readers think that trying deliberately to increase their repertoire in bed made sex more mechanical or impersonal, he assured them that while it might start out that way, "it makes us more, not less, receptive to each other as people," since it only works with compromise, give-and-take, and mutual caring.[40]

In part, his new book was an opportunity to say these things—about sex and sociality, about the need to stop worrying about what's "normal," about fantasy—that he had said many times already, but to a much wider audience. Who made up this audience? Not people who would find his suggestions disturbing; they would stay where they were, with, he said pointedly, "Reuben sandwiches."

For everyone else, the requirements were simple: willingness to have sex naked and spend some time at it, access to private premises and washing facilities, lack of aversion to such activities as "genital kisses," willingness to go beyond just one sexual trick, and love.[41] Alex was explicit that his book was for heterosexuals, but his intention, at least, was to create a guide for *couples* rather than individual men or women; the idea was for them to use it in collaboration. Outside the Hegelers' books, this was still unusual for the time.

Alex was writing a posture book with a difference. In 1971 the section of Weckerle's *Golden Book of Love* covering positions finally appeared in English, now somehow with six hundred positions, from a small New York publisher, Land's End Press.* Weckerle is sometimes thought to

* In 1937–38, an abridged, under-the-counter edition with just two hundred of Weckerle's positions had been published in New York under the title *Kinesthesia of Love*. G. Legman, *The Horn Book: Studies in Erotic Folklore and Bibliography* (New Hyde Park NY: University Books, 1964), 64.

have been a physical education teacher; one reason is that he organized the positions he described into categories ("Back Brace Group," "Table Group," "Hassock Gym-Mat Group") and sub-categories ("Frontal Positions," "Hip-Thigh Positions," "Bath Positions") related to anatomy and the type of acrobatics involved.** Some of his positions required actual gym equipment: mats, pull-up bars, rings, and climbing ropes, not to mention swimming-pool ladders, desks, and hassocks. A properly equipped space for male-female fun he called a "sexuarium."

Alex took a less mechanistic, more topical approach. He only detailed twenty-eight distinct positions and techniques, some of them lifted from Weckerle ("frontal," "flanquette," "croupade," "cuissade," "negrèsse"), some from other manuals ("horseback," "feuille de rose," "Viennese oyster"), and few of them especially gymnastic for a book on "advanced" lovemaking. "Few of the freak positions merit more than a single visit out of curiosity," he advised.[42]

Instead, his organizing principle would be the metaphor of a cookbook, divided into four sections. "Starters" covered basics like love, clothes, pubic hair, the penis, and the vulva. "Main Courses" included a variety of positions as well as erogenous zones from breasts and buttocks to navel and earlobes. "Sauces & Pickles" included more positions as well as anal intercourse, bondage and discipline, G-strings, feathers, and other variations. A final section, "Problems," was a catchall covering such matters as bisexuality, children, frigidity, rape, smoking, and venereal diseases.

Alex's tentative title for the book was "Cordon Bleu Sex." "A cookery book is a sophisticated and unanxious account of available dishes—culinary fantasies as well as staple diets," he wrote in the preface. "This book is an equally unanxious account of the full repertoire of human heterosexuality." The "full repertoire" meant more than plain-vanilla male-female sex, however. Both women and men have "traces" of a need to dominate or be dominated, and bondage offered a way to explore this: if done properly.[43] No one should be afraid to explore their bisexual side, even if they regard themselves as essentially heterosexual, since everyone has the capacity to respond to both sexes.

One good thing about foursomes and other group situations, Alex wrote, is that they provide an inducement to do so. The same goes for

** The new translation was illustrated with drawings; as depicted, many of the six hundred positions appeared less likely to lead to ecstasy than to a trip to the emergency room.

cross-dressing—some men are turned on by being laced into corsets, for example. And fetishes are not something to worry about unless they become all-consuming. "Perversion" Alex defined as "something antisocial which handicapped people use as a substitute for the sexuality from which their hangups debar them." But the commonest perversions, he explained, "are getting hold of some power and using it to kick other people around, money as a status activity, treating other people, sexually or otherwise, as things to manipulate, and interfering with other people's sex lives."[44]

Alex's discussion of bisexuality and cross-dressing was culturally in synch. London's first gay pride parade would be held less than three months before the book was released in America, on July 1, 1972 (about seven hundred people participated). Less than a week later, on July 6, David Bowie and his band would perform his song "Starman" on the BBC's *Top of the Pops*. During the three-and-a-half-minute performance, Bowie feigned seducing his guitarist, Mick Ronson, at one point getting down on his knees and applying his mouth to Ronson's instrument, as if to fellate it. The broadcast, and Bowie's entire, gender-bending persona, shocked much of mainstream Britain but had a seismic effect on countless British youth who were just beginning to define themselves sexually.

Sex was no less than "the supreme human experience," Alex declared, so it didn't have to be absolutely spontaneous. "Planning and thinking about sex is part of love." It started with fantasizing, then talking through a position or technique, then planning and rehearsing, much as dancers formulated their moves. That included masturbation: "A couple who can masturbate each other skillfully can do anything else they like." Since the body was a site of exploration, every aspect was important. Alex frowned on men and women washing away their natural odors, including with deodorants and douches, since natural odors could be a turn-on. Shaving off armpit hair, at least in a cool climate, he denounced as "ignorant vandalism."[45]

There is no such thing as too much sex, Alex urged; likewise impotence and frigidity are largely myths. Both men and women retain their sexual needs and functions their whole lives by adjusting to physical changes, such as a longer interval for a man to get an erection. A woman who couldn't seem to respond sexually didn't need a man to fret with her or make her anxious. She could explore her body on her own, fantasize, and figure out for herself what excited her, perhaps with the aid of a vibrator, then try to set it up with her lover.[46]

This was consistent with a complaint Alex had been making for several years: that too much research and advice on female sexuality was being handed down by academic men rather than the parties best able to do so—namely, sexually fulfilled women.[47] It also dovetailed with Masters and Johnson's findings in their 1970 *Human Sexual Inadequacy*, which strongly suggested that it was men's sexual hang-ups that prevented women from achieving sexual fulfillment, not the other way around, and with Shere Hite's later research, published in 1976 as *The Hite Report,* which found that clitoral stimulation, not penile thrusting during vaginal penetration, brought women to orgasm.

Good heterosexual sex must, above all, be a partnership, Alex reiterated throughout his book. "Nobody can possibly be a good lover—or a whole man—if he doesn't regard women as (a) human beings and (b) equals," he said flatly. "Finding out someone else's needs and your own, and how to express them in bed, is not only interesting and educative but rewarding, and what sexual love is about."[48]

ALL IN ALL, THE text he had produced was a good deal more enlightened than nearly any other guide, manual, or compendium of sexual instruction available at the time. But did he succeed? Did he produce a book that was truly liberating, or did he reinforce, consciously or not, some of the old prejudices and presumptions?

"Most writing about human sexuality, whether in journals or on walls, is the product of deep preoccupation," he had written in a 1959 article about Havelock Ellis. "I suspect that . . . inspired science, like inspired art, is generally compulsive—its merit depends upon how far the worker exploits the compulsion and how far the compulsion dominates the worker."[49] Like anyone else exploring the field, Alex's text was hugely affected by his own experience and preferences. Add to that the fact that most of the literature on sex dating back centuries—or millennia, in the case of some Indian texts he had studied—was written from a male perspective, and it was almost inevitable that his book would shortchange women's needs and desires, despite his intention not to do so.

"I have found this characteristic figure in nearly all of the 1970s sex manuals I looked into," feminist scholar Meryl Altman wrote a dozen years after Alex's book was published: "the affirmation of a new frankness, of a break with the repression of the past." This claim is made again and again "with no cumulative gain, in order to validate and create a discourse that may or may not be equally repressive."[50]

While he decentered the orgasm, Alex still made the phallus the center of attention. In a good sexual encounter, Alex said, the penis becomes like a third party or a child of the couple: "'their' penis." Not surprisingly, he also found the matrimonial or missionary position to be the fallback for any couple enjoying high-quality sex, because it's "uniquely satisfying": adaptable, effective for either tough or tender intercourse, easy to shift into or out of (for the man, that is). Other positions are chiefly useful "to delay his final orgasm while multiplying hers."[51] Either way, the drama is still largely centered on the "child" and its moods.

One of the innovative features of Alex's book was his incorporation of "bordel tricks" and fantasies—once thought of as obscene, deviant, and the province of professionals—into his couple's repertoire. Often, however, these tended to reinforce the presumption that dominance and submission were intrinsic to sex: "be the Sultan and his favorite concubine, the burglar and the maiden, even a dog and a currant bun, anything you fancy for the hell of it."[52]

These scenarios sometimes brought violence, or violent fantasies, into the situation. In his preface, Alex called these "symbolically aggressive games," but it wasn't always easy to tell what he meant by this or where he placed the boundary line. "Actual craving for pain (mental or physical) as a sex kick isn't uncommon," he wrote. "Good sex can be wildly violent but still never cruel." So can discipline or mild beating. "The sauna twig level is nearly enough for most straight couples, but people who really go for beating like it hard enough to mark the skin. . . . You can stick to the buttocks or cover the whole surface—back, belly, breasts, and even penis (careful!) and vulva. . . . For a genuinely decadent European sensation, you can use real birch twigs."[53]

Rape, at least as a fantasy, was fair game as well for sophisticated lovers. "Gagging and being gagged turns most men on," Alex advised. "Most women profess to hate it on prospect, but the expression of erotic astonishment on the face of a well-gagged woman when she finds she can only mew is irresistible to most men's rape fantasies." When something went wrong, it wasn't necessarily the perpetrator who was at fault, Alex more than suggested. "Many sex 'murders' are accidents overtaking women who treat partial strangulation as a kick," he warned, without revealing how he allegedly knew this. "Real" rape is, of course, "a frightening turn-off," but here again, whose fault is it? "Don't get yourself raped," Alex counseled, "i.e., [don't] deliberately excite a man you don't know well, unless you mean to follow through."[54]

Reading between the lines, these passages suggested what feminists were already pointing out: that fantasy was never just a place where malign scenarios go to be sublimated and die. Rather, it was a landscape across which heterosexual male dominance was being fought for and resisted, all the time. But Alex couldn't see this—a fantasy was a fantasy—and his pages on violent role-playing games would be among the most severely criticized in the book; he had already received some negative comments from people he asked to read the text prepublication.[55]

He wasn't arguing for literal dominance, of course. In his vision, violent game-playing and role-playing could go both ways. The woman could tie down the man, beat him, and dominate him, just as well as the other way around. And he was careful to set ground rules: nothing tied around the other person's neck; nothing pushed down into the throat; never leave anyone helpless alone, even briefly; and never play bondage games with someone you don't know or in groups.[56] But he betrayed his commitment to male-female mutuality in other ways.

It's the woman's responsibility to arouse the man, he asserted—never pressing the point about the man having a similar obligation—and so he spent a good deal of space advising her how to do so, not to mention on her appearance and presentation. "Because it is so important, a woman needs to guard her own personal perfume as carefully as her looks," he warned. Depilation is costly and not worth the trouble—except "if a girl has a lot of hair on her face." A bidet is okay for washing, but "showering looks better than sitting on a bidet like a battery hen." Only "a not over-intelligent whore" can be persuaded to beat a man hard during sex.[57] Nowhere did Alex offer any such patronizing advice on how the man can avoid turning off the "girl" with whom he's about to go to bed.

"Same-sex play" between either men or women was fine in Alex's book ("all people are bisexual"), and anal sex "is something which nearly every couple tries once." But he had no suggestions to make for same-sex positions or techniques. He hastened to assure his readers that attempting it didn't necessarily mean they were gay or lesbian, and he suggested that people who opt for the same sex exclusively are reducing, not widening, their experience. Despite his long support for gay rights, he continued in his new book to define homosexuality as a lack: "having some kind of turn-off towards the opposite sex."[58] As for lesbians, some "are simply women who have given up on men after a lifetime spent kissing frogs who failed to turn into princes," implying that the right man might be the remedy.[59]

In later years, Alex would ascribe his omission of gay and lesbian sex to lack of familiarity—"I haven't the expertise"—but that meant he hadn't bothered to acquire it. The files he had accumulated over two decades on sex education and practices contained very little about non-heterosexual activity.[60] Implicitly, Alex was discouraging gay people from identifying as a distinct community, even though increasingly that was their only option for asserting their rights and humanity. Elsewhere, he was more explicit about this.

When Micky Burbidge, a Gay Liberation Front activist, wrote in 1971 asking him to sign a letter asking the UK publishers of *Everything You Always Wanted to Know about Sex* to withdraw it on account of its anti-gay content, Alex declined, despite the fact that the signatories included Eustace Chesser and the well-known psychotherapists Charlotte Wolff, Lindsey Neustatter, and Anthony Ryle.[61] He gave only the flimsy explanation that, as he put it, "I don't counsel 'homosexuals,'" offering only to read the book and write privately to the publishers.[62]

The following year, the gay rights campaigner Alan Horsfall wrote, asking Alex's support for the Campaign for Homosexual Equality. Again he declined, arguing that the new group would "perpetuate the idea that 'homosexuals' exist and differ in an important fundamental [way] from non-homosexuals," adding that allowing same-sex partners to adopt children "seems to me a mistake."[63] Likewise, in a July 1973 review of *Loving Them Both*, a book on bisexuality by the novelist Colin MacInnes (*Absolute Beginners*), he found worrying "the tendency to create a category of 'bisexual' people who need special understanding." There are no homosexuals, bisexuals, or heterosexuals, he insisted, just people "whose behaviour is almost infinitely plastic." Any other perspective, he said dogmatically, would simply revive "the classificatory psychiatry of 1873."[64]

This may have been true so far is it went; some queer and feminist scholars have always been ambivalent about politics built around specific, perhaps limiting, self-definitions, which Judith Butler years later called "necessary errors of identity."[65] But they were "necessary" for the very good reason that they helped a stigmatized group of people step out of the shadows and claim their rights, and Alex was being unhelpfully dogmatic not to understand this.

Also dismayingly, he essentially agreed with David Reuben that "the commonest motive for becoming a regular streetwalking pro is an active dislike of males," although the "psychopathology" of most prostitutes was probably due to society's treatment of them. For centuries, governments and the medical establishment had stigmatized prostitutes as carriers of sexually transmitted diseases and used the anxieties this generated as leverage to control women's bodies and behavior. Alex was largely buying into this injustice.[66] Yet he also maintained a double standard when it came to the female partner. If you find out your man has seen a prostitute, Alex advised, try to find out why and be understanding.[67]

Like Reuben's guide, in fact, a good deal of what went into Alex's book were half-baked, very male opinions masquerading as authoritative advice. This went beyond the strictly male-female to include a smattering of stereotyped cultural references. Aside from "la negrèsse," "Japanese style" is sex on the floor with cushions, "numerous squatting or semi-squatting positions, a lot of bondage, and a preoccupation with extras and odd devices." The "Viennese oyster" is a woman who can "cross her feet behind her head, lying on her back." And "South Slav style," or "Serbian intercourse," is a kind of "mock rape."[68]

This terminology has much to say about the class assumptions behind the book. "Throughout," the cultural historian Rosalind Brunt noted, "appeals are made to the reader through the medium of good taste. This is to be 'the first explicitly sexual book for the coffee table' and sexual joy is metaphorically compared with what goes on in the worlds of concert-going, opera and ballet and the appreciation of fine wines"—and, of course, the culinary arts.[69] Alex was excavating techniques and positions salvaged from the underground of nineteenth-century forbidden erotic literature to provide these culturally aspiring couples with a full menu of aesthetic delights of the sexual variety.

That menu came with a lot of cultural undertow. In effect, it was a "re-presentation in contemporary guise of the familiar colonialists' bordello," Brunt pointed out, "and the couple's guide is the connoisseur of the place, a world-weary but refined gentleman—the Victorian sensualist." "Viennese oyster," "South Slav style," and "negrèsse" were a few of the exotic items—like tea from India and lion skins from Africa—that this pith-helmeted adventurer had brought back for the present-day couple's entertainment and delectation. In Alex's text, "the racist and imperialist elements of pornography are preserved—indeed, rehabilitated, through the apparently guilt-free language of 'cool.' . . . And just as the social context of the book is the imperial bordello, so bondage proves to be its main frame of reference."[70] Now middle-class couples could enjoy the same sophisticated pleasures as the jaded aristocrats of old.

Sexual sophistication actually had been an elite hobby much farther back than the Victorian era. The *Kama Sutra*, which is dated somewhere between 400 BCE and 300 CE, was written specifically for members of the Indian upper castes and was "really about the art of living," the Indologist Wendy Doniger, one of its translators, pointed out. "It tells us that anyone can live the life of pleasure—if they have the money."[71] Alex's text also appealed to class snobbery in a more contemporary way, however.

The historian of erotic publishing Jay Gertzman later argued that since *Joy* framed sex as a means for sophisticated—that is, middle class or affluent—individuals to please themselves and their partners, rather than a crude way to get off, it flattered its readers that they were different from those unsavory people who frequented prostitutes, massage parlors, and X-rated movies or bought skin magazines. Therefore they had no reason to feel any empathy when those establishments, their workers, and patrons were raided, shaken down, arrested, and run out of business by the police or the Mob.[72] While Alex's book helped to open up a more frank discussion of sex in mainstream society, it did so at the cost, perhaps, of creating new categories of "proper" and "improper" erotica, further marginalizing some of the people who had been most victimized by cultural puritanism.

The same distinction applies to Alex's treatment of pornography, which he defined simply as the "name given to any sexual literature somebody is trying to suppress." There were two kinds, he asserted. "Well done" porn described "feasible, acceptable and pleasurable sex activities" that couples could enjoy, or "fantasies which, though not feasible, turn them on." The other kind, featuring "antisocial fantasies about torture and so on," worried lawmakers but may have helped to keep "not very bright people"—or the lower social classes?—"from acting those fantasies out."[73] This was as far as his analysis went. He made no mention of the actual content of much porn, which was often highly degrading to women and sometimes involved children.

In this context, Alex's emphasis on sex as play could become a trap, as it did in the hands of *Playboy*, *Penthouse*, and other ostensibly sophisticated publications of the time. If you objected to any of the varieties of play he recommended, you were hung-up, uncool, a puritan. If there was really no such thing as "normal" when it came to sex, as Alex liked to assert, then everything was normal, and there was really no basis for telling your partner no. Otherwise, you were depriving him (or her) of an important outlet for (most likely) his fantasy, without which he might be more inclined to resort to "real" violence.

How did all this get mixed up with Alex's championing of sex as a building block of sociality?

THE COMMON DENOMINATOR, IN his mind, was biology. Attempting to explain why he had shuttled for so many years between the study of physiological aging and the exploration of sexual behavior, Alex once said that he regarded "biology as a whole as the study of behaviour."[74] Anything from sex to power relationships to eating habits fit into this definition, and so Alex could study and write about sexual practices, about the selection of sociopathic leaders (*Authority and Delinquency*), about the responses of *Lebistes* to different dietary regimes, and remain within his field of study as a biologist. Physiological fact and individual behavior, in the end, could not be studied in isolation from one another.

This was only becoming more so, Alex felt. In his preface, he mentioned that he was writing at a time "when primatology and classical human psychodynamics look like joining hands."[75] His mentor Herbert Read had argued that the intuitive element of art was a psychological process that had evolved along with human consciousness, which in turn was a product of humans' biological evolution.[76] Sex was somewhat the same, according to Alex: a psychological as well as a physical matter, and in both senses a product of evolution. Sociality was part of the same process, but it had to compete and find a balance with other drivers.

Later in his book, he noted that humans not only had the biggest brains of all the mammals, but that the human male had the largest penis. He borrowed this from Desmond Morris's *The Naked Ape*, a 1967 book of popular science that Alex had blurbed when it came out.[77] Morris, who knew Alex through academic circles and was the curator of mammals at the Zoological Society of London, examined how humans' biology influenced their social development.[78] He argued that many of their physical traits evolved to reinforce the male-female couple for child-rearing purposes—for example, that fleshy earlobes are erogenous zones that can provoke orgasm and that females' more rounded breasts evolved in part as a sexual signaling device, while face-to-face copulation cemented the bond between the partners.[79]

Morris's book became an international best seller (*Playboy* publisher Hugh Hefner co-produced a fictionalized film comedy version in 1973), and, while many scholars criticized its conclusions, it was a major text in what became known as sociobiology, or the study of the foundations of social behavior in biology and natural selection. Sociobiology itself would come under attack in the late '70s for allegedly encouraging eugenics and the biologizing of racism, among other accusations. But earlier, Alex and other biologists, brought up on the genetic research that scientists like Haldane had pursued and Read's ideas about the psychological and biological roots of art and other aspects of culture, weren't so ready to dismiss it.

He himself waded into this stream with an influential 1971 article in *Nature*, "Likelihood of Human Pheromones." The term "pheromone" had been coined to denote a substance that one individual produces and emits as a signal to other individuals in the same species. The pheromone stimulates the hormonal system, triggering a memory or behavior or alerting the target that the emitter is ready for sexual intercourse. In 1959 researchers showed that female silkworm moths emit a molecule that attracts the attention of males over a distance of miles: the first pheromone scientifically proven.

A widening circle of researchers plunged into the quest for pheromones in other species, and over the following decade they were discovered in insects and in mice, although proving their existence in higher primates was difficult since these species have more complex systems of signaling and reaction and respond to outside stimuli in less predictable ways. But the possibility that humans might communicate through pheromones piqued the curiosity of many biologists, including Alex.

In his *Nature* article, he noted that as far back as medieval times, people had identified odors like musk as "conceptuants," and that sex researchers since Havelock Ellis had been intrigued by the idea that certain body odors had "sexual releaser effects."[80] If human pheromones existed, Alex argued, they could open the door to control of endocrine cycles and even new types of "reproductive pharmacology. . . . We may live to see 'odor therapy' move out of the realm of fringe medicine, into a field with wider implications." Therapies using pheromones, which in animals could be as simple as a single molecule, could perhaps replace therapy using hormones, which are much more complex and have side effects that are harder to predict. Just as he had done in his books on gerontology, Alex digested virtually the whole existing literature on human pheromones and sized up the case for further research.

There were plenty of reasons to believe such things existed, he argued: for example, humans' obsession with controlling, suppressing, and altering body odor and the fact that they develop a strong body odor around puberty. Additionally, he said, humans have a set of supposedly nonfunctional organs that in other mammals might be regarded as part of a pheromonal system, including apocrine or sweat glands in the underarms, the pubic area, and other parts of the body.

Alex's paper helped focus the search for human pheromones on the sweat glands, even though scientists were finding other possible sources in other mammals. But his suspicion that they played some role in sexual arousal was strong enough that it informed his aversion to deodorants and the removal of body hair expressed in *The Joy of Sex*.

The trouble wasn't the search for human pheromones but the conclusions some people might draw if they did exist. What would female-to-male communication via pheromones be trying to "tell" the male? Or male-to-female? Or female-to-female? Or male-to-male? Creating a deterministic scenario around pheromones, perhaps involving a Darwinian imperative to reproduce, would be tempting and easy to put across.

Alex suggested nothing of the kind in his *Nature* article, but in his new book, he appeared to be receptive to sociobiological arguments. According to him, the violence and domination that riddled male-female sexual interaction could be sublimated and rendered harmless through fantasy and role-playing, and even used as a way to explore trust.[81] But that still meant that "intuition," "instincts," and biological inheritance imposed boundaries on what is possible sexually, Brunt argued. Alex was still telling his readers that "violence conforms exactly to the dictates of a man's essential sexuality" and that it "is literally bondage that keeps the pair-bond together, just as they are, forever."[82] Of course, there were other fantasies, other scenes the heterosexual couple could play that didn't involve dominance or violence, but, in Alex's telling, they weren't the most thrilling or intense.

George Orwell. Vernon Richards, Archive Berneri

George Woodcock.
Vernon Richards, courtesy
Queen's University Archives

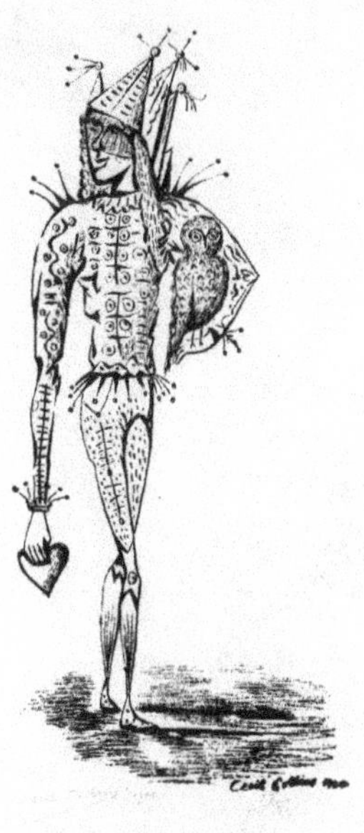

Cecil Collins, *The Fool.*
© Tate Images

Vernon Richards, Marie Louise Berneri.
Archive Berneri

Nick, Ruth, and infant Nick.
Family collection

Peter Medawar photo.
Bettmann/Bettmann via Getty Images

Alex Comfort lecturing (drawing)

J. B. S. Haldane photo.
Bettmann/Bettmann via Getty Images

Alex Comfort at Aldermaston march

Aldermaston marchers at Trafalgar Square

Alex Comfort and dinosaur. Family collection

Bertrand Russell photo. *Evening Standard*/ Hulton Archive via Getty Images

Alex Comfort, 1966. Mark Gerson

CHAPTER 15

Making *Joy* (1971–1972)

Much of the content of Alex's new sex manual chalks up easily to the times and his personal situation. The sexual revolution, which was already quite a few years old by the time he sat down to write what would become his most famous book, was already fastened into popular consciousness as a heterosexual affair, even if this was inaccurate. *Time* magazine's July 11, 1969 cover, "The Sex Explosion," depicted a gigantic fig leaf being unzipped to reveal a naked man and woman caressing. Pornography, to the extent it was a public issue, was still a club the Right used to bash the so-called permissive society, not a feminist concern, although this would change. The "everyone is bisexual" line may not have been all that helpful to a growing gay rights movement, but it was certainly an improvement over the culture of denial that had previously prevailed.

But Alex had promised more: an all-around sex guide that would correct the misinformation and alleviate the anxieties that other books perpetuated, give couples permission to enjoy sex as play—not psychodrama—and encourage them to form equal erotic partnerships, not continue the old dominant-submissive pattern. Instead, he smuggled male dominance back into the equation.

Neither was his text the most radical development in the opening up of human sexuality that was taking place at the time. For years, a motley collection of sex radicals on both sides of the Atlantic had been jumping into porn, prostitution, and so-called perversions to produce art—often using their own bodies as the surface—and concoct a raw, fearless, anarchic gutter version of utopia, rather than picking and choosing from the underground as Alex did. Despite his sanctioning of bondage games, Alex, the humanist, always aimed to make sex pleasurable, guileless, and unfearful: the farthest thing from these radicals who celebrated danger, transgression, and sometimes degradation. Eliminating anxiety could mean removing the wellspring of any number of acts that directly challenged publicly accepted morality. For Alex, fantasy was an aid to pleasure; for others, it was a field of battle in which old identities could be discarded and new ones forged.

Several years earlier, in her essay "The Pornographic Imagination," Susan Sontag was noting the arrival of a new politics of sexual identity that emphasized the culturally distinct elements of homosexuality, sadomasochism, and other outside-the-mainstream practices.[1] Perhaps these sexual rebels didn't want to be absorbed into a polymorphous melting pot, as Alex suggested, but for their liberation to take distinctive forms. Later Alex would discourage younger people from thinking of sex as a "performance," as a by-product of viewing pornography, but what about people whose ideal sexual experience was through performance or exhibition?

Alex couldn't endorse this new cultural turn, and probably never fully understood it, because it didn't fit into his humanist framework, though many found it profoundly liberating. David Wojnarowicz, who would emerge a few years later as an influential underground writer, performance and mixed media artist, and AIDS activist, was learning his trade as a Times Square hustler around the time Alex was writing his best seller. Marco Vassi, who Norman Mailer called "the foremost erotic writer in America" and a genuine "sexual explorer," was churning out hardcore porn novels while developing his notion of metasexuality, a condition beyond male-female heterosexuality or even bisexuality.[2]

In Amsterdam, Willem de Ridder, a Dutch member of the Fluxus art collective, had started *Hit Week*, a music magazine that quickly shifted into an anything-goes discussion of sex. In 1969, with the help of the British radical journalist and playwright Heathcote Williams; his girlfriend, model Jean Shrimpton; and the feminist writer Germaine Greer, who was then developing what would become her best seller *The Female Eunuch*, de Ridder relaunched his magazine as *Suck: The First European Sex Paper*. The openly pornographic publication had to be smuggled into the UK after officials banned it, and the publishing collective imploded after a handful of issues, but not before Greer contributed several incendiary pieces condemning missionary-position sex and critiquing every detail of male-female bodily contact from a feminist point of view.

In New York, Al Goldstein's underground tabloid *SCREW*, which started publishing in 1968, aimed primarily for a hetero male audience but was genuinely fascinated by every possible form of sexual behavior and was eager to thrust it in the faces of the middle-class citizenry. A classified ad in *SCREW* led to the coalescing of a group of people interested in sadomasochism who in 1970 formed the Eulenspiegel Society, which in turn spawned similar organizations in other parts of the country. Already in business in Manhattan's meatpacking district was the Hellfire Club, which had a strong S&M element but attracted every variety of hobbyist, from gay leather fetishists to coprophiliacs, and where virtually every human orifice was eventually explored. More exotically themed clubs followed.[3]

Not entirely coincidentally, in 1966, shortly before the Hellfire Club opened its doors, the first U.S. gender identity clinic opened, specializing in sex reassignment and transsexuality. Two years later, in London, *Penthouse* launched *Forum*, a magazine whose content consisted entirely of letters from readers discussing aspects of their sex lives. Three years later, *Forum* added a US edition that would build up a vast circulation.[4]

At the same time, European post-structuralist thinkers were analyzing the political and social role of desire through a more critical lens than Alex favored. Perhaps, suggested Gilles Deleuze and Felix Guattari in their influential *Anti-Oedipus* and Michel Foucault in studies like *Discipline and Punish*, sexual desire was not always and everywhere a liberating force. Perhaps, along with other forms of desire, it could be used to depoliticize the masses and blunt the edge of resentments along lines of class and wealth. Why should it automatically follow that, if the ruling class had more and better sex, they would relax their grip on power and usher in a cooperative utopia, as Alex had fantasized in *Come Out to Play*? or even tolerate the lower classes enjoying the same freedom? Just because the bourgeoisie were enjoying themselves more in bed didn't necessarily mean the rest of us would be free.

The sexual revolution was well on its way to becoming overtly political as well. It could be said to have exploded, almost literally, in the small hours of June 28, 1969, when a police raid on the Stonewall Inn, a Greenwich Village gay bar, ignited a riot, the torching of the bar, and a rebellion of the gay community against the casual brutality and abuse it had suffered for years. Gay and lesbian writers were already expressing themselves more openly in publications like *ONE* and the *Los Angeles Advocate*, which combined political writing with explicit art and images, but with Stonewall, the modern Gay Liberation Movement was born.

Plenty of women were taking up Alex's challenge to explore their own sexuality well before he laid it down. In 1968 Anne Koedt opened a fraught discussion of women's sexual response with her essay "The Myth of the Vaginal Orgasm," which declared that the clitoris is "the center of sexual sensitivity" and "the female equivalent of the penis" and that it "has no other function than that of sexual pleasure."[5]

The same year, Betty Dodson opened the first one-woman show of erotic art at a Manhattan gallery. In 1972, after renouncing romantic love, trying group sex and becoming disenchanted, she launched her soon-to-be-famous Bodysex workshops in which she helped women become more comfortable with their bodies and sexuality, including teaching better masturbation techniques. Soon after, Dell Williams would start her mail order business, Eve's Garden, specializing in vibrators and other sex aids, and then open a shop in Greenwich Village. In 1972, before *The Joy of Sex* was published, the young American poet Erica Jong was wondering why a woman couldn't write a novel as sexually frank as *Portnoy's Complaint*. Over lunch, her editor at Holt, Rinehart and Winston suggested she try writing a novel in the voice of her poems, and some months later she completed *Fear of Flying*.[6] The following year, Nancy Friday published *My Secret Garden*, her bestselling compilation of women's sexual fantasies.

The Pill had made much of this liberalization possible, although some key changes were still in the future. *Roe v. Wade* would not make legal abortion available in the United States until 1973, and home pregnancy tests would not be sold widely in America until 1977.[7] But the demand for information was expanding rapidly, just as Alex had predicted it would two decades earlier. In 1969 Boston's Emanuel College hosted a women's health seminar that pulled together the collective that, the following year, published a 193-page booklet titled *Women and Their Bodies*, which sold five thousand copies at thirty-five cents apiece. A year later, retitled *Our Bodies, Ourselves*, it would sell 250,000 copies, mainly through word of mouth, for the first time making reliable information about abortion, pregnancy, postpartum depression, and a variety of sex-related problems easily available to women.

THE PRECEDING WERE JUST some of the more visible elements of the radical sexual culture that was taking shape around the time Alex was writing his book and that revealed it as less than revolutionary outside most middle-class homes.

What he nevertheless had in common with many sex radicals of one variety or another was his emphasis on fantasy and experimentation, his admonition that couples establish a genuine give-and-take in fulfilling each other's needs and desires, and his urging women to explore their sexuality on their own. His book was genuinely sex-positive, unlike Reuben's and other sex manuals of the time, even though it wasn't entirely free of the old anxieties. It emphasized that sex must be a collaborative activity of equals, even if it didn't always point that way in the specifics.

Above all, Alex's voice—relaxed, conversational, unembarrassed—was something new and welcoming that would influence other popular writers on sex, including many more radical than himself, for decades to come. It's true that his book made very middle-class assumptions about its readers, with all the attached cultural baggage, but Alex was trying deliberately to appeal to the "domestic squares" whose lives he felt were changing more than they perhaps knew and who might be open, down the road, to a different social vision.

First, however, he had to get his book published. He had been writing about sex for well over two decades but had never produced anything this explicit. At the same time, he still hoped to secure funding and an institutional home for his "test-battery" on human aging and didn't want to tarnish his public image while he pursued the project. In April 1972 he replied to a letter from Albert V. Freeman, a Beverley Hills psychologist and member of the board of Sandstone, asking if he could put off accepting an offer to join the board. "At the moment I have an identity problem," he wrote.

> I am trying to get off the ground a big scientific project in the control of aging, and from past experience I am desperately anxious to stay Mr. Aging, while the Press (following some of my earlier writings) wants to make me Mr. Sex. If I'm Mr. Sex, every TV interviewer will want to talk about sex, including Sandstone, and not about aging, which is what I get on the program to propaganda for. Once the big push gets rolling without my having to shove, this may change.[8]

The expedient Alex hit upon to remain "Mr. Aging" was a fiction that he had not written the book, but only edited it; the authors were a couple, one of them a practicing physician, which was why they had to maintain their anonymity. "The final text incorporates the suggestions of several couples, plus a few experts."[9] The ruse served two other purposes as well; first, to make readers believe the book represented the female as well as the male perspective on heterosexual sex (one section,

"Woman (By Her for Him)," was supposedly written by the female author alone), and second, as a covert acknowledgment of Jane's role in its development.*

Alex was nevertheless aware that none of the established British publishers that had been issuing his novels, poetry, and scientific and critical volumes for more than thirty years would touch a sex manual, let alone one with illustrations, which was what he had in mind. Fortunately, the larger world of British publishing had changed a great deal in the preceding decade, becoming not only more receptive to his kind of sexual frankness but also more open to the sophisticated visual presentation he wanted.

The London book trade was still a small world, dominated by a tight network of editors and publishers drawn from the universities and sharing similar class backgrounds. The younger members of the circle had very different political and cultural leanings than their elders, however. Alcohol fueled a frantic social scene—it was the days of "alcohol and long lunches," remembered future Virago Press publisher Carmen Callil, who got her start in the business at this time.[10] To a lesser extent, so did illicit drugs. Marxism, in various forms, was fashionable—some of the younger editors and executives had discovered their political selves during the heyday of the Ban the Bomb movement—along with a desire to test the limits in sexual and cultural matters.[11] "Our hearts were young and gay and up the Establishment," Callil said.[12] At the same time, the rise of mass-market paperbacks—Penguin and Panther, in that order, were the biggest imprints—made it possible to issue cheap editions of popular titles, reissues, and new books that might appeal to specialized or cult audiences. Britain was publishing more books for a wider variety of audiences than it had in decades.

"The *Lady Chatterley* case changed everything—forever!" recalled John Boothe,[13] who was an editor at Panther Books when the landmark obscenity case was decided in 1960. Lawrence's novel sold a staggering three million copies in the next three months for Penguin, precipitating a rush into more sexually explicit titles.[14]

Boothe and his colleague William Miller, who became joint managing editors of Panther in 1962 and were determined to challenge

* Alex later credited Jane more publicly. In a 1975 interview he said, "My wife and I wrote it" ("An Interview with Alex Comfort, *Practical Psychology for Physicians*, January 1975). Jane likely had a hand in creating the book, from the inception of the notebook, but it's difficult to detect a voice other than Alex's very male one in the prose.

Penguin's dominance, leaped in, securing the paperback rights to translations of *The Kama Sutra* and another classical Indian text, *The Perfumed Garden*, both of which "sold hundreds of thousands of copies." Panther staked out a comparable slice of territory in the fiction department, publishing softcover editions of Henry Miller's previously banned Paris books as well as sexually provocative works by Jean Genet, William S. Burroughs, and Gore Vidal. In the fashion of the time, they also brought out important leftist texts, such as *The Beginning of the End: France, May 1968*, Angelo Quattrocchi and Tom Nairn's eyewitness account and analysis of the civil uprising in France that year. "Practically everyone we knew were . . . socialists, Marxists, Communists, or just liberal," Boothe recalled, "and we remained so all our lives."[15]

At the same time, the long-established, family-owned houses, such as Routledge, Thomas Nelson, Macmillan, and Duckworth, not to mention the university presses of Oxford and Cambridge, were being challenged by a new set of small, independent publishers. Some of these were headed by young fugitives from the traditional houses, driven alternatively by political idealism, stifled creativity, personal ambition, or a combination of the three. Pluto Press, a specialist in left-wing titles, launched in 1969; the similarly focused New Left Books (later Verso Books) was established by the staff of the *New Left Review* in 1970.

One young publishing exec who was striking out on his own was Alex's friend James Mitchell, the editorial director at Thomas Nelson, who in 1967 had brought out *The Anxiety Makers* and arranged the deal for Panther to issue Alex's Natural History of Society series in paperback. Two years later, Mitchell persuaded his bosses to publish the autobiography of Sir Oswald Mosley, because, he said, the prewar British fascist leader's life was interesting, and his views—which included forced repatriation of Caribbean immigrants—deserved a hearing. The book appeared but was not a success.

In 1969, Mitchell, who shared a bit of Oswald Mosley's brazenness if not his political views, left Nelson to start a new firm, Mitchell Beazley. Although it called itself a publisher and did publish some titles, its principal activity was book packaging. The concept—commissioning an author, collecting illustrations, then designing and producing the book to sell to other publishers in various markets—had been pioneered by the firm of Rainbird McLean in the early '50s. The advantage for both sides was a rational division of labor: the packager could focus on editing, design, and printing the book itself, while the publisher concentrated on sales, promotion, and distribution.

The packager typically earned back its investment via an advance from the publisher and a fee for services, including printing. Books produced this way were often cheaply assembled affairs: genre fiction, for example, written for a flat fee by sometimes anonymous authors, sometimes with a celebrity credited on the cover to increase sales. But Rainbird McLean enjoyed a dramatic success in 1963 with *Tutankhamen: Life and Death of a Pharoah*, a lavishly illustrated coffee-table book on the boy king that sold over two million copies in twelve languages.[16] Mitchell wanted to concentrate on this high end of the market, producing big, expensive, eye-catching books that he could sell as "co-editions" to publishers in markets around the world. Mitchell would come up with the concepts, find the authors, and peddle the entire package to publishers; John Beazley, a colleague at Nelson, would handle the business side; and Peter Kindersley, Nelson's talented art director, would supervise the look of the books.

The Natural History of Society series had languished at Thomas Nelson after Mitchell departed.[17] That had left Alex's Books and Broadcasts with no big projects in the works. But in August 1969, almost as soon as he was set up at his new firm, Mitchell wrote Alex asking for a volume on biology for what he described as "a series of concise, illustrated handbook-cum-encyclopedias."[18] Alex wasn't taken with the idea but wrote back suggesting a book on the social consequences of increased longevity.[19] That too fell by the wayside, but later that year they were discussing Alex's ideas for an "Encyclopedia of the Future," for which Mitchell wanted him to organize a team of top-level academic writers from around the world, and an "Encyclopedia of Human Biology" to be sold by mail order. These projects, too, failed to take off. But in the summer of 1971 Alex sent Mitchell a typescript of "Cordon Bleu Sex."

ASIDE FROM ALEX HIMSELF, James Mitchell would be the most important creative force behind the book that came to be titled *The Joy of Sex*, and their collaboration seemed a natural fit: the ambitious, mad-genius publisher and the brilliant but coolly rational author. "Alex Comfort was just the sort of man whose beliefs and philosophies James would have been attracted to," recalled John Boothe.[20]

Like Alex, Mitchell had all the expected credentials of the British establishment—both were graduates of Trinity College, Cambridge—but neither behaved like it. Mitchell's hyperactive personality and overdriven style of selling were out of place in the clubby, conservative world of British publishing, while Alex was contentious, intellectually assertive, and willing to stand on principle about even minor matters. Nevertheless—and again like Mitchell—there were lines he wouldn't cross, specifically when it came to anything that threatened his professional standing.

As Alex envisioned his book, text and graphics would complement each other to achieve a delicate balance between explicitness and good taste. It would require top-notch illustration and art direction: exactly what Mitchell Beazley was established to provide. Alex would also need a creative partner who was not afraid to run risks. This he felt he had in Mitchell himself.

"James was very mercurial and slightly anarchical," said Boothe, "but at the same time very talented. He could also be quite outrageous. 'Dangerous'—that's an exaggeration, but he could be slightly dodgy."[21] A closeted bisexual, he once wrote an entertaining account in the *Guardian* of his short-lived conversion and enlistment in Billy Graham's 1954 Greater London Crusade while a schoolboy at Winchester, involving a deep romantic crush in which, to young Mitchell, the charismatic evangelist "became indistinguishable from Christ."[22] (In a letter responding to Mitchell's piece, Alex commented, "Mr Graham's converts do not come to terms with such disturbing matters as their own sexuality or their childhood fears—they paste a religious ideology over them."[23])

Given to long, alcoholic lunches and all-night carousing on business trips, Mitchell was notorious for his antics at the Frankfurt Book Fair, then as now the premier international trade fair for publishing. He sometimes disappeared for hours or overnight, pursuing rough trade. Once, on an outing to a rowdy Frankfurt beer hall, he was invited on stage to conduct the oompah band that was providing entertainment. Wobbling up onto the bandstand, Boothe recalled, the "liquored up" Mitchell proceeded to offer the crowd a stiff-armed Nazi salute. His companions hustled him offstage and out the door before they could be thrown out.[24]

Mitchell could be a trial as well as an inspiration to his colleagues and would prove so for Alex. Along with his unpredictable personal style, however, he possessed a talent for spotting promising projects that would sell, not to mention concocting some himself, and a genius for packaging and promoting them. "Mitchell was basically a manic depressive bullshitter," his colleague Max Monsarrat recalled. "He was by turns effervescent with ideas and enthusiasm, carrying everyone along in his wake, charming and cajoling clients into huge orders and staff into huge effort; and then the next moment he'd be down, chewing you out and finding fault with everything. But, on balance, there were more than enough up times—perhaps because there were more than enough reasons to celebrate."[25]

The firm was successful from the start, scoring two big sellers, Patrick Moore's *The Moon Flight Atlas* and Hugh Johnson's *The World Atlas of Wine*, within the first two years of its existence. But Mitchell was itching for something more. He combined a nagging desire to outrage and a fearful need to keep his head down, not always in steady balance: "a sort of cross between a Labrador puppy and a bull in a china shop," as Monsarrat put it.[26] The first two books were popular but harmless, and they had nothing intrinsically to do with the social, cultural, and political upheavals of the '60s and early '70s. Mitchell could sell almost anything, but he wanted to sell something geared to cause a sensation.

That was what he saw in the pages Alex brought in 1971 to the firm's offices in Artists House, just off Charing Cross Road and next door, appropriately, to the huge Foyles bookshop. The authors, Alex said mysteriously, were a couple who lived "somewhere in the Mediterranean." He had merely edited their text and did not want his name to appear on it. Whatever its origins, Mitchell and his staff were intrigued. Mitchell, Kindersley, and the book's editor, Monsarrat, another Cambridge graduate who had just joined the firm, wondered at the range of positions and techniques and the wealth of sexual lore it dispensed, spanning India, Japan, Renaissance Italy, and the Paris of Toulouse-Lautrec.

Yet none of this seemed to weigh down the author's (or authors') voice in the least. Although the Mitchell Beazley team didn't know it at the time, he wasn't above pulling the reader's leg either. One item included under "Sauces & Pickles" was the "grope suit," described as "a diabolically ingenious gadget which has just come on the Scandinavian market to induce continuous female orgasm." "[The grope suit consisted of] a very tight rubber g-string with a thick phallic plug which fits in the vagina and a roughened knob over the clitoris. The bra has small toothed recesses in the cups which grip the nipples and is covered all over inside with soft rubber points. Once it is on, every movement touches a sensitive area—the result can be unbearable. Can be worn under the day clothes, if you can stand it."[27]The grope suit was a joke, as Alex later admitted.[28]

What really impressed Mitchell and his associates, however, was not so much the exotica as the voice conveyed in the words themselves. The text didn't read like other sex books, either smutty and leering or lethally clinical and dull. Instead, it was urbane, erudite, and entirely nonjudgmental.

That placed it right up Mitchell Beazley's alley. "The British were terrified of wine, and we demystified it," Tony Cobb, who later took over as art director, recalled. "That was the mission of Mitchell Beazley: taking complex or difficult topics and demystifying them while not diluting them for the audience."[29]

Monsarrat recalled that most of his colleagues at Mitchell Beazley had no premonition Alex's book would have the impact it did. By the time they received the typescript, Masters and Johnson's *Human Sexual Response* had already been a surprise best seller, *Everything You Always Wanted to Know about Sex* had hit number one on the *New York Times* Nonfiction Bestseller List, and *The Sensuous Woman* had followed suit. Sex had been selling for quite some time. Woody Allen was already preparing a parody film "version" of Reuben's book. What were the chances that another entry with another allegedly unique twist (a cookbook!) would repeat these successes?

The answer, from a commercial point of view, was that the earlier books all offered—however unreliably—mainly basic information and advice. Alex was offering a sex *manual*: an aboveground version of the kind of books that had been circulating for centuries through the mail, under the counter in bookshops (even some respectable ones) and porn shops, and privately among collectors and hobbyists, decked out, usually, with explicit drawings or photographs. Sex manuals were not even acknowledged to exist in polite circles, even in the days of the sexual revolution, and no respectable publisher in the industrialized world had ever produced and marketed one. Alex was proposing to take this ancient if disreputable genre to the great middle class.

John Beazley was unenthusiastic, concerned that a such a book could ruin the young firm's reputation. He also had a puritanical streak that set him apart from his colleagues. "I wouldn't publish a book that I couldn't show to my thirteen-year-old daughter," Kindersley remembered him saying.[30] Mitchell, however, recognized this as a challenge: to make the sex manual respectable. He won the argument. The book "tickled Mitchell's fancy, so 'that were decided upon,'" Monsarrat remembered.[31]

In August 1971 Books and Broadcasts, representing Alex, agreed to give Mitchell Beazley an option on worldwide rights to "Cordon Bleu Sex"—with any eventual contract to include "spinoff rights such as sex aids, posters, printed textiles, instructional media including films etc."[32] In October a more formal agreement was signed. Alex would receive 5 percent of Mitchell Beazley's net receipts on sales of the first fifty thousand copies, 10 percent thereafter, and 15 percent of royalty earnings on any non-illustrated edition that the firm might license in the future, plus 75 percent on translations.[33] Along with his own book, Alex agreed to act, uncredited, as consultant on another Mitchell Beazley project, *The Compleat Lover*, a coffee-table book of poems and other literary selections, art, and photos put together by Derek and Julia Parker, she a well-known astrologer who had published *The Compleat Astrologer* with the firm the year before, he the former editor of *Poetry Review* who had once given *Haste to the Wedding* a favorable write-up.[34]

Aside from the fact that it was a how-to rather than strictly an advice book, Mitchell could see something else that set Alex's text apart from the recent best-sellers. To claim authority—or just to find a respectable commercial publisher—the author of a sex book had to possess a medical or scientific credential, otherwise his or her motivation for writing about such a topic would be questioned. The result was that these books tended not only to be dreary reading but also to approach sex mainly as a set of problems. The reader must have a difficulty, abnormality, or hang-up such as frigidity or fetishes. *Our book will help to solve it!* Something similar was the case even with the franker quality fiction of the time. John Updike's *Couples* (1968) and Philip Roth's *Portnoy's Complaint* (1969), perhaps the most sexually uninhibited of recent mainstream works, found little or no joy in sex: mostly neurotic, if comic, despair. Above all, these books seemed plagued by a concern about whether certain sexual practices were normal or not, and they assumed the reader was anxious about this as well.

What appealed to Mitchell—and, he hoped, millions of others—was that Alex's book didn't assume there was anything wrong with its readers that needed fixing. As for what's normal or otherwise, it cheerfully dismissed the issue. "There is no norm in sex. Norm is the name of a guy who lives in Brooklyn," Alex liked to quip around this time.[35]

Although he had the scientific credentials, what he had written wasn't a counseling book, like Reuben's or even "J"'s, but a self-help book: an unashamed, do-it-yourself guide to sexual satisfaction much as *Our Bodies, Ourselves* was an unashamed, do-it-yourself guide to women's health. After his book became a best seller, Alex located its success not so much in the techniques and varieties of sex play that took up so many of its pages but in the fact that it "contained the essential human arouser, the element of permission and of fantasy—in this case, permission for concrete fantasies."[36]

The deal sealed, Mitchell and his team now had a collaborator: for he gradually dropped the pretense with them that he was not the author, though he still insisted that his name be kept off the book. Alex "was not the man to take kindly to invasive editing," Monsarrat recalled. "He was a combative person with little compunction at getting his own way." But the Mitchell Beazley team only got to know that side of him fully later on, after their first project together was a success, because they found virtually nothing that needed to be changed in his text. "The manuscript as it arrived was pretty much the text as it was published," recalled Monsarrat.[37]

The challenge was to come up with a design that provided a physical equivalent to Alex's text. If the typescript seemed to gracefully balance seriousness, humor, and eroticism, the trick was more difficult to turn visually. How to illustrate the book without making it look like pornography?

"We discarded the idea of using photographs," Alex recalled. "No matter how well they are done, they always tend to look like a peep show. One of the models is likely to have that 'How am I doing?' expression."[38] He and the Mitchell Beazley team decided instead to commission a set of black and white line drawings and color paintings, based on the positions Alex described in his text. The aim was to create tasteful, aestheticized versions of the pornographic illustrations that artists had been creating for centuries to depict acts that proper middle-class people would never before admit to having seen.

Kindersley hired a commercial artist, Charles Raymond, well known for his botanical illustrations, to do the paintings, and a busy but less established illustrator, Christopher Foss, to supply the drawings. Kindersley had worked with Raymond before. Foss had done illustrations for *Penthouse* and thus was no novice at nudes. The next step was to bring the two artists together with Alex, to decide, with Kindersley, exactly what positions to illustrate. The artists needed the author's guidance as to just how some of the positions worked. "He made me a bit nervous," Foss recalled, "because he had these missing digits on one hand, and he liked to use it to demonstrate manual things for us, which I found a bit unnerving: this rather crabby claw with a bit missing!"[39]

Photographs were still necessary as "artist's references" that Raymond could paint from and Foss could use to make his line drawings. Alex volunteered a set of smudgy black-and-white Polaroids of himself and Jane as well as "Our ABC, by John and Jane Thomas," which included descriptions and Alex's sketches of the positions they had attempted.

"He appeared with what seemed at the time to be really rather grubby little Polaroid pictures of him and Jane," Monsarrat recalled. "You could never really see very much, and they weren't very expertly taken. The one I really remember was her caressing his penis, which in close-up really looked quite bizarre and wasn't terribly clear what she was doing. And he produced it with great pride, saying this is exactly how it ought to be."[40]

The Polaroids were no good, so Kindersley tried cut-ups. "The first thing we did was to cut up magazines and try and make up different poses," he recalled, "but Alex was suggesting things we had never seen before or that magazines hadn't even thought of portraying. So we had to make these amalgams of different pictures—we want the legs to be a bit like this and we want the face to be a bit like this, and so on. The result was a sort of Frankenstein monster of reference, and it was really hopeless."[41]

Monsarrat spent some time "exploring the porn shops of Soho" in search of ready-made materials, but "there wasn't anything remotely suitable." Soho in the early '70s was at its seediest, replete with strip clubs, encounter parlors, and pornographic bookshops, but even the publications on sale in London's sex district hewed to fairly strict regulations: no penetrative sex could be depicted, and no erections. Alex's book would require both. It was possible, however, to hire models for a few pounds a session.

"My original intention was that we should not only have white people, we should have black people," Alex said several years later. "We should not only have young people, we should have couples of all kinds and all ages to show that love doesn't just belong to the young. But it wasn't feasible in view of the six weeks we had to do the illustrations."[42]

Monsarrat and Kindersley found a pair of models in Soho and set up a photo shoot, "but the results were unsatisfactory," said Kindersley. "Halfway through the pose, they would ask for an extra £100. They looked sleazy and were sleazy, to be frank. Looking at the photos, Charles suddenly said, 'I'll do it with my wife.'"[43]

It was not an obvious choice. Raymond and his German-born wife of a dozen years, Edeltraud, were not the sort of models one expected in erotic illustrations: that is, they clearly weren't teenagers or especially young adults, and they didn't look physically perfect. Charles was then in his late forties and Edeltraud her mid-thirties. In addition, Charles had long hair and a beard, and Edeltraud didn't shave her armpits or pubic hair, giving them both a hippy-ish look. On the other hand, they looked authentic: tender toward each other, at ease, communicating an unaffected eroticism. If Alex's goal was to give couples permission to enjoy themselves in bed without anxiety, the Raymonds bolstered the argument, sending the message that you could have "Cordon Bleu sex" even if you weren't glamorous, prodigiously endowed, or impossibly seductive. That, in turn, made the book less vulnerable to accusations that it was pornographic.

Charles, Edeltraud, and Chris Foss, who would take the pictures, set up shop in Monsarrat's third-floor flat in South Kensington to create the artist's references. The shoot took place over two cold days in the mid-winter of 1972, interrupted by the occasional power outage. London was far from the trendy, "swinging" capital of a few years earlier. Labor-management relations in the UK were reaching a level of animosity not seen in nearly half a century, and Mitchell Beazley was carrying out its experiment in erotic publishing in the midst of a wave of strikes and work stoppages, including a miner's strike that forced power rationing and occasional overnight shutdowns of the grid.

"I can't emphasize too much how grimy and dreary London was then," said Foss. "We would start at twelve, but we knew bloody well that come two o'clock that was it, and we had maybe fifteen positions to get through by five o'clock that evening." The light and heat would fail occasionally, rendering the photo sessions uncomfortable and halting. "There were warnings given that there would be power cuts at certain times during the day. But sometimes they came without any notice at all," Raymond recalled.[44] The photo shoots were hard physical work. "Some of these poses, you have to freeze for the photographer, and the tension and the concentration is very very tiring indeed. I was exhausted by the end of the session," said Edeltraud.[45]

Something was going right, despite the chaos, which may have had to do with the personalities involved. Thirty years later, Edeltraud recalled, "I just did what came naturally to me. I was in love with my husband. I did what we both enjoyed doing and had done for the last 12 years, so it was nothing very unusual what I did on that particular day."[46]

In reality, it wasn't quite so automatic. Charlie Raymond, despite his hirsute appearance, was a slightly reserved, almost formal presence. His wife enjoyed wearing sexy outfits and was quite comfortable with her body, but she also projected an underlying seriousness. Foss, on the other hand, who effectively directed the sessions, was a big, jovial man who couldn't help finding humor in nearly everything and quickly set his subjects at ease. "We had never met Chris before, but as the photo shoot went on, I think it turned into lovemaking, and the photographer just shot," Edeltraud said. "We got carried away, and Chris disappeared," Charlie added. The difference shows up in the drawings and paintings themselves, some of which are fairly mechanical renditions of poses described in the text and others tender scenes of a couple in genuine erotic embrace.

From "a huge amount of photos," Monsarrat, Kindersley, and Janette Place, the book's designer, selected over one hundred shots that would make it into the final design.[47] From these, Raymond and Foss created their paintings and drawings. The designers were enchanted with the results. They decided to place the fifteen paintings at the front of the book, portfolio-style, rather than illustrating specific poses. These scenes would depict the stages of a sexual encounter, accompanied by just a few words of text. The drawings would appear throughout the main body of the book, but Kindersley and Place decided not to tie all of them strictly to the descriptions of specific positions. Alex was enthusiastic when he saw the illustrations and some sample pages. The author's only quibble, Kindersley recalled, was with the positioning of the rope in a drawing that depicted some light bondage.

A few years earlier, Alex had written the introduction to *Art of the East*, a lavishly illustrated collection of essays on Asian erotic art. In it, he described Indian erotic art as "an art of acceptance which comes close to the idea of the new psychiatric humanism—lack of fear or surprise at one's impulses, coupled with rational control."[48] This is exactly what he hoped to impart in his sex manual, and, along with a desire to give the book an extra element of cultural validation, it prompted him to suggest adding a series of color plates of classical Chinese, Japanese, and Indian art depicting couples—all heterosexual—engaged in sex acts similar to those he described. "There was concern about the explicitness" of some of Raymond's and Foss's art, and "therefore we thought as a foil we would put in some of these ancient pictures," Kindersley remembered. "In a way, we were relating ourselves to the past. . . . We wanted to make the book feel as though it was related to a great tradition of explicit pictures."[49] Monsarrat knew where to get a selection of these works: Paul Raymond.

The King of Soho, as he was dubbed by the tabloid press, Paul Raymond (no relation to Charles) had his headquarters a short walk from Mitchell Beazley's offices, and his ex-girlfriend, as it happened, would shortly marry Monsarrat's brother-in-law. He was also the most notorious—or celebrated—smut peddler in Britain, a low-rent English

Hugh Hefner who established the first men's club in London to offer full-frontal, on-stage nudity, the Raymond Revue Bar, in 1958. By the early '70s, he was publishing what would be the first of a succession of sex magazines. All the while, he was buying up real estate in Soho that would eventually make him, reputedly, the richest man in Britain. Raymond was also an assiduous collector of Asian erotica, and when Monsarrat approached him about using some of the material in his holdings, he readily said yes. His contribution, needless to say, was not acknowledged in the book.[50]

The parties agreed that the book would be 240 pages, in a display format of 9¾ by 6¾ inches, including 48 pages of Charlie Raymond's paintings and Paul Raymond's art collection, and that the whole production should be ready for the printers by mid-February, anticipating publication in September.[51] Before Place had finished fitting the text and illustrations into the book design, Mitchell was off to sell his new product. He had Kindersley put together a twelve-page promotional brochure with a selection of the drawings and paintings and some sample text layouts. This, and Mitchell's compelling line of talk, would persuade publishers outside the UK to license the book from its creators.

Mitchell's first stop was the United States, where initially he had no luck. Random House and McGraw-Hill turned it down. Grove Press, which had shown some tentative interest, did likewise.[52] Publisher Barney Rosset found Alex's tone too jolly and healthy, accustomed as he was to the rather grim sex in Henry Miller, Hubert Selby, and other of his more avant-garde authors.[53] Michael Korda, editor-in-chief at Simon & Schuster, gave Mitchell a forceful no as well: curiously, perhaps, since he was about to publish his trendy first book, *Male Chauvinism and How It Works at Home and in the Office*. Playboy Press, which liked its women depilated and airbrushed, didn't take to Edeltraud's hairy armpits and privates, or Charles's beard, for that matter, and turned Mitchell down.[54]

"A lot of people, I think, were turned off by the illustrations," recalled Alan Mirken, president of Crown Publishers, the small firm that finally agreed to bring out the book in the United States. They may also have been concerned that major US booksellers and bookshop chains wouldn't carry it. Crown, a reprint house that had only recently begun releasing its own titles—"*How to Avoid Probate* had been our most successful book to that point," said Mirken—had a solution to that problem. Alongside its publishing arm, it owned Publishers Central Bureau, a mail order business. If Crown couldn't get enough bookshops to carry a sex manual with explicit illustrations, it could sell the rest of the print run through the mail, which was how most sexually explicit material had been sold for many years.

Crown was initially not taken with Charles's beard, but acquiesced when Mitchell Beazley insisted on retaining it.[55] The American publisher elected not to revise much of the text's British-style punctuation and spelling, however, or its terminology: a "showerbath" rather than the American "shower stall," for example. But Crown did contribute something to the book: its title.

"Nat Wartels [Mirken's uncle and the firm's founder] was the nicest, gentlest man I knew of," recalled Dick Snyder, then executive vice president at Simon & Schuster, "and the unlikeliest person to sit down with Mitchell Beazley about a book like this."[56] But Crown was well acquainted with James Mitchell, having already licensed several books from his firm. According to Mirken, when Mitchell showed him the brochure for the new book, Wartels said yes almost instantly. Since Crown lacked the deep pockets of its competitors, Wartels agreed to a first printing of only fifteen thousand copies and sold the large-format paperback rights to Snyder for Simon & Schuster's Fireside Books imprint for $250,000.[57]

But Wartels felt something was missing. The cookbook conceit was fine, he told Mitchell, but "cordon bleu" made it sound too rarefied and intimidating. Looking for something more accessible, he suggested they piggyback on the title of a perennial best seller—and another book that promised to put some sophisticated knowledge in the hands of everyday but interested people—Irma S. Rombauer and Marion Rombauer Becker's kitchen classic *The Joy of Cooking*, then in its fifth edition. Mitchell agreed, and so did Alex, since, he guessed, people were not "uptight" about food.[58] "I liked the idea of 'joy' versus problem," he later said. "The other writers treated sex as a problem."[59] He insisted, however, on retaining the "cordon bleu" conceit in the subtitle and in the text itself.

Altogether, Alex was delighted with Mitchell Beazley's work and the setting that had been created for his text. He was beginning to enjoy, as well, the prospect of getting the more audacious elements of his work in front of the public. In February 1972, he asked Crown to send the text of *Joy* to Bill Masters and Virginia Johnson for their comments. In a letter to Masters, still maintaining the fiction that he was only the editor, he noted particularly that the "Sauces & Pickles" section could change people's minds about what he referred to as "over aggressive and partialist impulses. . . . The authors aim to turn 'sadism' into playfulness, minor fetishes into additional resources to turn on a partner, bisexuality into one more human resource."[60]

None of which stopped the book from attracting non-US publishers. Mitchell and Alex Mosley, son of the fascist leader, whom Mitchell had hired as head of foreign sales, took their brochure and some sample spreads of *Joy* to the Frankfurt Book Fair in October, soon after Mitchell's trip to New York. The response was almost overwhelmingly positive. Mitchell Beazley licensed co-editions to publishers in nearly every western European market as well as other English-speaking countries—Australia, Canada, New Zealand—and Japan. That meant a substantial infusion of cash in the form of advances. For Alex, it meant his book would appear almost simultaneously around the world and begin generating royalties for him as soon as the non-Anglophone publishers could translate it.

In most markets, *Joy* appeared as Mitchell Beazley had designed it. The pains to which the firm had gone to mute any suggestion that it was pornographic had paid off. One exception was Japan, where the publisher insisted on redoing the illustrations to comply with a government prohibition against depiction of naked men. The publisher decided to replace the bearded man with an assortment of oversized flowers; the result was a series of illustrations of a blonde woman bearing no resemblance to Edeltraud, grappling with bunches of lilies, irises, and other flora.[61]

So eager was the response to his book that by the end of the year, after toying with author pseudonyms such as "Adam and Eve," "Him and Her," and "Dr. and Mrs. Chiron," Alex agreed to be credited as editor outside the UK.[62] That would make him available to promote the book in the United States, and Mitchell and Beazley went ahead and arranged for him to accompany them to a meeting in New York with Crown in January.[63] The only major market where the appearance of *The Joy of Sex* in any form was in doubt was its country of origin.

WHILE JOHN BEAZLEY HAD reluctantly gone along with packaging and licensing the book overseas, he would not permit Mitchell Beazley itself to publish it in Britain, for fear of prosecution. That set Mitchell off in search of another UK house to take it on. André Deutsch Ltd, whose authors at various times had included V. S. Naipaul, Norman Mailer, Philip Roth, and Jack Kerouac, considered the book seriously, but no deal resulted.[64] Months after Crown had signed on, then, and with the overseas publication date of September 1972 approaching, *The Joy of Sex* still had no UK publisher. Neither did it have a proper attribution attached to it in Britain, as Alex still would not allow his name on a UK edition. He even insisted to Mitchell that the eventual publisher not know of his involvement, for fear the information would get out in the media.[65] As Mitchell continued to shop the book under these awkward circumstances, Alex set about finding another well-known person to contribute an introduction as a further proof of respectability.[66]

The looming issue was what the British authorities would do to anyone who tried to bring out the book. The moralistic backlash led by figures like Mary Whitehouse and Malcolm Muggeridge was commanding more attention in the early '70s, and the new Conservative government of Edward Heath was happy to encourage it.

In 1971, at the very time Mitchell Beazley was gearing up to publish Alex's book, Martin Cole, a pioneering British sexologist, triggered a national scandal when he produced *Growing Up*, a twenty-three-minute sex education film that included footage of real sex acts. Cole had published a book the same year, *Fundamentals of Sex*, that also included explicit photos, but it was the prospect of his film being screened in classrooms that provoked most concern. The schools authority in Birmingham, the home town of "Sex King Cole," as he was dubbed in the tabloid press, banned the film, and it disappeared from circulation after only a few screenings.

Britain's humanist intellectuals supported Cole. The South Place Ethical Society had premiered his film at Conway Hall, distributing over four hundred free tickets.[67] But *Growing Up* drew condemnations from several members of Parliament and the Heath government, including the up-and-coming secretary of state for education and science, Margaret Thatcher. Its most vocal critic was Francis Aungier Pakenham, 7th Earl of Longford, one of the few hereditary peers who belonged to the Labour Party and one of the more eccentric figures in twentieth-century British politics.

Just after the *Growing Up* controversy hit its peak, Longford and a disparate collection of co-campaigners, including Muggeridge, the rock singer Cliff Richard, and Arthur Blessitt, an evangelist who had gained fame by traveling the world carrying a twelve-foot wooden cross, organized the Nationwide Festival of Light, a series of rallies against the commercialization of sex and the prominence of sex and violence in the media. The organizers succeeded in recruiting a broad range of denominations in support of their campaign, which was unexpectedly successful.

On September 23, 1971, supporters lit bonfires in some three hundred communities across Britain. Two days later, some forty-five thousand people jammed Trafalgar Square. After listening to a succession of speakers inveigh against a sex-saturated media and call on the nation to return to Christ, the crowd marched to Hyde Park to listen to more speeches and music by Christian performers.[68]

The Festival of Light advocated no specific political measures. Out of it, however, came Christian Action Research and Education (CARE), a political pressure group allied with Focus on the Family in the United States, which advocated for laws against abortion and gay rights.

Of more concern to Alex, James Mitchell, and John Beazley was another project that Longford launched several months before the festival, the Longford Committee Investigating Pornography, a panel he set up himself to test his case that pornography leads to violence, prostitution, and other sorts of human degradation. "Lord Porn," as the *Sun* dubbed him, paid the committee's expenses out of his own pocket and handpicked fifty-two members, including teachers, business executives, police and corrections officers, journalists, and two panelists from the pop music industry: Cliff Richard and Jimmy Savile, the radio DJ and *Top of the Pops* presenter (who would be exposed after his death in 2011 as a serial sexual predator).[69]

The committee proved a vast target for the Fleet Street tabloid press, especially when, just weeks before the Festival of Light, Longford led his troupe on a field trip to Copenhagen to investigate the effects of the abolition of censorship in Denmark. After sixteen months of such investigations, the Longford committee finally issued its report and recommendations in September 1972, just as *The Joy of Sex* was being released in most major markets. Like Alex's book, it sold well, although heavy press coverage and the bargain price of the report itself (60p.) must have helped. The committee had been roundly ridiculed by then, although some of its recommendations can be seen as ancestors of Section 28, the infamous Thatcher-era law against "promotion" of homosexuality by local authorities. Nevertheless, the committee created a most uneasy atmosphere for the team that had assembled the first detailed, explicitly illustrated mainstream sex manual. Combined with the massive turnout for the Festival of Light, it generated a strong public impression that Britain's moral masses were in revolt against the '60s culture, as popularly portrayed.

Whether or not the anti-porn crusade had a chance of latching on politically and creating new legislative restrictions, it emboldened the authorities to press charges against counterculture publications that seemed to deliberately blur the line between art and smut. In June 1971, the three editors of *OZ*, a satirical underground magazine, went on trial in London for "conspiracy to corrupt public morals," a charge that could mean a sentence of life imprisonment. The grounds were that they had run a sexualized parody of the comic strip character Rupert Bear. The case drew enormous attention in Britain. The publishers' barrister was John Mortimer, the novelist and creator of *Rumpole of the Bailey*, and celebrities including John Lennon and Yoko Ono joined street protests outside the central criminal court. The *OZ* editors—James Anderson, Felix Dennis, and Richard Neville—were convicted on lesser charges and sentenced to prison terms, as well as deportation for two of the three who were Australian citizens, although the convictions were overturned on appeal.**

OZ's readership declined precipitously once the media spotlight turned elsewhere, and the magazine folded two years later. Mitchell Beazley didn't have deep pockets and lacked the kind of flamboyant reputation that would enable it to exploit the publicity should *The Joy of Sex* attract prosecutors and anti-obscenity crusaders; a court case could ruin the young firm. Mitchell and his partners set up a shell company, Modsets Securities Ltd, to hold the rights, protecting their firm—they hoped—from prosecution once they were able to bring it out in the UK. In the contracts they offered Chris Foss and Charlie Raymond, they promised to pay court costs in case the artists were arrested.[70]

That still wasn't enough for John Beazley, who continued to worry that *The Joy of Sex* would ruin the firm. Mitchell was more of a risk taker but was also determined that the book become a mainstream success, not just another titillating sex manual to be sold under the counter, and he made sure its design fully reflected this. The book itself was a model of good taste, the text set in Optima, a subdued, sans-serif typeface sometimes used in academic journals, and the jacket without illustration of any kind. Out of the hundred-plus drawings in the book, only two depicted bondage (mild situations, at that). Charlie and Edeltraud, who disapproved of the practice, refused to be photographed for either of these illustrations, and Foss was forced to create them from other materials.[71]

On the other side of the Atlantic, Crown, despite its contract to publish *The Joy of Sex*, was also concerned about legal action. In 1967 the

** Felix Dennis went on to make a fortune as a publisher of magazines, including the egregiously sexist "laddie book" *Maxim*.

US Supreme Court had dismissed a case involving the arrest of a Times Square newsstand worker for selling two paperback sex novels with not a speck of redeeming social value between them. First Amendment scholars hailed the case as virtually ending book censorship in the United States.[72] A furious backlash began almost immediately, however. President Lyndon Johnson set up a Commission on Obscenity and Pornography to research the problem of smut and make policy recommendations. Richard Nixon won the presidency the following year promising, among other things, "a citizen's crusade against the obscene."

Two years later, a California mail-order publisher named Marvin Miller was convicted of distributing obscene materials through the postal system. The Supreme Court, under its new chief justice, Nixon appointee Warren Burger, agreed to review the case, which hinged on the issue of whether states and localities could apply their own "community standards" to the definition of obscenity. The court decided against Miller in 1973, opening the way for prosecution of the adult entertainment business in more conservative jurisdictions: a clear danger for publishers like Crown, a good chunk of whose business was by mail.

The Miller case made headlines and was watched carefully by the publishing industry leading up to the decision. In the wake of the Times Square decision, too, the Nixon administration had proved surprisingly adept at finding ways around the court's liberalizing pronouncement. The US Postal Service hired more mail inspectors, who used false names to order sexually explicit materials from addresses in conservative communities, then prosecuted the sellers in courts located in those communities. Legal fees alone could drive sex merchants out of business.[73]

Like the UK, then, the United States was experiencing a tug-of-war. What was increasingly, and visibly, a more permissive society was meeting tough resistance from conservative pressure groups that leaned ever more on cultural issues to build their political base. Publishers, as always, were on the front lines. In theory, the way had been paved for *The Joy of Sex* by *Playboy* and *Penthouse*, which were now sold on "legit" newsstands, but Alex's book was illustrated more explicitly than even they dared, despite its lack of photos. To allay Crown's concerns about possible legal trouble with the book, Mitchell Beazley added a lock of hair to one of Raymond's paintings, depicting Edeltraud fellating Charlie, to hide the detail in which her mouth met his penis, and the drawings that were to accompany the discussion of the technique were removed.[74] Alex later labeled the ploy "censorship" and insisted it was done without his permission.[75]

Even with that, Crown was still worried, and it decided to publish the book in two versions, illustrated and non-illustrated, in case the former proved too controversial. They were right to be concerned. Book clubs, which sold their offerings at special prices to subscribers, were a powerful force in American publishing at the time, and only two, both comparatively small, would offer *The Joy of Sex*: the Playboy Book Club and the Psychology Today Book Club. Playboy, oddly, had raised concerns about the drawings of fellatio, and in the end would only take the nonillustrated edition.[76]

Despite the efforts to keep it from coming across as pornographic or overly provocative, the book that publishers around the world brought out in fall 1972 was a breakthrough. For the first time, the general public was being offered a book by a mainstream firm that described the particulars of sexual play in detail and illustrated them explicitly. The era when people could purchase such material only through the mail, delivered in plain brown wrappers from marginal publishers, was about to end.

Charlie Raymond's portfolio of paintings set the tone for a presentation of heterosexual sex that was quite different from the underground publications of the past. "We wanted to have a real impact at the beginning of the book, to give this feel of a complete love-making episode," Kindersley recalled.[77] The first illustration depicted the couple about to kiss, along with these words from Alex: "The whole joy of sex-with-love is that there are no rules, so long as you enjoy, and the choice is practically unlimited." That set the stage for a variety of positions, from caresses to handwork to mutual oral stimulation, through to orgasm and a final painting of the couple relaxing, entwined. "Planning and thinking about sex to come is part of love. So is lying together in complete luxury afterwards."

While the text that followed covered an array of topics and variations, it retained the sophisticated but slightly wide-eyed tone of Alex's words. No matter how familiar you think you might be with the activity, Alex seemed to be reminding his readers, there is always room for fresh wonder at the great variety of sexual ways and means.

CHAPTER 16

Joy to the World (1972–1973)

"Crown reports that it has had enthusiastic response to 'The Joy of Sex' . . . and is considerably expanding its advertising program on the title," *Publishers Weekly* reported a month after the book arrived in US stores on October 30, 1972. "The book was published in two editions, illustrated ($12.95) and nonillustrated ($7.95), and the illustrated edition in particular is selling fast, with orders averaging 10,000 a week. Crown has gone back to press for a third 15,000-copy printing of the illustrated edition, bringing the number of copies in print to 45,000. In addition, there are 15,000 copies of the nonillustrated edition in print."[1]

Nineteen seventy-two was the year of Bloody Sunday in Northern Ireland, the floating of the pound sterling, a seven-week UK coal miners' strike, and Idi Amin's expulsion of fifty thousand Asians with UK passports. From May to December, Britain witnessed the trial of the Stoke Newington Eight, members of the Angry Brigade, an underground, anarchist-leaning group that had carried out a series of bombings—none of them lethal—over the preceding two years. Its targets had included embassies, banks, and the homes of members of the government. An earlier, separate trial had ended in the sentencing of one Angry Brigade member, Jack Prescott, to 15 fifteen years' imprisonment for "conspiracy to cause explosions."

Alex and numerous other prominent figures, including Germaine Greer, Kenneth Tynan, John Lennon and Yoko Ono, Peggy Seeger, and the writers Christopher Logue and A. Alvarez, joined in a statement protesting the Prescott verdict, which appeared to largely hang on his having hand-addressed three envelopes that were used to send out Angry Brigade communiqués.[2] During the subsequent prosecution of the Stoke Newington Eight, which resulted in ten-year sentences for four of the defendants, Alex wrote to the *Guardian* to complain that the press was not covering the trial—on its way to becoming the longest criminal trial in UK history—as actively as it ought to be, possibly due to "interference with the press by the establishment." "If anyone is taking the line that proceedings in which bombings are alleged should not be reported for fear that they might incite imitation," he wrote, "I think they are doing a disservice to justice."[3]

Elsewhere, the North Vietnamese Easter Offensive caught the American occupiers in the south flat-footed. President Nixon made history by visiting Communist China, then was reelected in a landslide.

Books with a spiritual or self-help bent dominated the bestseller lists. *Jonathan Livingston Seagull*, a novella by Richard Bach, was the year's top seller in the United States, according to *Publishers Weekly*, and *The Living Bible*, a paraphrase edition by Kenneth Taylor, was the biggest nonfiction title, followed by Thomas Harris's *I'm OK, You're OK*, Carlos Castaneda's *Journey to Ixtlan*, *Dr. Atkins' Diet Revolution*, and, interestingly, *Open Marriage: A New Lifestyle for Couples*, by George and Nena O'Neill.

Running through these titles was a focus on the self, a concern with one's own mode of living, that reflected some of the tensions and transformations in progress in the early '70s; the books offered various ways to either wall them off or adapt to them. Alex's book could be seen as part of the same trend, although his intentions were different. Perhaps for that reason, getting *The Joy of Sex* into major retail stores proved less of a problem than Crown had anticipated, starting on the West Coast.

The *Los Angeles Free Press* published a favorable review by Alex's friend Roy Walford, complete with excerpts from the book, almost as soon as it was published.[4] This helped put it in front of booksellers, but the *Free Press* was an underground weekly, not a mainstream publication. Bruce Harris, Crown's director of marketing, knew he had a potential hit when Ernie Greenspan, his sales representative on the West Coast, reported a meeting with Alan Kahn, the energetic, twenty-five-year-old buyer for Pickwick Books, a large regional chain with a multilevel flagship store on Hollywood Boulevard that boasted a strong celebrity clientele. Harris recalled, "Ernie asked me how many copies we were printing—that Alan wanted to buy the whole thing. I said 10,000—I didn't know exactly, so I made it up. Ernie says he'll take 8,500. It was a pretty gutsy move."[5]

Kahn, who would go on to build and run the B. Dalton Bookseller chain and then Barnes & Noble after the latter bought B. Dalton, was so convinced *The Joy of Sex* could be a big success for Pickwick that he persuaded his bosses, who were mildly shocked by the content, to take out a full-page ad in the book section of the *Los Angeles Times*—at about $9,000, an expensive proposition at the time. The ad, which Crown created and which several large New York booksellers ran in the major papers there as well, included a coupon that customers could mail in to order the book at a discount. "I think Nat Wartels and Alan Mirken respected my judgment, but they thought I went over the top peddling their book," Kahn later recalled. "But I think with the response, the orders for books, it was one of the most successful ads we ever ran. The response was enormous."[6]

"[Crown was] going with my gamble," Kahn said, "because if the books didn't sell—it was most of their print run—I could send them back and they'd have to sell them on remainder tables." Crown also footed part of the bill for the ads. Aside from his gut instinct, Kahn had two reasons for thinking Pickwick could make a success of *The Joy of Sex*. The first was what he expected to be a lack of competition. Before the advent of megastores like Barnes & Noble, a large chunk of trade books in the United States were sold by department stores, which maintained large book departments.

But Kahn figured many of these big rivals would not carry Alex's book, for fear of offending some of their customers, or else would display only dummy copies that Crown had printed up with a jacket but no text or illustrations inside, forcing customers to ask a clerk to pull a proper copy from behind the counter. "Pickwick had the actual book out in huge displays," Kahn remembered.*

A second reason for *Joy*'s success was *Human Sexual Response*. Kahn had started working at Pickwick when he was fifteen years old, and he had witnessed the sensation when Masters and Johnson's book was published in 1966. "That was really a technical book, but it sold like crazy. We couldn't keep it in stock." Masters and Johnson's follow-up, *Human Sexual Inadequacy*, achieved even greater mainstream success, landing the authors on the cover of *Time* and even eliciting an enthusiastic review in *Ladies' Home Journal*. Kahn could see that *The Joy of Sex* was aimed much more directly at a popular audience; it was written in

* An incident at one of Pickwick's rivals inspired Crown to hatch a typically '70s gimmick. Hearing that a man came into one bookshop, looked at the dummy copy, asked to buy ten, and insisted even when the clerk showed him a printed and illustrated copy, the publisher in 1974 issued *The Nothing Book: Wanna Make Something of It?*, a 160-page book of blank pages that became another big seller. A. M. Chaplin, "Safe Sex a Greater Concern in Updated Edition of 'Joy of Sex,'" *Baltimore Sun*, January 12, 1987.

an accessible style, and it was attractively illustrated. "I was young at the time, but I thought the illustrations were fabulous and tastefully done," he said. "The time was right. It was a no-brainer."

It helped that Alex had positioned *The Joy of Sex* as a self-help guide of sorts; by this time reviewers were friendlier and more accustomed to assessing books of this type. Starting with the publication of the first *Whole Earth Catalog* in 1968 and the first appearance of what would become *Our Bodies, Ourselves* in 1970 (*Women and Their Bodies*), self-help books with a practical, do-it-yourself bent—many of which, like *The Joy of Sex*, were written or edited by sometime political radicals and members of the counterculture—had carved out a robust new market niche. The last regular edition of the *Whole Earth Catalog*, in 1971, was a milestone in the commodification of the counterculture, becoming a million-copy bestseller and receiving a National Book Award for current affairs.[7] The first bound edition of *Our Bodies, Ourselves* that year, essentially a reprint of *Women and Their Bodies*, sold 250,000 copies (it would be republished in an expanded edition by Simon & Schuster in 1973).[8]

Several years before, a book like *The Joy of Sex* might not have been noticed in a major media outlet. Thanks in part to the success of these titles, and others of the self-help genre, this was no longer the case. The reviews themselves were largely excellent. *New York* magazine called Alex's book "the best thing of its kind ever published," and Anthony Storr in the *Washington Post* saw in it precisely what Alex had hoped people would see:

> This must be one of the least inhibited books on sex ever written. Like pornography, it arouses desire in the reader, but because it eschews the underhand, sly components which are the concomitants of puritanism, its impact is straightforwardly healthy. . . . The book contains a great deal of information about the so-called sexual perversions and abnormalities, yet it remains one of the cleanest and most straightforward books on sex ever to come my way. . . . So, tie each other up, wear the kinky clothes your partner fancies, do what you will, and all will be well.[9]

The *Houston Chronicle* praised the book for presenting its material "inoffensively and with humor, honesty, and directness."[10]

Some reviewers found Alex's book too programmatic, with its ethical prescriptions and obligations and its ban on deodorants. "*The Joy of Sex* makes the Talmud look like a manual for libertines," said Peter S.

Prescott in *Newsweek*.[11] But it performed the remarkable feat of earning approval equally from *Playboy, SCREW,* and Gloria Steinem's new feminist mass-monthly *Ms.* "[This] gourmet guide [is] not just another spicy nonbook with a clever title," Hugh Hefner's soft-core men's magazine enthused. "The volume is obviously the work of a man who knows his way around the kitchen and relishes his subject." *Playboy* did complain that the man in the illustrations was "hirsute to the point of resembling a naked cave dweller." And the sex described was "often kinky by American standards" (how so was not specified).[12] *SCREW*, on the other hand, found the illustrations a bit too tasteful and less earthy than the text ("cunnilingus is depicted, but the male figure looks as if he's praying to the female goddess"), although the entire package did a much-needed job of elevating the "lowly" sex guide.[13]

"This is not a sex manual for those with problems, but rather an aid for those who are at ease with the basics but want an alternative to chicken soup," wrote the *Ms.* reviewer. "The type is big enough for short passages to be read simultaneously by you and your partner and the $12.95 lavishly illustrated edition is worth the tab."[14]

What made the *Ms.* review especially noteworthy was that it combined its evaluation of *The Joy of Sex* with that of another new sex manual, *Cosmopolitan's Love Guide: The Ultimate Book*. The contrast was stark. Eschewing pictorials, editor Helen Gurley Brown, author of the 1962 best seller *Sex and the Single Girl*, had turned *Cosmopolitan*, the old Hearst monthly, into a *Playboy* counterpart for a female audience: a lifestyle magazine aimed at younger women who wanted to enjoy a more worldly and personally liberated life than their mothers, and who had, or hoped to have, the money to buy it. True to that mission, *Cosmo*'s "ultimate book" concerned itself "more with the grooming, hygiene, and consumerism that surround 'doing it' than with sex itself," *Ms.* commented.

The *Cosmo* book devoted much space to hawking various products that purportedly would help the reader create the perfect love nest for the man she wanted to snare. Beaded and chained breastplates were recommended for the large-breasted woman, frilly underthings were suggested for the boyish body, and fur throws were deemed "absolutely *de rigueur.*" *The Joy of Sex*, by contrast, devoted noticeably more space to how men could please women. *Ms.* noted approvingly the following passage: "If you haven't kissed her mouth, shoulders, neck, breasts, armpits, fingers, palms, toes, soles, navel, genitals, and earlobes, you haven't really kissed her."

Sex, for the *Cosmo* reader, took place in a perfumed hothouse, while for Alex's couple it was a much earthier experience. *Cosmo* "pimps for flavored douches," according to *Ms.*, while *The Joy of Sex* "recommends that armpit hair be left on and deodorant left off." Actual sex in the *Cosmo* guide was quite conventional, whereas, *Ms.* noted, the authors of *The Joy of Sex* didn't rule out group sex and suggested "that aggression can be utilized in sex to create intense and fulfilling sexual experiences [but only if you're sure you'd enjoy it]." *Ms.* had one pointed complaint: the book's use of the term "the pussy" to refer to "the female genitalia, *in toto*." Otherwise, "this book is meant for both partners—a substantial improvement in itself over both sex *Cosmo*-style and traditional, very male-oriented marriage manuals."

While its design and illustrations were critical to the book's appeal, the physical elements followed a path laid out in the text, creating a visual equivalent to the voice in the words. "What Dr. Comfort (how's that for a name?) and artists Charles Raymond and Christopher Foss have done is sponsor a witty, unprecedented guided tour of undressed sex action . . . that transports the plain old dirty book into the vicinity of the coffee table," wrote Larry Swindell, the *Philadelphia Inquirer's* book critic. "Reportedly *The Joy of Sex* has already become a thoughtful gift to newlyweds. Well, now."[15]

Not one reviewer so much as mentioned that the author was an anarchist and pacifist, or remarked on his argument about sex as an element in nurturing human sociality and cooperation. Alex had successfully smuggled some basic elements of anarchist thought and practice into his book but too subtly for them to be easily noticed. And his prior history in the UK hadn't penetrated America, even though he had been published sporadically in the States for almost thirty years.

What made the success of *The Joy of Sex* remarkable was the volume of competition it faced, for 1972–73 was the year sex broke for American book publishers eager to follow up on the success of David Reuben's Q&A guide, *The Sensuous Woman*, and *The Happy Hooker*, by former call girl Xaviera Hollander. Bookshops received a flood of titles including *The Civilized Guide to Extramarital Adventure*, *Out of the Closets: The Sociology of Homosexual Liberation*, *The Sex Book: A Modern Pictorial Encyclopedia*, and *The New Intimacy: Open-ended Marriage and Alternate Lifestyles*, along with such bigger sellers as *The Brothers System for Liberated Love and Marriage*, by advice columnist and TV personality Dr. Joyce Brothers; Hollander's *Letters to the Happy Hooker*; and *How to Find and Fascinate a Mistress*, by Will Harvey.

Reviewers also caught the difference in tone between Alex's book and these other titles. "When did you last have relations with a vacuum cleaner? . . . The anonymous authors of 'The Joy of Sex' . . . warn that numerous (male) accidents in the home have resulted from such intimacies, and that the damage can be devastating," was how critic Nora Sayre led off a roundup of sex books in the *New York Times* in February. Sayre judged *The Joy of Sex* by far the most "humane" and "literate" of the latest crop.[16] Other critics noted the entirely nonclinical tone of the text. "It spends less than one ratatouille's worth on frigidity, impotency, premature ejaculation—the standard fare of the more grim medical sex books," noted Ellen Goodman, the *Boston Globe's* reviewer. "The main course is rather the frills."[17] Of course, for Alex, that was exactly the point.

The book quickly attracted notice on TV as well as in print. Gene Shalit, film and book critic for NBC's *Today Show*, told his millions of viewers on November 6, 1972, that *The Joy of Sex* was a "beautiful" book filled with "fine drawings, many in color, and, again, all of them explicit." Its advice, he said, "is set down with exemplary taste."

The Joy of Sex made its debut on the *New York Times* list of nonfiction best sellers the week of December 10, and it first hit the number-one position thirty-three weeks later, the week of August 5, 1973. That week was surely a high-water mark for the lifestyle and self-help genre, since the top ten also included holdovers *I'm O.K, You're O.K.* and *Dr Atkins' Diet Revolution*, *How to Be Your Own Best Friend*, and the *Weight Watchers Program Cookbook*. But the first indication that Alex's book was more than just another popular title—that it was becoming part of a cultural phenomenon—surfaced in a roundup of best-selling sex guides that appeared in the *New York Times Book Review* in January.

"The 'No-nonsense' School vs. the 'Please-Give-Me-Back-My-Nonsense' School," by a Cambridge, Massachusetts, freelance writer named Mopsy Strange Kennedy, distinguished between two genres of sex books: the professional study, by the likes of Kinsey and Masters and Johnson, and the nonprofessional guides by such authors as Hollander and the anonymous J, usually based on personal experience. The former told the reader what had been clinically observed and, to some extent, what worked and what didn't (were multiple orgasms possible?). The latter, with at least a pretense of irreverence or insider confidence-sharing, encouraged the reader to treat sex as personal exploration.

Noticeably, Kennedy failed to assign *The Joy of Sex* to either category. But, in the third and fourth paragraphs of a front-page *Times Book*

Review feature, she described a ritual that quite a few people seemed to be performing in bookshops across the country.

> I have noticed a particular type of sidewinding—almost a dance—that goes on down the sex book aisle. People skulk along, pretending they think this is the Woman section, or the Psychology section, which are often placed tactfully side by side anyway, and then with a cavalier chuckle they pick up *Sex After Eighty*, which couldn't possibly apply to them yet, and have an indulgent little laugh, put it down, and then, humming and idly drumming their fingers to show how silly they realize they are continuing to be, . . . reach for *The Sensuous Woman*. . . .
>
> To show my mettle . . . I was obliged to reach for *The Joy of Sex*, the dirty copy (covered with dirt) they keep near the cash register and which I noticed was well thumbed. This I read for 10 full minutes in plain view of the entire store, lingering daringly over the most extravagant drawings of erotic Oriental upside down cakes.[18]

What many book shoppers were discovering was that *The Joy of Sex*, with its meticulous illustrations and detailed descriptions, was the most interesting book among the crop of sex titles to *look at*. Even when the store forbade customers to browse it except at the counter, doing so was a way to make a semi-subversive statement of sorts. You didn't just look at it; you *got away with* looking at it. As such, Alex and James Mitchell had succeeded at creating a product that was tasteful enough to make it into mainstream stores, but provocative enough that merely looking through it in public brought a mild thrill. The assistant manager of a B. Dalton bookstore in Pennsylvania's suburban Beaver Valley Mall told a reporter that women, especially, were working hard to deflect attention from themselves when they bought the book. "Either they will tell you it's a gift for a friend or they are giving it to their husband to read," she said. "We either get blushes, grins, chuckles, or else they try to act hard. Usually, the more nonchalant they act, the more obvious their embarrassment." Giving *The Joy of Sex* was a way to send a message, either subtle or unsubtle. "We had a few girls say they were buying the book for their boyfriends in hopes they will learn something, and some girls sending it to their ex-boyfriends as an insult to what they hadn't learned."[19]

Countless Americans, including many adolescents who couldn't buy the book themselves, encountered Alex's vision of un-anxious sex in various under-the-radar ways. "We didn't have the porn you have now," recalled Annie Sprinkle, the ex-sex worker, performance artist, and all-around sex radical and entrepreneur, who was eighteen at the time but already beginning to find her vocation. "The illustrations were pretty explicit. For a lot of people, it was the first porn or sexually explicit material they saw." Her parents were "pretty sex-positive," she said, and they had a copy.[20] This author first ran across *Joy* in The Emporium, a department store in downtown San Francisco, in stacks neatly displayed at the entrance to the book section. As a thirteen-year-old, it was easy enough to casually pick up a copy of *The Joy of Sex* and skim through it for five or ten minutes at a time while hordes of oblivious shoppers passed by, intent on locating the home furnishings department or the bridal registry. This being San Francisco, no one ever ordered me to put it down.

Dan Savage, years later the author of the bracingly frank syndicated advice column, "Savage Love," discovered *The Joy of Sex* in 1977, in a used bookshop near his parents' house in Chicago.

> I was thirteen years old and the store had five or six copies. I slunk off to a quiet corner of the store and read as much as I could in one sitting. And I didn't return the book to its proper place when I was done but hid it on a shelf where I was reading so one copy was sure to be there when I returned. [As for the illustrations], my parents weren't hippies, but my aunts and uncles were, and reading *The Joy of Sex* was like stumbling across a drawer of Polaroids of my extended family. There was not much about homosexuality—which interested me particularly. . . but I found much of Comfort's advice for women about men's bodies useful, and his open, breezy acceptance of sexual differences helped me to accept my own sexual difference.[21]

Previous generations had found their own sources of information about sex outside the porn shops, but with copies of Alex's book wending their way into respectable book outlets and onto middle-American coffee tables, information that directly addressed their questions was more available to teens in the '70s. Having grown up in suburbia in the '70s and '80s, the American novelist Jennifer Weiner has written that *Playboy* was not just a source of information about sex for boys. Often, it was the only thing easily available to show girls "what a pretty girl should look like: unless they sneaked a peek at the hairy, heedless lovers in *The Joy of Sex*."[22] Laura Berman, a sex and relationship researcher and professor at Northwestern University's Feinberg School of Medicine, wrote of finding a copy at age ten, under her friend Sarah's parents' bed:

"Like many other young people at the time, we pored through the pages. We were luckier than Sarah's parents, who—like mine—had grown up making do with *National Geographic* magazine."[23]

ALEX HAD PUBLISHED THIRTY books prior to *The Joy of Sex*. Some had sold moderately well, some had not, and many had been well received by critics. None had been greeted by the overwhelming, seemingly instantaneous success that met his new one, however, and certainly not in the vast American market. The sales just seemed to keep piling up. By the early months of 1973 it was clear that *The Joy of Sex* had legs. It was becoming a must-have or must-give book that would keep selling in quantity, perhaps for years. (Two years later, it had sold in the millions and was still regularly making the top five on major best-seller lists.) "The fact that it kept on selling was a total surprise to us," recalled Bruce Harris at Crown, "but I can see why. It was presented in an entertaining way, it was not threatening, and it was the '70s, so it hit a sweet spot in the culture. Great timing, and great *tone*: the tone of the book was playful and experienced. It said, 'These are not perversions. Try it, and if you like it, OK, or forget it.'"[24]

The book was moving the boundaries of publishing. Some months after Fireside issued the trade paperback edition, Dick Snyder was in Boston with a Simon & Schuster editor, Alice Mayhew, when they drove past a large, all-women rally. Some of the women were carrying copies of *Our Bodies, Ourselves*, still an alternative press publication. Snyder told the driver to stop and asked Mayhew to find out what was going on. Intrigued, she gave her card to several of the women and asked them to get in touch. In 1973 Simon & Schuster brought out the first commercial edition of the landmark handbook, which would sell more than four million copies in coming decades. "We were very confident that this one would be okay," Snyder recalled, despite the fact that *Our Bodies, Ourselves* contained sexually explicit illustrations, since the authorities had not complained when his firm issued *The Joy of Sex*.[25]

The air of mystery about *Joy* helped make it intriguing. The "authors" were never named, nor were the couple who revealed so much of themselves in the illustrations. American readers and media were curious at least to know who Alex Comfort was. Many, no doubt, were surprised to learn that ten of his books had previously been published in the United States, the first nearly three decades earlier (not to mention that he had already been advocating greater sexual freedom for a quarter-century). Still, some had trouble believing his name wasn't a pseudonym.[26]

Crown began to clear up the mystery when it summoned Alex for his first, short US book tour in early November 1972. Superficially, he was an odd choice to be the public face of a sex manual. "He was the most unlikely person you could ever think of as having a strong sex life," Peter Kindersley recalled.[27] "With his white hair and small build he looks rather like a leprechaun," one journalist wrote of him, while another, less kindly, described him as "shaped like a sack of dog food with long hair."[28]

He never seemed to be without a cigar, which gave a rough edge to his voice , but also lent him an air of informality—a "cheery brusqueness"—even in starchy settings.[29] His voice—or, to be more precise, his conversation—seemed to precede him, honed by more than twenty-five years addressing radio and TV audiences in the UK. If he wasn't a glamorous presence, that only made him attractively disarming as a pitchman for a graphic sex manual: ideal for the promotional circuit of personal appearances, radio and TV talk shows, and newspaper and magazine interviews.

The itinerary began in Los Angeles, where Pickwick's publicity campaign was proving successful, with an interview by Jean Sharley Taylor at the *Los Angeles Times*. The first few weeks of sales reports had left Alex bursting with enthusiasm and more than ready to offer American readers the kind of pithy provocations British audiences had long expected of him. He arrived in the *Times* waiting room fresh off the plane from London, equipped with the morning's papers and a copy of his book. Taylor noted his dubious fashion sense: "His mustard wool blazer gleamed with gold buttons; his shirt and tie were mismatched red and white prints. One foot bobbed lyrically as he read."[30]

"Wow!" he said, when asked about his book's success. "Every single advance publicity copy we sent out has been ripped off by somebody. We keep sending seconds. . . . I couldn't find a copy in Los Angeles this morning; luckily a boatload is coming."

What did the editor of the new best seller—if Taylor spotted subterfuge, she did not bring it up in her article—think of the state of sexual education and counseling? "I organized the book because of the extremely poor standard of counseling going on. . . . We have all suffered terribly from nonplaying coaches, physicians who don't know the answers and psychiatrists who've had no sexual experience."

Asked about the book he regarded as his principal rival and foil, Reuben's *Everything You Always Wanted to Know about Sex*, he replied with a humorous assault on the medical profession: "I am convinced that people who become medical students are even more hung up than the others. It's not quite that they go into medicine to find out where babies come from, but almost. . . . This book aims to reassure people about the hangups doctors don't understand."

Why anyone should worry about what other people do in the bedroom was beyond him, when there were so many other terrible things going on in the world, many of them perpetrated by the government of the country he was currently visiting: "What I say is that these things are kids' games. The real perversions are stealing from your neighbors and dropping napalm."

What about the illustrations? Was producing the book fun? Embroidering a bit, Alex told Taylor, "The couple began having such a good time that as they were getting on with it, they threw out the photographer and locked the door."

Alex emphasized, as he often would in coming years, that his book wasn't only for the young: "People stop having sex the way they stop riding bicycles, because it looks silly, they have arthritis or they haven't a bicycle." On the other hand, he had little to say about gay sex: "I don't want to knock it, I simply don't have the experience of it."

Above all, *The Joy of Sex* was not for "swingers" but for "square people," said Alex, who Taylor predicted was on his way to becoming "the Dr. Scholl of the pillow set." The ethics of sexual lifestyles would have to wait for another book, he added, suggesting a sequel might be on the way.

The present book was already selling briskly when the *Times* profile, headlined "Sex Manual sans Plain Brown Wrapper," appeared in the Sunday edition on November 5, but the interview gave it a significant boost. "After that, we started to see sales coming fast, orders flying in," recalled Alan Mirken at Crown. Marian Behrman, Crown's publicity director, happily circulated copies of the article to journalists, bookshops, and distributors all over the country.[31] This helped garner further newspaper and magazine reviews, which continued to appear well into the following year.

"Alex Comfort, M.B., Ph.D.," was becoming a familiar figure in major newspapers, on American radio and television (always as "*Dr.* Alex Comfort," the seal of approval displayed up front), and as a name to invoke for either proponents or enemies of the new sexual freedom.

Previously, his public-speaking experience in the United States had been limited almost completely to academic and scientific gatherings, but he addressed his new American popular audience confidently, like the practiced media personality he was. In interviews, his tactic consistently was to deflect criticism of the book by refocusing attention on its popularity and implicitly questioning why anyone would be so sex-obsessed as to spend time complaining about it. This approach seldom failed to charm.

"*The Mike Douglas Show* ran in New York yesterday," Behrman wrote him in September 1973, "and everyone in the office watched it with glee. I can't tell you how great it was and how magnificent you were—witty, warm, charming—it was a real delight! If you ever give up medicine, you could be a TV star."[32]

On a promotional trip to Toronto in January 1973—Canadian customs held the book up for four days before it was passed by the federal Ministry of Health[33]—he told reporters, "There haven't been any complaints from little old ladies . . . except ones who haven't seen the book yet." He claimed, "[*The Joy of Sex*] has to be the most ripped-off book in circulation," and he noted that close to half a dozen copies hadn't reached Johnny Carson, who quipped on *The Tonight Show*, "What joy of sex?"[34] Asked if members of his own family had read the book, Alex replied, on more than one occasion, that his ninety-one-year-old father had done so. "You're the only fellow who'd have the cheek to write it!" he quoted the elder Alexander as saying. "I heard most of that stuff in the office as a young man."[35]

Alex hadn't lost his knack for provoking at the same time that he reassured, and now that he had a large audience he was eager to widen the conversation. Previously, in *Sex and Society* and other books and articles, he had always stood by the institution of the family, even when he questioned the dogma of strict monogamy, and in *The Joy of Sex* too he had kept his distance from the more radical wing of the sexual revolution. But now he was moving further in that direction, and he thought perhaps his audience was ready for it. In December 1972, with momentum still building behind *Joy*, he published an article, "Sexuality in a Zero Growth Society," in *Center Report*, the newsletter of the Center for the Study of Democratic Institutions in Santa Barbara, in which he argued that the so-called traditional family was rapidly becoming "folklore."

Contraception, he wrote, had for the first time separated "the three human uses of sex—sex as parenthood, sex as total intimacy between two people ('relational' sex), and sex as physical play ('recreational' sex)." "Worthy" sex no longer had to be either relational or "an expression of a wish for children." For some, to be sure, parenthood and relational intimacy would remain the most "central satisfactions" of sex. For others, "one or more primary relationships will be central, but will not exclude others, in which the recreational role of sex acts as a source of bonding to supply the range of relationships formerly met by kin—an old human pattern in which sexual contacts were permitted between a woman and all her husband's clan brothers, or a man and all of his wife's titular sisters. In the zero population growth world we are all 'clan brothers' and will have to find ways of expressing the hippy ideal of universal kinship."[36]

Alex was suggesting that the traditional family could be replaced by a wider, less possessive circle of intimacy, although in his telling, the male stood to reap the biggest benefit. We weren't there yet, he acknowledged, but we were making progress. "Unless the result disturbs children and leads to a backlash generation, the genuine insight present in 'swinging' by the bored and the unrealized could expand into something far more like institutionalized sociosexual openness."[37]

The readership of *Center Report* was more academic than the public buying *The Joy of Sex*. Nevertheless, the newsletter, which had a circulation in the tens of thousands, was flooded with letters, most of them outraged. Alex's speculations were "balderdash," the author "a pathetic creature" who was proposing to "wipe out the basic tenets of Judeo-Christianity," bury the ideal of romantic love, and turn society into "another gang on the night out." "Obviously after a long weekend of random indulgence in pot, bourbon and other delicacies, a group of you got together to write this nonsensical spoof," one correspondent concluded.[38] It got worse when a slightly revised version of Alex's article appeared in *Medical Opinion* magazine. "This idiot, Comfort, is advocating the broken home," one reader wrote in. "My advice . . . is that he get in touch with Margaret Meade [*sic*] for a few wild weeks of 'tabooless sexual expression' and leave the kids alone to form happy families."[39]

Alex was unfazed. "The fact is that both the traditional, property-based, and the sentimental views of marriage have had it," he replied. "A concerned and candid look at, say, the family in California doesn't uphold the view that everything in the middle class marital garden was lovely until Comfort came along and soured it."[40]

The controversy helped keep Alex in the news and, no doubt, boosted sales of *The Joy of Sex*, especially after *Time* magazine published an interview with him on swinging: "In the years to come, Comfort predicts, more and more couples may turn to group sex for satisfactions once sought only in traditional patterns of family living."[41] "Sexuality in a Zero Growth Society" quickly became one of the most widely reprinted articles ever to appear in *Center Report*.[42] A larger audience got to read it in *Newsday*, the suburban Long Island newspaper, under the provocative title "Sex Has a Future—and How!"

ALEX HAD ALWAYS ASSUMED that if his book was going to be attacked, it would be for the sections on bondage and fetishes: "aggression in sexuality."[43] At first glance, this might appear puzzling.

Bondage, leather, and representations of sadomasochism had something of a vogue in early-'70s Britain, spurred by the increasingly visible gay subculture; the popularity of movies like Ken Russell's *The Devils* (1972) and *Mahler* (1974), with their S&M-inflected imagery and pumped-up themes of power and domination; and the outré, proto-punk clothing designs, replete with straps, harnesses, and zippers, of Vivienne Westwood and Malcolm McLaren. The psychiatric establishment had yet to catch up, however. Sadomasochism and bondage were still classified as "perversions" in the American Psychiatric Association's *Diagnostic and Statistical Manual of Mental Disorders*, as was homosexuality. As a medical practitioner, Alex would have known that to appear to sanction it—even as fantasy or role-playing—would be to invite serious professional criticism. The first such began in the UK, where *The Joy of Sex* hadn't even been published yet.

Launching the attack in spring 1973 was Alex's old nemesis David Holbrook, by now an ex-member of the Longford Committee. When Holbrook heard that the sex manual that was sweeping the States would soon be published in Britain, he wrote a full-page critique of the book for the *Daily Mail*. Alex had reduced sex to pure sensation, he charged, turning couples into "dehumanized nothings" and eliminating the "quality of transcendence and creativity" that makes marriage unique. He zeroed in on the "Sauces & Pickles" section of *Joy*, which, he alleged, advised the man to "improve his sex performance by gagging his wife or tying her up" and instructed him to "go out and cut birch twigs and make a bundle to birch her with."[44]

Holbrook was especially disturbed that Alex had recently edited a counseling book titled *Man and Woman* for the UK's Marriage Guidance Council, a comparatively liberal, forty-five-year-old organization that provided advice to couples on sex and other aspects of relationships.[45]

Without citing a single passage from *Man and Woman*, he asked how it could be that Dr. Comfort was recognized "as a 'progressive' expert on sex"? "Is it not high time for an inquiry, at national level, into the powers now influencing this council, and into the whole racket of 'sex technique' books and counselling?"

Throughout the article is the suggestion that the problem was not just books like *Man and Woman* and *The Joy of Sex* but also people in authority who had become much too accepting of such productions. A couple of months later, in a letter to *The Listener* in response to one of Alex's contributions, Holbrook wrote that he had been asked by Gershon Legman to help place a review of *The Joy of Sex*—hardly a complimentary one—in a British periodical. Holbrook claimed to have approached "half a dozen Fleet Street editors" about the piece. "None dared publish it," he wrote.[46] His implication: some sort of conspiracy against anyone expressing qualms about the new sexual freedom.

Holbrook's letter came as a surprise to Alex, who had included Legman on a list of people to whom Mitchell Beazley should send review copies of his book. Only a few months earlier, Alex had written to the eccentrically learned American to ask how he was getting over an eye condition, and Legman had written back asking him to send along any good long-playing records of eighteenth-century classical music if he had them lying around.[47] Other than that exchange, however, Alex had been out of touch for several years with his friend, some of whose notions of the social and psychological role of sex were very different from his own.

"Normal" sexuality, Legman felt, had become deformed by violent perversions that included almost anything other than a few variations on plain-vanilla heterosexual intercourse and oral sex and by a barely repressed hatred of women, something Legman, a devout Freudian, felt was closely related to homosexuality, of which he strongly disapproved. Nor was he fond of the '60s counterculture that Alex found so hopeful. The review Legman wrote of *The Joy of Sex*, and which Holbrook was trying to put before the British public under the headline "The Joys of Perversion," was an all-out, nearly unhinged denunciation, composed, judging from the tone of it, in a fit of sputtering outrage. His erstwhile friend's book was "the first kinky sex-technique manual on the market," Legman declared, after which he focused almost entirely on the few pages on bondage and related practices.

Until *The Joy of Sex*, Alex had never written about sadomasochism or other sexual practices that involved rough play and power relationships, and the entries "Bondage," "Discipline," "Fighting," "Chains," and "Boots," whatever their faults, took up less than fifteen pages of the book. He understood too that genuine sadists existed, and that they were dangerous people. And he was clear that fantasy should never go beyond the line of consent or devolve into genuine violence. None of this would have mattered to a dogmatist like Legman, who never criticized the more fundamental element of male dominance that ran through *The Joy of Sex* since, as a heterosexual traditionalist, he had no quarrel with it. Alex was fortunate enough that his former friend could not find a publication willing to carry his diatribe.

Not immediately, anyhow. A backlash against *The Joy of Sex* from the puritanical Right was less than a couple of years away, but in the meantime Alex had only Holbrook's attacks in the daily press to respond to. In a brief reply to Holbrook's letter in *The Listener*, he pointed out that "the book he attacks me for editing is, as he says, not yet available here for readers to judge: this could be one reason for the reluctance of editors to print unsolicited and abusive reviews of it circulated by Mr Holbrook." As for *The Joy of Sex* being "the first kinky sex-technique manual," "the statement Mr Holbrook attributes to Gershon Legman (author of *Oral Sex* and *The Rationale of the Dirty Joke*) about its promotion is quite simply untrue."[48]

"[Holbrook himself] habitually advocates love, tenderness and mental health in terms which express hostility, fear, and excitement," Alex wrote. But he sensed that he and Holbrook, and even Lord Longford, weren't really on opposite sides; each, in his own way, was concerned about the demeaning of human relations in a capitalist society. He wrote letters to both, attempting to find some common ground. In his letter to Holbrook, he explained that he was not promoting the confusion of sex with violence but rather arguing that "the human capacity for play, in the sexual situation, has as its function the resolution of this dangerous confusion." The "whole text" of *The Joy of Sex* "was very carefully constructed with this aim in mind," he said, and was "not part of a conspiracy to devalue affectional sex—rather the reverse."[49]

Longford never responded to Alex's letter. A long correspondence with Holbrook followed.** But it got nowhere, running aground on

** When a reader in Aberdeenshire wrote an angry letter to Alex, stating that she would rather "rot with leprosy" than put his "male chauvinistic" book in front of her daughters, it was Jane who wrote back, telling her that *The Joy of Sex* was the result of their partnership and that their sexual relationship was one of "utter joy."

Holbrook's insistence that certain acts were "perversions," that pornography was an unalloyed, dehumanizing evil, and that a preoccupation with the "details" of sex was "sick."[50]

From the vantage point of a half-century later, the criticisms that Holbrook and Legman aimed at Alex and his book suggest a male counterpart to the dogmatic arguments that the radical feminist Andrea Dworkin later made against pornography and sadomasochism, and that led her eventually into an unlikely alliance with the political right.[51] All four denied that a boundary can exist between violent fantasies and violence itself, between playacting aggression and the real thing. Since then, bondage and S&M have become the stuff of performance art, comic fodder for writers and directors from Woody Allen to Judd Apatow, and the sales hook for titillating romances like E. L. James's *Fifty Shades of Gray* trilogy.

This only points up the distance that mass culture has come from the days when *The Joy of Sex* was a best seller. Whereas Alex's professed purpose was to remove anxiety from sex, critics like Holbrook, reacting to a decade of cultural upheaval that seemingly had undermined the very notion of the family, thought the opposite. For them, it was necessary to suppress fantasy, to bring anxiety back. The debate concerning pornography's social impact has not gone away, but it's less likely to be treated as a simple matter of male dominance and female disempowerment. Alex had written a book for a less anxious age. Paradoxically, the fact that it was published in a time somewhat more so—when reading and acquiring *Joy* was still a mildly transgressive act, despite its wide availability—may have boosted its popularity.

CHAPTER 17

Divorce (1973)

Alex contacted Holbrook personally because he disliked "shouting at a distance," he wrote, but that may not have been the only reason. Holbrook was wrong that publication of *The Joy of Sex* in Britain was imminent. Instead of coming out in the spring of 1973, as originally planned, publication had been moved to 1974, almost two years after the book's US debut. Alex, meanwhile, was maintaining a far more subdued profile at home regarding his best seller than he had in the United States.

Not until shortly after the book appeared in America did Mitchell Beazley find a British publisher: Quartet Books, which would not even be officially in business until the spring 1973. James Mitchell and John Beazley had known Quartet's principals, John Boothe and William Miller, from their days at Panther Books, and both firms were founded with an eye to putting nontraditional material in front of the public in innovative formats. Quartet agreed to pay Mitchell Beazley a £6,000 advance, stipulating a 10 percent royalty for the author. The book would have an initial print run of twenty-five thousand copies: larger than the number Crown had committed to but still relatively small for the UK. It would be costly to produce and Quartet therefore expected to assign it a high cover price.

Boothe recalled that when he and Miller saw an early impression of Crown's US edition in fall 1972, they knew immediately that it was "too good an opportunity" to pass up. "We wanted a major title" to help launch the firm's first list the following spring, Boothe later recalled. "[The book] was in keeping with the things we had done at Panther . . . [but] we knew there were certain risks, which was why we sought legal advice."[1]

Despite the historic decisions in the *Lady Chatterley* and *Last Exit to Brooklyn* cases, nobody was safe from some level of harassment. In

Alex's words, the UK remained a country where "any psychopath [could] lodge a complaint."[2] Accordingly, Quartet approached the Director of Public Prosecutions (DPP) through lawyers to determine if the authorities were likely to charge the publisher under the obscenity laws. They would not, provided the Asian erotic art plates were omitted. "Given *Joy*'s known worldwide success, the authorities would have looked stupid to ban the book on the illustrations, and would certainly have lost a prosecution," Boothe reasoned.[3]

However, when Quartet tried to bring some twelve hundred copies into the country from Mitchell Beazley's Netherlands-based printer, Smeets, for prepublication promotion and sale at Gatwick Airport, they were seized by HM Customs and Excise and destroyed by a local judge's order. That meant Mitchell Beazley and Quartet would have to find a printer in the UK, a more expensive proposition for a book that would already be costly to produce. As packager and publisher considered how to overcome this latest hurdle, Alex suddenly set another in their path.

He had always been a trifle reluctant to publish the book in the UK; at one point, he got a commitment from Mitchell to keep his name off entirely, even as editor, or communicate his authorship to any outside publisher, pleading the "nuisance value" of being identified as a "sex guru."[4] Now he demanded, through Mitchell Beazley, that Quartet delay publication of *The Joy of Sex* in Britain for at least year.

"It was a blow," Boothe remembers. "It had a financial effect on us." Quartet was licensed as publisher for six years in the UK and the Commonwealth of Nations except Canada but was anticipating the lion's share of sales coming from Britain. Without what was expected to be one of its most prominent titles—a book that was already a publishing phenomenon in America—Quartet would have to dig further into its start-up capital to get through its first year. Given Alex's new status as Mitchell Beazley's most successful author, however, Mitchell and his colleagues were unwilling to argue with him, especially when he told them that if they attempted to publish the book in the UK, he would be obliged to say publicly, if asked, that he had advised against it.[5]

From the start, Alex had been concerned that *The Joy of Sex* not be regarded as smut, or damage his reputation; that had been avoided in the U.S., but even there, he found himself in a minor spat with Crown when the publisher did a test mailing of a marketing leaflet for the book, at about the same time it appeared on the bestseller lists, that he regarded as "disgusting trash." He demanded it be redone, and Crown complied.[6]

As to his native land, he was even more sensitive. In a letter to Bill

Masters, Alex argued vaguely that "opinion" was not ready for *The Joy of Sex* in the UK, and that the only path to publishing it there successfully would be to first secure "massive endorsement" from one or more respected counseling bodies. *Joy* had received a positive blurb from Mary Calderone, a former Planned Parenthood physician and leader in the fight to legalize abortion who had founded the Sex Information and Education Council of the United States (SIECUS) in 1965. But no such organization existed in the UK at the time. Lacking such an endorsement, the book would surely meet a storm of protest, and Alex hadn't the time to engage in a fight over it, he said.[7]

None of this was quite sufficient explanation, however. Alex had no reason to fear prosecution: Quartet had already determined this would not happen. His professional reputation was protected by the fiction that he had not written the book, only edited it. But his personal life was about to change significantly: he was getting a divorce.

His dual relationship with Ruth and Jane was now a dozen years old, and for a long time, when he wanted to let someone into his confidence, he had taken an impish pride in divulging the unconventional arrangement.[8] The routine they had fallen into—Alex spending weekends in Loughton with Ruth, weeknights with Jane at her flat in London—still held in the early '70s, although his time in Loughton was becoming more sporadic. So far as his colleagues and coworkers at UCL were concerned, Ruth was still his wife, and they continued to attend official and social functions related to his work as a couple. Jane often accompanied him on trips to conferences and other professional appointments outside the country, of which there were many. They had also acquired a separate group of friends who saw them socially in London.[9]

The arrangement had never been as untroubled as Alex liked to make out, however, particularly at the outset. Nick recalled "arguments and scenes" between Alex and Ruth, in some of which he had intervened to keep the peace. Later Alex would complain to his son about the difficulty of maintaining households with two different women. But for years now, each of the three had gotten something out of this peculiar compromise.[10]

It was Jane who finally decided to press the issue, Nick believed, at about the time *The Joy of Sex* was being readied for publication. When their relationship began in 1960, sex was the precipitant, and Jane was happy to be Alex's muse as his preoccupation with the theory and practice of physical love grew over the next decade. But his new book was to a considerable degree the product of their relationship, and, as work on it proceeded at Mitchell Beazley, the expectation grew that it could be a major success. As such, it was likely to draw attention to Alex's personal life, including his unconventional domestic arrangements. From Jane's point of view, it was time to demand that Alex at last make up his mind between her and Ruth.

Matters may have been a bit more urgent than that, however. On January 24, 1972, Jane had appeared at Clerkenwell Magistrates Court and was ordered to pay a fine of £1 for being drunk in public the night before in Leverton Road, close to her old flat in Lady Margaret Road. Most likely, she had spent the night in jail.[11] No other evidence points to a significant drinking problem at this stage, but Jane was becoming increasingly dependent emotionally on Alex and less able to be apart from him for days at a time. When he rather abruptly presented Ruth with divorce papers to sign, one weekend in the spring of the following year, Alex said by way of explanation, "Jane needs me more."[12]

Alex's professional circumstances were in flux as well. His grant from the Medical Research Council was ending, and he was making no progress at convincing an institution in the UK to fund his test-battery project on aging. He had been making noises for months about leaving UCL after more than twenty years and moving to America. He had hoped to apply for a new, federally funded position directing research on aging, but Congress decided not to create the job. He even supplied an introduction to *Free Beaches: A Phenomenon of the California Coast*, a text-and-photos coffee-table book on nude beaches, published by Santa Barbara–based Capra Press. While he had no definite plans, Alex was clearly moving into another phase of his life and career, and Jane wanted to make sure she was unequivocally a part of it.

In later years, Alex was less smug about his arrangement with Jane and Ruth and was able to allow that there had always been problems. "For a long time, I was living with two women," he said in a 1994 interview with the *Independent*.

> It didn't work very well, they were both in eruption the whole time. . . . I lived in two different houses. I used to tootle over every morning and pick up Wife No 2 and take her to work. I don't recommend it. . . .
>
> I was trying to be a decent husband to both of them, and I couldn't. I could have left Ruth, I suppose, but I didn't like to leave her because Nicholas was still at school. And the other woman, who I was equally fond of, who wanted me to live with her—and I used

> to go on holidays with her. It was only latterly, toward the end of the period, that it became possible for me to settle it up. I did the best I could, that's all I can say.

How did he "settle it up?" the interviewer asked. "By divorcing Wife No 1, and marrying Wife No 2."[13]

A great mess of feeling is packed into these words: love, selfishness, shame, regret, and the very English form of detachment that allowed him to continue such an awkward domestic routine for so many years, despite the pain it caused. In his December 1972 article in *Center Report*, Alex had written quite differently about the kind of relationship he had established with Ruth and Jane, and it's worth savoring the contrast.

> Our society has . . . virtually institutionalized adultery: a growing number of spouses permit each other complete sexual liberty on the conditions that there shall be no 'involvement' and that the extracurricular relations are not brought to their attention. It is beginning to institutionalize ritual spouse exchange. This is more honest . . . the partners, instead of excluding each other, share in the arrangement.[14]

It was a great irony; while Alex could write smoothly and credibly about the potential of an open relationship—or at least a tacitly open one—he hadn't been very good at making it work in his own life. He hadn't succeeded in creating an "institutionalized" form of adultery; he had merely taken twelve long years to decide which woman he wanted to be married to. Alex was, of course, being disingenuous to insist that only "latterly" could he resolve the three-way relationship. He could have done so at almost any time.

Here was another irony: that a man whose political philosophy placed such strong emphasis on personal responsibility could not bring himself to make a responsible choice between the two women in his life. So long as Ruth and Jane were willing to put up with his indecision, however, the arrangement suited Alex because of the boost it gave to his ego. At Cambridge he had genuinely fallen in love with Ruth—but in part because she had fallen in love with him and thereby made him feel lovable. Years later, Jane had made him feel desirable, and their affair allowed him to think he was actually living in the new world of open and enlightened sexuality he was describing in his books. He, as well as Ruth and Jane, had paid a price, and not only in the "eruptions" that punctuated their lives.

"I did the best I could, that's all I can say." A note of desperation creeps out of these words, as if even he didn't really believe it, and perhaps never did.

On April 30, 1973, *Time* magazine noted cheekily in its "Milestones" column that Alex Comfort, "biologist, gerontologist, and author, and lately one of science's most approving analysts of group sex," had divorced his wife of twenty-nine years. Despite the trials of the past dozen years, it was not at all what Ruth had wanted. She still loved him, and had gotten used to her place in the three-way arrangement. Her status as Alex's wife was still important to her. It came as an unexpected shock when Alex came home one weekend as usual but with divorce papers for her to sign. She dreaded the attention the breakup might bring, although family and close friends had known for years that they hadn't been living a traditional marriage.[15]

The split was difficult as well for Alex, who didn't want to see Ruth completely pass out of his life. He promised he would always take care of her. "I don't think she ever had any doubt about that," recalled Nick, who first heard about the split from Ruth. "She trusted him completely."[16]

Doing his best after his fashion, Alex cast about for some way to spare Ruth as much unpleasantness as possible. Given the notoriety it was already achieving in America, he knew the release of *The Joy of Sex* in the UK would greatly embarrass his soon-to-be ex-wife. One way Alex could accommodate her was to delay publication until well after the divorce took place. The financial inconvenience was worth it to him.

Accordingly, he wrote to James Mitchell on December 5, 1972, well before he brought the documents to Ruth, asking him to either postpone Quartet's publication of the book or else repurchase the rights, leaving Quartet an option for a future deal. Otherwise, he said, "it may foul up the possibility of what would otherwise be an uncontested divorce."

Quartet agreed to the buyback and option in exchange for a £2,000 payment in compensation and a £6,000 interest-free loan to tide the firm over until *The Joy of Sex* could finally be published in the UK, in September 1974. Quartet meanwhile would go ahead and publish the book elsewhere in the Commonwealth in June 1973, as planned.[17]

Alex was correct about Ruth's opinion of his book. While she kept the Loughton house in the divorce settlement, she did not ask for any share of the earnings from his best seller. In the short run, Alex got what he wanted: a relatively routine divorce and remarriage with little public attention. The divorce from Ruth was barely reported in Britain, and only a few short notices appeared when he and Jane were married at

Islington Register Office on June 8. None mentioned that he was the author of a phenomenal best seller in America.

LIFE WAS CHANGING PROFOUNDLY for one of Alex's good friends as well. In 1973, after years during which he was barred from travel to the West for conferences or other scientific gatherings, Zhores Mevedev at last received permission from Soviet authorities to accept a one-year position at the National Institute for Medical Research in London. Soon after he arrived with his wife and son, he was summoned to the Soviet embassy, where his passport was seized and he was stripped of his citizenship. "[Alex] was the only person I knew," Medvedev recalled, "so for the first few weeks in London, we met frequently. He helped me to open an account at the bank, showed me how the banks worked, helped me to meet with a publisher, and to be at ease with British life. It was the first time I was making a life in a foreign country, and Alex was a person who I used to ask how to do this and that."[18]

Medvedev was surprised that Alex didn't seem to have a large laboratory of his own at UCL, and his office was messy, cluttered with boxes and piles of papers in various stages of being packed up. Alex informed his friend that he was leaving for the United States to become senior fellow in biology at the Center for the Study of Democratic Institutions (CSDI), and he asked Medvedev if he would like to take over the unpaid position in the Zoology Department at UCL that he himself had occupied since his Medical Research Council grant had run out, and which Medvedev could turn into a paying position by applying for a grant. Medvedev decided to stick with his new job at the National Institute for Medical Research, where a mutual friend, Robin Holliday, was doing work on aging in cellular cultures that intrigued him.[19]

On June 4, just days before his remarriage, Alex had begun putting out word to colleagues and friends about his move to California.[20] The CSDI had been established in 1959 by Robert Maynard Hutchins, the educational philosopher and former head of the University of Chicago and the Ford Foundation, backed initially by funds from the latter. Its mission was to sponsor public policy research projects, but Hutchins reorganized it in 1969 as a West Coast approximation of Princeton's Institute for Advanced Studies or All Souls College, Oxford. The center was "a latter-day Platonic Academy," in the words of one participant, with twenty distinguished scholars and scientists.[21] Alex already lent his name to the revamped institution as an associate. Although no responsibilities or compensation came with the title, he had spent more and more time there over the next couple of years, culminating in a fellowship offer.

Hutchins described the CSDI as "an organization of men who are free of any obligation except to join in the effort to understand the subjects they have elected to study."[22] That description, plus a relatively generous $35,000-a-year stipend and the center's location—a forty-three-acre mountaintop estate overlooking the Pacific Ocean in Santa Barbara—were certainly strong inducements to Alex. He had labored at UCL for more than twenty years, never earning an entirely secure living from his scientific work, despite his contribution to the university's reputation. His long research project on aging in guppies was winding down, bringing to a close his major laboratory work in gerontology.

The Joy of Sex changed his prospects completely. For the first time, substantial royalty income from one of his books was coming in, and increasingly it appeared he could anticipate quite a bit more in coming years. But he was also exposed for the first time to the UK's top marginal income tax rate, which in 1971 had been cut from about 90 percent to a still-high 75 percent. It would be raised to 83 percent in 1974. That confiscatory rate only applied to income over £20,000 a year—a snugly middle-class level at the time—but the resulting bill could be quite a shock to a taxpayer who had never been in that bracket before, which is why a bevy of British celebrities, from the Rolling Stones to Michael Caine and Sean Connery, were establishing residences elsewhere in these years.

Scrambling for a tax shelter would seem out of character for a person with Alex's political and social principles, but he never apologized for it, and, like many others who came into sudden wealth from a less-than-affluent background, he had his reasons. He could not be sure how long *The Joy of Sex* would continue to sell, not to mention any subsequent books—he was already working on a sequel for Mitchell Beazley, he told Bill Masters[23]—and so he had no way of knowing how long he would remain a high earner. Jane was leaving her librarian post and was undecided whether she would take another job in California. Additionally, Ruth was retiring from her job as a social worker, and Alex intended to support her to whatever extent her small pension did not. He himself had no pension. On balance, it made sense for him to preserve as much as he could of his windfall. Six months before the book appeared in America, already anticipating a big success, he was working with his accountant to set up an arrangement whereby his non-UK earnings could be held in a "Sterling-area bank outside the U.K," such as in the Cayman Islands.[24]

His new employer had a solution. Alex would assign 30 percent of his royalties from *The Joy of Sex*, or an estimated $150,000 in the first twelve months and more thereafter, to the CSDI.[25] The legal rationale was that Alex had written the book later than 1969, when the center had begun to list him as an associate, and that he had written some portions at the center itself.[26] Supposedly that gave the center some rights to the book, which Alex had only discovered after it became a best seller. Whatever the case, the assignment of royalties would reduce Alex's UK tax bill; out of the proceeds, the CSDI would pay Alex's salary and use the remainder to cover other operating expenses.[27]

The deal was concluded in an agreement dated July 31, with Alex engaged to assume his new role at the beginning of January.[28] It was a boon for the center as well as its newest fellow, since the CSDI was struggling financially under Hutchins's not-very-firm grip, which Alex appears not to have been aware of at the time.[29] In fact, the gambit would prove far more problematic than he anticipated. But, for the moment, the center meant not only a practical, tax-advantaged way to dispose of his book earnings but also a broader field of study and strong institutional recognition of his accomplishments.

Not to mention an attractive new home. Alex now had friends in both the San Francisco and Los Angeles areas, including John and Barbara Williamson and several others at Sandstone, who had been delighted by *Joy* when he brought a copy to the retreat soon after it was published.[30] "If Sandstone Retreat had been recognized as a university, *The Joy of Sex* would have been required reading," Barbara said later.[31] He still took every opportunity to visit Marilyn and Irvin Yalom at their home in Palo Alto. Like so many Britons before him, from Robert Louis Stevenson to Aldous Huxley and David Hockney, he found the weather a welcome change from England, with its "wet and wintry" climate.[32]

His excitement came through clearly when he and Jane lunched with Nick in the summer of 1973 and he told his son about the reception *The Joy of Sex* was receiving in the States and of his plans to move. He was elated, Nick recalled; the book was going to be *big*, he predicted. Jane was enthusiastic too, although the prospect of starting a new life with Alex, rather than the specific location, was what most appealed to her.[33]

The popular reception *The Joy of Sex* was enjoying—and that Alex himself encountered on the book tour circuit—provided a further inducement. He had never experienced anything like it in Britain, despite his presence on TV and radio, and he was coming to enjoy being a celebrity. Americans seemed eager to absorb the perspective he had been trying for years to disseminate in his own homeland. While Britain in the '70s was quite different from the prewar society in which he had grown up, the backlash represented by the *OZ* case and the Longford Committee suggested that his chances of acceptance in the United States—particularly in California—were much greater when it came to his sexual, social, and political views.

Alex publicly announced his impending arrival in a June 4 letter to the Forum for Contemporary History, a Santa Barbara group he had visited on previous trips. The following month, the *Los Angeles Times* republished it as an opinion piece.[34] In it, he explained why, aside from lower taxes, an eminent British biologist and writer would want to live in the often derided land of fruits and nuts. Citing "the weather and the gentle, candid women who seem to grow there like oranges," he also noted that "from its foundation, the United States has been something of a social laboratory" and that California was "the place par excellence for a human biologist." While Europeans liked to deride such phenomena as Forest Lawn Cemetery, the Manson family, and Haight-Ashbury, Alex wrote, California also "had or has Marcuse, Maslow, Esalen and the Center for the Study of Democratic Institutions." It had "some of the openness and the assimilative powers of India. [It] digests the stuffiest and most culture-proud immigrants and makes them into Californians."

The "home of extremes," California was also full of "empiricists with no traditional nerves": people who approached each problem afresh and made up their own traditions as they went along. "What strikes me about California," Alex wrote,

> is that it is at grips with the cardinal problems of our time—reconciling technology with conservation, freedom with planning, revolution with stability and liberty and in particular, thinking with feeling. . . . Now that we are starting to preserve forests rather than fell them, any would-be pioneer has to use his ax on sacred cows and conventional notions rather than on timber. He has to construct his own intellectual cabin, not live at the airport hotel. My California friends, scientific or lay, are adepts at this, and I respect the way in which they have transmuted a physical into an intellectual tradition.

Admittedly, his acquaintance with the state's people—and with Americans, despite his frequent visits there—was limited, but Alex was determined to broaden it once he made his move. Gesturing at the recent reelection of Richard Nixon, he wrote,

> I know virtually nobody who voted for a President who was elected by a very large majority. . . . All my close friends are university people. Nearly all are 'liberals' rather than 'conservatives'; nearly all are Jewish. I know few American Catholics, for example. I know few American Blacks. I know no American farmers, and not many businessmen, one Nisei family who are old friends, and lately a community of Lutherans. This is something which, if I live in America, I can remedy, not merely with colleagues. In California, too, I think it is easier than elsewhere, for the demarcations between interests and ethnic traditions, though drawn, are not defended.

Alex sketched an idealized view of California if not the entire United States. Some of his *Los Angeles Times* readers no doubt were flattered, others mildly baffled that he could so easily glide over a legion of social, racial, economic, and environmental problems in a populous and complex state. Herbert Marcuse, writing in response to Alex's letter, found his characterization of America "so obviously and naively false . . . that it does not deserve any comment. The whole thing seems to me highly embarrassing!"[35]

Not altogether wrongly, however, Alex saw America, and California in particular, as a vast laboratory populated by a less straitjacketed society than the one that had raised him. And he knew it was time for a change. Seventeen years earlier, Jack Haldane had resigned the chair he had held for almost a quarter-century and moved to India, desiring the benefit of the warmer climate—he could observe the yellow-wattled lapwing from his backyard in Calcutta—and finding the Congress Party government's state-socialist model of development more in keeping with his own political philosophy. He called India "the closest approximation to the Free World." Visiting him there the early '60s, Alex had noted that dapper Jack, now in Indian dress, was sometimes mistaken in the streets for a Hindu holy man.[36]

Alex likewise wished to move to California not just to cut his UK tax bill but also to go native in a place where he imagined the future was being born. "To be a 'progressive' in America," he wrote, "in the true sense of seeing society in continuous change, one needs to stay with Franklin, Jefferson and the others. They have managed better than previous nation-makers to stay disturbingly relevant." For a "wandering scholar," as Alex called himself, who had reached a crossroads but was still ambitious, receptive, and full of ideas, California seemed the perfect place to touch down. It remained to be seen whether California, and America, had a place for him.

CHAPTER 18

California (1973–1975)

In early October 1973, Alex cleared out the office at UCL that he had occupied for more than twenty years and flew to California to house-hunt. He was to formally join the staff of the CSDI in January. "I'm going because I've been offered a good job," he said matter-of-factly to *Inside London*, which headlined its story, "Comfort Joins Brain Drain." "I don't want to comment further. It would be bad-mannered of me to say any more while I am still waiting for my visa, I'm going to California on a visitor's visa." It was said, the paper reported, that he wanted to be out of Britain when *The Joy of Sex* was published there, "to avoid the inevitable publicity."[1]

He quickly found a house, at 683 Oak Grove Drive in Montecito, just outside Santa Barbara: an eleven-year-old, ranch-style house on one acre of land perched on a hillside facing toward the Pacific, surrounded by oak trees and with a central patio, four bedrooms, and a studio off the garage with skylights and bookshelves that Alex could use as his home office. The house also had a stable and corral, should he and Jane want to own horses (which they would not). Fronting their new home was a rock garden with succulent plants rather than a lawn and flower beds: the farthest thing from either Alex and Ruth's cozy suburban English home in Loughton or the flat he had shared with Jane in Kentish Town. So too was the listed price of the house: $375,000 in cash, affordable thanks to Alex's sudden change of fortune.

Montecito and Santa Barbara seemed curious places for an English anarchist to fetch up. An hour and a half drive north of Los Angeles on the Pacific Coast, they had a long association with the Hollywood film industry, both as shooting locations and the home of many celebrities. At the time Alex and Jane moved in, wealthy Santa Barbara's most-discussed residents were Pat and Bill Loud and their five children.

The prosperous Louds had agreed to let a film crew make a twelve-part, cinema vérité-style documentary of their lives, which caught many of the tensions and dissatisfactions in a seemingly ideal American household, including Pat's dramatic demand for a divorce. Sometimes called the first reality TV show, *An American Family* screened on public television from January to March 1973, drawing ten million viewers and sparking an outpouring of earnest commentary about the decline of the institution it was examining, the impact of media on character, and the price of affluence. Alex would seem to have stepped right in the middle of the social disruption he had discussed in "Sexuality in a Zero Growth Society."

But Santa Barbara was also full of well-educated people, including some of Alex and Jane's compatriots, who were still enchanted with the California dream and glad to welcome the best-selling author and his wife to their new home. Kenneth Rexroth, who had written so perceptively about Alex and the other Neo-Romantics in the '40s—and a fellow anarchist to boot—was now living in Montecito and teaching at the University of California, Santa Barbara. John Burton, an expatriate British poet and artist living in Santa Barbara, called California "the New Hellas" and invited Alex to stop by for "a moment of quiet reflection and an avocado lunch." Alan Watts, another UK expatriate and a well-known popularizer of Eastern philosophy, warned him that Californians were "busy smoggifying and bulldozing this gorgeous territory, and setting up suburbs quite as abominable as anything in North London"—presumably unaware that Alex had grown up in one of those suburbs—but still advised him to "come while it lasts" and help "stop the rot."[2]

On the professional side, the *Journal of the American Geriatrics Society* quickly invited him to join its editorial board.[3] But Alex would be spending most of his time in his new office at the think tank—sometimes jokingly called "El Parthenon"—that Hutchins had set up overlooking the ocean.

"For people like me," Alex had written in his *Los Angeles Times* opinion piece, "it's far, far better to be surrounded by freaks than by squares."[4] He was referring to the popular image of Southern California society, but he might have had the center in mind as well, or even Hutchins himself, who had built up a reputation as a leading American educator and intellectual without ever quite earning it.

Prior to World War II, as president of the University of Chicago, Hutchins had championed the "great books" approach to molding future leaders through Socratic dialog and exposure to the great (exclusively

Western) minds of the past. He spoke in favor of returning higher education to a vaguely medieval structure based on his reading of Thomas Aquinas while railing against empiricism and positivism: the practical and philosophic traditions in which Alex had grown up.[5] Hutchins had opposed United States entry into World War II, but on his watch the first nuclear reactor—a critical component of the Manhattan Project—was built under the stands of the university's sports stadium.

The CSDI in Santa Barbara grew out of the Fund for the Republic, a civil liberties group backed by the Ford Foundation, that Hutchins headed in the '50s. The very different and rather poorly defined aim of the center was to bring together the "best minds" in an ongoing dialog, building on the model Hutchins had promoted at the University of Chicago and producing, it was hoped, breakthroughs in government, philosophy, science, futurology, and any other field the fellows considered important. Every weekday at 11:00 a.m., they would gather, along with visiting fellows, in a large room on the center's campus for another installment of the ongoing conversation; once back in their offices they would churn out papers, lectures, and articles for the *Center Magazine* and other publications.

This was all supposed to yield some super-enlightened version of the truth, but without a better defined set of objectives, the energy at the center could yield either nothing or a great deal of visionary vapor. Edward Engberg, a CSDI fellow in the late '60s and early '70s, compared it to the Mudfog Society for the Advancement of Everything, the parody of high-minded Victorian learned societies that Charles Dickens concocted for a set of humorous sketches. A 1969 *New York Times* story on the center described the daily meetings:

> No subject is too vast for their attention, no project too visionary for their concern. They daily deal with concepts as grand as universal law, and as remote as the users of the most distant seabed. In this echoing think tank, the accent is liberal and the optimism unbounded. . . . One of the fellows—Episcopal Bishop James A. Pike . . . says that he even communicated with his dead son, an assertion that the other fellows pass over in uncharacteristic silence. The one woman—Elisabeth Mann Borghese—perfected yet another form of communication: She says she taught her dog to type.[6]

These New Agey elements aside, the center was a fairly typical product of the optimistic postwar period of American ascendancy, when US governmental, military, and academic elites, deeply in synch, felt completely confident of their ability to design and execute the future of the earth and the human race. And it did attract some accomplished individuals. Elisabeth Mann Borghese, when she wasn't drilling her dog at the typewriter, was a respected environmentalist and expert on maritime law. Alex quickly bonded with the political scientist Harvey Wheeler, coauthor of the nuclear-disaster novel *Fail-Safe* and later a pioneer in online learning, who shared his intense interest in the junction between sociology and biology and approached his level as a polymath. Wheeler had published a book in 1971, *The Politics of Revolution*, in which he argued that humanity's survival would depend on a new coalition between radical activists and radical scientists.[7] Another friend at the center was Peter Ritchie-Calder, a British journalist, socialist, and former comrade in the CND.

The Ford Foundation covered much of the center's set-up costs and its budget in the early years. But with its nebulous objective, even Hutchins, a champion fund-raiser, had trouble supporting its generous budget and keeping its lavish property maintained after the Ford money tapered off. He also had trouble finding people to fill the ranks of the fellows, especially after he effectively canceled several ostensibly lifetime positions upon reorganizing the center in 1969. Soon, the CSDI started selling off acreage to pay its bills.[8] Hence, Alex's agreeing to join in 1973 was both a boost to the center's prestige and visibility and a financial godsend.

What was Alex doing in such an institution, with its strongly elitist ethos, aside from sheltering his earnings from *The Joy of Sex* and rationalizing a move to California? At fifty-three, he was done with laboratory work, but in the near term he wanted the center to be a base from which he could catalyze the project for statistical research in human aging that he had been trying to get off the ground for the past six years. That meant, paradoxically, that aside from the new home, new office, and new marriage, his life didn't change much. His round of conferences, addresses, and lectures had mostly been in the United States for some time, and these continued, and he was still busily developing ideas for articles and books, some scholarly and some, with the encouragement of James Mitchell, popular. Jane was now retired and he was helping her develop her own writing projects too.

Zhores Medvedev was a guest of the center for three days and found it a bit dazzling. Celebrities and dignitaries such as UN ambassadors passed through, and the talk was on a consistently high level. Alex, who conducted a question-and-answer session with him on "Science in the USSR" and the situation of dissidents, was hardly the most famous person in the room. "He seemed very relaxed, cheerful, settled," Medvedev recalled. "He had a nice office, an assistant, a library, and the possibility of doing anything he wanted."[9]

In October 1974, ten months after Alex and Jane moved in, the Canadian literary critic and scholar Hugh Kenner, who had taught at the University of California, Santa Barbara, until the preceding year, published a long profile of Alex in the *New York Times Sunday Magazine*.[10] One of the few extended pieces ever written about him during his lifetime, it foregrounds the torrent of talk, ideas, snatches of poetry and limericks that Alex customarily unleashed on his guests, along with an overflowing good humor. Not everyone liked this side of his personality. Betty Dodson, when she ran into him at Sandstone, found him "a very boring man, very full of himself, . . . [who] loved to hear himself talk."[11] Kenner clearly disagreed.

"Eyebrows arching above his cigar, Alex Comfort grins in delight" as he summarizes the plot of *Come Out to Play* to his guest. "Iron-gray hair curls above the collar of his blue jumpsuit," the trouble-free attire he had recently adopted; "take three, and you needn't wash shirts." His head "is shaggily massive. His face mobile. A jag of rapid talk—paragraphs at a breath—escapes the pursed lips, somehow bypassing the waggling cigar." As Alex describes his fictional alter ego, Dr. George Goggins, his interviewer begins to feel in the presence of "a somewhat enlarged Peter Sellers."

Kenner had followed Alex's earlier literary career, and this performance, he felt, would have "nonplussed" the critics who engaged with the very serious young novelist and poet. Even Alex's disability was a source of amusement: "When he came to practice obstetrics," Kenner wrote, "he found the attenuated hand with its mobile thumb 'very useful for performing uterine inversions.'"

Alex showed Kenner his most precious possession: a large green safe containing thousands of paper slips divided by tabs, comprising a career in biological study and research. "My 25-year archive, quite irreplaceable," he said of it. "I had that safe especially made to be fireproof. Half-inch steel plate, and it weighs 800 kilos. In England, it took four men to carry it out."

Rattling about the Santa Barbara house, Kenner questioned his subject about nearly every topic or occupation that Alex had delved into for the preceding three decades: poetry, Neo-Romanticism, and the fact of death; sexual behavior; authority and disobedience; gerontology and aging; anarchism; the American political system; Highgate and Cambridge. Perhaps inevitably, since his subject was English literature, Kenner brought up social class. "I have none," Alex replied flatly. "My parents were middle class, my grandparents were working class. I went to school on scholarships, not on privilege. And I felt no sense of being classed, none whatsoever."

It would have been fair to ask whether people who felt thus were still less common in England than the social transformations of the postwar years suggested, and that this might have been one reason Alex moved out of the country, but Kenner didn't bring it up. Instead, he asked how an anarchist could find the American political system acceptable and of what Alex's anarchism currently consisted.

It was the system's responsiveness to protest, Alex answered—a disgraced Richard Nixon had resigned as president just two months earlier. He did still consider himself an anarchist. "It's a fact of experience," he said, "that no political doctrine is ever fulfilled in the form in which it is preached. It simply forms an amalgam with what was there already. . . . So I continue to advocate anarchy, not to bring about anarchy, but hoping to modify in the anarchic direction whatever already exists." If his old colleagues at Grey Walls Press would have been surprised by the ebullient Alex of 1974, so might his comrades from Freedom Press and the DAC have been taken aback by the squishy way the author of *Art and Social Responsibility* engaged with his political principles.

AT THE TIME HE spoke with Kenner, *The Joy of Sex* showed no signs of fading from view. In the second half of 1973, the hardcover edition had battled for the top position on the *New York Times* nonfiction best-seller list with two other self-help books, *Dr. Atkins' Diet Revolution* and *How to Be Your Own Best Friend*, by Mildred Newman and Bernard Berkowitz. Alex's book notched eleven weeks at number one, and it remained in the top ten almost the entire first half of 1974, then continued to sell strongly. Simon & Schuster would print 2.63 million copies of the trade paperback edition, putting it in competition with Jacqueline Susann's steamy novel *Once Is Not Enough* and the latest edition of the *Guinness Book of World Records* (although nowhere near the 7.1 million copies Bantam printed of the mass market paperback edition of William Peter Blatty's *The Exorcist*). By February 1975, nearly all of that print total was sold, and *Joy* had been at the top of the trade paperback best-seller list for thirteen months, making it, according to *Publishers Weekly*, one of the most successful books ever issued in that format.[12]

The book remained firmly in the public conversation. New Yorker cartoonist William Hamilton name-checked it multiple times. In one cartoon, a middle-aged man asks his wife, who is cooking, about a book on the kitchen counter: "Hey! What the hell are you cooking? This is 'The Joy of Sex'!" Gossip columnist Earl Wilson asked Paul Newman, being honored by the Film Society of Lincoln Center, why he was sporting a beard. Was it for his next movie? "Yeah, it's *The Joy of Sex*," Newman quipped. "I think I ought to have a beard for a porno picture."[13]

The title itself, in other words, had already become a cultural reference point, a punch line packing a set of meanings that everybody, seemingly, understood as soon as they heard it. When Gulf & Western Industries, owner of Paramount Pictures, announced it was buying Simon & Schuster, the *San Francisco Chronicle* couldn't help leading, "The conglomerate that brought you 'The Godfather' on film will soon be bringing you 'Joy of Sex' in paperback."[14]

In July 1974 the wire services picked up a story about a distributor that mistakenly sent twenty-five copies of *Joy of Sex* to a Webster Groves, Missouri, convent school instead of twenty-five copies of *The Joy of Cooking*. "Thus far, there hasn't been a single utterance from the school," the item reported. When the Plainedge Public Library on Long Island announced a brown-bag lunch discussion of Alex's book, the *Farmingdale Observer* noted, "Leading the discussion will be Barbara Draimin, an instructor in the SUNY Stony Brook course, Human Sexuality. Those attending should bring a sandwich."[15]

Abigail Van Buren, the advice columnist, caught the book in its intended spirit when she answered a "Dear Abby" letter from "Mixed-Up Kid," who complained that his or her parents had "started to act like they just got married," including reading *The Joy of Sex* and asking each other if they wanted to "try something new," which the writer found "disgusting." "Dear Abby" replied: "Responsible sex is joyous, and it's perfectly respectable."[16]

The book had already received one of its highest pop-culture compliments in 1974, when the humor magazine *National Lampoon* published a book-length parody entitled *The Job of Sex: A Workingman's Guide to Productive Lovemaking*, which the editors promised was "based on the practical, on-the-job experiences of hard-working orgasm technicians under the supervision of sex industry professionals." The pocket-sized paperback included a reasonably precise parody of Alex's preface to *Joy* ("You don't get high production, Grade A quality orgasms by trial and error, any more than you make an intercontinental ballistic missile by 'just tinkering about'"), and it was arranged similarly, with alphabetized entries on such thoroughly immature topics as "acting like apes," "underpants," the "vibrator-blender," "geodesic sex," "otter flopping," "towel-snapping," and something called the "Bulgarian swan dive."

Brian McConnachie, who edited the book, later recalled that the text took some six weeks to assemble; a "young man and woman" were hired to pose for photos that served as reference for a set of Chris Foss-esque illustrations. The first printing sold some one hundred thousand copies, which McConnachie considered "pretty good," and he said he received a "very nice letter from either Alex Comfort or his editor, congratulating us. Usually, we would have expected a threat of a lawsuit."[17]

James Mitchell had truly shaken up the publishing trade, and never more so than with the scale of the new book's success and notoriety. "Mitchell Beazley were these bright stars that suddenly came soaring into a rather gray firmament," said Chris Foss, who was approached by another publisher to illustrate a competing volume soon after *Joy* made a splash (Mitchell Beazley scotched the deal).[18] "We were all astonished at the success of the book. We were all going along in our funny little gray world, and suddenly this obscene amount of money came in! That's how I bought my first brand-new motorcar."[19]

Mitchell, true to form and with some help from Alex, was soon hatching or considering numerous ideas for capitalizing on the notoriety of *The Joy of Sex*. Ever since Hugh Johnson's wine encyclopedia notched one of the firm's first big triumphs, Mitchell and Johnson had been turning out new editions and spin-offs from the original, with great success. Less than six months after *Joy* first appeared in the United States, Mitchell and Alex were planning a sequel and had already started discussing a *Joy* film, possibly a spoof along the lines of Woody Allen's *Everything You Always Wanted to Know about Sex* adaptation. They began scouting for someone interested in making the movie, and after seeing an early cut of Jonathan Dana's *Sandstone* documentary, Alex enthusiastically recommended him as the director, although Mitchell never pursued the suggestion.[20] In summer 1975 they retained a Hollywood agency, Adams, Ray & Rosenberg, to represent them with the studios, stipulating that any deal had to include a $10,000 payment to Alex for his services as consultant.[21]

The film idea hung fire for a long while, but another scheme, for a *Joy of Sex* magazine, built momentum fast. Alex wanted it to be attached to a university or a reputable research institution, and initially, the Sexuality Information and Education Council of the United States (SIECUS) was interested in forging a link.[22] In early 1975 Alex and Mitchell found a London-based publisher, New Perspectives, and began working out a royalty deal for Alex to endorse the magazine and serve as contributing editor.[23] Joyce Fleming, an editor at *Psychology Today*, was to serve as day-to-day working editor, but then the board of SIECUS decided not to participate.[24] In May 1975 Mitchell Beazley pulled the plug on the project, at least for a year, pleading the need for austerity in the face of a global financial crisis.[25] The magazine scheme was never revived.

Another proposal, from an American outfit called Software Productions, to market sweatshirts with the *Joy of Sex* typographic design and even a *Joy* coloring book, ran up against Mitchell's concerns that this could violate the rights of Crown and Mitchell Beazley. Amid these efforts to extend the property, Mitchell decided in June 1974 to trademark the title *The Joy of Sex*. His immediate concern was that Playboy Enterprises or another organization might try to use the title before Alex and Mitchell Beazley could get their own magazine out.[26]

Care of Crown Publishers, Alex was receiving a large if not overwhelming volume of fan mail: some 150 letters within a little less than two years of *Joy*'s release, mostly asking where to get some of the sex aids described in the book.[27] Some were less than complimentary. A Mrs. Dick Jackson of Houston wrote to complain that her daughter had left home after surreptitiously reading *Joy* (Alex suggested in reply that perhaps lack of communication between the two had something to do with it).[28] At the opposite end of the curve, a woman from Maine wrote, "[*Joy*] underlined and re-confirmed many of the things I learned in therapy. . . . I've read alot [*sic*] of books about sexuality and ended up throwing books like *Any Woman Can* [by Alex's nemesis, David Reuben] out the window. Yours is the book that makes me feel proud and joyful about my own sexuality."

By some time in the middle of its second year on the best-seller lists, however, the right-wing morality police caught up with Alex and his book, which they seem to have missed earlier. Richard Lyman, president of Stanford University, condemned *The Joy of Sex* and other self-help books on the *Chronicle of Higher Education* campus best-seller list as "junk" and "inhumane letters," urging students to exercise "aesthetic conservatism" in choosing their light reading.[29]

Such attacks turned serious in July 1974, just seven months after Alex became a US resident, when the board of trustees of the public library in Mount Laurel, New Jersey, demanded the resignation of the librarian, Naomi Piccolo, who had received *The Joy of Sex* in a routine order with other bestsellers and placed it on a shelf of medical books. That apparently put Piccolo under scrutiny, even after she agreed to keep the book behind the librarian's desk, where young children couldn't access it. When the board decided to remove her anyway, she wasn't told the specific reason.[30]

The Mount Laurel case put *Joy* in a broad category of books that reportedly were removed from American public library shelves that year, including Kurt Vonnegut Jr.'s anti-war novel *Slaughterhouse-Five*, Philip Roth's *Portnoy's Complaint*, Eldridge Cleaver's memoir *Soul on Ice*, and even Edgar Lee Masters's half-century-old poetry collection *The Spoon Rover Anthology*. Some librarians blamed the uptick in censorship on the Supreme Court's ruling the year before in *Miller v. California*, allowing local authorities to define obscenity according to "community standards."[31]

"It's worse now than it has been in many years," said Judith Krug, director of the American Library Association's Office for Intellectual Freedom. "Libraries around the country spent much of 1974 waging anti-censorship battles at the state and local levels," it was reported the next year.[32]

The attacks briefly attained national scale in the summer of 1975 when the Senate Judiciary Committee took up the Criminal Justice Reform Act, a revision of US criminal code that shocked civil libertarians by including stringent government secrecy rules that could permit the prosecution of whistle-blowers and journalists who exposed official wrongdoing. Sponsored by a frighteningly wide assortment of senators, the bill's grab bag of provisions included the requirement of a physician's prescription to purchase big sellers like *The Joy of Sex* and *Penthouse* magazine.[33] But that item didn't stay in the bill long, and the push for a revamped criminal code collapsed amid disagreements between Democrats and Republicans.

By then, the last bulwark against *Joy* had fallen. Alex's tacit embargo on the book's British publication ended a year after it had been available in the United States, and Quartet Books was finally able to issue it in the UK in March 1974. Quartet arranged for an initial printing of twenty-five thousand copies by William Collins in Glasgow, with a highish cover price of £6.50,[34] and initially it was only a modest success.

As in the States, it received mostly excellent reviews. The *Evening Standard* picked a reviewer it must have thought perfect for the assignment. Sam Hutt, a Cambridge-educated doctor, had opened the UK's first cannabis clinic, providing marijuana tinctures to wean addicts off heroin, then became physician to members of the Who, Pink Floyd, and the Rolling Stones before launching a second career as Hank Wangford, country singer. "The basis of the whole book is PLAY," Hutt readily grasped, "something which tends to get lost in the process of growing up." His only quibble was with the UK edition's subtitle, which dropped the Cordon Bleu reference to become "A Gourmet Guide to Lovemaking." That, said Hutt, suggested the search for "super-performance rather than the ideal participation which is the real theme." He also objected to the cover price: "What about the workers?"

Others disagreed. The *Observer*'s anonymous reviewer predicted, "[*The Joy of Sex*] will replace fear of sex with nausea [brought on by its] sick-making . . . sub-pornographic illustrations [and] French brothel expressions" (not to mention the author's "nasty" obsessions with "multiple orgasms and bondage").[35] The sensational, and sensationally moralistic tabloid *News of the World* treated the book as "some kind of recipe-for-orgies," a UK reader informed Alex.[36]

Some British publications shrank from reviewing the book at all. Carmen Callil, who had worked with William Miller and John Boothe at Panther Books before they set up Quartet, was doing book publicity on the side to help her new venture, the feminist publisher Virago Press, get on its feet. One of her assignments was the UK edition of *Joy*. She and her team did "an amazing job of prepublication promotion," Boothe recalled four decades later.[37] Callil remembered "almost nothing about it"—except for "the rude letters I got from literary editors around the country, who found it disgusting: most particularly Christopher Small of the *Glasgow Herald*, who loved to cock a snoot [thumb his nose]."[38]

Some of the fears that had beset Mitchell Beazley and Crown when the book appeared in the United States were coming true in the land of its author's birth. Some UK media would not take advertising for *The Joy of Sex*, Boothe recalled. "[W. H. Smith, then] the all-powerful bookseller chain and newsagent, wouldn't stock it, while those that did tended not to display it. We were told it was a target for stealing or having the illustrations torn out."

Monetary success came when Quartet brought out a large-format paperback at £2.50. The publisher then "pulled a fast one" and produced a mass market paperback edition, with no color illustrations, which it could sell at £1.95, even though its contract with Mitchell Beazley was only for a color edition. "We didn't tell them until a couple of days before publication," Boothe recalled, "when I took John Beazley to lunch and gave him a copy. Nothing was or could be said by John or Mitchell Beazley."[39]

That wasn't the end of the troubles for *Joy* in Britain. When W. H. Smith at last agreed to carry the cheap paperback, the DPP office changed its mind about the book and served a forfeiture order under the Obscene Publications Act on the bookseller and the publisher, barring them from challenging the decision in court. "It's not very nice to find the police making idiots of themselves," Alex commented from California, adding grandiosely: "This book is being read by the whole of the civilized world." The DPP action was later reversed, however, and the mass market edition of *The Joy of Sex* would sell some eight hundred thousand copies in the UK by 1980. Just four months after the book finally saw the inside of British bookshops, in July 1974 its follow-up, *More Joy: A Lovemaking Companion to "The Joy of Sex,"* appeared in America.

Alex, who had been hard at work on it when he and Jane moved to the States, told Hugh Kenner that the new book was "about interpersonal relationships," and aside from a few entries on "masturbation," "positions," "giving head," and "simultaneous orgasm," it devoted much less space to technique than the previous book had. Its purpose, instead, was to take a step back and describe how reliable forms of contraception had changed the approach couples could take not just toward sex but also toward wider aspects of their relationship, encompassing "the re-examination of fidelity, with religio-social dogmas, personal feelings, fantasy needs, and the deeply proprietorial attitudes of one another enjoined on husband and wife by the priest, the neighbors, folklore and the attorney."

That mouthful made *More Joy* less a sequel to *The Joy of Sex* than to *Sex in Society*: a full-on endorsement of radical sexual liberation and "the extraordinary power" of gourmet sex "to transform us, as citizens of an ex-puritan culture, to our own good."[40] "No other bedroom manuals go anything like that far," Kenner declared.

This was a departure from the argument Alex had been making for years, that an end to state violence and obedience to "delinquent" authority was the key to better sex, rather than the other way around, and which had set him apart from sexual utopians like Wilhelm Reich.[41] Partly responsible for his change of view was the rise of the '60s counterculture, which appeared for a time to be leaving behind many of the older generation's assumptions about human relations, along with much of its politics, and embracing a seemingly boundless vision of personal growth potential. The more time Alex spent in California, starting in the late '60s, the more he internalized this, and nothing pushed him further in this direction than Sandstone.

ALEX HAD BEEN TO John and Barbara Williamson's retreat in Topanga Canyon several times before he and Jane moved to Montecito, and they had even gone together on occasion. Jonathan Dana found Jane quieter than Alex, "more British," and very likeable.[42] On one visit, and with Alex's enthusiastic encouragement, Jane had sex in the downstairs room with a twenty-three-year-old ex-Marine.[43] By the time they relocated, however, Sandstone in its original incarnation no longer existed.

Homeowners' associations and other more conservative forces in the area—an unincorporated stretch of Los Angeles County—had been waging a campaign for several years to rid Topanga Canyon of Sandstone and three other "growth centers," or nudist colonies. Finally the county denied John Williamson and Ed Lange, who operated Elysium Fields, a nearby nudist colony, license to operate a growth center on the grounds that their establishments were a "detriment to public welfare"—and filed a criminal case against them. Stanley Fleishman, the civil rights attorney who had argued the *Miller* case before the Supreme Court, won a reversal from the California Court of Appeals in April 1972.[44]

It was a significant legal ruling and a victory for the Williamsons but a costly one. They had initially hoped to find wealthy backers for Sandstone, but these never materialized. To keep it operating, they and their core group of residents had therefore relied on club memberships and other fees, but these never generated enough cushion to sustain a major expense like a lawsuit, and the Williamsons had put all their personal capital into the retreat.

On top of that, the county case threw John, whose presence sustained much of the atmosphere that drew people to Sandstone, into a depression. He spent much of his time in a motor home on the grounds, and he and Barbara devoted more of their energy to searching for a new property on which they could launch the next phase of their experiment in intentional community, for which they had always regarded Sandstone as proof of concept.

In December they accepted an offer for the Topanga Canyon property, announced its closing, and on December 28 held a going-away party. Alex, still completing the move from the UK, was not there. By the following March, the Williamsons had taken an option on a couple of hundred acres along the Flathead River in Montana and decamped for their new home.[45]

That didn't stop Alex from giving Sandstone a prominent place in his new book, since he had come to see the retreat and its core community as an embodiment of his hopes for a less authoritarian, less anxious way of life. Much of what went into *More Joy* was based on his observations there, and he devoted eight pages, with illustrations, specifically to a description of the place as well as a behavioral analysis of its effect on residents and visitors. What he liked about Sandstone was its openness. At other purported sensitivity centers that combined workshops and seminars with sexual encounters, he wrote, a high proportion of visitors "have the air of going through a lot of psycho-makework and verbal behaviors when the real object of the exercise is to get laid." At Sandstone, on the other hand, "one could quite frankly go to get laid—but with that out of the way, participants were surprised to find that sensitivity, encounter and a good deal of genuine self-education quite often followed." What the place was most like was not a brothel but "a wholly relaxed home," where the keynote was "innocence once the freakout produced in strangers by openness was over."[46]

Alex had always preached the ills of anxious sex, and in this respect, Sandstone seemed to him to have cracked the code. Jealousy subsided, playfulness and childishness reemerged, "low-dominance" individuals of both sexes developed greater self-esteem, and stereotypes about age were punctured, all because couples got used to the notion of having sex openly, in company. Most important, Alex said, "was the exorcism of all the custodial anxieties of conventional marriage." While "there were a few bad trips" when, for example, one partner went downstairs and the other found himself or herself alone, "these would be cured by learning that all things usually come to him or her who waits."[47]

While all this seemed very new to an English visitor, and even to many Americans at the time, Sandstone, minus its more contemporary trappings, fit easily into a tradition of intentional communities going back more than a century in the United States, many of which adopted a less proprietary approach to marriage and sex.[48]

Sandstone was a similarly utopian experiment, with an added dash of futurism. Alex learned more about this in his conversations with

John Williamson, the blue-eyed, soft-spoken visionary who concocted it. Others who got to know Williamson in these years used words like "intense," "complex," "deep," and "a mystery" to describe him. But he was really a kind of anti-guru—Church of Scientology founder L. Ron Hubbard was his idea of evil.[49] Weaving a fabric of theory around Sandstone and the more ambitious successor community he had conceived, called "Project Synergy," he avoided, as much as possible, exercising a leadership role. Lacking a high school degree, he had become an engineer while in the military and worked on the Polaris missile program before starting his own company. He spoke little about his past, and some Sandstone habitués spun fantasies that he was a CIA agent or a trained killer. Because he talked so little—Barbara was his only close confidant—he "could seem sinister one day, saintly the next, and with no apparent effort his mood altered the atmosphere of the entire house and influenced everyone within it," Gay Talese wrote.[50]

What did Williamson intend with his experiments in human relations? His thinking was an uneasy synthesis of ideas bubbling up in the nexus between the academic world and popular culture in the postwar decades, some of which were close to Alex's and some not, ranging from Abraham Maslow's humanistic psychology and anarchism's focus on small, autonomous communities to the proto-New Age theorizing of the French scientist and philosopher Pierre Theilard de Chardin to cybernetics, systems analysis, libertarianism, apocalyptic fears, and the science fiction of Robert Heinlein. *Stranger in a Strange Land*, Heinlein's 1961 novel about a gifted human raised on Mars who founds a religion whose inner circle of attractive, polyamorous men and women recruit outer circles of ordinary members and financial backers, could have been a rough aspirational model for the Williamsons' retreat. "Heinlein would have loved Sandstone," said Peter Lert, a DJ, recording engineer, and frequent visitor.[51] John Williamson's favorite book was Ayn Rand's 1957 cult novel *Atlas Shrugged*, in which a group of railroad and steel barons and "men of the mind" lead a strike against a tyrannical, bureaucratic government.

Out of all this, Williamson developed an analysis which he delivered in talks across the country once Sandstone became well known. Briefly, he believed that human society had become too complex, no longer fostered effective communication, and by the mid-'70s would fall into "violent confrontations" leading to an ecological disaster and a "massive human regression to more simplistic tribal societies." One branch of society would hurtle into "wholesale destruction." The other, "positive" branch would develop new, improved tribal structures and continue the process of human evolution. For it to succeed, however, would require much better communication: not just verbal but also "kinesthetic," which involved "touch, body contact, and most importantly, sex."[52]

Williamson, in other words, was on a mission to rescue the salvageable portion of the human race from apocalypse. Sandstone was the trial run and Project Synergy the scaled-up version, which he estimated would cost $10 million to develop in Montana.[53] (He never was able to raise the money, perhaps in part because his outline of the project was too vague for many people to comprehend.)

Magi Discoe, who was a core member, recalled that it was understood that Sandstone was "just the first stage of a project to form an intentional community."[54] But John and Barbara kept their politics mostly to themselves, recalled Lert,[55] and it's doubtful that Alex or many other visitors realized they were part of a libertarian survivalist scheme to save a self-selected elite remnant of humanity from certain extinction. None of Williamson's more extreme ideas pop up in anything Alex wrote about the retreat, nor do they in Talese's eventual book, *Thy Neighbor's Wife*, much of which is about the Williamsons and their circle. Day to day, John was too busy maintaining the property and fielding questions about nudity, open sexuality, and his relations with county officials to talk much about his more grandiose schemes.

Besides which, many of the residents and guests found Sandstone terrifically rewarding just as it was. Betty Dodson, according to Talese, called it "probably the only place in the nation where recreational sex could be indulged in by women in a pleasant and open environment."[56]

Magen O'Farrell, who lived there with her mother from ages ten to twelve—the only child ever at the retreat—and was mentored by another member, Sally Binford, toward a career in anthropology, later had only good things to say about her time at Sandstone. "I loved it," she recalled. She stayed away from the main house on Wednesday and Saturday nights but "wasn't at all shocked" by the nudity and physicality she observed at other times. "If people were naked and affectionate in other places, that was beautiful and that's what I was being taught at the time."[57] She participated in Sandstone's Monday night "family meetings," generally was treated like an adult, and never experienced any inappropriate behavior from the other residents or guests. John she found "warm and funny"; he would spend time and tell jokes and sometimes talk to her about more complex topics, "like a grandfather teaching a granddaughter."

Wiliamson's ideas were not the only thing Alex didn't notice about Sandstone. Another was the hard work it demanded. The retreat was at high risk from forest fires, which required constant clearing of brush. Once a raging fire almost forced the residents to evacuate; the place was saved by an ingenious outdoor sprinkler system John had devised. Mudslides were another pressing problem, and two bulldozers seemed to constantly be in use. When a reporter from *Rolling Stone* asked John what his job was at the retreat, he replied, "I move rocks." Cooking, cleaning, food shopping, processing paperwork, and keeping the grounds in immaculate condition occupied most of the residents' time between the Wednesday and weekend parties. What Alex saw was the show put on for guests like himself.

Mostly what Alex missed—as did most of the legion of journalists and self-appointed experts who wrote about the retreat—was the deeper dramas that periodically consumed the inner Sandstone community. The Williamsons were trying to put together a select group of people who could embody the tightly knit lifestyle they envisioned, which they felt was necessary to survive the coming "violent confrontations." But that lifestyle was a work in progress. When core members disagreed or wanted to move on from open sexuality or simply wanted to be somewhere else, all-too-familiar emotions like jealousy, resentment, and possessiveness popped back up.

John's approach "was very much 'my way or the highway,'" recalled Magi Discoe. "If you left, he washed his hands of you." When she fell in love with a member of the documentary film crew and announced she was moving to the San Francisco Bay Area with him, John ordered her off the property and barred her from reentering. She had no money at the time, barely any clothes or other possessions, and had to start all over with the help of friends outside the community she had come to love.[58] Later, Barbara recalled only vaguely that Magi "couldn't face the truth."[59]

On at least one occasion, matters turned violent and John decided to call a meeting. A resident had barricaded herself in her room for weeks when her jealous boyfriend began to abuse her physically. John listened to both sides and ordered the man, with whom he was close, to move out. "I will not, or ever, allow this type of behavior at Sandstone," he said. "It's not what it's about."[60] This speaks to the Williamsons' commitment to sexual equality—Barbara would not tolerate demeaning language or behavior toward women—but also to the difficulty of achieving their ideal of open, non-possessive sexuality.[61]

Such incidents never made it into Alex's account of Sandstone in *More Joy*, although all occurred during the period when he was visiting often, perhaps because he was more interested in the concept than in the details. "I don't think he ever got into the politics of the place," recalled Marty Zitter, a core member who was Sandstone's ebullient de facto outreach director. But he found Alex's description of the retreat in *More Joy* "just spectacular": "there was very little to add on the subject."[62]

Sandstone was in many ways a considerable success. It didn't yield the permanent community the Williamsons had hoped for, but most people who spent extended time there found the experience unique and rewarding and continued to think so years later. What Alex seemed not to understand was that the retreat owed its success largely to the style and personalities of the Williamsons and the commitment of some of the core members, like Marty Zitter and Magi Discoe, rather than to a well-thought-out structure or John's apocalyptic futurism. Alex mistook Sandstone for the beginnings of a new politics of human relations when it really embodied an escape from politics: a temporary one.

MORE JOY, NEVERTHELESS, WAS full of ideas and notions Alex would have encountered during his weekends in Topanga Canyon. "Proprietary" feelings toward one's partner were on the way out. Jealousy ("Othello and all that") was a social convention that people learn. "Secure and communicating couples which include each other in all their fantasies and pleasures aren't jealous." Open sex and mutual observation could cure a lot of hang-ups: penis size, for instance. "Primary relationships" between couples were not necessarily threatened by "secondary relationships," since no two people could be entirely sufficient unto each other.[63] Not surprisingly, then, Alex devoted a great deal of space to sharing—not the same thing as swapping partners, he insisted, and not always "group sex" as such—and "extended sexuality," sexual encounters between three or more people.

More Joy went further than its predecessor in urging couples to shake off traditional roles and assumptions in sex play. It contained a fair amount of advice on anal sex (but no illustrations of the act). It also delved deeper into against-the-grain fantasies: "Try experiencing maleness if it doesn't specially attract you, or femaleness if you're self-consciously male." Aggressive types could experience helplessness by way of bondage, less assertive types might try completely controlling their partner. Men should be able to turn on and satisfy a woman without an erection but too often were not. "Unfulfilled biological drives toward motherhood" in childless women were pure folklore. Alex inveighed against common assumptions that people with disabilities do not want or need sex and that older people lose their sex drive, and he argued strongly that society do more to accept and accommodate them.[64] He also warned against con artists posing as sex therapists, a profession his earlier book was doing much to encourage.

The focus was still largely on heterosexual couples, however, and the emphasis on male needs. Boys needed to learn to recognize "predatory" behavior in the opposite sex. If a girl inadvertently turns a boy on, she should let him show her how to give him an orgasm by hand. "Being deeply penetrated by a man you love and trust," Alex assured his female readers, "is about the best of all feminine experiences." Sexually speaking, alcoholism was mainly a problem in that it makes getting an erection more difficult, leading to "habitual impotence." Women should consider plastic surgery if they no longer turned on their partner, Alex said, but he suggested nothing of the sort for men. And an entry on sexual surrogates focused entirely on surrogates for men.[65]

Other misconceptions and prejudices carried over from *More Joy*'s predecessor, along with some new ones. An entire section on special needs and problems failed to mention rape as an issue between the sexes, just as Alex had neglected to do in *The Joy of Sex*. Alex stuck to his argument about homosexuality, contending that the Gay Liberation Movement was wrong to reinforce the "totally erroneous idea that there are two kinds of people, gay and straight." In his new book, he dismissed the idea that Black men have larger genitals than white men as "bunk." But in a short section entitled "Soul Power," he added the cringe-inducingly dubious compliment that Black culture had never lost its "body sense" compared to its white counterpart and wasn't "physically uptight." "Many black people are better at sex than anxious Wasps," he added, "for the same reason that they dance much better."[66]

Rather like John Williamson with his speculations about future human communities, Alex in *More Joy* was trying to describe the sexual etiquette and possibilities of the near future, at least for hetero couples. "What the authors say here about couple relationships and nonpossession," he wrote in the preface—again Comfort was billed as "editor"—"represents roughly what the equivalent of respectable middle-class morality will approve in about ten years' time."[67] Unlike Williamson, he was describing what he expected to be a wholesale change of practice for society in general, or at least the broad middle class, not the way forward for an elite remnant of a society that was about to collapse.

Just the same, *More Joy* was a more ambitious book than *The Joy of Sex*. It was a guide for couples in a new era of greater sexual freedom. Alex split it into sections and alphabetical entries, just like the previous book, and devoted a good deal of space to issues like hostility, aggression, selfishness, and performance. As always, the emphasis was on relieving anxiety from the practice of sex. He offered advice on depression, prostate health, sex for people with weight issues, and resources such as behavior therapy, meditation, and psychoanalysis.

The heart of the book, however, was the nearly forty-page section titled "Couples and Others," which including sharing, swinging, threesomes, and Alex's description of Sandstone. Two years earlier, *The Joy of Sex* had barely touched on these matters. Now Alex was making open or extended sexuality a major part of the menu. For the first time, this led to serious problems with his publishers.

Working with the Mitchell Beazley crew on *Joy*, Alex "was all sweetness and light," recalled Max Monsarrat, his editor on both books. But when he turned in the manuscript of *More Joy* to Mitchell Beazley and Crown, the latter "wanted major changes in the text, and Alex was truculent," Monsarrat said. The revisions were nearly all in "Couples and Others," and Monsarrat found himself in the position of go-between, conveying objections and suggestions back and forth between the parties, even traveling to the States to meet with Alex on the West Coast and Nat Wartels on the East Coast during one especially troublesome stretch. Wartels and Crown were adamant, and Alex "could be very abusive," said Monsarrat. "He took a bit of time to think that somebody might have a better idea than he did."[68]

The subject of open relationships was neither a new one, nor did it pop exclusively out of Alex's experience at Sandstone. The movie *Bob & Carol & Ted & Alice* had been a hit in 1970, and even as Alex was writing *More Joy*, the book *Open Marriage: A New Lifestyle for Couples* was rising on the best-seller lists. But the stakes were higher this time. Since *The Joy of Sex* was a hit, Crown was paying more for the right to bring it out in the United States, and the first hardback printing would be 250,000 copies, far beyond the 15,000 the publisher had initially produced of *Joy*.[69] That made Crown leery of any complications.

After a good deal of diplomacy on Monsarrat's part, the two sides compromised. Rather than making wholesale changes, Alex inserted some qualifiers into the text—"probably," "can be," "tend to be"—along with warnings that not every couple share the same preferences or degree of curiosity. A couple should not go into a threesome or foursome "as amateur therapists, or persuade people to share, even at the least sexual level, because they think it would do them good," he wrote.[70]

Crown and Mitchell Beazley would see more of the stubborn, abrasive side of Alex's personality in coming years, but the text he had turned in to them had the same disarmingly relaxed, humorous tone as *Joy*. Nowhere did he go so far as to suggest the replacement of the traditional family with something like "universal kinship," as he had in "Sexuality in a Zero Growth Society" a couple of years earlier. *More Joy* was still a book for couples, even if they chose to define the term in a more open-ended way.

Accordingly, Mitchell Beazley stuck faithfully to the design it had created for *The Joy of Sex*. Charlie Raymond again supplied a section of paintings, and Chris Foss was back with drawings of a couple in action, only this time the illustrators' names appeared on the cover, and a pair of younger, more conventionally attractive models replaced Charlie and Edeltraud. One drawing, taken from a photo, of couples lounging in the living room at Sandstone, included a recognizable John Williamson, watching amiably from his perch by the fireplace, and several drawings included more than one couple. Cover design, typefaces, and layout all remained the same, and Alex again was credited only as editor.

More Joy appeared officially on September 10, 1974, two years after its predecessor, but was already in a second printing by then. Some three hundred thousand copies had shipped by publication date, Crown reported. Whereas only the *Playboy* and *Psychology Today* book clubs had picked *The Joy of Sex* for their members, *More Joy* was embraced by the powerful Literary Guild, guaranteeing that millions of middle-class households would be tempted to acquire a copy through the mail.[71] It went on to become the fourth-largest nonfiction bestseller of the year in the United States, according to *Publishers Weekly* (the top spot went to Marabel Morgan's *The Total Woman*, an extremely unliberated set of suggestions for how a woman could please her man).[72]

When critics reviewed *More Joy*, the amount of space devoted to "sharing" didn't escape them, and neither did a passage under the heading "Selfishness," in which Alex let himself expand on the power of better sex to liberate society. "People who have eroticized their experience of themselves and the world are, on the one hand, inconveniently unwarlike," he asserted—"they'd rather stay and make love than kill Vietnamese or Hungarians—and, on the other, violently combative in resisting goons, political salesmen, racists and 'garbage' people generally who threaten the personal freedom they've attained and want to see others share." These "garbage" people, who ruled "most great powers," he diagnosed as suffering from an "inability to eroticize and hence humanize their experience," while "money-grubbing and power-hunting" were due to "early distortions of body image and of self-esteem."[73]

The originality of Alex's earlier analyses of political power had given way to simplistic psychologizing and a reductive assertion that more of the right kind of sex equals less violence and oppression. "This is not only fuzzy thinking cast in hackneyed language," said *SCREW*'s Michael Perkins, in one of the sharpest reviews of the new book, "not only a simple-minded rendering of the ideas of Herbert Marcuse in *Eros and Civilization*, it is fascistic—'garbage' people?—and condescending ('they themselves have sex')." *More Joy* was "obviously written in a rush, to capitalize on a market situation," Perkins concluded.[74]

Most reviewers said little to nothing about Alex's attempts to wring a political message out of his sexual teachings, although several others joined Perkins in wondering who the "garbage people" were. Some critics who had praised *The Joy of Sex* thought the author had gone too far in his latest offering. "The emphasis on adding some extra people into the recipe would send most of us McDonald's types to the Rolaid counter," concluded Ellen Goodman in the *Boston Globe*.[75] In the *Los Angeles Times*, Digby Diehl, the books editor, had praised the "wholesome, balanced approach to sexual possibility" in *The Joy of Sex*, but took *More Joy* to task for "trying to make some fairly exotic minority sexual tastes sound as though any couple left huddled cold and alone in the isolation of their private bedroom is missing out on the rest of America who are all watching, swinging and swapping."[76]

These reviews at least approached the book sympathetically. Perkins thought it "useful" despite his criticisms. This time around, however, Alex had not caught conservative book critics off guard. Whereas few had been aware enough of *The Joy of Sex* to write about it, several actually decided to review *More Joy*. The most widely read was most likely an unsigned review in *Time*. Written as a letter to Alex from a housewife named "Betty Jo," it was a mercilessly sarcastic rip on Alex's "selfless" expedition to watch people make love at Sandstone, his "touching tale of the crippled man who carries on a fulfilling sex life with his big toe," his urging heterosexual men to explore their bisexual side, and his suggestion that batacas (soft, cloth-covered, plastic-foam bats) could be fun to play with in bed.[77]

The author may not have realized that she (or he) had permission to discuss some of these matters in a mainstream newsweekly, even in a humorous tone, because of the efforts of Alex and the women and men who had preceded him to extend the bounds of acceptability in mainstream publishing. The aim of the *Time* review was to show up Alex's books as another example of the snobbism of America's coastal elites: their contempt for "normal" people and "housewives" like Betty Jo, who nevertheless could spot their ludicrousness a mile away. "Your *Joy* books got raves from big sex experts in California, and . . . some people in the Midwest are actually showing up at bookstores [to buy it]." But Betty Jo was distressed that Alex advised acceptance when a daughter learned to masturbate, and the reviewer couldn't help expressing impatience with his willingness to join *Penthouse* in "yammering away on the sex life of amputees."

Why the hostility, especially from a magazine like *Time*, which profited from its coverage of trends like the sexual revolution? One reason may have been the quickening of the cultural backlash that had always been rumbling barely beneath the surface and was simultaneously finding ways to coopt the trend.

Nixon, who resigned the presidency weeks before *More Joy* appeared, had never tired of appealing to the conservative Silent Majority that supposedly remained loyal to him. Feminists and the gay and lesbian communities were demanding their rights and mainstream acceptance, sometimes successfully, but cultural reactionaries were using opposition to these movements as a rallying point, and arguably succeeding far more at making sexuality a political issue. Soon afterward, "secular humanism" would become a bogeyman of fundamentalist Christians and their allies, directly targeting intellectual figures like Alex.

Phyllis Schlafly had already launched her crusade against the Equal Rights Amendment to the Constitution, and America was just a few years away from the launch of pop singer Anita Bryant's antigay "Protect America's Children" campaign, the foundation of the evangelical pressure group Moral Majority, and the election of Ronald Reagan. Mainstream media like the *New York Times*, the *Washington Post*, and the big newsweeklies were becoming concerned—especially after taking a prominent role in investigating and exposing Nixon's crimes—that they might be losing the confidence of Middle America. That being the case, a popular book promoting sexual freedom looked like fair game for cheap satire.

More Joy received plenty of good reviews, and as a publishing venture it scored Alex and his collaborators another success. But it could not repeat the phenomenon that was *Joy*. It climbed into the upper regions of 1974 best sellers despite only coming out in September, but at the end of the year it left booksellers somewhat disillusioned because they had overordered it.[78] That didn't stop Simon & Schuster from printing one million copies of the book in trade paperback format the following May, including fifty thousand boxed sets of the two books, and supporting the launch with a $50,000 advertising campaign. The paperback, its title modified to *More Joy of Sex*, also sold well, but when it faded, the original was still occupying space on the best-seller lists.[79]

Why was *More Joy* not a longer-lasting success? Alex and Mitchell Beazley had opted to stick as closely as possible to the look, feel, and tone of their first book, rather than produce something dramatically different. This guaranteed them strong performance from its successor but not outperformance. Chris Foss felt the illustrations lacked the "warmth and lucidity" of those in the first book. The models had less personality than Charlie and Edeltraud, on top of which Chris was given reference photos to draw from, rather than being allowed to take them himself. As a result, he didn't have the chance to develop a rapport with his subjects, Overall, he found the second book visually "rather bland."[80]

The first book's novelty, too, was beginning to wear off. Sex books were flooding mainstream bookshops on the heels of *Joy*, cutting into *More Joy*'s trade. Erica Jong recalled that after her sexually explicit novel *Fear of Flying* became a breakout softcover bestseller in late 1974, Dick Snyder at Simon & Schuster suggested she write a sex book from a woman's perspective: *The Joy of Women*, perhaps. Jong turned him down, concerned that she might become too firmly typecast as a sex writer.[81] Ironically, the years following the publication of the original *Joy* also saw a boom in sex manuals aimed at a conservative Christian audience; while they endorsed good sex as a natural feature of a good marriage, they reinforced all the older assumptions about premarital virginity, the man's primacy in the relationship, and the woman's body as the locus of most sexual problems.*

Once readers had *More Joy* in their hands, they found that it wasn't a sex manual. It only introduced a few new positions and techniques.

* Two of the most popular of these books, which sold in the millions, were *The Total Woman* by Maribel Morgan (1973) and *The Act of Marriage: The Beauty of Sexual Love* (1976), by Tim and Beverly LaHaye. Amy DeRogatis, "What Would Jesus Do? Sexuality and Salvation in Protestant Evangelical Sex Manuals, 1950s to the Present," *Church History: Studies in Christianity and Culture*, March 2005. Tim LaHaye, a hard-right evangelical pastor, would later co-author the wildly successful *Left Behind* series of Christian doomsday novels.

Most of the book, including "Couples and Others," was devoted to the place of sex in other aspects of a couple's lives. This was exactly as it should be, commented Eleanor Links Hoover in *Human Behavior* magazine. "[Comfort] pokes more deeply into our widespread confusion over the expectations we place on love, marriage and relationship," she noted perceptively. "He suggests that now that sex is no longer such a hang-up for many, relationship is where our taboos lie."[82]

Alex may have been wrong to suggest that Sandstone was the future of the American household, and he certainly exaggerated the political implications of the loosening sexual culture. He was wrong especially to think that liberation for gay, lesbian, and other gender-nonconforming people was not or should not be the next stage of the sexual revolution, when it already was. But he was correct that household patterns were shifting, that the pattern of people's sexual lives was changing, and that these changes were introducing people to new possibilities and fresh anxieties that would not go away, despite the failure of mainstream culture and the law to keep up. This was a more complicated message than the one he had delivered in *Joy* and less likely to resonate with as large a public.

IN AN INTERVIEW WITH an Associated Press reporter in January 1975, Alex announced that he would be writing no more sex manuals. "I think we've about exhausted the subject," he said. He would, however, be writing a book on aging: one that might help to shape a "generation of old people who are totally militant and won't take anything from anybody."[83]

Less than a couple of months after *More Joy* appeared, he had embarked on a course of lectures, panel discussions, and media interviews around the United States that advertised his shift from sex to aging. He was as engaging and amusing as ever, especially when taking questions from audiences, but while he still answered questions about sex and sexual behavior—and was at last admitting that he had written, not just edited, *Joy* and *More Joy*—his announced subject was old age.[84]

In conversation, he toggled back and forth between two aspects of the topic: the need to pursue research on life extension, and the need for society—especially the medical profession—to improve its treatment of elderly people. On the first point, he urged the scientific community to take up research on the aging process that could yield faster results: the "test-battery" method he had been advocating for years. He exhorted his audiences to write to their members of Congress to demand funding for the new National Institute of Aging, which he hoped would take this approach.[85] On the second, he called for a change in American cultural attitudes toward the aged, who were too often pigeonholed as "unintelligent, uneducable, unemployable and asexual."[86]

Sometimes he had to press the point. "I've practically given up on lecturing about sex," he told an audience at Lutheran Hospital in Baltimore in May. "You can all read, after all." When questions related to *The Joy of Sex* persisted, he said, "I want you to understand, this is not the only book I've ever written. It's just the only one I managed to sell."[87]

As it happened, the next book of Alex's to appear in the United States was about sex as well: the belated American publication of *Come Out to Play*, his dozen-year-old satire of NATO and the British class system in which he created the world's first sex clinic (albeit fictional) and proposed the ultimate aphrodisiac. The satire was dated and probably too culturally specific for most America readers, but Crown brought it out anyway in hopes of reaping some further sales off *Joy*'s success.

Anatole Broyard, the redoubtable *New York Times* book critic, pounced on the novel—characters, plot, satire and all—and suggested that "full sexual satisfaction had eliminated [the author's] superego-dictated need to write well."[88] Other reviewers were kinder, but the most balanced evaluation came from Tom Dowling of the *Washington Star*: "[*Come Out to Play*] holds up as prophecy and fails as wit. . . . [Its] cleverness depends entirely on a public that would be astounded to see a book like 'The Joy of Sex' in the drugstores. That public no longer exists."[89]

One reason for reissuing the book may have been that Alex still hoped to sell his yarn to Hollywood. "For my hero, I took the world's biggest know-it-all. Some people said it was autobiographical," he told an interviewer in April. "We're getting interest from moviemakers on it." "I could see Peter Sellers in the role of the hero," he said, just as he had a dozen years earlier.[90]

Cheap paperback publishers were flooding the market with knock-off sex books, and another of Alex's earlier titles, *Sex in Society*, at last found a US publisher at about the same time: Award Books, which added some mildly titillating illustrations of a couple in action that had nothing to do with the text but suggested the look of *The Joy of Sex*. A banner across the cover announced that this was "the only fully illustrated edition" of a book that contained not a single description of a sex act. Simultaneous with its reissue of Alex's book, Award was publishing *The Sensuous New Yorker* by Bernhardt J. Hurwood, which it hailed as "the hot underground guide everyone's talking about."

The two reissues consumed little to none of Alex's time, but another matter was competing for his attention just as he was attempting to relaunch himself in the field of aging. In May, less than a year and a half after joining, he left the Center for the Study of Democratic Institutions and demanded it return $93,000 in royalties from sales of *The Joy of Sex*. He would not be handing over the additional $61,600 estimated for the remainder of the year. The CSDI had received the money in accordance with the deal Alex had worked out before joining full-time, under which he turned over 80 percent of royalties on the book and took a salary in return.

The think tank's financial situation had become desperate, and Malcolm Moos, who had taken over from Hutchins as president the previous June, had been unable to raise funds to shore it up. After a fierce fight, the CSDI board rejected a plan by Moos, that Alex had supported, to drastically pare back the staff and fellowships and remain in Santa Barbara. Instead, it opted to sell its headquarters and reestablish the center with a very small staff at the University of Chicago, with Hutchins back in charge, while keeping a small group in Santa Barbara mainly to publish the *Center Report*. To make the move, it was counting on Alex's money, and so it would keep him on as the sole full-time senior fellow, dismissing all the others. That was not acceptable, he told an Associated Press reporter after the board voted. By reorganizing and moving to Chicago, they were effectively breaking their contract with him. "The center no longer exists. What there is here now is humbug, a pretense," he said. "My attorneys are demanding the return of funds and we will sue in the event they don't return them."[91]

The CSDI's collapse made national headlines and caused a great deal of alarm in Santa Barbara, where a citizens' group, fearing the loss of jobs and spending it pumped into the local economy, unsuccessfully asked the state attorney general to look into blocking the move.[92] The fight between the various factions was bitter, hyperbolic, and played out in full public view. Alex's fury came across each of the many times he spoke to reporters on the subject. Asked why matters had taken such a turn, he replied, "For exactly the same reason Satan was expelled from heaven. Certain people got carried away by their sense of injured merit."[93] He was referring, at least partly, to Hutchins, for whom he had lost nearly all respect. "This is an attempt to rip off my money," he told the *New York Times*. "Hutchins and the rest of the board bear as much relationship to the Center as Al Capone and his men do."[94]

Harry Ashmore, a Pulitzer Prize–winning journalist and board member in the Hutchins camp, replied to Alex's attacks by accusing him of having "spent too much time doing field work on his books." "It has addled his brain," he added.[95]

In July Alex followed up on his threat, filing a $406,000 lawsuit in US District Court in Los Angeles, including $250,000 in damages plus $63,000 in severance pay, against the Fund for the Republic, the center's governing body. When the CSDI announced the reorganization and the dismissal of the other fellows, it had effectively destroyed the intellectual environment Alex had been promised, the suit charged. Therefore, it had breached its contract and legally dissolved itself as defined in the contract. He also alleged that the CSDI had made false statements to him about its financial prospects and the severance payments he would be entitled to if it dissolved.[96] In October, the CSDI countersued for $3.08 million, alleging in federal court that Alex had published *More Joy* specifically to cut into sales of *The Joy of Sex*, thereby depriving the CSDI of income, and had defamed it in the news media. He had done so, moreover, while employed by the center and using its "facilities and staff to accomplish said work."

Through his lawyer, Alex denied all the allegations.[97] The following February, he amended his complaint, accusing the CSDI of misleading him about its financial condition when it lured him. He was not an iota less angry about the entire matter. In his filing, he described the management and control of the center as "not in the nature of a democracy, but . . . a monarchy or oligarchy beset with machinations and intrigues more typical of a Byzantine house of ill repute." He upped his demand for damages to $506,320.[98]

As the two lawsuits slowly crawled through the court, Alex, Harvey Wheeler, and another ex-center fellow, John Wilkinson, a former professor at the University of California, Santa Barbara, and an early leader in computer forecasting, announced in September 1975 that they were setting up a new think tank in Santa Barbara, the Institute for Higher Studies (IHS).[99] In interviews and a rather pompous document outlining their plans, they described not a typical research center but "a continuing project of prevision" that nonetheless sounded like a new and improved version of Hutchins's creation, geared to help them raise money for specific projects they wanted to launch. Joining them was Richard Lewis, a veteran television producer, to develop TV documentaries and dramatizations that would bring the fellows' ideas to a wider audience. It was a project Wilkinson had been hatching with Moos at the CSDI before Hutchins announced the reorganization.[100]

Pointedly, the IHS opened an office in a building on Garden Street in downtown Santa Barbara—the exact opposite of the isolated, Shangri-la-like setting Hutchins had created for his center and a sign that, unlike Hutchins, Alex's crew would welcome community input. It would also be more democratically run: a "self-governing cooperative community of Fellows," all of its property and assets vested in the IHS "as a commonwealth," according to a press release.

Ideas for taking their work to the broader public that the trio of fellows discussed with a reporter from a local paper in October included "a national sex anxiety test with audience participation," conducted by Alex; a documentary TV series on human biology, also with Alex; and a "network adventure series teaching science fact through science dramatization." The IHS reported that it was negotiating with KCET, the public broadcasting station in Los Angeles, about "various TV show possibilities," but nothing was yet decided. Other planned spin-offs included a scholarly quarterly, tentatively titled *Social Biology and Social Science*, and conferences, starting with a weekend event at UC Santa Barbara titled "Future Think—1976 to 2176," with Alex discussing life extension and the aging process.

Alex was hoping the IHS would serve as the institutional catalyst for his long-hoped-for test-battery project on human aging as well as a new study of what he called "the biology of religion," but how was he to find the necessary donors at a time when a seasoned fund-raiser like Hutchins had failed to save his own organization? The IHS proposed wooing a core group of some one hundred "charter patrons" who would have the privilege of attending its programs and receiving autographed copies of limited editions of the papers it produced. It would also be offering consultancy services—stemming, for example, from Alex's work on aging—to corporations engaged in relevant activities, including annual executive seminars at the institute. Alex promised, however, that the IHS "will not be a champagne operation" and donor money would be spent responsibly, another dig at the free-spending Hutchins.

That said, Alex knew that assembling a critical mass of donors would take time. Meanwhile he had someone at hand eager to work with him on new projects with the potential to score another popular success. James Mitchell was riding high with the triumph of the *Joy* books and wanted Alex to remain part of Mitchell Beazley's brain trust. The firm was now paying him a monthly consulting fee, but in May, three months after the CSDI imploded and Alex quit, they signed an agreement by which the firm would convert that fee into a more generous salary related to expected earnings on his next book. He would also get a photocopy machine for his home office paid for by Mitchell Beazley, along with expenses and secretarial assistance as needed. The deal went through numerous revisions to protect him from the UK tax collector, and Alex would be free to meet any existing obligations, such as editing *Experimental Gerontology*, without any involvement from Mitchell Beazley.[101]

Over the next several months, they discussed several new projects, including a book on religion, which they referred to informally as "The Joy of God"; a new collection of poetry; and an ambitious, multivolume general encyclopedia that Mitchell was keen to produce with Alex as consultant, talent scout, and contributing author. Mitchell was also eager to extend the franchise that the *Joy* books had launched. He already had authors lined up to write *The Joy of Gay Sex* and *The Joy of Lesbian Sex*, which Mitchell Beazley would produce and Crown would publish in 1977, and he wanted Alex to work with him on a comprehensive *Joy of Sexual Knowledge*.

But Alex wasn't interested in developing that sort of material. In November he wrote Mitchell, "I am not putting my name to any more sex books of any kind." (Despite that statement, there were two exceptions: a book on sex for disabled people and an edited anthology of erotic poetry.) "This is absolutely essential image-wise," he explained. Otherwise he would be accused of cheap exploitation, and attention would be diverted from his work on aging. He might be willing to come back to sex later, "but not until at least 3 major bestsellers on other topics have been interposed."[102] He seemed awfully sure that he had more mega-successes in him, and Mitchell Beazley seemed to agree. In August, Alex had turned in a first draft of his next book, *A Good Age*, a kind of guidebook and manifesto for the elderly, which Mitchell himself called "splendid" and "saleable."[103]

CHAPTER 19

The Geriatrician (1975–1980)

Alex had been writing intermittently about the condition and treatment of the aged since he published his article "On Gerontophobia" in 1967, and he had debunked the myths about sexuality among the elderly in *The Joy of Sex* and *More Joy*. Now he was in America, where an upsurge of activism among seniors had been ongoing for some years. The American Association of Retired Persons (AARP), a lobbying and advocacy organization, was founded in 1958 and had some thirty million members by the early '70s.

In 1970, a more radical group, the Gray Panthers—officially, the Consultation of Older and Younger Adults—was founded in Philadelphia by Maggie Kuhn, an activist and retired social researcher for the United Presbyterian Church. The Panthers included many veterans of the labor struggles of the '30s and also made a point of reaching out to teens and young adults, aiming to build a cross-generational movement for social justice. Initially the Panthers adopted a decentralized organizational structure that delegated power to local networks and developed a shared leadership arrangement instead of a hierarchical structure. Some of the local networks included clinics and other resources for self-help. Their social and political agenda included nationalizing transportation and the oil industry, opposing nuclear energy and "the concentration of corporate power," and defending Social Security and Medicare against attacks from the right.[1]

The Panthers were a much smaller organization than the AARP, but their six thousand or so members were intensely involved, and they helped change the way American society viewed the aged. Kuhn insisted on talking about sex among the aged and denounced the practice of shunting them into nursing homes and elder communities, which she tagged as "glorified playpens" if not worse. The Panthers knew how to get their point across. In August 1975 they organized a guerrilla theater action outside an American Medical Association convention in Atlantic City, New Jersey. In one skit, a doctor auctioned off old people to nursing homes: the Kill 'Em Quick Home, the One Nurse Home, the Way to Heaven Home, and so on.[2]

Soon after he moved to the United States, Alex made friends with Kuhn and began speaking at Gray Panther meetings and conferences. He also made the acquaintance of Robert N. Butler, the American psychologist and gerontologist who had coined the term "ageism" and was a close ally of the Panthers. In 1975 Butler wrote a detailed and devastating survey, *Why Survive? Being Old in America*, that framed the treatment of elderly people as not a series of problems to be corrected individually but a comprehensive social injustice. Discrimination in the job market and housing, the nagging presence of poverty, the shocking conditions in nursing homes, victimization of older people by both scam artists and respectable businesses, and above all the patronizing attitude of government and the medical establishment all got a thorough review in Butler's book, which won the 1976 Pulitzer Prize for General Nonfiction.

Reviewing the book for the *Washington Post*, Alex called *Why Survive?* "a crushing indictment . . . the best and most informed exposé so far [of America's mistreatment of the aged]," a book "every American of every age should read," if only because most people would at some point become old.[3] Alex's new book, *A Good Age*, was quite different, however: a manifesto and advice manual for the elderly and people about to enter old age, combined with a summary of current biological research on aging. Alex set it up along the same lines as the *Joy* books, in the same conversational voice and with an introduction followed by a series of alphabetized entries on everything from arthritis and erections to quackery and rip-offs.

People didn't become old, he argued. They were "created" old by a society that wanted them out of the way and invisible. The result was a host of folktales, misconceptions, and harmful attitudes about the elderly that needed to be exploded. Some of these he had discussed elsewhere—that sexuality ended in old age, rather than continuing for both men and women—and others he compiled from his own and others' research: that older people were naturally passive and quietist; that they wanted to die (usually it's "what the relatives clamor for, not the patient"); that the aging process could be reversed (it could only be slowed down); that the brain and memory deteriorate with age; that masturbation in old age was infantile (it's a "healthy gesture of life-affirming defiance").[4]

Cumulatively, these misconceptions were causing the elderly to be isolated, pacified, "unpeopled," and "ejected from a citizenship traditionally based on work."[5] All of this often contributed to a poor self-image and depression among older people: what Alex called "sociogenic aging." *A Good Age* offered practical advice, such as how to spot con jobs like fraudulent arthritis remedies, design a balanced diet, be prepared for drop attacks (sudden falls) or spells of dizziness, insist on benefits one is entitled to, and know when to be concerned about overmedication. Smokers, he counseled, should give it up, or at least switch from cigarettes to a pipe, as he had recently done.

Embedded throughout the book was a program, very close to the Gray Panthers' activist philosophy, for how older people could resist the place society was forcing them into. It started with cultivating the personal quality he had long valued more than almost any other. "The bloody-minded person kicks shins, telephones the media, writes letters and takes the door frame with him or her when assailed by the forces of faceless society," he wrote. "Bloody-mindedness is an index of self-respect."[6]

Concerned about the quality of a nursing home? Pose as a potential investor and listen carefully to what the proprietors say about "the low costs, high profits and high turnover." Annoyed by neglectful relatives? Pick up the telephone but make the call collect—"for their education, not your benefit." Media and everyday conversation shape people's attitudes toward the elderly, and when demeaning portrayals or references crop up, they require pushback. "In entertainment, any time you see a senior depicted as a clown by virtue of age, pick up the phone," he said. "Never let 'old' go past when it's used as put-down. . . . If you alter people's verbal behaviors, you alter them." The objective was to break down the psychological distinction between older and younger people in general. Alex argued for a campaign to strike the word "age" from public documents, except for statistical or record purposes, in the same way that the use of race and religion was being minimized.[7]

Elderly people were encouraged not to accept disengagement as their lot. Alex urged them instead to take collective action, including "becoming a lobby strong enough to harass public authorities for action" on their concerns. "Leisure is a con," he charged. Hobbies are fine, but "a hobby is no good as a substitute for engaged living." Continued engagement throughout life—including political engagement—is normal. It had only come to seem otherwise in the industrial era of wage labor, atomized households, and forced retirement. To reclaim it must include political action by the elderly themselves. "The only way older people . . . can fight poverty," Alex wrote, again reflecting the Gray Panthers' philosophy, "is by organization and by militancy." But he also urged the elderly to see their struggle as part of a larger one. "Much more than in some other countries, . . . poverty among old Americans is not so much a special issue as part of the general issue of social justice and the common wealth, carried into old age."[8]

With minimal encouragement from government and capital, older people could launch second careers or do nonprofit work, Alex wrote, but he also encouraged them to provide group-based services in their communities. "You don't need to live in a commune to rationalize your living through bulk buying, shared housing, mutual help and shared investment," he argued, "and these things, which must be administered, generate employment." Because it's noncompetitive, mutual aid "can be a new and enlightening experience for people who haven't tried it."[9]

Alex's dedication to *A Good Age* was "To my father on his ninety-third birthday," although Alexander had actually died in October 1975, while the book was still coming together. Alexander had lived at Havengore in New Barnet right to the end, still passionate about cricket, and still serving on the management committee of Coram's Fields. He had taken the train down to King's Cross and walked to a management committee meeting. There was a heatwave, and on the way home from the station he felt too exhausted to make the climb and stopped at a friend's house on Bulwer Road to get a lift. He revived, but died in his sleep the same day.[10]

The book Alex dedicated to his father was in part a manifesto advocating that elderly people and their supporters launch a new social movement in America. But Mitchell Beazley was not ready to move much beyond the design it had used successfully for the *Joy* books, and *A Good Age* accordingly came out in dimensions similar to its predecessors, with an uncluttered layout and a stark white dust jacket decorated only with a quote from Alex's introduction: "This book is not only for the now old. All people, of all ages, need the basic facts."

That statement betrayed a concern that Alex's new book might not appeal to as broad an audience as *Joy* and *More Joy*. So Mitchell Beazley and the author gussied it up with highlighted quotations about age from famous authors and a series of illustrations and capsule biographies of high-achieving elders: Bertrand Russell, Maggie Kuhn, Josephine Baker, Nadia Boulanger, even Mao Tse-tung (as his name was then typically spelled). Crown launched a promotional campaign for its best-selling author when *A Good Age* came out in October 1976, including big ads in the *New York Times* and the *Times Book Review*, the *Los Angeles Times*, and other major papers, backed by interviews and profiles in *Publishers Weekly*, the *New York Times*, the *Houston Post*, and others.

When it came to reviews, the results were extremely gratifying. Anatole Broyard, who had trashed *Come Out to Play* the year before in the *New York Times*, recommended Alex's new book. After two books about the joy of sex, "Dr. Comfort has progressed quite naturally to the joy of age," he wrote. And while he thought Alex's exhortations that middle-aged and elderly people should launch second careers were too optimistic, he praised the book for debunking so many myths and prejudices about age.[11] *Time*, which had likewise panned *More Joy*, also praised *A Good Age* for challenging conventional wisdom and demanding a full social role for the elderly.[12] The *New York Times Book Review* found that the humanistic vein that characterized the *Joy* books carried over to the new one and called the book "at once poetic, passionate, gently ironic, humane—and lucid, practical, tough-minded, and detailed."[13] When the book was published in the UK the following year, the critics there also greeted it warmly.

Elder activism and campaigns for the rights of the aged were reaching high-water marks in the mid-'70s, and activists embraced Alex. He had already been lecturing frequently about aging and the need to devote greater resources to elder care, especially since leaving the CSDI, but the new book upped the volume of invitations, including from congressional bodies addressing aging.

A Good Age was not a best seller, although it sold in the tens of thousands. Unlike *The Joy of Sex*, it was far from the only book of its kind. *Prolongevity*, *Vigor Regained*, and (inevitably) *Everything You Always Wanted to Know about Aging* were a few of the other titles in competition, most of them offering more practical advice on such matters as diet and exercise. Another reason may have been that the audience Alex's book addressed was unclear. Was it aimed at anyone who was or would eventually become elderly? At social workers, geriatricians, and others who treated and counseled the aged? Some sections, such as a long one on gerontology, were typically clear and accessible, but whether a popular audience would find a rehearsal of current biological theories of old age interesting was debatable. Yet the book's audience-friendly format—with its superficial entries on feet and hair and its entertaining if thin capsule biographies—didn't recommend it to scientists, doctors, or social workers as a serious text.

Alex had written an informative, consciousness-raising book, but its natural audience was already being addressed passionately by Butler in *Why Survive?* and by the Gray Panthers and other elder advocacy groups. Alex's profile got a boost from the good press that *A Good Age* received, but that wasn't enough to generate *Joy*-level sales. For the author, however, the book represented the first step in what he hoped would blossom into a campaign to vastly improve medical care for the aged.

The poor quality of geriatric care—or its virtual absence—was a problem that had preoccupied him for some time. He had first noticed it, he told some of his audiences, during World War II in England, when nurses were drafted into service and those who proved incompetent or untrustworthy in the acute care wards were shunted off to look after the elderly.[14] Among doctors, geriatrics "was for a long time looked upon as just another branch of embalming."[15] While matters were improving in the UK and some Western European countries, geriatrics in the States was still a direly understaffed and undervalued field; it would not be recognized as a specialty there until 1978, in fact.*

In the course of the year since he left the CSDI, Alex had taken up two unpaid part-time positions: as a consultant in the Department of Pathology at the University of California Medical Center at Irvine, and on Irvin Yalom's recommendation, lecturer in psychiatry at Stanford. The first focused on training medical students in physical treatment of the aged, and the second on their psychological condition. The latter meant he traveled regularly to Palo Alto to lecture, staying with the Yaloms while he was there, but Alex complained he was used "only as an alumni fund-raiser."[16] In 1977, he took on a third post, as consultant and lecturer in geriatric psychiatry at the Veterans Administration Brentwood Hospital in Los Angeles, which had the first inpatient psychogeriatrics unit in the VA system. He would continue to teach geriatrics for the rest of his working career in America.

He still pressed from time to time for his "test-battery" project to determine the causes of aging but now considered geriatric care a more urgent problem—and, perhaps, one he was more capable of addressing. "I intended when I emigrated to go on working on gerontology," he told a correspondent in April 1978, "but revised my priorities when I saw

* Susan Aronson, *Elderhood: Redefining Aging, Transforming Medicine, Reimagining Life* (New York: Bloomsbury Publishing, 2019), 137.An Austrian-born American physician, Ignatz Leo Nascher, coined the term "geriatrics" in 1909. "The idea of economic worthlessness instills a spirit of irritability if not positive enmity against the helplessness of the aged," Nascher observed, just as Alex and many others would later.

that outside the [Veterans Administration] and the Jewish Hospitals there *was* no geriatrics."[17]

It was an uphill struggle, Alex often complained, and it occasionally brought out something arrogant and patronizing in him. "We have a vast job here teaching the peasants what it is about," he wrote a European correspondent in 1980.[18]

He laid out the problem in a short section on doctors in *A Good Age*. Doctors were trained without much attention to the feelings they would develop about their work, he argued. They developed "an activist fantasy, of the St.-George-and-the-Dragon type."[19] This prompted them to focus on people who could "get well" rather than those tending to be less gratifying, provoking an "odd hostility to the old" in many of them. The problem was especially bad in American medical schools, which seldom taught geriatrics, even though treating the elderly was quite a different business from pediatrics. Older people react differently to drugs, Alex pointed out. Pneumonia could produce fits in babies, for example, an acute illness with fever and delirium in adults, and no symptoms at all in the elderly, except confusion. The latter might be shuffled off to a mental or chronic ward, when simply treating the pneumonia might clear up the problem.

In fact, "there is no more interesting branch of medicine than geriatrics," Alex wrote. "The intern who ignores an elderly patient with many symptoms as a 'geriatric crumble' is abusing his vocation." The need for good geriatricians would only grow as the population aged, and already more than 70 percent of prescriptions in America were written for old people. To serve the changing profile of patients, Alex envisioned, medical care would have to be decentralized, with accessible walk-in clinics and mobile offices replacing big medical centers. Care would have to be community-based, closer to patients and their needs, rather than centralized under the control of government or insurance companies. House calls would once again become part of how doctors tended to and treated their patients, and in-home care prioritized over long-term institutionalization. Every old person would need a primary-care physician, a geriatric specialist for referral, and access to a high-quality geriatric assessment hospital.[20]

None of this could happen without nurturing a new generation of trained, dedicated geriatricians. Alex had a plan for doing so. In a 1977 letter to a colleague, he recommended the creation of one or more geriatric centers of excellence to develop a cadre of "already excellent physicians," whose training would also include "a sojourn of exchange in Europe."[21] They would then be sent out to incorporate geriatrics into the general repertoire of internal medicine. As a first step, he hoped to set up a conference through the IHS, either in Santa Barbara or Washington, that would include physicians and health care administrators. Alex also suggested adding a British expert ("geriatrics in Britain, like opera in Italy, is well worth the export market") and getting the support of Robert Butler, who was now head of the National Institute on Aging (NIA). "Our institute has the advantage that it is neutral ground, not part of any medical school," Alex wrote. The total cost would be around $20,000 and would yield a book or taped lectures that the NIA could circulate in support of the program he was describing.

Months later, nothing had come of his scheme, and he conceded that he was still "pretty much a one-man band" on the subject. He expressed annoyance that too much attention in the aging field was going to faddish pursuits like cryonics—the freezing of human bodies in hopes of bringing them back to life at a later time—and not enough to the kind of basic care he felt the elderly most needed.[22]

But he was working to find support in higher places. In April he asked Maggie Kuhn, who was meeting with the new First Lady, Rosalynn Carter, and the new secretary of health, education and welfare, Joseph Califano, to give them copies of *A Good Age* and a paper he had written on mental health care for the aged, which she did. Kuhn also urged Connie Hirschman, a member of the President's Commission on Mental Health, to get in touch with Alex and read his paper.[23] In June Alex wrote to Stansfield Turner, the new head of the Central Intelligence Agency, who had earlier hosted him at a conference at the Naval War College in Newport, Rhode Island, enclosing a copy of *A Good Age* and suggesting to the new spy chief the need to "get geriatrics on the European model into the U.S. medical curriculum."[24] The following March he sent his book—autographed—to Rep. Claude Pepper of Florida, chair of the House Select Committee on Aging, in hopes of gaining the powerful congressional leader's ear.[25]

Nothing appears to have resulted from these contacts, but Alex was pursuing other angles as well. In February 1978 the Ethel Percy Andrus Gerontology Center at the University of Southern California invited him to speak to its faculty and students. The Andrus Center, named after the founder of the AARP, was the research arm of the USC Leonard Davis School of Gerontology, the first of its kind in the United States. Alex accepted at once but also raised the possibility with James Birren, the executive director, of setting up an exchange program between the USC Medical Center and the Royal College of Physicians and Surgeons in Glasgow. He had already spoken with Sir William Ferguson Anderson, president of the college, and assured Birren that Anderson would help if he could. The matter was urgent, he wrote. If a shortage of geriatricians were to develop in the United States, "every quack will put up a shingle, and when that is a failure, Europe and Canada will be brain-drained with damage to their excellent geriatric services."[26]

With these gambits failing to pay off, Alex decided he needed a stronger institutional base for himself: a much stronger one than the IHS supplied. As early as January 1976 he had confessed to James Mitchell that the institute "has absolutely no funds to meet its bills."[27] In August 1977 he brought up the possibility of a full-time position in a letter to Lissy Jarvik, a friend and professor at UCLA who had set up the inpatient psychogeriatrics units at UCLA Medical Center and then at the Brentwood VA hospital, and had recommended him for his consultancy at the latter.[28]

A great deal of Alex's frustration in trying to relaunch himself in America after the CSDI debacle surfaces in this letter. "I am just about tired of constant travel and lecture," he complained. His unpaid positions at Stanford and Irvine largely consisted of being trotted out to "talk to alumni or serve to thicken out grant applications." Did Jarvik see any chance of his obtaining a "regular, faculty teaching job" at UCLA? He was reluctantly willing to leave Santa Barbara if necessary and was sounding out other schools and institutions, including the Texas Research Institute for Mental Sciences in Houston, which included biochemistry and gerontology in its mission.

Alex groped for reasons why he hadn't been able to secure such a post. "My problem is that I have no idea how to set about getting considered for some job such as Associate Dean of Curricula in human biology or professor of gerontology and geriatrics," he confessed to Jarvik. "In England these things go via the grapevine, not by direct solicitation—here I believe you have academic placement agencies!"

Len Hayflick chalked his friend's failure up to jealousy and resentment. "At Stanford, I tried to help him, but Stanford never gave him a proper appointment," Hayflick said. University president Richard Lyman took a dim view of *The Joy of Sex*, and this must have hurt Alex's chances. But Hayflick thought the matter ran deeper, at Stanford and elsewhere. "It was fear," he said years later. "The faculty of these institutions were scared to death of this brilliant mind. They felt threatened by him, and the great success of his book certainly would have been an element. It speaks to the ignorance and stupidity of some of these people."[29]

One practical matter standing in his way was his lack of a license to practice medicine in the United States. Getting one, even for a professional with impressive credentials in his native country, was not a simple matter, and it took years for Alex to navigate the process. Another element, possibly, was the attention he had drawn with his suit against the CSDI, which was not likely to endear him to image-conscious academic department heads. Although he never mentioned this as an issue in his job hunt, Alex's case—he was now asking $1 million, including damages—had exposed his carefully guarded financial arrangement with the center, suggesting he might not be a reliable team player at another institution.

US District Judge David W. Williams began hearing the case of *Alexander Comfort v. The Fund for the Republic* on Tuesday, October 26, 1976, in a nearly empty courtroom in Los Angeles. Harvey Wheeler and John Wilkinson testified on Alex's behalf, and a board member and a former secretary-treasurer of the center also answered questions.[30]

Williams handed down his verdict on November 23, and it didn't offer much vindication to either side. The judge agreed that the CSDI had breached its contract with Alex and voided it; the center would have to return the royalties it had received from *The Joy of Sex*. But Williams ruled that Alex had not been defrauded, hinting instead that the two sides had colluded in a fraud, and therefore denied his request for damages and severance pay. Calling the two parties' deal an "unholy contract," he stated, "The men on Eucalyptus Hill were uncomfortable with Comfort's scheme, but the thought of adding him to the staff, plus having him effectively pay his own salary was tempting. The shabby pact was one in which Comfort untruthfully represented that he had written 'Joy' in the United States and under the auspices of the Center while using its facilities. The Center winked at the fraud."[31]

The CSDI was entitled to 20 percent of royalties on the book sold outside the UK only up to May 10, 1975, when Alex left, the court ruled, while the balance was due to Alex, plus 7 percent interest from the date the funds were withheld. The copyright on *The Joy of Sex* would be reassigned back to him as well. Hutchins said he was "relieved" by the court's decision. Alex made no public statement, but he had succeeded in stopping the center from using his money to foot the bill for Hutchins's reorganization scheme. This victory came at the price of some damage to his public reputation, however.

ALEX WAS NEVER ENTHUSIASTIC about personal profiles. He once turned down a request to be the "castaway" on an episode of the popular

Radio 4 program *Desert Island Discs*, in which the guest chooses eight recordings, a book, and a luxury item to take with them into exile. When *Fortune* magazine contacted him in October 1977, proposing to include him in a feature on best-selling authors, he turned down the request. "I don't appreciate publicity as a person, as opposed to publicity for ideas expressed," he said. Besides, he didn't have time for an interview. "I am up to my neck in teaching geriatrics, and I am already nine books ahead of JOY. . . . I need best-selling author treatment like a hole in the head."[32]

It would be some time before his search for a proper academic job bore fruit, and, as the Carter administration tightened its belt, the chances of catalyzing a great leap forward in geriatric medicine receded. That didn't stop him from putting out more information that could improve training in the field, however, and so he pursued the project with a string of books and papers over the second half of the decade. One was a new edition of *The Biology of Senescence*; others addressed the gaps he perceived in medical practice, mostly relating to gerontology but covering some related areas as well; still others went much further afield. By now, he had several years under his belt teaching and consulting on geriatrics, internal medicine, and psychiatry, his first experience in these areas since he had joined UCL a quarter-century earlier.

Sexual Consequences of Disability was an edited volume he brought out in 1979. Of the twenty-three chapters, he wrote five. Up to that time, almost nothing had been published on the subject in textbooks on medicine or surgery, one reviewer found: little on sex for patients with heart trouble or on drugs that interfere with sex, and no mention of the fact that one of the benefits of a successful hip replacement might be that a person could enjoy sex again.

Alex's book addressed all of these, along with arthritis, mastectomy, strokes, renal disease, multiple sclerosis, diabetes, spinal injuries, impotence, and gynecological problems, among others. For example, he laid out a set of prescriptions for patients with heart problems who want to have sex without risking a seizure, touching on alcohol, exercise, and diet. The subject had a personal aspect as well. Alex's entire career was a triumph over the disability he had endured since the accident that removed most of the fingers of his left hand at fifteen, yet he had never before written about the problems disabled people faced, including the attitudes and assumptions of the rest of society. The new book was his first attempt to make a contribution.

Why had there been so little prior research on sex among people with disabilities? Just as with the aged, Alex blamed cultural attitudes that doctors and therapists had absorbed, such as an unrealistic emphasis on physical beauty and strength as an index of desirability. "The sexual needs of such people are better minimized or ignored, rather than discussed, for fear of embarrassing them—by which we mean they embarrass or disturb us," he wrote. Hospital staff and relatives all too often were relieved when patients with disabilities gave up on sex and would just as soon do nothing to remedy the frustration and loss of self-worth that could result.[33]

Sexual Consequences of Disability was published by the George F. Stickley Company, a small Philadelphia press that specialized in medical and health care books, and it was aimed at doctors and therapists. It had its weaknesses, reviewers pointed out, including an emphasis on physical as opposed to psychosocial problems and on disabilities in men rather than women.[34] The first chapters in the book were on penis function and impotence, for example. Alex blamed this gap on inadequate data on women and the fact that male sexual functioning was more easily observed, and most reviewers were impressed that researchers were finally taking seriously an issue that physicians had neglected if not completely ignored. They did not note that, like the *Joy* books, the book said next to nothing about gay men or lesbians.

Less than a year after *Sexual Consequences of Disability* came out, Alex produced another textbook, *Practice of Geriatric Psychiatry*, but this time he had written the whole thing himself. It was one of less than a handful of books published in the United States on the subject. It was also the first medical text Alex had fully authored since *First-Year Physiological Technique* more than thirty years earlier, and it was as surprisingly readable and often entertaining as that short book had been.

A certain amount of psychiatric savoir-faire was needed in any kind of medical practice, Alex argued, but with older patients it was absolutely necessary. "However much physical and mental health interact in the young," he wrote, "in the older patient, they are wholly inseparable for practical and clinical purposes."[35]

Often the lines between the two were blurred, and a physical problem could mask a mental problem, or vice versa. Depression was commonly undiagnosed, dementia was misdiagnosed, and it could be difficult to tell a patient who was truly depressed from one who was mainly neurotic. Because older patients' nerves "are as raw to perceive prejudice as those of a persecuted minority," doctors need to ask themselves, with each new patient, "What are this person's sources of self-worth?" and take care also to sound out the attitudes of the nursing and junior staff toward aged people.[36]

Practice of Geriatric Psychiatry covered a host of topics: depression and dementia; hypochondria; problems—like sexual behavior—related to loss of privacy; sleeplessness, including something called "Goldwyn's syndrome," in which patients exhibited "disturbance in glorious technicolor, including noisy insomnia"; bereavement; and doctors' legal duties, including assessing mental competence and the need for guardianship. Alex made it clear that he was fully aware how trying some patients could be. "Floridly disruptive tactics may reflect real brain damage, psychosis or mania," he cautioned, "or be the endpoint of a lifetime of manipulative behavior (one can imagine Madame Bovary in a nursing home)." The hypochondriac, "like Milton's Satan, has a sense of injured merit—responsibility for his sufferings is projected onto others, others are not appropriately sympathetic, only incompetence prevents cures. His medical knowledge may be volubly expressed."[37]

The toughest aspect of treating geriatric patients, however, could often be dealing with unsympathetic or uncomprehending hospital staff and family members, and this subject gave Alex an opportunity to expand on some views he was developing on the duties of a doctor. "The area of medical ethics, and of gauging responsibilities to the law and to the patient, is probably the only area of medical practice in which the physician has a professional duty to be arrogant," he wrote. "Cultivate in all matters private and confidential to the patient a memory and a record system which, if improperly raided, are like [the] Bellman's map, a perfect and absolute blank."[38]

Alex's larger purpose in writing the book, building on the proposals he had made in *A Good Age*, was to provide a basis for better geriatric training in America. At the time, there was only one professorship in geriatric medicine in the United States, compared with fourteen in the UK, and no professorship in geriatric psychiatry. He expanded on the suggestions he had already made for improving the situation: setting up assessment centers where doctors could tease apart elderly patients' physical and psychological problems and combining these with "day attendance centers" that could function as clubs, social and meal centers, and monitoring points while relieving family members of some of their responsibilities. With these resources, more aged people stood a better chance to keep living at home rather than in institutions.

Finally, he wanted to see geriatric care integrated into general medical practice, not confined to specialists and social workers. The elderly should be able to rely on their primary care physicians as the first place to go for treatment, just as younger people did. That would mean making geriatric psychiatry a normal part of medical education. "No single reform would be more beneficial than the inclusion of geriatric questions in the medical licensure examinations," he wrote.[39]

Practice of Geriatric Psychiatry was written quickly. Some sources referred to in the text did not appear in the bibliography, and he contradicted himself in some of the more technical sections. Important topics like delirium, or acute confusion, were left out. But Tom Arie, a friend of Alex and a pioneer in psychogeriatrics in Britain, called it a tour de force, citing its "innumerable sharp insights, new angles on technical points, and . . . sheer readability." While it wasn't a basic textbook for entry-level students in the field, Arie wrote, "I would much sooner see someone read just this book than a more comprehensive 'sounder' text—for Comfort's book will turn people on."[40]

ALEX'S VISION FOR GERIATRICS, like the Gray Panthers', was as much political as practical, and it fit in with the anarchist's traditional preference for decentralization, cooperation, and community control. What were his politics, and did they differ from the ideas he had formulated during World War II and the immediate postwar years?

A few months before he moved to the United States and joined the CSDI in Santa Barbara, Alex had written an article for the *Center Magazine*, "Latterday Anarchism."[41] In it he claimed that anarchists "aim at a standard of inner-directed social responsibility high enough to exceed the normal demands of citizenship," making clear that his political vision was still rooted in the individual and individual psychology, rather than social or economic theory. But the established order—the State and capitalism—were approaching a crisis, he argued, because fewer and fewer people still believed that their goals could be achieved by legislation "or could be reached by voting for the established parties or just hoping that the very human tendency to use power as abusive play therapy will just somehow go away."

The pattern of life had become one of "frustration with inefficiency, crowding without sociality, high input without communication." A solution would require organization and consensus, but the established order was not capable of supplying either. In earlier times, governments appointed a tribune or an ombud to look after the interests of the common people or the public good; no such offices existed anymore. The writers of the US Constitution had attempted to create a system that would prevent abuse of power, but they had failed. World government was not the answer; it would mean only "bigger and better pigs acting in collusion (as they already do unofficially)." Neither was the answer classical liberalism, which placed its faith in the rule of law to protect individual rights. The law would always be abused to advantage a self-interested elite. Yet a complex society made some form of human organization necessary.

The solution, Alex proposed, was "adhocracy." The futurist Alvin Toffler had coined the term in his 1970 best-selling book *Future Shock*, referring, rather vaguely, to an information-rich, nonhierarchical organization with a highly flexible design that allowed it to detect and respond to change rapidly, including by redesigning itself. Adhocracy later became a popular notion with business management consultants, but for Alex it implied a leaderless structure that could generate "non-paternalistic, non-directive solutions."

What made him feel that this alternative form of human organization was possible, when the state-capitalist system had been building and solidifying itself for centuries? Humans had evolved culturally beyond the need for rigid social and political structures, Alex argued. "The new men of 2000 are ungovernable by anyone," he wrote, and anarchism was the only ideology that suited them. "We anarchists no longer tolerate authority for its own sake, or tolerate its use as play therapy; we will not tolerate solutions which override minorities or discount human emotional needs; we will not tolerate the irrational use of property, which is a special branch of power; and we are determined to be heard, not killed off through psychopathology or inadvertence."

Adhocracy was anarchism, Alex was saying, and anarchism was less an ideology than a set of principles. Those principles would lead to a more rational world, "as far as man is able to inhabit one":

> a zero-growth environmental economy, where planning is important but popular participation is also provided for, where all automobiles are Rolls-Royces because they have to be non-expendable and are bought like real estate, where there are no bigger, faster, or noisier aircraft, only optimal aircraft . . . and where research and development are geared to judgment and thought, with emotional insights thrown in, rather than geared to paranoiac technology. There is also, as a safety measure in case any latter-day Hitlers get any ideas, a militant, articulate, and non-coercible public.

Adhocracy might produce not a pure anarchism or a pure democracy but instead a mixture, "empirically justified because it has grown in response to reasonable needs and the overriding need to make power subject to protest." Revolution, which too often swapped one coercive system for another, would give way to "constant and unrelenting extra-institutional militancy."

"Latterday Anarchism" was consistent with the political thought Alex had put forth in the '40s, grounded in scientific humanism, with the addition that rational solutions for society need to take human emotional needs into account. It was also a remarkably optimistic statement, arriving as both the Vietnam War and the Nixon administration were reaching their squalid ends, the British government was in a pitched battle with labor, and a structural crisis in the global financial system was giving neoliberalism the opportunity to assert itself in policy circles. Alex was just as uninterested as ever in addressing developments like these in a detailed manner. He put a great deal of emphasis on "rationality" without explaining why it would logically lead in the direction he favored. But he was correct to point out that human survival would depend on getting rid of current systems of government—of human organization—that were incapable of organizing to address the problems facing them except in a self-serving way.

"Latterday Anarchism" was, in other words, an Alex Comfort production. In his review of *Practice of Geriatric Psychiatry*, Tom Arie had noted that one didn't read Alex for the most meticulous, detailed, authoritative account of any subject but instead for his flashes of insight and the provocative way he presented them. "Everything he says (and the way he says it) is lively, stimulating, often right on the mark, [and] sometimes plainly wrong, occasionally silly," Arie wrote, while recommending the book enthusiastically.

The one area in which Alex was consistently meticulous and authoritative was gerontology, where the 1964 edition of *The Biology of Senescence* was still a basic text. But even here, Alex's years-long effort to build a public base of support for the study of aging sometimes caused him to push the envelope too far.

In a 1971 article for *Playboy*, he had predicted that in the next ten to twenty years, research would prove whether dietary restrictions or other experiments could increase the period of human vigor. "By the year 1990, we will know of an experimentally tested way of slowing down age changes in man that offers an increase of 20 percent in life span," he predicted. Uncertainty about this would depend only on the amount of money and energy that went into the project. "Dietary tricks or maintenance chemicals"—possibly antioxidants to mop up free radicals that otherwise would damage cells—would be the agents involved, and they would be simple and cheap, possibly cheaper than antibiotics.[42] Gerontologists were fast approaching the point at which the necessary research could be done, Alex was saying, and the rest would simply be application.

Some of his colleagues found this a bit misleading or at best overly optimistic. "Dietary tricks" would indeed be tricky to devise; calorie-restricted regimes were found to stunt growth in mice, for example, and nobody knew how long one would have to follow them for any effect on vigorous life to show up. The behavior of free radicals was still not well enough understood for anyone but Alex to consider antioxidants an imminent solution. Yet, in a 1974 interview, Alex said firmly, "I believe we could slow down human aging now. We know how to do it."[43]

"That was when I gave up on him as a scientist," said an "eminent lab man" who spoke with Hugh Kenner for his *New York Times Magazine* profile. Running the battery of tests for which Alex had hoped for years to get funding was not yet worthwhile, this person concluded, because it wasn't yet clear what should be tested. In the same 1974 interview Alex stated as fact that humans have pheromones "that are specific oral stimuli," when he knew this was not established.[44]

That didn't mean he had nothing to contribute. "The systematic body of knowledge; the broad overview; the prediction of areas apt to be productive of results; and—he writes so well!—the potent voice to stir people" all these Alex had over almost anyone else in the field of gerontology, another of Kenner's interviewees said.[45]

Alex was on firmer ground, then, when he decided it was time to prepare another edition of *The Biology of Senescence*. Routledge had let the second edition go out of print in 1973, and Alex assumed—correctly—that the rights had reverted to him.

He quickly got to work, despite a bad recurrence of migraines, anticipated that the third edition would be about one-third longer than the second, and by August 1976, he was able to report that his revision was practically done.[**]

It would be another three years before the book appeared, however, from the Netherlands-based international publisher Elsevier. Once

**AC, letter to Robert Maxwell, August 15 and August 31, 1976. Alex was finally coming to grips with the need to use less sexist language. In a letter to the copy editor of the new *Biology of Senescence*, he wrote that he thought he had worked this out "sensitively enough to pass" and that he had tried particularly "not to convey that the doctor is male and the troublesome patient female." AC, letter to Diane Huggins, July 25, 1979.

again reviewers greeted the new edition as the most comprehensive work yet written on the subject. The core of the book was still Alex's chapters comparing the longevity of different species, from protozoans to invertebrates to humans, and he had produced the largest and most authoritative tables on these ever assembled. Much more was known by the late '70s about methods of gerontological measurement and also about the pros and cons of the various theories of aging, and Alex covered all of these comparatively and in depth.

After reviewing and assessing all the current theories, he remained optimistic about the possibility of increasing life span. In fact, he was a bit more hopeful than he had been just a few years before. Soon, a ninety-year-old would be able to expect to live as vigorously as a present-day seventy-year-old.

The third edition of *The Biology of Senescence* was richer and more wide-ranging than the previous editions. Alex included a discussion of premature aging syndromes, a fuller review of the changes that characterize "normal" aging, and, of course, a chapter on his test-battery proposal. He also made an intriguing proposal for a new line of research: aerospace gerontology. Skylab, the first US space station, had been launched in 1973, and a semipermanent space shuttle was scheduled to launch in 1981, meaning that humans would soon be spending extended periods of time in outer space.

If the National Aeronautics and Space Administration wanted to send senior scientists and technicians—not just young, fit adults—it would need to test candidates' response to unconventional forms of stress such as acceleration, weightlessness, and reentry over the entire adult life span. This could yield valuable data for geriatricians and gerontologists. A large-scale study of humans' response to weightlessness, Alex suggested, could show whether it worsened calcium loss or, on the positive side, allowed subjects to expend less energy, since resisting gravity accounts for much of the energy requirement of organisms. Too much bed rest was known to be bad for older patients; perhaps reduced gravity could be an alternative.

Aerospace gerontology was partly a selling point for Alex's test-battery project. Understanding the components of biological aging could enable NASA to send people of a wider range of ages on its missions, while including gerontologists on space missions, possibly together with lab animals like mice, could help them pinpoint new therapies that would improve the lives of older people.[46]

Its bibliography remained the most remarkable features of the new

Biology of Senescence: some eighteen hundred references, including almost all the essential literature on biological gerontology stretching back to 1498.*** If Alex didn't have or know of it, seemingly it didn't exist. In keeping up with a field that appeared to be entering a boom period with the establishment of the National Institute on Aging, he had produced "a model in scholarship and thought," a reviewer in the *Quarterly Review of Biology* concluded.[47] N. K. Coni, a Cambridge geriatrician, in *Annals of Human Biology*, called it "the definitive account . . . pleasingly presented, well written, and painstakingly researched."[48] Alex's ability to write lucidly and engagingly on the subject was still unsurpassed. Len Hayflick, in a review in the *Journal of Social and Biological Structures*, praised the new edition's literary style as much as its scientific content, calling Alex "our most literate gerontologist."[49]

WHILE ALEX WAS PREPARING his new books on disability and aging, he was also producing a series of lectures and papers, aimed initially at his students at Stanford and VA Brentwood, on the social role of the physician. He collected these in 1980, along with some earlier pieces, in another book, *What Is a Doctor? Essays on Human and Natural History*. Some of the best and most intellectually powerful pieces he ever wrote, they took off from the argument he had made a decade earlier in *Nature and Human Nature* about the need for humans to recover the "emotional technology" they had lost in controlling their physical environment, and which had enabled an understanding of themselves as part of a social and natural world.

Ten years later, Alex was calling for a complete rethinking of the physician's role, based on "a radically new world-view which is both scientific and empathetic." Doctors, who were so often tempted to think of themselves as gods or parents in their relationships with their patients and even their colleagues, would now have to see their patients as partners, and they would need to see their task not just as managing and curing diseases and other complaints but also as healing in a larger sense. They would have to wake up to the fact that they were psychiatrists almost as much as medical practitioners, since a countertransference takes place between patient and doctor similar to the one that occurs in

*** *De vita libri tres* (Three Books of Life), by the Italian humanist Marsilio Ficino; the second book is on prolonging life.

psychoanalysis—and because one of the physician's tasks would inevitably be to reconcile the patient to mortality.

The starting point would be for physicians to understand their own fears and anxieties, because these would inevitably trigger reactions to their patients that would inform their treatment. Alex broke down the elements of the physician's practice into four: expertise, the technical areas of medicine learned in medical school and developed thereafter; insight into the fantasies and anxieties the doctor projects onto the patient; wisdom, which is simply a sensitivity to the ordinary but diverse realities of human experience and the patterns they generate; and all these three combined to produce sound clinical judgment on the best thing for the patient to do.

"You cannot teach clinical judgment, though it is contagious, but you can encourage it," Alex wrote. There was reason in the European habit of referring to medicine as an art as well as a science.[50]

Pressures like social anomie, the weakening of the family, and the decline of religion placed new demands on the physician, some emotional, which made it hard to rely exclusively on technology or expertise to do the job. All this was disorienting, because the physician was naturally uneasy in the face of problems that were incurable and that harked back to the profession's origins in shamanism ("the expertise which deals with the interface between the self and the not-self").[51] If they didn't want to resort to mumbo-jumbo, they would need to understand much better the site of human anxieties and neuroses and even illness: the brain.

Harnessing computers to medicine would be no real help if they fell in the hands of "scientoids" who only wanted to reduce the physician's job to tabulating symptoms and dispensing prescriptions. But they could offer a great deal of help if programmers could construct models that unraveled the multitude of comparison-patterns the brain generated and that drive so much of human activity, and analyzed them in ways we could understand.

Such models, which could literally "tell us how we function," were, of course, a long way off, but Alex argued that medicine was reaching a point where it could no longer treat the body as merely "a biochemical-mechanical system."[52] Physicians would have to stop acting as if their job was to pursue human health as one pursued "the health of the automobile, by regular inspection and repair by a technical expert." To do so they would have to acquire a much greater knowledge of the systems of human emotion and impulse while taking care to avoid the "mixture of magic and marshmallow" that would later be described as New Age.

This would enable the physician to play a pivotal role in society's development going forward. "I believe that the real psychiatric and philosophical problem of modern societies lies in adjusting the balance between thinking and feeling," Alex wrote. "This is especially true of medicine, which tries as no other specialty to be both rational and insightful," he noted, "[and has the capacity] to understand our emotions without denying them."[53]

That understanding would have to include some idea of where our emotions and impulses come from: for what purpose they evolved. Accordingly, Alex waded into one of the most controversial scientific topics of the decade: sociobiology. Attempts to find a foundation for social behavior in biology and natural selection had always been problematic, but they flared into a full-scale set-to in 1975, when the eminent American naturalist E. O. Wilson, sometimes called "the new Darwin," published *Sociobiology: The New Synthesis*, in which he claimed that behaviors like altruism, nurturing, and aggression were part of humans'—not just animals'—biological inheritance.

Wilson was immediately attacked for endorsing or at least giving respectable cover to biological justifications for elitism, authoritarianism, or racism, although this was clearly not his intention. On one occasion, a protester at a conference where Wilson was speaking threw water on him while others chanted, "Wilson, you're all wet."[54] Alex defended Wilson and other scientists who were exploring the subject as doing serious and ethical work, which he differentiated from the "barroom biology" of racists and quasi-fascists whose entire method was to analogize human behavior with that of the lower animals.

The trick was to know where to draw the line. There are "biological invariants," Alex argued, such as that men can't give birth or suckle infants and that their sex role depends on an erection. But, he added, this "doesn't affect the fact that 'sex roles,' and even more remarkably gender roles, in humans are demonstrably learned, and that the override from learning can transcend, or at least seriously confuse, genetic, hormonal and anatomical determination."[55]

Understanding "the override"—the routine ability of humans, as opposed to most animals, to overcome biological programming through learning and example—was the crucial difference, for Alex, between responsible social biologists and the "barroom" variety. This was part of what made humans social animals. Even when it could be determined for what purpose certain biological mechanisms evolved, thanks to the human brain and nervous system, that purpose didn't completely define the potential of that mechanism—or of human society. The override, in other words, was a biological tool that humans had evolved, perhaps uniquely: the ability to short-circuit other aspects of their biology. At some point in our history, it had taken over, and we had switched "from genetic to cultural transmission of behaviors."

That didn't mean humans had stopped evolving, only that they did so differently. "We shall not 'evolve' into leglessness through using motorcars," Alex wrote, "even if these render congenitally legless people able to survive, . . . but we may change ourselves by intervention, purposive or accidental." Humans can do this by learning and by absorbing cues from one another. Sociobiology, he argued, was the proper name for the study of this cultural process, which was as much a component of human evolution as the biological and had nothing to do with "charlatanisms" like eugenics.[56]

Being a physician, Alex argued, didn't require being a social biologist, but it did mean understanding the override. Because the materials it worked with were more cultural than biological, that mechanism included the "emotional technology" that Alex liked to emphasize. In his papers on the physician and sociobiology, he was stretching the boundaries of the empiricism, positivism, and scientific humanism that were his intellectual heritage in an attempt to make them a force for human liberation. That liberation would include breaking down the wall between doctor and patient and making hard science compatible with a broader social empathy.

ALEX WAS IN THE midst of a flurry of writing and publishing. All told, he would have eight books published in 1979 and 1980, either alone or in collaboration. Freed from laboratory research and the confines of Hutchins's think tank, and still without the academic post he desired, he had only to spend a day or two a week at VA Brentwood and an occasional day at Stanford to satisfy his institutional commitments. He was maintaining a strenuous public speaking schedule, however. In February 1976 he addressed the Council of State Governments on suggested state legislation for the elderly. In October 1977 he and Maggie Kuhn participated in a seminar series, "Survival for Seniors," at the University of Minnesota. The same month he gave three workshops at the Indiana Governor's Conference on Aging.[57] The following February he testified before the House Subcommittee on Aging on "life extension and tomorrow's elderly."[58]

Despite the demand for his presence, his fight with the CSDI, which sold its real estate and affiliated with UC Santa Barbara after its implosion, had left him bitter. In a March 1978 letter to Peter Medawar, he supplied a quick, one-sided account of the affair: the center was "a swindle," it had tried to accuse him of "operating a tax fraud," and the judge was scared of Hutchins or he would have run the miscreant out of town. "Soon after, before I could consider filing perjury charges, he died, and is said to have been buried vertically in a posthole 'because he was too cheap to purchase a horizontal grave.'"[59] In September 1979, three years after the court's judgment came down, Black Rose, an anarchist publishing collective in Boston, wrote Alex asking if he would be interested in writing a book or article on the "Joy of Anarchist Sex." His reply was noncommittal, but he added that he might one day write a "Joy of Politics—How to Get Even."[60]

That said, Alex was settling into life in Montecito. He and Jane fixed up the Oak Grove Drive house in '60s "hippie style," Marilyn Yalom recalled, with Indian wall hangings and a bedroom with a very large bed.[61] He had converted the stable, corral, and adjoining ground behind the house into a large vegetable garden, which he repeatedly expanded, adding an irrigation system. (He had particular success with squash and tomatoes.) "Shoveling shit was always an expertise in our family," he wrote one friend, while to another he suggested, "'The Joy of Vegetables' might make a book."[62] His practical side emerged when he rewired the station wagon he and Jane bought to include a beeping warning system when the car backed up—an innovation at the time, aimed at preventing collisions, but that startled some of his visitors. His creative side was on display in a stuffed desk drawer in his home office, which he told Len Hayflick was where he kept his unfinished plays and poems.[63]

Alex retained a new Santa Barbara–based law firm, Seed, Martin & Mackall, soon after the CSDI case concluded. He would need their services quite a bit in the years to come. His main business was with the senior partner, Harris Seed, whose specialties included working with authors (his clients included Margaret Millar and Ross Macdonald, the crime novelists). Seed's colleague John Mackall remembered Alex coming to the office fairly often, generally in a tweed sport jacket and smoking his pipe, to which nobody in the office seemed to object. Never in a hurry, he would have long conversations—"he expected a *conversation*, not an American-style get-to-the-point conversation"—with Seed, who got on well with his client and found it a point of pride to have Alex's business. "Harris had an incredible range of experience and communicated well about the law and human nature," said Mackall. "I'm sure that's why they liked and enjoyed each other."[64]

Having been a long-time ham radio operator in Britain, Alex embraced citizens band radio in the United States, where CB was mushrooming in popularity. Once he had acquired a set, he became a volunteer for REACT (Radio Emergency Associated Communication Teams), which monitored Channel 9, the frequency reserved for emergency communications, and notified drivers in his area of trouble ranging from breakdowns to brushfires to sick sea lions.

The community clustered around CB appealed to Alex as a form of mutual aid. Its practitioners included plenty of cranks, he admitted in a letter to the editor of the magazine *New Scientist*, in response to an article about operators in the UK, where it was still in its infancy, but it wasn't all "recreational funny folks who use a weird jargon and adopt comic nicknames." Operators halved response time from police and emergency services on the sometimes dangerous north–south highway and in the Santa Barbara Channel, he claimed, while doing a little to "reinstate a sense of local community which small-town and large-town America both need."[65]

One aspect of his life was done with, however, seemingly for good. When Barbara and John Williamson closed and sold Sandstone at the end of 1972, some longtime members and friends of the community, including Alex, were disappointed. Alex suggested strongly that after the Williamsons moved, the remaining members in the Los Angeles area try to restart it.[66] In 1974, Paul Paige, an ex-Marine and Gestalt therapist who had been a regular visitor to Sandstone, put together the financing to purchase and reopen the retreat.

Paige hired Marty Zitter as a general manager; one of Marty's first moves was to approach Alex about becoming scientific adviser to the new incarnation. Alex agreed; he was especially eager to explore how "the Sandstone experience" could be of help to old people and the disabled, he told Marty.[67] Paige then engaged him as a featured speaker, along with Gay Talese and Al Goldstein of *SCREW*, at a fundraiser titled "A Day with Gay and an Evening of Comfort Exploring Alternate Life Styles."

But Alex wasn't pleased with the changes Paige had made in the retreat. Aside from more than doubling the annual membership fee to $500, he envisioned it as a more structured community than had the Williamsons: more along the lines of Esalen, with yoga classes, Gestalt clinics, massage, and assorted workshops.[68] He also wanted Sandstone to provide actual sex therapy, similar to what Masters and Johnson offered at their clinic in St. Louis, except that the "therapy" would happen, vaguely, within the community rather than as a separate, professional program. Alex found this ethically dubious and suggested to Paige that he partner with a university department of psychiatry to run a separate program at Sandstone and make referrals.[69] Paige never responded, although Marty approached—unsuccessfully—USC, UCLA, and several East Coast universities for support, and Alex eventually wrote Marty asking that he no longer be listed as a sponsor on the retreat's literature. It closed its doors for good in 1976.[70]

Alex was already distancing himself from Sandstone, however. While she had gone with him to the retreat several times, Jane had found it "more than she could take," Alex wrote to Marty in April 1976. "[Because of this,] I have not been able to visit, much to my regret. . . . You know how much I myself got from the Sandstone experience . . . I was only sorry Jane didn't find it as rewarding." The community in Topanga Canyon had been an important and happy discovery for him, and he would never find anything to replace it.

Jane was having more difficulty than Alex adjusting to life in California. Initially she was "taken by the scene," Marilyn Yalom said, but Sandstone especially made her feel that she didn't belong: not attractive enough, not culturally in synch, and perpetually in her husband's considerable shadow. (While Gay Talese recalled meeting her there several times, she doesn't appear at all in *Thy Neighbor's Wife.*)[71] Alex made efforts to include her when he was interviewed, but either he couldn't help but take over, or she retreated when the interviewer tried to draw her out. When *Oui*, *Playboy*'s somewhat racier sister publication, interviewed Alex after the publication of *More Joy*, he mentioned that he and his wife had together written *The Joy of Sex*—but the interviewer identified her as Ruth Muriel Harris, married to Alex since 1943.[72]

Jane felt increasingly alone. Her mother died in 1977, her father had been dead over a dozen years, and she had little other family, leaving only Alex for support. Another problem, perhaps, was some people's skewed expectations. Surely the fiftysomething author of *The Joy of Sex* would have a sexy younger wife. Zhores Medvedev, who first met Jane some months before she and Alex emigrated, recalled, "His second wife was not a model. When I met her, I was surprised. I thought she would be a younger girl."[73]

One thing Alex could do was encourage Jane to write. They had reestablished Books and Broadcasts as an American concern, and discussed with James Mitchell the possibility of her putting together an anthology titled "The Joy of Love," but this died despite some early interest from Crown.[74] They then proposed a "middle-of-the-road book" to be titled "Romantic Love" or "Building a Life Together." Herb Michelman, an editor at Crown, came up with a list of topics the book would cover, including compatibility ("lifestyle of each participant must be similar"), sports, finances, shopping, problems ("individual and mutual"), sex, leisure, and recreation.[75]

That project too never materialized, but Mitchell quickly suggested another: a book on sex for adolescents. Initially Alex proposed finding authors in the United States who had more expertise than he, and that he edit it. "I cannot afford to appear to be cashing in on a sex series," he said.[76] After a meeting with Mitchell in New York in July 1977, however, he changed his mind (and his earlier decision to forgo writing more sex books) and agreed to write it himself.[77] Jane soon came aboard as coauthor; it would be their first official collaboration.

The new book deal also served to smooth Alex's relationship with his publishing collaborator. Mitchell's hyperactive marketing mind knew no bounds in the wake of the *Joy* books' success. The crown jewel of the firm's 1977 catalog was the four-volume *Joy of Knowledge Encyclopedia*, which he had driven his staff mercilessly to produce and for which Alex had provided a good deal of editorial assistance as well as text. It appeared the same year in the United States in the guise of the one-volume *Random House Encyclopedia*. But the Mitchell Beazley catalog also included *Joy of Art*, *The Joy of Music*, and the multivolume *Joy of Living Library*, not to mention the UK edition of *A Good Age*.

Alex's fingerprints were all over the firm's products, in other words, but Alex and his friend James, both habitually determined to get their way, were not working together easily. Misunderstandings cropped up due to the time difference between California and the UK and Alex's inability to meet with Mitchell at will. More seriously, Mitchell was looking for frankly commercial projects that he could produce quickly, and Alex, while he wanted to oblige for monetary reasons, was thinking in other directions. At the time he left the CSDI, he was working on an ambitious sociobiological study of religion. Mitchell envisioned a "Joy of Religion" for a popular audience, which Alex showed no enthusiasm to write.[78] Mitchell wanted an *Encyclopedia of Sex*, but Alex was leery of producing something that might be too much like the *Joy* books. Another project, tentatively titled "The Future," was a persistent topic of conversation between them, but nothing appears to have ever been written for it.

Barely a year after their new relationship began, Mitchell was getting restless. "I don't know how you feel," he wrote, "but I certainly feel that the thing is not working at the moment and that MB as a company is not getting value for money for the retainer which we are paying you!"[79] Alex wasn't about to take the blame. "Don't resent it if I say that I think things are proving a little too much for you," he replied. He considered his retainer to be monies that Mitchell Beazley paid him in place of an advance on *A Good Age*, and so a non-issue. He disliked Mitchell's presumption that he operated as an idea factory for cheap quickies. "It is not reasonable to expect me to put in work on a project a week," he complained, "unless I see ongoing action at your end on the projects already offered."[80] And he found some of Mitchell's ideas—for example, that he contribute a chapter to a forthcoming *Bed and Bath Book* on how to fit out a bedroom "for gourmet love-making"—silly and beneath him.[81]

Alex was uneasy too about two new Mitchell Beazley projects, *The Joy of Gay Sex* and *The Joy of Lesbian Sex*. Mitchell had found first-class authors for both: psychologist Charles Silverstein and a not-yet-well-known novelist, Edmund White, for the first; Emily Sisley, a clinical psychologist, and novelist Bertha Harris, both important in developing lesbian consciousness in the '70s, for the second. Silverstein had written *A Family Matter*, a book for parents of gay children, and had played a major role in persuading the American Psychiatric Association to replace the "Homosexuality" entry as a mental disorder in its *Diagnostic and Statistical Manual* with "Sexual Orientation Disturbance": a first step on the road to its outright removal in coming years.

Both books were constructed similarly to Alex's, the text organized alphabetically by topic and illustrated with line drawings and a portfolio of color paintings. The expected audiences were different, and not just in regard to sexual preference. For *The Joy of Gay Sex*, White recalled imagining "a closeted, deeply religious person from the Midwest" who wanted not just a sex manual but also something about the gay community and lifestyle, a very different person from the middle-class, relatively sophisticated straight couple Alex had had in mind. "We were determined to use dirty words, not medical words," White recalled.[82] Unlike Alex as well, "We wanted it to be pornographic," said Silverstein, fully expecting that readers would want to use it as a visual aid for masturbation.[83]

When Mitchell broached to Alex the subject of gay and lesbian versions of *Joy*, his first reaction was to insist, once again, that there are no "gay people," only "homosexual behaviors, which people may or may not elect to use."[84] After he had a look at the manuscripts, noting that his advice hadn't been followed, he insisted that his name not be associated with them and strongly suggested that the "Joy" titles not be used and that "Living Gay" and "Living Lesbian" be substituted, otherwise he and Mitchell Beazley would be seen as cashing in. He also suggested getting the advice of several better-informed people than he for each of the books, perhaps Quentin Crisp for the gay book.[85]

Once he had more time to read them, his attitude softened. Both were well written and publishable, he assured Mitchell. But he was afraid White and Silverstein's book, in particular, "clearly reflects an idiosyncratic, gay-swinger lifestyle" that might not represent the majority of gay men. "In particular, the plug for amyl nitrate as a sexual turnon [*sic*] is to my mind ill-advised."[86] Once again he urged Mitchell to test other people's reactions, both gay and straight, if he wanted to avoid public outrage.

He needn't have worried. Both Mitchell Beazley and Crown, which published the gay and lesbian books in the United States, were even more concerned about provoking legal action than they had been with Alex's books. Silverstein and White recalled that they were not allowed to use the words "shit" and "cock," to include a section on teenagers, or to devote more than a paragraph or two to sadomasochism. On the other hand, Mitchell specifically refused to allow a section on sexually transmitted diseases, because it would have been "a turn-off." He also excised a bibliography of books on gay topics. While *The Joy of Gay Sex* met some resistance from booksellers and trouble with customs authorities in Canada and the UK, and didn't sell up to Mitchell's aspirations, both books were successful with their target audiences and contributed to the mainstreaming of gay and lesbian sexuality.[87]

By the time they appeared in print in the spring 1977, Alex and Jane were at work on their book of sexual advice for adolescents, tentatively titled "One plus One." In a 1975 interview, Alex was asked at what age sex education for children should start. "The earlier the better," he replied, "and before the child is at an age to understand it." How many parents had shown their children *The Joy of Sex*, he wondered? "It wasn't meant for children, but it certainly won't hurt them."[88] The new book was a bit more precisely aimed at ages eleven and upward—anyone without sexual experience—and as such it drew not just on Alex's experience writing about sex but also on Jane's earlier career counseling children and their parents.

The Facts of Love, as it was finally titled when it appeared in 1979 in the United States, started from the same ethical place as Alex's *Sex in Society* sixteen years earlier—namely, that only two things were forbidden: recklessly producing an unwanted child, and abusive or inconsiderate sexual behavior generally. The authors also took care to explain in detail the importance of birth control, much as Alex had done, to considerable objection, on the BBC shortly after *Sex in Society* came out. He and Jane emphasized the element of sociality that had now been part of his approach for decades: sex is something that two people did for one another; find out what the other person enjoys the most and let them know what you want, and don't hurry (because people aren't "vending machines").[89] The words "unselfish" and "caring" appeared often.

Jane and Alex encouraged children to explore their bodies, both for their own enjoyment and to begin to understand what sex between two people feels like. Masturbation, including mutual masturbation, "is the natural way of testing the equipment." Abortion they treated briefly and matter-of-factly, as a way to stop an unwanted pregnancy early on but not as an excuse not to take precautions when having sex. This being the *Roe v. Wade* era, the legal status of the procedure was not an issue.[90]

Throughout the book, Alex and Jane took a sex-positive attitude. Thanks to better contraception, there was no longer any justification for waiting until marriage to have sex, they told their young readers. Maturity level was the important thing, and they urged teens not to rush into it. But sex is "one of the most enjoyable things we do," they wrote. Boys' first ejaculations feel "better than anything they ever felt before," and being naked together "is one of the pleasantest things lovers do." Sex is play, and fantasies—"being Pharoah or a prostitute or a Roman emperor"—are part of the play. The only rule is that these be fantasies both partners enjoy,[91] and the book included a section on contraceptives.

Some fantasies of "straight people" are about "homosexual play," Alex and Jane noted, and *The Facts of Love* mercifully left out Alex's hobbyhorse about gay people versus gay behavior. It described how gay and lesbian people have sex and assured the reader that having such an experience didn't automatically make them something they didn't want to be. Sex roles were learned, not innate, and one couldn't tell a gay from a straight person just by looking at them. Societies that deplored and punished homosexuality were the peculiar ones, not those that accepted it.[92]

Once again, Mitchell Beazley opted for a plain white jacket and tasteful drawings, à la their earlier *Joy* creations and *A Good Age*. There were no sensual paintings, but the illustrations included nude images of a boy and a girl, detailing their anatomy. As always with Alex, the point was to present the subject of sex in a matter-of-fact, unworried, reassuring manner: nothing to be embarrassed about here, plenty to enjoy responsibly. This came through in the uniformly good reviews it received. "[*The Facts of Love*] will smooth some anxious young brows," the *Washington Post* concluded under the heading, "The Junior Joys of Sex."[93]

Sex education had come a long way since *Sex in Society*, and Jane and Alex's book may have suffered commercially from society's having caught up with some if not all of their views. No critic objected to the book's deliberate ambiguity as to the age when sex ought to be allowed—it clearly wasn't urging teens to wait until adulthood—nor to its condoning of same-sex experimentation. But the '60s and '70s had seen a boom in publications designed for parents planning "the talk" with their adolescents—*The Teenage Body Book* came out at about the same time—and the Comforts' contribution didn't stand out dramatically. Like many of the competing books, it was sometimes a bit too earnest and wide-eyed for early teens who often knew more than their parents suspected by the time they discussed the subject (a review in the *Los Angeles Times* criticized its "isn't-growing-up-wonderful drawings").[94] Young adult novels like Judy Blume's much-banned *Forever* (1975) were already telling teens fairly frank stories about the introduction to sexuality, providing something spicier than what Alex and Jane offered.

While *The Facts of Love* missed the best-seller lists, Alex was eager to extend the property into other realms. In a letter to his and Mitchell Beazley's Hollywood agent, Lee Rosenberg, about the time the book appeared, he suggested an educational "video treatment" of the book, along with a cable TV series based on *Come Out to Play* ("a kind of sexual *MASH*") and another based on *The Joy of Sex*, which Norman Lear, producer of *All in the Family* and other hit shows, was considering at the time.[95] The latter suggestion prompted Alex to check with Rosenberg as well on the fate of a *Joy of Sex* movie comedy. Paramount had taken out an option on a big-screen adaptation, and in 1976 Mitchell heard from Simon & Schuster that the studio had decided in principle to go ahead with it.[96] But the wheels, typically for Hollywood, ground slowly. In February 1978 an item in the *Evening Standard* reported that the actor and "Beyond the Fringe" comedian Dudley Moore was working on a script for Paramount, possibly starring actress Tuesday Weld, his wife.[97] But then the project seemed to go fallow again.

WHILE THESE IDEAS CHURNED in Alex and James Mitchell's correspondence, Mitchell Beazley and Crown were preparing another, much less commercial Comfort release: his first collection of poetry in seventeen years. Poetry was a specialty of neither firm, but at least initially they thought the name of the author of *The Joy of Sex* on such a book could move some copies.

Alex had written little poetry since *Haste to the Wedding* was published in 1962 and no longer produced anything as ambitious as *Elegies* or *The Signal to Engage*. But in 1973 Philip Larkin published the *Oxford Book of Twentieth Century English Verse*, including Alex's exchange of wartime poems with Orwell. In his preface, Larkin indicated that his selections would be something less than traditional, making room for any fine or historically significant poem, not just for the poets who had the greatest careers.

That resulted in some odd choices, critics complained, including some poems that were not the authors' best. One critic was Alex's old comrade from *NOW* and Freedom Press, George Woodcock. In the *Sewanee Review*, Woodcock complained that the Comfort/Orwell *Tribune* poems from 1943 were "quite untypical and very bad Byronic dialogue," adding that he remembered both writers regarding the poems lightly, "as no more than a literary lark."[98]

Most surprising was a review in *The Listener* by the Movement poet Donald Davie, who had once denounced the Neo-Romantic poets for their "diffuse and sentimental verbiage," "hollow technical pirouettes," and "surrender to subjectivity." Davie agreed with Woodcock, lamenting that "from Alex Comfort, Larkin takes, not any example of Comfort's admirably elegant erotic poems, but a piece of polemical doggerel contributed under pseudonym to *Tribune*; and this so, apparently, to print as a rejoinder to similar doggerel by George Orwell. Thus the professional poet, Comfort, is sacrificed to the amateur, Orwell."[99]

Shortly after Larkin's anthology appeared, Alex told Mitchell Beazley that he wanted to publish a new collection, but assembling one took some time. He already had the "Vienna Poems" that he had written in the late '60s to Madeleine Jenewein: impressions of the city, its imperial past haunting its post-imperial present; a fantasy of flying over the city with his lover; an ode to love "outside time"; a scene between two lovers in which she begs off on account of a "rigid hymen" and his being "unquiet." In one, he addressed his younger and older selves and wondered which came first.

And so I love women he did not know,
think thoughts he did not think, and am to him
son to his father, father to his son,
a son or father but unsure of which.
I wonder where the man I was is gone?[100]

These aren't Alex's best poems, but they reveal the self-doubt lurking in a man in his late fifties who had experienced sudden, unexpected success and was no longer entirely sure his life was proceeding as it ought to. Would the deeply serious young English poet of the '40s have recognized the ebullient sex guru of the Santa Barbara years? Wordsworth had famously written, "The Child is father of the Man," but perhaps the relationship was not so clear, Alex suggested.

The new collection contained two other sections. One group consisted of poems composed in something close to Alex's earlier, Neo-Romantic rhetorical style, full of observations and musings on mortality. The last section, Alex titled "Anacreontica" after the ancient Greek poet Anacreon, noted for his witty, ironic, yet joyful lyrics on love. These poems have more of the playful spirit he revealed in *Haste to the Wedding* (and that Donald Davie had admired):

Love, don't forsake all others
dancers like us were never made
to keep ourselves to ourselves
though lack of jealousy erases
four-fifths of European literature[101]

Another, untitled poem in this group is one of the most personal Alex ever wrote: a tribute to the women he had slept with:

I have a childish fantasy
that they will come, all of them, when I am
expiring or condemned or something similar
in Indian file, with candle in each hand
blue-eyed Ruth who bore me a son,
and little, loving Jane whose heart almost consumed her
my wives, these, and my muses after them
two Marilyns, the tiny and the buxom,
two Lisas, Madeleine, then sundry creditors
and Anne the seeker bringing up the rear[102]

All hurt and wrong have disappeared or been put aside in this tableau—Alex's unfaithfulness, the unhappiness he had caused Ruth and Jane—in favor of gratitude and reconciliation. Each woman eyes him "kindly," and he is "not chauvinist but grateful" that they had honored him "with their wild affections." Some of the women in Alex's fantasy are familiar; one of the Marilyns was no doubt Marilyn Yalom; one of the Lisas may have been Lisa Hammel, a *New York Times* reporter who had interviewed him twice after *The Joy of Sex* appeared; Madeleine was Madeleine Jennewein; and Anne may have been a Santa Barbara friend of Alex and Jane whom they mentioned several times in letters.

That leaves the other Lisa, the other Marilyn, and the "sundry creditors." Who were they? And did Alex actually have sex with all of these women, or was much of this merely male vanity? He was a fundamentally honest person but could at times be an unreliable guide to details of his own life, in part because for him the past was always just a prologue to his latest project. He appears never to have revealed who the mystery women were.

The one element that knitted these diverse poems into a collection, however, was Alex's persistent preoccupation with death. In his second novel, *The Almond Tree*, one of his characters says, "I've only found two certainties—things you can't reach and things you can't avoid. The inevitable and the unattainable." The inevitable is death and the unattainable, he says, is "knowing what to do next and why to do it." More than three decades later he was still wrestling with this conundrum, only the problem was less purely philosophical now.

In one of the last poems in the new collection, he seemed to find an answer, informed perhaps by his therapeutic work with the aged. Love is "quantity, yard, mile, the push of continuity," we've been taught to believe. "But dying people / have a more lucid outlook upon that; / they learn another mode, that now is now. / God breaks each moment to create the next." Some things are not parallel but "perpendicular to time."[103] We should experience them as an eternal now.

Alex titled his new book *Poems for Jane*. But Jane—"little, loving Jane whose heart almost consumed her"—is mentioned only twice. Any clear references in the rest are to other women. Aware of this, Alex added a dedicatory poem in which he observed that "wives have a harder stint than mistresses / muses or mermaids." In these poems, he says, "I mostly didn't write about you— / you're the residual legatee. / It is to you that poems finally come."[104] Hardly the most gallant dedication that Alex had ever made, it was still a sign that he regarded his days of modest sexual adventuring to be behind him. He, as much as his poems, was Jane's inheritance.

As a publishing project, *Poems for Jane* offered proof that Mitchell Beazley and Crown no longer knew what to do with their polymathic author. The publishers began work on the book in 1975 and assigned Charlie Raymond to illustrate it. This time around, however, Alex didn't like Raymond's work, finding it didn't convey the atmosphere he wanted ("crassness and a decadentism are the last things I'd have forseen [*sic*] from him").[105] Instead, he asked Mitchell to consider his friend Reg Butler. Mitchell Beazley had "already spent a lot of money in text setting, commissioning of illustrations and reproduction work," James Michell wrote, and was anxious that the book go forward.[106]

But it wouldn't be published until four years later, in late 1979, just a few months after *The Facts of Love* appeared. One critic reviewed both books in the same article. There were no illustrations, but the book was produced in the same dimensions as the *Joy* books and *A Good Age*, on thick stock and with heavy borders at the top and bottom of each page. The effect was like that of a large Hallmark greeting card—a far cry from the austere designs that Grey Walls Press and Routledge had created for his poetry in the '40s—except that a Hallmark recipient would probably not have known what to make of the poems' classical allusions, occasional explicit sexual descriptions, and persistent grimness ("Shelley and Rilke met / themselves—a premonition / of death or madness, but / for me most commonplace").[107] Neither the book nor its dust jacket contained a single reference to the author's most famous book, the one thing that might have attracted the larger audience at whom Mitchell Beazley seem to have aimed with their design.

Alex called *Poems for Jane* "my best book of poems by far," but few agreed out of the few who reviewed it.[108] Kenneth Seib, an English professor at Fresno State College who was familiar with his earlier work, compared him to William Carlos Williams—another doctor-poet—in that they shared a "certain perception and sensitivity derived from everyday experience with birth, death, and human frailty." Alex's verse was "highly crafted, carefully balanced and cooly [*sic*] detached," Seib found.[109] Agnes McDonald, a poet and teacher at North Carolina State University, criticized the "sappy California, let's-love-everybody flavor" of the book—she must have overlooked the presence of death in nearly every poem—and rightly took him to task for persistently referring to women as "girls."[110]

Life and Times in NW1: Fully Stretched

Zhores Medvedev photo. Fotos International/ Archive Photos via Getty Images

James Mitchell photo. Mark Gerson

Chris Foss drawing. © Chris Foss / Artists Rights Society (ARS), New York / DACS, London

Alex *More Joy* photo. © Historic Images

Maggie Kuhn photo. Photo Researchers/Archive Photos via Getty Images

Alex Comfort smokng a pipe.
Family collection

Michael Randle.
PA Images / Alamy Stock Photo

Alex and Jane Comfort. Family collection

Alex Comfort later in life. Family collection

CHAPTER 20

I and That (1974–1980)

Mitchell Beazley and Crown brought out one more Comfort title in 1979: the book that Alex and James Mitchell had been referring to in their letters back and forth as "The Joy of God." Mitchell must initially have expected something along the lines of his Hugh Johnson wine guides or the firm's popular titles for foodies and music lovers, because the plan was to illustrate it extensively, in Mitchell Beazley's patented format. What Alex delivered instead was a densely argued treatise on human identity and phenomenology, which he organized much as he had *Authority and Delinquency in the Modern State* thirty years earlier. Understandably, the publishers didn't expect much commercial success from *I and That: Notes on the Biology of Religion*, and it shows in the production: the design is unattractive, typos abound, the index is skimpy, and, about three-quarters of the way through the book, a block of text of indeterminate length was dropped prior to printing.

But *I and That* was one of the most impressive intellectual achievements of Alex's career and the biggest step yet in his lifelong effort to understand what it meant to be human. It was in writing the book that he "began to get an overall view of the whole thing," he later said. "I began to see what the picture on the jigsaw puzzle actually represents."[1] He dedicated the book to his "gurus," J. B. S. Haldane and P. C. Mahalanobis, the scientific eminence who had first invited him to India in 1962 and introduced him to Sanskrit literature and philosophy. In it he marshaled a decade and a half of quiet study in religion and the philosophy of science, his reading of William Blake's visionary poems (which had fascinated him since his days as a young poet), and his own scientific knowledge of the brain and other parts of the nervous system to synthesize a new understanding of the elements that make up the self, or the "I"—the "inner 'someone'" we each feel to be our essence—and the "not-I" or "That" with which it interacts.[2]

He started by proposing to answer three questions: What is religion, biologically speaking? What are the origin and function of the "oceanic feeling": the sensation of eternity and unity or oneness with the universe that we get from such experiences as meditation, trances, dreams, hallucinogens, religious rituals and celebrations, consciousness-raising sessions, and sex? And why do so many humans from so many different cultures seek such experiences?

Alex's interest in these questions had several sources. As a scientist with an interest in sociobiology, he understood religion to be a part of the human experience; therefore, it must have a biology, which had yet to be explored. Oceanic states were commonly associated with most religions, at least in their formative periods, so they too must be understood. And he himself had experience of them. When he hit upon a scientific discovery or solution, the sensation wasn't always just satisfaction at work well done. Sometimes, he found, it was a momentary but "total euphoriant experience," an "orgasm-like feeling of well-being" comparable to an oceanic state.[3]

There was something more personal as well. The migraines, characterized by numbness and "dream scintillations"—visions of shining shapes—that had plagued him in his twenties and thirties, visited him rarely now, and he never got anything like an "oceanic" sensation from them.[4] But he had come to regard them differently. His were often preceded by what he called "aurae of impending discovery or insight," intimations of *gnosis*, or divine insight.[5] He knew these emanated from his brain circuitry, not some supernatural source, but that too encouraged him to better understand their biological purpose.

Alex first approached the subject of oceanic states in a 1969 article, "On Ecstasy and Originality," about the neurology of thinking, in which he discussed the connection between creative inspiration and seemingly methodical activities like scientific research. He took a further stab in a paper he delivered at a 1974 conference during his last months at the CSDI, "The Changing Role of Religion in Contemporary Culture," on the nature and role of oceanic experiences. Much of this paper found its way into *I and That*.

At about the same time, a diverse collection of thinkers were pondering a similar nexus of topics: the mind, the self, phenomena outside the self and the body, and the way they all interact. In his 1972 book, *The Natural Mind*, the future alternative medicine guru Andrew Weil discussed how to coordinate intellect and intuition more fruitfully. Two years later, Robert M. Pirsig published *Zen and the Art of Motorcycle*

Maintenance: An Inquiry into Values, which argued for a healing of the mind-body dualism in Western consciousness. Linguist and anarchist Noam Chomsky's 1975 *Reflections on Language* summarized for a popular audience his theory that the human mind has an innate ability to understand and produce language. A year later, Julian Jaynes published *The Origin of Consciousness in the Breakdown of the Bicameral Mind*, which attempted to pinpoint the cultural beginnings of individual consciousness as a "learned behavior."

All of these (and many other) contributions were concerned with how the mind works, but Alex wanted to find out specifically how it creates the I. What induced him to weigh in was a belated study of physics while he was at the CSDI that challenged the positivism he had imbibed as a student.

Physics differs from objective sciences like biology because, unlike them, it can't be easily visualized.[6] Einstein's theories of relativity had forced a recognition that time and space are relative, not absolute relationships, prompting a reevaluation of standard Newtonian physics. Two other important scientists affected Alex more fundamentally, however. One was Ernst Mach, whose physics held that relative motion must be the basis of any valid finding, and that any observed phenomenon must be explainable according to the distribution of matter in the universe, not absolute space and time.[7] Werner Heisenberg went further, concluding, when discussing subatomic particles, that we could no longer speak of particles themselves but only of "our knowledge of them." When we speak of nature in present-day science, we do not mean objectively observed nature "so much as *a picture of our relationships with nature*," since "by its intervention science alters and refashions the object of investigation."[8]

What Alex gathered from these perceptions was that any description of nature, including of time and space, was actually a description not of a concrete reality but of a contingent and shifting relationship that the scientist—the "I," in this case—not only observes but also participates in. If he wants to understand the I as a biological reality, he must understand it not as a thing but as a system or relationship.

In *I and That*, Alex offered a hypothesis inspired by systems theory: Consciousness and identity are generated in the brain through the interaction of two "channels" or faculties. Channel 1 interacts intimately with "That": everything outside the self, including the other parts of the human body. It sops up experience and sensations, generating perceptions, intuitions, and patterns of perceptions, constantly and at lightning speed. Channel 2 scans these outputs, picks and chooses among them, ending up with information and ideas that it understands logically and can express through language. The I, or self, appears in the nanosecond, which Alex called the "delay element," during which Channel 2 receives and analyzes each perception and pattern of perceptions from Channel 1 and fits it into a structure.[9]

What emerges is not just our comprehension and understanding of the world (and the universe) but also our body image—the mental impression we create of ourselves—our personal inclinations, the peculiar way each of us observes and analyzes information, our psychology, our ways of interacting with nature and other humans, and many other components of our individual identity. The I is not a thing, a "transcendental core or hot-spot of being" but rather the product of a system: a "point of view . . . dimensionless and virtual . . . round which experience is structured."[10] It is a constantly shifting and expanding field generated by the interplay between Channel 1 and Channel 2. This means the "That" that the "I" observes is constantly shifting as well. In this sense, Alex proposed, the mind is a sort of miniature version of the cosmos, a microcosm or "inner-space world" corresponding to the physical universe in which planets, solar systems, other heavenly bodies, and their respective electromagnetic fields constantly shift positions in relation to each other.[11] "What the mystic contemplates, and sees to be related to the universe," Alex said in his earlier paper, "On Ecstasy and Originality," "is in fact his own mental process."[12]

Alex was not insisting that he was right about this hypothetical system. "[But] though it is probably wrong, it lies in the right universe of discourse and something like it is probably right." Either way, it helped him to understand many elements of human experience, especially religion. This he defined as a range of behaviors "by which humans deal with their impression that 'the universe addresses us,' and by which they attempt to structure relationships and dialog with the not-human": animals, rocks, sun and rain, spirits or deities, and most importantly the "inner That of the human nervous system and its software." This range of behaviors is colored by a strong human tendency to "project human-like responses into the not-human, so that it may be conversed with." It embraces everything from the monotheistic faiths to shamanism, and from nature worship to objective observation ("the religion of our own culture").[13]

"All theologies and cosmologies," therefore, "are descriptions of man, not of God or gods," and they reflect "the multiplicity of the experience of self."[14] Religion could include other tool kits we use to understand our world, such as those of contemporary objective science, but it had its genesis, according to Alex's model, with early humans' experience of what Freud called "oceanic states": the province of mystics and shamans and the one occasion when the universe—the not-human—seems to "answer back."

Oceanic states could be spontaneous or self-generated, as in meditation, trances, religious rituals, and even practices like sadomasochism that are really about altering identities and manipulating body image. The common denominator is that "the strong sense of distinction between I and not-I is summarily suspended."[15]

The emotional appeal of the oceanic experience lies in the "conviction of one-ness" it imparts, Alex wrote.[16] This may have been a factor in the evolution of human society, he suggested. However illusional oceanic experiences may be—no great understanding or wisdom necessarily emerges from them, even though they can create an expectation of this—they are compelling and create lasting impressions. In a highly social species with a long infancy and childhood and an elaborate mental life, a deep psychological feeling of belonging "to the world, to other animals, to people, to ourselves" is critical, otherwise our environment might appear alien to the point of intolerability. But it's not easy to impart or maintain. Oceanic experiences—a sort of "jackpot combination" in the human machine for some if not all people—reinforce this essential feeling of belonging.

Scientism and formal, ritualized religion are the means humans have developed to channel the oceanic into structures that produce rules and ethical codes, by interpreting the visions and sensations that arise from it, Alex proposed. In so doing, however, they force it into narrower channels, restrict or suppress it, since on its own, the oceanic is "religion-disturbing." This is necessary up to a point; ethics make life with other humans endurable, a linear perception of time is a useful if sometimes overused convention, and powerful tools like mathematics require an objective self or I that can take an intellectual problem and experience it as external and observable.

Besides, oceanic experience has its problematic elements, Alex cautioned. "The experimental mystic must be occupationally oblivious to common convention," he wrote. "When good he may be very very good (like St Francis) and when bad, homicidal (like Charles Manson or Gilles de Rais)."[17] Moreover, mysticism and the intuitive would never be able to replace hard science even when it comes to understanding mysticism and the intuitive. Scientists like Einstein and Heisenberg wouldn't have got as far as they did with physics that problematizes objective observation if they hadn't themselves been adept at objective observation.

But formal religion—Buddhism, Hinduism, the monotheistic faiths—has a way of becoming consumed by rules and strictures, pushing experience—including the oceanic—aside in favor of squabbling over the literal versus symbolic aspects of its belief systems. "It is the religions which believe themselves to be the repositories of ethics" that have probably committed the worst atrocities in human history, Alex argued, not the antinomians who reject law, morality, and religious norms. The result of organized religion is "a Taj Mahal erected over the altered I-states of the shaman and the seer" and a war in which the medieval Christian mystic Meister Eckhart, the "witches" of the sixteenth and seventeenth centuries, and "even Dr Timothy Leary" are all casualties.[18]

Blake, "a cultural innovator of giant stature," had arrived at many of the same conclusions the better part of two hundred years ago, Alex noted. Some of these turn up in Hinduism as well, particularly the understanding that the perceived universe is the product of the "illusion" of I-ness. What Blake and the Tantric mystics had in common, Alex found, was a recognition that intuitive and objective experience, which so often seem in conflict, actually complement each other: "indispensable allies in the creation of a holistic philosophy."[19] A combination of the Hindu tradition and the British empiricism he had been born into could help us understand on a personal, not just a theoretical level, the new conception of self that physics was producing.

Medicine was the practical activity that could play the greatest role in developing this new understanding, Alex argued, since it's the one that "most concerns itself with body, body image, [and] physical self-experience." Efforts to understand the wiring of the mind that brought together the internist and the neurologist—biofeedback, for example—could reveal ways that humans' mental states and self-perception affect them physically, along with techniques for altering those effects.[20] Along the way, these efforts might help us develop techniques for encouraging the kind of imaginative leaps that lead to breakthroughs in art, science, and many fields in between.

Alex was not getting religious. "Buddhists are not theists," he said, "and if you look at the original teaching, it's not a religion. It's a form of extremely transcendental humanism."[21] In *I and That*, he had produced a rational, humanist argument for taking mysticism seriously as both an aspect of the human mind and a way to comprehend it, so long as mysticism was understood as a human, biological phenomenon, not something supernatural or an excuse for rejecting rationalism.

He had also come back around to one of his earliest philosophical concerns. In *Art and Social Responsibility*, he had declared a heightened awareness of death—of the end of I-ness—to be one of the chief characteristics of modern society. Fearing death in the absence of a religious faith, people were tempted to throw in with the State and the forms of authoritarianism it nurtured, like fascism, which promised them a new sense of belonging, even a kind of immortality.

Positivism had never offered Alex a satisfactory approach to the questions that death raised, only a "realistic stoicism."[22] Art was one possible protest against death, as was resistance to authority, he argued in *Art and Social Responsibility*, but in *I and That* he provided a more substantial answer: that acceptance of death—of the end of I-ness, as he now understood it—can bring a better experience of the world and of oneself.

How so? Alex quoted his late comrade Bertrand Russell's 1903 essay "The Free Man's Worship," that only on absolute acceptance of the individual's inevitable annihilation, "on the firm foundation of unyielding despair, can the soul's habitation henceforth be safely built." Curiously enough, Alex argued, "the consequence of real death is that all experience is sacral because it is limited and irreversible—only an immortal or an inordinately long-lived organism could afford a secular category of experience."[23] This echoes the "reverence for life" that another early influence, Albert Schweitzer, emphasized, and was still not too far removed from the scientific humanism of Julian Huxley, who had argued that "man's most sacred duty is to realize his possibilities of knowing, feeling, and willing to the fullest extent."[24]

Samuel Johnson had said, "Depend upon it, sir, when a man knows he is to be hanged in a fortnight, it concentrates his mind wonderfully." Why not, Alex was replying in effect, concentrate the mind for one's whole lifetime, treating all of that life with the seriousness, or sacrality, it deserves? The prospect of death sets off "a motivated and engaged introspection of what I-ness is." This is something he found in Blake, in Russell, and in some of the Indian sages. The job of any "healer"—shaman, physician, psychiatrist—must be not just physical healing but also to help bring about this important "attitude adjustment."[25]

I AND THAT IS a surprisingly accessible, clearly written tour through a complex and fascinating subject. Except for a few lapses—Alex sometimes refers to the I as the "homuncular I" or the "Cartesian observer"—it keeps jargon to a minimum, assumes no prior knowledge, and is readable—with care—by anyone interested in digesting a novel theory of human identity. It received very little notice in mainstream media, likely in part because neither Mitchell Beazley nor Crown had much notion how to promote such a book.

But its natural audience of scientists and philosophers took note. "Running through Comfort's book is much of the turbulence, self-contradiction and real excitement that belongs to a phase of growth and self-transcendence," the zoologist J. C. Poynton wrote in *Theoria: A Journal of Social and Political Theory*, particularly in its mixing and merging of traditionally Eastern and Western thinking. "Anyone not taking the plunge into this turbulence with Comfort is surely missing a period of intellectual transformation without parallel in cultural history."[26]

Alex would have been most pleased by a glowing review by Peter Medawar in *The Sciences*. In a letter thanking him for the review, he mentioned that his old boss was "much in my mind" when writing the book ("in the form 'I wonder what Medawar would say about this style of philosophy?'").[27]

While *I and That* was about mysticism, it was not mystical, Medawar wrote, but brisky matter-of-fact. He also found it to be a symptom of something larger: "a reaction against positivism which is becoming fairly widespread even among some of its erstwhile champions."[28] This reaction was due at least partially to many positivists' stubborn insistence that any questions science can't answer—What are we all here for, anyway? What is the point of living?—are non-questions. Alex was arguing that these questions could be understood in a scientific context—and must, since they are clearly aspects of the human experience, which is what science sets out to comprehend.

Which was not to say that Alex hadn't taken on a subject with a lot of trip wires attached to it. The sociologist Hans Mol, who made a particular study of religion as a social experience, called *I and That* "a crucial step forward toward a new psychology of religion" but faulted it for ignoring the fact that religion is more than just the product of a neurological "delay network." It also integrates communities, clans, tribes, ethnic groups, and nations, working through rites of passage, charisma, and conversion experiences: all social phenomena.[29]

Poynton suggested that in trying to establish a less "linear" understanding of human consciousness and its relationship to the not-I, Alex's Channel 1/Channel 2 hypothesis might itself be over-mechanistic. How far was Alex really willing to go in questioning modern humanity's conception of reality? He still regarded the human brain as an indispensable part of awareness, and he dismissed out-of-body experiences, and the near-death experiences reported by Elizabeth Kübler-Ross, the psychiatrist renowned for her work with the terminally ill, as "illusions." In doing so, how did he know he wasn't falling back on strict positivism in reaction to something his gut instinct told him was implausible?

Alex never offered a rebuttal to these objections, but he might have pointed to the subtitle of his book: <u>Notes</u> *on the Biology of Religion*. He was offering a path forward, not a set of definitive answers. He never denied there was a social element, particularly in modern organized religions, and he wasn't offering a catalog of certified oceanic experiences. More research would be required for that.

Further complications arose, however, in a largely positive review by Antonio de Nicolás, a professor at the State University of New York, Stony Brook, with a specialty in Hindu philosophy. De Nicolás's article appeared in the *Journal of Social and Biological Studies*, the academic journal that the IHS had launched in 1978, with Alex's friend and colleague, Harvey Wheeler, and the British biologist James F. Danielli as editors and Alex on the advisory board. The following year, the institute, which had never been well funded, ended all its activities except publishing the journal.[30]

De Nicolás found *I and That* "theoretically sophisticated, empirically sound, practical, and due to its subject matter and approach, humanly explosive."[31] The biological study of culture and religion was bound to become an important field in coming years, he said, which ought to make *I and That* "a seminal book." Scientists and philosophers of science would have to delve deeply into how the human nervous system was coded to create the worlds humans know and experience and would have to take religion, in the broadest sense, seriously as a component of humanness.

But de Nicolás also thought the book overgeneralized. The experiences of I and not-I that Alex described were all based on language and language structures—"the code of the nervous system"—and these were not the same in every culture; therefore, every culture's experience of I and not-I was not the same either. Aristotle and Descartes did not view the I in the same way, for example, while in Hindu thought the I had various meanings depending on the grammatical case one used. Alex was wrong to pile up "all of the different experiences of the 'I' as one, with one kind of rationality."

This raised further questions. Do the I and the not-I speak the same language? De Nicolás thought not ("in the language of 'I' *substance* is primary; in the language of 'not-I' *movement* is primary"), suggesting that their relationship was more complicated than Alex realized. And what about the practical applications of Alex's hypothesis? If his structural model of how the I is produced in the interface between Channel 1 and Channel 2 was plausible, and the oceanic could be cultivated to work more systematically with the analytic mind, then "there are large resources of body-manipulation which could be tapped" to yield greater knowledge and inspiration, Alex suggested.[32] De Nicolás agreed: "The biological study of religion could liberate humans from codings in the nervous system" that could prove to be "shackles of human freedom."

That would depend on who was doing the manipulating, however. Once the systems Alex hypothesized were better understood, couldn't they be exploited to shackle humans even further, to wire in more tightly anything from brand loyalty to cultural chauvinism to unthinking loyalty to the State? *I and That* didn't address these questions, but, if they had been put to him, Alex would likely have responded that the biological study of religion was not something science could avoid in any case, since Mach, Heisenberg, and quantum physics—the often mysterious realm that opened up when scientists began examining the physical properties of atoms and subatomic particles—had decentered objective observation.

Many scientists, whether or not they fully understood it or accepted its findings, felt that quantum physics had opened up the possibility of re-asking fundamental, even metaphysical questions that Newtonian science had seemingly settled. Alex believed his theories about the I, its relationship to the non-I, and the place of oceanic experience in human identity were not something that concerned only scientists and philosophers. If he was anywhere near right, they amounted to an expansion of the "universe of discourse," and he was eager to recast them in a form that non-adepts could understand. He started the job while he was still finishing *I and That*.

IN DECEMBER 1977, ALEX wrote his old UK agent, David Higham, that he had been "surprised to find myself writing novels again." He had produced a trilogy of science fiction or fantasy novels, his first venture into the genre, and was having trouble placing it. Neither Crown nor Mitchell Beazley were interested—the novels were "boring and not my best work," Alex said he had heard from James Mitchell—and he was in negotiation with a small California publisher for the US rights, but he wanted to test it in Britain and other markets as well.[33]

Unlike Mitchell, Higham and his associates found the trilogy "a brilliant tour de force" that "might well appeal to a wider public," and they set about shopping it to the major UK houses.[34] Higham suggested, however, that it would have better luck if presented as a single novel, and Alex agreed. He titled the combined work *Tetrarch*, after one of his characters, a fantastic primeval horse with sharp teeth and claws that saves its masters on more than one occasion (the name was the same as that of a champion Irish thoroughbred of the early twentieth century).

Just as *Come Out to Play* had been unlike anything Alex wrote in his earlier span as a novelist, *Tetrarch* was a completely different proposition from that satirical piece. In outline, it slightly resembled C. S. Lewis's *Chronicles of Narnia*: a couple pass through a mysterious doorway (rather than entering a wardrobe) and enter an alternate realm of time and space where they survive a series of adventures and ordeals before returning to their home in the present.* But instead of founding his story on Anglo-Catholic theology, Alex used the cosmology Blake laid out in his prophetic poems, in which humanity is situated at the crossroads of four great realms: Urizen (intellect or reason), Luvah (passion), Tharmas (sensation), and Los (imagination), with wisdom as a balancing of all four.

In *Tetrarch* a couple, Edward and Rosanna, once they pass through the doorway, discover that they are adepts and that they have a mission to fulfill in and between the four realms: helping the people of Los to recover a crystal that holds the secrets of the universe from the bloodthirsty ruler of the techno-fascist kingdom of Verula. Los is a kind of anarchist paradise, in which the army is a vehicle for play therapy, people have to be conscripted into government—since no one who desires power is actually fit to hold it—sex is an element of everyday social bonding, and the inhabitants' conventional greeting is "Have you loved well?" The tale moves along at a brisk pace and ends with a satisfying outcome to Rosanna and Edward's quest, but Alex found plenty of

* Another possible comparison is with Madeleine L'Engle's 1962 novel *A Wrinkle in Time*, with its mixture of fantasy and physics.

occasions to seed it with mild eroticism, Blakeian mysticism, and elements of quantum mechanics.

Higham surely saw *Tetrarch* as a promising item for readers who had reread Tolkien enough times and yearned to lose themselves in a similarly serious fantasy world. For their benefit, Alex included a diagram breaking down the Losian religion; a Losian grammar, vocabulary, and script; and a map of the four realms. Unlike those in his earlier novels, however, the characters don't fill out—their dialogue all sounds more or less like Alex's voice—and he frequently lapses into barely explained jargon. "You're assuming real time is the objective state?" one character suddenly asks. "Aren't both explicates equally real? Or is this an Everett-Wheeler-Graham model?"[35]

Alex had been writing books, essays, papers, and novels at a lightning clip for several years. Along with *Tetrarch*, he sent another complete novel to Higham, titled "Tiger Tiger," a comic tale of a British biologist from an Anglo-Indian military family who goes back to India and finds he is a natural Tantric yogi and can remember events of his past lives. He was also writing a historical novel about the Roman emperor Nero's physician. Higham enjoyed "Tiger Tiger" but advised against shopping it until he sold *Tetrarch*.[36]

Not surprisingly, then, and in spite of the attention Alex paid to sketching in the Losian language, *Tetrarch* showed signs of haste. A reader's report to Ross-Erikson, a Santa Barbara publisher that had agreed to issue it in the United States, complained that the story rushed from one scene to another as if the author was impatient to get through it and that Alex hadn't fleshed out his description of Losian society or developed some of the intellectual themes of the book. But Alex could be as stubborn as ever. When Ross-Erikson turned the manuscript over to an editor, he rejected the suggested changes outright, declaring that the editor "doesn't know his ass from a hole in the ground, and should jump into one or the other of them before he tries to teach me my business," demanding that the publisher print the text "as approved by me and without alteration."[37] The deal with Ross-Erikson fell through.

Higham failed to find a major UK publisher to take on the novel. Aside from the manuscript's textual deficiencies, he was hampered by Alex's having sold the US rights separately, which made it less attractive to major houses that typically acquired worldwide rights. In March 1978 David Higham died, and, while his associates carried on, the firm gave up on shopping *Tetrarch*.

Two years later, Shambhala, an independent publisher in Boulder,

Colorado, specializing in books related to Buddhism and personal growth, brought out the novel in the United States without popular success. Sales were hampered in part by the decision of B. Dalton-Pickwick, which had purchased the chain that had done so much to make *Joy* a success, not to advertise *Tetrarch*. Another problem: its one review in a mainstream publication, a *Los Angeles Times* piece by William Fadiman, a critic and veteran Hollywood script supervisor, couldn't have been harsher.[38] Fadiman called Alex's prose "a gallimaufry of contemporary slang, scientific jargon and the usual quota of neologisms seemingly inherent in extraterrestrial fiction" and tagged it "an also-ran in the science-fiction sweepstakes."[39] In a letter to Shambhala editor-in-chief Sam Bercholz, Alex speculated that Fadiman, the brother of literary critic Clifton Fadiman, might have been a Hutchins sympathizer during his court battle with the CSDI.[40]

Alex finally secured a UK publisher for *Tetrarch*—Wildwood House, which had been established less than a decade earlier by two former Penguin editors—around the time it appeared in the United States, and when it finally came out in Britain, in 1981, it fared much better with critics there. The *Daily Telegraph* called it "a well-sustained adventure narrative," and the *Observer*, in a science fiction roundup, praised *Tetrarch* as "a rattling good adventure yarn" set in "an alternate world at right-angles to our own."[41] Alex had hopes of striking a movie or television deal ("a lulu of an adult *Star Trek* with Alan Alda cast as the hero"), suggesting the puppets used in the then-recent sci-fi film *The Dark Crystal* as a clue to the appropriate visual style.[42] But in neither the United States nor the UK could Alex's publishers strike a deal for a mass market paperback edition of the book, denying it the backbone of the science fiction-fantasy readership.[43]

TETRARCH, AT LEAST, WAS published. "Tiger Tiger" never was. In the United States, Shambhala turned the novel down as being too British, even before *Tetrarch* appeared in print.[44] In the UK, Alex offered the book to his old publisher, Routledge, to no avail, then to Wildwood and Maurice Temple Smith, his old editor at Eyre & Spottiswode, who now had his own publishing house. The campaign devolved into a comedy of errors. The copy Alex sent to Wildwood got lost at the publisher; the copy sent to Temple Smith never arrived. When a fresh copy got to Wildwood, editor Oliver Caldecott initially liked the book, but on closer inspection he told Alex it needed work. On top of that, given the economic pinch in the UK, Wildwood had decided to hold off on new contracts and commitments, at least until *Tetrarch* had had a chance to prove itself. That included reissuing Alex's earlier novels, which they had discussed.[45]

In just a few years, Alex had gone from a best-selling author with a strong brand name to a writer of seemingly scattershot books who had to struggle to get published. He was trying, with some difficulty and annoyance, to do something about it. In January 1980, he had written to Nat Wartels at Crown, behind James Mitchell's back, proposing that he deal directly with Crown on his next books. His contract with Mitchell Beazley, which had paid him a retainer, had lapsed, he said, since the firm had not renewed it, and so he was free to strike a new deal directly with his publisher. He was unhappy with the co-editions that were Mitchell Beazley's bread and butter: the carefully designed books, like *The Joy of Sex*, which it then sold to multiple publishers around the world. Alex felt he could get a better deal under a standard publishing agreement, and this was how he had recently sold *Tetrarch* and was still trying to sell "Tiger Tiger."

Wartels agreed and offered Alex an annual option fee of $10,000 for exclusive first rights to any popular or general book he completed going forward, excluding fiction and technical or clinical works. Once each topic was accepted, Crown and the author would hammer out a contract.[46]

Mitchell, of course, was not happy when he learned that his deal with Alex—which he apparently did not realize had lapsed—was over. He especially took offense when Alex wrote him, apologizing jokingly for his act of "adultery."[47] "Adultery," Mitchell wrote back bitingly, "does not usually matter in relationships very much if both parties are adult[;] what does matter is a fundamental breakdown of relationship."[48] Alex was offering one possible book, on death and dying, to Crown that he had already discussed extensively with Mitchell Beazley. On top of that, he had been peppering the firm with letters demanding more thorough accounting of sales and his share of the proceeds from his books.

All this left Mitchell feeling that Alex was taking out any number of unrelated frustrations on him and his firm. "We have had quite a flow of fairly peremptory abusive or near-abusive cables and instructions and counter-instructions from your side on matters where you have drifted into presuming that over here we were acting in ways inimical to you and/or Jane," Mitchell wrote. Referring obliquely to the Hutchins lawsuit, he went on: "I have got the feeling in recent months that we might just possibly be becoming your new targets for projected aggression of the type which you do, as the historical record shows, occasionally lapse into with people you work with. Please don't turn us into your bogie people: all of us at MB are on your side."

In explaining why he was not going to make any future deals with Mitchell Beazley, Alex opened up to Mitchell about his current, frustrating personal situation. After three long years of lobbying, he had finally landed a faculty position at UCLA, as adjunct professor in the Neuropsychiatric Institute, teaching psychiatric residents. But it came with no salary. "I have now no paid job," he told Mitchell. "I am accordingly dependent for income for the rest of my life on funds passing through the books of one publisher. In spite of your solid position, this is an unacceptable business hazard. Any reasonable adviser would have to tell me to diversify, especially since I am not likely to equal the success of JOY with any other book—which makes it my sole means of support. Don't forget I have to take a 15–20 year view allowing for wars, pestilences and Acts of God."[49]

He hastened to add that any new deals he made would have no effect on his existing business with Mitchell Beazley, including any new editions of the *Joy* books or *A Good Age*, or any spinoffs from them. These "we should develop to the full. I very much hope that they prove profitable to both of us."

It is tempting to think that Alex had spent the past half-dozen years running from the success of his best seller. He had publicly announced his shift from sex writer to old-age authority, written several specialized books for doctors and geriatricians, published a challenging volume on the self and the biology of religion, a sci-fi/fantasy novel, and even a new poetry collection. Was he embarrassed by his popular success and anxious to reestablish himself as a serious scholar and writer? He was already putting the finishing touches on a sequel to *I and That*, delving further into physics and self-perception.

The short answer is no. Alex had been writing on geriatrics since the mid-'60s and developing his thinking on sociobiology, religion, and the self since he first visited India and became familiar with Hindu philosophy earlier in that decade. His earnings from the *Joy* books and his position at the CSDI—whatever its defects—had given him the opportunity to pursue these interests full-time. Particularly after his break with the center, Alex had attempted to support his more serious projects with popular titles he cooked up with James Mitchell. *A Good Age* had been aimed at the best-seller charts, *The Facts of Love* at steady mainstream success. *Tetrarch* was intended to appeal directly to a large and expanding sci-fi/fantasy audience. And he was working on his novel about Nero, which he hoped would attract the crowd who had made the 1976 TV adaptation of Robert Graves's novels about the emperor Claudius a popular success. It too had TV potential, he guessed.[50]

But none of these projects had worked nearly as well as the parties had hoped, and Alex's relationship with his publishing partner had always been difficult. Mitchell was a human bulldozer and Alex a stubborn, prickly author who increasingly reacted badly to interference from those he regarded as uninformed. Given his lower profile as a literary property, however, Alex may have been fooling himself that he still had the upper hand with either Crown or Mitchell Beazley concerning his future books. He only knew he no longer was in demand as he once had been.

Alex was still invited occasionally as a guest on television talk shows. In a letter to Sam Bercholz at Shambhala, volunteering to promote *Tetrarch*, he noted, "Usually I am preceded by Zsa Zsa [Gabor] and followed by a talking dog which had a sex change operation." In the UK he had been nearly a household name on BBC radio and TV, speaking on sex, old age, literature, and politics. In the United States, it seemed, his opinion was in demand on only one topic, and he was tiring of answering the same questions the same way, over and over.

He was supremely annoyed when Gay Talese's long-awaited book on the sexual revolution, *Thy Neighbor's Wife*, was published and instantly hit the best-seller lists with its depiction of "nude biologist Dr. Alex Comfort," "traipsing" among the naked bodies at Sandstone. Talese had then had the effrontery to use Alex's name to promote the book—a "rather obnoxious farrago," Alex complained to Bercholz.[51] ("Gay Talese brings home the real meaning of the sexual revolution," a display ad for the book boasted, "from Hugh Hefner and Alex Comfort to the ordinary men and women who tell the fascinating stories of their own sexual liberation.") Asked about the book's portrayal of himself, Alex replied, "The only reason he wrote that is because I refused to give him an interview. I believe in leaving Gay Talese to God."

Finished, more or less, with his latest spate of writing projects, Alex cast about for other ways to reengage. He fired off a letter to Carl Sagan, creator and host of the popular public television series *Cosmos*, trying to interest the astronomer in a new series confusingly described as "expounding both quantum logic and the influence of the

Boolean, non-superposition-seeing, human brain on the shape of physics."[52] He also wrote to Oliver Sacks, who had just published a book on migraines, but to no apparent reply.[53] Neither did he hear back from Sen. Alan Cranston of California, to whom he wrote offering his services as an advisor on legislation related to aging research and old-age policy.[54]

Alex's first stabs at projects under his new relationship with Crown—a "Physicians' 'Joy of Sex'" advising doctors how to use the book in medical practice, a series of guides for doctors in developing countries—went nowhere with the publisher.[55] And the proposals and inquiries he got were not always to his liking. In August 1980, two professors at Harvard Medical School asked him to contribute a "reflective essay" to a volume, later published as *Psychedelic Reflections*, describing what he had learned, as a nonexpert, from psychedelic drugs.[56] Alex replied that he had no experience whatsoever with psychedelics, which he regarded as "a rather risky way of promoting experiences obtainable by more physiological routes."[57]

HOWEVER FRUSTRATING HIS INTERACTIONS with the larger public, there was always *Joy*. The book remained a genuine cultural and publishing phenomenon. While it had slipped off temporarily one or twice, it had otherwise held a spot on either the US hardback or trade paperback *New York Times* best-seller lists for more than seven years. In May 1980 it was still number five on the trade paperback list, just behind Richard Nelson Bolles's *What Color Is Your Parachute?* But Mitchell was concerned that it would soon fade and wanted to pursue creating a new edition as well as develop a line of "educational short films on video" based on the book. Additionally, Alex had good news in February from Mitchell about the long-gestating *Joy of Sex* film: Paramount was at last ready to "do something about" the project, in partnership with the producers of the enormously successful frat-house comedy, *National Lampoon's Animal House*. He hoped that Alex would work with him on all of these ideas, rather than responding with "one of your one-up snappy or sneery letters."[58]

Alex was interested, but cautious; Mitchell was better off waiting another five of six more years before attempting to reinvent their money-spinner. He wasn't sure, either, how a video series could be structured that wouldn't cross the line into pornography. As for the comedy film, he was skeptical Paramount could come up with a good script: "'Monty Python and the Joy of Sex' would be something else."[59]

In September 1980 another offer came in, this one from Jac Holzman, the founder of Elektra and Nonesuch Records, who was now investing in home video and cable television properties. He wanted to "translate" *Joy* for the emerging videocassette and video disc markets.[60] Alex said he would consider any proposal, but an educational video would have to be sponsored by a reputable professional group—for instance, the American Psychiatric Association or the College of Family Physicians—and he would be extremely wary of any product that wasn't as tasteful as the original book.[61] Holzman withdrew the offer.[62] But Mitchell was now dying to get some sort of new *Joy of Sex* product onto the market, and he persisted with the idea of a video series for, he hoped, the BBC. Alex suggested he find an eminent professional association in the UK to act as sponsor before taking it any further.[63]

Mitchell was not happy being told to slow down. In his reply, he reminded Alex that Modsets, the shell company that Mitchell Beazley had set up to hold the rights to *The Joy of Sex*, also held the video rights. "You seem to imply," wrote Peter Mead, another director of the firm, "that you have a right to approve and/or dictate the form of the adaptation and neither is the case." Mitchell Beazley had decided to proceed with a video version of the book. Alex was welcome to be "further involved," but the adaptation would go ahead in any event.[64]

Alex threw all the leverage he had into his response. "Be realistic," he wrote. "I don't think that a version or adaptation from which the author publicly dissociates himself would be a great financial success." Mitchell Beazley had been acquired just weeks earlier by American Express, the credit card company.[65] "As a shareholder, I would feel obliged to raise at the shareholders' meeting of American Express the whole question of that corporation's subsidiaries being involved in the production of sexually explicit video material. . . . Quite apart from that, I have a public responsibility in regard to a book which people have come to respect, and I will go to any length to avoid having it discredited, exploited, or my own professional standing damaged."[66]

But then Alex added a note that epitomized the sometimes comic clash of personalities between himself and James Mitchell. "I don't know what we are arguing about at this time," he confessed, because he had not yet received any detailed proposal for a video from Mitchell. Would it be pornographic? Would it be entirely tame? Who really knew as yet? Nevertheless, Alex shot off a copy of Mead's letter to his lawyers, noting that the argument arose "from the fact that I am anxious to prevent them turning JOY into an explicit live-sex movie" and hinting that the BBC's lawyers—if the network got involved with the video—could help to hold Mitchell in line.[67]

MITCHELL BEAZLEY NEVER PRODUCED the video series, but the exchange of ultimatums, threats, and temper tantrums drove Alex's relationship with his sometime publishing partner to a new low. He had just produced some of the best work of his career in the form of *I and That* and the newer essays in *What Is a Doctor?*, he had a position at UCLA—if nonpaying—yet nothing seemed to be going right for him professionally.

He was also spending an inordinate amount of time worrying about his tax status. Much of his correspondence with Wildwood involved finding out how the Inland Revenue would treat his earnings—such as they might be—from *Tetrarch*.[68] When the prospect of a British documentary series based on *The Facts of Love* arose, he cautioned his prospective UK agent, Hughes Massie, that he and Jane had to limit the time they spent in England to avoid changing their domicile.[69] He was also shopping for brokers who could suggest new ways to shelter his income. Amid a drastic spike in inflation in the United States, he looked in particular for a way to convert his and Jane's American retirement account into a Swiss bond account in Zurich.[70]

As with most else, once Alex spent a bit of time researching these matters, he got creative. In September 1980 he suggested that Harris Seed put together "a syndicate of offshore earners" such as himself, to which they could assign their forward earnings. "The dodge," he said, "would be to create a simulacrum of a bona-fide multinational so close that it was not distinguishable by the Courts. This could be a highly profitable operation for the managers, who could take a moderate service fee." If his attorney wanted "a partner—or an accomplice—let me know."[71] Nothing, fortunately, came of this dubious scheme.

Paralleling Alex's practical and professional frustrations was a troubled life with Jane. Several years into their US residency, the two were living a curiously solitary existence. They had few close friends in Santa Barbara and few visitors. Most of Alex's communication was by mail or phone. Jane had never had many friends and was only making new ones in their new home through her husband. Alex and Len Hayflick were getting to know each other better, for example, and Jane got on well with Len's wife, Ruth; the couples visited back and forth in Santa Barbara and Palo Alto.[72] But Jane was increasingly unhappy.

Alex's family noticed a degree of isolation as well. Nick and his wife, Deborah, and their young daughter had moved to Washington, DC, in 1976, when Nick was sent by the *Daily Telegraph* to cover Queen Elizabeth II's bicentennial tour and then to cover Congress, the Pentagon, energy, and aerospace. Alex and Jane visited the family numerous times in Washington, often when Alex was on the East Coast for a conference or speaking engagement.[73] But they never extended an invitation to visit them in California. When Nick had a chance to visit the West Coast on one occasion, they begged off.[74]

Nick moved his family back to London two years later when he joined the *Telegraph*'s political staff ahead of an upcoming general election, and Alex and Jane came over to visit. Jane had grown close to Deborah and helped her with her newborn second child, a son, John.

Early in 1980 Jane had a blepharoplasty—removal of excess skin from the eyelids—and Alex wrote to Joseph "Pete" Reidy, an eminent plastic surgeon he had known at St Andrew's Hospital in Billericay early in his medical training, now retired, about the possibility of getting her a full facelift in the UK (they did not follow through). She tried dieting. Fourteen months later, Alex wrote to their personal physician—the letter was marked confidential—suggesting some options for adjusting Jane's medications for depression when he next saw her.

She was already taking Amoxepine, which is used to treat major depression, and another drug, Flurazepam, for insomnia. Now Alex was suggesting she take Nardil—the drug he was on for his migraine attacks—plus, as needed, Chlorpromazine, also known as Thorazine, which was used to treat schizophrenia, manic depression, and other psychotic disorders. Their doctor filled the prescriptions. When Jane had a bad food reaction, including higher blood pressure, from eating New Zealand spinach, possibly on account of its chemical makeup, Alex gave her some Chlorpromazine but then asked the doctor to prescribe phentolamine shots that they could keep around the house, in case the drug brought on very high blood pressure.[75]

Jane was clearly suffering from severe depression, sometimes crossing over into worse episodes, and Alex was trying everything he could to treat it medically. The difficulty of doing so is compounded when the patient drinks too much, as Jane did. What was odd about Alex's letters to their doctor is that he never mentioned drink—even though he would have known that combining Flurazepam, for example, with alcohol can be life-threatening. The tone of his letters too was breezy and professional. "Jane was, as I suspected, working up to a sharpish attack of depression," he wrote on one occasion, almost as if his wife was suffering from a flu rather than a more fundamental unhappiness. Nor did he say anything about how Jane's troubles were affecting him.

In August 1981 Alex wrote a letter to *The Lancet*, laying out his theory that some of the chemicals in New Zealand spinach had caused Jane's high blood pressure, again without mentioning alcohol.[76] He was seemingly sweeping the deeper background of the episode out of sight. But he couldn't keep it completely suppressed.

In the early years after he and Jane moved to America, Marilyn and Irvin Yalom and their children remained Alex's best friends there, and the couples visited back and forth frequently, despite the distance between Santa Barbara and Palo Alto. On a visit shortly before Alex and Jane were married, Marilyn took Jane to the Stanford Shopping Center to pick out her wedding outfit—a pink dress—and the two maintained at least a superficial friendship. The Yaloms' youngest son, Ben, whom Alex had known almost since birth, came to stay with him and Jane in Santa Barbara for an extended visit in the late '70s. Ben had always loved talking with Alex, who addressed him more as a mature person than a child, and he remembered that Jane always treated him fondly and was "very warm and supportive" of Alex.[77]

Alex was always the center of his friends' attention, however. Jane "seemed a rather a dim person," Eve Yalom, Marilyn and Irv's oldest child, recalled. "I remember her sitting in the garden, reading. I couldn't figure out why he was with her." In the early '80s her disposition changed. One day at breakfast in Santa Barbara, with no clear provocation, she picked a quarrel with Marilyn over Marilyn's having sent her children to day care while she was working. Jane thought "parking a lot of children" with a supervisor was a terrible idea. Marilyn replied that she had raised four children this way and, like many other married women, had to work to support them.

But she was shocked by Jane's outburst, which seemed out of proportion to the topic. Jane was "very nasty, explosive, irrational," Marilyn recalled. Later she took a walk with Alex on the beach. "He was troubled by what had transpired, but he was very loyal to her and wasn't about to abandon her."[78]

That was the last time the Yaloms saw Alex for some years. Jane clearly wanted nothing more to do with the family, and particularly with the woman she appeared to regard as her rival. The break may have relieved some of Jane's insecurity about her life with her husband in a new country, but for Alex it meant the end of one of the closest friendships of his life.

ALEX'S RELATIVE ISOLATION IN America included generally staying out of political conflicts, sensibly out of concern for his resident status. This was, of course, a great change from his former life in Britain. When the Santa Barbara Renters Rights Coalition, which included the local chapter of the Gray Panthers, wrote him in 1980 asking his public support for a new rent control measure, he and Jane declined, offering this as an excuse. (They did, however, point out that rent control was only a stopgap; what was really needed was an end to tax shelters on speculative real estate deals and "proper municipal housing on the European model.")[79]

Aside from producing the third edition of *The Biology of Senescence*, Alex had been less involved in gerontology since his move as well. Zhores Medvedev noticed the change in 1977, when their mutual friend, Bernard Strehler, a pioneering biogerontologist at the University of Southern California, organized an International Biogerontology Conference in San Francisco, and Alex was not there. "Most people in the field were very anxious to attend," Medvedev recalled.[80] Alex was no longer publishing in academic journals on the subject either.

He still considered himself part of the research community on aging, however. That relatively small world was the epicenter of a major scandal beginning in 1975, when Len Hayflick was accused by the National Institutes of Health of profiting from the sale of a strain of normal human fetal cells he had developed. The dispute only ended after six years in an out-of-court settlement of the parties' lawsuits against each other. The settlement was a landmark that helped establish the rights of individual scientists and researchers to share in the profits that universities and corporations were reaping from the boom in biotech discoveries and innovations.

Alex stood by his friend from the start, demanding that the journal *Science* allow Hayflick to respond to the allegations against him in its pages, recommending him for jobs, and marshaling other prominent scientists to speak up on his behalf. "I know this can't be true," Alex told Hayflick, "because I understand the man, regardless of what he's accused of."[81] In 1979, he dedicated the third edition of *The Biology of Senescence* to Hayflick, with the inscription "IN CVIVS CALVMNIATORES MINGIMVS": meaning roughly, "We piss on those who defame." In 1987 he contributed a glowing recommendation when Hayflick applied for an adjunct professorship in anatomy at the University of California, San Francisco. The appointment marked the final restoration of his friend's reputation after a dozen years in the wilderness. In his recommendation letter, Alex couldn't resist getting in a final dig at "the palace eunuchs at the N.I.H."[82]

Flourishes like that were cropping up more frequently in Alex's letters, which had become longer and chattier and revealed more of his personality since his move to the States and the end of his responsibilities as a laboratory researcher. Writing to friends or even professional colleagues, he was more liable to offer his opinion on a multitude of subjects, criticize individuals and institutions, and share more than previously about his and Jane's plans.

In March 1982, in the ninth year of his US residency, he finally received his license to practice medicine in California. But what would he do with it? He wanted a paying job, and the next step would be a residency, repeating the routine he had gone through nearly forty years earlier in London. He was teaching and consulting on internal medicine in the family medicine residency program at Ventura County Medical Center, a program affiliated with UCLA. He enjoyed the work but was also thinking about neuropsychiatry, which he had been teaching for several years at UCLA. Now he had the possibility of doing a residency and actually practicing it.

But that could take three years, by which time he would be sixty-five. And his plans were changing. In a letter to Milton Greenblatt, his boss at the UCLA Neuropsychiatric Institute, he mentioned that he expected to go back permanently to the UK once he reached retirement age, placing his and Jane's trust in the National Health Service rather than Medicare to see them through their later years. Perhaps, he suggested, he would wait until he returned to Britain, where he could obtain a diploma in psychological medicine and begin practicing more quickly.[83]

In a letter to a friend a month later, Alex revealed that he and Jane had bought property in Cranbrook, Kent, some sixty miles from London, where some of the Comfort family had lived in past centuries. The land included an apple orchard called Fightingcox Farm, and they were looking for a house to buy.[84] In July 1983 Alex began consulting a London solicitor as to how they could make the move while maintaining legal residency in the United States, to avoiding incurring higher taxes.[85] In September, writing to Peter Medawar, he said they were "preparing to come home," although probably not for another year at least. Aside from wanting nothing to do with the American "sickness industry" in their old age, Alex was keen to return to the "collegial atmosphere" he had known in British academia and had never really enjoyed in the United States.[86]

They had considered other options. Alex had thought about relocating to Ireland, and he later told George Woodcock that "if Canada had been a smidgeon warmer" he and Jane might have considered going there.[87] It's possible that Jane's unhappiness influenced their choice of England, although he didn't say so in his letters. At home in Montecito, they were addicted to BBC television dramas. They got their global news from the BBC World Service and their American news from *The Economist*, Alex liked to say.

Moreover, he had never left off reviewing books for the *Guardian* and firing off letters to the British papers whenever he needed to scratch a political itch. His politics had changed very little over four decades. A November 1981 letter to *The Economist* argued for the UK and its European neighbors to divorce themselves from Reagan's increasingly aggressive foreign and defense policy and declare themselves neutral in the Cold War.[88] Often his rhetoric turned Swiftian: in another letter to *The Economist* he noted that "missiles that are not heat- or radar-seeking but [rather] caudillo-seeking," in the service of "selective and well-deserved tyrannicide," could be justifiable.[89] He was as fiercely opposed as ever to nuclear weapons and the arms race, denouncing, in a February 1985 letter to the *Times* of London, the Thatcher government's "poodle policy" in endorsing Reagan's enormous Star Wars missile-defense program. Alex also denounced the prime minister's relentless determination to push through the costly Trident submarine program to expand and upgrade the UK's own nuclear warfare capability.[90]

That said, his desire to return to England is not clearly explainable. He was still a comparatively young sixty-two-year-old, had taken the trouble to acquire a California medical license, was going for a ham radio license in the state, and was happy to be working at an excellent nearby teaching hospital for pay. In some ways, his life in America was finally starting to come out right. Jane, on the other hand, had few friends and very little to do there. She volunteered at the stroke center at Santa Barbara Cottage Hospital and made rugs and other items for the senior center, but Alex was still constantly traveling on speaking engagements, and even when he was home her depression often paralyzed her. The answer, perhaps, was a return to their old home, even if not right away.

In the meantime, they could work together on another writing project. This turned out to be the strangest and most uncharacteristic work in Alex Comfort's long publishing career. *What about Alcohol?* is a 26-page booklet, with illustrations, that Alex and Jane wrote and published in 1983 through the Carolina Biological Supply Company as part of a series of booklets on science. Aimed at high school students, the text reads less like the work of a responsible scientist than something written by an early-twentieth-century temperance crusader. Along with some scientific data, Alex and Jane hammered home a checklist of the horrors of drunkenness that seemed to equate even moderate consumption with alcoholism. Abstinence is the only certain strategy for avoiding the disease, they concluded flatly.

The publisher sent the booklet to the National Association of State Boards of Education (NASBE), which was preparing a set of teaching guidelines on alcohol, and received back a sharp rebuke for publishing "such an unbalanced piece of work." The NASBE noted particularly the pamphlet's reliance on scare tactics, "notoriously ineffective in producing desirable behavior in young people." Young readers would "recognize the exaggerations and lack of substance," and "[an opportunity to] capture their interest, increase their factual knowledge, and develop their decision making skills [will] have been lost."[91]

Rejection by a group like the NASBE was enough to sink a textbook, let alone a modest booklet like *What about Alcohol?* Carolina Biological Supply forwarded a copy of the letter to Alex and Jane, who wrote to the NASBE, but they only reiterated the points that had alarmed the group to begin with.[92] They intended their booklet "to counteract the unbalanced emphasis on 'sensible drinking' which repeatedly surfaces in educational programs," they said, since a responsible decision to drink is "not so much impossible as unreal." Indeed, any person who takes up alcohol is playing "straightforward Russian roulette"; those who don't become alcoholics are merely "lucky." For the NASBE to "play pat-a-cake with so serious and preventable an epidemic disease" was "quite wrong," the Comforts insisted.

What had persuaded Alex to embark on a campaign against alcohol? He had never been much of a drinker, but never before had he spoken out against it. At the end of their letter, he and Jane noted that their primary interest in writing the booklet had been their engagement in geriatric medicine. "Geriatrics stand on the foundation of life-styles which are set in youth," and even moderate alcohol consumption can result in "chronic brain and liver disease," they wrote. But this is not very convincing. While the letter was signed by both Comforts, the voice is Alex's, and it's tempting to guess that the entire project was a backhanded attempt to prod Jane to give up alcohol. If "scare tactics" wouldn't work on American teens, perhaps they would work on one of the coauthors.

Alex was nevertheless genuinely alarmed by the degree of alcoholism he was encountering in the United States. In an article in *The Lancet* a year later—a considerably more level-headed piece of writing than the booklet—he noted that at the Ventura County hospital, where he was now attending rounds, some 40 to 50 percent of the medical caseload was directly alcohol-related, and probably more in trauma surgery. The same arguments that governments and nonprofits were making for keeping narcotics and other recreational drugs illegal applied with equal force to alcohol, he pointed out. "Our attitude toward alcohol is basically not evidential but sentimental, rather as we are slow to admit that a family member is delinquent or insane. If cocaine is an Edwardian roué, marijuana a grubby counterculturalist, and LSD a crazy with a knife, alcohol is a beloved if disreputable old uncle whose peccadilloes are excused because he is friendly and keeps a good cellar."[93]

Alcohol had no place in a technological society, Alex argued, in which automobiles were the referred means of conveyance and substance abuse was endemic. To address the problem, Alex suggested offering tax advantages for the production of wine with 2 percent or less alcohol, for example, while jacking up taxes on stronger alcoholic beverages. He also urged doctors to set an example of not drinking, just as fewer and fewer of them smoked.

Alex was venturing into territory he knew little about, or had not come to terms with in his own life. The idea that alcoholism is a disease he dismissed as a "catch phrase," since the disease "disappears in the absence of alcohol." Yet his wife had a serious drinking problem bound up with an underlying struggle against depression. Alcoholism in general was never as simple a problem as Alex seemed to think, and neither was Jane's.

As they began to solidify their plans to return to England, he was still working with her doctor to adjust her medication levels. Suffering from insomnia and intense anxiety in April 1983, around the time *What about Alcohol?* appeared, she was still taking Nardil; Chlorpromazine, sometimes in "full antipsychotic doses"; Temazepam, for insomnia; and Lorazepam, which treats anxiety but also seizures. Writing to her doctor, Alex said she had been under "a great deal of stress over the past year (repeated infections, workmen, no domestic help, etc.)" but mentioned nothing about her drinking.[94] Later that year, after a visit by Alex and Jane to Nick and his wife Deborah and their children in London, Deborah noted that the levels in their liquor bottles had gone down substantially: their first inkling that there was a problem.[95]

The summer of the following year, Alex and Jane visited England again to scout out a place to live. During their trip, Jane had a breakdown—the details are not clear—and had to be hospitalized. Alex, at a loss, went back to the States before she was released, telling Nick, "The last thing she needs is me around." It was the first time he had spoken to his son about his wife's condition. His Englishness may have had something to do with the delay in doing so. "He was a very considerate man and didn't like to bother other people with his problems," Nick recalled.

Jane stayed with Nick and Deborah briefly following her release and before returning to California.[96] Back home, she began taking lithium and L-tryptophan, suggesting the diagnosis was now bipolar disorder.[97] While she seemed better on her return to Montecito, within a few months she was suffering from night terrors, nighttime muscle twitches, and sleep-walking.[98] A doctor they had seen in the UK couldn't understand these new developments and only suggested—again—rejiggering her medications.

CHAPTER 21

Reality and Empathy (1980–1984)

At times, attending to Jane could be nearly consuming, pushing Alex's work and his still-heavy travel schedule to the side.[1] But he was absorbed in another project as well.

In an interview several years later, Jane observed that the composition of *I and That* had marked a "sudden break" in Alex's thinking. Previously they had talked about "everything under the sun." Now, when her husband wanted to discuss his intellectual pursuits, it was "that": the confluence of physics, religion, phenomenology, and the self. Alex agreed that his work had become more focused since he began to "get a grip on general philosophy rather than on specific topics."[2] A variety of longtime interests, from psychology to medicine to sociobiology, were converging.

Immediately after completing *I and That* he had written *Tetrarch*, which attempted to popularize the ideas in that book through sci-fi fantasy. He then resumed work on a sequel to *I and That*, titled *Reality and Empathy*, and he completed a first draft in 1980. It was an even more complex work, and he had more difficulty getting it into print. The style was "fairly light-hearted," he said.[3] "The trouble is that when you mix math, psychiatry, oriental religion, cosmology and the kitchen sink in one book, publishers don't like it."[4]

Oxford University Press turned it down, despite an enthusiastic reader's report from Peter Medawar.[5] Alex tried Basic Books, a unit of Harper & Row that published brainy nonfiction, touting *Reality and Empathy* as "the first no-nonsense modern book about metaphysics for the intelligent teen-ager."[6] When that approach failed, he tried the Academic Press (publisher of the *Journal of Social and Biological Structures*). He said—less than accurately—that the book did not contain "a lot of inaccessible algebra" and conceded that it would not be another *Joy of Sex* commercially, and the answer again was no.[7] It took Alex three years to find a publisher, State University of New York Press, and *Reality and Empathy* finally appeared in June 1984.

The book was spawned in a series of academic papers and lectures Alex gave his psychiatric residents at UCLA and Brentwood VA hospital, on how and why humans form world models: hypotheses and structures of conviction ranging from Darwinism and natural history to monotheism and from psychoanalysis to quantum mechanics. We do so for a variety of reasons, he argued: natural inquisitiveness, a need to make sense of our surroundings, and, most importantly, to come to terms with "the basic feature of the human condition"—"foreknowledge of our own mortality." All world models, he wrote, "ultimately comment on existential anxiety."[8] A good one enables us, collectively or spiritually, to reassure ourselves that death, in the end, has no dominion.

Metaphysics, Alex continued, is the study of these world models, and his larger purpose was to persuade practitioners of "hard" sciences like biology to take metaphysics seriously again after a long period when many had been disinclined to think about "first principles" like being, identity, and time.

In this, he had to walk a fine line. Ever since quantum physicists had observed that atoms and subatomic particles don't behave like the solid objects we're used to in the everyday, "macro" world, and that the distinction between particles and waves was blurry at best, physics had been moving into uncharted territory. New concepts were often impossible to visualize, and a motley crew of occultists, parapsychologists, and pseudo-mystics threatened to take over the popular discussion and understanding of the subject. Alex liked Haldane's observation, "Nature may not only be odder than we think, but odder than we can think" and quoted it twice in *Reality and Empathy*, but he still had to convince his colleagues that he wasn't asking them to hand over the keys of the kingdom to crackpots.[9]

A good deal of work by respectable researchers, especially over the preceding couple of decades, was suggesting the direction that new world models might take. Alex cited Bell's theorem, introduced by physicist John Stewart Bell in a 1964 paper, which proposed that the measurable attributes of an atom were determined not just by events happening nearby but also by events so far away that their influence had to travel faster than the speed of light. Reality must be nonlocal, and all systems must have interacted at some time in the past, Bell concluded.[10]

Around the time Alex was writing *I and That*, the American scientist David Bohm, currently at Birkbeck College in London, was developing a theory called "implicate and explicate order," which held that reality is underpinned by an "implicate" order of structures and processes that can be expressed mathematically. These structures and processes are a "superposition," meaning they can be, paradoxically, in multiple states at the same time, until they are observed, or explicated. "Explicates" are everything else: electrons and other quantum particles, extending to larger phenomena like space and time, that arise from the implicate order and become observable to us.

Bohm claimed that the patterns of the implicate order, which could be remote in time and space, explained the odd behavior of subatomic particles. The upshot, in theory, was that reality—the entire world or universe, at the implicate level—is a seamless, measurable whole.[11]

Is there a way to think about that unity in the recognizable physical world? There is, Bohm said. Holograms are photographic images that mimic three-dimensionality, allowing the viewer to see the photographed object from many angles. Their special feature is that every region of the hologram contains the whole, undivided image. Bohm and the Stanford psychologist and neurosurgeon Karl Pribram theorized that the implicate order was like a hologram in that all parts of the brain contain all the information contained in the whole. Something similar might apply to the universe as a whole, which may actually consist of multiple universes plotted into one another, the American theoretical physicist John A. Wheeler and two colleagues suggested.[12]

Alex was especially taken with a paper by the Czech-Austrian logician Kurt Gödel arguing that, given the laws of relativity, "now" cannot exist as a distinct slice of space-time. Past, present, and future must exist *en bloc*: all together, at once. Gödel imagined a rotating universe, in which "the local times of certain observers cannot be fitted together into one unified world time."[13] Change, Alex gathered from this, is not an objective but a subjective phenomenon, "not a thing but a way-of-seeing."[14] Alex took this insight of Gödel's to clear the field for the kind of theorizing that Bell, Bohm, and Pribram seemed to be moving toward, in which—in an extremely general sense—a unified system underlies both the physical and the mental worlds.

Another wrinkle was supplied by a mathematician at the University of Illinois, Chicago, Louis Kauffman, and a Chilean biologist and neuroscientist, Francisco Varela, who together invented the iterant, an algebraic situation in which two seemingly opposite phenomena oscillate, appearing to the viewer alternately. An example would be a limitlessly oscillating sequences of plus and minus signs, in which it's unknown which of the two begins or ends the sequence. The iterant is neither one nor the other, but both at the same time.[15]

"The iterant is what the mind is generating constantly when it tries to observe something," Kauffman later said, and Alex was taken with it as a counterpart, in the world of higher mathematics and logic, to Bohm's implicate and explicate order: another kind of superposition. Kauffman and Varela had published their initial paper on the iterant in the *Journal of Social and Biological Structures*, and Kauffman started a correspondence with Alex after Harvey Wheeler asked him to respond to a comment Alex made on it.[16]

Yet another explorer who was traveling in much the same territory as Alex was Douglas Hofstadter. In 1979, while Alex was writing the first draft of *Reality and Empathy*, Hofstadter published *Gödel, Escher, Bach: An Eternal Golden Braid*, an extraordinarily successful book about how consciousness and the self emerge from hidden neurological mechanisms.[17] The book brilliantly laid out some very difficult concepts for the general reader—Alex called it "the most entertaining book ever written on mathematical logic"—and was rewarded with both a Pulitzer Prize and an American Book Award.[18]

Like some of the other thinkers whose work Alex was building on, Hofstadter, a physicist and cognitive scientist at Indiana University, described a system that was more than the sum of its parts. He compared the workings of the mind to an ant colony, a complex system in which a single ant brain carries no information about more than a few activities yet joins teams that operate according to signals generated by an underlying formal structure of rules to carry out often very complex tasks. The human brain, Hofstadter said, "has a formal, hidden hardware level," perhaps analogous to Bohm's implicate order: "a formidably complex mechanism that makes transitions from state to state according to definite rules embodied in it."[19]

In a hypothesis paralleling the Channel 1/Channel 2 system that Alex had proposed in *I and That*, Hofstadter described the mind as a hierarchical system and explained consciousness as the product of a "strange loop": a feedback pattern running from top to bottom and from bottom to top of the hierarchical layers, always arriving back where it started. Along the way, the strange loop produces "ideas, hopes, images, analogies, and finally consciousness and free will."[20]

Neither in *Reality and Empathy* nor anywhere else did Alex compare Hofstadter's strange loop to his own hypothesis in *I and That*. He was more interested in encouraging other scientists to investigate current world models and develop new ones that brought physics, metaphysics, and the natural sciences together. Hofstadter's analogy of the ant colony suggested that he was moving toward a model in which the "I" might not be contained only in a single human brain but instead over numerous ones, an idea he embraced in a later book, *I Am a Strange Loop,* that Alex would likely have appreciated, had he lived to read it.[21] But Alex did have one significant criticism. Hofstadter's theory, he said, failed to incorporate the inconvenient fact that the mechanisms that presumably produce the strange loop—the central nervous system, physiology, and finally atomic physics—are all formulated and understood by the mind: the very thing they presumably activate.[22]

The mind habitually looks for causation; this is one of the tools it uses to build world models. But does causation exist in nature or only in the human mind? Alex likened the mind to a computer game consisting of a black box and a video display terminal. The terminal allows the player to control space ships traveling across the screen. The ships collide and explode, shoot each other down, and protect themselves from each other, all at the player's command. The game's "sole object is to exhibit correlations to the players, so that they can aim." Yet, there are no "real" correlations on the screen: just numerical relationships "implicated" in the circuitry of the black box and "explicated" on the screen display. There is no one-to-one correspondence between the space ships, asteroids, and other pseudo-objects the player sees on the screen, and the modulated pulses that the black box produces; no matter how much mayhem occurs on the screen, the black box's wiring stays immobile.[23]

So it is, Alex argued, with the many observations, comparisons, and analyses the mind generates: all are the product of an inherently problematic observer that incessantly creates new models with which to view nature, including of the body it inhabits. "All 'critiques' of reality have to be carried through the system which generated the model of phenomenal reality in the first place."[24]

It was this paradox that drew Alex into the dense subject matter of *Reality and Empathy*, Lou Kauffman, who soon began a lively correspondence with him, later speculated. "Maybe part of this comes not so much from physics as his interest in studying the relationship between people's psychology and medicine and the Eastern mystical traditions," Kauffman said, because, like quantum physics and the higher math connected to it, "those points of view involve leading logic into paradox . . . . Alex, in his book, is quite unabashedly playing in a world of associations that lets him move freely among these different ideas."

Rather than trying to explain away the paradoxes that Bell and Bohm had discovered, which Eastern traditions tend to accept, Alex started by asking another question: is the mind—the observer—really separate from the underlying, unified system of reality, be it Bohm's implicate-explicate order or the circuitry of some universal black box? Some scientists had already gone a long way in the latter direction, Alex noted. In a 1946 interview, the British physicist and mathematician Sir James Jeans had said, "I incline to the idealistic theory that consciousness is fundamental, and that the material universe is derivative from consciousness, not consciousness from the material universe. . . . In general the universe seems to me to be nearer to a great thought than to a great machine. It may well be, it seems to me, that each individual consciousness ought to be compared to a brain-cell in a universal mind."[25]

That speculation prompted one critic to respond, "Jeans going off the deep end," and Alex was not saying he agreed with it. But he did suggest it was worth investigating whether the brain wasn't "in some way plugged into this fundamental structure," making consciousness not a secondary capacity but "as primary and as fundamental as matter." Perhaps not, but given that quantum physicists and investigators like Bell, Bohm, and Hofstadter had unsettled some of the givens of Newtonian science, "the question itself no longer makes scientific nonsense, because it no longer runs counter to the prevalent understanding of physics."[26]

One possibility, which Alex derived from Bohm, was that mental activity and physical reality were structurally similar and "shared a similar algebra at the implicate level." In other words, the same mathematical processes that underpinned one, underpinned the other. Mathematics, then, was the means of exploring the nature of both the mind and the physical world. If we can't "view" the implicate order, we can feel around in it using the tool kit—"polynomials, spinors, matrices, etc. etc."—that mathematics supplies.[27]

If the relationship he was suggesting was valid, Alex speculated, it was possible that the human mind was not locked into its "computer game" after all but had abilities to comprehend and explore the implicate order that it normally filtered out: in other words, to investigate world models without all the subjective baggage of the I. "If there are available states of mind in which such complex models, instead of being computed, are directly perceived as we normally perceive in terms of conventional space and conventional time," Alex said, "it would be a blockbuster . . . what is now relevant only to models in physics would become existentially relevant to all." This, he noted, "is what mystics and other cultivators of oceanic states have always claimed."[28]

For example, black holes—the mysterious areas in space-time that are so dense their gravitational pull sucks in everything—might become comprehensible to us directly, not just through algorithms. Non-physicists could "empathize" this new way of perceiving the universe, instead of relying on mathematics to express it. Once they did, they might begin to notice other singularities or "sore-thumb-type anomalies, not in the remote world of microphysics or cosmology, but in actual experience."[29] If space-time existed *en bloc*, would that have implications for the theory of evolution? Since the brain is composed of matter, but matter is a less stable affair than previously assumed, what is doing the thinking: about space-time or anything else?[30]

The way to start investigating these questions was by attempting to describe the behavior of the implicate order in metaphorical—that is, mathematical—terms. This would enable the development of testable hypotheses that would yield practical results, Alex hoped. He suggested two steps for doing so. First, examine existing models in physics to see if they have "psychological and psychophysical consequences which are fundamental and not simply self-referent"; second, get the model-making of physics back in step with sciences such as evolutionary biology and neuropsychology. End the split between modern physics and the natural sciences.[31]

Doing so, however, would mean asking some "disreputable questions." Is there any point, for example, in devoting serious research to instances of synchronicity, what Carl Jung and the Austrian physicist Wolfgang Pauli described as circumstances that appear meaningfully related yet lack a causal connection? Should scientists seriously investigate parapsychology, what Alex defined as "any phenomena which might suggest that mind is a primary, not a secondary explicate"? And what if that meant honoring with critical attention people who claimed to bend spoons with their minds, communicate information directly from their mind to another's, or have precognitive dreams?

For the most part, Alex said, the answer is yes to all these questions. While many or most people in the spoon-bender camp would prove to be frauds, so did many people operating in the hard sciences, and, besides, some interesting effect might emerge, "even if the investigators do not appear to have hold of the right end of the stick."[32] It was also worthwhile for contemporary scientists to look again at the classic texts of Hinduism and Buddhism, which analyzed the self in somewhat the same decentered, contingent way he was proposing, and the work of the Renaissance alchemists—the "Department of Premature Intuitions and Near Misses," as he called them—some of whom had some inkling of what became quantum logic but lacked the math or the computing power to pursue it usefully.[33]

What did Alex guess researchers would learn from such inquiries, particularly about the relationship of mind to matter? "Mental processes," he wrote, "might be patterned by the grain of nature, and our perception of the grain of nature might be patterned by our mental processes: in other words, rather than treating them as a chicken and egg, we should see them as mapping into one another." The good news, he said, was that world models were being demystified. Thanks to the scientific revolution, more and more "cosmological, eschatological, and psychological statements" were "coming in the reach of testing." Those that truly had nothing to offer and no basis in reality were quickly tested and dismissed.[34]

A further piece of good news was that Hindu and Buddhist philosophical practice could be enlisted in the program. "A systematic pursuit of oceanic perception, starting with traditional methods, might help us in intuiting how a thing-less or holographic universe might look," even though the logic of that experience would then have to be "reduced to mathematical form" just to see if it made practical sense.[35]

ALEX WAS FIRST ATTRACTED to this immense subject by the parallels he perceived between Indian philosophy, Blake's worldview, and the discoveries emerging from quantum physics. That led him to two popular of books: Fritjof Capra's 1975 *The Tao of Physics* (published in the U.S. by Shambhala and in the UK by Wildwood, the same houses that brought out *Tetrarch*) and Gary Zukav's 1979 overview of the new physics, *The Dancing Wu Li Masters*. In its jacket copy for the book, SUNY Press claimed that *Reality and Empathy* was a grand theoretical synthesis. In reality, it was an invitation to other researchers to pursue what Alex thought was the future of science: the bringing-together of modern physics—not visually representable but suggesting "a more fluid range of possibilities" than the old rational-mechanical model—with the natural sciences and psychology. For the first time, consciousness would be seen as an essential aspect of the universe, not just a byproduct of human physical processes. As it happened, this was exactly what Capra himself would challenge future researchers to attempt when he issued a fifth edition of his book, 26 years later.[36]

A larger public might find *Reality and Empathy* compelling as well, Alex thought, because people were always excited by such stuff as science fiction, black holes, cosmological epics, and archetypal symbols, both serious and fanciful. "People like any good story of which the moral is that things are not as they seem, and that marvels are not dead," he wrote, channeling some of the pitches he used to sell publishers on his novels.[37]

He was not fooling himself about his book's commercial prospects, however. He knew it was a tough read. To some correspondents, he described it as "skull-splitting," and he warned others that it "summarily turns most readers into frogs." Unlike *I and That*, some chapters contained a daunting load of math, and the whole text was more heavily weighted with scientific jargon than the earlier book.

He balanced out these negatives, to a degree, with his usual lively prose and a series of semi-comic dialogues, sprinkled as interludes throughout the text, that explained some of his tougher concepts in more down-to-earth terms: a device Hofstadter had used in *Gödel, Escher, Bach*.

In *Reality and Empathy*, a lion and a unicorn step down from the British coat of arms to argue over scientific method. To provide some notion of what the mind could do if it got past the distinction between I and not-I, Alex invented Gezumpstein, a "demon" who has no a priori human ideas or methods, can see past, present, and future *en bloc*, and exists mainly to generate new world models. Gezumpstein's ideas and intuitions take the form of balloons—or "poppers," after the philosopher Karl Popper—which the demon keeps safe in a wooden box. Sometimes he sells them to mathematicians, who take them to play with outdoors, with mixed results.

"Every balloon which is reasonably well-formed . . . is serviceable," Gezumpstein says. "You could play with some of them on and off for several of your centuries. Even let one down and blow it up again years later." Some, of course, prove less serviceable than, say, Euclid's or Newton's, and when removed from the box, just pop. But none is "popper-proof."[38]

The dialogue that strikes the most personal note is a psychiatric session in which the analyst is God, the patient Adam. Their sessions are scheduled every five hundred years. At their 1983 meeting, Adam demands that she (God) reveal why he can't come back inside the

Garden of Eden. God replies, "You *are* in the Garden. Nobody ejected you from it. Certainly not I. But we constructed you very carefully, with a great deal of circuitry to spare, and the circuitry itself carried with it the option of using it. It has two quite different logics, in fact. It also carried a built-in option of choice, and under its own program it selected the second of these logics, the desire to know objectively."

Adam never left Eden; he chose to reshape it into a "learning-knowledge-analysis system" that included a new dimension, time, with which God, in her infinitude, has some trouble empathizing. Did I therefore invent the universe? Adam asks. No, says God, "I created a recursive infinity of universes, and you, as a result of eating the apple, picked one of them." Adam took his choice and "constructed a world view [God] never intended." God recommends that Adam see her again in one hundred years.[39]

REALITY AND EMPATHY IS not as engaging a book as Hofstadter's—Alex had a bad habit of "saying everything at once," in long summary sentences, one reader remarked—but he tried.[40] What the two have in common is the spectacle of an extraordinarily restless and inquisitive mind wrestling with the role of the mind itself in the universe. In Adam's psychiatric session, Alex posed his book's most fundamental question: to what extent is the human mind either a creator or a subject of the body and the world it inhabits? What he didn't ask—and neither did Hofstadter or the other investigators Alex drew on and challenged—was whether we would want Adam and his descendants, who are clearly all scientists, to fulfill their desire to know objectively. What would that knowledge be, and what would they do with it?

In his reader's report on the book, Medawar criticized it as a bit too long and in need of tightening up. But Alex's writing, as always, was well worth reading, he said: "and would, I think, be thought to be so by . . . a circle wider than his existing admirers, among whom I count myself."[41] SUNY Press did a better job of producing *Reality and Empathy* than Crown had done with *I and That*; there were few typos and no unforgivable blocks of missing text. But *Reality and Empathy* received only one major review, in the scientific journal *Nature*. The reviewer was Martin Gardiner, the mathematician and former writer of *Scientific American's* popular "Mathematical Games" column. Gardiner was a great skeptic and the author in 1960 of a best-selling annotated edition of *Alice's*

Adventures in Wonderland and *Through the Looking Glass* that teased out the mathematical riddles and jokes Lewis Carroll had implanted in the books.

With a rave review in *Scientific American*, Gardiner had helped make *Gödel, Escher, Bach* a great publishing success. His review of *Reality and Empathy* was cooler, in part because he felt it took too tolerant an attitude toward the kind of junk science—parapsychology, Lamarckism, telepathic dreams—that he had spent much of his career debunking. While he found Alex's general line of argument astute enough to follow it out, he also thought it could have been more clearly presented. "The book is stimulating, funny, quirky and marred by a rambling, repetitious, disjointed organization," Gardiner concluded. "Although I learned much, I finished the book with a dizziness from its endless zigzags."[42]

Gardiner's review echoed distinctly Tom Arie's review a year earlier of a very different book, *Practice of Geriatric Psychiatry*, which Arie had called "lively, stimulating, often right on the mark, sometimes plainly wrong, occasionally silly." Both point up a curious fact of Alex Comfort's long and varied career. For decades, he had been writing stimulating, sometimes brilliant books on fields in which he was essentially a self-trained amateur. *Reality and Empathy* was no different.

He was not an expert on mollusks; it was a hobby he had picked up collecting shells as a child that stretched into something more serious. He was not a political scientist, but his anarcho-pacifist convictions during the war had compelled him to tackle the subject anyway. He was not a sexologist; sexology was still a vaguely defined field full of dubious self-appointed experts at the time he decided to investigate and help set it right. He was not a trained gerontologist but had been invited to become one by Peter Medawar—and succeeded. He was not a geriatrician or geriatric psychiatrist but decided to make himself into one when he found there was a need. He was only a self-taught scholar of Indian literature and philosophy, to the annoyance of some with real credentials in the field, but he pursued it anyway, and it informed his later work.

He had never before been a philosopher of science either. And he was not, like Hofstadter or John Wheeler or Kauffman, a physicist or higher mathematician—two subjects he had struggled with in school—just an enthusiastic student once he took an interest, who was nevertheless able to arrive at some valuable insights and establish a useful perspective on these fast-developing fields. Lou Kauffman was impressed on meeting him that he was able to discuss complex subjects that Kauffman had mastered through years of training and application, at the same level but in his own way. *Reality and Empathy* influenced Kauffman's own work; rereading it years later, he found it just as sound as he had initially and still considered it a potentially great contribution to scientific thought.[43]

THE FIELD OF STUDY Alex had been pursuing in his latest book was where he had decided to concentrate much of the rest of his career. He seemed to be signaling this when, the same year *Reality and Empathy* was published, he announced that he was stepping down as editor of *Experimental Gerontology*. Len Hayflick would take his place. Later that year he donated his sex archives to the Kinsey Institute, including his microfilm of Weckerle's *Golden Book of Love*, and gave his library of books on gerontology, geriatrics, and related fields to the Royal Society of Medicine in London. He had already donated his letters through 1973 to UCL when he moved to the States. Two years later, he would give his collection of mollusks to the National Museum of Ireland.

This deaccessioning was connected with Alex and Jane's return to England, where they expected to move into a smaller house and would not have room for a large library. But they suggest too that he was clearing the decks to focus his work more narrowly. One field was the mind, the self, and the nature of religion; the other was a new iteration of his work in geriatrics.

In 1980 Alex had speculated with a former colleague who now headed the St. George's University School of Medicine in Grenada about producing a "copiously illustrated" book for Mitchell Beazley on medical care in poorer nations that had little health care infrastructure, taking as a model the "barefoot doctors" who were trained to provide basic medical services in post-revolutionary China. The project never came together, but in November 1983 Alex went to India, partly to speak on the forthcoming *Reality and Empathy* and partly to discuss with his old acquaintances at the Indian Statistical Institute the possibility of creating a geriatric teaching curriculum for developing countries.[44] He visited India again two years later, this time with Jane, and planned more, possibly regular trips after that.[45]

Alex had conceived the idea of a geriatric training program using videocassettes in 1981, when he proposed it to Robert Maxwell at Pergamon.[46] His desire to develop a reputable product in this area was one of the reasons he had fought with Mitchell Beazley about its plans to produce a video spinoff of *The Joy of Sex*.[47] As he continued to think it through, the project became more ambitious. It wasn't just that developing nations tended to have poor health care infrastructure—too few doctors, too few clinics, too little of other resources—but also that social arrangements were different from those in Europe and the United States, Alex said, "It will be of no use sending doctors to Britain or America to learn geriatrics as practiced in teaching hospitals with the type of social services that exist there if, when they go home, they will have to think in terms of the village or the extended family."[48] Geriatrics, to be useful in developing countries, would have to be adapted to their way of life and available resources.

Alex had been training geriatricians in teaching hospitals for half a dozen years, and serving as a "traveling friar," proselytizing for geriatrics as a medical discipline, ever since coming to the United States, at conferences, in speaking engagements, and even before Congress, and he now felt his work in this context was done. In a talk a few months before his departure for England in April 1985, he said he was pleased with the progress being made in gerontology, especially in Alzheimer's research. His test-battery approach to speeding up research on the effects of aging had never taken hold, however. Alzheimer's studies had had better success attracting financial support, especially from Congress, because they involved a headlining disease that affected millions of people, like cancer, whereas general research on aging offered no definite payoff over any estimated time frame.

Alex admitted he had been too optimistic when he first came to America: "I thought then that because so many politicians were old, and so many rich men who were growing older were worried about their aging, there would be a gathering rush to fund experimental gerontology. There has not been because those people when they did fund anything tended to fund quacks and not people who have been doing serious research."[49]

He was still concerned too about the prospects for geriatrics in America in the Reagan years, despite the energy he had put into it. Geriatric care in the United States was organized largely as social services, he noted, and its "multitier structure"—with federal, state, local, and voluntary levels—made it extremely difficult to integrate them, whereas in the UK, to which he was returning, "one telephone call will usually turn on all the social services." Coupled with "the Neanderthal interpretation of laissez faire—that social services should be provided as grudgingly as possible"—this meant that while a great deal of money was spent, much of it never reached the people for whom it was intended.

Americans could be very kind, Alex observed, but "if you try to put a penny on the sales tax to pay for social services, it is vigorously resisted and even categorized as 'Communistic.'"[50]

Given the political difficulties he had encountered in the States, it made sense to Alex to direct his efforts at places where geriatrics and research on aging were newer, less institutionalized, and less ideologically fraught. India would be the hub, and the UK would be his jumping-off point. First, however, he had to finish his relocation to England.

By January 1985, Jane was feeling healthy enough that Alex was able to take her on holiday to Jamaica.[51] The previous fall they had bought a small house in Ventura, a larger city a half-hour drive down the coast from Santa Barbara. The property included a "detached unit" they intended to use as a residence when they visited, while renting out the main house.[52] This would allow them to maintain their residence in California for tax purposes after they moved back to the UK. At about the same time, they listed their house in Montecito for sale. The deal closed the following April, and they moved into their new home, in Cranbrook, toward the end of the month.[53]

Cranbrook was a small, picturesque old Kentish town, dominated by a large, 170-year-old working windmill set on top of a hill in the middle of town. Alex and Jane's new home, located just in front of the mill and not far from the High Street and therefore known as Windmill House, gave them an overlook of some nice parkland.[54] On the property as well was a smaller house, Tilvern Cottage, which Alex could use as his office.

The cottage was also part of the Comforts' elaborate tax planning. Alex was still doing much of his writing and speaking under the Books and Broadcasts corporate label, which was now located, officially, at the Ventura house. Tilvern Cottage would be the Books and Broadcasts UK office, which Alex took care to state on its letterhead. Copyrights on *More Joy* and the other books he had produced while living in the United States would remain there. His earnings from *The Joy of Sex* had always been on Mitchell Beazley's UK copyright, and they would remain so, although Alex had explored the possibility of transferring them to the firm's US subsidiary.

The critical matter, of course, was to make sure the Inland Revenue accepted that the Comforts were still US residents for tax purposes. In reply to a questionnaire from the department two years later, Alex maintained that his home, office, and business interests were still in California, that he was still "deeply involved" in training family medicine residents at Ventura hospital, and that he still held his adjunct professorship at

UCLA. He needed an outpost in the UK to "continue his research," which involved studying general medicine and hospital services there in order to apply the results to his course for residents.[55] But in future, he proposed to visit only during the summer "as he now finds the English winters to be harsh." When he retired or found travel too arduous, he said, he planned to stop coming to England entirely.[56]

None of this was untrue so far as it went. Alex had encountered many frustrations in the States; the latest had come not long before he returned to England, when he was declined permission to sit for the psychiatry boards in California because he hadn't been a psychiatry resident, despite the fact that there were no geriatric psychiatry residencies available and he was himself teaching residents in family practice.[57] But he wanted to maintain his connections in the United States and planned to be there often, since he was still in demand as a speaker and conference participant.

JAMES MITCHELL DIED ON March 12, 1985, at age forty-five, less than two months after Alex moved back to England. He had left a powerful mark on publishing, especially with his contributions to *The Joy of Sex*. "He took a huge risk at that time, and came up with a brilliant solution about how to publish it," Duncan Baird, one of his colleagues at Mitchell Beazley, later said.[58]

Mitchell had often complained that working together would have been easier if he and Alex hadn't been separated by a continent and an ocean, and by the time of his death they hadn't completed a major project together in five years and were sometimes not on speaking terms. Almost to the end, Mitchell was determined to produce a video version of *The Joy of Sex*, spurred by the huge success of Jane Fonda's series of workout tapes, but was stymied by Alex's refusal to endorse or contribute to it.[59]

Alex in turn was frustrated by Mitchell's lack of enthusiasm for his own ideas for extending the *Joy* brand. Two years earlier, they had discussed a *Joy of Sex* game for couples—a kind of Monopoly in which each would draw a card in turn with suggestions for their partner drawn from the book—pitched as a wedding or anniversary present. "One would just get these out for the Christmas market," he proposed. "As a test of marketability, I suggest approaching not only bookshops, but Frederick's of Hollywood (which sells lingerie, posture books and 'soft' erotics)."[60] Helpfully, he supplied a sketch of what the package might look like. Alex brought up the idea again a year later, but neither Mitchell nor Crown in the United States took much interest.[61]

The *Joy of Sex* movie—ten years in the making—had finally premiered in the summer of 1984 and was a big disappointment to Alex and to Mitchell Beazley. In 1980 Matty Simmons, the producer of *National Lampoon's Animal House*, had engaged John Hughes, a *Lampoon* writer, to turn out a screenplay. Hughes came up with a set of loosely joined humorous sketches, taking off from topics in the book. Alex had a good meeting with Simmons, read the script and was enthusiastic ("with the right casting it ought to beat *Jaws* and *The Exorcist* combined").[62] He noted some suggestions in the margins of the script, but generally gave it his blessing and offered to help promote the film.[63]

Somewhere in the bowels of Hollywood, however, Hughes's script was dropped—he would quickly move on with great success to a series of coming-of-age comedies, including *Sixteen Candles* (1984), *The Breakfast Club* (1985), and *Home Alone* (1990)—and replaced by one that attempted to follow the lead of the teenage sex farces popular of the early '80s, notably *Fast Times at Ridgemont High*. *National Lampoon*'s involvement ended, and, while "Based on the book 'The Joy of Sex'" appeared in the credits, Alex's name did not. In addition, the title was shortened slightly to *Joy of Sex*, further distancing it from the book. "Join this gang of madcap characters on a boisterous and unpredictable journey into the topsy-turvy world of rampaging teenage hormones," a promo beckoned, in a tone guaranteed to drive Alex to fury, when the film was released and then quickly relegated to video.

"Smarmy and lackluster and charmless," the *Philadelphia Inquirer* concluded.[64] Precious few critics had anything more positive to say. To Alex, it was simply "that appalling film."[65]

While there was nothing much to be done about the movie, Alex upon his return to the UK was finally ready to work on revised editions of *Joy* and *More Joy*. Mitchell, in the year before he died, got his art director, Tony Cobb, working on some new illustrations in hopes of giving the book "the '80s edge which it now needs visually." At one point they tried bringing Charlie Raymond back as a model, his beard shaved off, but that didn't seem to do the trick.[66]

After Mitchell's death, Alex's relations with Mitchell Beazley could have been expected to improve; the tone of letters between the two parties suggests they did. The firm's principals had bought it back from American Express, and Alex began sending his *Joy* revisions to the new editor-in-chief, Jack Tresidder, soon after he was settled into Cranbrook. Tresidder was soon discussing opportunities for him to promote the book, perhaps including a high-visibility magazine profile.[67] Alex wasn't prepared to go much further, however, without discussing some fundamental changes in his contractual relationship with the firm.

Ever since his wrangle with Mitchell about the proposed *Joy* video, he had been unhappy with the arrangement. He did not own the rights to either *Joy* or *More Joy*, and, while he had made a small fortune from the books, he felt his publisher was shortchanging him. He wanted a new contract, under terms that were more to his advantage. Mitchell Beazley had made a lot of money off his work, he wrote Tresidder, but he couldn't get a paid medical job, despite which it was somehow assumed that he "had a yacht, a staff of secretaries, and should work for free."

"Mitchell Beazley owes me a raise," he insisted, "especially since the initial muddle landed me with a $250,000 lawsuit."[68] Giving him one "might shorten poor old James' sojourn in purgatory, or get him a better reincarnation, according to your theological taste."[69] In two long letters to Tresidder and another director, Duncan Baird, Alex laid out the history of his contractual relationship with the firm, as he understood it, starting with some poor advice he had received from "a not very bright lawyer" when he had first offered *The Joy of Sex* to Mitchell and also including the welter of agreements that had resulted from his old arrangement with the CSDI in Santa Barbara. The bottom line was that under a standard publishing agreement, he felt he would be receiving around 10 percent of the published price of the *Joy* books, whereas under his deal with Mitchell Beazley he was receiving far less, in part because his share came out of the net profit on the book, not the sales price.

Baird's colleague Peter Mead wrote back explaining Mitchell Beazley's view. The vast majority of sales of the *Joy* books came from the licensed paperback editions, he pointed out, and the royalty on these was based on the published sales price. That royalty was paid by Simon & Schuster to Crown, which then remitted 50 percent to Mitchell Beazley, who then paid Alex his share. As for the hardback editions, Alex did indeed get a smaller percentage, but it was on every copy that Mitchell Beazley delivered, including review copies, damaged copies, and copies given away. So the co-edition deals that the firm was used to working out were not that disadvantageous for its authors after all. On top of which, Mitchell Beazley couldn't simply rewrite its contracts with Crown, Simon & Schuster, and its partners in other countries simply because Alex wanted them to.[70]

That, curiously, seems to have satisfied Alex, whose complaints to Tresidder and his colleagues cease at this point in the correspondence. Much of what Mead said was borne out in the royalty statements the firm was now sending to Alex regularly; in California he had often complained that he was not receiving these or that they arrived late. And since he was now living in the UK and coming by Mitchell Beazley's London offices occasionally while the new editions were under production, there was more opportunity to sort out misunderstandings in person.

Preparing the new editions of *Joy* and *More Joy* proceeded smoothly, in part because so little was actually changed, at least in the first book. After some attempts to revise the illustrations, Tresidder and his colleagues decided to leave them largely as they were. Alex's revisions to *Joy* were minor, but the text of *More Joy* needed considerable work because AIDS was now a full-blown, impossible-to-ignore epidemic. In 1985 8,406 people died of the virus in the United States, more than in all the preceding years since it had been discovered, bringing the total to 16,458, according to the Centers for Disease Control, while many times that number were infected with HIV.[71] Mitchell had been concerned about overemphasizing AIDS and letting it take over the revised book; at the same time, he wanted to be sure the subject was covered properly and the revised edition didn't come across as an invitation to promiscuity. Alex argued that it wouldn't do to simply add a short chapter to a text that urged openness toward anal sex, group sex, and swinging without any attached warnings.[72]

He debated whether to ask Mitchell Beazley to withdraw existing copies of the book and scrub the revised edition. Instead, in June 1986, with the pages of the new *More Joy* already in the film stage, he asked Tresidder to remove four entries—"Sandstone," "Sharing," "Swinging," and "Threesomes"—and add new copy to "Massage" that he would provide, along with smaller revisions to other parts of the book.[73] He also wanted a general statement of caution tipped into all existing copies of the original editions still going out ("The advice and/or information included in this book should be considered in light of the present understanding of new health risks") and new copy added to the Italian edition of *The Facts of Love*, which Mitchell Beazley was getting ready to issue.

Tresidder persuaded Alex to minimize his revisions. "Sandstone" was out, but "Sharing" and "Swinging" remained, with some new warnings acknowledging that these arrangements weren't for everyone, and he added strong warnings about AIDS to "Threesomes." Most importantly, he added a long section to the introduction, "Beyond Advanced

Lovemaking," summarizing current knowledge about AIDS and its dangers, which, he acknowledged, were now "the most pressing concern in the management of our sexual behaviors." Impulse sex was now unacceptably dangerous, anal sex was to be avoided, and knowing one's partner's sexual history was a must. While AIDS was incurable, the best way to avoid it was through "an intelligent change in our behaviors based on accurate knowledge."[74]

Crown, for one, was glad of the changes and the cautionary note, even though they held up the release of the new *More Joy* until the following year. Moreover, the new edition would bear the words, "Completely revised and updated" on its cover. But Alex was now quite anxious that no one who bought his books should misunderstand his intention. With the new *Joy* out and the republication of *More Joy* still months away, he wrote Alan Mirken at Crown, concerned that copies of the original editions were still being sold; Mirken assured him they were not and that he had canceled an order for *More Joy* as soon as he heard that a new edition was underway.[75]

When the new *Joy of Sex* appeared, it had been fourteen years since the first edition was published. In the interval, the book had sold 5.5 million copies in the U.S. alone, including some 1 million in hardback, and *More Joy* had added another 1.5 million.[76] While Alex's revisions were necessary to keep abreast of the health and social changes AIDS had wrought, they did little to deepen the books as guides to better sex. If anything, Alex and Mitchell Beazley strove to keep them as much the same as possible. The design and illustrations—except for those related to Sandstone and topics like "Sharing"—were identical to those of the earlier editions when the new *Joy* and *More Joy* hit bookshops and book club lists in late 1986 and early 1987, respectively, in the United States and the UK.

As a publishing matter, the biggest change was that the new editions dropped the pretense that an unnamed couple had written them, without fully ascribing authorship to Alex. His name appeared on the cover and title page of each but without the word "by" preceding it, while in his preface to the new *Joy* he never explicitly says he wrote it. The change provoked next to no comment, since anyone familiar with the books had already assimilated the fact that Alex had written them.

Crown noted in January that the new *Joy* was "selling steadily," and Alex and his publishers were pleased to find that, despite the plethora of sex manuals and advisories it now competed with, it still had a strong cultural resonance. Its persistent strong sales, the *Baltimore Sun* commented, "probably says quite a bit about the persistent vitality of some of the book's liberal notions of sexuality, despite the setbacks of AIDS and a more conservative political climate."[77]

While the sexual revolution of the '60s and '70s had met plenty of resistance even at the time, the backlash was building up considerably in the present decade. Reagan's attorney general, Ed Meese, was a strenuous prosecutor of pornography. Still fresh at the time Alex was revising his books was the Meese Report, which called for a federal crackdown on distribution of obscene content and urged citizens' groups to picket stores that sold such materials (but not *Playboy* or *Penthouse*, which the courts had ruled were not obscene). In the UK, the indefatigable Mary Whitehouse prodded the Thatcher government to shove through the Commons an Obscene Publications (Protection of Children, etc) (Amendment) Bill. It included a detailed laundry list of "obscene" activities that would have made *The Joy of Sex* and most other sex manuals illegal.[78]

Yet Dr. Ruth Westheimer, the popular sex columnist and broadcaster, could still recommend *Joy* to a woman who wrote in that she had just learned to have an orgasm after thirty-four years of marriage and wanted advice to improve her sex life.[79] On a far grimmer note, about the time the new *More Joy* came out, a man in Citrus County, Florida, on trial for sexually abusing his eleven-year-old stepdaughter and her twelve-year-old friend, claimed that the stepdaughter had concocted the details of the charge by reading *More Joy of Sex*, which her mother had left in the house. He was convicted anyway.[80]

Bruce Harris, Crown's publishing director, allowed that the two books had had to change with the times but emphasized that the changes were in response to AIDS, not a cave-in to the Reaganite and Thatcherite reaction. "Sex hasn't changed that much," he said, "but Alex Comfort, the author, felt that in terms of things that were happening, especially diseases, [a revision was necessary]." In 1972 Alex's message had been "try anything," Harris noted, whereas now he was "pointing out the risks" of some forms of sexual activity.[81]

A long interview in the *Daily Telegraph* demonstrated that AIDS had not shaken the essential message of Alex's book, so far as he was concerned. He came to his meeting with reporter Jane Ellison wearing a conservative, charcoal-gray three-piece suit and spoke in his usual rapid-fire manner, with a pipe, as usual, fastened between his teeth. His books were not out of step with the times, he told Ellison, because sex could still be fun despite AIDS. And he was as concerned about the harm that excesses of moral indignation could do as he was about the epidemic itself. "People have been very unkind to Aids victims," he said. "Wait until a few members of the Cabinet get the disease—and it won't have to be for some form of unorthodox behavior—and then see how attitudes start to change."[82]

Anal sex should be "on hold," he allowed, and threesomes, swinging, and "any sexual involvement with unknown quantities" were now "wildly imprudent." As far as he knew, his old friends at Sandstone "have all got scared and gone home." But he refused to follow Ellison's lead when she suggested that his books bore some responsibility for the spread of AIDS. "I only describe the physical and factual aspects of sex," he answered. "We must make the . . . choices of who our partners are for ourselves." As for Dr. Comfort specifically, "my own habits are in fact most uninteresting."

AIDS was a consuming topic by the time the new *Joy* and *More Joy* appeared. A flood of books had hit the market, starting with *AIDS: The Epidemic* in 1983 from St. Martin's Press. In June 1987, with Alex's books well launched, a survey by *Publishers Weekly* turned up more than 130 books and other bibliographic references about AIDS. With new information about the medical, legal, and political ramifications of the crisis appearing constantly, the number would certainly grow.

Given the level of concern, Alex was being asked why he had waited so long to revise his books. He replied, a bit disingenuously, that he had been following developments and keeping his publishers informed all along. "As soon as material has become available I have passed it on to them," he told the *Sunday Telegraph*.[83]

Whatever the case, he had not been ignoring the epidemic. He first wrote about it in a 1982 letter to *The Lancet*, and in a June 1, 1983, letter to a medical colleague he argued that the cause of AIDS "could well be a specific virus." For several years he had been appealing for the development of a safe and reliable "genital antiseptic" to counter sexually transmitted diseases, and he called for it more frequently as the AIDS crisis grew.[84]

In October 1986, after the Thatcher government formed an interdepartmental Ministerial Cabinet Committee on AIDS, chaired by Viscount Whitelaw, the de facto deputy prime minister, Alex wrote him, pointing out that "a very crude antisepsis proved very effective in the control of STD's" during World War I, but that "partly through public disapproval of measures which could be represented as making promiscuity safe," the search for a better one had gone no further. "May I very strongly urge the Commission to raise the idea of renewing this research with its scientific advisers?" Alex wrote. "There is a chance here of a safe and rapidly available accessory weapon, and I find it hard to understand why it has not been more widely suggested. The danger of AIDS is so serious that it would outweigh any anxieties about individual hypersensitivity."[85] The committee appears not to have taken up the idea.

At the same time, Alex pitched a new book on AIDS to Tresidder at Mitchell Beazley, but the publisher turned it down. Sales of their 1985 book *Sex and Your Health* had been "abysmal," and Tresidder was afraid a separate AIDS book by Alex would only steal sales from the new *Joy* and *More Joy*.[86]

CHAPTER 22

Emperors and Philosophers (1984–1991)

That Alex was not able to secure a foothold in the AIDS discussion underscores the difficulty he had reestablishing himself in the British medical and scientific establishment following his return. After years proclaiming the National Health Service as superior to the US "sickness industry," he was unable to secure a full-time practice under the NHS and had to settle for a contract as a part-time locum consultant in psychiatry, which went into effect in the fall of 1986, nearly a year and a half after he had settled into Cranbrook. It was as a locum that he had first begun practicing medicine on his own, more than forty years before.

His stature in the larger scientific community remained high, however. Soon after his return to the UK, he helped an Indian gerontologist, Madhu Kanungo, obtain a grant from the Nuffield Foundation to continue his work after Banaras Hindu University stopped supporting his research group.[1] In 1986 the Royal Society of Medicine made its inaugural presentation of the AC Comfort Memorial Award to a young geriatrician; Alex had endowed the award, named for his father and consisting of a cash prize of at least £200 and a contribution toward the cost of publishing the winning paper.[2] He received a steady flow of invitations to lecture on gerontology and geriatrics from UK universities and institutions in India, although he no longer followed the latest research or wrote about these subjects regularly.

In 1987 King's College London, which had an unusually large number of staff involved in aging studies, established a new research and teaching unit, the Age Concern Institute of Gerontology, and invited Alex to join its advisory council, which he quickly agreed to do.[3] The year before, Cambridge had decided to establish a chair in clinical gerontology and asked Alex to recommend candidates for the position.[4] He replied that he couldn't make any suggestions since he had just come back after eleven years in America. But he was delighted that the university seemed inclined to combine basic research with clinical work that could lead to a significant treatment breakthrough, "not so much to attract further funding as to establish the first clear link between research gerontology and geriatrics, which would benefit both."[5] As always, Alex was keen to persuade both scientists and the people who held the purse strings that basic research on aging wasn't a waste of money but was superior to the piecemeal, disease-specific approach as a way to achieve major improvements in vigor as people aged.

The irony was that, on account of either his age—he was 65 on his return—or his extended absence from the UK, Alex was no better able to find a full-fledged institutional position back home than he had been in the United States. He was reestablishing himself in England in other ways, however. Soon after he moved back, he exchanged letters and had lunch with Fred Marnau, his old friend from the Grey Walls Press days. "*Tetrarch* is on my bedside table soon to be read," Fred told him.[6] He also revived his friendship with Bob Greacen, with whom he had edited *Lyra* at Grey Walls and who was about to move to Dublin as the recipient of a lifetime stipend as an important Irish poet. ("You should live there," he counseled Greacen; "it keeps the poetry coming."[7]) Alex was still a ham radio enthusiast, and soon after his arrival he joined the West Kent Amateur Radio Society, volunteering to address the members on CB radio in America and other topics.[8]

Britain's anarchist community heard that Alex was back and quickly made contact with him. A workers' cooperative in Swansea asked him to speak at the opening of their new book and coffee shop.[9] In October 1985 he was invited to address the Anarchist Discussion Group at the Mary Ward Adult Education Centre in London, which Nicolas Walter had founded a couple of years prior. Prompting the invitation was a letter Alex had written to the *Guardian* a month earlier, about MI5's recent rescue from Moscow of Oleg Gordievsky, an ex-KGB bureau chief in London who had provided information covertly to MI6.[10]

Gordievsky was said to be prepared to out a number of moles in the ranks of British Intelligence, but Alex questioned why he hadn't done so already. Perhaps, he suggested, "Mrs. Thatcher needed an Intelligence coup to impress Washington . . . if we are to get even one foot in the Star Wars trough." Could it be that, as the next general election approached, the ex-Soviet spy would out National Mine Workers president Arthur Scargill, Social Democratic Party leader David Owen, and the director-general of the BBC as "full Colonels in the KGB?"[11]

Before his move back to Britain, Alex had told a number of people, half-jokingly, that he was doing so to "have a crack at Mrs. Thatcher," who was busy prodding Reagan not to work with Soviet leader Mikhail Gorbachev to abolish nuclear weapons.[12] To a friend at the Indian Statistical Institute, he wrote, "When the Raj was kicked out of India it went home and started lording it over its own people—Mrs. T. is an old-style intolerable memsahib of a kind only too familiar in India fifty or sixty years ago. Wouldn't surprise me if we need to start an Independence movement in London!"[13]

He followed through on his return, commencing a steady barrage of letters to the *Guardian*, *Times*, *New Statesman*, *Daily Telegraph*, and *Independent*, most taking the government to task for its subservience to US foreign policy and questioning the wisdom of Europe's involvement in NATO and the Cold War and nearly always poking fun at the regime's naked opportunism and inhumanity. He hadn't lost his capacity for the outrageously telling turn of phrase; the Bomb had turned Britain into a "military outpost of the US," he wrote in a 1987 *Guardian* piece, leaving the nation committed to a defense policy "based on penis envy rather than operational needs."[14] Sometimes he suggested more sinister purposes. In a letter to the *New Statesman* about the same time as his *Guardian* letter, he wondered if there wasn't a CIA contingency plan "to destabilize any British government which threatens to change the rules." "Such a plan is militarily inevitable and historically credible," he wrote. "By buying this 'special relationship' to a point which makes it a vital American military interest we have also bought the likely promotion of a Mr (or Ms) Pinochet, P.C., M.P., in the event that a party committed to disengagement from the Reagan jehad [*sic*] is, or looks like being, elected."[15]

Happily, Alex had returned to a Britain much of which was again disposed to listen to such arguments. The CND had undergone a dramatic revival in the early Thatcher years and its membership was surging. This time around, however, direct action, which had never met with full acceptance when Alex and others had pushed for it in 1960s, was central to the movement. The UK disarmament movement was commanding international attention thanks to the Women's Peace Camps, the series of occupations and civil disobedience actions in opposition to the placement of nuclear missiles at the RAF's Greenham Common base. And for a time, it seemed the movement might bend the political establishment to its will.

In 1986, when Labour Party chief Neil Kinnock briefly advocated Britain's unilaterally stripping itself of nuclear weapons, Alex wrote him a supportive note, but in a letter to the *Guardian* he wondered if "it would not be too paranoid in the modern world to see the faces of Allende and Dubcek looking over [Kinnock's shoulder]."[16] (After Labour lost the general election the following year, the party abandoned disarmament.) The following year, when Friends of the Earth launched a campaign to halt the construction of the Sizewell B pressurized water reactor and reevaluate the emergency plans connected with all of Britain's nuclear facilities, Alex signed an open letter in support, joining a procession of celebrities including ex-Beatles Paul McCartney and George Harrison, the Who's Pete Townsend, Martin Amis, Alan Bennett, John Fowles, Emma Thompson, Paul Theroux, Polly Toynbee, and Jeremy Irons.[17] (Construction of the new reactor went ahead as planned.)

In general, Alex preferred sarcasm and satire in his attacks on Thatcher's grimly transformative rule. The voice in his letters after his repatriation, which often prompted supportive comments from other readers, is more like that of Dr. Goggins of *Come Out to Play* than the morally severe Dr. Comfort of World War II and the early Cold War. In 1987, when the Commons discussed bringing back capital punishment, Alex announced in the *Guardian* his plan "to launch a British Executions Corporation. . . . We would anticipate that capital will come chiefly from the advance sale of worldwide cable television rights. At one blow we could also revive the fortunes of British football by providing a novel entertainment for the half-time interval, though we would, if the supply of contracts is sufficient, expect eventually to erect our own stadium."[18]

Sometimes humor wouldn't quite do, however. When Freedom Press was preparing to celebrate the centenary of its newspaper, *Freedom*, Nicolas Walter, who had once called Alex "the true voice of nuclear disarmament" and was still an active member of the collective, invited him to contribute to a special issue. Alex's offering, "Letter from America," appeared in October 1986 and was as morally serious as anything he had ever written. After eleven years in the States, "it is distinctly strange to find oneself living in a colonial country, with armed police, lathi-charges and trumped-up charges as appropriate responses to trade unions, and the promise of rubber bullets to come. . . . What is new to British history is the shadow of the Marcos pattern: a country full of foreign troops and foreign nuclear bases, with a client government drawing its support and its guidelines from Washington."*

* "Lathi-charges" were baton charges by police in British India to break up crowds and demonstrations.

As an anarchist, Alex was "not vastly interested in elections." But should an anarchist be anti-American? Having lived there and seen the Reagan administration at close quarters, he had to say, "[no] more than one should be anti-Semitic because of Begin and Ariel Sharon." Americans included Jesse Helms and Jerry Falwell but also Daniel Berrigan and the Committee in Solidarity with the People of El Salvador. "Liberty is by no means dead in America, though in some areas it always has been on life support. There is quite possibly more direct action there than here." The UK had the Official Secrets Act while the United States had the First Amendment.

It was when America looked abroad that it became most dangerous. Since Gorbachev's "attempts to inject some rational self-interest into superpower relations [ran into] Reagan's frank paranoia," Alex wrote, "the United States is possibly the more dangerous and certainly the more accident-prone of the two Tar Babies." Neutralization of Europe was still the best hope for preventing a further nuclear arms race, just as Alex had said it was forty years earlier, and he suggested that such a thing was not an impossibility. "Reagan will not be forever," he predicted, "and the American Right could salutarily be tipped into isolationism—i.e., getting its finger and its weapons out."

Freedom Press wasn't done with Alex. Walter asked if he would agree to a reprint of some of his writings from the '40s, including all or part of *Art and Social Responsibility*, in a new Libertarian Classics series along with works by the likes of Thoreau and Wilde. The publisher also wanted to include some of his verse in an anthology of twentieth-century anarchist poets.[19] He agreed to both requests.

Vernon Richards, now seventy-three and still active at Freedom Press (and running an organic market gardening operation on a two-and-a-half-acre allotment), was delighted that Alex had returned and urged him to write a new book on the relevance of anarchism to society at the end of the twentieth century. But he was pessimistic about the future of radical publishing.

In the '40s, publishers like Freedom had brought out politically challenging books easily and quickly and found a healthy readership for them, just as more literary houses like Grey Walls had with new poetry. Freedom was still succeeding with some titles like Colin Ward's *Anarchy in Action*, Richards told Alex, but in the '80s, in a market increasingly dominated by a small group of big corporate-backed publishers, things were different. "All the indicators are that apart from bestsellers, booksellers will only order single [copies] for customers so far as our kind of titles are concerned."[20] Whereas a favorable review of a Freedom Press book in a prominent publication might once have netted an additional hundred copies sold, perhaps ten more might sell in 1987. A recent feature article in the *Independent* about the state of publishing had analyzed the problem and concluded: "too many books are chasing too few buyers at too high a price."

Freedom Press, Richards told Alex, was surviving by building up a backlist that might find its way into greater circulation down the road, and through a group of supporters, Friends of Freedom Press, which now owned its building and bookshop at 84b Angel Alley in Whitechapel. He guessed he could be excused for expanding on his problems, Richards told Alex in his letter: "It's so many years since we last met and, after all, those years were very exciting and I imagine we really thought we might help change the world."

Even in the depths of the Thatcher era, Alex was far less pessimistic than his old publisher. "I haven't written recently on anarchism qua anarchism," he replied, "because it is a general background to all my thinking (fish don't write essays on water?)." But if he were to write a new book on the subject, he said: "It should be a specific examination of what [anarchist-] inspired thinking offers the 21st cent. and how far there is a certain inevitability of a. implicit in areas like technology: it is interesting that competitive Victorian models in biology are shifting towards synergistic models at a more fundamental level than Kropotkin foresaw."[21]

How did Alex define anarchism—*his* anarchism, some forty years after he had first avowed it? "I might take the line that a. isn't political," he said, "meaning that although in some instances it points to direct political action, e.g. in the structuring of local resistance, viewed against any going political system it is a critique of politics with both revolutionary and evolutionary implications."

As always for Alex, anarchism was embedded in direct action and personal resistance. How were present-day anarchists to make a difference? Alex was still not inclined to stand for election, support candidates for office, or otherwise throw in his lot with mainstream state politics, he told Richards. The strategy, instead, should be to test the limits of "negative intervention in non-a. politics, viz., to stop governments from doing things, committing atrocities, and ripping people off," the target to be decided case by case. He had often toyed with the idea of a "Joy of Politics," he wrote. "It could be libelous, seditious, sarcastic, and just about a real picture of what goes on in the political circus and how to baffle it: and bearing in mind that mockery often works better than exhortation it could be influential."

Alex didn't comment on his friend's frustrations as a publisher, but he had his share of related concerns. Only a few years earlier, he had told Mitchell Beazley he would be writing no more books on sex until he'd notched three best sellers in other fields, but now he was struggling to find publishers for anything other than further iterations of *Joy*. He had given up on getting his Indian novel, "Tiger Tiger," published and had just about lost hope for a satirical novel he had finished shortly before returning to England that fleshed out his scenario of a CIA plot to destabilize an antinuclear British government.

"Walsingham's Drum," named for Queen Elizabeth I's spymaster, Sir Francis Walsingham, was "Le Carré with a twist," Alex said. Through a neat piece of computer hacking, British patriots and leftists foil Washington's plot to stop the UK from kicking out American missile bases and pulling the country out of NATO. The main character is an ex-cryptographer from Turing's wartime team at Bletchley Park, now a history don fascinated by Elizabethan intrigue and Walsingham's efforts to frustrate the queen's enemies.[22]

Seeking a publisher for the novel, Alex had contacted the Dianne Coles Literary Agency in London, which replied that they had very little chance of placing it. Alex's occasional tendency to write fast and without much regard for anything but the idea in his head was once again defeating his fiction. The manuscript was "less of a novel than a semi-fictionalized prediction of what could happen as a result of our present foreign policy," agent Jim Reynolds told him. Missing were a strong plot and flesh-and-blood characters with credible emotions, as opposed to a collection of "rather shadowy representatives of the Service, Parliament, and technological know-how." The story was too slow-moving and lacked the dramatic denouement that would qualify it as a political thriller.[23]

Reynolds's evaluation was on the mark. "Walsingham's Drum" had a sketchy feel that suggested Alex had produced the novel more to sell a television adaptation than for its own sake. Indeed, he sent a pitch letter to BBC Channel 4 shortly after he mailed the manuscript to the Coles agency, in hopes the story would not be "banned under the Poodle Policy."[24] The network turned it down.

ALEX HAD BEGUN WORK on a new cycle of poems, tentatively titled "Mikrokosmos," early in the decade, entering eight completed sections in Sotheby's International Poetry Competition in 1982.[25] (It did not win.) It started out as an autobiographical sequence, but as he continued to tinker with it and his expeditions into mathematics, quantum physics, and the self expanded, the poems took a detour into "a mixture of mathematical physics and Buddhism."[26] Inevitably, perhaps, he was finding no luck getting "Mikrokosmos" published, nor an edition of his collected poems he was hoping to see in print. When he wrote Bob Greacen in June 1986 asking if he knew of any Irish publishing houses that might be interested in the latter, Faber & Faber had just turned him down—there was not enough material "of quality" to justify a full collection, they said.[27]

The following year, however, Alex finally found a new firm to publish his fiction. Colin Haycraft had run Gerald Duckworth since shortly after the retirement of Mervyn Horder, who had brought out *Sexual Behaviour in Society* and *Sex in Society* decades before. Haycraft was an ex-Oxford classicist who was most interested in producing learned books, but who made money for his firm by publishing Oliver Sacks, A. N. Wilson, and the celebrated novels of his sometime paramour Beryl Bainbridge.[28] In 1987 he agreed to publish *Imperial Patient*, Alex's novel about Nero, which had been gestating for the better part of a decade.

The first-person narrator of *Imperial Patient* is Callimachus, a Greek doctor and something of a psychoanalyst, whom Nero summons to Rome covertly when his wife, Octavia, fails to produce a child. Callimachus becomes his friend, adviser, and is present at Caesar's (apparent) death and cremation in AD 68. As a piece of historical fiction—Alex's first—the novel paints a lively portrait of educated Greek and Roman society at the time, including medical circles and the fantastically corrupt and self-indulgent imperial court. Alex loaded it with historical figures who don't directly figure in the story of Nero's ill-fated reign, including Petronius, author of the *Satyricon*; Josephus, the Romano-Jewish general and historian; and the Greek philosopher Apollonius of Tyana, all of whom lived around the same time, plus more directly relevant figures like Seneca the Younger, Stoic philosopher and Nero's tutor.

Nero had always been one of the most reviled Roman emperors, thanks initially to the stories included in Suetonius's *Lives of the Caesars*, most notoriously that the emperor deliberately burned Rome to the ground to make room for a vast new palace, the "Golden House," and played his fiddle while watching the conflagration. *Imperial Patient* attempted to rehabilitate Nero, but only partially.

In Alex's telling, Nero is not the culprit behind the fire. He leads the effort to curtail it, extends compensation to the victims, and attends a music lesson only when he is no longer needed on site. He is maneuvered into having his mother and wife killed only after his mother, Agrippina, tries to poison him, and in any case these crimes were dismissed by most Romans at the time as a family affair. Having assumed the emperorship at age sixteen, Nero is petulant and self-indulgent but also intelligent, educated, and generally opposed to violence. Seneca and some of his other advisors hope to mold him into a philosopher king, but they are thwarted by the emperor's moods and whims and by the plotting of the Senate, whom Nero takes pleasure in snubbing.

Alex pictures Nero as a sensitive, damaged youth born to a brutal father and a ruthlessly ambitious mother, who rejects their values and prefers to see himself not as an emperor but rather as a poet, singer, and performer in the Greek tradition he loves. "I'm a Greek like you," he tells Callimachus. "I love music: it's about the only thing I do love. I hate bloodshed and Roman thuggery. I didn't want to be Caesar—that was mother's idea. I wanted to work in music drama. That's what I was trained for. I'm good." Alex's Nero aspires to somehow bring the two guises together to uplift a corrupt and tyrannical empire by performing in public and staging mammoth triumphs and spectacles; these make him popular with the masses but further offend the Senate.[29] He fails, of course, but Alex's last chapter leaves open the possibility that he faked his death and escaped to Rhodes to live as a musician.

Alex once said that *Imperial Patient*, and its portrait of Rome and the Romans, was his response to his years in America. Callimachus is clearly a stand-in for Alex, and his scorn for the Romans—and fear of them—echo the patronizing attitude that many upper-strata English had always felt for Americans. Even some of the more erudite figures in Alex's novel speak this way. "A swordfighting, slave-killing goon" is Seneca's description of a typical Roman.[30] Rome's response to the Jews' brewing rebellion against imperial rule reads like a premonition of Washington's brutal war in Vietnam, with a different outcome.

Alex completed *Imperial Patient* after he wrote *Reality and Empathy*, and it's informed by his hunch that Roman and Greek scholars and mystics had been asking the same questions as he about time and space, the self, and the mind. Nero longs to become an initiate of the Eleusinian Mysteries, the secret rites symbolizing the eternity of life that the Greeks practiced in the city of Eleusis. He also wants to have something like an oceanic experience, which his counselors think would be too dangerous (he might decide he is a god). Alex's Callimachus and Apollonius had each lived in India and studied with "a guru of the Vedic religion" (Apollonius lives in "a kind of ashram"), and they discuss "the subdivision of the One into the Many," a concept that suggests Bohm's implicate and explicate order. [31] Seneca had read and appreciated some of the classic Hindu texts as well, in Alex's telling.

These aspects of the novel feel shoehorned in, and *Imperial Patient* sometimes reads less like a historical romance novel than a fast rummage through Late Classical intellectual preoccupations, but it is also lively, funny, and a vivid revisionist account of a notorious period in Roman history. "The most interesting things here are the diversions from [the] narrative in which the author's own richly idiosyncratic preoccupations are indulged," concluded a very positive review in the *London Review of Books*.[32]

Alex made no attempt to write ancient-sounding dialogue—the characters all speak like Oxbridge scholars and undergraduates—but this makes the story more accessible and reinforces the parallels between Nero's time and the current age. And Alex's research on the period has gained support over the years. In 2020 the English historian John Drinkwater published a new biography, *Nero: Emperor and Court*, which debunked many of the myths and suppositions that had grown up around the emperor. He was not a great persecutor of Christians; the Golden House was for the people, not just the court; he tried to keep his civil service graft-free; and his poetry was actually fairly good.

Alex had a larger point in retelling the story of Nero, however, about the impossibility, in the end, of attempting to transform a calcified state, using the tools of power it affords, without simply reproducing it. Ascending to supreme power at age sixteen, Nero was "going to have somehow to master the Machine, its goons, its warehouses, its professional armies, its brainless Tradition, and its vast size: or be killed or assimilated by it," Callimachus says. "I couldn't get over the size and ponderousness of the apple and the pathetic rottenness of the core."[33] Arthur Salmon, an American academic who published a study of Alex's fiction and poetry in 1978, noted that in his work, "the struggle against death and power is, in Freudian terminology, partly the struggle of Eros against forces of biological and social disintegration."[34] This is certainly true in *Imperial Patient*.

The reviews were mostly good when the novel appeared in the UK in June 1987, shortly after the revised edition of *More Joy* hit the stores. "Most Roman revivals are wearisome affairs and this one does well to prove an exception," the political journalist Norman Shrapnel said in the *Guardian*, producing "the best read of the week."[35] Alex's novel unsnarled some hideously complex Roman politics, said the critics, who found his portrait of the hapless emperor persuasive. "In the end, Nero is found most guilty of force-feeding culture to his people who like nothing better than to watch a few gladiators hack each other down the middle before lunch," wrote Diana Hutchinson in the *Daily Mail*.

When Alex set about writing *Imperial Patient*, the BBC had just produced a very successful television miniseries based on Robert Graves's novels *I, Claudius* and *Claudius the God*, a wallow in decadence about the emperor who preceded Nero. Two years before his novel came out, he had been shopping the idea to the network's drama department.[36] Jonathan Powell, head of series/serials, drama, television, declined the offer. Bearing in mind the success of *I, Claudius*, he wrote back, "We would need stronger material before venturing back into roman [*sic*] times once more." But he said he would be happy to look at the book itself once it was available.[37] Alex went ahead and sent Powell the manuscript, describing his Rome alluringly as "very like Dallas or Los Angeles—rich, squalid, bumptious and dangerous": made for '80s TV, that is.

Powell was not convinced. While he found the book interesting and engrossing ("[its] interpretation of history is remarkable to say the least"), he guessed that BBC viewers would not buy it. Nero's killing his wife and his mother would make him "an irredeemably unsympathetic hero with whom an audience would lack sympathy."[38] The realities of ancient Rome evidently were too brutal for the BBC, it seemed.

Alex does not appear to have approached the network again after *Imperial Patient* was published, although Haycraft at Duckworth sent them a copy.[39] One reason may have been that the novel did not sell well, in spite of good if not abundant reviews. But pushing his intellectual creations into different media had become a habit with Alex. In 1984 he had pitched the idea of a film or TV miniseries based on *Tetrarch*. Though unsuccessful, his argument that "adult fairy tales [were] a market that would appeal even more than THE JOY OF SEX" would later be proved correct by the success of the *Lord of the Rings* films and the *Game of Thrones* TV series. [40] He was mulling over a new book, a sequel of sorts to *Reality and Empathy*, on modern science as a form of religion, and passed the idea of a documentary adaptation to the BBC, but received no response.[41]

His failure to crack the network where he had once been a staple was beginning to wear on him. He pitched the science series through Roger Van Zwaanenberg, who ran a new small publishing house, Zwan Books, that had reissued *Authority and Delinquency* and was interested in bringing out a book tied in to the series. In a letter to Van Zwaanenberg, Alex grumbled, "The BBC should bloody well know who I am—I've done enough work for them in the past, including umpteen talks, a series on humanism, scientific TV programmes, and 'One Pair of Eyes.' You might hint tactfully that they take a look at their files."

Alex was still appearing regularly in periodicals, reviewing books for the *Guardian* and *The Lancet*. But what he really wanted to do, as he settled into life in Cranford, was continue the work he had begun with *Reality and Empathy*—and not just on his own.

He was taken with the notion, dating to seventeenth-century pamphlets describing the mythical Rosicrucian Order of scholars, of an "Invisible College" of like-minded scholars and scientists who met to share ideas outside the accepted intellectual boundaries of the time. The idea may have been an inspiration for the founding of the Royal Society of London in 1650. Since then, an Invisible College has been an ingredient in numerous conspiracy theories, but Alex had in mind a group of scientists who shared a common interest in the kind of ideas he was putting forth in *Reality and Empathy*.

In a 1982 letter to Ian Stevenson, a University of Virginia psychiatric researcher who studied the cases of people who claimed to recall past lives, Alex wrote, "I hope that on some occasion we can get a suitable body . . . to convene an Invisible College including not only physicists, computer men, yogis and parapsychologists but also some far-out mathematicians. . . . It would be extremely funny if one day the [artificial intelligence] people build their super-mind-simulating computer and find it is picking up some of these signals and is, effectively, possessed."[42]

In an article the following year in the journal *ReVision*, Alex put out a more public call for a society that could consider every eccentric idea, examine them all with scientific rigor, and see if a new scientific world model emerged.[43] In a letter to a friend at the Royal Society of Medicine, he described *Reality and Empathy*—yet to be published—as "a sort of controversial prospectus" for such a working group, which could include David Bohm and assorted Jungians, yogis, and skeptics.[44]

Alex was still corresponding regularly with Lou Kauffman at the University of Illinois, Chicago; the two were considering writing a book on iterants together.[45] Martin Zwick, a biophysicist at Portland State University who studied systems theory and methodology, and Christopher

Chapple, an Indologist at Loyola Marymount University, were writing back and forth with Alex as well and, as such, were candidates for his Invisible College. In 1987 another potential member sought him out: Alison Watson, a young British scholar who had just completed a thesis that dovetailed with much of his thinking about physics and metaphysics. She too hoped to see "the long overdue reunification of philosophy, science, and that 'perennial philosophy' at the heart of all religions."[46]

Alex was delighted to hear from Watson and wrote back that the time had come for a convocation "not of Rosicrucians, but of those who realise that philosophy is once more natural philosophy."[47] These would be scholars who adopted a model of nature and the physical universe as an organic phenomenon rather than a kind of machine. He thought he might have found such a body when Kauffman and others introduced him to the Alternative Natural Philosophy Association (ANPA), a group set up at Cambridge in 1979 to develop a modernized natural philosophy.

The founders of the ANPA included physicist Ted Bastin, mathematicians Clive W. Kilmister and John Amson, American theoretical physicist H. Pierre Noyes, and physicist, linguist, and mystic Frederick Parker-Rhodes. Their common denominator was that they all straddled physics and mathematics, were keen to better understand the nature of space-time, and were happy to go beyond the boundaries of Newtonian physics. Bastin proposed that physical space is not a continuum but a finite set of points, a theory that might bridge the gap between the theory of relativity and quantum physics. A possible way to prove this was the "combinational hierarchy," a complex model of basic particle processes that Parker-Rhodes had developed.[48]

Alex was delighted to make contact with ANPA and quickly began corresponding with most of its core members. In the fall of 1987 he attended their annual conference at Cambridge, and he would participate regularly thereafter. He was especially taken by Parker-Rhodes's conception of space, in which he found, unsurprisingly, some elements paralleling classical Buddhist philosophy.[49] His letters to the group bubble over with enthusiasm for their project, coupled with preemptive admissions of his status as an interloper.

"My math is incredibly patchy," he warned in a 1987 letter to Bastin. "I can't 'do' e.g. formal matrix algebra, but oddly I find higher math easier to follow than lower. It's a bit like using a computer without knowing how to wire it. . . . [At the upcoming ANPA conference,] it will become me to keep my mouth shut and be instructed!!"[50]

The ANPA group, for their part, were happy to have Alex join. "It is my belief," Bastion wrote him, "that our model has the power to free the life sciences from the limitations in hypothesis making that they take over with their unbelievably automatic acceptance of the old [Newtonian] physics as commonsense." He too wanted to "get the physicists and the philosophers into real contact," which hadn't proved easy. Getting biologists to the table would prove even tougher, because they would want to know what natural philosophy could do to help them address problems in their own field.

Alex, as a biologist and psychologist, could perhaps help bridge the gap.[51] "My prime interest is in how minds abstract phenomena," he said in a letter to Parker-Rhodes. "I think physicists are going to have to address neuropsychology, and psychologists are going to have to take some of your materials on board in talking about the nature of 'mind.'"[52]

PHENOMENOLOGY AND QUANTUM MECHANICS weren't taking up all of Alex's time. He had chalked up the low sales numbers for *Imperial Patient* to its being a "scholarly piece about ancient history," forgetting his own boasts that it could duplicate the sensation of *I, Claudius*. He still had a contract with Duckworth, and in October 1987, just as the Black Monday stock market crash was rippling across the world, he delivered to his publisher another novel, a satire about a computer-hacking plot to destroy the British ruling class.

The new novel was no kind of history lesson, he told Duckworth. "It is politically vicious enough to start a row," he said. If they were lucky, they could get it out synchronously with another financial crisis.[53] If it didn't sell, he told Colin Haycraft in the brash, scolding manner that James Mitchell had come to loathe years before, it would be the publisher's fault. "Get a competent publicity agent on the job, on results commission," he advised. "I know it's quite vain to suggest you plant the necessary news stories, send copies to the appropriate people, get to radio and TV shows, etc. etc. You don't. So get someone who can and will. Unless you actually like spending money producing books you can't be bothered to sell."[54]

The novel, titled *The Philosophers*, came out in June 1989, four years after William Gibson published *Neuromancer*, the novel that made cyberpunk a conspicuous genre, and it shares some qualities with Gibson's dystopian tale. The main character (and Alex's stand-in), David

Knight, is a lecturer in philosophy at an unnamed university. His father, with whom he has little in common, is a wealthy London financier.

David lives in a South Asian and Caribbean neighborhood of London plagued by violent police and racist National Front thugs, echoing the brutal politics of an ultra-Right Tory government presided over by a prime minster referred to alternately as the Witch of Endor and the Grocer. Working people are being impoverished and their communities hollowed out, refugees are held in detention before being shipped back from whence they came, everything of value is seemingly for sale to American and Japanese corporations, and the financial class is happily enriching itself, shifting assets around while making nothing of value.

The plot reads like a better version of the one Alex had concocted for "Walshingham's Drum." One of David's students, who learned computer hacking from an alumnus of Turing's wartime codebreaking crew, goes to work for David's father and devises a plan to undermine the corrupt financial edifice and drive the Grocer from office. It involves exposing a web of corporate insider dealings and finally crashing the pound. His job gives him access to a mainframe computer, from which he plants viruses in those of other banks and financial concerns in London and elsewhere, assisted by David, his new wife, and several of his other students—including a high-end prostitute, two Catholic priests, and a woman who operates an underground railroad for refugees.

The plan goes off smoothly: the government falls (the Grocer seeks political asylum in apartheid South Africa), and Britain, climbing out from under the digital rubble, begins to put a non-speculative economy back together. David and his wife Sarah resettle in Sligo, in the shadow of Benbulbin, where they cultivate their garden while working for a Japanese-backed institute researching ways to talk to extraterrestrials.

Alex said at the time that he wrote *The Philosophers* in "a sheer attack of spleen."[55] But like *Tetrarch*, which folded in some of the ideas that Alex was simultaneously developing in *I and That*, *The Philosophers* references quantum physics and other matters from *Reality and Empathy*, although without turning the plot into a demonstration in higher math. Like *Come Out to Play*, the story is wish fulfillment: Alex's vision of how a corrupt and inhuman regime could be overthrown by clever, nonviolent people leveraging their enemies' greed against them, skipping class war, bloody revolution, and the power struggles that typically follow.

Along the way, he had plenty of fun lampooning Thatcherite Britain and the new class of financial predators and opportunists who seemed to take over the country in the '80s. In one episode, David and his crew spoil a photo op for the Grocer at a hospital for disabled children when they teach the children to sing the following lyrics, to the tune of "What a Friend We Have in Jesus," to the visiting PM:

> All those spivs and snobs and wankers,
> all the yuppie middle class,
> all those inside-dealing bankers
> hunker down to kiss your ass.
> When the IRA gets lucky
> we will scrape you off the floor—
> shut the lid and pull the handle
> hear that canting voice no more.[56]

The underlying issue, which gives *The Philosophers* its title, is David's argument with himself over how best to engage politically and morally: by being a bodhisattva, who seeks awakening out of compassion for humanity, or by being a ninja? By practicing loving-kindness, or by meeting oppression with violence? The answer is a little of both: "half time as the ninja, half time as the bodhisattva."[57]

Weeks before the book was released, Alex couldn't stop quarreling with his publisher. Haycraft had illustrated the book jacket with a Renaissance relief of Plato and Aristotle debating, against a drab, greenish-gray background. "Pull this idiot jacket and substitute another," Alex demanded. "If your talent for deliberate sabotage was as great as for the accidental variety, you could go far."[58] Haycraft did not relent, and the jacket went out as he had intended it.

Its cover art didn't keep the eminent critic Christopher Wordsworth from giving *The Philosophers* a fine review in *The Guardian*. "Loathing and contempt have fueled more bad tracts than they have good fiction," he cautioned, "but put an archaic sense of humour in the tank, pump the tyres with some Greco-Buddhist air . . . as Alex Comfort does in *The Philosophers*, and enjoy the stimulating ride." "[*The Philosophers*] may not convert our rulers to philosophy as Plato hoped," Wordsworth predicted, "but the itching powder should make a few of them scratch even if they are not yet ready to think."[59]

That was what Alex was hoping for. His great fear, he said in an interview just before the novel was published, was that it wouldn't prove "spiteful" enough, wouldn't cause enough of a row, and would be ignored, "like most novels I write."[60] Unfortunately it was largely ignored, despite Wordsworth's praise. *The Philosophers* was not widely reviewed, and it failed to sell.

TOWARD THE END OF *The Philosophers*, David and his friends note a news item about an explosion at a US air base in England that knocks out three F-111 fighter bombers on the ground but also damages an adjacent house. They deplore it as the work of "cowboy activists" operating from good motives but little seriousness of purpose.[61] Just before the novel appeared, Alex was drawn back into an episode of cowboy activism more than twenty years in his past.

In 1987 a book titled *George Blake, Superspy*, came out. Penned by H. Montgomery Hyde, an ex-MP and prolific writer (he was delisted by the Ulster Unionist Party after he spoke in favor of the Wolfenden report's proposed decriminalization of homosexuality), the book identified Michael Randle and Pat Pottle, Alex's old comrades from the Committee of 100 and the Direct Action Committee against the Bomb, as the parties who had helped convicted spy George Blake escape prison in 1966 and flee to the Soviet Union. British intelligence had known their identities for some time and never pursued them, possibly because the case would have been too embarrassing. But in the aftermath of Hyde's book, some 110 Tory MPs signed a motion demanding that Randle and Pottle face criminal charges.

Alex had declined to assist the Blake escape when Randle approached him about it at the time, but over the years his name had percolated below the surface as someone who might have knowledge of it. After Hyde's book came out and the case was reopened, he, the actors Vanessa Redgrave and Bernard Miles, the Rev. John Papworth (who did shelter Blake after his breakout), and at least ten others were mentioned in the press as possibly having information of interest to Special Branch, which had reopened the case.[62]

Alex still tended to believe that Blake was a double agent, whose escape MI6 had engineered to implant him in Moscow as its informant, and that his friends had been taken in. He laid this out in an article for the *Daily Telegraph* that was never published, but in January 1989, as the case against Randle and Pottle was gaining traction and they were writing their own book about the Blake episode, Alex was interviewed by journalist Barrie Penrose in the *Times* of London. It was the first time he had ever spoken publicly about the case.

They "didn't have the brains to see" that the authorities might have been using them, he said of Randle and Pottle. "A lot of those chaps were as worried as doves and as harmless as serpents. If they'd have got caught it would have harmed CND. I thought they might be being got at through Blake. They wouldn't see an intelligence stunt coming if it had a label on it."[63] Penrose's article went on to say that Alex might become "the key to whether Randle and Pottle are brought to trial" and that Scotland Yard considered his prior knowledge of the plot as critical since it supported the claim that Randle had tried to recruit other activists for the prison break.

When Alex saw the article, he dashed off a letter to the *Times* complaining about the use of the phrase "CND supporters organized the escape" since, other than Randle, he had no knowledge of anyone else connected with CND having been part of the plot or knowing any details of it.[**] The *Times* didn't run his letter, and when Randle saw Penrose's article, with Alex's belittling characterization of him and Pottle, he was stunned but too immersed in preparing their legal case to respond.

He replied a year and a half later, when the case was further advanced, asking why Alex had seen fit to use such "contemptuous" language about him and Pottle. "Are these terms in which to speak to someone you yourself say you regarded as a friend and colleague?" He particularly cherished, he said, a postcard Alex had sent to him the first time he was imprisoned, after the DAC's 1958 occupation of a US nuclear missile site at Swaffam. The card quoted the St. Crispin's Day speech from Shakespeare's *Henry V*—"and gentlemen in England now a-bed / Shall think themselves accurst they were not here!" and was signed "Warmest congratulations and solidarity—Alex Comfort.'" If he still meant what he had written then, Randle said, "I think you owe me some explanation now."[64]

Alex wrote back that what he had said about some CND members being "as worried as doves and as harmless as serpents" hadn't referred to Randle or Pottle. He meant Ralph Schoeneman, an American-born CND and Committee of 100 organizer who had been close to Bertrand Russell to the extent, some said, of exercising undo influence over him. "However much I disagree with your decision to get involved I hope

** AC, letter to the editor, *Sunday Times* (London), January 29, 1989. In their book, Randle and Pottle said only that they obtained £200 "from a personal friend" to fund the caper. Michael Randle and Pat Pottle, *The Blake Escape: How We Freed George Blake—and Why* (London: Harrap Books, 1989), 60.

you are not penalised for it," Alex wrote. But he was firm on his basic point: Randle and Pottle's freelance decision to break Blake out of jail had "placed nuclear disarmament at very grave risk" since it might have given ammunition to those who wanted to represent activists "as being in cahoots with either of the international tar babies—which they were not."[65]

A year later, Randle and Pottle's case finally went to trial at the Old Bailey; they represented themselves. The judge disallowed their argument that Blake's life and mental stability had been under imminent danger in prison, or might have been over time, and prevented them from presenting some evidence and calling some witnesses on national security grounds.[66] They were released in a dramatic case of jury nullification, however, when the jurors disregarded the judge's instructions and voted to dismiss all the charges. Asked why he thought they did so, Pottle replied, "I think common sense, straightforward common sense." Blake, who gave videotaped testimony that Randle and Pottle had not been in touch with the Soviet authorities at the time of his escape or received any money from Moscow, said he remained "deeply grateful" to them.[67]

ALEX'S TIME WAS TAKEN up less with politics than with his efforts to get various literary and media projects off the ground. He was still trying to find a publisher for his collected poems, without success.[68] He had toyed with pitching a television documentary version of *Reality and Empathy* since before the book was published.[69] In 1990 he sent a proposal to IDT Television for a film of the book. He proposed fleshing out three key assertions:

- Time doesn't flow, it only looks as if it does.
- Quantum theory has upended our world, introducing noncausality, interconnectedness, nonlocality, and the fact that observation affects what is observed.
- Reality is not what we see around us; what we see is a complex mental construct derived from phenomena.

Alex was proposing an ambitious series à la Carl Sagan's *Cosmos*, including a roundtable discussion between biologists, physicists, and psychologists: a mini-version of his Invisible College. But who would watch it? "If anyone thinks I'm overrating the audience," Alex said, "remember that Stephen Hawking on Time, Roger Penrose on Mind, and Douglas Hofstadter on recursive systems have all proved bestsellers." And there was plenty of public interest in Hindu and Buddhist philosophy, "which both chimes in with and has influenced quantum physics."[70] IDT did not respond.

Alex hoped to produce a revised edition of *I and That*. The rights to the book had reverted to him by 1990, and he wanted to expand it to include the discussion of modern science as a normative religion that he had been turning over in his head for some while, along with other revisions. A question had been looming: if ethics enter the universe with humanity—with the human mind—then how do we make sense of the evolution of both mind and ethics from a premoral universe? Alex thought he could address this question from a hard scientific rather than a theological perspective.[71] Tessa Strickland, editorial director at Random House's UK-based Rider Books imprint, suggested he devise a way to update *I and That* and incorporate it into the "more scientific" *Reality and Empathy*.[72] Instead, he stuck with his original idea of expanding *I and That*, and in fairly short order, turned in a set of revisions to Rider. Most of the new material simply clarified or expanded on the original text, but it also included a new subsection on the origins of the idea of reincarnation and a discussion of the relationship between mathematics and physical reality.

The most important addition was a new final chapter, drawn from a lecture he delivered to the South Place Ethical Society in September 1990, in which he called upon scientists to confront the "reshuffling of the entire pack" that quantum physics demanded. "I do not expect to see us enter the twenty-first century with ... the nature of consciousness and observerhood in its present scientifically and philosophically unsatisfactory state," he wrote. "There are too many converging factors, from computer science to experimental physics, which make the conventional wisdom less and less satisfactory."[73]

Scientists and mystics, at least in the non-theistic Vedic and Buddhist traditions, would have to work together, using a combination of objective observation and intuitive experience to arrive at a satisfactory picture of the universe and humans' place in it, Alex argued. That didn't mean a return to traditional religion; "no religious formulation will ever again serve unless it passes science as gatekeeper," he said.

Instead, "we are embarking on quite a new kind of intellectual adventure, one in which neither myth nor math will have primacy though both will be involved." The result, Alex hoped, would be a new "scientific humanism quite unlike what we have so far meant by scientific humanism, one which treats cocksure reductionism at least as toughly as our fathers treated Christian dogma."

Other projects dragged on. In 1987 Alex updated *A Good Age*, with revised text on Alzheimer's, sexuality, hypothermia, high blood pressure, and poverty, plus a new entry on dementia, but it was three years before it came out, in paperback, published by Pan Books in the UK and Crown in the United States, with the perky new title *Say Yes to Old Age!*[74]

Once again Alex was running up against the reality that the most salable thing about him was his authorship of *The Joy of Sex*. Occasionally he feared it was the only thing he would be remembered for. "I wish people would wait to write my epitaph until I am dead," he wrote a prospective interviewer as early as 1982. "Otherwise, it is like putting a tumbler over a cockroach, and finding it has moved on. My main need at the moment is to get untangled as a sex guru, standardbearer for Californianism, etc. etc."[75] In a 1989 interview, he called the book "a bit of an albatross, because it was entirely a side project." It was "purely the luck of the draw" that it sold better than his other books, he said.[76]

He was still getting proposals for a video version of *Joy* and was still responding in the same fashion. Typically he vetoed any "live-photographic version," which would simply be pornography, while an "informative video" on sex education for adults would have to consist mostly of on-camera discussions with couples. "Any discussion with us would require a firm contract, our artistic control, and top dollar up front," he told one supplicant. "We have found by experience that our business conditions weed out most would be producers!"[77]

Alex had earlier discussed with Mitchell Beazley writing another, more serious book looking at human sexual behavior from an anthropological perspective. That idea had gone by the boards with James Mitchell's death, but Alex continued to think about it, along with the possibility of turning it into a film or television documentary. In 1987 he got the chance to make a film, working with SC Entertainment, a Toronto-based production company. Run by producers Syd Cappe and Nicolas Stiliadis, SC was a prolific manufacturer of low-budget horror movies and thrillers and the occasional educational documentary.[78] The new film would explore the factors that make human sexuality distinct from that of other mammals. Alex was to write and perform the narration and appear on camera with other experts.

Signs of trouble emerged in May, when SC Entertainment published an ad for the film that used *The Joy of Sex* in the title without clearing it with Alex. When Mitchell Beazley and Paramount, which still had an interest in the *Joy* film, got wind of it, they complained to him, and he reminded Cappe that, under their agreement, the film was to have nothing to do with his book and that it was not his intention to "sanction an exploitation film." He also demanded to see a complete script before the movie was finalized.[79] They settled on the title *The Sexiest Animal*.

Alex expected SC to produce a documentary of a caliber to be shown on British TV, but the rough cut, which he viewed in January 1988, was anything but. While his narration largely survived, and several other experts duly appeared, visually the film came close to soft-core porn. A long segment with former porn star Gloria Leonard, a staged sex scene, short sequences from X-rated movies, and a frolic on a beach with a naked couple took up much of the running time, along with leering footage of swingers and gay men, none of which was connected more than tangentially with Alex's script. The narrator himself appeared, dressed in a safari outfit and filmed at various off-kilter angles.

Alex was incensed, although it's difficult to understand how he could have failed to find something amiss during filming. "The director has clearly gone all-out for the cable-sleaze market," he said in an angry letter to Cappe, suggesting that he had been deceived in agreeing to participate. He insisted that the segment on swingers, which was irresponsible during the AIDS crisis, be removed, along with "all the soft-core film clips." And he warned that unless the film was redone from top to bottom, he would have nothing to do with promoting it.[80] "If my name is used in advertising or promoting it or, in general, other than as one of the contributing speakers," he warned, "I will take energetic measures to repudiate such use."[81]

He suffered little embarrassment, despite his appearance on screen, as the film sank quickly into the VHS video bins and was forgotten. But Alex was still taken with the idea of a documentary on the anthropology of human sexual behavior. A few months after his fracas with SC Entertainment, he proposed it to his old acquaintance Desmond Morris, who had continued writing on human and animal behavior since the success of his book *The Naked Ape* in 1967. Morris was also a veteran broadcaster who often paired his TV documentaries with books—and vice versa.

Alex suggested a series for Channel 4 on "the comparative biology of human sexual behaviour in the light of new work," followed by a "painless" book for the lay reader. Topics could include continuous sexual receptivity as a distinguishing human trait, fetishes and other releasers, jealousy, the origins of homosexuality, and the possible role of pheromones in human behavior. Together, Alex said, "we could sell it, and do it in words of one syllable but not four letters."[82] "That letter sums him up," Morris said years later of Alex: "every line a new idea in it."[83]

Morris had always liked and respected Alex and found they had much in common. Morris had been a surrealist painter early in his career, at the same time Alex was writing about painting; he still had a copy of Alex's short book on Cecil Collins's work. Both had been research scientists as well as broadcasters; both had achieved great success with one best-selling book; and both were interested in expanding biology's reach to include more aspects of the human. Morris shopped Alex's idea to his contacts at the BBC "but it wouldn't take off," he recalled.[84]

Alex's persistent identification with his best seller had its gratifications, however. In August 1987 he got a phone call from Jack Harte, head of the newly founded Irish Writers' Union, asking if he would come to Ireland to speak in support of the union's fight against literary censorship in the republic. Since a few years after independence, Ireland had labored under a strict censorship regime that caught thousands of books in its net, including modern classics like *The Grapes of Wrath*, *The Catcher in the Rye*, *Catch-22*, and the early novels of Edna O'Brien. That regime had been moderated in 1967, when book bans were limited to twelve years, after which they had to be renewed.

The Joy of Sex had never been published in Ireland but was not under a censorship order in 1987 when it suddenly appeared on a new list of prominent titles that also included Angela Carter's novel *The Passion of New Eve* and a book of erotic art: evidently a move by some extreme members of the Censorship Board to flex their muscles. The Writers' Union was taken by surprise and decided to launch a legal and public relations campaign against the board.

Bob Greacen, now living in Dublin, suggested Harte get hold of Alex and ask him to get involved. Initially Alex said no. "The English interfered in the affairs of Ireland far too long," he told Harte, "and I have too much respect for the Irish to go over there now and start telling you what to do. I have total confidence in your ability to sort out this matter for yourselves."

Harte tried another ploy. "Robert tells me you were part of the literary scene in Dublin when you were here in the '40s. Would you be interested in coming over to give a poetry reading?" "I would be delighted to give a poetry reading in Dublin," Alex replied.[85]

The reading was set for October 6 at Buswell's Hotel in Dublin, across the road from the Dáil Éireann and a frequent venue for literary events. The agreement was that he would not talk about *The Joy of Sex*—which he was happy enough not to—but would read from the still-gestating "Mikrokosmos" along with some earlier poems about Ireland. A quartet would provide musical interludes. Harte and the Writers' Union blanketed the Irish media with notices about the event, taking care to note they were organizing it both to honor Alex's literary achievements and to "highlight the injustice whereby a serious book by a serious author can be banned without explanation, without a complaint against it being made known, and without the author being given an opportunity to defend his work."[86]

That generated a flurry of interview requests when Alex arrived in town. "It's not for me to say what should or should not be banned in Ireland," he told the *Sunday Press* diplomatically. "I don't want to add to the controversy except to say that I am against censorship altogether, whether of the sort that exists in Ireland or the political censorship they are trying to introduce in Britain."[87]

"The reading was packed," Harte recalled, and Alex's selections, laced with references to everything from quantum physics and mathematics to pacifism to the allure of Sligo, held the audience engrossed. He did not once mention *The Joy of Sex*.[88]

The Writers' Union's campaign paid off. Two years later, the ban on *Joy* was removed after an appeals board agreed that it did not undermine support for the institution of marriage.[89] While publications providing information on abortion and birth control were still banned for many years, the Censorship Board otherwise beat a retreat, and no further books were banned in Ireland for indecency or obscenity.[90]

HIS READING AT BUSWELL'S was one of the nicest experiences he'd had in years, Alex told Harte, inadvertently highlighting the frustrations he had experienced since his return to England.[91] In the years that followed, one novel had flopped, another was about to follow suit, *The Sexiest Animal* had proved a mistake, and none of his other film or broadcast ideas was panning out.

Life in Cranbrook was narrowing as Jane's drinking continued and as she became ever more dependent on Alex. Cicely Hill, a neighbor who moved in near the Windmill House some three years after they arrived, noticed that Alex did the daily shopping and a great deal of the cooking and was generally much more often seen in public than his wife. Hill became friendly with them and visited their home several times. Conversation with Alex was always on some interesting topic, with Jane coming in occasionally with remarks and asides. When she talked at length, Hill said, "her conversation was rather broken up," and for long stretches "she would disappear and was just not there." She was "clearly not all together," and Hill got the impression of "a very seriously troubled person."[92]

Earlier in 1989 David Goodway, a lecturer at the University of Leeds, contacted Alex for a series of interviews that he planned to use in a book on the British poets of the '40s. Goodway, a professed anarchist who had been influenced by Alex's writings, was the author of *London Chartism, 1838–1848*, a well-received history of the movement, and he was now intending to write a history of British Neo-Romanticism. He visited Alex and Jane at the Windmill House several times in March and April, lunched with them at Alex's favorite Indian restaurant in town, and ended up covering far more than the early years of Alex's literary and political career. Jane was present for most of the conversations, supplying tea and occasionally stepping in when Alex, as sometimes happened, had trouble recalling the details of something that had happened decades ago.

Their talks offer a snapshot of Alex's projects, perspectives, and feelings at the time about his life and accomplishments. By now he had been essentially a full-time writer for a decade and a half, and he was more frustrated than ever by publishers' confusion at the range of genres and subjects his work encompassed.

"I act like a vacuum cleaner," he said with a laugh, "and sweep up various things which happen to be on the floor, and then you have a department which puts them together and hands them out . . . . [But] if you do that, it drives publishers crazy because you're not really classifiable." Jane remarked that when she was a librarian at LSE, she once found *Authority and Delinquency in the Modern State* catalogued under "Juvenile Delinquency."[93]

At one time, Alex said regretfully, the culture of literature and publishing wasn't so constrained. "Descartes wrote about politics, religion, philosophy, and mathematics. Goethe wrote about the theory of vision, evolution, the evolution of the vertebrate skull, and wrote poetry, plays, and novels. Leibniz wrote not only a lot of mathematics, he also wrote a treatise on the relationship between religion and government. It's not unusual for people to have written about more than one thing." But they had more trouble doing so in the twentieth century.

What was he working on? "I've got almost a chest-full of essays," he told Goodway, "some of which have been published, the rest scattered around in other places." But he didn't feel they merited pulling together into a new collection. He was still trying to get "Mikrokosmos" published. "I've started to try to write poetry about mathematics," he said, "[but] it gets to the point where you can't expound what you're talking about over linearity and timelines and experience without losing the audience." Only scientists and philosophers would read *Reality and Empathy*, and TV didn't seem to want a *Cosmos*-type approach to quantum physics and the self. Perhaps he could convey his ideas more impressionistically, in verse—not that he was working hard at it.

"Poetry comes in fits. I'm not writing any at the moment, but it doesn't mean I won't." He was waiting to hear from Andrew Motion, poetry editor at Chatto & Windus, about "Mikrokosmos" and a "Collected Poems." He had the setup for a new work of fiction, however. It didn't yet have a title or much of a story, but it would dramatize some of the ideas in *Reality and Empathy*, much as *Tetrarch* had embodied his thinking in *I and That*. Its premise: A group of scientists send a mathematician on a space shot. He is disabled but small enough to fit in the vessel they have designed, "and he says he's just as happy sitting in the spacecraft as sitting in a wheelchair." Neither does he mind being alone with his computer, making calculations and contemplating the nature of physical reality versus the one his brain maps out. "I'm not quite sure where to take the story after that," Alex confessed. "I've written a few pages."

He was still "thinking hard" about writing a book that would treat science as a religion, "establishing if it has any creed other than not having a creed and how are you to integrate that with current philosophical and religious ideas," his latest notion for how to follow up *Reality and Empathy*. That prompted Goodway to ask how Alex's ideas on natural science had changed since the late '40s and his *Pattern of the Future* broadcasts, when he had disturbed religious Britons with his positivist views.

"*The Pattern of the Future* was a criticism of one particular interpretation of religion," Alex replied, "a rather naïve type of theism which I would still be prepared to reject in those terms." Due to recent advances in physics and the understanding of space-time, however, the concept of the nature of reality had changed. "It's now much more like . . . the Hindu-Buddhist idea, the Maya"—the world as a "vibration of consciousness." But if he felt scientific positivism underrated the complexity of reality, given that quantum physics had undermined the traditional understanding of material reality, "some sort of humanism"—as yet undefined—was still valid.***

"I'm a very un-psychic and un-mystical character," he added. "I don't have massive pre-conscious experiences of any kind. Some people do, and tend to intuit the thing bodily, but not me."

Colleagues at the Royal Society of Medicine encouraged him in his efforts to pull together an Invisible College exploring the links between physics, mathematics, and biology, and he was an enthusiastic member. Now that he was practicing again as a locum in geriatric psychiatry, he had also, at long last, joined the British Medical Association, a group he used to rail against for opposing the establishment of the National Health Service in the '40s.

He remained a member of both the Peace Pledge Union and the Campaign for Nuclear Disarmament, going back close to forty-five years and thirty years, respectively. But the only campaign he was on at the present was "a general campaign against Thatcherism." And his feelings about direct action, including political violence, were as provocative as ever.

"As a pacifist," he said, "I'm opposed to war on the ground that violence organized by the state never really produces the object it's supposed to. I think assassination's far more discrete. The only trouble is that, historically, assassinations usually kill the wrong people. And it's much more often being perpetrated by the Right on the Left. People like Rosa Luxemburg got popped off, people like Hitler didn't."

But popular violence had its place. Alex recalled an appearance on an American TV talk show in 1978. A neo-Nazi group had applied to march through Skokie, a Chicago suburb that was the home of many Holocaust survivors. "The Nazis had the right to march and produce a provocation," Alex said, but in addition "every right-thinking citizen had the right to go beat their skulls in. Because those bastards have it coming."

On the other hand, Alex disagreed that direct action for its own sake was ever a good idea. "You've got to think it out carefully and do

*** He also worried that positivism encouraged humans to dissociate themselves dangerously from the rest of nature. In the text for an unpublished, revised edition of *I and That*, he wrote that "the positivist humanism of our time ... asserts that if Man is not God, he is the only available candidate for that position."

something which really makes the government look ridiculous or does them damage. If you want to be guerrillas, you need a sense of humor, which they don't usually have." His model in this, and one of his great heroes, was Michael Collins, the Irish guerrilla leader against the British occupation who helped win independence in 1921 as much by disrupting the courts and tax collection as through targeted raids and assassinations. Always he sought to catch the British occupiers flat-footed and make them look ineffectual. Alex loved to tell stories about Collins almost as much as he did about Jack Haldane, and he recounted a couple for Goodway.

"It sounds like you've plenty to keep you busy in retirement," Goodway suggested. "What's retirement?" Alex replied. "I mean, I'm only doing what I've always done." At the time he was finding it difficult to work on the follow-up to *Reality and Empathy*, but being surrounded by various projects in different stages of completion was his normal state. "I never know what I'm going to do next," he said. "It's just what comes along. Maybe something that has to be done. Or it may be something that I haven't thought about yet but which will bubble up in due course. When it does, it writes itself very fast. I may eventually get too old to do that, but you never know how many more fits there are coming. I think there might be some more in the queue."

Alex, nevertheless, was thinking about his legacy, a subject he had neglected to discuss in *A Good Age* and his other writings on elderhood. The impulse may have come in part from his response to the death in October 1987 of Peter Medawar, whose health had gradually deteriorated since his stroke in 1969. The two had never been personally very close, but Medawar had been part of his life, professionally and intellectually, for more than thirty-five years. Together they had helped orient gerontology as a legitimate field of research, and later Medawar's defense of a more imaginative approach to scientific speculation had anchored the thinking that Alex poured into *I and That* and *Reality and Empathy*. Medawar had also been the presiding spirit of the brilliant collection of researchers, including Haldane and John Maynard Smith, to which Alex had belonged at UCL in the '50s and '60s.

Alex and Jane attended the memorial service at Westminster Abbey, along with Bernard Levin, Desmond Morris, Karl Popper, Isaiah Berlin, David Attenborough, and other luminaries. "You know how much we all admired his wit and fortitude," Alex wrote in a letter to Medawar's widow, Jean. "Peter's reputation as scientist and a philosopher is secure, and so is his defence of the imaginative aspect of science. He rightly warned against confusing it with poetry, but at the same time he asserted that the resources of artistic and scientific insight are the same."[94] Later, Alex and Jane visited Medawar's grave at St Andrew's Church in Alfriston, East Sussex, where Jane reported that he was very moved.[95]

One advantage to living in Cranbrook, he told Jean, was its proximity to Alfriston, and Medawar's resting place. Subsequently, he asked several people if they could help him find a literary executor.[96] He was also inquiring with UCL whether it would take his papers subsequent to his move to the United States in 1973.[97] He was the largest single benefactor to an appeal for books to replace those destroyed at the Bucharest University library during the 1989 Christmas uprising against the Ceauşescu regime in Romania: seven tonnes (some 15,000 pounds), "the result of a mass clear-out of his house to give himself living room," the *Times* reported.[98]

He and Jane were making their wills and had decided to transfer the eleven hectares of orchard and farmland they had bought near their home to the Woodland Trust. It was being seeded to form what would be known as Comfort's Woods. By the spring of 1990, at least one thousand seedlings were in place or had established themselves, including sweet chestnut, ash, and oak, and Alex noted happily that a large bird population was frequenting the area. Plans called for further planting the following winter.

The trust was doing a splendid job, Alex wrote the regional officer. The former owners' farm next door was being converted to residences, he noted. "We may have prevented any future move to use the Swattenden Lane frontage for yuppie housing, which would not have been impossible knowing the pressure on Cranbrook to expand."[99]

INEVITABLY, DURING HIS INTERVIEWS, David Goodway asked Alex if further editions of *The Joy of Sex* were to be expected. As long as interest in the topic persisted, he replied. "I have a feeling the interest can go on for centuries, like *Gray's Anatomy*." He could see himself continuing to revise the book, he said resignedly, "until I'm dead and gone, or until somebody does a better one in a quite different climate."[100]

It wasn't his idea to do another revision of the book, however, just four years after the last one had appeared. *Joy*'s sales, despite the steadying influence of the 1986 edition, were not trending up. Yet Alex's books remained a profitable corner of Mitchell Beazley's backlist, and the firm was keen to find new ways to exploit it and protect it from competition. Sales director David Hight observed that other major publishers were now issuing illustrated sex guides and manuals, and Mitchell Beazley and Crown were missing out by sticking too closely to the original 1972 edition. Rather than just making a few editorial additions and adjustments to keep the book up to date, as they had done a few years earlier, Hight said, why not completely revise and refresh it for the '90s?[101]

Alex was not taken with the idea initially. But he met with Jack Tresidder and Tony Cobb, who had been art director since Peter Kindersley left in the mid-'70s, and with whom he was familiar, and agreed to the plan. Tresidder, an ex-journalist and prolific ghostwriter, would do much of the rewriting, in close consultation with Alex. Cobb would completely redesign the book, to be titled *The New Joy of Sex*.

The process was "really smooth," Cobb recalled, in contrast to the turbulent James Mitchell period. "We were all singing from the same sheet. [Alex] really did respond to what we wanted, and we didn't come up against any brick walls with him."[102] He was "a most extraordinary man with the widest range of intellectual interests, in sometimes surprising areas of study," said Duncan Baird, Mitchell Beazley's publisher and managing director, remembering a lunch at which Alex held forth on "tantric philosophy and the fourth dimension. He was also very open to considering innovations, such as the then-novel idea of producing a CD-ROM or CD-I version of the book."[103]

As it happened, Tresidder did little to no ghosting, because the text of the *New Joy* remained largely the same as in the 1986 edition. He and Alex reorganized the entries to start with physical characteristics like breasts, buttocks, skin, earlobes, and penis ("Ingredients") before moving on to "Main Courses," "Sauces," and "Venues" (e.g., beds, bathing, and motorcars) and ending with health and other issues ("frequency," priapism, birth control, etc.). Alex added new entries on fidelity, safe sex, and anal intercourse and expanded the section on AIDS he had included in the 1986 edition, but not a single new position appeared. He also made some small but very necessary changes in wording: "girls" became "women," a sarcastic reference to "the Women's Lib bit" became "sexual equality," the entry on fighting now warned, firmly, that one should never put up with "real violence," and the reference to "men's rape fantasies" in the "Bondage" entry disappeared.

The introductory essay, "On Advanced Lovemaking," changed very little, except for a couple of added paragraphs addressed to disabled readers. "If you happen to be disabled in any way, don't stop reading," Alex urged. "In sex, as in other activities, physical disability is an obstacle to be outwitted."[104]

The biggest difference in the text was an entirely new preface by Alex that looked back on the nearly twenty years since the first edition was published and assessed the changes they had wrought in social attitudes toward sex. "Counsellors have come to realize that sex, besides being a serious personal matter, is a deeply rewarding form of play," he wrote. "One can now read books and see pictures devoted to sexual behavior almost without limitation in democratic countries." The change was still ongoing, however. "It takes more than 20 years and a turnover in generations to undo centuries of misinformation." While sex-related books, newspaper columns, TV shows, and counseling services were proliferating, the "new glasnost" still included much that was "anxious, hostile or over the top."

Alex was pleased to see that a healthy acceptance of sexual equality was taking hold, but he was careful to explain what he meant by this in practice. Dominance wasn't something to be eliminated but something to share, he argued: "letting both sexes take turns controlling the game." "Sex is no longer what men do to women and women are supposed to enjoy," he added. It can be a "loving fusion" or a situation in which "each is a 'sex object'" ("both are essential and built-in to humans"). Play, he said—as always—is the way to work all this out. Men must learn to stop domineering and women to "take control in the give and take of the game rather than by nay-saying."

There was a presumption in this that women were too apt to shut down men's harmless fantasies. But Alex's basic message had remained the same, echoing the one that Havelock Ellis, Marie Stopes, Alfred Kinsey, and Masters and Johnson had been urging for nearly a century: that what people needed above all was "accurate and unbothered information." The availability of this, he said, and the degree of resistance by "the minority of disturbed people" who rejected it, "is an excellent test of the degree of liberty and concern in a society."[105]

The new text complete, Mitchell Beazley set about redesigning the book. Cobb and Tresidder agreed that the old drawings and paintings, while daring for their time, now seemed a bit staid and formal. It was also time to introduce more color into the product. Cobb recalled approaching David Hockney about doing the illustrations, but the California-based British painter turned down the assignment. In place of Chris Foss's line art, they commissioned John Raynes, a painter and illustrator trained at the Royal College of Art, to produce a series of textured chalk drawings in black and sepia of a couple engaged in sex; instead of Charlie Raymond's paintings, the reader would see chapter breakers consisting of cautiously erotic black-and-white close-up photos of the couple caressing.

The process that followed was quite similar to the one that Mitchell Beazley had devised in the early '70s.[106] One of the principals knew someone who had just bought a house but had not yet moved in, leaving it only partially furnished: perfect for a home photo shoot. They found a young Australian couple—a nurse and a carpenter—who were willing to pose for the photos that would supply the chapter breakers and the references for Raynes's drawings, provided their identities were kept strictly private.[107] Simon McMurtrie, the twenty-five-year-old editor who had just taken over as managing director, kept the photos under lock and key in his office, and the couple's names were never revealed. The photo sessions took a month to complete.

Cobb and Tresidder had noticed that Charlie Raymond and Edeltraud rarely smiled in the 1972 illustrations. In the new images, the new and clearly younger couple did, and the effect was warmer, producing a sense of fun that the first edition sometimes lacked. The designers augmented this with amusing drawings of the couple taking a bath together ("soaping one another all over leads naturally to better things") and making love in a rocking chair (awkwardly, from the look of it). To Alex's satisfaction, Mitchell Beazley and Crown overcame some of the qualms they had had in the early '70s about displaying certain types of sexual activity. In the new edition, the man is shown massaging the woman's vulva, and she is shown taking his penis into her mouth.**** The woman, doubtless at Alex's insistence, did not shave her underarms or pubic hair.

Perhaps the most telling visual difference between the old and new *Joy* was the absence of the plates of Asian erotic paintings that the designers had interspersed throughout the original edition. Including fine art in a sex manual for the '90s appears never to have come up. Presumably, a guide to better lovemaking no longer needed the additional cultural validation.

At each step, Tresidder showed Alex samples and got his approval. While suggesting the original design in some ways, the book they

**** Mitchell Beazley had overcome its fears in another respect as well. Whereas the rights to the first edition had been held by a shell company, Modsets Securities Ltd, to protect the firm from prosecution, the new one was copyright Mitchell Beazley International.

produced had a very different feel. A new typeface was introduced, and the pages had far less white space. A close-up photo of a couple kissing centered the book jacket, giving it a less austere look than the older version. "Alex Comfort, M.B., D.Sc.," was for the first time unequivocally the author, not editor, and he declared himself as such in the first line of the preface.

The result, arguably, was a bit of sleight-of-hand. Mitchell Beazley had created a book that looked and felt very different from the old version, but the actual text was not "completely revised," as it claimed, because most of the material didn't need to be. There simply wasn't anything additional to say, even twenty years on, about the Viennese Oyster, for example. Yet everybody involved, including Alex, felt they had come up with a product that truly brought *The Joy of Sex* into the '90s.

IN SEPTEMBER 1990 ALEX received a card from an old friend: George Woodcock, editor of *NOW* during the war and member of the Freedom Press circle. Woodcock had moved back to Canada in 1949 and subsequently established himself as one of the country's leading writers. He was still an anarchist, having published *Anarchism: A History of Libertarian Thought and Movements* (1962), which was for a long time the standard book on the subject in English, as well as biographies of Pierre-Joseph Proudhon, William Godwin, Oscar Wilde, and Peter Kropotkin. Woodcock was writing to thank Alex for his excellent review of two volumes of autobiography he had published.[108]

Alex had visited Woodcock in Vancouver years earlier but had lost touch with him since moving back to England and was glad to reestablish contact. In a letter back, sent just before Christmas—one of the last long letters he ever wrote—he commiserated about the lack of attention Woodcock's autobiographies were receiving from critics and lamented his own lack of success at getting two of his novels and his collected poems published.[109] Thinking of the fatwa that the Iranian mullahs had recently inflicted on Salman Rushdie for writing *The Satanic Verses*, and omitting mention of *The Joy of Sex*, Alex supposed that he himself would have to insult Islam if he was to get a hearing.

He was still furious at the very thought of Margaret Thatcher ("may the Devil choke her") but couldn't help being hopeful about the future of Russia, where the Soviet regime was disintegrating. "With the collapse of the Uncle Joe circus the Russians, always thorough and always anarchist by tradition, in spite of autocracies, aren't going to embrace populist capitalism, or not for long," he predicted. "Interesting to see whether from being merely ungovernable they vote with their feet and simply bypass government: same thing in parts of S. America."

As always, he was full of hope, rightly or wrongly. The world, or at least part of it, was coming around to his understanding of sex as play and a vital ingredient in developing sociality. The new physics was inspiring an overhaul of humans' understanding of reality and the self, if only slowly. One by one, the world's peoples would throw off the yoke of the State. Surely these developments would continue to play out, and he would live to see at least some of them come to fruition.

CHAPTER 23

Confinement (1991–2000)

In his Christmas latter to George Woodcock, Alex mentioned that he and Jane would be traveling once again to India in January. They had been there several times since their move back to England; Alex was intrigued by a statistical anomaly that showed lower incidence of Alzheimer's among Indians, and he had been corresponding about it with gerontologists there and in the United States for several years. They were looking forward to a pleasant trip, assuming the crisis precipitated by Iraq's invasion of Kuwait didn't get in the way.[1]

It didn't, and Alex and Jane were in India for much of the subsequent Gulf War. When they got home, Alex reported to Nick that both of them had suffered food poisoning on their travels. He still hadn't shaken it, and Jane was in bed with a virus.[2] Nevertheless, in early February, father and son met for lunch at the Athenaeum Club.

Nick's career and Alex's absence in America had meant they were out of touch for long stretches of time, but after Alex and Jane's return they saw each other more frequently. Nick had worked at an assortment of UK papers, much of the time with the *Daily Telegraph* and reporting on Parliament. In early 1991, he was at the *European*, the "first European newspaper" launched by Alex's old publisher, Robert Maxwell.

Nick had acquired a passion for cricket from his grandfather Alexander, and for railroads from Alex. Like his father, he had published his first book while still in his teens: a thirty-two-page history of *The Mid-Suffolk Light Railway*, which, to Alex's delight, was well-received by rail fans. Nick would publish further editions over the years.[3]

Nick's personal life had not always gone smoothly. He and Deborah had separated in 1984 and divorced in 1988. The breakup was difficult for Alex and Jane as well. Jane was close to Deborah, and both she and Alex were fond of Alex's grandchildren, Caroline and John, and worried how the split would affect them. Alex, who seldom interfered, urged

Nick to get therapy and offered to help pay for it.[4] When Nick remarried in 1990, Alex welcomed his new daughter-in-law, Corinne, but Jane took the news more than badly. She and Nick had always got on well, but now she faulted him for not waiting until his children were grown to leave Deborah, and she stopped seeing or speaking to him entirely.[5]

Such was the family situation the day Alex met Nick at the Athenaeum. Returning home, he resumed work on a talk he was to give in April at a conference on nursing homes in Australia; it was to be his first visit there. He was still using a typewriter but had told Nick he was on the verge of buying his first computer.

On February 15, 1991, he suffered a brain hemorrhage. Less than two weeks later he had a stroke and had to be airlifted from Cranbrook to Brook General Hospital in London, where emergency surgery saved his life. Once he was stable, he was transferred to Tunbridge Wells Hospital in Pembury, which served the Cranbrook area. His mind was clear, but he had a bad tremor, which made it difficult for him to sign his name to a power of attorney for Jane.

Alex's plight caused Jane's world to collapse. She stayed with Deborah while her husband underwent surgery but then suffered a breakdown and was admitted to Farnborough Hospital in Orpington. Later she was moved to a ward near Alex's in Pembury, but by the end of March was back home in Cranbrook.

Nick was keeping apprised of the situation through Tony Colville, Alex and Jane's solicitor, and he wanted to help, but Jane wanted him kept away. Until she moved back home, she was concerned that he might try to get into the Cranbrook house, and she asked Colville to warn him off.

In May Alex was moved again, to Hawkhurst Community Hospital in Cranbrook itself, which provided some rehabilitation, but he wasn't making much progress. He was asking Jane to have his passport renewed, but could talk only slowly and understanding him was often difficult. Then in September he suffered a second stroke, and his right side was partially paralyzed, although the tremor subsided. He was moved a fifth time, to the Royal Hospital and Home in Putney, which specialized in rehabilitation and long-term care for patients with complex neurological disabilities, and where he was looked after by John Wedgwood, a geriatrician he had known at Trinity College.

Jane was determined, nevertheless, to bring Alex home. She made plans to rig the house with railings for him get about, and to convert the dining room into a downstairs bedroom.

ALL THIS WHILE, MITCHELL Beazley was moving forward with production of *The New Joy of Sex*. The firm was in some turmoil itself at the time. In 1987 the directors, including James Mitchell's widow Janice, had sold the firm to Octopus Publishing Group, which similarly specialized in glossy, eye-catching, large-format books. The purchase price, £2 million, made it a big acquisition for Octopus, which was then only three years old. Three years later Octopus provoked the resignation of Janice Mitchell and several other directors when it moved Mitchell Beazley out of its longtime offices and into Octopus's own headquarters in Michelin House, in South Kensington, signaling a loss of autonomy. Several important authors reportedly threatened to find another publisher, but Simon McMurtrie, the new managing director, was able to reassure them and avoid an exodus.[6]

On the production side, a near-panic developed around the *New Joy of Sex* while art director Tony Cobb was preparing the reference photos. The Australian couple who served as models had to return home, forcing Cobb to rush the process along. Jane, meanwhile, was insisting on controlling communication with Alex through Tony Colville while Mitchell Beazley was trying to get his approval for the drawings and other aspects of design. She was especially upset in August, when an item in the *Times's* "Diary" column reporting that the revamped *Joy* was on the way, inferred that it was discussing AIDS for the first time, when the 1986 edition had already done so. (She drafted but then didn't send a complaining letter.)

Otherwise, prepublication publicity proceeded smoothly. A feature in the *Sunday Telegraph* about another new book, *The Magic of Sex* by Miriam Stoppard, paused to mention the imminent appearance of *New Joy*, mourned the retirement of the "bearded Seventies character and his Woodstock partner," but added, "surely, Dr. Comfort's book stands as an unimprovable classic for anyone who needs to know about sex."[7]

When *New Joy* appeared in September, riding a large print run, it benefited from a price war between retail booksellers that favored big titles like Alex's. At the Dillons chain's shop on London's Gower Street, "giggling customers" found "light relief" thumbing through the "prominently displayed and discounted *The New Joy of Sex*," the *Sunday Telegraph* reported.[8] Soon the book was showing up among the top five sellers reported by other UK chains, including W. H. Smith.[9]

Reviewers were split between those who had never liked *The Joy of Sex* to begin with and those who greeted it like the welcome return of an old friend. *Newsweek* was generally positive, although its critic, David

Gelman, was sharp enough to notice that the substance of the book was not much changed and "repeats the hedonistic philosophy of the old."[10] When the conservative *Sunday Telegraph* got around to critiquing the book, the unsigned critic complained that it still described "all manner of unspeakable acts . . . in the same relentlessly jaunty tone," including "urination," "bondage," and "prostitution," "without a whiff of disapproval," making the *New Joy* a "pleasureless, unerotic" experience. Alex was "like Hugh Hefner with a Ph.D.," and the original edition would have been better left alone as "a historical curiosity, a window onto a bygone age." Much fun was had at the expense of Alex's assertion that the big toe and the armpit could be sources of erotic pleasure.[11]

Crown and Mitchell Beazley were prepared for this line of attack. "If someone can get [satisfaction] using their big toe, then we need to know this," Crown editor Erica Marcus said. With the AIDS crisis in mind, she added, "This is a book filled with alternatives to basic intercourse. It's perfectly suited to these times."[12]

Given the pall that the epidemic had cast, the new book was needed "to reintroduce the idea of joy," said Bruce Harris, who had been Crown's director of marketing when the original edition came out and was now an executive at its new parent company, Random House. "Everyone has been so concerned about the serious issues, so it was time to emphasize the sense of happiness in sex that is eternal."[13] Sex is still a banquet, Alex assured his readers, even in a section on AIDS, with "practically unlimited" choices.

The publishers were anxious to let potential customers know that, aside from addressing the epidemic, most of the changes in the new edition were in the design and illustrations. The new couple were "more contemporary, less like the flower children of the 1960s and '70s," Tony Cobb told *Newsday* from the Frankfurt Book Fair, where he was making overseas deals. "They are meant to seem more like an average young couple of the 1990s."[14]

That said, some reviewers felt that something was lost. "We loved the old 'Joy,' and we were a little puzzled that anyone felt a need for a new one," said the *New Yorker's* Adam Gopnik, especially since Alex's original "covered its subject with an encyclopedic thoroughness that could only be described as Borgesian." The difference, again, was the illustrations. The older models had not been perfect physical specimens; they were older, less toned, their bodies "as white and slack and unmuscled as those of snowmen."[15] But Raymond's and Foss's paintings and drawings of them had radiated desire, intimacy, and a kind of blunt realism.

The new couple, by contrast, were "just entertaining themselves." The man had "ridge upon ridge of muscle . . . like a Calvin Klein model," his hair was blow-dried and moussed. The woman had "delicate, refined features, and a small wardrobe of lace lingerie, and a look of gentle, distanced amusement at the acrobatics they undertake." The furnishings depicted in Foss's original drawings were almost nonexistent: a simple bed, a chair, and very little else. The new couple, Gopnik observed, had nice things: flowers in vases, a big brass bed, pictures on the bedroom walls, and "Conran's-style bathroom accessories" (no surprise, since Mitchell Beazley produced a line of home design and decoration books for designer-retailer Terence Conran).

Gopnik was onto an essential difference between the two projects. The first *Joy of Sex* aimed to deglamorize the act, to make the point that "Cordon Bleu sex" was in reach of everybody. *New Joy*, design-wise at least, was intended to restore some of the allure, to encourage readers to imagine themselves as the attractive people in the book and to be living their lives. "Sexual behavior," Alex said, "probably changes remarkably little over the years"; it's the "degree of frankness or reticence" that changes. Probably so, but the way sex is sold changes from one era to the next. After leafing through *New Joy*, a glance at the first edition reveals again how dramatically new it looked and how merely pretty its successor was.

What the launch of *New Joy* lacked was Alex himself, who had done so much to sell the original book in America when its publishers needed an engaging presence to make it acceptable to the middle-class public. He was still recovering, however, and Crown and Mitchell Beazley instead made their executives available to the media. They also came up with some clever marketing gambits. A series of advertisements in the British tabloids featured inspirational quotes from Alex ("Sex is no longer what men do to women and women are supposed to enjoy. Sexual interaction is a loving fusion"). And on Boxing Day 1991, viewers of the top-rated soap opera *EastEnders* saw a copy of *New Joy* under one character's Christmas tree.[16] Rupert Murdoch's free newspaper *Today* ran a three-part, condensed serialization.[17]

The publishers' efforts, along with the book's sheer familiarity, paid off. Crown's initial, thirty-two-thousand-copy US print run of *New Joy* sold out quickly, and the book hit the US and UK best-seller lists within weeks of its release, then lingered in top-ten lists in both countries well into the following year. "It was a very successful relaunch," Cobb recalled. "Sales were better than some people thought they would be, and most were very happy with it."[18] Crown and Mitchell Beazley followed up with a pocket-sized edition two years later, minus the photo portfolio.

ALEX FOLLOWED THESE HAPPY developments from the Royal Hospital and Home, where he was still ensconced. Jane, alone in Cranbrook and drinking heavily, was trying to keep a grip on Alex's business affairs, but her efforts mostly consisted of badgering the team at Mitchell Beazley. In October she took up again Alex's complaint about the low level of royalties he received on the *Joy* books and asked Colville to enlist the Society of Authors in getting them hiked to 10 percent. It was "absolutely iniquitous," she told him, that the firm was protesting it couldn't pay more because the book was "difficult to sell."

Cicely Hill, Alex and Jane's neighbor, continued to see Jane from time to time. Once she asked Cicely's help with arrangements for lunch for someone coming to visit. "When she spoke of Alex, she was very intense," Hill recalled, "but a lot of the time, she was vague and absent."[19]

The renovations Jane had planned were never made. John Doheny, Alex's friend at the University of British Columbia, didn't know of his condition and tried to call him at home in early November. He talked with Jane instead and found her "distraught, exhausted, and very worried." He wrote to Alex, "She said she didn't want to live without you."[20] On November 11, 1991, she told Colville she expected to have Alex back in the house by Christmas, with an attendant. Several times she had to be walked home from the pub at the nearby George Hotel. On November 28, after trying to reach her unsuccessfully for two days, Colville called the police, who broke into the house along with a social worker. They found Jane dead in an armchair. A postmortem showed the cause was a brain hemorrhage.[21] She was seventy years old.

Colville informed Alex at the Royal Hospital and Home and Nick at work. Nick passed on the news to Ruth, who had sold their old home but was still living in Loughton, in a house that had formerly belonged to her sister Alison and Alison's husband. Upon hearing that Jane had died, Ruth responded with a single word: "Oh."[22] Later Nick was surprised to learn that Jane had left him a modest amount in her will.

Alex and Jane had planned to have a woodland burial—with only natural materials covering them and no embalmment—in Comfort's Woods, but they hadn't yet received planning permission, so Alex asked

Colville to help expedite the process with the local council. On January 22, Alex and Nick attended her burial, which included a service by Canon Collins of St Dunstan's Church, with whom Jane and Alex had been friendly.

Jane's death brought Alex a mixture of grief and relief, Nick recalled.[23] She loved him completely and had always been unequivocally on his side, and this inspired in him a deep sense of obligation and commitment. He was also, to use a word not yet current, an enabler. As time went on, and Jane's world narrowed, Alex had found himself filling nearly all of it—and discovered that he did not have the emotional resources to rebalance the relationship. He could do nothing to help her overcome her depression or her addiction—perhaps he never really understood the sources of her unhappiness—and he could not imagine leaving her, so he simply did his best to accommodate her, day to day. A highly intelligent person whose life's labor was to understand human beings, he was, ironically, probably never fully able to comprehend the human who was closest to him.

Alex was doing better physically, although he still needed a great deal of assistance. The following month, he was able to move from the Royal Hospital and Home to an apartment in Fitzwilliam House in Highgate, not far from his boyhood school and a half-mile from Nick and Corinne's home with their son, Alex, Nick's third child.

Fitzwilliam House was an elder care facility with small private apartments and a nursing facility attached. Alex would live there, more or less satisfactorily, for the next five years, looked after by an attendant. He had his books—including *The Joy of Sex* in an assortment of languages—and an old manual typewriter, and could receive visitors. But his eyes couldn't focus together properly, making it difficult to read except in large print.[24] And he could only type with the thumb of his damaged left hand, since his right side was paralyzed.

Alex's affairs were in some disorder following the months in which Jane had tried to take charge of them. Nick now had power of attorney, and early in 1992 he and Corinne flew to California to meet with Alex and Jane's lawyer and banker and sort matters out. Hoping to stay in the detached unit next to the Ventura house, which had been unoccupied for years, they found it a mess—"infested with insects"—and checked into a hotel instead. When they showed up at Alex and Jane's bank, they found that an account Alex used to make alimony payments to Ruth was about to go into overdraft. They moved money from another account to avoid an embarrassing holdup. They also put the Ventura property on the market; a year later, it would be sold. Back home, they rented out the Cranbrook house for a year, then sold it, along with Tilvern Cottage, where Alex had had his office.[25]

All of this helped to unwind the convoluted web of tax dodges that Alex had labored to create. British tax law was no longer as onerous as it had been in the '70s, so there was less of a rationale for many of these arrangements: for instance, keeping the Ventura house as Alex's "permanent" residence. In 1996 Nick also shuttered Books and Broadcasts, which had still existed as a US company after Jane died.

Alex remained concerned about taxes, however. In 1993 David Goodway got in touch with him about collecting a volume of his political writings for Freedom Press. Alex agreed readily, but through Tony Colville he insisted that the book include a disclaimer in order to maintain the appearance that he was no longer making a living from writing. The note duly appeared opposite the table of contents, in which Goodway stated that Alex had "graciously given me permission to reprint works written by him" but that "all necessary work on this volume has been carried out by me."

Published in 1994 as *Writings against Power and Death*, the book collected articles, reviews, pamphlets, and radio talks, mostly from the '40s, along with Alex's "Letter after America" from *Freedom* and a long essay he had written for a 1983 collection about Orwell. Most of these had been out of print for thirty years or longer, including "October 1944," "Peace and Disobedience," "Art and Social Responsibility," and "Social Responsibility in Science and Art," some of which had nevertheless been finding their way into the hands of anarchists and activists of other stripes.

Writings against Power and Death was not widely reviewed, but it did get a fine short write-up from the *Guardian*'s book critic, Nicholas Lezard. Alex's authorship of *The Joy of Sex* might give some people an excuse to be "sniffy" about him, Lezard said. "[But] if his pacifism during WWII makes one feel uneasy, [his] rigour and consistency and the Orwellian clarity of his prose . . . make him very worth reading indeed."[26]

Some people were reading Comfort apart from *The Joy of Sex*. The same year, 1994, Freedom Press brought out the collection that Vernon Richards had first discussed with him in 1987, *Visions of Poesy: An Anthology of 20th Century Anarchist Poetry*. Several of Alex's poems appeared, along with work by Rexroth, Patchen, Allen Ginsberg, Lawrence Ferlinghetti, Herbert Read, Adrian Mitchell, and George

Woodcock, among others. In 1995 *Authority and Delinquency in the Modern State* was translated and published in Italy for the first time, with an introduction by Eduardo Colombo, a well-known Argentine anarchist living in exile in France. Also in 1995 Alex's edition of *The Koka Shastra* was translated and published in Japan, although he was unable to supply a new preface, as requested. The following year, "Letter to an American Visitor" was included in the massive *Faber Book of War Poetry* (in a section headed "Pacifism").

More importantly for Alex himself, *Mikrokosmos*, the cycle of poems he had written several years before, was finally published in 1994, by a new firm, Sinclair-Stevenson. Several of the poems appeared in the *New Statesman and Society* just before the book itself came out.

The poet of *Mikrokosmos* is the poet of *Haste to the Wedding* and *Poems for Jane*—terse, technically accomplished, witty—rather than the one who produced *The Signal to Engage* and the other '40s volumes, with their Neo-Romantic rhetoric. The new book was not among Alex's best, but it is entertaining, straightforward, and full of learning and echoes of his beloved Greek and Roman lyric poets, and it reveals more of the author's self than any of his earlier collections.

Some of the poems—most do not have titles—are peppered with autobiography: his youth as a precocious reader, Ireland and Benbulbin, sex, his endless years as a scientific "traveling friar," a scan of his life as it slowly turned toward the speculations on the self in *I and That* and *Reality and Empathy*.

> among the gimcracks in the cart
> the intellectual and the horny
> somewhere, I found, I had picked up
> a guidebook to the whole weird journey
>
> perhaps I bought the thing
> in a hotel from off the shelf
> could be, an offbeat Gideon Bible—
> perhaps I wrote the thing myself[27]

Alex had earlier described *Mikrokosmos* to Lou Kauffman as "a mixture of mathematical physics and Buddhism." The title suggests his notion of the mind as a kind of mini-cosmos or "inner-space world," and he was trying, often successfully, to express in verse this and some of the other ideas he had set down in his two difficult books.

John Wheeler says our thinking made the world—
stars, fossils, protons, dinosaurs, the lot:
the fox that comes and goes like a thin courtier,
grass, water, girls' breasts, and galaxies, old age

we make these things out of a pile of That—
they are our algorithms and not God's,
and making them we make their histories
even that fiery start of Space and Time[28]

He never got a chance to write the sequel to *Reality and Empathy* that was to treat modern science as a form of religion. But he may have intended his new collection as part of the same overall project: to make the new conception of space-time that he was exploring empathic, as natural a way of thinking about the reality humans inhabit and help create as the older, linear way. Poetry could help him do it:

in which the 'I' is neither ghostly nor spiritual
in which the mind outranks the tangible order
in which the mind outlasts the skeleton
because it makes the tangible unreal world.[29]

What took him hundreds of pages to explore in prose, Alex tried to boil down to something concrete and plainspoken:

We say, there is an end to everything—
there'll be a last time that the moon will rise
even a last time that we lie together . . .

But then these things are unreal anyway
they simply are. We make things 'first' or 'last':
Time's how our heads work—so is Sequence . . .
God sees such firsts and lasts all in a heap
What's real is the coherent superposition.[30]

Alex seems to have wondered sometimes what kind of expedition he had joined. "My colleagues called us Falstaff's Army / and left us studiously alone." Who were his companions? "A mystic and a Trappist monk / two yogis and a statistician / (I'd like some more biologists)." But never fear:

Here come the physicists at last
two yaks, three pony-loads of gear.
The walk has been well worth the blisters
I'm interested how I came here.[31]

The image brings to mind the Cecil Collins painting Alex had admired nearly fifty years earlier, *Three Fools in a Storm*, and his own comment that the painting obliges "the possessors of minds to set up in business as Fools forthwith." But he seasoned his book with other subjects: a reflection on Ingres's portrait of Mme. Moitessier; another, much grimmer, on the 1979 killing of Lord Mountbatten by the IRA, not far from where Alex and his family used to vacation in Mullaghmore; even an appreciation of the beauty of fish. Alex's longtime subject closes *Mikrokosmos*: a suggestion of what death might mean if reincarnation were real.

Masks and garments will be new
(what you abandon is well worn)
and with no memory of me
or what transpired, or being born

waking into some other part
you'll not recall the closing door,
expect my knocking, and deny
that you and I have met before.[32]

MIKROKOSMOS WAS NOT REVIEWED. Nick recalled that soon after publishing Alex's book and a handful of other volumes of verse, Sinclair-Stevenson went out of the poetry business entirely. Neither was Alex having any luck with one remaining publishing project. The same year *Mikrokosmos* and *Writings against Power and Death* appeared, he received back the manuscript of his revised version of *I and That*, which he had sent to Rider Books four years earlier; a change of editors at the firm had left the project an orphan, and the new team decided not to publish it.[33]

Still, his most famous book was keeping him before the public—or at least the popular media. Television interviews and personal appearances were out of the question, but that didn't mean journalists with a story in mind couldn't come to him.

Conversations with the media were never easy, however. Reporters encountered a frail, white-haired man, neatly turned out in suit and tie, sitting stiffly in a large armchair that dwarfed him. He was trying to get back to walking, but the odds were against it. His mind was as sharp as always, but his eyes still couldn't focus properly, and the torrent of words that had formerly poured out was blocked by his paralysis. He was forced to speak in terse sentences that sometimes came across as brusque and impatient. He had never been terribly happy being profiled, and he anticipated correctly that his interviewers wanted to talk mainly about one thing, which he characterized, nearly every time it came up, as the "albatross."

"He long ago wrote his own script for interviews on *The Joy of . . .* ," reporter Liz Hunt noted in a 1996 profile in the *Independent*, "and decided what questions he would or wouldn't answer. Journalists who depart from the script are treated courteously but abandoned until they realise their error and refrain from ad libbing."[34]

An interview two years earlier in the same paper, headlined "The Grand Old Man of Sex," had been occasioned by the CD-ROM release of *The New Joy of Sex*. "Comfort is, according to your taste, a Timothy Leary figure or a Cyril Connolly figure—or a poor man's Jonathan Miller," reporter Ian Parker analogized. He was on firmer ground with the following: "[Alex] is undoubtedly one of the last of his kind. He has had the kind of highly prolific, HG Wells-stye, renaissance-man-in-tweeds career whose support requires both great self-confidence in moving between subjects, and a more generous culture of book publishing than exists today."[35]

Alex was eager to persuade his readers that "there is some straightforward connection between good sex and a good society," Parker asserted, extrapolating from the plot of *Come Out to Play* and greatly oversimplifying Alex's position. "Vietnam and Belsen can be accounted for by uninteresting sex." "Well," Alex replied, playing along, "it made them an awful lot easier. If people were really keen on what they did at home, they wouldn't have wasted their time going to Vietnam."

Alex opened up, for the first time publicly, about his complicated relationships with Jane and Ruth. "It didn't work very well, they were both in eruption the whole time," he recalled. "I was trying my best to be a decent husband to both of them, and I couldn't." He didn't want to leave Ruth while Nick was at school. Only later did he resolve the situation by "divorcing Wife No. 1, and marrying Wife No. 2." Thus did he sum up his awkward navigation of the two most important relationships of his life.

"You haven't asked me anything about poetry, I'm interested to notice," Alex pointed out, hopefully, as the interview was winding down. Parker asked whether he should he have started with that topic. "Oh, absolutely," Alex replied. "It's the only thing I've done that will be remembered. When all the rest has gone down the tubes, if the poetry's any good, it remains." He had still not found a publisher for his "Collected Poems."

Ruth and Alex had been on friendly terms since soon after their divorce; they talked often by phone although they seldom saw one another. But the interview in the *Independent* threw their relationship badly off kilter. Ruth had settled happily into a very private life. She had never wanted to have anything to do with *The Joy of Sex* and never took any money from Alex related to it, beyond her alimony.[36] Now she was angry at having the painful arrangement her husband had maintained for a dozen years dragged out in public, and she let him know it. Nevertheless, at Christmas in 1995, Nick and Corinne hosted Alex and Ruth—their first meeting in years—and the occasion passed in friendly fashion.

He didn't bring up his private life again when the *Guardian* profiled him in 1996, prompted by Mitchell Beazley's release of a limited-run, twenty-fifth-anniversary edition of the original *Joy*, but once again reporter John Illman called him "the grand old man of sex." Alex took some pride, however, in the changes that his book had helped bring about. "The sexual climate today is more open," he said, in spite of the pall cast by AIDS, so much so that many younger people had no clear idea of what it was like before the sexual revolution. "People can and do talk about sex. They talk about it with their doctors, and oddly enough, even with their partners. I recall a woman who didn't want to go to the antenatal clinic because she didn't want people to know she had been having sex with her husband."[37]

The most sympathetic interview Alex enjoyed in these years—in the sense that the interviewer understood his point of view—was never published. H. B. (Tony) Gibson was a British psychologist and anarchist who had first met Alex in the '40s through the Freedom Press group. In the '90s he was conducting a series of interviews with older British anarchists, including Vernon Richards, Colin Ward, and George Woodcock, which he hoped to publish in a book, "Kindling the Phoenix Nest."

Gibson's interview provided a snapshot of Alex's current perspective and the ways it had evolved since he had first emerged as a writer and political thinker. He had no doubts about the anarchism he had embraced during the war years, he said. But his political philosophy was his own. He called himself an anarchist because the label fit the perspective he was already evolving at the time, not because he had been converted by the writings of Kropotkin, Malatesta, or the other "classical" anarchists, or his close contemporaries, like Colin Ward, whom he had never read.

Alex told Gibson that he had come to find it more apt to call himself a Buddhist, though only in a philosophic sense. He did not believe in God, and Buddhism was not a theistic religion. "I'm inclined to believe that the universe was designed by a mind," he explained, "and I'm inclined to believe that my mind is part of it. In other words, that we're all gods. That, I think, was Buddha's view." But other of the world's religions were moving in somewhat the same direction, he said. "Christianity has got less and less theistic and more unorthodox." "Extreme fundamentalist views one doesn't encounter very often," he observed overoptimistically; "they are a sort of fringe."

He still considered himself a pacifist, and he stuck by his position during World War II that there was less to choose between the British and the German ruling elites than met the eye. ("Hitler was worse than I thought," he did admit.)

A good deal of melancholy crept into Alex's conversation. He had given up on marrying again, he told Parker, because no one would take on someone who spent his day sitting in a "bloody chair." He still had his vigorous mind, but "no one marries a brain."[38] He was not lacking for female companionship, however. He had a warm relationship with Nick's wife Corinne and sometimes dictated new poetry to her from his armchair. In October 1995, with the help of his aide, Linda, he was able to take a two-week cruise along the coast of Alaska and then California, stopping in Santa Barbara to rendezvous with Marilyn and Irv Yalom. Also accompanying him was Anna van Loon, a younger woman he had met in Santa Barbara before moving back to the UK, and to whom he had made a small legacy in his will.

The Yaloms had visited Alex twice in his apartment at Fitzwilliam House, and they urged him to write poetry. But his visit to Santa Barbara was, for them, a sad occasion. Alex was "well taken care of," Marilyn recalled, but required a wheelchair and rarely left the motel where he was staying. Sightseeing along the coast, he didn't get out of the car. They went to a pierside seafood restaurant for lunch, and Alex confessed to Marilyn that Jane had made it impossible for him to continue seeing her or her family after their quarrel. Saddest of all, she sensed that his infirmities had crushed his once irrepressible spirit. No longer in command of books and words, around which he had built so much of his life, he'd "lost his sense of adventure," Marilyn said. "He was simply surviving."[39]

But he was trying. The following January, Alex had a holiday in Madeira, accompanied by Linda and Corrine and his seventeen-month-old grandson, Alex. On another occasion, Nick took Alex and young Alex on a one-day jaunt to Paris to celebrate the elder Alex's birthday.

His condition was worsening. A month after the Madeira trip, he had a third stroke and spent two weeks in Whittington Hospital recovering. Afterward he moved back to Fitzwilliam House but to the intensive nursing wing. Later that year, he transferred to Brooklands Nursing Home in Banbury, Oxfordshire, near where Nick and his family had moved, but returned to Whittington Hospital in early May, 1997, after a fourth stroke. Nick put the Fitzwilliam House apartment on the market, since Alex clearly could not live in London any longer, and in the spring of 1998 he moved to Chacombe House, a retirement home in Banbury, where he had a private room, a view of parkland, a shelf full of books, and twenty-four-hour nursing care.

ALEX HAD ALWAYS CONDUCTED a large part of his life by correspondence, and this had not changed, except that it was now enormously difficult for him to respond. He was receiving a steady stream of letters and requests for interviews, articles, blurbs, book reviews, advice, and autographs, from people who knew him well and others who knew nothing of his physical condition.

In January 1992 his longtime friend from the University of Southern California, biogerontologist Bernard Strehler, sent him a new paper in which he posited a theory of how memory storage takes place in the brain and where the experience of "selfness" arises. How can one explain in scientific language, he asked, the fact of subjective experience and its reality to each of us that experiences it? "Alex, I hope that you will respond to the puzzle I have outlined," Strehler wrote. "I think it is one of the major puzzles of the Universe and I would like to solve it in your company, if possible."[40] It's easy to imagine how eagerly Alex would have wanted to join Bernie Strehler in tackling the problem, but there was nothing he could do.

A producer at CBS News wrote asking him to participate in a project on "aging and the process of rejuvenation," the latter part of which would certainly have struck him as dubious.[41] A TV production company in London wanted his views on the sex education video business for a Channel Four program it was putting together.[42] A British journalist, Linda Grant, was writing a book on women and the sexual revolution and wanted to arrange an interview.[43] David Peat, a Canadian physicist writing a life of David Bohm, had read *Reality and Empathy* and wanted to know more about Alex's views on Bohm.[44]

In 1995 another production company was developing a television documentary series for the BBC on anarchism, "from Lao Tse to the present day," and wanted to secure his involvement.[45] A biologist at the University of Leeds requested a photo of Alex for a new book on the biology of aging.[46] BBC Scotland was preparing a documentary on Muriel Spark and wanted to know how contemporaries reacted to her expulsion from *Poetry Review*.[47] The *Guardian* wanted to repeat the exercise that *Horizon* had conducted fifty years earlier, getting one hundred published novelists' and poets' response to a questionnaire on how they managed to survive financially; would Alex care to do it again?[48] The answer, usually via Nick or Corinne, was generally no, or else the inquiries went unanswered.

In 1998, the CND held a fortieth anniversary screening of the Free Cinema documentary of the first Aldermaston March at the British Academy of Film and Television Arts and invited Alex to attend. When he couldn't, his comrades offered to send him a copy of the film.[49] The following year, his coeditor on *Poetry Folios*, Peter Wells, now a painter living in Suffolk, proposed that they produce a short anthology of the best poems they had published. Wells told Alex he could turn this out on an old-fashioned letterpress he had available, much as they had the first issue of *Poetry Folios*, fifty-five years earlier.[50]

Still, Alex couldn't shake the "albatross"; in 1997, when the publishing consultant Diagram Group announced its Oddest Title of the Year at the Frankfurt Book Festival, the winner was *The Joy of Sex: Pocket Edition*. And the queries stemming from his best seller only seemed to get more personal as the years passed. A couple in Malawi wanted to improve their sex life and therefore wanted Alex to send them a copy of *The New Joy of Sex*. A man in Philadelphia, having read the original edition, wanted to know where he and his wife could receive "intensive sexual instruction" ("If need be, then direct us to Abyssinia, or an Arab or Middle Eastern nation"). A woman in Spring Valley, New York, enjoyed the *New Joy* but hoped Alex could tell her where she and her boyfriend could acquire the "equipment, sex toys, and vibrators" he mentioned, as these were not available in their town. A man in Aberdeen wanted Alex's advice on treating his erectile dysfunction. A woman of fifty-three in Sheffield wanted to know how she might regain her sex drive and save her marriage.

Earlier he would have written back to these people, protesting that he wasn't a sex counselor and warning them to be careful in a field full of charlatans. Now he had to leave most if not all of these letters unanswered.

Some old friends were writing him steadily, expecting no reply, in hopes their letters would cheer him up: John Doheny; Robert Greacen, who dedicated a volume of autobiography to Alex and sent him a copy, via Nick; and Caleb Finch, a gerontologist at USC who Alex had known since the '60s.[51] Len Hayflick stayed in touch with Nick as well as Alex, anxious for news of his friend and occasionally sending copies of recent papers on aging.[52]

Len and his wife visited Alex at Fitzwilliam House in 1996 and then again two years later, after he had moved to Chacombe House. The second time, Zhores Medvedev came with them. Following his most recent stroke, Alex wasn't able to move much, and speech had become more difficult. When Medvedev and the Hayflicks arrived, Len recalled, "We were devastated." Alex was sitting on a sofa in his room, and every five minutes would say "Help!" It was nearly the only word he spoke. At one point, his friends went to find a nurse, thinking something was seriously wrong. Alex was always yelling "Help," the nurses explained, and they had learned to ignore him.

"We left in anguish," Len recalled, "and a feeling of helplessness knowing that we would never see Alex again."[53]

The situation wasn't as dire as they thought. Alex was well taken care of, and Nick and his family were nearby to visit and advocate for him. But Alex's was a lively mind trapped in a body that had betrayed him. Without anything else to do, Nick observed, he could dramatize, sulk, "play mind games" with his doctors and nurses, and generally act the victim, this despite spending his days in a facility that many elderly people would envy. After advocating for years for the rights and dignity of the aged, he found himself in a situation that even the best care and treatment could do little to alleviate.

BILL FORBES, A BIOLOGIST and statistician at the University of Waterloo in Ontario who had known Alex for years, wrote to Nick in 1994, asking if he could help with a project that Forbes and Len Hayflick had hatched: a festschrift in honor of Alex's contributions to gerontology. Could he supply the names of people his father regarded as friends or esteemed colleagues to contribute to the collection? Three years later, Forbes was able to tell Alex that he and Len were preparing a double issue of *Experimental Gerontology* for the first half of 1998 to publish the papers. There would be twenty-one contributors, and Alex was invited to add an essay of his own. He was delighted, although he couldn't supply anything, replying in a note typed with his left thumb, "I can't get over the idea of a festschrift. Thank you and Len very much, and excuse the lousy typing."

The special issue included contributions from scientists who had known Alex for nearly their whole careers, including Hayflick and Forbes; Caleb Finch; Takashi Makinodan and Roy Walford of UCLA; Avril Woodhead of the Brookhaven National Laboratory; Denham Harmon of the University of Nebraska; Richard Adelman of the University of Michigan; and Robin Holliday, a biogerontologist now working for the Australian government. Alex would have been especially pleased by an article by Tom Kirkwood of the University of Manchester, highlighting his pursuit of a "test-battery" for measuring the short-term effects of aging and reviewing recent progress in identifying the biomarkers that should be used to carry it out.[54]

Alex had never managed to secure major financial support for what he had come to regard as the Holy Grail of gerontology, but at least it was being pursued piecemeal. And he would have agreed vigorously with Adelman's article, which criticized the National Institute on Aging for funding Alzheimer's research at the expense of more comprehensive study of aging.[55]

Many of the contributors had read one or another edition of *The Biology of Senescence* early in their careers, only meeting the author later on. "After later meeting and having the honor of working with Alex, I realized the book was really only mildly interesting when it was compared with the man himself," Forbes wrote.[56] "There was always more to Alex than seemed possible, and this extended even to music," wrote Finch, who was an accomplished Appalachian fiddler. "Once I spent an afternoon at the 1974 NICHD [National Institute of Child Health and Human Development] Summer Course with the Biology of Aging in Duluth, swapping fiddle tunes: I'd whistle Appalachian versions, and then Alex would hoot out regional equivalents from different parts of England."[57]

The festschrift didn't stick entirely to aging studies. It also included a paper by his former colleague Harvey Wheeler on Alex's study of I-ness and the oceanic in *I and That*, a piece by Antonio de Nicolás on the interplay of biology and culture in that book and *Reality and Empathy*, and even an essay on the critique of authoritarianism in *Imperial Patient* by a Canadian scholar, Ira Sobkowska-Ashcroft.

Inadvertently, perhaps, they were all bearing out something that Alex had said fifty years earlier. In *The Novel and Our Time*, his 1948 literary manifesto, he wrote, "[The novel] is an observational form of art. It has both drawn upon and contributed directly to psychology, social anthropology, and even physics and biology."[58] Implicitly, he had been arguing for years that these branches of science were all "observational forms of art" as well, that they owed as much to inspiration and imagination as any creative activity. Collectively, his colleagues seemed to recognize this as well.

ALEX HAD SUNDAY LUNCH regularly with Nick, Corinne, and their son Alex, who lived just on the other side of Banbury. The nursing home brought him over by ambulance and picked him up for his return.

On Sunday, March 26, 2000, less than two months after his eightieth birthday, Alex came for lunch as usual. Talk was ever more difficult, but when Nick asked him the name of Bellerophon's horse, he quickly responded, "Pegasus."

Afterward Nick remembered that he had intended to show his father a DVD of Neil Jordan's film, *Michael Collins*, with Liam Neeson in the role of one of Alex's political heroes. It would have to wait for another time. Later that afternoon, the matron from Chacombe House called to tell Nick that Alex had had a heart attack and was being taken to Horton General Hospital. He and Corinne hastened over, but Alex was gone by the time they arrived. Four weeks later, Ruth Harris Comfort died. Alex was buried alongside Jane in Comfort's Woods, where a marker bears both their names.[59]

CONCLUSION

Afterlife

Not every one of the stories that make up a person's life finishes before they die. One of Alex's stories only closed in 2003, three years afterward.

The List

At some point during the early Cold War years, George Orwell began keeping a notebook listing people he suspected of being either communists or morally squishy when it came to totalitarianism. Some were writers, artists, and celebrities not personally known to him; some were people he knew and didn't like; others were people he knew and liked but didn't trust. In May 1949, just months after applying the final touches to *Nineteen Eighty-Four*, Orwell sent an abbreviated list of thirty-eight names to Celia Kirwan, a friend who had taken a job with the Information Research Department (IRD) of the Foreign Office.* Kirwan had asked him for the list in order to warn British diplomats at the United Nations, who were approaching writers and artists to help them counter Soviet propaganda, against individuals deemed unreliable.[1]

One of these was Alex Comfort. About his friend's alleged collaborationism, Orwell wrote, "Potential only. Is pacifist-anarchist. Main emphasis anti-British. Subjectively pro-German during war, appears temperamentally pro-totalitarian. Not morally courageous. Has a crippled hand. Very talented."[2]

What did this somewhat cryptic entry mean? "Potential only" clearly meant that Orwell saw Alex as only "potentially" pro-Soviet,

* Orwell finished the novel at the end of 1948. Julian Symons, introduction to *Nineteen Eighty-Four*, Everyman's Library (New York: Alfred A. Knopf, 1992), xix.

"not morally courageous" that he had never explicitly denounced the Soviet regime: "*the* test of intellectual honesty," Orwell once asserted. "Pro-German" and "anti-British" fit with Orwell's conviction that anyone who did not wholeheartedly embrace the war effort was effectively on the side of the enemy. By adding the word "subjectively," Orwell went further, implying that Alex wasn't a patsy of the Germans but was actively on their side—this despite the fact that Alex never wrote a sympathetic word about Hitler's regime. "Appears temperamentally pro-totalitarian" would have alluded to Alex's anarchism and Orwell's argument that anarchists tended in the direction of conformist tyranny.

In 1996 the Foreign Office released documents verifying that the list existed, although one Orwell biographer had already mentioned it in 1980, and a truncated version appeared in the twenty-volume *Complete Works of George Orwell* in 1998. Peter Davison, who edited the series, and had written back and forth with Alex about some details of his correspondence with Orwell, left his name out, along with those of seven other individuals who couldn't be traced or who were still alive at the time. By then, Alex was disabled and living at Chacombe House. Nick Comfort didn't recall his father ever knowing that Orwell had included him on the list, a full copy of which only surfaced in 2003.[3]

Had he known, Alex would likely have been taken aback. At the time Orwell was compiling the list, they were still associated together on the Freedom Defence Committee, and while they had disagreed angrily about pacifism during the war, in the following years both had expressed opposition to nuclear armaments and written in favor of European neutrality in the Cold War. "I counted Orwell as a friend," Alex wrote in 1983, and Nick recalled that his father always spoke of Orwell with great respect.[4]

The assertions Orwell made were not very different from the accusations he had hurled at Alex and other anarcho-pacifists during the war. But now he was making them known in a letter directed to the IRD, a cog in Britain's Cold War propaganda apparatus.

Alex, in his wartime writings, had never offered support to the Soviet regime or to Marxist-Leninism in general. Nor had he ever expressed hostility to Britain or its people, only to the state and its government. He had been the victim of pro-Soviet leanings in the British cultural world early in the war, when the Unity Theatre canceled the premiere production of his anticapitalist dystopian play, *Cities of the Plain*.

Whatever he knew or thought he knew, Orwell seems to have been oblivious—or chose to ignore the fact—that sharing his personal observations with a state intelligence service was quite different from attacking or sparring with his intellectual opponents in the pages of *Tribune*. The list itself is a remarkably thrown-together affair, especially for a writer so often praised for the analytic precision of his prose and his intense concern about the misuse of language for political purposes. The names range from Charlie Chaplin to Nicholas Moore, and from J. B. Priestley and historian E. H. Carr to Isaac Deutscher, the ex–Communist Party member and biographer of Stalin and Trotsky.

"A glance through the contents pages of *Labour Monthly* and other Stalinist publications could well have provided a better list of fellow-travelers," Orwell scholar Paul Flewers concluded.[5]

All of these people were either publicly prominent or occupied sensitive positions and had, at one time or another, expressed sympathy with the Soviet Union, however limited—all, that is, except Alex. While he was already known in intellectual circles in the '40s for his poetry, fiction, and political writings, Alex was by no means a celebrity, and his day job was not politically sensitive. He was also the only anarchist to appear on the list, although Orwell included a notation "? Anarchist leanings" next to the name of Moore, who actually identified as a Marxist in a general sense.[6] Others Orwell knew well, including Alex's fellow anarchists George Woodcock and Herbert Read, do not appear, even though Read, in particular, was a frequent guest on the BBC.

Why was Alex included while Read and Woodcock were not? For one thing, Woodcock and Read were closer friends with Orwell than Alex ever was. And, unlike them, he stepped up his political agitation after the war ended. At the same time that he was dissecting the pathology of power in *Authority and Delinquency*, he continued to call on artists and writers, in *Art and Social Responsibility*, to embrace disobedience to a "barbarian" society directed by delinquents in positions of leadership. As Orwell grew more concerned about the possibility that fellow travelers could undermine Western resolve in the struggle against Soviet communism, he again perceived Alex, despite their friendship, as he had during the war: as a witless apologist and a threat to national morale.

When the existence of Orwell's list became known, and later when the notebook list was partially revealed in the *Complete Works*, many scholars and political commentators expressed shock and anger. Others excused Orwell, arguing that the Soviet Union was indeed a totalitarian menace and that he wasn't denouncing the people he named as security risks, only as individuals who should not be recruited to counter Soviet propaganda.[7] It's more than probable, the Cold War historian Timothy Garton Ash argued, that the IRD did nothing at all with the list other than not ask the enumerated individuals to write anything. Alex was once again a guest on the BBC in 1947, and the network continued to host him frequently on both radio and TV for decades.

But the matter is not so simple, because the IRD itself was not as innocuous an organization as some supposed. Its budget was voted on in secret, and its purpose, according to one former employee, "was to produce and distribute and circulate unattributable propaganda."[8]

The department compiled "factual" reports and briefs that it then passed on to sympathetic members of the British intelligentsia to recycle in their own writings. Knowing who was reliable and unreliable for this work was valuable information that the intelligence services would certainly have wanted to possess. Adam Watson, the IRD's second-in-command, later told historian Frances Stoner Saunders that while the "immediate usefulness [of Orwell's list] was that these were not people who should write for us, [their] connections with Soviet-backed organizations *might have to be exposed at some later date*."[9]

The IRD's mission later evolved in more dubious directions. "By the late 1950s," Garton Ash wrote, "according to someone who worked for British intelligence agencies at that time, IRD had a reputation as 'the dirty tricks department' of the Foreign Office, indulging in character assassination, false telegrams, putting itching powder on lavatory seats, and other such cold war pranks."[10]

While Orwell's carelessly assembled memo was not a blacklist—he wasn't seeking to get anyone fired—it brought Alex and dozens of others to the attention of a state intelligence apparatus that might abuse that information. And while many of these individuals were already strongly identified as leftists, being tagged as unreliable by another prominent writer of the Left could only have put them at greater risk, given the atmosphere of the time.

Numerous explanations have been offered as to why Orwell did what he did, including failing health. When he remembered Orwell years later, Alex detected something else about him: a certain naïveté and a certain overconfidence in English political culture. Focusing on institutional Britain's response to the rise of fascism, and just how reactionary the nation's leadership might in fact have been, he wrote, "[Orwell] had no love of these institutions, judged by their performance, but he was as profoundly English as Churchill, and Englishness imposes rules even on revolution. . . . He would have been the last person to agree that politics were governed by the rules of cricket, but the unconscious assumption remained that the 'bosses,' the opposition, though they might commit barbarities, weren't cannibals. If that were not so, if there were no limits to what Tory Britain would do to defeat change, then we were headed for political Gehenna."[11]

While Alex had little difficulty believing that any unit of the State was capable of such things, Orwell couldn't conceive that the leaders of the nation he loved might share some of the same sociopathic impulses as the Nazis. This may be the essence of the personal and political differences between the two. The fact that Alex never knew Orwell had named him and thus never had a chance to answer back to the distorted mini-portrait Orwell painted is one of the minor but telling injustices of the Cold War era.

Obituaries

Political vendettas of the '40s did not figure in the response to Alex's death in March 2000. The "albatross" was all that most obituary writers seemed to care about.**

Some headlines in major newspapers in the United States, Canada, and the UK: "'Joy of Sex' Author Alex Comfort Dies at 80" (*Washington Post*), "Comfort and Joy: Sex Handbook Writer Dr Alex Dies Aged 80" (*Mirror*), "Alex Comfort, 80, Dies; a Multifaceted Man Best Known for Writing 'The Joy of Sex'" (*New York Times*), "Alex Comfort Helped the Uptight Unwind about Sex" (*National Post*), and "Alex Comfort: Dazzling Intellectual Whose Prolific Output of Novels, Poetry and Philosophy Remains Overshadowed by a Sex Manual" (*Guardian*). This is at least partially understandable. At the time he died, *The Joy of Sex* reportedly was still among the five best-selling titles at venerable Hatchards of Piccadilly, jostling with *Hot Sex: How to Do It* by Tracey Cox and a new edition of the *Kama Sutra* by Anne Hooper.[12]

Quite a few notices produced various items of misinformation about their subject, some new, some old. They said, for instance, that *The Silver*

** None noted the intriguing fact that Alex had died on the same day as another legend of the London environs, the punk-era singer and songwriter Ian Dury, nor that one of Dury's best-known songs, "Billericay Dickie," about a sexually braggadocious Essex lad, name-checked the town where Alex had his fateful meeting with Wrey Gardiner in the summer of 1941.

River and *Song of Lazarus* were novels; that Alex had lived at Sandstone (he only visited); that he gave away most of the money he earned from *The Joy of Sex*; and that his working title for the book, "Cordon Bleu Sex," was changed because the owners of the copyright objected.[13] They said that he claimed only to have edited the book in order to sidestep an obscenity charge (it was his publishers, not Alex, who were worried about this) and that he was a "pioneer of the promiscuous society" and "uninhibited hedonism."[14] (He always insisted that he was only describing what was going on, not willing it into being.)

Some of the obituaries and summations were more probing. The *Independent* ran a piece headlined, "Alex Comfort: The Last Positivist?" in which John Pilgrim, the sociologist and writer and former skiffle musician, recalled, "It was Comfort's anarchism and the parallels he drew with psychology and sociology that took some of us into those disciplines."[15] Adrian Mitchell, in the *Guardian*, remembered when he first read Alex's poems, during the Korean War: "[They] shook me. I studied them and learned them; so did many of my generation of poets—at least those who preferred the hot prophecy of Comfort's *Art and Social Responsibility* to the pronouncements of Eliot."[16] Robert Greacen remembered his old friend with these lines in *Poetry Ireland Review*:

> Memory on memory—London, Dublin, Essex
> I still can hear the cataract of words.
> Sane doctor in a world gone mad.
> How can I find words to honour him,
> Dear Alex, friend, poet, hero, anarchist?

Plenty of attacks followed his death as well, generally on the same grounds that David Holbrook and other cultural conservatives had assailed him in the '60s, well before *The Joy of Sex* was published: that his thinking undermined marriage and replaced tenderness and love with superficiality, overindulgence, and callousness. The *Daily Mail* accused him of "emptying sex of all moral and emotional significance," leaving as his "malign legacy" a "cold and gloomy swamp of violence, antagonism, despair, loneliness and irresponsibility."[17] A quarter-century on, conservatives still found Charlie and Edeltraud Raymond's appearance in *The Joy of Sex* offensive. The manic controversialist Julie Burchill, in the same paper, called Charlie "a priapic, bearded, shaggy-pelted Neanderthal."[18] On the other side of the Atlantic, the journalist David

Frum, in the *Wall Street Journal*, pegged Alex as taking "the view that modern society's excessive emphasis on hygiene and grooming detracts from sexual pleasure," noting his disapproval of "deodorants, hairspray and shaving."[19]

Some of the sex advisers who had followed in Alex's wake were happy to eulogize him, however. "I would never have been able to say the things I said about sex without Dr. Comfort's paving the way ahead for me," Dr. Ruth Westheimer wrote in *Time*. "[His book] was an incredible tool that every sex therapist used at one time or another to help teach clients how to make sex fun and enjoy it to the fullest."[20]

Nick, in a feature in the *Daily Telegraph*, tried to set the record straight in his own way, describing an upbringing that was hardly a mini-Sandstone. "I probably heard less talk of sex than the average child," he wrote. "[My father's] idea of sex education was to race through the most basic facts of life when I was 12—and then only after my school had sent him a missive about 'personal hygiene.' During my teenage years, he did very little to fill in the gap."[21]

New *Joy*

Nevertheless, Nick oversaw another revision of *The Joy of Sex*, on the thirtieth anniversary of the original book's publication. This one was illustrated with photos as well as drawings of the performing couple. "The bearded Kris Kristofferson look-alike and his stern Frau have been replaced by a buff gym rat and a slightly over-cheerful brunette," the *New York Post* noted. The new edition promptly sold one hundred thousand copies in the United States upon its release during the 2002 holiday season.

Once again, the revisions were light, and some observers seemed to have noticed, after a long delay, the book's emphasis on intimacy. "It's the perfect antidote to 'Sex and the City,' the *Post*'s Bridget Harrison reported a friend telling her. "Sex is so hard-edged and artificial these days."[22]

Clearly the book still had legs, and so, as the decade neared its end, Mitchell Beazley decided that a really thorough updating of its biggest title was in order: by a woman. In 2007 the firm selected—with Nick's input—Susan Quilliam, an advice columnist and relationship psychologist from Liverpool who had been acquainted with the original book since it came out.

It was a risky move, since the market by this time was flooded with sex guides, from *The Low-Down on Going Down* to *Blow Him Away* to *Sex: How to Do Everything*, by "Em & Lo," which spawned a TV series (and was published by Doring Kindersley, the firm established by Peter Kindersley, original designer of *The Joy of Sex*, after he left Mitchell Beazley). Paul Joannides, author of the comprehensive and well-received, eight-hundred-plus-page *Guide to Getting It On*, was already preparing the sixth edition of his book. The story of the various editions of *The Joy of Sex* had itself entered into popular culture. In 2005 Meg Wolitzer had published *The Position*, a novel about a highly sexualized couple who write a *Joy*-like book that embarrasses their children, who, thirty years later, must decide whether to reissue it.

But somehow Alex's book had never stopped shocking some people. In March 2008, as Mitchell Beazley and Crown were preparing for publication, the public library board in Nampa, Idaho, decided to pull *Joy* and *The Joy of Gay Sex* from their shelves. In September, after a storm of protest and a threat by the American Civil Liberties Union to sue, the board restored both books.[23]

That same month in the UK and the following January in the United States, *The Joy of Sex: The Timeless Guide to Lovemaking*, by Alex Comfort and Susan Quilliam, was published (with a cover advertising "The Ultimate Revised Edition"). It retained the bulk of Alex's text but also included a grab bag of forty-three new or expanded entries on such matters as vibrators and other sex toys, self-esteem, Internet and phone sex, hormones, pheromones, sexual resources for the aged and disabled, the clitoris, "transsexualism," striptease and other forms of foreplay, and the G-, A-, and U-spots. Gone were Alex's jokey references to sex on a motorbike, the (fictional) grope suit, and "mock rape." A great deal of new information on sex from a woman's point of view was what made the book genuinely new: not just female orgasm but also sex during pregnancy, complications of anal sex, and sexually transmitted diseases.

The book was well reviewed and was a modest best seller, but some critics complained, once again, that the couple in the illustrations were too conventionally attractive. Looking back, it seemed there had been something oddly charming about Charlie and Edeltraud. "Once you remove those memorable drawings and Comfort's batty, phallocentric prose," wrote the *New Yorker*'s Ariel Levy, "what you are left with is something that bears little resemblance to the subversive, explosive original. 'The Joy of Sex' redux becomes generic—*Cook's Illustrated* with boobies."[24]

The Revolution Continues

Perhaps, these reviews suggested without quite saying so, *The Joy of Sex* was simply too much of a period piece to ever be successfully updated. But some of Quilliam's text, and some of her remarks in interviews promoting the new book, undermined this conclusion.

"I don't think there has ever been more need for [sex] education," she told the *Times* of London, "because we're living in a society which is far more sexualized than when Alex Comfort was writing. At the same time, I know people in their thirties who still don't know about the importance of the clitoris."[25] More information was available than ever, but people were being bombarded with explicit images, impossible-to-achieve standards of performance, and a tangle of contradictory misinformation, Quilliam told the *New York Times*.[26] In the new book, she argued that one thing missing from the greater sexual openness of the early twenty-first century was the "unashamed ability to see sex as play."

These were the same issues that had prompted Alex to write about sex in the first place, which suggests that his writings, broadcasts, and public conversations about sex over a period of fifty-plus years, including *The Joy of Sex*, had had disappointingly little social impact. This conclusion is too simple, however. Too much had happened in the fifty-some years after the book first appeared on the best-seller lists and the forty-some since AIDS became a public health crisis.

The sexual revolution itself was far from being reversed. The Centers for Disease Control's statistics showed that as of 2015, 89% of American women and 90% of men aged 15-44 who had ever been married had engaged in premarital sexual intercourse while 62% of women of reproductive age used a contraceptive.[27] A great deal of new research was focusing—finally—on female desire and sex drive, much of which decentered traditional, phallocentric sex, although most doctors continued to be woefully undereducated on such seemingly basic maters as the anatomy of the clitoris.[28] The sexual desires and needs of the elderly and disabled too had finally caught the attention of researchers and counselors, as evidenced by a number of new books and sex aids hitting the market that catered to disabled people.[29] Sexual practices were changing, spotlighted by a stream of coverage in the mainstream media of polyamory (the subject of a cable-TV reality series in 2012–13), open marriages, hookups, and invitation-only sex parties.

Much of the hysteria about bondage and sadomasochism once directed at *The Joy of Sex* was subsiding as well. *Fifty Shades of Grey*—the novel, the movie, and their sequels—brought it to the cultural multiplex, while the *Diagnostic and Statistical Manual of Mental Disorders*, the bible of psychiatric medicine, downgraded these practices from "paraphilic disorders" to mere "paraphilias" (unusual sexual interests).[30]

The biggest changes, however, have centered on and been generated by the LGBTQ+ communities. Growing acceptance and legal sanction of gay marriage removed a host of civil disabilities from gay and lesbian people. Beyond this, nontraditional sexual relationships became more common, shattering the once-rigid boundaries of gender and even what constitutes "sex." In surveys, younger people were more apt to come out as trans, bisexual, or gender-fluid.[31] Meanwhile, advances in assisted reproduction enabled groups of three, four, or more adult "poly-parents" to make a baby and raise the child together, as Alex had predicted in 1973 in "Sex in a Zero Growth Society": only now, it seemed, the softening of the hetero norm would play an important role in pushing along the development he had anticipated.[32]

As for *The Joy of Sex*, arguably it had succeeded at Alex's original goal: giving couples permission to enjoy themselves in bed without anxiety and explore their fantasies and identities together, without self-consciousness or embarrassment. The book contributed to the positive changes of the next five decades, in part through the guides and manuals that succeeded it, even those that criticized Alex's book. One of the best received was Cathy Winks and Anne Semans's *Good Vibrations Guide to Sex*, which first came out in 1994. In it they singled out for criticism Alex's treatment of a certain sex toy ("vibrators are no substitute for a penis").[33]

But what's striking about their book is how much of its playful, practical approach traces back to *The Joy of Sex*. "People need good sex books," the authors said. "Access to accurate sex information helps us to understand ourselves better and to build more intimate relationships. Not to mention that sex is just good, clean fun—and the more you learn about it, the more fun it becomes."[34]

Yet, while Winks and Semans paid tribute to several "sex-positive . . . educators, activists, and entrepreneurs" in their book, they never mentioned Alex, his best seller, or any of his other writings on sex as influences or inspirations.

While *The Joy of Sex* undoubtedly had a powerful and lasting effect on the culture, both overtly and covertly, progress in the realm of sexual freedom seemed to take one step backward—at least—for every two steps forward in the decades that followed. These years were punctuated by a succession of moral panics that contributed to keeping sex a focus of fear and anxiety: over pornography in the '70s and '80s; "HIV monsters" in the '80s; day care centers; sex trafficking; child abuse, predation, and "grooming," especially by homosexuals; Internet porn; sexting among teens; and trans and gender-fluid identification, to name a few.

Informed, un-anxious sex education, which Alex held to be vital to the development of greater equality between the sexes in the bedroom, faced an intensifying culture war from the right, at least in the United States. The percentage of teens receiving any kind of sex ed was dropping, and in many states sex education was being replaced by ineffective "abstinence-only" classes, saturated with fear and misinformation.[35] ("[Premarital] sex is like pre-chewed chewing gum," one instructional piece opined. "Is that what you want to present to your husband?"[36]) In the absence of better or just more available sex education, online porn—another dispenser of anxiety, competitive pressure, and reinforcement of sexist attitudes—was becoming the classroom for many younger people.

The backlash never succeeded in changing people's actual behavior any more than Mary Whitehouse's outrage over Alex's advice about condoms had yielded a downturn in teenage sexual activity in the '60s. But it created a great deal of anxiety and distress, and heightened the odds that an individual's choices and personal circumstances could lead to tragedy.

In the United States, pressure groups initiated a movement to remove "age-inappropriate" books from school and public libraries, reenacting the campaigns against *The Joy of Sex* forty-some years earlier. In 2022 the US Supreme Court overturned *Roe v. Wade*, the 1973 ruling that had recognized abortion as a constitutional right.. It was widely expected that birth control would soon be under legal threat too.[37]

Looking for ways to understand and respond to what had every appearance of a war on sex, some observers on the left and in the anarchist movement put forth an analysis similar to the one Alex had propagated for decades. Sociologist Lisa Wade, discussing a new mode of sexual interaction in her 2017 book *American Hookup: The New Culture of Sex on Campus*, concluded that hooking up wasn't the problem. The problem was the culture surrounding it, which was aggressively heterosexual, alcohol- and drug-fueled, and violent.

Where did that culture come from? "How Capitalism Created Sexual Dysfunction" is how journalist JoAnn Wypijewski titled a 2020 essay on the commodification of sex.[38] Neoliberalism "profoundly reshaped not only economic relationships, but our relationships with each other," the British economist Noreena Hertz wrote in her 2021 book, *The Lonely Century*, echoing Alex's analysis in *Barbarism and Sexual Freedom*. "It fundamentally changed how we saw each other and the obligations to each other that we felt, with its valorizing of qualities such as hypercompetitiveness and the pursuit of self-interest."[39] Alex had made the same argument decades earlier in *Barbarism and Sexual Freedom*.

British critic Jacqueline Rose widened that analysis to connect violence against women to State violence in her 2022 book *On Violence and On Violence Against Women*. "Reckoning with the violence of the heart and fighting violence in the world are inseparable," she wrote.[40] In a review in the *New York Times*, Parul Sehgal understood Rose to be arguing that "there is no border between us and the world. . . . [Her book] is an invitation to a radical kind of responsibility." This recalls Alex's emphasis on individual responsibility, including through resistance to the State and its demands.[41]

Because of the role sexual behavior plays in nurturing sociality, Alex maintained that it is bound up with every other form of relationship between humans. In 2010 the British anarchist scholar and activist Jamie Heckert asked similarly, "How is it that we are meant to spend much of our day being told what to do, or perhaps telling others what to do, and then go home and be capable of listening with care to the desires of another, to our own desires and to negotiate sex as equals?"[42]

Must we overthrow capitalism and the State before we can achieve anything like real equality in sexual relations? Yes, Alex argued, but in order for that to take place we must first instigate a social revolution, and the bedroom is one of the places where that must happen, which was one reason he wrote *The Joy of Sex*. "If we are able to transmit the sense of play which is essential to a full, enterprising and healthily immature view of sex between committed people, we would be performing a mitzvah," he declared in that book.[43]

Years later, as mainstream educators and counselors cast about for ways to make sex less anxious, aggressive, and hurtful at a time when accurate instruction was rare and fresh revelations of sexual abuse in entertainment and the professions sparked the #MeToo movement, they often echoed Alex's conclusions. What was needed for good sex, novelist Hayley Phelan wrote, was "two empowered individuals liberated and secure enough to explore each other's impulses, to listen to each other, and ask for what they want—even if that includes permission to *not* ask for what comes next."[44]

What about the Rest?

In 2012 it was reported that Super Linda, a restaurant in New York's trendy Tribeca that had become a popular place "to watch rich men flirt with young women," was offering a cocktail called the Alex Comfort (rum, sloe gin, orange juice, bitters).[45]

If nothing else, *The Joy of Sex*—"the albatross"—was maintaining itself, along with Alex's name, as a cultural meme. In the 2012 movie *Beginners*, a couple played by Ewan McGregor and Mélanie Laurent find a copy of *The Joy of Sex* ("it's a sort of classic American thing," he tells her) in a used bookshop and scour it for tips that might enhance their sex life. In 2014's *Sex Tape*, another couple, also hoping to revitalize their sex lives, video themselves trying every position described in the book—and then the video falls into the hands of a porn distributor. In the Oscar-nominated 2016 comedy-drama *Captain Fantastic*, an off-the-grid couple (Viggo Mortensen and Trin Miller) give their six-year-old a copy of *The Joy of Sex* when she asks them where babies come from.

In 2015 the British conceptual artist Julie Verhoeven created a video installation, *The Art of the Joy of Sex*, for the Institute of Contemporary Arts (of which Alex and Herbert Read had been among the original sponsors). She assembled the show, captured in a documentary, using wearable soft sculptures that a pair of models donned, creating tableaux that took off from Chris Foss's drawings for the book. "What was so attractive about the book," Verhoeven recalled, was "the sense of fun, irreverence, honesty and evident commitment to highlighting the humour and quirks of sex. . . . It helped me be more fearless, more brazen and less conformist." It still struck her as phallocentric; she found this element "amusing and annoying but ripe to respond to and highlight."[46]

Another guise in which Alex's name lingered in popular culture, curiously enough, was as a songwriter. One of his protest songs from the Ban the Bomb days, "One Man's Hands," for which Pete Seeger had supplied the music, was recorded numerous times, including by Seeger, Odetta, the Highwaymen, and the Chad Mitchell Trio, and it was a hit for the Japanese pop singer Rutsuko Honda.*** A snippet from Honda's version, Nick Comfort learned in 2010, had become a popular ringtone in Japan. In succeeding years, Nick received royalties sufficient "to have a good dinner every six months."[47]

But what about the rest of Alex? A 1974 *New York Times* profile was headlined "Will the Real Alex Comfort Please Stand Up?" He was a novelist, poet, activist, scientist, essayist, sexologist, but Alex as poet and novelist is hidden today. His novels, stories, and poetry collections are all out of print. His fiction is ambitious, contentious, full of ideas, and contains a great deal of fine writing. *The Power House*, *On This Side Nothing* and *A Giant's Strength* ask questions about the individual's relationship to the State that very few other novelists aside from Orwell and Camus have asked, and they are still rewarding reading. His later satirical novels are funny, well-paced, topical yarns—too topical to have lasting appeal, and because they were written in a hurry they feel rushed and their characters sketchy. *Imperial Patient* looks at the individual/State bond, this time from the point of view of a man imprisoned and betrayed by the power placed in his hands, and few other historical novels impart as vivid a sense of the richness of intellectual life in the Greco-Roman world.

Alex wanted to be remembered as a poet, and one or two of his poems continue to be included in new anthologies. The latest of these, in 2021, was *Apocalypse: An Anthology*, a three-hundred-plus-page collection devoted to the movement that flourished alongside the Neo-Romantics in the '40s, stretching the definition to include Dylan Thomas, W. S. Graham, and even Philip Larkin and Ted Hughes. In 2022 a symposium titled "Apocalypse Poetry: Visionary Modernist and Expressionist Poetry of the 1930s and 1940s" was held at Sheffield Hallam University.

Most of the interest in Alex's poetry has focused on the lush, highly symbolic verse he published early in his career, leaving aside the wittier, more concise poems he wrote later. Some major poets who discovered his work when they were younger, like Adrian Mitchell, still loved it for its refusal to stifle emotion and its fierce political and social engagement, but their number has never been large. That's not to say that Alex's poetry should not be read. It's uneven, but his language is rich and beautiful and full of feeling, and he conveys a deep love of nature.

*** "One man's hands can't tear a prison down / Two men's hands can't tear a prison down / But if two and two and fifty make a million / We'll see that day come 'round / We'll see that day come 'round."

The Conquest of Aging

"Nobody ever had a full inventory of what Alex knew, or what he forgot," Caleb Finch once said.[48] But Alex didn't expect to cut a towering figure as a scientist after he was gone. From his early days watching trains pass through Monken Hadley Common and collecting mollusk specimens in the Orkneys, Madeira, Ireland, and elsewhere, to his years collecting statistics on human and animal mortality at UCL, he had always been more a close observer than an investigator, and old-age research was still getting its footing when he began his work in the field. He fully expected his findings to be melded into the general body of knowledge about aging, and his name to appear mainly in footnotes. But researchers who had learned the field from his books or who had collaborated with him or encountered him at conferences still spoke of Alex with a certain reverence reserved for pioneers.

Gerontology remained one of the most perplexing areas in science, because figuring out the biology of aging meant understanding so much of what the human body does, plus the external factors that affect it. Far more was known about aging twenty years after Alex died than was understood when he was writing any of the three editions of *The Biology of Aging*. But he would probably have been dismayed to know that the number of credible theories—the proliferation of which he believed had held the field back in its early decades—had not shrunk and that the increased focus on research at the DNA and cellular levels had not produced a consensus on causes and treatments.

Alex had argued for years that fundamental research was more likely to yield big improvements in vigor and longevity than a piecemeal approach centered around specific diseases and conditions. This was increasingly recognized in the decades after he died, precisely because more age-related diseases were being identified as more people lived into very advanced years. "There is an urgent need to find apt interventions that slow down aging and reduce or postpone the incidence of debilitating age-related diseases," a paper in *Aging and Disease* concluded in 2018.[49]

Something along the lines of the "test-battery" approach that Alex had advocated began to be adopted in the years after he died. One study tracked a large cohort of people born in 1972 and 1973 in Dunedin, New Zealand. The researchers recorded biomarkers such as kidney and liver function, dental health, and the condition of subjects' immune and metabolic systems, along with more traditional measures like balance, coordination, hand grip, and cognitive abilities. The results, it was hoped, would enable researchers to determine how fast each person's body was aging and whether their condition was affected by genetics, lifestyle, environment, or some combination of these.[50]

Some of the specific factors Alex had highlighted as possible elements in anti-aging therapies—antioxidant intake, limiting calorie intake, physical exercise—were being validated by further research. Several studies found that lack of antioxidants was a factor in many age-related diseases, including arthritis, dementia, stroke, cancer, vascular diseases, obesity, and osteoporosis.[51] Alex had also stressed the need for aging studies to link with overall research on human health, since many of the factors that speed aging in later years may have their origin as far back as early childhood. A 2018 study found that babies exposed to high levels of air pollution while still in the womb could be at risk of premature aging.[52]

These developments would have delighted Alex. Less than thrilling to him would have been the boom in venture capital-fueled aging research that began in Silicon Valley and its satellites a few years after he died. High-tech moguls, investors, and assorted immortality-seeking *übermenschen* including Amazon's Jeff Bezos, Google's Sergey Brin and Larry Page, PayPal cofounder Peter Thiel, Oracle boss Larry Ellison, and venture capitalist Laura Deming sank hundreds of millions of dollars into a wave of new research, much of it involving gene editing. Their money capitalized a half-dozen or more new biotech companies with ambitious goals to crack the code of aging.

This made media stars of a bevy of researchers and futurists who sounded like the "disrupters" their patrons fancied themselves to be and whose work often yoked some solid experimentation to an over-optimistic understanding of a very complex field. Aubrey de Grey, a much-quoted English biologist, liked to compare the body to a car in need of a tune-up and pinpointed "seven types of physical damage" that, if repaired, would allow humans to reach "longevity escape velocity" and live a thousand years or longer.[53] In 2015 an international group of researchers published a paper titled "It Is Time to Classify Biological Aging as a Disease," as if the process was somehow not natural to the human condition.[54]

Such talk, and the money it attracted, would surely have reminded Alex of the rejuvenators who had touted treatments with monkey glands decades earlier and whose antics had threatened to discredit the work of serious gerontologists. Sorting out the crackpot and faulty theories from the valid findings, which he had hoped to accomplish with *The Biology of Senescence*, was still a nagging difficulty. Alex had been accused of overoptimism on occasion, but he argued that aging was "comprehensible and probably controllable," not that it could or should be eliminated.[55]

Above all, he would have asked the latest generation of immortality peddlers to examine their motives. In *Art and Social Responsibility* he had warned that in a modern culture of vast alienation, fear of death and accompanying feelings of personal powerlessness encourage individuals to escape through violence or by losing themselves in fascism, the State, or religious fanaticism—in other words, to flee from any sense of responsibility toward each other. Death may seem like an irrationality, he wrote in *Nature and Human Nature*, but "it is also part of the predicament which makes us human and which gives us, among other things, the sense of pity which is part of our sociality and our moral achievement as a race."[56]

The Elder Crisis

In the '60s Alex was one of the few gerontologists who also concerned themselves with the treatment of the elderly by their families, the medical establishment, and society in general. When he moved to the United States, he found the situation of the aged there especially bad, and he worked to change it. He saw this as a political issue. "No pill or regime known, or likely, could transform the latter years of life as fully as could a change in our vision of age and a militancy in attaining that change," he wrote in *A Good Age*, granting militancy the same level of importance as the change itself.[57]

Would he have been pleased with what he saw in America in succeeding decades? Geriatric psychiatry was the area in which he practiced, and he spent a great deal of his time in America training doctors in the field. It was making progress. By 1997, two years before he died, the American Board of Psychiatry and Neurology reported that some 2,360 psychiatrists held its certificate in geriatric psychiatry. Several peer-reviewed journals had also been established in the field.[58] In 2019, however, the American Medical Association reported that only 1,265 geriatric psychiatrists were active in the United States. One out of six was based in New York State, while two states—Mississippi and North Dakota—had none.[59]

As for geriatric medicine, in 2015, 97 percent of all medical students in the United States did not take a single course in the subject, the *New York Times* reported. According to the American Geriatrics Society, ideally there should be one geriatrician for every 300 aged people, but in 2015, at the then-current rate of growth, there would only be one for every 3,798 older persons by 2030.[60]

Some experts were already calling this imbalance a crisis. Susan Aronson, a geriatrician who wrote on the subject, argued that a "vicious cycle" had arisen "wherein geriatricians focus on the oldest, frailest, and most neglected old people, an approach that makes the specialty seem narrow compared to pediatrics or adult medicine . . . . That self-imposed restriction in turn makes geriatrics easier to dismiss." Few doctors know much about aging, she added in her 2019 book *Elderhood*, which means medical care may harm or kill old people "in ways and numbers far beyond what gets reported."[61]

Alex had seen a crisis coming before he left America for England. Something would have to give: either more geriatricians would have to appear, or the existing ones would have to train other doctors—and institutions—to treat the elderly. Otherwise, elderly people wouldn't get the care they needed to have satisfactory lives or even, in many cases, to stay alive.

"The elderly are going to be the big consumers, and they pack much more punch than most of them realize," he said in 1984, "not just because of the Gray Panthers but also because [the senior lobby] is a lobby with a lot of experience and skill. . . . I think that we are going to see the old adopting a very major activist role in this society, far more so than they have done in the past."[62]

"Bloody-mindedness"

Alex's love of bloody-mindedness—the kind of stubborn contrariness he had admired in Jack Haldane, the kind he wanted to see among the elderly—was more than an attraction to troublemakers and eccentric personalities; it was a manifestation of his faith in direct action, as the anarchist David Graeber defined it: "the defiant insistence on acting as if one is already free."[63] This is perhaps the thread that ties together Alex's thought and activism, from his Cambridge days to his final writings and from his literary output to his political theory and even his geriatric teaching and practice.

"Our best hope," he told BBC listeners in 1960, at the height of the Ban the Bomb campaign, "is not in stern enthusiasms but in the combativeness of the ordinary man in defence of the things he is always being encouraged to think unworthy—his skin, his food, his sexual relationships, his pleasures. . . . If we could exchange the courage which is willing to annihilate the entire race on principle for a little intelligent cowardice in office, and above all for an intelligent love of pleasure, it would be of great value."[64]

This is sensible and inspiring, but it may be a little too easy. Even people who admire Alex's work have questioned whether his vision of enlightened collective self-interest is sufficient basis for a practical political philosophy. Historian David Goodway, who knew Alex, offered three criticisms: first, that it's centered almost entirely on the notion of disobedience; second, that it offers no theory of history or even "any significant sense of history"; and third, that Alex didn't develop his anarchist thought any further to fill in these gaps after he published *Authority and Delinquency in the Modern State* in 1950.[65] In his 1974 *New York Times Magazine* profile, Hugh Kenner passed judgment on Alex's political philosophy as follows: "Political freedom, in Dr. Comfort's view consists in freeing oneself from the neurotic need to submit to authorities. It's as pat, the way he outlines it, as a page of Euclid. Utopians are great simplifiers."[66]

Was he a naïve utopian? Alex's comrade from the Freedom Press days, George Woodcock, compared him with Proudhon, who, when a traveler from England expressed admiration for his "system," is said to have replied irritably, "My system, sir? I have *no* system!" Alex was not a utopian, Woodcock argued in a keenly written analysis of his old friend for the anarchist scholar Max Blechman's anthology series, *Drunken Boat*, because his concerns were always rooted in the present: in opposition to indiscriminate wartime bombing, in the struggle for nuclear disarmament, in opposition to American imperialism, in his support for proper treatment of the elderly. He wasn't a "populist demagogue," but he "had a great faith in the people's ability to manage their affairs, though he never quite explained how."

As an anarchist, he was closer to the English radical tradition than to "the continental insurrectionary one," Woodcock concluded. Like many English radicals going back to Thomas Paine and even earlier, much of his political analysis appeared in pamphlets or newspapers with small circulations, like *Freedom* and *Peace News*. In them he wrote "as passionately as if he were addressing millions," and in this he echoed "the great British pioneers like Winstanley and the more extreme Levellers, William Godwin and William Hazlitt."****

Alex was always an anticapitalist, despite his success as an author, and never denied that a class system existed or that class struggle was necessary. But he came to political consciousness during the interwar years, when it was obvious that even a revolution based on class struggle could impose its own kind of tyranny as long as it maintained itself through the mechanism of the State. Inevitably it would end up subordinating human liberation to the continuing task of building the State.

In a preface to Harold Barclay's 1982 *People without Government: An Anthropology of Anarchism*, Alex defined anarchism as "that political philosophy which advocates the maximization of individual responsibility and the reduction of concentrated power—regal, dictatorial, parliamentary: the institutions which go loosely by the name of 'government'—to a vanishing minimum."

Alex was not a political scientist. What he attempted throughout his political writings was to provide an ethical basis for practical social and political action: a "signal to engage," as he titled one of his poetry collections. In this, he resembled his sometime friend Orwell, with personal "responsibility" playing a role in his ethic similar to "decency" in Orwell's. "The rejection of authority as a social tool is an attitude, not a programme," he wrote in his preface to Barclay's book.

> Once adopted it patterns the kind of solutions we are predisposed to accept. Nor in order to be an anarchist does one need to wait until society shares the same attitude. Anarchists do not plan revolutions—but when they become numerous, and the type of thinking which underlies the social organization of . . . small groups . . . becomes common, the thinkers constitute active, unbiddable and exemplary lumps in the general porridge of society. If numerous enough, they begin to affect the types of choices which societies make. Mutual aid begins to constitute a serious alternative

**** George Woodcock, "Manifestations of English Anarchism," unpublished manuscript, January 13, 1995. Gerrard Winstanley (1609–76) was an English Nonconformist reformer, proto-anarchist, and cofounder of the True Levellers, or Diggers, a group that during the English Civil War occupied privatized property to turn it back into common land for collective cultivation and sharing. William Godwin (1756–1836), another English proto-anarchist, was the author of the pioneering critique of the State, *An Enquiry concerning Political Justice* (1793). William Hazlitt (1778–1830), the great essayist, was known for his scathing attacks on establishment political figures.

> to administrative services, [and] general dissatisfaction begins to turn into civil disobedience.

This was perhaps the clearest summary Alex ever gave of his political program, and it fits snugly with the nonprescriptive approach that anarchists have adopted since the time of Proudhon and Kropotkin. As he became more engaged as an activist, he saw that the labor movement, which was supposed to be the engine of class struggle and human liberation, was either unwilling to join in opposition to war and nuclear armaments, or else unable because of the political alliances it had forged. That forced him, along with other postwar anarchists including Dwight Macdonald and Paul Goodman, to look elsewhere for the precipitating force that would move humanity out from under the State and capitalism.

A social revolution would have to come before a struggle for political power, he argued, and that revolution would have to be fought in and for the individual. He laid out the elements in his postwar writings, including education in the specific problems of the current system, experiments in communal living, pressure to increase worker control of production, psychiatry, and above all, public resistance to authority.

What did this mean in practice? "Comfort's stress, like Gandhi's, lay on disobedience and evasion as cultivated by the Good Soldier Schweik, which seemed to him a revolutionary virtue," George Woodcock concluded.[*****] Disobedience will come, Alex argued, when "ordinary" people lose the shame that a State-based society inculcates in them at the thought of ditching heroism, patriotism, status, and faith in favor of defending the things that matter—their skin, their food, their sexual relationships, their pleasures—and recognizing their responsibility to each other as individuals.

Alex was sketching out an extremely ambitious project of social change that humans would have to undertake without any institutional support but that was necessary to save the race and their world. He was calling not for revolution as it's ordinarily understood, but rather for a kind of flexible and ongoing insurgency that could extend from the workplace to public spaces and the household.

"We are likely in our time to see many local and neighborhood exercises whose form is classically anarchist," Alex wrote in 1982, "plus a

***** George Woodcock, "Manifestations of English Anarchism." Schweik was the genial trickster hero of Czech anarchist Jaroslav Hašek's eponymous satirical antiwar novel (1921–23).

growing tide of protest, some principled, some merely exasperated, in which anarchist modes of action and thought may be embodied. A society in which protest is fully effective has no need of a set revolution."

That logic has since informed the movement against corporate globalization, the Occupy encampments and protests, the Arab Spring, the #MeToo movement, and the mass refusal to serve that Vladimir Putin ignited when he called up hundreds of thousands of Russian reservists for his war in Ukraine in 2022. All of these bespeak Alex's creed of radical personal responsibility. Remembering the ill-treatment of refugees in Britain during the war that spurred him to write his first novel, he would have applauded the activists who stood up to their governments' xenophobia when refugees streaming into Europe from Afghanistan and Syria were harassed and deported.

Habitual bloody-mindedness is certainly not an entire liberatory program, but it appears to be the ethical first step, and sometimes, at least in passing, society gives the bloody-minded their due. In 1994, by which time Alex was living under care at Fitzwilliam House, a Conscientious Objectors Commemorative Stone was installed at Tavistock Square in London. Its inscription reads, "To all who have established and are maintaining the right to refuse to kill. Their foresight and courage give us hope." He would have been pleased.

An underlying unity

Anarchism was fundamental to Alex's quest to reconcile the individual and the collective. This was a personal and a professional or political mission, stemming from his need to understand and embrace human community.

Under his mother's tutelage, he had acquired impressive intellectual equipment but less of an intuitive feeling of belonging than most other children. His intellectual skills nevertheless were what was available to him to achieve that feeling. In this, and in spite of the warm, affable personality he always displayed, he was a bit like Thomas Jerome Newton, the alien scientist living surreptitiously among humans in Walter Tevis's 1963 novel *The Man Who Fell to Earth*. Asked how he feels about his hosts, Newton replies, "Oh yes, I love you, certainly. . . . I may be more like you than I am like me. . . . After all, you're my field of research, you know. I've studied you all my life."[67]

Lou Kauffman later observed that Alex may have been taken with the implicate-explicate model in physics in part because it proposed a reality that was not only deeper but implied an underlying unity in the nature of the universe. "In *Reality and Empathy*, he's trying to redefine humanism in a certain sense," Kauffman said, and the model he was proposing implied a more empathic relationship between humanity and the rest of nature. The intersection of physics, phenomenology, and the study of the mind, which promised to pull in psychology, mathematics, and his own field of biology as well, suggested to him that the mind is where this occurs: where we really become human.

Many accomplished scientists and powerful institutions appeared to agree with him. Harnessing artificial intelligence and more powerful computers, the BRAIN Initiative (Brain Research through Advancing Innovative Neurotechnologies), a twelve-year, public-private research initiative announced by the White House in 2013, aimed to map the human brain, including its physical structure, its patterns of activity, and what researchers called the "connectome": the connections that form the self. By the end of the decade, the private sector was pursuing similar projects. Google reportedly hoped to create a kind of Google Earth of the brain that could zoom in on the firing of a single neuron. Ominously, IARPA (Intelligence Advanced Research Projects Activity), the research arm of the US Office of the Director of National Intelligence, was funding its own project on neural networks.[68]

There was still a crucial dimension of mind that these exercises were unlikely to capture, however. In 2014 Evan Thompson, a professor of philosophy at the University of British Columbia, published a highly praised book, *Waking, Dreaming, Being: Self and Consciousness in Neuroscience, Meditation, and Philosophy*, that covered some of the same ground Alex had in *I and That*. Like him, Thompson pointed out that neuroscience depends on objective, third-person descriptions of brain scans, removing the subjective experience that our self and our knowledge of the world depend on. He argued for taking seriously Vedic (Hindu) and Buddhist contemplative practice—meditation—as a way to understand subjective experience. Like Alex, he urged scientists to investigate out-of-body and near-death experiences: not to endorse the idea that consciousness may transcend death but to understand what actually happens when the brain dies, shuts down temporarily, or resuscitates. "The waking world isn't outside and separate from our minds," Thompson wrote. "It's brought forth and enacted through our imaginative perception of it."[69]

Since then, other scholars have stepped into essentially the same landscape Alex explored. The blurry boundary zone between the physical mind, mental perception, and the oceanic has become much livelier. The "Mind and Life Dialogues," later organized as the Mind & Life Institute, had already begun in 1987 with the participation of neuroscientist Francisco Varela and the Dalai Lama. Future cognitive scientists will also have to be skilled in meditation and phenomenology, neuroscience, psychology, and mathematics, Thompson predicted,[70] just as Alex suspected they would.

"Theorizing about religion's origins is now a cottage industry," the anthropologist Melvin Konner said in his 2019 book *Believers: Faith in Human Nature*.[71] Konner, like Freud, linked the persistence of religion to the "'oceanic' feeling of the newborn infant dissolving its own boundaries, merging with the mother and the world."[72]

Neuroscientist Anil Seth, in *Being You: A New Science of Consciousness* (2021), took that idea one step further. The human brain is a "prediction machine," he argued, making "best guesses" of the causes behind the sensory inputs it receives. The evolutionary process that produced this "controlled hallucination" aimed to "enhance our survival prospects," not to provide humans "a transparent window onto an external reality."[73] Like Alex, Seth wanted to break down the tradition, dating from Descartes, that treats the body (including the brain) and the mind (intelligence) as two separate things, and instead explore them as interlocked aspects of human biology. "The essence of selfhood is neither a rational mind or an immaterial soul," he wrote. "It is a deeply embodied biological *process*, a process that underpins the simple feeling of being alive that is the basis for all our experiences of self, indeed for any consciousness at all."[74]

In the decades after Alex's death, scientists were also following something like the path he had laid out in *Reality and Empathy*—and producing evidence that backed up that book's speculations. One of the precipitating factors in Alex's project had been Bell's Theorem, which argued that the measurable attributes of an atom could be determined by events almost infinitely far away. Bell described an experiment that would test the idea. In 2015 scientists at Delft University of Technology in the Netherlands announced they had "entangled" two electrons, 1.3 kilometers apart, and shared information between them.[75]

Then in 2022, three physicists—an American, John F. Clauser; France's Alain Aspect; and an Austrian, Anton Zeilinger—won the Nobel Prize for another series of experiments that bolstered the theory of quantum entanglement. Clauser showed that a hidden variable couldn't explain away the "spooky action at a distance" that Bell had theorized, and Aspect and Zeilinger performed further experiments that closed loopholes left by Clauser's efforts.[76]

Alex would likely have been fascinated by the British physicist Roger Penrose's comprehensive 2004 book, *The Road to Reality*, which explored new ways to understand the relationship between the physical and mental worlds. He would have been challenged as well by *Existential Physics*, a popular book published by the theoretical physicist Sabine Hossenfelder in 2022. Not at all ironically, Hossenfelder, a very logically-minded thinker, argued that much of what physicists claim are theories are actually speculation as pure as any mystic's intuitions. So-called theories of what made the Big Bang possible are "modern creation myths written in the language of mathematics."[77] She categorized them as "ascientific," meaning they can't be proven or disproven by science.

Could the world have been created by a single being? Could it be that humans all live inside a gigantic simulation? There's no way to prove one or the other, Hossenfelder concluded, because we have never observed them. That throws the researcher back on the nature of experience and the ways humans can broaden or deepen it, as Alex had suggested.

Polymath

Some of his friends wished, not so secretly, that Alex Comfort could have been more of one thing and less of many others. In a 1980 interview Kenneth Rexroth said of him, "It is very tragic that he should have turned to writing vaguely dirty books for married couples which are translated into several hundred languages. Alex Comfort is a very beautiful poet, though his newest book of poetry [most likely, *Poems for Jane*] which I have here wasn't very strong. We were closely associated after the war, when he was an anarchist, at least in those days."[78]

Nicolas Walter, who had once called Alex's "the true voice of nuclear disarmament, much more than that of Bertrand Russell or anyone else," published a review of *Writings against Power and Death* in 1994 in *Freedom* in which he lamented, "His creative gifts seem to have failed him in the 1950s, and his social and scientific writing steadily deteriorated after the 1960s. His ideas became increasingly mystical and his writings became increasingly mystifying."[79]

Others disagreed. Dannie Abse, like Alex a poet as well as a physician, had written a "Letter to Alex Comfort" around 1950 in which he compared cold, rigorous, systematic scientists like Koch and Ehrlich to those who trust more to inspiration: "the unkempt voyagers," like "butterflies drunk with suns."

> You too, I know, have waited for doors to fly open, played
> with your cold chemicals, written long letters
> to the Press; listened to the truth afraid, and dug deep
> into the wriggling earth for a rainbow with an honest spade.
>
> But nothing rises. Neither spectres, nor oil, nor love.
> And the old professor must think you mad, Alex, as you rehearse
> poems in the laboratory like vows, and curse those clever scientists
> who dissect away the wings and haggard heart from the dove.[80]

At the time, Alex was just turning thirty and had yet to delve into gerontology, geriatrics, pheromones, phenomenology or the mind, science fiction, or the comic novel. But the pattern was already clear. Abse was happy enough with his portrayal a quarter-century later that he included it in his *Collected Poems.*

Early in his career, when Alex decided to call himself a Romantic, he meant the term in several specific ways: awareness of death and tragedy, sensitivity to the tension between humans and the rest of nature, concern for individual freedom and self-expression, and assertion of individuals' responsibility to each other. Looking back, however, his entire career places him in the overall tradition that began with the first self-identified Romantics in the early nineteenth century, those responding to another impulse: to see the world as a connected whole.

The nineteenth-century German philosopher Wilhelm von Humboldt thought his brother Alexander, the naturalist, the greatest mind he had ever come across, because he was able "to see chains of things." Filling notebooks with thousands of entries, the poet and mystic Novalis aimed to "unite everything," the historian Andrea Wulf has written: "from music to physics, poetry to chemistry and philosophy to mathematics." "The sciences must all be poeticised," he once wrote to another polymath, Friedrich Schlegel, who replied, "Yes, why not?"[81] The philosopher Friedrich Schelling held that nature and the self are identical, and Alexander von Humboldt saw all nature as bound together in "a wonderful web of organic life."[82]

Likewise, Alex sensed nature and humanity as a connected network; his project was to understand the human, and its place within that network. He saw the novel as a way to observe nature and society; he insisted that science, like art, requires inspiration; he defined human biology to include virtually anything relating to the human, including poetry, sex, religion and mystical experience; he insisted that sex teaches us about sociality, not just pleasure and childbearing; and he longed for a new Invisible College that could explore the links between physics, mathematics, and biology.

This way of looking at reality came naturally to Alex, who wrote in *The Silver River*, at age seventeen, that the real world is "where philosophy and religion are natural, indisputable phenomena, and where all the great discoveries of mankind, from birth to relativity are set in their proper place as manifest appurtenances of a rational, undefiled universe." He wrote this on a journey to South America that he spent partly collecting mollusk specimens, bringing to mind the travels in Spanish America and the United States that gave Alexander von Humboldt the material for his monumental scientific studies.

Anarchism, Alex's chosen political stance, was another product of the Romantic rebellion, alongside Humboldt's natural philosophy. While Humboldt was not an anarchist, a clear line can be traced from him to Alex by way of the nineteenth-century anarchist geographers Peter Kropotkin and Élisée Reclus. Alex once called anarchism "a very total empiricism, almost a non-ideology," and it had in common with Romanticism an interest not in "absolute truth" but rather in the "process of understanding."[83] Anarchism's refusal, likewise, to be pinned down to a specific, prescriptive social program or blueprint matched Alex's own reluctance to move from political ethicist to political scientist.

By the end of his life, it was once again common to see the human as a whole, but only insofar as it could be reduced to an algorithm or a predictive model. The one large project that occupied Alex's polymathic career, across all his interests and professions, was too diverse for that; it fed on complexity, not reduction. And it could seem a bit archaic, redolent of a time when alchemists talked about universal knowledge and the Philosopher's Stone. Publishers, academics, and even some of his anarchist comrades were no longer sure in later years what to make of him or how his work could possibly fit together (except, of course, when he was writing about sex). But in an age when nature is under relentless attack, humans increasingly treated as assets, not individuals, and nuclear war once again conceivable, perhaps Alex and the tradition to which he belonged suggest an alternative

Notes

Major archival sources for Alex Comfort's correspondence cited here are: University College London (the large majority, as well as the Herbert Read papers); the Kinsey Institute for Research in Sex, Gender, and Reproduction, Indiana University (most correspondence related to sex research); the Harry Ransom Center at the University of Texas, Austin (correspondence with editors, publishers, and other British authors of the 1940s); the Archive of British Printing and Publishing at Reading University (correspondence related to *The Koka Shastra*); the University of Bradford (correspondence with the Direct Action Committee and the Committee of 100 and their members); and Bishopsgate Library (correspondence with the Peace Pledge Union and its members). Unless otherwise noted, all interviews were conducted by the author.

Unpublished Comfort manuscripts are housed at University College London. David Goodway shared with me his copy of the manuscript of Wrey Gardiner's unpublished memoir, "The Octopus of Love."

Preface

1. Lisa Hammel, "Will the Real Alex Comfort Please Stand Up?" *New York Times*, June 2, 1974.
2. Matthew Sweet, "The Final Joy of Alex Comfort: Death," *Guardian*, December 28, 2012.
3. Interview with Leonard Hayflick, February 17, 2022.
4. AC, "None but My Foe to Be My Guide," in *The Signal to Engage* (London: George Routledge & Sons, 1946), 22.

Chapter 1: Nonconformists (1920–1932)

1. AC, "Trains with Faces," *London Calling*, November 12, 1953.
2. Ian Jack, "The Railway Hobby," *London Review of Books*, January 7, 2021.
3. Nicholas Comfort, *Copy! A Life in Print, Parliament and Far Flung Places* (London: Nicholas Comfort, 2021), 12.
4. Chris Richards, emails to author, November 22, 2021, and January 6, 2022.
5. Nicholas Comfort, *Copy!*, 13.
6. Ibid., 12.
7. Ibid.

8. Interview with Nicholas Comfort, September 4, 2021.

9. AC, "My mother in my father's arms—," *Poems for Jane* (New York: Crown, 1979), 20.

10. Ibid.

11. Máirtín Ó Catháin, "'A Nation of Shopkeepers': The Real Lost History of British Anarchism?," *Anarchist Studies*, September 21, 2021, https://anarchiststudies.noblogs.org/article-a-nation-of-shopkeepers-the-real-lost-history-of-british-anarchism.

12. A.P. Baggs, Diane K. Bolton, Eileen P. Scarff, and G. C. Tyack, "Enfield: Social Life," in *A History of the County of Middlesex*, vol. 5, *Hendon, Kingsbury, Great Stanmore, Little Stanmore, Edmonton Enfield, Monken Hadley, South Mimms, Tottenham*, T. F. T. Baker and R.B. Pugh, eds. (Oxford: Oxford University Press, 1976), 239–41, http://www.british-history.ac.uk/vch/middx/vol5/pp239-241.

13. Interview with Nicholas Comfort, September 4, 2021.

14. AC, interviewed by David Goodway, March 16, 1989.

15. Cited in Horace Mann, *Religious Worship in England and Wales* (London: George Routledge, 1854).

16. John Maynard, *Victorian Discourses on Sexuality and Religion* (Cambridge: Cambridge University Press, 1993), 36.

17. Susan Crosland, *Tony Crosland* (London: Jonathan Cape, 1982), 8.

18. Nicholas Comfort, *Copy!*, 8.

19. AC, interviewed by David Goodway, March 16, 1989.

20. Nicholas Comfort, *Copy!*, 9.

21. "Wise did wonders": Kathleen Burk, ed., *War and State: The Transformation of British Government, 1914–1919* (London: Allen and Unwin, 1982), 151.

22. AC, interviewed by David Goodway, March 16, 1989.

23. Ibid.

24. Robert Graves and Alan Hodge, *The Long Weekend: A Social History of Britain 1918–1939* (1940; repr., London: Penguin Books, 1971), 11.

25. Ibid., 21.

26. Graves and Hodge, *The Long Weekend*, 105.

27. Lesley A. Hall, *Sex, Gender and Social Change in Britain since 1880* (New York: St. Martin's Press, 2000), 30–31, 55–57.

28. Ibid., 30–31, 122–27.

29. AC, *The Anxiety Makers: Some Curious Preoccupations of the Medical Profession* (New York: Dell, 1970), 171.

30. Graves and Hodge, *The Long Weekend*, 109.

31. AC, interviewed by David Goodway, March 16, 1989.

32. Nicholas Comfort, email to author, June 24, 2018.

33. Comfort, *Copy!*, 13.

34. AC, letter to David Goodway, October 1988, cited in David Goodway, *Anarchist Seeds beneath the Snow: Left-Libertarian Thought and British Writers from William Morris to Colin Ward* (Liverpool: Liverpool University Press, 2006), 241.

35. AC, interviewed by H. B. (Tony) Gibson, October 13, 1992.

36. See Martin Ceadel, *Semi-Detached Idealists: The British Peace Movement and International Relations, 1854–1945* (Oxford: Oxford University Press, 2000).

37. Geoff Dyer, *The Missing of the Somme* (London: Phoenix Press, 2001), 73.

Chapter 2: The Prodigy (1932–1941)

1. Nicholas Comfort, *Copy!*, 40.
2. Interview with Timothy Dickinson, July 7, 2010.

3. AC, interviewed by David Goodway, March 16, 1989.
4. 3rd term report, 1933 (AC's first at Highgate).
5. AC, interviewed by David Goodway, March 16, 1989.
6. AC, interviewed by David Goodway, March 16, 1989.
7. Nicholas Comfort, *Copy!*, 14.
8. AC, interviewed by David Goodway, March 16, 1989.
9. Nicholas Comfort, email to author, September 4, 2021.
10. Crosland, *Tony Crosland*, 9–10.
11. Paul Rowntree Clifford, "The Legacy of Norman Goodall," *International Bulletin of Missionary Research*, October 1988.
12. AC, interviewed by David Goodway, March 16, 1989.
13. Nicholas Comfort, *Copy!*, 14.
14. Ibid.
15. "Speech Day 1936," *Cholmelian*, December 1936.
16. AC, "The Spell," *Cholmelian*, June 1938.
17. "Schoolboy Writers," *Times Literary Supplement*, December 5, 1936.
18. AC, *The Silver River* (London: Chapman & Hall, 1938), 8, 10.
19. Ibid., 42.
20. Ibid., 101.
21. Ibid., 68.
22. Ibid., 90–92.
23. Ibid., 126, 142.
24. Ibid., 163.
25. AC, interviewed by David Goodway, March 16, 1989.
26. Caroline Moorehead, *Troublesome People: The Warriors of Pacifism* (Bethesda, MD: Adler & Adler, 1987), 22.
27. Martin Ceadel, *Semi-Detached Idealists*, 290.
28. Leyton Richards, *The Christian's Alternative to War: An Examination of Christian Pacifism* (London: Macmillan, 1929), 143–44.
29. Graves and Hodge, *The Long Weekend*, 211.
30. Ibid., 328.
31. See Ellen Wilkinson, *The Town That Was Murdered* (London: Victor Gollancz, 1939).
32. Arthur Waugh, letter to AC, November 12, 1937.
33. Alexander Waugh, *Fathers and Sons: The Autobiography of a Family* (New York: Nan A. Talese/Doubleday, 2004), 229.
34. Ibid., 53, 261.
35. Arthur Waugh, letter to AC, November 23, 1937.
36. Arthur Waugh, letter to AC, March 25, 1938.
37. Arthur Waugh, letter to AC, Lady Day (March 25), 1938.
38. "An Interview with Alex Comfort," *Practical Psychology for Physicians*, January 1975.
39. AC, *The Silver River* (London: Chapman & Hall, 1938), 7.
40. Ibid., 43–44.
41. AC, interviewed by Arthur Salmon, August 7, 1974.
42. AC, interviewed by David Goodway, March 16, 1989.
43. Albert Schweitzer, *The Philosophy of Civilization* (Buffalo: Prometheus Books, 1987), 317.
44. Albert Schweitzer, *Out of My Life and Thought* (Baltimore: Johns Hopkins University Press, 1998), 156–57.
45. Quoted in George Seaver, *Albert Schweitzer: The Man and His Mind*, rev. ed. (New York: Harper & Brothers, 1955), 151.

46. Kenneth Rexroth, introduction to *The New British Poets: An Anthology*, Rexroth, ed. (New York: New Directions, 1947), xxviii.
47. *The Cholmelian* 50, no. 273 (March 1936), 505.
48. *The Cholmelian* 50, no. 278 (June 1937), 716.
49. *The Cholmelian* 51, no. 282 (February 1938), 86.
50. Nicholas Comfort, *Copy!*, 453.
51. *The Cholmelian* 51, no. 284 (June 1938), 132–33.
52. Nicholas Comfort, email to author, October 2, 2021.
53. *The Cholmelian* 51, no. 287 (December 1938), 208.
54. Second and third terms reports, 1937.
55. *The Cholmelian* 51, no. 286 (November 1938), 181.
56. AC, interviewed by David Goodway, March 16, 1989.
57. Nicholas Comfort, *Copy!*, 16.
58. Ibid.
59. Peggy Xu, "The Ritualized Extravagance of Cambridge," *New York Times*, January 10, 2021.
60. See A.S.F. Gow, *Letters from Cambridge 1939–1944* (London: Jonathan Cape, 1945).
61. G. E. Moore, *Principia Ethica* (Cambridge: Cambridge University Press, 1903).
62. E. M. Forster, "What I Believe," in *Two Cheers for Democracy* (London: Penguin Books, 1965), 64.
63. Bertrand Russell, "In Praise of Idleness," *Harper's Magazine*, October 1932.
64. AC, interviewed by David Goodway, March 16, 1989.
65. S. Peter Dance, "Comfort and Joy among the Snails of Chaldon," *Mollusc World*, no. 24 (November 2010).
66. Robert Skidelsky, *John Maynard Keynes*, vol. 2, *The Economist as Saviour, 1920–37* (New York: Allen Lane/Penguin Press, 1994), 293, 514–15.
67. T. E. B. Howarth, *Cambridge between Two Wars* (London: Collins, 1978), 71–27, 209–24.
68. Comfort, *Copy!*, 16.
69. AC, interviewed by David Goodway, March 16, 1989.
70. Evelyn Waugh, letter to AC, June 29, 1939.
71. Gow, *Letters from Cambridge 1939–-1944*, 7, 33, 51–52.
72. AC, "Cellar," first published in *The Listener* (date unknown), reprinted in *France and Other Poems* (London: Favil Press, 1941).
73. Peter and Leni Gillman, *"Collar the Lot!" How Britain Interned and Expelled Its Wartime Refugees* (London: Quartet Books, 1980), 25.
74. Gow, *Letters from Cambridge 1939—1944*, 44–45, 78.
75. Ibid., 59, 107, 60.
76. Nicholas Comfort, *Copy!*, 22
77. Ibid., 21; "Slight, curly-haired": ibid.; AC and Jane Comfort, interviewed by David Goodway, March 16, 1989.
78. AC, interviewed by David Goodway, March 16, 1989.
79. AC, letter to Arthur Salmon, September 11, 1980.
80. AC, interviewed by David Goodway, March 16, 1989.
81. Nicholas Moore, letter to Arthur Salmon, November 6, 1980.
82. Nicholas Moore, "At the Start of the Forties," *Aquarius*, nos. 17–18 (1986–87).
83. Ibid.
84. AC, interviewed by David Goodway, March 16, 1989.
85. "Reviews," *New English Weekly*, April 2, 1941.
86. Arthur Waugh, letter to AC, January 23, 1941.
87. AC, *No Such Liberty* (London: Chapman & Hall, 1941), 22.

88. Ibid., 108–9.
89. Peter and Leni Gillman, "*Collar the Lot!*" 5, 153, 163, 225.
90. Ibid. 173–76.
91. Arthur Waugh, letter to AC, January 23, 1941.
92. J. G. Gatfield, letter to Arthur Waugh, February 14, 1941.
93. J. G. Gatfield, letter to AC, February 26, 1941.
94. Arthur Waugh, letters to AC, February 15 and 22, 1941.
95. "PPU History in Context," Peace Pledge Union, http://www.ppu.org.uk/ppu/history1.html, cited in Nicholson Baker, *Human Smoke* (New York: Simon & Schuster, 2008), 196.
96. J. G. Gatfield, letter to AC, February 26, 1941.
97. Arthur Waugh, letter to AC, February 22, 1941.
98. Arthur Waugh, letter to AC, February 26, 1941.
99. F. W. Walker, letter to AC, March 10, 1941.
100. "Fiction," *Spectator*, July 4, 1941.
101. Harold Brighouse, "Five New Novels," *Manchester Guardian*, June 29, 1041.
102. Frank Swinnerton, "Shadows of War," *Observer*, June 29, 1041.
103. "A Refugee's Complaint," *Times Literary Supplement*, date unknown.
104. Arthur Waugh, letter to AC, July 27, 1941.
105. AC, interviewed by David Goodway, March 16, 1989.
106. Nicholas Comfort, *Copy!*, 16-17; Wrey Gardiner, "The Octopus of Love: An Autobiography," unpublished manuscript, 228.
107. AC, interviewed by David Goodway, March 16, 1989.
108. Ibid.
109. Nicholas Comfort, *Copy!*, 27.
110. Interview with Nicholas Comfort, September 4, 2021.
111. Interview with Nicholas Comfort, November 14, 2021.
112. Nicholas Comfort, *Copy!*, 19-20. Preceding and following account of Ruth's family draws from this source.
113. Nicholas Comfort, *Copy!*, 22.
114. Nicholas Comfort, *Copy!*, 19.
115. AC, interviewed by David Goodway, March 16, 1989.
116. Interview with Nicholas Comfort, September 39, 2015.

Chapter 3: Poets and "Conchies" (1941–1942)

1. Wrey Gardiner, "The Octopus of Love: An Autobiography," unpublished manuscript, 212.
2. AC, interviewed by David Goodway, March 16, 1989.
3. Nicholas Comfort, *Copy!*, 22.
4. Arthur Waugh, letter to AC, July 17, 1941.
5. AC, interviewed by H. B. (Tony) Gibson, October 13, 1992.
6. Derek Stanford, *Inside the 'Forties: Literary Memoirs 1937–57* (London: Sidgwick & Jackson, 1977), 41, 51.
7. Arthur Salmon, *Alex Comfort* (Boston: Twayne, 1978), 30.
8. Unity Theatre, letter to AC, August 20, 1941.
9. AC, letter to Henry Treece, September 3, 1941.
10. AC, letter to Henry Treece, September 11, 1941.
11. Herbert Read, letter to AC, September 1, 1941.
12. AC, letter to David Goodway, March 24, 1989.
13. AC, *The Almond Tree: A Legend* (London: Chapman & Hall, 1942), 205.

14. Ibid., 155.
15. AC, interviewed by David Goodway, March 16, 1989.
16. AC, *The Almond Tree*, 208.
17. Arthur Waugh, letter to AC, October 18, 1941.
18. Arthur Waugh, letter to AC, October 27, 1941.
19. Arthur Waugh, letter to AC, December 6, 1941.
20. D. J. Taylor, *Orwell: The Life* (New York: Henry Holt, 2003), 272.
21. Richard Overy, "Pacifism and the Blitz, 1940–1941," *Past and Present*, no. 219 (May 2013): 202–5.
22. George Orwell, "No, Not One," *Adelphi*, October 1941, in *The Collected Essays, Journalism and Letters of George Orwell*, vol. 2: *My Country Right or Left, 1940–1943*, ed. Sonia Orwell and Ian Angus (London: Penguin Books, 1971), 195–201.
23. AC, letter to George Orwell, July 16, 1942, in *George Orwell: A Life in Letters*, selected and annotated by Peter Davison (New York: Liveright, 2010), 202.
24. Caroline Moorehead, *Troublesome People*, 193.
25. Ibid., 171.
26. Richard Overy, "Pacifism and the Blitz," *Past and Present*, no. 219 (May 2013), 219–20, 225.
27. "PPU approved of pacifists": *Peace News*, April 26, 1940, cited in Martin Ceadel, *Semi-Detached Idealists*, 409.
28. Nicholas Comfort, *Copy!*, 20.
29. Richard Church, "A Creative Novelist," *John O'London's Weekly*, July 17, 1942.
30. Edwin Muir, "New Novels," *The Listener*, August 13, 1942.
31. J. G. Gatfield, letter to AC, July 14, 1942.
32. "Formidable": AC, letter to Arthur E. Salmon, August 28, 1980.
33. Richard Schofield, email to David Goodway, October 17, 2021; Derek Stanford, *Inside the Forties*, 90.
34. Donna Hollenberg, *A Poet's Revolution: The Life of Denise Levertov* (Berkeley: University of California Press, 2013), 63.
35. Wrey Gardiner, letter to AC, April 16, 1941.
36. Wrey Gardiner, "The Octopus of Love: An Autobiography," unpublished manuscript, 173–74.
37. Ibid., 180.
38. Jason Scott-Warren, email to author, September 25, 2014.
39. George Woodcock, *The Crystal Spirit: A Study of George Orwell* (New York: Minerva Press, 1966), 14; George Orwell, letter to Stephen Spender, April 15, 1938, cited in Bernard Crick, *George Orwell: A Life* (Boston: Little, Brown, 1980), 243.
40. Nicholas Moore, "At the Start of the Forties," *Aquarius*, nos. 17–18 (1986–87).
41. J. F. Hendry, "Writers and Apocalypse," in *The New Apocalypse: An Anthology of Criticism, Poems and Stories* (London: Fortune Press, 1939), 11.
42. J. F. Hendry, letter to the editor, *Contemporary Literature*, February 7, 1972.
43. AC, letter to Arthur E. Salmon, August 28, 1980.
44. AC, letter to Arthur E. Salmon, August 25, 1980.
45. AC, letter to Arthur E. Salmon, August 28, 1980.
46. Derek Stanford, *Inside the Forties*, 85–87.
47. AC, interviewed by David Goodway, March 16, 1989.
48. Derek Stanford, *Inside the Forties*, 87–88.
49. Nicholas Moore, letter to Arthur Salmon, February 6, 1980.
50. Alan Smith, "Grey Walls Press," *Antiquarian Book Monthly Review*, September 1986.
51. Wrey Gardiner, *The Dark Thorn* (London: Grey Walls Press, 1946), 74, 45.

52. Wrey Gardiner, "The Octopus of Love: An Autobiography," unpublished manuscript, 181.

53. Robert Greacen, interviewed by Pagan Kennedy, 2006.

54. Herbert Read, preface to *Lyra: An Anthology of New Lyric*, Alex Comfort and Robert Greacen, eds. (Billericay: Grey Walls Press, 1942), 10–11.

55. Cyril Connolly, "New Poets," *Observer*, May 3, 1942.

56. Clement Greenberg, untitled poetry roundup, *Partisan Review*, November 1942.

57. AC, letter to Henry Treece, August 13, 1941.

58. "Margarine manufacturer": George Woodcock, *Letter to the Past: An Autobiography* (Toronto: Fitzhenry & Whiteside, 1982), 214.

59. Henry Treece, letter to AC, August 31, 1941.

60. AC, "Out of What Calms," *Poetry London*, no. 7 (October/November 1941).

61. Kathleen Raine, "Poetry," *Manchester Guardian*, August 28, 1942.

62. Desmond MacCarthy, "New Writers," *Sunday Times*, December 27, 1942.

63. Arthur Waugh, letter to AC, August 20, 1942; John Lehmann, letter to AC, October 3, 1941.

64. AC, "Letter from Safety," in *Lyra: An Anthology of New Lyric*, ed. Alex Comfort and Robert Greacen (Billericay: Grey Walls Press, 1942), 21–22.

65. Connolly in *Horizon*, Orwell in "Inside the Whale," cited in Sherrill Tippins, *February House: The Story of W. H. Auden, Carson McCullers, Jane and Paul Bowles, Benjamin Britten, and Gypsy Rose Lee, under One Roof in Brooklyn* (New York: Mariner Books, 2006), 53.

66. George Orwell, "London Letter," *Partisan Review*, January 5, 1941, in *The Collected Essays, Journalism and Letters of George Orwell*, vol. 2: *My Country Right or Left, 1940–1943*, ed. Sonia Orwell and Ian Angus (London: Penguin Books, 1971), 72.

67. John Lehmann, *I Am My Brother* (New York: Reynal, 1960), 109.

68. See Linda M. Shires, *British Poetry of the Second World War* (New York: St. Martin's Press, 1985), 1, 24.

69. Nicholas Moore, "At the Start of the Forties," *Aquarius*, nos. 17/18 (1986–87).

70. Linda M. Shires, *British Poetry of the Second World War* (New York: St. Martin's Press, 1985), 19, 54.

71. AC, "Another Poet Answers Back," letter to *John O'London's Weekly*, March 13, 1942.

72. AC, "On Interpreting the War," *Horizon* 5, no. 29, May 1942.

73. Herbert Read, "The New Romantic School," *The Listener*, April 23, 1942.

74. George Orwell, "Pacifism and the War," *Partisan Review*, July 12, 1942, in *The Collected Essays, Journalism and Letters of George Orwell*, vol. 2: *My Country Right or Left, 1940–1943*, ed. Sonia Orwell and Ian Angus (London: Penguin Books, 1971), 265.

75. AC, interviewed by David Goodway, March 16, 1989.

76. See Mark Antliff, "Pacifism, Realism, and Pathology: Alex Comfort, Cecil Collins, and Neo-Romantic Art during World War II," *Modernism/Modernity* 27, no. 3 (2020).

77. David Mellor, *A Paradise Lost: The Neo-Romantic Imagination in Britain 1935–1955* (Oxford: Lund Humphries, 1987), 109.

78. George Woodcock, *Letter to the Past: An Autobiography* (Toronto: Fitzhenry & Whiteside, 1982), 214.

79. AC, letter to Arthur E. Salmon, August 28, 1980.

80. "*New Directions*" refers to the American publisher's semi-annual anthologies. AC, letter to Jon Bayliss, undated, 1942 or 1943.

81. Linda M. Shires, *British Poetry of the Second World War* (New York: St. Martin's Press, 1985), 68.

82. Cited in Woodcock, *Letter to the Past*, 210.

83. Ibid., 234.

84. AC, "Wartime Ballet," *NOW*, no. 6 (Summer 1941).

85. Woodcock, *Letter to the Past*, 235–36.

86. George Orwell, "London Letter," *Partisan Review*, March/April 1942, in *The Collected Essays, Journalism and Letters of George Orwell*, vol. 1: *My Country Right or Left, 1940–1943*, ed. Sonia Orwell and Ian Angus (London: Penguin Books, 1971), 211–14.

87. AC, "Pacifism and the War," *Partisan Review*, September/October 1942, in *The Collected Essays, Journalism and Letters of George Orwell*, vol. 1: *My Country Right or Left, 1940–1943*, ed. Sonia Orwell and Ian Angus (London: Penguin Books, 1971), 259–61.

88. Vera Brittain, "Humiliation with Honour," in *One Voice: Pacifist Writings from the Second World War* (New York: Continuum, 2005), 44–45.

Chapter 4: The Neo-Romantic (1942–1943)

1. Henry Treece, letter to AC, December 9, 1942.

2. AC, "Hands On in Clinical Training," *The Lancet*, September 29, 1984.

3. Nicholas Comfort, *Copy!*, 22.

4. Herbert Read, letter to AC, July 19, 1942.

5. "New Poetry in War-Time," *Times Educational Supplement*, December 22, 1942.

6. Michael De-la-Noy, *Denton Welch: The Making of a Writer* (New York: Penguin Books 1986), 157.

7. Arthur Waugh, letter to AC, August 20, 1942.

8. Denton Welch, letter to AC, January 5, 1943.

9. Herbert Read, letter to AC, September 25, 1942.

10. Michael De-la-Noy, *Denton Welch*, 148–49.

11. AC, interviewed by Arthur Salmon, August 7, 1974.

12. AC, letter to Herbert Read, November 3, 1943.

13. Graham Greene, "Herbert Read," in *The Lost Childhood and Other Essays* (Harmondsworth: Penguin Books, 1962), 159.

14. Derek Stanford, *Inside the Forties*, 26–27.

15. Cited in Jason Harding, *The "Criterion": Cultural Politics and Periodical Networks in Inter-War Britain* (Oxford: Oxford University Press, 2002), 122–23.

16. Herbert Read, "Poetry and Anarchism," in *Anarchy and Order: Essays in Politics* (Boston: Beacon Press, 1971), 104.

17. Herbert Read, *Poetry and Anarchism* (London: Faber & Faber, 1938), 87.

18. Cited in James King, *The Last Modern: A Life of Herbert Read* (New York: St. Martin's Press, 1990), 168–69.

19. AC, "English Poetry and the War," *Partisan Review*, March/April 1943.

20. Derek Stanford, *Inside the Forties*, 23.

21. AC, letter to David Goodway, October 1988.

22. AC, "Imagination or Reportage?" *Readers News*, January 1946.

23. AC, letter to Henry Treece, undated, 1941.

24. AC, interviewed by David Goodway, March 16, 1989.

25. Lois Gordon, *Nancy Cunard: Heiress, Muse, Political Idealist* (New York: Columbia University Press, 2007), 282.

26. AC, letter to Nancy Cunard, January 17, 1946.

27. AC, "Imagination or Reportage?" *Readers News*, January 1946.

28. See Robert Gildea, *Fighters in the Shadows: A New History of the French Resistance* (Cambridge MA: Belknap Press/Harvard University Press, 2015).

29. Andre Maurois, review of *The Power House*, *Chicago Sun Book Week*, April 1, 1945.

30. H. R. Kedward, *Occupied France: Collaboration and Resistance 1940–1944* (New York: Basil Blackwell, 1985), 50.

31. George Orwell, "The Meaning of Sabotage," January 29, 1942, BBC radio broadcast, in *Orwell: The Radio Broadcasts*, ed. W.J. West (London: Duckworth/British Broadcasting Corporation, 1985), 77–79.

32. AC, "An Exposition of Irresponsibility," *Life and Letters Today*, October 1943, in *Writings against Power and Death*, ed. David Goodway (London: Freedom Press, 1994), 32.

33. AC, "Art and Social Responsibility," *NOW* 2 (1944), 42–43.

34. AC, *The Power House* (New York: Viking Press, 1945), 131.

35. Ibid., 10–11.

36. AC, "Art and Social Responsibility," revised and republished in *Art and Social Responsibility: Lectures on the Ideology of Romanticism* (London: Falcon Press, 1946), 19.

37. AC, *The Power House*, 459–61.

38. Arthur Waugh, letter to AC, August 23, 1942.

39. AC, letter to Henry Treece, undated, 1942.

40. AC, "The Politics of Lying-In," *Medical Opinion*, December 1971.

41. AC, "Letter from Ireland," *Horizon* 7, no. 40 (April 1943). Quotations from next two paragraphs are also from this source.

42. AC, "The Politics of Lying-In," *Medical Opinion*, December 1971.

43. AC, "Cepaea Nemoralis L. in the Dartry Mountains," *Journal of Conchology* 22 (1944), 80–82.

44. AC, letter to Robert Greacen, June 7, 1986.

45. Des Nix, "The Joy of Being Comfort," *Sunday Press*, October 4, 1987.

46. AC, letter to *Tribune*, April 2, 1943.

47. Quoted in Eric Laursen, *The Duty to Stand Aside:* Nineteen Eighty-Four *and the Wartime Quarrel of George Orwell and Alex Comfort* (Oakland: AK Press, 2018), 27–32.

48. Richard Overy, "Constructing Space for Dissent in War: The Bombing Restriction Committee, 1941–1945," *English Historical Review* 131, no. 550 (June 2016).

49. AC, letter to *Tribune*, April 16, 1943.

50. John Atkins, "Excerpts from Interesting People I Have Known," http://www.winamop.com/interest1.htm.

51. AC, "Letter to an American Visitor, by Obadiah Hornbooke," *Tribune*, June 4, 1943.

52. David R. Costello, "'My Kind of Guy': George Orwell and Dwight Macdonald, 1941–49," *Journal of Contemporary History* 40, no. 1 (January 2005).

53. Cited in Edmund Wilson, "Archibald MacLeish and the Word," in *Classics and Commercials: A Literary Chronicle of the Forties* (New York: Vintage Books, 1962), 3.

54. Clement Greenberg, letter to AC, December 12, 1942; Dwight Macdonald, letter to AC, April 12, 1943.

55. John Atkins, "Excerpts from Interesting People I Have Known," http://www.winamop.com/interest1.htm.

56. George Orwell, letter to AC, July 15, 1942, in *George Orwell: A Life in Letters*, selected and annotated by Peter Davison (New York: Liveright Publishing, 2010), 200.

57. AC, letter to George Orwell, July 16, 1942, in *George Orwell: A Life in Letters*, selected and annotated by Peter Davison (New York: Liveright Publishing, 2010), 201–2.

58. George Orwell, letter to AC, August 26, 1942, in *The Complete Works of George Orwell*, vol. 13: *All Propaganda Is Lies*, ed. Peter Davison (London: Secker & Warburg, 1998), 496–97.

59. Cyril Connolly, "Frost, Raine, and Fog," *Observer*, July 25, 1943.

60. George Orwell, letter to AC, July 1943, in Orwell, *George Orwell: A Life in Letters*, selected and annotated by Peter Davison (New York: Liveright Publishing, 2010), 213–14.

61. Alexander Waugh, *Fathers and Sons*, 263–64.

62. AC, letter to Catherine Waugh, June 28, 1943.

63. Herbert Read, letter to AC, July 6, 1943.

64. Herbert Read, letter to AC, September 9, 1943.

65. Herbert Read, letter to AC, July 27, 1943.

66. T. Murray Ragg, letters to AC, October 8, 14, and 26, 1943.

67. Nicholas Comfort, *Copy!*, 22.

68. AC, "For Ruth," *Elegies* (London: George Routledge & Sons, 1944), 27.

Chapter 5: Blacklisted (1943–1945)

1. Reprinted in AC, *Writings against Power and Death*, ed. David Goodway (London: Freedom Press, 1994), 31–36.

2. Martin Ceadel, *Pacifism in Britain*, 236.

3. Vera Brittain, "One Voice: A Collection of Letters," unpublished manuscript, cited in Y. Aleksandra Bennett, introduction to Brittain, *One Voice: Pacifist Writings from the Second World War* (London: Continuum Books, 2005), xx.

4. "I am a coward": Stephen Spender, letter to AC, January 25, 1944.

5. AC, "The Progress of Cultural Bolshevism: A Communication," *Partisan Review*, Spring 1944.

6. Stephen Potter, "You want the best poetry. . . ," *Radio Times*, December 3, 1943; AC, "The Portable Forge," *The Listener*, April 20, 1944.

7. AC, letter to Nancy Cunard, October 27, 1944.

8. AC, letter to Alec Craig, undated, 1944.

9. George Orwell, letter to AC, November 29, 1943, in *The Complete Works of George Orwell*, vol. 16: *I Have Tried to Tell the Truth*, ed. Peter Davison (London: Secker & Warburg, 1998), 9–10.

10. George Orwell, "As I Please," *Tribune*, July 28, 1944.

11. "Mass Bombing Foes Rebuked by Roosevelt," *New York Herald Tribune*, April 26, 1944.

12. William L. Shirer, "Propaganda Front: Rebuttal to Protest against Bombing," *New York Herald Tribune*, March 12, 1944.

13. Y. Aleksandra Bennett, introduction to Vera Brittain, *One Voice: Pacifist Writings from the Second World War* (London: Continuum Books, 2005), xix.

14. AC, "Art and Social Responsibility," *NOW* 2 (Spring 1944).

15. John Rowland, "The Academy, 1944," *The Freethinker*, May 25, 1944.

16. Julian Symons, "Literature and Reaction," *Tribune*, September 5, 1944.

17. Rhys J. Davies, letter to AC, October 6, 1944.

18. W. P. Rilla, letter to AC, October 6, 1944

19. Rhys J. Davies, letter to AC, October 10, 1944.

20. W. P. Rilla, letter to AC, October 12, 1944.

21. W. P. Rilla, letters to AC, October 16 and 18, 1944.

22. Robert Speaight, letter to AC, October 23, 1944.

23. Herbert Read, letter to AC, December 8, 1944.

24. Ian Whittington, *Writing the Radio War: Literature, Politics and the BBC, 1939–1945* (Edinburgh: Edinburgh University Press, 2018), 19.

25. S. Gorley Putt, "Elegies," *Time and Tide*, October 24, 1944.

26. H. Peschmann, "Hopes and Elegies," *New English Weekly*, September 14, 1944.

27. AC, "Fifth Elegy," *Elegies* (London: George Routledge & Sons), 19.

28. Peter J. Conradi, *Iris Murdoch: A Life* (New York: W. W. Norton, 2001), 179.

29. Ad, *New Statesman and Nation*, October 14, 1944.

30. V. S. Pritchett, letter to AC, June 1944.

31. Kate O'Brien, "Fiction," *The Spectator*, September 29, 1944.

32. Richard Church, "The Power and Ambition of Youth," *John O' London's Weekly*, October 6, 1944.

33. "The Power House," *New Statesman and Nation*, October 14, 1944.

34. Richard Aldington, undated private letter, in AC papers. University College London.

35. "Popular Novels," *Liverpool Post*, October 3, 1944.

36. "Best Books of the Year," *John O' London's Weekly*, December 29, 1944.

37. AC, "October 1944, *NOW* 4 (Fall 1944).

38. AC, letter to Henry Treece, undated, ca. 1942–43.

39. Wrey Gardiner, *The Dark Thorn*, 193, 75, 176.

40. Interview with Nicholas Comfort, September 30, 2015.

41. Murdoch cited in Peter J Conradi, *Iris Murdoch: A Life*, 268–69.

42. AC, letter to Henry Treece, September 14, 1941.

43. Robert Greacen, unpublished interview by Pagan Kennedy, 2006.

44. Wrey Gardiner, *The Dark Thorn*, 74, 70–71.

45. Charles Hamblett, "A Summing Up," *Tribune*, April 27, 1946.

46. Derek Stanford, *Inside the Forties*, 96.

47. Ibid., 97.

48. AC, letter to Martin Seymour-Smith, March 4, 1944.

49. Emanual Litvinoff, letter to AC, February 12, 1946.

50. John Atkins, "Excerpts from Interesting People I Have Known," http://www.winamop.com/interest1.htm.

51. Wrey Gardiner, "The Octopus of Love: An Autobiography," unpublished manuscript, 110, 112.

52. AC, "Art," *New English Weekly*, March 2, 1944.

53. AC, introduction to *Cecil Collins: Paintings and Drawings (1935–1945)* (Oxford: Counterpoint Publications, 1946), 10.

54. Cited in Mark Antliff, "Pacifism, Realism, and Pathology: Alex Comfort, Cecil Collins, and Neo-Romantic Art during World War II," *Modernism/modernity* 27, no. 3 (2020).

55. Wrey Gardiner, *The Dark Thorn*, 44–45, 53.

56. Oscar Williams, letters to AC, April 12, June 20, 1943.

57. Alf Evers, *Woodstock: History of an American Town* (Woodstock, NY: Overlook Press, 1987), 400–419.

58. Holley Cantine, letter to AC, June 15, 1943.

59. Henry Miller, letter to George Woodcock, July 22, 1944, cited in Woodcock, letter to AC, September 16, 1944.

60. Henry Miller, letter to AC, January 26, 1945.

61. Caresse Crosby, letter to AC, July 19, 1945.

62. James Gifford, *Personal Modernisms: Anarchist Networks and the Later Avant-Gardes* (Edmonton: University of Alberta Press, 2014), 131.

63. Kenneth Rexroth, letter to AC, June 18, 1945.

64. James Gifford, *Personal Modernisms*, 35.

65. Philip Rahv, letter to George Orwell, July 20, 1943, cited in David R. Costello, "'My Kind of Guy': George Orwell and Dwight Macdonald, 1941–49," *Journal of Contemporary History* 40, no. 1 (January 2005).

66. Kenneth Rexroth, letter to AC, June 18, 1945; Rexroth, letter to John Q. Burch, Conchological Club of Southern California, July 12, 1946.

67. Kenneth Rexroth, introduction to *The New British Poets*, xi.

68. Kenneth Rexroth, letter to AC, June 18, 1945.

69. Holly Cantine, "The Mechanics of Class Development," *Retort*, Winter 1942.

70. James Tracy, *Direct Action: Radical Pacifism from the Union Eight to the Chicago Seven* (Chicago: University of Chicago Press, 1996), xiii–xiv.

71. Ibid., 126.

72. George Woodcock, *Letter to the Past*, 246–47.

73. Ibid., 245.

74. See Gerrard Winstanley, *The True Levellers Standard Advanced: Or, The State of Community Opened, and Presented to the Sons of Men* (1649), https://www.marxists.org/reference/archive/winstanley/1649/levellers-standard.htm.

75. Dennis Hardy, *Utopian England: Community Experiments 1900–1945* (London: E. & F. N. Spon, 2000), 22–24, 42–46.

76. John Quail, *The Slow Burning Fuse: The Lost History of British Anarchists* (London: Paladin Books, 1978), 287–93, 305–6.

77. Colin Ward, "Obituary: Vernon Richards," *Guardian*, February 4, 2002.

78. Ibid., 281–83.

79. Herbert Read, letter to AC, September 9, 1944.

80. George Woodcock, *Letter to the Past*, 265.

81. AC et al., "The Freedom Press Raid," letter to *New Statesman and Nation*, March 3, 1945.

82. Stephen Richards Graubard, "Demobilization in Great Britain following the First World War," *Journal of Modern History* 19, no. 4 (December 1947).

83. David Lamb, *Mutinies: 1917–1920* (Oxford: Oxford Solidarity, 1977), 9.

84. "More severe": see Angus Calder, *The People's War, 1939–1945* (New York: HarperCollins, 1979); and Paul Addison, *The Road to 1945: British Politics and the Second World War*, rev. ed. (London: Pimlico, 1994).

85. The National Archives, extract from Special Branch Fortnightly Summary no. 41, July 15, 1942, cited in Carissa Honeywell, "Anarchism and the British Warfare State: The Prosecution of the War Commentary Anarchists, 1945," *International Review of Social History* 60, no. 2 (2015).

86. Reprinted in *War Commentary*, April 21, 1945; cited in Carissa Honeywell, "Anarchism and the British Warfare State."

87. Douglas Fetherling, *The Gentle Anarchist: The Life of George Woodcock* (Vancouver: Douglas & McIntyre, 1998), 41–42.

88. AC et al., "The Freedom Press Raid," letter to *The New Statesman and Nation*, March 3, 1945.

89. Carissa Honeywell, "Anarchism and the British Warfare State."

90. George Woodcock, *Letter to the Past*, 268.

91. Ibid., 267.

92. Ibid., 283.

93. Ibid., 266.

94. AC, letter to Herbert Read, March 2, 1945.

95. AC, letter to *The Listener*, May 19, 1945.

96. George Woodcock, *Letter to the Past*, 267–68.

Chapter 6: Against the Cold War (1945–1949)

1. Kenneth Patchen, letter to AC, March 25, 1945.
2. AC, "Criminal Lunacy Exposed," *War Commentary*, August 25, 1945.
3. George Orwell, "You and the Atomic Bomb," *Tribune*, October 19, 1945.
4. AC, "Us and the Atom Bomb," *Tribune*, October 26, 1945.
5. AC, "An Anarchist View: The Political Relevance of Pacifism," *Peace News*, December 7, 1945.
6. Editors' Note, *Conscientious Objector*, September 1945.
7. T. Murray Ragg, letter to AC, October 16, 1944, including telegram from B. W. Huebsch to Ragg; Huebsch, letter to AC, March 9, 1945.
8. Noted in Ben Huebsch, letter to AC, March 9, 1945, and in Marguerite Young, "Comfort's Work," *The Conscientious Objector*, date unknown, 1945.
9. Diana Trilling, "Fiction in Review," *The Nation*, March 31, 1945.
10. Francis Hackett, "Books of the Times," *New York Times*, March 22, 1945.
11. John Chamberlain, "The New Books," *Life*, date unknown, 1945.
12. Harry Hansen, "War as Madness," *New York World-Telegram*, March 16, 1945.
13. T. Murray Ragg, letters to AC, April 6, April 27, and May 1, 1945; February 28, 1946.
14. Marguerite Young, "Comfort's Work," *Conscientious Objector*, date unknown, 1945.
15. Randall Jarrell, "Verse Chronicle," *The Nation*, December 29, 1945.
16. AC, interviewed by David Goodway, March 16, 1989.
17. AC, "Song for the Heroes," in *The Signal to Engage* (London: Routledge, 1946), 17.
18. AC, "The Song of Lazarus," in *The Signal to Engage* (London: Routledge, 1946), 31–32.
19. David Gascoyne, ed., *Outlaw of the Lowest Planet* (London: Grey Walls Press, 1946).
20. AC, "None but My Foe to Be My Guide," in *The Signal to Engage* (London: Routledge, 1946), 22.
21. Richard Church, "Good Poems of To-day," *John O'London's Weekly*, July 25, 1947.
22. "Legal reasons": T. Murray Ragg, letter to AC, May 7, 1945.
23. See Peter Baker, *My Testament* (London: John Calder, 1955).
24. Cited in Hilary Spurling, *Paul Scott: A life of the Author of "The Raj Quartet"* (New York: W. W. Norton, 1990), 158–59.
25. Muriel Spark, *A Far Cry from Kensington* (Thorndike, ME: Thorndike Press, 1988), 29.
26. Alan Smith, "Grey Walls Press," *Antiquarian Book Monthly Review*, September 1986.
27. T. Murray Ragg, George Routledge & Sons, letter to AC, May 7, 1945.
28. This and what follows in AC, "Art and Social Responsibility," in *Art and Social Responsibility: Lectures on the Ideology of Romanticism* (London: Falcon Press, 1946), 16–37.
29. Julian Symons, "Responsible People," unknown publication, February 27, 1948.
30. Margaret Willy, "Man and Cosmos," unknown publication, date unknown; in AC papers, University College London.
31. "Art and Anarchy," *Birmingham Post*, December 3, 1947.
32. "The Listener's Book Chronicle," *The Listener*, June 3, 1948.

33. "Adrian Mitchell Interviewed by John Rety," *Freedom*, January 24, 1998.

34. AC, "Romanticism, Primitivism and Kitsch-Culture," in *Art and Social Responsibility: Lectures on the Ideology of Romanticism* (London: Falcon Press, 1946), 62–63.

35. V. S. Pritchett, undated letter to AC, June 1944.

36. Arthur E. Salmon, *Alex Comfort* (Boston: Twayne, 1978), 87–88.

37. AC, *Darwin and the Naked Lady* (New York: George Braziller, 1962), 95.

38. In *Twentieth Century Authors: First Supplement* (New York: H. W. Wilson, 1955), 21.

39. Stevie Smith, "Short Stories of All Kinds," *John O'London's Weekly*, November 2, 1947; Olivia Manning, "Short Stories," *The Spectator*, December 9, 1947.

40. Kenneth Rexroth, introduction to *The New British Poets*, xxviii.

41. Derek Stanford, *The Freedom of Poetry: Studies in Contemporary Verse* (London: Grey Walls Press, 1947), 75.

42. See David Higham, *Literary Gent* (New York: Coward, McCann & Geoghegan, 1978), 199–232.

43. David Higham, letters to AC, May 31 and June 6, 1945.

44. AC, letter to Henry Treece, undated, 1945.

45. Interview with Nicholas Comfort, November 14, 2021.

46. Nicholas Comfort, *Copy!*, 23.

47. Nicholas Comfort, *Copy!*, 26.

48. AC, "Questionnaire: The Cost of Letters," *Horizon*, September 1946.

49. Ibid.

50. Roy A. Church, *The Rise and Decline of the British Motor Industry* (Cambridge: Cambridge University Press, 1995), 39.

51. Nicholas Comfort, *Copy!*, 26–27.

52. AC, interviewed by David Goodway, March 16, 1989.

53. *Peace and Disobedience*, *Peace News* pamphlet, 1946.

54. W. Albert Noyes, "The British Atomic Energy Act," *Bulletin of the Atomic Scientists* 2, nos. 11–12 (1946).

55. "Did No Wrong, Nunn May Insists; 'Hopes to Serve Fellow Men,'" *New York Times*, December 30, 1952.

56. Nicholas Comfort, *Copy!*, 12-13.

57. AC, "Congenital Syphilis in an Infant Treated with Penicillin," *The Lancet*, October 6, 1945.

58. Interview with Nicholas Comfort, September 4, 2021.

59. AC, "Fate of the Foreskin," *British Medical Journal*, February 4, 1950.

60. AC, "Childhood Advisory Clinics at Camberwell," *The Lancet*, October 11, 1947.

61. "Modern Fiction," *Times Literary Supplement*, July 24, 1948.

62. AC, "Social Aspects of Censorship and Pornography," *NOW* 8 (May–June 1947).

63. George Orwell, "Raffles and Miss Blandish," *Horizon*, October 1944, in *The Collected Essays, Journalism and Letters of George Orwell*, vol. 3: *As I Please, 1943–1945*, ed. Sonia Orwell and Ian Angus (London: Penguin Books, 1971), 246–60.

64. AC, "Literary Sadism and the Origins of Miss Blandish," *NOW* 7 (February/March 1947).

65. AC, "Plague and Quarantine," *Tribune*, September 10, 1948.

66. Laura Marris, "Camus's Inoculation against Hate," *New York Times Book Review*, August 9, 2020.

67. AC, "Keep Endless Watch," *Reader's News*, December 1950.

68. AC, letter to Wayne Burns, cited in Arthur E. Salmon, *Alex Comfort* (Boston: Twayne, 1978), 82.

69. AC, interviewed by David Goodway, March 16, 1989.
70. AC, *The Novel and Our Time* (London: Phoenix House, 1948), 41.
71. AC, *On This Side Nothing* (New York: Viking Press, 1949), 149.
72. Ben Huebsch, letter to AC, July 30, 1948.
73. Charles Poore, "Books of the Times," *New York Times*, January 15, 1949.
74. Richard McLaughlin, "Always on the Run," *Saturday Review of Literature*, January 29, 1949.
75. Mary Sutphen Hurst, "Africa as Two Novelists See It," *New York Times Sunday Book Review*, January 9, 1949.
76. George J. Becker, "The Ghetto as Myth," *Commentary*, March 1949.
77. AC, "Whither Israel?" *New Israel*, Summer 1948, in AC, *Writings against Power and Death*, ed. David Goodway (London: Freedom Press, 1994), 104–6.

Chapter 7: The Anarchist (1947–1951)

1. Cited in Stefan Collini, "Beebology," *London Review of Books*, April 21, 2022.
2. Callum G. Brown, *The Battle for Christian Britain: Sex, Humanists and Secularisation, 1945–1980* (Cambridge: Cambridge University Press, 2019), 4, 22.
3. Mary Webb, *My Apprenticeship* (London: Longman's, Green, 1926), 54, 83.
4. AC, *Sex in Society* (London: Pelican Books, 1964), 18.
5. "Cold Comfort," *British Weekly*, December 15, 1949.
6. AC, *The Pattern of the Future: Four Broadcast Talks* (London: Routledge & Kegan Paul, 1949).
7. Ibid., 27.
8. Ibid., 29, 33, 34.
9. Ibid., 40–41.
10. Ibid., 45–46.
11. Ibid., 51.
12. BBC internal memos cited in Callum G. Brown, *The Battle for Christian Britain*, 131.
13. AC, *The Pattern of the Future*, 53.
14. Martin Armstrong, letter to the editor, *The Listener*, July 28, 1949.
15. R. G. Walford for the BBC, letter to AC, July 12, 1950; Mrs. B. H. Gray, BBC, letter to AC, July 22, 1950.
16. Paul Scott, Falcon Press, letter to AC, August 11, 1948; Norman Franklin, Routledge and Kegan Paul, letter to AC, November 10, 1948.
17. H. P. Laird for the London Hospital Medical College, letter to AC, July 18, 1949.
18. AC, *First-Year Physiological Technique* (London: Staples Press, 1948), 45.
19. "First-Year Physiological Technique," *The Lancet*, October 23, 1948.
20. "Urban Life 'Barbaric': Oxford Talk on Sexual Ethics," *Oxford Mail*, May 31, 1947.
21. AC, "Sexual Abnormality and the Law," *The Lancet*, November 8, 1947.
22. James H. Jones, *Alfred C. Kinsey: A Public/Private Life* (New York: W. W. Norton, 1997), 564.
23. Lesley A. Hall, email to author, August 29, 2021.
24. A. C. Kinsey, W. P. Pomeroy, and C. E. Martin, *Sexual Behavior in the Human Male* (Philadelphia: W. B. Saunders, 1947).
25. AC, "The American Male," *New Statesman and Nation*, June 19, 1948.
26. AC, "The Kinsey Report," *Freedom*, May 1, 1948.

27. See, for example, Mary Astell's *A Serious Proposal to the Ladies* (1694) and Sarah Scott's *A Description of Millennium Hall* (1762), described in Lyman Tower Sargent and Lucy Sargisson, "Sex in Utopia: Eutopian and Dystopian Sexual Relations," *Utopian Studies* 25, no. 2 (2014).

28. David Goodway, *Anarchist Seeds beneath the Snow*, 59-60.

29. Marie Louise Berneri, "Sexuality and Freedom," *NOW* 5, 1945; David Goodway, *Anarchist Seeds beneath the Snow*, 207.

30. Interview with Nicholas Comfort, September 4, 2021.

31. Lesley A. Hall, "'The English Have Hot-Water Bottles': The Morganatic Marriage between Sexology and Medicine in Britain since William Acton," in *Sexual Knowledge, Sexual Science: The History of Attitudes to Sexuality*, eds. Roy Porter and Mikulas Teich (Cambridge: Cambridge University Press, 1994), 362–63.

32. AC, *Barbarism and Sexual Freedom: Lectures on the Sociology of Sex from the Standpoint of Anarchism* (London: Freedom Press, 1948), 8.

33. Ibid., 6–8.

34. Ibid., 48.

35. Ibid., 55.

36. Ibid., 25, 7, 61.

37. Ibid., 61–62.

38. See D. J. Taylor, *Lost Girls: Love, War and Literature, 1939-51* (London: Constable, 2019).

39. "Barbarism and Sexual Freedom," *The Medical Officer*, August 25,1949.

40. Alfred C. Kinsey, letter to Freedom Press, October 10, 1949.

41. Mervyn Horder for Gerald Duckworth & Co., to AC, February 2, 1949.

42. Quoted in Mervyn Horder for Gerald Duckworth & Co., to AC, March 3, 1949.

43. Lesley A. Hall, *Sex, Gender and Social Change in Britain since 1880*, 136–37.

44. Cited in Jeffrey Weeks, *Sex, Politics & Society: The Regulation of Sexuality Since 1800*, second edition (London: Longman, 1981), 253.

45. Alan Petigny, "Illegitimacy Social Psychology, and the Reperiodization of the Sexual Revolution," *Journal of Social History* 38, no. 1 (Fall 2004).

46. James M. Gregory, "Internal Migration: Twentieth Century and Beyond," in *The Oxford Encyclopedia of American Social History* (New York: Oxford University Press, 2012), 540–45.

47. Birth Control Federation of America, Inc., annual report 1939; cited in Alan Petigny, *The Permissive Society: America, 1941–1965* (New York: Cambridge University Press, 2009), 111.

48. Hera Cook, *The Long Sexual Revolution: English Women, Sex and Contraception 1800–1975* (Oxford: Oxford University Press, 2004), 184.

49. See Murray Watson, *Invisible Immigrants: The English in Canada since 1945* (Winnipeg: University of Manitoba Press, 2015).

50. AC, *Sexual Behaviour in Society* (New York: Viking Press, 1950), 75–76.

51. Ibid., 7.

52. AC, letter to the editor, *The Lancet*, January, 1949; "Sex Education in the Medical Curriculum," *International Journal of Sexology*, Winter 1950.

53. AC, *Sexual Behaviour in Society*, 79, 27.

54. Ibid., 80, 154.

55. Ibid., 139.

56. Ibid., 149.

57. Ibid., 108.

58. See Susan K. Freeman, "Postwar Sex Education and the Roots of White Male Sexual Entitlement," *Notches: (Re)marks on the History of Sexuality*, October 13, 2016.

59. Frank G. Slaughter, "Why We Are as We Are, *New York Times*, April 22, 1951.
60. "Sexual Standards," *The Times Educational Supplement*, June 16, 1950.
61. Dannie Abse, "Sex in the Sick Society of Today," *Public Opinion*, May 12, 1950.
62. Dachine Rainer, "Book Reviews," *Retort* 4, no. 4 (Winter 1951).
63. Dick Kisch, "Doctor's Sex Proposals Jolt British Conventions," *Daily Telegraph*, May 14, 1950.
64. Data cited in Callum G. Brown, *The Battle for Christian Britain*, 31.
65. Paul Bloomfield, "The Horse before the Cart," *Time and Tide*, date unknown, 1950.
66. Alfred C. Kinsey, letter to Freedom Press, October 10, 1949.
67. AC, "Contraceptives in Slot Machines," *The Lancet*, date unknown, 1949.
68. Cyril Bibby for the *International Journal of Sexology*, letter to AC, April 7, 1950.
69. Paul Reiwald, *Society and Its Criminals*, trans. T. E. James (London: William Heinemann, 1949), 166, 296.
70. Ibid., 296.
71. AC, "Criminals and Society," *Freedom*, December 24, 1949.
72. David Goodway, *Anarchist Seeds beneath the Snow*, 241; Peter Marshall, *Demanding the Impossible: A History of Anarchism* (Oakland: PM Press, 2010), 594.
73. AC, *Authority and Delinquency in the Modern State: A Criminological Approach to the Problem of Power* (London: Sphere Books, 1970), 11.
74. Mikhail Bakunin, "Power Corrupts the Best" (1867), http://dwardmac.pitzer.edu/Anarchist_Archives/bakunin/bakuninpower.html.
75. AC, *Authority and Delinquency in the Modern State*, 21.
76. Ibid., 43.
77. Ibid., 110.
78. "Working classes strike more often": ibid., 99.
79. Ibid., 103-4.
80. Ibid., 80–81, 119-20.
81. AC, "1939 and 1984: George Orwell and the Vision of Judgment," in *On Nineteen Eighty-Four*, ed. Peter Stansky (New York: W. H. Freeman, 1983), 17.
82. Julian Symons, introduction to George Orwell, *Nineteen Eighty-Four*, Everyman's Library (New York: Alfred A. Knopf, 1992), xx.
83. AC, *Authority and Delinquency in the Modern State*, 116–19.
84. Hyman Levy, "The Marxist View of Liberty," *The Listener*, December 7, 1950.
85. AC, letter to the editor, *The Listener*, December 21, 1950.
86. Hyman Levy, letter to the editor, *The Listener*, January 4, 1951.
87. AC, letter to the editor, *The Listener*, January 11, 1951.
88. Margery Fry, "A New Slant on the State," *Tribune*, date unknown.
89. "The Listener's Book Chronicle," *The Listener*, February 1, 1951; "Corruption by power," *Liverpool Post*, October 17, 1950.
90. E. G. Pratt, secretary, National Association of Probation Officers, letters to AC, February 10 and February 17, 1951.
91. Walter A. Linden, "Authority and Delinquency in the Modern State," *Journal of Criminal Law, Criminology, and Police Science* 42, no. 3 (September–October 1951).
92. B. R. Hinchliff, "Authority and Delinquency in the Modern State," *British Journal of Sociology* 2, no. 2 (June 1951).
93. Morris Ginsberg, "Authority and Delinquency in the Modern State," *British Journal of Delinquency* 1, no. 3 (January 1951).
94. Thomas Blass, *The Man Who Shocked the World: The Life and Legacy of Stanley Milgram* (New York: Basic Books, 2004), xix.

95. Stanley Milgram, *Obedience to Authority*, 188.
96. George Orwell, "Notes on Nationalism," *Polemic*, October 1945.
97. Reprinted as "Delinquency" in *Freedom*, [fall 1951].
98. Herbert Read, letter to AC, January 25, 1951.
99. AC, letter to Herbert Read, January 27, 1951.

Chapter 8: The Public Intellectual (1949–1956)

1. AC, letter to Herbert Read, January 27, 1951.
2. AC, "*Hygromia conctella* (Draparnaud) in England," *Journal of Conchology*, no. 23 (1950).
3. S. Peter Dance, "Comfort and Joy among the Snails of Chaldon," *Mollusc World*, no. 24 (November 2010).
4. Interview with Gabe Maletta, July 23, 2010.
5. British Empire Cancer Campaign, letter to AC, June 8, 1950.
6. Peter Medawar, letter to W.A. Sanderson, Nuffield Foundation, July 5, 1950.
7. Leslie Farrer-Brown, Nuffield Foundation, letter to AC, November 30, 1950.
8. W.A. Sanderson, letter to AC, August 10, 1951.
9. Peter Medawar, *Memoir of a Thinking Radish* (Oxford: Oxford University Press, 1986), 127.
10. Samanth Subramanian, *A Dominant Character: The Radical Science and Restless Politics of J. B. S. Haldane* (New York: W. W. Norton, 2020), 277.
11. Peter Medawar, *Memoir of a Thinking Radish*, 124.
12. Ibid., 123, 127.
13. Interview with Nicholas Comfort, November 19, 2021.
14. Adrian Mitchell, "Poetry Explodes—Adrian Mitchell Tells the Story of the Oral Poets," *The Listener*, May 14, 1970.
15. "Poets at Work," *Daily Herald* (London), August 20, 1953.
16. Ruth Prothero, letter to AC, August 4, 1962.
17. Alan Smith, "Grey Walls Press," *Antiquarian Book Monthly Review*, September 1986.
18. AC, letter to Wrey Gardiner, February 9, 1955.
19. Martin Stannard, *Muriel Spark: The Biography*, 140–41.
20. Derek Stanford, "A Mug's Game," unpublished memoir, cited in Martin Stannard, *Muriel Spark: The Biography*, 142.
21. "Go with the young moderns": Wrey Gardiner, "The Fiery Forties," *Poetry Review*, Autumn 1962.
22. Robert Conquest, ed., *New Lines* (London: Macmillan, 1956), xii–xiv.
23. Ted Hughes, interviewed by Ekbert Faas, *Ted Hughes: The Unaccountable Universe* (Santa Barbara: Black Sparrow Press, 1980), 202; cited in Heather Clark, *Red Comet: The Short Life and Blazing Art of Sylvia Plath* (New York: Alfred A. Knopf, 2020), 412.
24. AC, *And All but He Departed* (London: Routledge & Kegan Paul, 1951), 44.
25. Ibid., 63–64.
26. Ibid., 62–63.
27. AC, interview by David Goodway, March 16, 1989.
28. Ibid.
29. Herbert Read, letter to AC, June 18, 1945; George Woodcock, *Letter to the Past*, 282–83.
30. Herbert Read and AC, "No Annihilation. . .," letter to the editor, *New Statesman and Nation*, February 9, 1951.

31. Herbert Read, letter to AC, February 22, 1951.

32. Ibid.

33. "Napalm Bombs," letter to the editor, *Times* (London), July 8, 1952.

34. Sybil Morrison, *I Renounce War: The Story of the Peace Pledge Union* (London: Sheppard Press, 1962), 76–77.

35. Rose Grant, "12 Famous Writers in Peace Call," *Daily Worker*, April 25, 1951; "Writers Define Their Peace Aims," *Times* (London), date unknown, 1951.

36. "If Hitler were alive today. . . ," *Daily Worker*, July 23, 1951.

37. AC, letters to the Home Secretary, March 31 and May 8, 1952.

38. C. N. Ryan, Home Office, letter to AC, May 22, 1952.

39. AC, letter to the editor, *News Chronicle* (London), November 23, 1950.

40. Sybil Morrison, for the PPU, letter to AC, July 10, 1951.

41. Dorothy Glaister, letters to AC, October 30 and November 14, 1950; J. Norman Glaister, letter to AC, August 13, 1951.

42. Gilbert Phelps, for the BBC Talks Department, letters to AC, November 27 and December 2, 1952.

43. AC, "Social Responsibility in Science and Art," *The Listener*, November 29, 1951.

44. Callum G. Brown, *The Battle for Christian Britain*, 133.

45. AC, "Under Tension, *The Lancet*, October 9, 1948.

46. AC, "The Challenge of Science," *Tribune*, December 24, 1954.

47. AC, "Britain and the Soviet Union," *Peace News*, November 17, 1950.

48. AC, "Collective Security," *Peace News*, January 26, 1951.

49. AC, "The Korean Situation," letter to the *New Statesman and Nation*, June 28 1951.

50. AC, "Is It to Be Unconditional Surrender Again?," *New Statesman and Nation*, September 14, 1951.

51. "End the Cold War," *Peace News*, July 25, 1952.

52. David Leeming, *Stephen Spender: A Life in Modernism* (New York: Henry Holt, 1999), 182.

53. Stephen Spender, "The Fear Neurosis," letter to the editor, *New Statesman and Nation*, September 1951.

54. AC, letter to the editor, *New Statesman and Nation*, September 1951.

55. S. E. Parker, "Britain and the USSR," letter to the editor, *Peace News*, December 12, 1950.

56. AC, *A Giant's Strength* (London: Routledge & Kegan Paul, 1952), 199–200.

57. A. M. Turing, "Computing Machinery and Intelligence," *Mind* 49 (1950).

58. Herbert Read, letter to AC, February 22, 1951.

59. Ibid.

60. AC, letter to Herbert Read, June 28, 1951.

61. AC, interviewed by David Goodway, March 16, 1989.

62. Arthur Calder-Marshall, "New Novels," *The Listener*, September 18, 1952.

63. Philip Toynbee, "Over-Indulgence," *Observer*, date unknown, 1952.

64. "*A Giant's Strength*," letter to the editor, *New Statesman and Nation*, October 4, 1952.

65. AC, "McCarthyism: The Impact on Europe," *The Nation*, April 11, 1953.

66. Eleanor Roosevelt, "My Way," syndicated column, November 2, 1951.

67. Vera Brittain, letter to AC, June 10, 1951.

68. AC, letter to Vera Brittain, June 19, 1951.

69. Vera Brittain, letter to AC, June 20, 1951.

70. Robert Greacen, "The Militant Pacifist," *The Humanist*, November 1958.

71. T. F. Fox, letters to AC, December 7, 1956, and December 8, 1950.

72. Interview with Nicholas Comfort, November 19, 2021.

73. Nicholas Comfort, *Copy!*, 341; AC, letter to L. V. Komarov, September 2, 1958.

74. T. F. Fox, "Russia Revisited: Impressions of Soviet Medicine," *The Lancet*, October 9 and October 16, 1954.

75. AC, "Russia Revisited," letter to the editor, *The Lancet*, October 30, 1954.

76. AC, "Closing a Breach," *The Lancet*, December 12, 1954.

77. Julian Huxley, *Memoirs* (New York: Harper & Row 1970), 201–3, 282–85.

78. See Gary Werskey, The *Visible College: The Collective Biography of British Scientific Socialists of the 1930s* (New York: Holt Rinehart and Winston, 1978), 292–98.

79. Peter Medawar, *Memoir of a Thinking Radish* (Oxford: Oxford University Press, 1986), 129.

80. AC, "Closing a Breach," *The Lancet*, December 12, 1954.

81. Barbara McPherson, for the Society for Cultural Relations with the USSR, letters to AC, December 14, 1956, and January 7, 1957.

82. AC, letter to unknown recipient, March 31, 1957.

83. AC, letters to Pierre Emmanuel, December 18 and December 31, 1959; Pierre Emmanuel, letter to AC, March 14, 1960.

84. Samanth Subramanian, email to author, January 8, 2022.

85. AC, unpublished manuscript, 1955 or 1956.

86. Nicholas Comfort, *Copy!*, 454.

87. AC, letter to Herbert Read, November 12, 1956.

88. "Labour Meeting Slates Eden for 'Betrayal of U.K., U.N. and Humanity,'" *London Gazette*, November 28, 1956.

89. AC and Herbert Read, unpublished letter to the *New Statesman and Nation*, December 12, 1956.

90. AC, letter to unknown correspondent, March 31, 1957.

Chapter 9: Science and Sex (1952–1958)

1. Nicholas Comfort, *Copy!* 29.
2. Robert Greacen, email to Pagan Kennedy, 2006.
3. Interview with Nicholas Comfort, November 19, 2021.
4. Ibid., 27.
5. AC, interviewed by David Goodway, March 16, 1989.
6. Nicholas Comfort, "The facts of life about my father," *The Daily Telegraph*, March 30, 2000.
7. Interview with Nicholas Comfort, November 19, 2021.
8. Nicholas Comfort, *Copy!*, 28–32.
9. AC, interviewed by H.B. (Tony) Gibson, October 13, 1992.
10. Nicholas Comfort, *Copy!*, 316.
11. "She didn't share": Robert Greacen, email to Pagan Kennedy, 2006.
12. Thomas Dalby, for Hutchinson and Co. (Publishers), letters to AC, November 2 and 30 and December 11, 1959.
13. Interview with Nicholas Comfort, November 19, 2021.
14. Paul Gray, *The Immortalization Commission: Science and the Strange Quest to Cheat Death* (New York: Farrar, Straus and Giroux, 2011), 205.
15. Zhores A. Medvedev, "An Attempt at a Rational Classification of Theories of Ageing," *Biological Reviews* 65 (1990).
16. Jonathan Weiner, *Long for This World: The Strange Science of Immortality* (New York: Ecco, 2011), 89–92.

17. Ibid., 39; Michael R. Rose, *The Long Tomorrow: How Advances in Evolutionary Biology Can Help Us Postpone Aging* (New York: Oxford University Press, 2005), 15.

18. J. B. S. Haldane, *New Paths in Genetics* (New York: Harper & Brothers, 1942), 193–94.

19. P. B. Medawar, *An Unsolved Problem of Biology* (London: H. K. Lewis, 1952), reprinted in Medawar, *The Uniqueness of the Individual*, 2nd rev. ed. (New York: Dover Publications, 1981), 41–54.

20. Cited in Jonathan Weiner, *Long for This World*, 184.

21. See P. B. Medawar, *An Unsolved Problem of Biology* (London: H. K. Lewis, 1952).

22. AC, *The Process of Aging* (New York: Signet, 1964), 89.

23. Tiago Moreira and Paolo Palladino, "Ageing between Gerontology and Biomedicine," *Biosocieties* 4, no. 4 (2009).

24. Robin Holliday, "Alex Comfort: Clearing the Way for Future Research," *Experimental Gerontology* 33, nos. 1–2 (1998).

25. AC, letter to Wrey Gardiner, February 9, 1955.

26. Mary Banwell, née Sydenham, letter to AC, November 18, 1986.

27. AC, interviewed by David Goodway, March 16, 1989.

28. "Interview: John Maynard Smith on ageing research," *Biogerontology* 1, September 2000.

29. E. A. L. Gueterbock, for UCL, letter to AC, March 8 1960.

30. Interview with Nicholas Comfort, November 15, 2021.

31. Ralph Powell, Evans Medical Supplies Ltd, letter to AC, March 26, 1954.

32. Nicholas Comfort, email to author, March 12, 2008.

33. AC, interviewed by David Goodway, March 16, 1989.

34. Robin Holliday "Alex Comfort: An Appreciation," *Biogerontology* 1, September 2000.

35. AC, *The Biology of Senescence*, 3–4.

36. G. P. Bidder, "Senescence," *British Medical Journal*, September 24, 1932.

37. AC, *The Biology of Senescence*, 14, 4.

38. Ibid., 189–91.

39. Ibid., 197–98.

40. Ibid., 193–94.

41. Interview with Caleb Finch, May 14, 2018.

42. "Growing Old," *British Medical Journal*, September 8, 1956.

43. Gerald Gruman, "The Biology of Senescence," *Isis* 48, no. 4 (December 1957). "An important monograph": Gerald J. Gruman, "A History of Ideas about the Prolongation of Life: The Evolution of Prolongevity Hypotheses to 1800," *Transactions of the American Philosophical Society*, New Series, vol. 56, pt. 9 (1966).

44. William F. Forbes, "Editorial," *Experimental Gerontology* 33, nos. 1–2 (1998).

45. N. Bland, for the CIBA Foundation, letter to AC, July 16, 1958.

46. W. S. Bullough, for the British Society or Research on Aging, to AC, January 27, 1958.

47. AC, letters to L.V. Komarov, September 2 and 18, 1958.

48. AC, "Mortality and the Nature of the Aging Process," *Journal of the Institute of Actuaries* 84, no. 3 (December 1958).

49. Martin Stannard, *Muriel Spark: The Biography*, 78–97; Michael Lister, "Muriel Spark and the Business of Poetry," *Agenda*, December 2004.

50. Allan Hepburn, "*Memento Mori* and Gerontography," *Textual Practice* 32, no. 9 (2018).

51. AC, *The Biology of Senescence*, vii.

52. AC, "By Laodicean out of Lady Chatterley," *The Listener*, December 29, 1960.

53. Z. A. Medvedev, "Alex Comfort (1920–2000) Known and Unknown: A Personal Account," *Experimental Gerontology* 35 (2000).

54. AC, "Coat-Colour and Longevity in Thoroughbred Mares," *Nature*, November 29, 1958.

55. AC, "By Laodicean out of Lady Chatterley."

56. Ibid.

57. BBC Audience Research Department, "Audience Research Report," December 6, 1960.

58. AC, "The Effect of Age on Growth Resumption in Fish (*Lebistes*) Checked by Food Restriction," *Gerontologia* 4 (1960); "The Longevity and Mortality of a Fish (*Lebistes reticulatus*, Peters) in Captivity," *Gerontologia* 5 (1961); "Effect of Delayed and Resumed Growth on a Longevity of a Fish (*Lebistes reticulatus*, Peters) in Captivity," *Gerontologia* 8 (1963).

59. AC, "The Life Span of Animals," *Scientific American*, August 1961.

60. Eunice Thomas Miner, for the New York Academy of Sciences, letter to AC, May 31, 1960.

61. James Henderson, for the University of London, letter to AC, October 24, 1962.

62. Avril D. Woodhead, "Aging, the Fishy Side: An Appreciation of Alex Comfort's Studies," *Experimental Gerontology* 33, nos. 1–2 (1998).

63. AC, interviewed by David Goodway, March 16, 1989.

64. Robert S. W. Pollard, for the Marriage Law Reform Society, letter to AC, April 6, 1951.

65. "This plague": Simon Jenkins, "Make Mine a Glass of Cannabis Wine, Thank You," *Guardian*, October 19, 2018; prison stats: "Homosexuality and Prostitution: B.M.A. Memorandum of Evidence for Departmental Committee," *Supplement to the British Medical Journal*, December 17, 1955.

66. D. J. West, *Homosexuality* (London: Gerald Duckworth, 1955).

67. AC, "Homosexuality," *The Lancet*, September 24, 1955.

68. "Homosexuality and Prostitution: B.M.A. Memorandum of Evidence for Departmental Committee," *Supplement to the British Medical Journal*, December 17, 1955.

69. AC, "Reflections on the B.M.A. Committee's Report on Homosexuality and Prostitution," *The Lancet*, January 21, 1956.

70. "Homosexuality Should Not Be a Crime," BBC Home Service, September 4, 1957.

71. Home Office, "Report of the Committee on Homosexual Offences and Prostitution" (London: Her Majesty's Stationery Office, 1957).

72. AC, "Homosexuality and Common Sense," *Tribune*, March 14, 1958.

73. A. E. Dyson, letters to AC, February 26, April 23, June 6, June 7, July 15, and November 5, 1958.

74. AC, "Unmarried Parenthood," *The Lancet*, January 26, 1957; E. C. Cordeaux, "Unmarried Parenthood," *The Lancet*, February 16, 1957.

75. AC, "Censorship Favours Abnormality," *Manchester Guardian*, March 9, 1959.

76. AC, "Havelock Ellis To-day," *Observer*, February 1, 1959.

77. Anon. [G. Legman], *The Limerick: 1700 Examples with Notes, Variants and Index* (Paris: Les Hautes Etudes, 1953).

78. *United States of America v. 31 Photographs 4-3/4 by 7 Inches in Size and Various Pictures, Books and Other Articles*; Wardell B. Pomeroy, for the Institute for Sex Research, letter to AC, March 4, 1958.

Chapter 10: Make Love, Not War (1956–1962)

1. AC, "The Individual and World Peace," *Resistance*, June 1954.
2. AC and Herbert Read, unpublished letter to the *New Statesman and Nation*, December 12, 1956.
3. Pat Arrowsmith, letter to AC, April 30, 1958.
4. Herbert Jehle, letter to AC, November 9, 1957; AC reply, undated.
5. Lawrence S. Wittner, "Blacklisting Schweitzer," *Bulletin of the Atomic Scientists*, May/June 1995.
6. AC, "The Individual and World Peace," *Resistance*, June 1954.
7. "Motley 4,000 Begin H-Bomb Procession," *Daily Telegraph*, April 5, 1958.
8. Walter E. Spradbery, letter to AC, April 10, 1958.
9. *Rip Bulkeley, Pete Goodwin, Ian Birchall, Peter Binns and Colin Sparks, "'If at First You Don't Succeed. . .': Fighting against the Bomb in the 1950s and 1960s,"* *International Socialism*, Winter 1981.
10. Interview with Nicholas Comfort, March 5, 2008.
11. Cited in Christopher Driver, *The Disarmers: A Study in Protest* (London: Hodder and Stoughton, 1964), 71.
12. George Woodcock, "Anarchism Revisited," *Commentary*, August 1968.
13. Charles Wheeler, for the British Broadcasting Corporation, letter to AC, March 27, 1958.
14. "One activist": interview with David Goodway, March 6, 2008.
15. Dorothy Frith, for the Campaign for Nuclear Disarmament, letter to AC, November 17, 1958.
16. "Bases Part of Dulles' Precaution against Peace, Doctor Says," *Eastern Daily Press*, April 12, 1958.
17. April Carter, for the Direct Action Committee against Nuclear War, letter to AC, October 20, 1958.
18. April Carter, for the Direct Action Committee against Nuclear War, letters to AC, May 5, May 9, and May 15, 1958.
19. "Motley 4,000 Begin H-Bomb Procession," *Daily Telegraph*, April 5, 1958.
20. Ibid.
21. AC, *Are You Sitting Comfortably?* (SING, 1961).
22. W. Leader, for Topic Records, letter to AC, June 26, 1958.
23. Pete Seeger, letter to AC, December 7, 1961.
24. Pete Seeger, letter to AC, April 1962.
25. Tuli Kupferberg, letter to AC, September 24, 1962.
26. Interview with Nicholas Comfort, November 19, 2021.
27. "Comfort and Niemöller Call for Action against Nuclear War," *Peace News*, April 25, 1958.
28. AC, "The Rebellion against Suicide" (text of April 20, 1958, PPU address), *Peace News*, May 2, 1958.
29. Sybil Morrison, Peace Pledge Union, letters to AC, January 27 and 30, 1959.
30. *Rip Bulkeley, Pete Goodwin, Ian Birchall, Peter Binns and Colin Sparks, "'If at First You Don't Succeed. . .,'"* *International Socialism*, Winter 1981.
31. Wendy Butler, for the Direct Action Campaign against Nuclear War, September 15, 1960; G. Michael Scott, Bertrand Russell, letters to AC, September 16, 1960.
32. Christopher Driver, *The Disarmers: A Study in Protest* (London: Hodder and Stoughton, 1964), 115.
33. AC, unpublished text, February 2, 1961.
34. Pendennis, "Sitters and Striders," *Observer*, September 19, 1961.
35. Andy B. Stroud, for Stroud Productions, letter to AC, April 8, 1964.

36. Pendennis, "Sitters and Striders," *Observer*, September 19, 1961.
37. Interview with Michael Randle, June 2009.
38. Peter Dawson, letter to AC, May 31, 1961.
39. Nicholas Comfort, *Copy!*, 455.
40. "Wire-Tapping Denied by Police," *Daily Mail*, September 12, 1961.
41. AC, unpublished article, 1989.
42. "Prison for Lord Russell and 31 Others," *Daily Mail*, September 13, 1961.
43. AC, *Are You Sitting Comfortably?* (*SING*, 1961); quoted in Ian Parker, "The Grand Old Man of Sex," *Independent*, October 2, 1994.
44. "Prison for Lord Russell and 31 Others," *Daily Mail*, September 13, 1961.
45. "Police Win Battle of Trafalgar Square," *Daily Mail*, September 18, 1961.
46. Caroline Moorehead, *Troublesome People*, 225.
47. Ann Jellicoe, letter to Ruth Comfort, September 13, 1961.
48. Marnau: Nicholas Comfort, letter to AC, September 12, 1961; Agnes (May) Harris, letter to AC, September 16, 1961.
49. AC, "News from Prison," *Peace News*, September 22, 1961.
50. Interview with Nicholas Comfort, March 5, 2008.
51. Nicholas Comfort, *Copy!*, 456.
52. Interview with Michael Randle in "Stop Calling Me 'Dr Sex,'" BBC Radio 3 documentary, September 3, 2013.
53. Murray Sayle, letter to AC, November 2, 1961; "Mystery Voice Starts Hunt for Radio Pirates," *Stevenage Pictorial*, February17, 1962.
54. AC, "Nuclear Pirates on the Air," *Peace News*, May 25, 1961.
55. Interview with Michael Randle in "Stop Calling Me Dr. Sex," BBC Radio 3 documentary, September 3, 2013.
56. AC, "Nuclear Pirates on the Air," *Peace News*, May 25, 1961.
57. Tom Baistow, "Let's Be Honest about Sex," *Daily Herald* (London), July 22, 1963.
58. Interview with AC, excerpted in "Stop Calling Me 'Dr Sex,'" BBC Radio 3 documentary, September 3, 2013.
59. Gerald Leach, letter to AC, November 18, 1961.
60. Anne Randle, letter to AC, November 5, 1967.
61. Cited in James King, *The Last Modern*, 300–301.
62. "Ban the Lot!": Caroline Moorehead, *Troublesome People*, 228.
63. Tony Judt, *Postwar: A History of Europe Since 1945* (New York: Penguin Press, 2005), 256.
64. Caroline Moorehead, *Troublesome People*, 226-–28.
65. Gerald Leach, letter to AC, November 18, 1961.
66. Cecil A. Franklin, for Routledge & Kegan Paul, letter to AC, May 18, 1951.
67. Norman Franklin, for Routledge & Kegan Paul, letter to AC, August 14, 1953.
68. Ian Parker, "The Grand Old Man of Sex," *Independent*, October 2, 1994.
69. AC, interviewed by David Goodway, March 16, 1989.
70. Ibid.
71. Interview with David Goodway, March 6, 2008.
72. AC, *The Power House*, 459-61.
73. Norman Franklin, *Routledge and Kegan Paul: 150 Years of Great Publishing* (London: Routledge, 1998), 22.
74. Herbert Read, letter to AC, September 30, 1960.
75. David Higham, letter to AC, November 17, 1960.
76. Interviews with Andrew Temple Smith, March 9, 2017, and March 30, 2017.
77. Cited in letter from David Higham to AC, February 17, 1961.
78. Jane Henderson, letter to AC, November 28, 1960.

79. Julian Huxley, letter to AC, January 4, 1962.

80. Humphrey Carpenter, *A Great Silly Grin: The British Satire Boom of the 1960s* (New York: Public Affairs, 2000), 10–12, 154–57. "Explosion onto the scene": Nicholas Comfort, *Copy!*, 43.

81. Letters from Donald MacLean to AC, February 25, March 3, and April 1, 1962.

82. Quoted in Patrick M. McGrady Jr., *The Love Doctors* (New York: Macmillan, 1972), 288.

83. See, for example, Bertrand Russell, *Marriage and Morals* (London: George Allen & Unwin, 1929).

84. Charles Radcliffe, "The Seeds of Social Destruction," *Heatwave*, no. 1 (July 1966).

85. Herbert Read, letter to AC, November 7, 1960.

86. It soon appeared as well in two anthologies, *A Garland for Dylan Thomas* and the Borestone Mountain Poetry Awards' *Best Poems of 1960*.

87. Harold Drasdo, "Alex Comfort's Art and Scope," *Anarchy*, no. 33 (November 1963).

88. Arthur E. Salmon, *Alex Comfort* (Boston: Twayne, 1978), 135–36.

89. AC, "After You, Madam," in *Haste to the Wedding* (London: Eyre & Spottiswoode, 1962), 15.

90. A. Alvarez, "With Passion and Reserve," *Observer Weekend Review*, May 6, 1962.

91. Derek Parker, "Person and Place," *Poetry Review*, Winter 1963.

92. Richard Kell, "Collections of British Poetry 1962," *Critical Survey*, Spring 1963.

93. AC, *Haste to the Wedding* (London: Eyre & Spottiswoode, 1962), jacket.

94. AC, "The Individual and World Peace," *Resistance*, June 1954.

95. Nicholas Comfort, email to author, September 2, 2021.

96. Interview with Nicholas Comfort, December 17, 2014.

97. Nicholas Comfort, "The facts of life about my father," *The Daily Telegraph*, March 30, 2000.

98. Nicholas Comfort, email to author, September 21, 2022.

99. Desmond Pond, letter to AC, July 19, 1960.

100. Pagan Kennedy, *The Dangerous Joy of Dr. Sex and Other Stories* (Santa Fe: Santa Fe Writers Project, 2008), 11.

101. David Goodway, interview with Jane Henderson Comfort, March 16, 1989.

102. Interview with Nicholas Comfort, December 17, 2014.

103. Interview with Nicholas Comfort, June 26, 2015.

104. AC, *The Joy of Sex* (New York: Crown, 1972), 14.

105. AC, "Communication," in *Haste to the Wedding* (London: Eyre & Spottiswoode, 1962), 17.

106. Interview with Nicholas Comfort, December 17, 2014.

Chapter 11: The Controversialist (1961–1965)

1. R. G. G. Price, "Come Out to Play," *Punch*, November 22, 1961.

2. "An Interview with Alex Comfort," *Practical Psychology for Physicians*, January 1975.

3. AC, *Authority and Delinquency in the Modern State*, 116–19.

4. Gerardo A. Andújar, letter to AC, December 15, 1959.

5. AC, *Darwin and the Naked Lady: Discursive Essays on Biology and Art* (New York: George Braziller, 1961), 74.

6. Quoted in Samanth Subramanian, *A Dominant Character*, 273.

7. Quoted in William DeJong-Lambert, *The Cold War Politics of Research: An Introduction to the Lysenko Affair*, 150.

8. Samanth Subramanian, *A Dominant Character*, 291.

9. J.B.S. Haldane, letter to AC, November 21, 1961.

10. AC, "Mood of the Month—XIII," *London Magazine*, November 1959.

11. AC, "Eastern Approaches," *Manchester Guardian*, January 4, 1959.

12. AC, "What 'P. C. M.' Did for Me," *Samvadadhvam: House Journal of the Indian Statistical Institute* 19, no. 1.

13. AC, letter to Krishna Dronamraju, February 24, 1983.

14. In "Portrait of J. B. S. Haldane, narrated by Lord Ritchie-Calder," *The Listener*, November 2, 1967.

15. Quoted in David Feller, "Conversation with Alex Comfort," *Oui*, December 1974.

16. Nicholas Comfort, *Copy!*, 43.

17. Tom Baistow, "Let's Be Honest about Sex," *Daily Herald* (London), July 22, 1963; AC, letter to "O'Neill," March 14, 1966.

18. Maurice Temple Smith, letter to AC, November 30, 1961.

19. Mervyn Horder, letter to AC, August 3, 1962.

20. AC, letter to W. G. Archer, February 18, 1963.

21. AC, "Lessons of the Kama Sutra," *20th Century*, Spring 1963.

22. W. G. Archer, letter to AC, February 18, 1963; letter to Rayner Unwin, February 25, 1963.

23. W. G. Archer, letter to Rayner Unwin, February 25, 1963.

24. Rayner Unwin, letter to W. G. Archer, March 6, 1963.

25. W. G. Archer, letter to Rayner Unwin, March 28, 1963.

26. Rayner Unwin, letter to AC, April 25, 1963.

27. AC, letter to Rayner Unwin, June 21, 1963.

28. W. G. Archer, letter to Rayner Unwin, June 21, 1963.

29. W. G. Archer, letter to Rayner Unwin, November 7, 1963.

30. Bruce Hunter, for David Higham Associates, letter to Rayner Unwin, November 12, 1963; Rayner Unwin, letter to Malcolm Barnes, November 25, 1963.

31. W. G. Archer, letter to Rayner Unwin, December 12, 1963.

32. Abe Yagoda, "When *Lady Chatterley's Lover* Ran Afoul of Britain's 1959 Obscenity Law, the Resulting Case Had a Cast Worthy of P. G. Wodehouse," *American Scholar*, Autumn 2010.

33. Rayner Unwin, letter to AC, December 31, 1963.

34. "One of the most-pirated books": Wendy Doniger, "Redeeming the *Kama Sutra*," excerpt, March 11, 2016, *Literary Hub*, https://lithub.com/redeeming-the-kama-sutra.

35. Rayner Unwin, letter to W.G. Archer, July 2, 1964.

36. Tandem: Ralph Stokes, for Tandem Books, letter to Joy Hill, George Allen and Unwin, March 4, 1965.

37. Robert Harben, letter to David Higham, December 3, 1965.

38. AC, *The Koka Shastra: Being the Ratirahasya of Kokkoka and Other Medieval Indian Writings on Love* (London: George Allen and Unwin, 1964), 134.

39. "Marriage Manual," *Sunday Telegraph*, June 14, 1964.

40. AC, letter to David Higham, March 14, 1964.

41. Alec R. Clark, for G. Ernest Clarke & Co., letter to AC, May 19, 1964.

42. Nicholas Comfort, *Copy!*, 62–63.

43. AC, interviewed by David Goodway, March 16, 1989.

44. Mervyn Horder, letter to AC, May 8, 1962.

45. David Higham, letter to AC, April 26, 1962.

46. Mervyn Horder, letter to AC, August 21, 1962.

47. Malcolm Muggeridge, "The Slow, Sure Death of the Upper Classes," *Sunday Mirror*, June 23, 1963.

48. Callum G. Brown, *The Battle for Christian Britain*, 156.

49. See Paula Rabinowitz, *American Pulp: How Paperbacks Brought Modernism to Main Street* (Princeton: Princeton University Press, 2014).

50. AC, "Where Freud Had Feared to Tread," *Washington Post Book World*, September 3, 1971.

51. Edna O'Brien, *Country Girl: A Memoir* (New York: Back Bay Books, 2012), 121–27.

52. Edna O'Brien, *The Love Object: Selected Stories* (New York: Little, Brown, 2015), 170.

53. Cited in Hera Cook, *The Long Sexual Revolution*, 326.

54. Many states in the United States continued to ban contraceptives until the Supreme Court's 1965 decision in *Griswold v. Connecticut*.

55. Alan Petigny, *The Permissive Society: America, 1941–1965* (New York: Cambridge University Press, 2009), 127–30.

56. Hera Cook, *The Long Sexual Revolution*, 112–13, 268, 288.

57. AC, *Sex in Society*, 17, 54.

58. Ibid., 80, 162, 165.

59. Ibid., 168–69.

60. Ibid., 146–47.

61. Ibid., 127.

62. Ibid., 111, 108–9.

63. Ibid., 95, 97, 154.

64. See John Money, Joan G. Hampson, and John Hampson, "An Examination of Some Basic Sexual Concepts: The Evidence of Human Hermaphroditism," *Bulletin of the Johns Hopkins Hospital*, October 1955.

65. AC, *Sex in Society*, 42.

66. Ibid., 136.

67. "Some readers noticed": see Canon G. B. Bentley, "The New Morality: A Christian Comment," in *Sexual Morality: Three Views*, Richard Sadler, ed. (London: Arlington Books, 1964), 43, 55.

68. AC, *Sex in Society*, 117, 89.

69. Ibid., 124–26.

70. Ibid., 132.

71. Ibid., 144, 122.

72. Ibid., 161.

73. A.S., "... or tolerance and good sense," *Sunday Times* (London), May 12, 1963; Peter Worsley, "The Healthiest Human Sport," *Guardian*, May 10, 1963.

74. Derek J. G. Holroyde, for the BBC, letter to AC, June 27, 1963.

75. Maurice Richardson, *Observer Weekend Review*, July 21, 1963.

76. Derek J. G. Holroyde, for the BBC, letter to AC, July 17, 1963.

77. Cited in Callum G. Brown, *The Battle for Christian Britain*, 154.

78. "The Harm Sex Talk Can Do ... by a Peer," *Daily Express*, date unknown, 1963.

79. Oliver Hunkin, for the BBC, letter to AC, July 19, 1963.

80. "No Comfort for B.B.C," *Sunday Telegraph*, July 21, 1963.

81. Tom Baistow, "Let's Be Honest about Sex," *Daily Herald* (London), July 22, 1963.

82. "Dr. Comfort Says It Again," *Daily Mirror*, November 16, 1963.

83. Ian Charlton, letter to the editor, *Evening Standard*, December 2, 1963.
84. "Cleric's Comments," *Barnet Press*, April 1, 1964; Mary Crozier, "Monitor on BBC TV," *Guardian*, March 16, 1963.
85. Callum G. Brown, *The Battle for Christian Britain*, 289.
86. M. L. Burnet, for the Ethical Union, letter to AC, July 16, 1963.
87. Joan Harvey, letter to AC, July 19, 1963.
88. Leslie A. Bell, letter to AC, July 19, 1963.
89. Nicolas Walter, "Disobedience and the New Pacifism," *Anarchy*, no. 14 (April 1962).
90. Pietro Ferma for the CIRA, letters to AC, late June–July, 1960.
91. AC, letter to Vito S. Goudo Jr., August 25, 1959; Gerardo A. Andújar, letter to AC, April 1, 1959; Colin Ward, letter to AC, May 9, 1959; Cesar Milstein, letters to AC, June 3 and September 6, 1959; Vito S. Goudo Jr., letters to AC, August 20 and September 15, 1959; Vito Luis Landolfi, letter to AC, September 15, 1959; Marta Guastavino, letter to AC, June 29, 1960.
92. B. Stansbury, letter to AC, July 1, 1963.

Chapter 12: "Emotional Technology" (1965–1971)

1. AC, letter to "Miss Voice," January 25, 1965.
2. AC, "Our William Blake," *Guardian*, December 3, 1970.
3. AC, "The Art of the Possible," *The Listener*, March 24, 1960.
4. AC, "A Technology of the Emotions?" in Paul A. Senft, ed., *The Human Context* (Dordrecht: Springer, 1968).
5. AC, interviewed by David Goodway, March 6, 1989.
6. Anthony Burgess, "Coming to the Crunch," *Guardian*, November 4, 1966.
7. AC, *Nature and Human Nature* (London: Wiedenfeld and Nicolson, 1966), 145.
8. Ibid., 181.
9. Ibid., 206.
10. AC, "The Professional," review of P. B. Medawar, *The Art of the Soluble*, *Guardian*, February 17, 1967.
11. Anthony Burgess, "Coming to the Crunch," *Guardian*, November 4, 1966.
12. David L. Edwards, "A Humanist on Man," *Catholic Times*, December 9, 1966.
13. AC, "A Technology of the Emotions?."
14. Ibid.
15. AC, Tasks for the Underground," *Guardian*, December 6, 1968.
16. AC, "Two Cultures No More," *Guardian*, May 16, 1968.
17. AC, "Chance and Necessity: Monod's Evolutionary Position," *Meanjin Quarterly*, September 1972.
18. "One Pair of Eyes: Dr. Alex Comfort, A Traveller in the Dream Time," BBC2: June 3, 1967, post-production script.
19. "Traveller," *Morning Star*, June 7, 1967; Michael Billington, "Stimulating Weekend TV," *Times* (London), June 5, 1967.
20. H. G. Wells, Julian Huxley, and G. P. Wells, *The Science of Life* (New York: Doubleday Doran, 1931), 503.
21. See Mary Ziegler, "Eugenic Feminism: Mental Hygiene, the Women's Movement, and the Campaign for Eugenic Legal Reform, 1900–1935," *Harvard Journal of Law and Gender* 31 (2008).
22. Gordon Wolstenholme, ed., *Man and His Future: A Ciba Foundation Volume* (Boston: Little, Brown, 1963), 342, 352–53.

23. Ibid., 342, 288–89.

24. AC, "Genes before Customs," *Guardian*, September 9, 1969.

25. "Rationalistic exploration of feeling": AC, "Completely Human," *Guardian*, June 7, 1968.

26. Krishna Dronamraju, email to author, July 11, 2015.

27. Krishna Dronamraju, interview with author, September 15, 2015.

28. AC, *Ageing: The Biology of Senescence* (New York: Holt, Rinehart and Winston, 1964), 231.

29. AC, *The Conquest of Ageing* (Saskatoon: University of Saskatchewan, 1968), University Lectures 16.

30. AC, *Ageing: The Biology of Senescence* (New York: Holt, Rinehart and Winston, 1964), 266, (quote), 254–63.

31. AC, *The Process of Ageing* (New York: Signet, 1965), 114–15.

32. Ibid., 39–40.

33. Ibid., 19.

34. Ibid., 133–35.

35. AC, interviewed by David Goodway, March 16, 1989.

36. AC, "Science and Longevity," *Guardian*, March 31, 1966.

37. AC, "Life Can Begin at 40," *Sunday Times Magazine*, November 12, 1967.

38. Paul Bulleit, "Goal of Expert on Aging Isn't Fountain of Youth," *Louisville Courier-Journal*, April 6, 1968.

39. "Slowing Down Aging Forecast," *Saskatoon Star-Phoenix*, October 5, 1967.

40. Quoted in Beverley Jackson, "By the Way," *Santa Barbara Chronicle*, July 25, 1969.

41. "Comfort on Ageing," *Catholic Herald*, October 4, 1968.

42. AC, "New Cures for Old Age," *Washington Post Book World*, November 3, 1968.

43. AC, "Faust, Prometheus, and Methuselah," *Meanjin Quarterly*, June 1969.

44. "Expert Looks at the Search for Eternal Youth," *Oxford Mail*, September 9, 1968.

45. Malcolm Muggeridge, "Condemned to Life," *Observer*, September 5, 1965.

46. AC, "Life Can Begin at 40."

47. AC, *The Process of Ageing*, 132–33.

48. Bertrand Russell, letters to AC, October 8 and 17, 1966; AC, letter to Russell, October 12, 1966.

49. AC, "On Gerontophobia," *Medical Opinion and Review*, September 1967.

50. See Erdman Palmore and Kenneth Manton, "Ageism Compared to Racism and Sexism," *Journal of Gerontology*, July 1973.

51. Carl Bernstein, "Age and Race Fears Seen in Housing Opposition," *Washington Post*, March 7, 1969.

52. Robert N. Butler, "Age-ism: A New Form of Bigotry," *Gerontologist*, December 1969.

53. Cited in Moira Martin, "Medical Knowledge and Medical Practice: Geriatric Medicine in the 1950s," *Social History of Medicine*, December 1995.

54. J. L. Halliday, letter to AC, March 28, 1950.

55. Dorothy Porter, "The Decline of Social Medicine in Britain in the 1960s," in *Social Medicine and Medical Sociology in the Twentieth Century* (Amsterdam: Editions Rodopi, 1997), 112–13.

56. AC, *The Conquest of Ageing*.

57. Peter Medawar, letter to the Medical Research Council, January 29, 1969.

58. P. B. and J. S. Medawar, *The Life Science: Current Ideas in Biology* (New York: Harper & Row, 1977), 159.

59. AC, letter to Marilyn Yalom, December 17, 1968.

60. See P. B. Medawar et al., "Aging," *The Listener*, July 18, 1971.

61. Tiago Moreira and Paolo Palladino, "Ageing between Gerontology and Biomedicine," *Biosocieties*, December 2009.

62. Luigi Ferrucci, "The Baltimore Longitudinal Study of Aging (BLSA): A 50-Year-Long Journey and Plans for the Future," *Journals of Gerontology: Series A, Biological Sciences and Medical Sciences*, December 2008.

63. AC, "Must We Grow Old?" *Sunday Times* (London), February 17, 1963.

64. J. W. Hollingsworth, A. Hashizume, and Seymour Jablon, "Correlations between Tests of Aging in Hiroshima Subjects—An Attempt to Define 'Physiologic Age,'" *Yale Journal of Biology and Medicine*, August 1965.

65. AC, "Test-Battery to Measure Ageing in Man," *The Lancet*, December 27, 1969.

66. AC, "Gerontology—Implications for Future Mortality Experience," *Transactions of the Faculty of Actuaries* 32, no. 235 (1969–71).

67. AC, "Basic Research in Gerontology," *Gerontologia* 16 (1970).

68. AC, I. Youhotsky-Gore, and K. Pathmanathan, "Effect of Ethoxyquin on the Longevity of C3H Mice," *Nature*, January 22, 1971.

69. John G. Cartwright, Gottlieb Duttweiler Institute for Economic and Social Sciences, letters to AC, May 26 and June 2, 1971.

70. AC, "The Selling of Soft Science," *Medical Opinion*, April 1972

71. P. B. Medawar and others, "Aging," *The Listener*, July 18, 1971.

Chapter 13: The Traveling Friar (1964–1970)

1. Samanth Subramanian, *A Dominant Character*, 140–44.

2. In "Portrait of J. B. S. Haldane, narrated by Lord Ritchie-Calder," *The Listener*, November 2, 1967.

3. AC, "Completely Human," *Guardian*, June 7, 1968.

4. Dan Callahan, letter to AC, January 6, 1968.

5. AC, letter to Dan Callahan, January 9, 1968.

6. AC, "I wonder where the man I was is gone—. . .," in *Poems for Jane*, 42.

7. Quoted in Hugh Kenner, "The Comfort behind *The Joy of Sex*," *New York Times Sunday Magazine*, October 27, 1974.

8. AC, letter to Marilyn Yalom, February 19, 1969.

9. Quoted in Beverley Jackson, "By the Way," *Santa Barbara Chronicle*, July 25, 1969.

10. "Nick . . . joined CongSoc": Nicholas Comfort, *Copy!*, 49.

11. Quoted in Jerry LeBlanc, "The Joy of Alex Comfort," *Milwaukee Journal*, April 25, 1975.

12. AC, *Poems for Jane* (New York: Crown, 1979), 26.

13. Ibid., 62; Madeleine Jenewein, letter to AC, date unknown, 1967.

14. Marilyn Yalom, letter to AC, January 18, 1968.

15. Marilyn Yalom, interviewed by author, June 9, 2009.

16. AC, "By the gate of the garden. . .," in *Poems for Jane*, 54.

17. AC, "Young Sir or Madam, though you are not mine. . .," in *Poems for Jane*, 51.

18. Interview with Eve Yalom, July 15, 2009.

19. Interview with Marilyn Yalom, February 19, 2009.

20. Interview with Marilyn Yalom, June 9, 2009.

21. "Alex's encouragement": interview with Irvin Yalom, June 9, 2009.

22. Interview with Leonard Hayflick, February 17, 2010.
23. AC, letter to Marilyn Yalom, November 13, 1971.
24. AC, letter to Marilyn Yalom, August 12, 1968.
25. Marilyn Yalom, letter to AC, undated, probably early 1973.
26. "Nudes in Post—MPs Call for a Ban," *Sunday Times* (London), December 7, 1964.
27. Sir Richard Acland, letter to AC, November 28, 1964.
28. AC, "Reading about Sex," *Guardian*, December 15, 1968.
29. AC, letter to the editor, *Guardian*, March 1, 1965
30. Iris Murdoch to Brigid Brophy, in *Living on Paper: Letters from Iris Murdoch 1934–1995*, ed. Avril Horner and Anne Rowe (Princeton: Princeton University Press, 2015), 307–8.
31. Bob Guccione, letter to AC, March 24, 1965.
32. David Higham, letter to AC, December 30, 1965.
33. AC, "Sexual Response," *The Lancet*, May 7, 1966.
34. AC, "Venus Observed," *New Statesman*, May 6, 1966; "Sexual Response," *The Lancet*, May 7, 1966.
35. AC, letter to William Masters, August 25, 1966.
36. W. H. Masters, letter to AC, September 2, 1966.
37. Lesley A. Hall, *Sex, Gender and Social Change in Britain since 1880*, 30–31, 175.
38. "Dialogue on Sex and Morality" (extracts from *Sex and Morality*), *Guardian*, October 17, 1966.
39. David Holbrook, "The New Morality and Pornography," *Catholic Herald*, November 18, 1966.
40. AC, "The 'New Morality,'" *Catholic Herald*, December 9, 1966.
41. David Holbrook, "The 'New Morality' and Pornography: David Holbrook Replies to Dr. Comfort," *Catholic Herald*, December 16, 1966.
42. "Words of Comfort," *Observer*, January 1, 1967.
43. Minutes of Books and Broadcasts Ltd board meeting, March 3, 1966; AC, letter to R. G. Davis-Poynter, April 27, 1971.
44. Phyllis and Eberhard Kronhausen, letter to AC, January 4, 1967.
45. AC, *The Anxiety Makers: Some Curious Preoccupations of the Medical Profession* (New York: Dell, 1970), 192.
46. Ibid., 186–87.
47. "Doctors and Anxiety," *Birmingham Post*, June 17, 1967.
48. Michael Rapoport, "Knocking on Open Doors," *Morning Star*, June 22, 1967.
49. Anthony Storr, "Horror of the Body," *Sunday Times* (London), June 18, 1967.
50. Malcolm Bradbury, "Are We Less Naïve?" *The Listener*, July 13, 1967.
51. Charles Rycroft, "Awful Warnings," *Observer*, July 30, 1967.
52. AC, *The Anxiety Makers*, 198–99.
53. Gordon Fielden, letter to Robert Harben, June 17, 1965.
54. AC, "The Great Agrippa," undated synopsis.
55. Minutes of Books and Broadcasts Ltd board meeting, August 14, 1966.
56. Minutes of Books and Broadcasts Ltd board meeting, October 19, 1966.
57. AC, letter to Morton Grosser, December 10, 1968.
58. AC, letter to Irving Sarnoff, December 2, 1968.
59. Laboratory of Molecular Radiology, Institute of Medical Radiology, letter to AC, February 20, 1968.
60. Interview with Zhores Medvedev, February 18, 2010.
61. Z. A. Medvedev, "Alex Comfort (1920–2000) Known and Unknown: A Personal Account," *Experimental Gerontology* 35 (2000).

62. Interview with Zhores Medvedev, February 18, 2010.
63. Ibid.
64. Interview with Zhores Medvedev, February 20, 1968.
65. Ruth Prothero, letter to AC, August 4, 1962.
66. AC, "Can't Labour Do Better?," *New Statesman*, March 12, 1965.
67. Gerald Frost, "Journal de Combat of the Cold War," *The Critic*, April 2020.
68. AC, "Third Opinion," *Guardian*, May 12, 1967.
69. John Wain, "In Support of 'Encounter,'" *Guardian*, May 13, 1967.
70. Michael Randle and Pat Pottle, *The Blake Escape: How We Freed George Blake—and Why* (London: Harrap Books, 1989), 245–58.
71. Ibid., 52.
72. Interview with Michael Randle, June 2009.
73. Barrie Penrose, "Author Knew of Spy Escape Case; Michael Randle and Pat Pottle," *Sunday Times* (London), January 29, 1989.
74. Michael Randle, letter to AC, June 20, 1990.
75. Henry Hemming, "Confessions of a Lunchtime Spy," *Wall Street Journal*, May 8–9, 2021.
76. Michael Randle and Pat Pottle, *The Blake Escape*, 168–83.
77. AC, "Dangerous Men," *Guardian*, October 13, 1967.
78. Anne Randle, letter to AC, November 5, 1967; *Guardian*, November 24, 1967.
79. Terry Chandler, letters to AC, October 17, 1967, and March 8, 1968.
80. Neville Armstrong, letters to AC, February 23 and March 8, 1967.
81. "Suggested to him by James Mitchell": John Calder, letter to AC, February 16, 1967.
82. AC, letter to John Calder, February 16, 1967.
83. John Calder, letter to AC, February 17, 1967.
84. "Free Thinkers Unite! The Hat Will Be Passing Among You," *Daily Mirror*, April 18, 1967.
85. John Calder, letter to AC, November 27, 1967.
86. "John Calder: 'The Reformers Are Fighting,'" *Illustrated London News*, April 13, 1968.
87. AC, letter to Fritz Verzar, December 8, 1967.
88. AC, "The 'Leonardo da Vinci Syndrome,'" *Medical Opinion*, September 1971.
89. AC, letters to David Carver, both November 21, 1967.
90. AC, "Medvedev's Patriotic War against the Pigs," *Guardian*, July 29, 1971.
91. AC, "Who's crazy?," *Guardian*, November 25, 1971.
92. Helen Hall for Michael Murphy, letter to AC, February 20, 1970.
93. Theodore Roszak, letter to AC, February 25, 1970.
94. Theodore Roszak, letter to AC, March 17, 1970.
95. Theodore Roszak, letter to AC, April 10, 1971.
96. Nahum Waxman, letter to AC, November 14, 1969.
97. AC, letter to Marilyn Yalom, June 21, year unknown [pre-1973].
98. AC, letter to Marilyn Yalom, April 10, 1970.
99. Roy L. Walford, letter to AC, March 26, 1968.
100. Pat McGrady, letter to AC, March 3, 1970.
101. Patrick M. McGrady Jr., *The Love Doctors* (New York: Macmillan, 1972), 288.
102. Interview with Jennifer O'Farrell, February 5, 2019.
103. "Middle-class ostentatious": interview with Jonathan Dana, March 22, 2018.
104. AC, letter to Albert V. Freeman, April 4, 1972.
105. AC, letter to Marty Zitter, September 30, 1972.
106. AC, "Nudes—Who's Eccentric?" *Reflections* 1, no. 3 (1966).

107. AC, ed., *More Joy of Sex: A Lovemaking Companion to* The Joy of Sex (New York: Simon & Schuster, 1974), 159.

108. Interview with Jonathan Dana, March 29, 2018.

109. Interviews with Barbara Williamson, March 16 and June 28, 2018, and February 19, 2019.

110. Interview with Peter Lert, September 10, 2019.

111. Interview with Barbara Williamson, February 13, 2019.

112. Interview with Jonathan Dana, March 22, 2018.

113. Gay Talese, *Thy Neighbor's Wife* (Garden City, NY: Doubleday, 1980), 349.

114. "Freaked all the guys out": interview with Barbara Williamson, March 16, 2018.

115. Interview with Betty Dodson, November 15, 2013.

116. AC, message to the Peace Pledge Union Conference, *The Pacifist*, April 1969.

117. AC, "The Anti-Pig Movement," *Guardian*, May 22, 1969.

118. AC, "A New Sensibility," *Center Magazine*, April 1971.

119. AC, "Approaching the Watershed," *Guardian*, October 10, 1969.

120. AC, "The Shift in Awareness," *Guardian*, June 10, 1971.

121. AC, *"What Rough Beast?" and "What Is a Doctor?"* (Vancouver: Pendejo Press, 1971).

122. AC, "The Shift in Awareness," *Guardian*, June 10, 1971.

Chapter 14: Sex for Pleasure (1963–1971)

1. Julian Huxley, "The Faith of a Humanist," *Woman's Hour*, BBC Radio, March 15, 1960.
2. Interview with Nicholas Comfort, September 4, 2021.
3. AC, *The Koka Shastra*, 75.
4. AC, *Sex in Society*, 155.
5. AC, *The Koka Shastra*, 60.
6. AC, letter to Gershon Legman, May 16, 1966.
7. AC, *The Koka Shastra*, 66; *Sex in Society*, 17.
8. John Doheny, letters to AC, May 3, 1963, August 14, 1964; Wayne Burns, letter to AC, December 20, 1967.
9. Susan Davis, "Eros Meets Civilization: Gershon Legman Confronts the Post Office," in Alexander Cockburn and Jeffrey St. Clair, eds., *Serpents in the Garden: Liaisons with Culture & and Sex* (Petrolia and Oakland CA: Counterpunch and AK Press, 2004), 253–70.
10. AC, letter to Gershon Legman, August 11, 1949.
11. Gershon Legman, letter to AC, November 14, 1949.
12. AC, review of *The Horn Book: Studies in Erotic Folklore and Bibliography*, *Folklore*, Winter 1964.
13. Gershon Legman, letter to AC, May 20, 1966.
14. AC, letter to Gershon Legman, May 23, 1966.
15. Gershon Legman, letter to AC, May 20, 1966.
16. Gershon Legman, letter to AC. May 20, 1966.
17. AC, letter to Gershon Legman, May 23, 1966.
18. Gershon Legman, letter to AC, May 25, 1966.
19. Gershon Legman, letter to AC, December 5, 1966.
20. David Higham, letter to Neville Armstrong, March 29, 1965.
21. Maria Popova, "The Book That Taught Vonnegut about Sex," *Atlantic*, December 6, 2012.

22. Kari I. Nordberg, "The Circulation and Commercialization of Sexual Knowledge: The Celebrity Sexologists Inge and Sten Hegeler," in John Östling et al., eds., *Circulation of Knowledge: Explorations in the History of Knowledge* (Lund: Nordic Academic Press, 2018), 56–67.

23. Ibid., 65.

24. Inge and Sten Hegeler, "Sex Mechanics: *Penthouse* Interview," *Penthouse*, October 1971.

25. "An ABC of Love," *Observer*, February 2, 1969.

26. Jack Booth, "Med Students Get Comforting," *Philadelphia Bulletin*, date unknown.

27. J, *The Sensuous Woman* (New York: Dell, 1971), 27.

28. "Two weeks to write": Linda Deutsch, "From Sex to Senior Citizens," *State* (Columbia, SC), January 27, 1975.

29. AC, *The Joy of Sex: A Cordon Bleu Guide to Lovemaking* (New York: Crown, 1972), 150.

30. Interview with Max Monsarrat, November 18, 2009.

31. Lesley A. Hall, "'The English Have Hot-Water Bottles': The Morganatic Marriage between Sexology and Medicine in Britain since William Acton," in *Sexual Knowledge, Sexual Science: The History of Attitudes to Sexuality*, ed. Roy Porter and Mikuláš Teich (Cambridge, UK: Cambridge University Press, 1994), 362–63.

32. AC, *The Joy of Sex*, 15.

33. Ibid., 51.

34. Ibid., 9.

35. Amy DeRogatis, "What Would Jesus Do? Sexuality and Salvation in Protestant Evangelical Sex Manuals, 1950s to the Present," *Church History: Studies in Christianity and Culture*, March 2005.

36. "On Right and Wrong," *Church Times*, October 10, 1966.

37. AC, *The Joy of Sex*, 78.

38. Ibid., 14, 11.

39. Kildare Dobbs, "Author of *The Joy of Sex* 'a Sort of Travelling Friar,'" *Toronto Star*, April 15, 1974.

40. AC, *The Joy of Sex*, 118, 11.

41. Ibid., 9.

42. AC, *The Joy of Sex*, 140.

43. Ibid., 6, 167.

44. Ibid., 182, 223, 174, 231, 247.

45. Ibid., 73, 96, 174, 124, 138, 112.

46. Ibid., 220, 237.

47. AC, "A Girl Needs a Father," *The Listener*, April 16, 1973.

48. AC, *The Joy of Sex*, 103, 16.

49. AC, "Havelock Ellis To-day," *Observer*, February 1, 1959.

50. Meryl Altman, "Everything They Always Wanted You to Know: The Ideology of Popular Sex Literature," in *Pleasure and Danger: Exploring Female Sexuality*, ed. Carole S. Vance (London: Pandora, 1989), 116–17.

51. AC, *The Joy of Sex*, 80–81, 133.

52. Ibid., 85.

53. Ibid., 246, 103, 159.

54. Ibid., 169–70, 241, 248.

55. AC, letter to Lester A. Kirkendall, June 16, 1972.

56. AC, *The Joy of Sex*, 170.

57. Ibid., 110, 228, 106, 246.

58. Ibid., 158, 223.

59. Cited in M. E. Melody and Linda M. Peterson, *Teaching America about Sex: Marriage Guides and Sex Manuals from the Late Victorians to Dr. Ruth* (New York: New York University Press, 1999), 174.

60. Author's examination of AC files at Kinsey Institute, September 2013.

61. Michael Burbidge, letter to AC, November 7, 1971.

62. AC, letter to Michael Burbidge, November 9, 1971.

63. AC, letter to Allan Horsfall, March 28 1972.

64. AC, "All Sorts and Conditions," *Guardian*, July 5, 1973.

65. Judith Butler, *Bodies That Matter: On the Discursive Limits of "Sex"* (New York: Routledge, 1993), 221–22, 229–30.

66. Cynthia Gorney, "Locking Her Up," *New York Times*, August 5, 2018. See also Scott W. Stern, *The Trials of Nina McCall: Sex, Surveillance, and the Decades-Long Government Plan to Imprison "Promiscuous" Women* (Boston: Beacon Press, 2018).

67. AC, *The Joy of Sex*, 248.

68. Ibid., 195, 216, 211.

69. Rosalind Brunt, "'An Immense Verbosity': Permissive Sexual Advice in the 1970s," in *Feminism, Culture and Politics*, Rosalind Brunt and Caroline Rowan, eds. (London: Lawrence and Wishart, 1982), 161.

70. Ibid., 164.

71. Wendy Doniger, "A Fresh Look at India's Erotic Classic," *Wall Street Journal*, March 19–20, 2015.

72. Jay Gertzman, email to author, April 1, 2022.

73. AC, *The Joy of Sex*, 204.

74. AC, interviewed by Kenneth Hudson, "Towards a Technology of Human Behaviour?" *The Technologist*, date unknown.

75. AC, *The Joy of Sex*, 7.

76. See Herbert Read, *The Meaning of Art* (Baltimore: Penguin Books, 1967).

77. Desmond Morris, *The Naked Ape: A Zoologist's Study of the Human Animal* (London: Jonathan Cape, 1967).

78. Interview with Desmond Morris, March 16, 2016.

79. "The Naked Ape Steps Out," BBC News, October 12, 1967.

80. AC, "Likelihood of Human Pheromones," *Nature* 230 (April 1971).

81. David Feller, "Conversation with Alex Comfort," *Oui*, December 1974.

82. Rosalind Brunt, "'An Immense Verbosity,'" 167.

Chapter 15: Making *Joy* (1971–1972)

1. Susan Sontag, "The Pornographic Imagination," *Partisan Review*, Spring 1967.

2. Mailer cited in John Heidenry, *What Wild Ecstasy: The Rise and Fall of the Sexual Revolution* (New York: Simon & Schuster, 1997), 192–93.

3. Ibid., 160–61.

4. Ibid., 101, 63–64.

5. Anne Koedt, "The Myth of the Vaginal Orgasm," in *Notes from the First Year* (New York: New York Radical Feminists, 1968).

6. Interview with Erica Jong, December 7, 2020.

7. Pagan Kennedy, "The Pregnancy Test Scandal," *New York Times*, July 31, 2016.

8. AC, letter to Sandstone Foundation, April 4, 1972.

9. AC, *The Joy of Sex*, 6.

10. Interview with Carmen Callil, May 13, 2015.

11. John Boothe, email to author, May 19, 2015.
12. Interview with Carmen Callil, May 13, 2015.
13. John Boothe, email to author, June 3, 2015.
14. "Three million copies": Geoffrey Robertson, "The Trial of *Lady Chatterley's Lover*," *Guardian*, October 22, 2010.
15. John Boothe, email to author, May 19, 2015.
16. John Powell, "Somewhere over the Rainbird," *New Scientist*, January 11, 1979.
17. R. G. Davis-Poynter, letter to AC, March 18, 1971.
18. James Mitchell, letter to AC, August 1, 1969.
19. James Mitchell, letter to AC, August 14, 1969.
20. Interview with John Boothe, May 21, 2015.
21. Ibid.
22. James Mitchell, "How I Loved Billy," *Guardian*, June 1, 1966.
23. AC, "Doctor Graham and His Converts," *Guardian*, June 10, 1966.
24. Interview with John Boothe, May 21, 2015.
25. Max Monsarrat, "Mitchell Beazley: My Role in Their Rise and Fall," unpublished manuscript, 2008.
26. Ibid.
27. AC, *The Joy of Sex*, 189.
28. Hugh Kenner, "The Comfort behind the Joy of Sex," *New York Times Sunday Magazine*, October 27, 1974.
29. Interview with Tony Cobb, November 17, 2015.
30. Peter Kindersley, email to author, April 13, 2015.
31. Max Monsarrat, "Mitchell Beazley: My Role in Their Rise and Fall."
32. AC, letter to James Mitchell, August 16, 1971.
33. James Mitchell, letter to AC, May 11, 1972.
34. James Mitchell, letter to AC, October 1, 1971.
35. Comment made "during a panel discussion on fetishism, open marriage, transvestism, etc.," quoted in untitled news brief, *San Antonio Evening News*, December 5, 1974.
36. AC, letter to David Holloway, October 30, 1979.
37. Max Monsarrat, "Mitchell Beazley: My Role in Their Rise and Fall."
38. Jack Schnedler, "'The Joy of Sex,' Our Hottest Bestseller," *Chicago Daily News*, May 29, 1974.
39. Interview with Christopher Foss, in *The Joy of Sex*, documentary (Twenty Twenty Television, broadcast December 18, 2000).
40. Interview with Max Monsarrat, in *The Joy of Sex*, documentary (Twenty Twenty Television, broadcast December 18, 2000).
41. Interview with Peter Kindersley, in *The Joy of Sex*, documentary (Twenty Twenty Television, broadcast December 18, 2000).
42. Quoted in David Feller, "Conversation with Alex Comfort," *Oui*, December 1974.
43. Interview with Peter Kindersley, October 26, 2009.
44. Interview with Charles Raymond, in *The Joy of Sex*, documentary (Twenty Twenty Television, broadcast December 18, 2000).
45. Interview with Edeltraud Raymond, in *The Joy of Sex*, documentary (Twenty Twenty Television, broadcast December 18, 2000).
46. Ibid.
47. "Huge amount of photos": interview with Peter Kindersley, October 26, 2009.
48. AC, introduction to Philip Rawson, *Erotic Art of the East: The Sexual Theme in Oriental Painting and Sculpture* (New York: G. P. Putnam's, 1968), 21.

49. Cordelia Hebblethwaite, "How the Joy of Sex Was Illustrated," BBC World Service, October 26, 2011.

50. Interview with Max Monsarrat, November 18, 2009.

51. James Mitchell, letter to AC, December 1, 1971.

52. Dick Seaver, letter to AC, May 20, 1971.

53. Michael Rosenthal, *Barney: Grove Press and Barney Rossett—America's Maverick Publisher and His Battle against Censorship* (New York: Arcade, 2017), 9.

54. Interview with Peter Kindersley, October 26, 2009.

55. Max Monsarrat, email to author, November 3, 2022.

56. Interview with Dick Snyder, April 15, 2014.

57. AC, letter to Alan Harrington, September 26, 1972; Franklynn Pearson, "The Big Publishers in Publishing," *Publishers Weekly*, date unknown.

58. Quoted in David Feller, "Conversation with Alex Comfort," *Oui*, December 1974.

59. Quoted in Jerry LeBlanc, "The Joy of Alex Comfort," *Milwaukee Journal*, April 25, 1975.

60. AC, letter to William Masters, February 9, 1972.

61. *The Joy of Sex*, documentary (Twenty Twenty Television, broadcast December 18, 2000).

62. AC, letter to James Mitchell, October 1, 1971.

63. James Mitchell, letter to AC, December 1, 1971.

64. James Mitchell, letter to AC, May 5, 1972.

65. AC, letter to James Mitchell, May 5, 1972

66. James Mitchell, letter to AC, May 5, 1972.

67. Callum G. Brown, *The Battle for Christian Britain*, 190.

68. Amy C. Whipple, "Speaking for Whom? The 1971 Festival of Light and the Search for the 'Silent Majority,'" *Contemporary British History* 24, no. 3 (2010).

69. Jonathan Green and Nicholas J. Karolides, *Encyclopedia of Censorship*, rev. ed. (New York: Facts on File, 2005), 329.

70. Interview with Christopher Foss, March 27, 2015.

71. Interview with Charles and Edeltraud Raymond, in *The Joy of Sex*, documentary (Twenty Twenty Television, broadcast December 18, 2000).

72. Gay Talese, *Thy Neighbor's Wife*, 398–401.

73. Ibid., 388–89.

74. Peter Kindersley, email to author, April 13, 2015.

75. AC, note to Linda Roberts, November 1977.

76. AC, letter to Hugh Hefner, date unknown, 1972; "Crown Reports. . . ," *Publishers Weekly*, October 30, 1972.

77. Interview with Peter Kindersley, in *The Joy of Sex*, documentary (Twenty Twenty Television, broadcast December 18, 2000).

Chapter 16: *Joy* to the World (1972–1973)

1. "Crown Reports. . . ," *Publishers Weekly*, October 30, 1972.

2. Full-page ad, "People Seeking Justice for Prescott and Purdie," *The Guardian*, January 27, 1972.

3. AC, "Stoke Newington Eight," *The Guardian*, September 9, 1972.

4. Roy L. Walford, "The Joy of Sex," *Los Angeles Free Press*, September 22, 1972.

5. Interview with Bruce Harris, July 30, 2014.

6. Here and following paragraphs: interview with Alan Kahn, August 7, 2014.

7. Sam Binkley, *Getting Loose: Lifestyle Consumption in the 1970s* (Durham, NC: Duke University Press, 2007), 125.

8. Our Bodies Ourselves, "History," http://www.ourbodiesourselves.org/history.

9. Anthony Storr, "'Bed Is the Place to Play,'" *Washington Post*, October 2, 1972.

10. James McCary, "Uninhibited and Adventurous Sex," *Houston Chronicle*, October 22, 1972.

11. Peter S. Prescott, "Please Don't Come in the Garden, Maude," *Newsweek*, August 1973.

12. "The Joy of Sex," *Playboy*, November 1972.

13. Michael Perkins, "The Joy of Sex," *SCREW*, December 12, 1972.

14. M. Petchesky, "*Cosmopolitan's Love Guide* and *The Joy of Sex*," *Ms.*, November 1972.

15. Larry Swindell, "The Joy of Sex," *Philadelphia Inquirer*, date unknown.

16. Nora Sayre, "Ahh!" *New York Times*, February 11, 1973.

17. Ellen Goodman, "Here's a Coffee Table Number. . . ," *Boston Globe*, March 11, 1973.

18. Mopsy Strange Kennedy, "The 'No-nonsense' School vs. the 'Please-Give-Me-Back-My-Nonsense' School," *New York Times Book Review*, January 14, 1973.

19. Rick Wasko, "'The Joy of Sex': Controversial Book Attracting Readers," *Beaver County (PA) Times*, July 5, 1974.

20. Interview with Annie Sprinkle, November 2, 2018.

21. Dan Savage, "The Doctor of Love," *New York Times Magazine*, January 7, 2001.

22. Jennifer Weiner, "The Innocence of Playboy," *New York Times*, October 18, 2015.

23. Laura Berman, "The Joy of Sex, Updated," *Wall Street Journal*, April 27, 2015.

24. Interview with Bruce Harris, July 30, 2014.

25. Interview with Dick Snyder, September 30, 2015.

26. "Will the real Alexander Comfort please stand up? Come on. There can be no such person." Ana Carter Smith, letter to the editor, *Center Report* (Center for the Study of Democratic Institutions), April 1973.

27. Interview with Peter Kindersley, in *The Joy of Sex*, documentary (Twenty Twenty Television, 2001).

28. Ruthe Stein, "Sex with Comfort," *San Francisco Chronicle*, November 1, 1975; Jon Franklin, "Author (4 Million Copies) Sheds Daylight on Sex," *Chicago Sun-Times*, May 14, 1975.

29. John F. Baker, "Dr. Alex Comfort," *Publishers Weekly*, October 18, 1976.

30. This paragraph and the following: Jean Sharley Taylor, "Sex Manual sans Plain Brown Wrapper," *Los Angeles Times*, November 5, 1972.

31. Interview with Alan Mirken, May 2, 2014.

32. Miriam Behrman, letter to AC, September 13, 1973.

33. Allan J. Stormont, General Publishing Limited, letter to AC, November 24, 1972.

34. Lotta Dempsey, "New Book Encourages Sex for Mature," *Toronto Star*, January 4, 1973.

35. Kildare Dobbs, "Author of *The Joy of Sex* 'a Sort of Traveling Friar,'" *Toronto Star*, April 18, 1974.

36. AC, "Sexuality in a Zero Growth Society," *Center Report* (Center for the Study of Democratic Institutions), December 1972.

37. Ibid.

38. Various respondents, "First Class Mail," *Center Report*, April 1973.

39. George B. Murphy, letter to the editor, *Medical Opinion*, September 3, 1972.

40. AC, "Alexander Comfort Replies to His Critics," *Center Report*, August 1973.

41. "Swinging Future, *Time*, January 8, 1973.

42. Editor's note, *Center Report*, April 1973.

43. Jean Sharley Taylor, "Sex Manual sans Plain Brown Wrapper," *Los Angeles Times*, November 5, 1972.

44. David Holbrook, "Does the Marriage Council Need Some Guidance?," *Daily Mail*, April 6, 1973.

45. Stuart Jeffries, "Relate: 75 Years of Marriage Guidance," *Guardian*, October 26, 2013.

46. David Holbrook, "Joys of Sex," *The Listener*, May 10, 1973.

47. Gershon Legman, letter to AC, January 4, 1972.

48. AC, letter to *The Listener*, May 10, 1973.

49. AC, letter to David Holbrook, May 11, 1973.

50. David Holbrook, letter to AC, May 31, 1972.

51. See Amia Srinivasan, "Short Cuts," *London Review of Books*, October 6, 2022.

Chapter 17: Divorce (1973)

1. Interview with John Boothe, May 21, 2015.

2. Quoted in David Feller, "Conversation with Alex Comfort," *Oui*, December 1974.

3. John Boothe, email to author, June 5, 2015.

4. AC, letter to James Mitchell, May 7, 1972; James Mitchell, letters to AC, May 8 and May 24, 1972.

5. AC, letter to William Masters, November 16, 1972.

6. AC, letter to Nat Wartels, November 30, 1972; Herbert Michelman, letter to AC, December 1, 1972; AC, letter to Herbert Michelman, December 5, 1972.

7. AC, letter to William Masters, November 16, 1972; AC, letter to John Beazley, November 16, 1972.

8. Interview with Marilyn Yalom, June 9, 2009.

9. Interview with Nicholas Comfort, December 17, 2014.

10. Interview with Nicholas Comfort, June 26, 2015.

11. Jane Henderson court papers, courtesy of Nicholas Comfort, March 9, 2022.

12. Interview with Nicholas Comfort, December 17, 2014.

13. Ian Parker, "The Grand Old Man of Sex," *Independent*, October 2, 1994.

14. AC, "Sexuality in a Zero Growth Society," *Center Report*, December 1972.

15. Interview with Nicholas Comfort, June 26, 2015.

16. Interview with Nicholas Comfort, September 30, 2015.

17. John Boothe and William Miller, letter to James Mitchell and John Beazley, December 12, 1982.

18. Interview with Zhores Medvedev, February 18, 2010.

19. Interview with Zhores Medvedev, February 23, 2010.

20. AC, letter to the members of the Forum for Contemporary History, June 4, 1973.

21. Harvey Wheeler, "Alex Comfort's Biology of Ontology: Implications for Gerontology, Phenomenology and the Philosophy of Science," *Experimental Gerontology* 33, nos. 1–2 (1998)

22. John. D. Lowry, "'Think Tank' Thinks Economy," *Dispatch* (Lexington, DC), July 9, 1975.

23. AC, letter to William Masters, October 19, 1972.

24. AC, letter to "Ramsay," March 3, 1972; James Mitchell, letter to AC, May 3, 1972.

25. "Royalties and 'Joy of Sex,'" *Washington Post*, May 14, 1975.

26. AC, letter to "Ramsay," March 3, 1972.

27. AC, letter to A. Leithead, Wilkinson Kimbers & Staddon, Solicitors, January 1974.

28. AC, letter to L.A. Kirkendall, August 20, 1973.

29. Edward Engberg, "Hutchinsland," *New Republic*, July 21, 1979.

30. Interview with Barbara Williamson, June 28, 2018.

31. Barbara Williamson, email to author, November 10, 2022.

32. AC, letter to Marilyn Yalom, December 17, 1968.

33. Interview with Nicholas Comfort, July 13, 2015.

34. AC, "Taking Comfort in California's Variety," *Los Angeles Times*, July 15, 1973.

35. Herbert Marcuse, "No Comment," *Journal of the Forum for Contemporary History*, July 2, 1973.

36. Krishna R. Dronamraju, "On Some Aspects of the Life and Work of John Burdon Sanderson Haldane, F.R.S., in India," *Notes and Records of the Royal Society of London* 41, no. 2 (June 1987).

Chapter 18: California (1973–1975)

1. "Comfort Joins Brain Drain," *Inside London*, October 11, 1973.

2. John Burton and Alan Watts, "Get It While It's Hot," *Journal of the Forum for Contemporary History*, July 2, 1973.

3. Charles E. Lyght, letter to AC, September 17, 1973.

4. AC, "Taking Comfort in California's Variety," *Los Angeles Times*, July 15, 1973.

5. Martin Gardner, "The Strange Case of Robert Maynard Hutchins," in *The Night Is Long: Collected Essays, 1938-1995* (New York: St Martin's Press, 1996), 510–15.

6. Cited in Edward Engberg, "Hutchinsland," *New Republic*, July 21, 1979.

7. Harvey Wheeler, *The Politics of Revolution* (Berkeley: Glendessary Press, 1971), ix, 304.

8. Edward Engberg, "Hutchinsland," *New Republic*, July 21, 1979.

9. Interview with Zhores Medvedev, February 23, 2010.

10. Hugh Kenner, "The Comfort behind *The Joy of Sex*."

11. Interview with Betty Dodson, November 13, 2013.

12. "Comfort on Aging," *People*, February 2, 1975.

13. Earl Wilson, "Tribute to 'Paul Good ... uh, Newman,'" *Philadelphia Daily News*, May 7, 1975.

14. Milton Moskowitz, "'Godfather' Meets 'Joy of Sex," *San Francisco Chronicle*, February 18, 1975.

15. "Plainedge," *Farmingdale Observer*, February 13, 1975.

16. "Dear Abby," *Staten Island Advance*, February 7, 1975.

17. Interview with Brian McConnachie, October 12, 2015.

18. Interview with Chris Foss, November 22, 2022.

19. Interview with Chris Foss, March 27, 2015.

20. AC, letter to James Mitchell, April 5, 1974; interview with Jonathan Dana, May 10, 2022.

21. Edward Blau, Pacht, Ross, Warne, Bernhard & Sears, letter to Lee Rosenberg, Adams, Ray & Rosenberg, August 7, 1975; Lee Rosenberg, letter to Tom Moore, Pacht, Ross, Warne, Bernhard & Sears, August 8, 1975.

22. James Mitchell, letter to AC, September 27, 1974.

23. Richard Holme, letter to AC, January 14, 1975.

24. Fleming: Richard Holme, letter to AC, February 17, 1975; SIECUS: Mary S. Calderone, letter to AC, November 18, 1974.

25. James Mitchell, letter to AC, May 12, 1975.

26. James Mitchell, letter to AC, June 26, 1974.

27. Hugh Kenner, "The Comfort behind *The Joy of Sex*."

28. AC, letter to Mrs. Dick Jackson, August 21, 1973.

29. "Inhumane Letters," *Library Journal*, March 15, 1975.

30. Rod Nordland, "Jersey Librarian's Ouster Another 'Peyton Place,'" *Philadelphia Inquirer*, July 28, 1974.

31. Tommy Miller, "Book Banning Increase Attributed to Court Rule," *San Francisco Chronicle*, October 6, 1974.

32. "Censorship and Its Effects on Libraries," *Gaffney (SC) Ledger*, April 23, 1975.

33. Glen Elsasser, "Pressure Strong for Secrecy Bill," *Philadelphia Inquirer*, June 15, 1975.

34. Interview with John Boothe, May 27, 2015.

35. "Other New Books," *Observer*, March 21, 1974.

36. B. Lynn Barber, letter to AC, August 25, 1973.

37. Interview with John Boothe, May 27, 2015.

38. Interview with Carmen Callil, May 13, 2015.

39. Interview with John Boothe, May 27, 2015.

40. AC, *More Joy of Sex: A Lovemaking Companion to* The Joy of Sex (New York: Simon & Schuster, 1974), 80–81.

41. See, for example, Andrew Lester, "'This Was My Utopia': Sexual Experimentation in the 1960s Bay Area Radical Left," *Journal of the History of Sexuality*, September 2020.

42. Interview with Jonathan Dana, March 22, 2018.

43. Interview with Al Gentry, July 9, 2018.

44. Skip Ferderber, "Sandstone: Closeup of a Unique Lifestyle," *Los Angeles Times*, April 6, 1972.

45. Barbara Williamson with Nancy Bacon, *An Extraordinary Life: Love, Sex and Commitment* (Bloomington IN: Balboa Press, 2013), 124–132.

46. AC, *More Joy of Sex: A Lovemaking Companion to* The Joy of Sex (New York: Simon & Schuster, 1974), 159–60.

47. Ibid., 165, 161.

48. See Gay Talese, *Thy Neighbor's Wife* (Garden City, NY: Doubleday, 1980), 296–300.

49. Interview with Jonathan Dana, March 29, 2018.

50. Gay Talese, *Thy Neighbor's Wife*, 289.

51. Interview with Peter Lert, September 10, 2019.

52. John Williamson, *Project Synergy: An Outline and Abstract*, pamphlet, 1970; "Sexuality and Social Stability," abstract of presentation delivered at 1970 Kirkridge Conference on New Life Styles and Changing Community; and *A Brief Answer to an Often Asked Question*, Sandstone pamphlet, 1970.

53. Interview with Barbara Williamson, March 16, 2018.

54. Interview with Magi Discoe, March 23, 2018.

55. Interview with Peter Lert, September 10, 2019.

56. Gay Talese, *Thy Neighbor's Wife*, 513.

57. Interview with Magen O'Farrell, August 7, 2018.

58. Interview with Magi Discoe, March 23, 2018,

59. Interview with Barbara Williamson, March 30, 2018.

60. Interview with Jennifer O'Farrell, December 12, 2022.

61. "Barbara would not tolerate": interview with Barbara Williamson, March 30, 2018.

62. Interview with Marty Zitter, June 26, 2018.

63. AC, *More Joy of Sex*, 153–55, 136, 152.

64. Ibid., 191–92, 128, 122, 210, 214.

65. Ibid., 54, 107, 125, 208, 215, 203.

66. Ibid., 111, 90.

67. Ibid., 7.

68. Interview with Max Monsarrat, November 18, 2009.

69. Interview with Max Monsarrat, April 24, 2015; "*More Joy*: A Lovemaking Companion to *The Joy of Sex*," *Publishers Weekly*, July 22, 1974.

70. AC, *More Joy of Sex*, 174–75.

71. "*More Joy*: A Lovemaking Companion to *The Joy of Sex*," *Publishers Weekly*, September 30, 1974.

72. Leslie Cross, "Still More Books—and a Sleeper," *Milwaukee Journal Sentinel*, February 23, 1975.

73. AC, *More Joy of Sex*, 132.

74. Michael Perkins, "The Joy Ploy," *SCREW*, October 7, 1974.

75. Ellen Goodman, "A Bossy Tone in Sex Advice," *Boston Globe*, October 4, 1974.

76. Digby Diehl, "Cold Comfort," *Los Angeles Times*, October 27, 1974.

77. "More Tidings of Comfort and Joy," *Time*, October 7, 1974.

78. Lila Freilicher, "Post-Christmas Returns Generally Low; Art and Gift Books the Exception," *Publishers Weekly*, February 3, 1975.

79. "Close on the Heels of Its Success. . . ," *Publishers Weekly*, May 26, 1975.

80. Interview with Chris Foss, November 22, 2022.

81. Interview with Erica Jong, December 7, 2020.

82. Eleanor Links Hoover, "Far Out," *Human Behavior*, January 1975.

83. Linda Deutsch, "From Sex to Senior Citizens," *State* (Columbia, SC), January 27, 1975.

84. "He and Jane had written *Joy*": David Feller, "Conversation with Alex Comfort," *Oui*, December 1974.

85. Jon Olson, "Turning Back the Clock," *Daily Pilot* (Orange County, CA), February 9, 1975.

86. Janet Chusmir, "A Little Comfort on Problems People Make," *Miami Herald*, January 21, 1975.

87. Jon Franklin, "Author (4 Million Copies) Sheds Daylight on Sex," *Baltimore Sun*, May 23, 1975.

88. Anatole Broyard, "There's Not Much New in 'Come Out to Play,'" *Baltimore Sun*, May 2, 1975.

89. Tom Dowling, "Novel Whose Time Has Passed," *Washington Star*, May 4, 1975.

90. Jerry LeBlanc, "The Joy of Alex Comfort," *Milwaukee Journal*, April 25, 1975.

91. "Man Wants Sex Manual Royalties," *Nashville Tennessean*, May 14, 1975; "Demise of the Center, *Time*, May 26, 1975.

92. Jerry Rankin, "'Joy of Sex' Royalties Playing Major Role in Center Dispute," *Santa Barbara News-Press*, May 7, 1975.

93. Charles Foley, "When Great Minds Fall Out," *Observer*, June 1, 1975.

94. "Supporter Threatens to Sue Coast Study Center on Its Plan to Move," *New York Times*, May 12, 1975.

95. William Trombley, "Strife Leaves Think Tank in Shambles," *Los Angeles Times*, May 26, 1975.

96. "Comfort Sues Center, Seeks $406,000 in Damages, Royalties," *Santa Barbara News-Press*, July 26, 1975; Jerry Rankin, "Center Suit Complains of Second Comfort book," *Santa Barbara News-Press*, October 22, 1975.

97. Jerry Rankin, "Center Suit Complains of Second Comfort book."

98. Jerry Rankin, "Wheeler Suit against Center Charges Malicious Harassment," *Santa Barbara News-Press*, February 29, 1976.

99. William Trombley, "Strife Leaves Think Tank in Shambles," *Los Angeles Times*, May 26, 1975; Jerry Rankin, "Institute for Higher Studies," *Santa Barbara News-Press*, October 26, 1975.

100. Jerry Rankin, "Institute for Higher Studies," *Santa Barbara News-Press*, October 26, 1975.

101. Edward Blau, letter to James Michell, June 6, 1975; James Mitchell, letter to AC, August 7, 1975.

102. AC, letter to James Mitchell, November 6, 1975.

103. James Mitchell, letter to AC, January 5, 1976.

Chapter 19: The Geriatrician (1975–1980)

1. See Roger Sanjek, *Gray Panthers* (Philadelphia: University of Pennsylvania Press, 2011).

2. AC, *A Good Age* (New York: Crown, 1976), 152.

3. AC, "No Country for Old Men," *Washington Post Book World*, May 25, 1975.

4. AC, *A Good Age*, 30, 77, 129.

5. Ibid., 14–16.

6. Ibid., 45.

7. Ibid., 154, 204, 63–65, 141.

8. Ibid., 81, 115, 160.

9. Ibid., 186.

10. Nicholas Comfort, email to author, October 2, 2021.

11. Anatole Broyard, "Books of The Times," *New York Times*, November 10, 1976.

12. "The Joy of Aging," *Time*, November 8 1976.

13. H. Jack Geiger, "Some Comfort for Old Age," *New York Times Book Review*, November 28, 1976.

14. Quoted in Mary Ann Seawell, "Exposing Myths about the Elderly," *Palo Alto Times*, April 4, 1977.

15. Quoted in J. C. Martin, "The Best Is Yet to Be . . . and Is Long Way Off," *Arizona Star* (Tucson), October 2, 1977.

16. AC, letter to "Dr Reavin," February 5 1978.

17. AC, letter to "Doctor Jeghers," April 15, 1978.

18. AC, letter to "Dr Trimmer," July 14, 1980.

19. AC, *A Good Age*, 66.

20. Ibid., 67–68.

21. AC, letter to "Dr Seixas," April 6, 1977.

22. Cryonics: J. C. Martin, "The Best Is Yet to Be . . .."

23. Maggie Kuhn, letter to AC, May 10, 1977.

24. AC, letter to Stansfield Turner, June 16, 1977.

25. Claude Pepper, letter to AC, March 1, 1978.

26. James Birren, letter to AC, February 9, 1978; AC, letter to James Birren, February 14, 1978.

27. AC, letter to James Mitchell, January 9, 1976.
28. AC, letter to Lissy Jarvik, August 26, 1977.
29. Interview with Leonard Hayflick, February 17, 2010.
30. Jerry Rankin, "Center and Dr. Comfort Square Off for L.A. trial," *Santa Barbara News-Press*, October 29, 1976.
31. Quoted in Dorothy Townsend, "'Joy of Sex" Author Wins Suit on Royalties Contract," *Los Angeles Times*, November 24, 1976.
32. AC, letter to the editor, *Fortune*, October 3, 1977.
33. AC, ed., *Sexual Consequences of Disability* (Philadelphia: George F. Stickley, 1979), 1, 3.
34. Ronna Krozy, "Sexual Consequences of Disability," *American Journal of Nursing*, November 1979.
35. AC, *Practice of Geriatric Psychiatry* (New York: Elsevier, 1980), vii.
36. Ibid., 26, 19, 63–64.
37. Ibid., 77–78.
38. Ibid., 84. "Bellman's map": from Lewis Carroll's 1876 mock-epic poem "The Hunting of the Snark."
39. Ibid., 93.
40. Tom Arie, "Practice of Geriatric Psychiatry," *Age and Ageing*, January 1983.
41. AC, "Latterday Anarchism," *Center Magazine*, September/October 1973.
42. AC, "To Be Continued," *Playboy*, November 1971.
43. Quoted in David Feller, "Conversation with Alex Comfort," *Oui*, December 1974.
44. Ibid.
45. Hugh Kenner, "The Comfort behind *The Joy of Sex*."
46. AC, *The Biology of Senescence*, 3rd ed. (New York: Elsevier North Holland, 1979), 313–18.
47. Christian Holinka, "The Biology of Senescence," *Quarterly Review of Biology*, December 1979.
48. N. K. Coni, "The Biology of Senescence," *Annals of Human Biology* 7, no. 3 (November 3, 1980).
49. Leonard Hayflick, "The Biology of Senescence," *Journal of Social and Biological Structures*, April 1980.
50. AC, *What Is a Doctor? Essays on Medicine and Human Natural History* (Philadelphia: George F. Stickley, 1980), 5.
51. Ibid., 9.
52. Ibid., 21.
53. Ibid., 60–61.
54. Bill Trott, "E. O. Wilson, Naturalist Dubbed a Modern-Day Darwin, Dies at 92," Reuters, December 27, 2021.
55. AC, *What Is a Doctor?*, 161.
56. Ibid., 167-68.
57. John W. Riggle, letter to AC, February 3, 1978.
58. Ronald A. Sarasin, letter to AC, February 9, 1978.
59. AC, letter to Peter Medawar, March 8, 1978.
60. Richard Mandel for Black Rose, letter to AC, September 1, 1979; AC, letter to Black Rose, September 6, 1979.
61. Interview with Marilyn Yalom, February 19, 2009.
62. AC, letter to Ian MacNeill, August 26, 1980; AC, letter to "Pat," September 4, 1980.
63. Interview with Leonard Hayflick, February 17, 2010.
64. Interview with John Mackall, March 29, 2016.

65. AC, letter to *New Scientist*, July 24, 1979.
66. AC, letter to Marty Zitter, September 30, 1972; Ralph Yaney, letters to AC, January 5 and May 9, 1973.
67. AC, letter to Marty Zitter, March 14, 1974.
68. Gay Talese, *Thy Neighbor's Wife*, 518–20.
69. AC, letter to Paul Paige, date unknown, 1974.
70. AC, letter to Marty Zitter, April 12, 1976.
71. Gay Talese, email to author, November 21, 2016.
72. David Feller, "Conversation with Alex Comfort," *Oui*, December 1974.
73. Interview with Zhores Medvedev, February 18, 2010.
74. James Mitchell, letter to AC, April 30, 1976.
75. Herbert Michelman, letter to James Mitchell, July 12, 1976.
76. AC, letter to James Mitchell, July 17, 1977.
77. AC, letter to James Mitchell, July 24, 1977.
78. James Mitchell, letter to AC, October 17, 1975.
79. James Mitchell, letter to AC, July 9, 1976.
80. AC, letter to James Mitchell, July 17, 1976.
81. Iain Parsons, for Mitchell Beazley, letter to AC, December 8, 1977.
82. Interview with Edmund White, November 18, 2015.
83. Interview with Charles Silverstein, November 13, 2015.
84. AC, letter to James Mitchell, July 17, 1976.
85. AC to Bruce Hunter, May 14, 1977.
86. AC, letter to James Mitchell, June 6, 1977.
87. Interviews with Charles Silverstein, November 6 and November 13, 2015, and Edmund White, November 18, 2015.
88. "An Interview with Alex Comfort," *Practical Psychology for Physicians*, January 1975.
89. AC and Jane Comfort, *The Facts of Love: Living, Loving and Growing Up* (New York: Crown, 1979), 9, 46.
90. Ibid., 42, 73.
91. Ibid., 78, 40, 87, 103.
92. Ibid., 84–86.
93. Mary Breasted, "The Junior Joys of Sex," *Washington Post*, November 11, 1979.
94. Melanie Kubale, "The Birds and the Bees in Words and Pictures," *Los Angeles Times*, September 30, 1979.
95. AC, letter to David Sheehan, October 24, 1979; AC, letter to Lee Rosenberg, October 25, 1979.
96. James Mitchell, letter to AC, April 30, 1976.
97. "Moore's Comfort," *Evening Standard*, February 16, 1978.
98. George Woodcock, "Old and New Oxford Books: The Idea of an Anthology," *Sewanee Review*, Winter 1974.
99. Donald Davie, "Larkin's Choice," *The Listener*, May 29, 1973.
100. AC, *Poems for Jane*, 42.
101. Ibid., 63.
102. Ibid., 52.
103. AC, *The Almond Tree: A Legend*, 155, 68.
104. AC, *Poems for Jane*, 5.
105. AC, letter to James Mitchell, date unknown.
106. James Mitchell, letter to David Higham, September 4, 1975.
107. AC, *Poems for Jane*, 33.
108. "My best book": AC, letter to James Mitchell, undated.

109. Kenneth Seib, "Poems for Jane," *Fresno Bee*, December 30, 1979.

110. Agnes McDonald, "Gentle McCarthy, Glossy Comfort," *News and Observer* (Raleigh NC), September 30, 1979.

Chapter 20: *I and That* (1974–1980)

1. AC, interviewed by David Goodway, March 16, 1989.
2. AC, *I and That: Notes on the Biology of Religion* (New York: Crown, 1979), 12.
3. AC, "On Ecstasy and Originality," in *The Human Context*, vol. 1 (Dordrecht: Springer, 1969).
4. AC, letter to Oliver Sacks, December 15, 1980.
5. AC, "On Ecstasy and Originality."
6. AC, *I and That*, 17.
7. See Ernst Mach, *The Science of Mechanics*, translated by Thomas J. McCormack, 4th edition (Chicago: Open Court, 1919).
8. Werner Heisenberg, *The Physicist's Conception of Nature* (New York, Harcourt, Brace, 1968), 15, 28–29.
9. AC, *I and That*, 56, 33.
10. Ibid., 12.
11. "Inner-space world": ibid., 107.
12. AC, "On Ecstasy and Originality."
13. AC, *I and That*, 57, 107, 69, 14.
14. Ibid., 107, 104.
15. Ibid., 102, 34–35.
16. Ibid., 132.
17. Ibid., 132.
18. Ibid., 134, 84, 134.
19. Ibid., 122, 112, 126–27.
20. Ibid., 145, 146.
21. AC, interviewed by David Goodway, March 16, 1989.
22. AC, *Reality and Empathy: Physics, Mind, and Science in the 21st Century* (Albany: State University of New York Press, 1984), xv.
23. AC, *I and That*, 141.
24. Julian Huxley, "The Faith of a Humanist," *Woman's Hour*, BBC Radio, March 15, 1960.
25. AC, *I and That*, 141, 149.
26. J. C. Poynton, "Alex Comfort on Self and Religion: A Case Study in Mergence of Eastern and Western Thinking," *Theoria: A Journal of Social and Political Theory*, no. 54 (May 1980).
27. AC, letter to Peter Medawar, undated (1979 or 1980).
28. Peter B. Medawar, "Rational Mystic," *The Sciences*, December 1979.
29. Hans Mol, "I and That," *Journal for the Scientific Study of Religion* 19, no. 4 (December 1980).
30. Harvey Wheeler, "Alex Comfort's Biology of Ontology: Implications for Gerontology, Phenomenology and the Philosophy of Science," *Journal of Social and Biological Structures* 33, nos. 1–2 (1998).
31. Antonio T. de Nicolás, "Notes on the Biology of Religion," *Journal of Social and Biological Structures*, April 1980.
32. AC, *I and That*, 153.
33. AC, letter to Nat Wartels, January 1, 1980; AC, letters to David Higham, December 2, 1977 and January 11, 1978.

34. David Higham, letter to AC, January 14, 1978.
35. AC, *Tetrarch* (London: Wildwood House, 1981), 130.
36. David Higham, letter to AC, February 7, 1978.
37. AC, letter to George Erikson, September 1, 1978.
38. Samuel Bercholz, letter to AC July 23, 1980.
39. William Fadiman, "Science Fiction from Alex Comfort," *Los Angeles Times*, June 22, 1980.
40. AC, letter to Samuel Bercholz, July 26, 1980.
41. Nina Bawden, "Recent Fiction," *Daily Telegraph*, May 28, 1981; Kelvin Johnston, "Science Fiction," *Observer*, May 17, 1981.
42. AC, letter to Oliver Caldecott, October 23, 1980; AC, letter to James Brabazon, January 23, 1983.
43. Oliver Caldecott, letter to AC, October 16, 1980.
44. AC, letter to Norman Franklin, January 28, 1980.
45. Oliver Caldecott, letter to AC, December 11, 1980.
46. Nat Wartels, letter to AC, February 28, 1980.
47. AC, letter to James Mitchell, February 21, 1980
48. James Mitchell, letter to AC, February 28, 1980.
49. This paragraph and the following: AC, letter to James Mitchell, March 13, 1980.
50. AC, letter to Nat Wartels, November 23, 1980.
51. AC, letter to Sam Bercholz, June 6, 1980.
52. AC, letter to Carl Sagan, November 18, 1980.
53. AC, letter to Oliver Sacks, December 15, 1980.
54. AC, letter to Dan Perry, special assistant to Sen. Alan Cranston, September 29, 1980.
55. AC, letters to Nat Wartels, November 23 and December 11, 1980.
56. Lester Grinspoon and James B. Bakalar, letter to AC, August 6, 1980.
57. AC, letter to Lester Grinspoon, August 18, 1980.
58. James Mitchell, letter to AC, February 29, 1980.
59. AC, letter to James Mitchell, March 25, 1980.
60. Irwin E. Russell for Jac Holzman, letter to AC, September 4, 1980.
61. AC, letter to Irwin E. Russell, September 10, 1980.
62. Irwin E. Russell for Jac Holzman, letter to AC, September 28, 1980.
63. AC, letter to James Mitchell, November 20, 1980.
64. Peter Mead, letter to AC, December 16, 1980.
65. "Business Briefs," UPI, November 18, 1980.
66. AC, letter to Peter Mead, December 29, 1980.
67. AC, letter to "Gordon," December 29, 1980.
68. See Oliver Caldecott, letter to AC, October 16, 1980.
69. Letter to Aubrey Davis, Hugh Massie, December 17, 1980.
70. AC, letters to The Manager, E F. Hutton Inc., September 1980; Walter O. Sellers, Merrill Lynch, October 12, 1980; "Mr. Holt," Merrill Lynch, October 25, 1980; and Frank J. McNerney, Merrill Lynch, November 8, 1980.
71. AC, letter to Harris Seed, September 5, 1980.
72. Interview with Leonard Hayflick, February 17, 2010.
73. Interview with Nicholas Comfort, August 10, 2022.
74. Nicholas Comfort, email to author, June 24, 2018.
75. AC, letters to Wendell D. Klossner, June 10 and August 3, 1981.
76. AC. letter to the editor, *The Lancet*, August 5, 1981.
77. Interview with Benjamin Yalom, July 2, 2009.
78. Interview with Marilyn Yalom, June 9, 2009.

79. Joel Goldberg, letter to AC, April 17,1980; AC and Jane Comfort, letter to Joel Goldberg, April 24, 1980.
80. Interview with Zhores Medvedev, February 18, 2010.
81. Interview with Leonard Hayflick, February 11, 2010.
82. AC, letter to H. J. Ralston III, August 16, 1987.
83. AC, letter to Milton Greenblatt, March 25, 1982.
84. AC, letter to "Frances," April 18, 1982.
85. Keith Harrison, letter to AC, July 14, 1983.
86. AC, letter to Peter Medawar, September 6, 1983.
87. AC, letter to George Woodcock, September 18, 1990.
88. AC, letter to the editor, *Economist*, November 11, 1981.
89. AC, letter to the editor, *Economist*, May 20, 1982.
90. AC, letter to the editor, *Times* (London), February 24, 1985.
91. Karen W. Powe, National Association of State Boards of Education, letter to Phillip L. Owens, Carolina Biological Supply Company, May 11, 1983.
92. AC, letter to Karen W. Powe, National Association of State Boards of Education, October 3, 1983.
93. AC, "Alcohol as a Social Drug and Health Hazard," *The Lancet*, February 25, 1984.
94. AC, letter to Wendell D. Klossner, April 15, 1983.
95. Interview with Nicholas Comfort, August 10, 2022.
96. Nicholas Comfort, email to author, June 26, 2021.
97. AC, letter to Alec Coppen, August 13, 1984.
98. AC, letter to Alex Coppen, December 31, 1984.

Chapter 21: *Reality and Empathy* (1980–1984)

1. Interview with Nicholas Comfort, August 10, 2022.
2. AC and Jane Comfort, interviewed by David Goodway, March 19, 1989.
3. AC, letter to Jane Isay, Basic Books, July 9, 1980.
4. AC, letter to Louis H. Kauffman, November 10, 1981.
5. Peter Medawar, letter to "Henry," March 29, 1982; AC, letter to Medawar, September 6, 1983.
6. AC, letter to Jane Isay, Basic Books, July 25, 1980.
7. AC, letter to The Academic Press, November 11, 1982.
8. AC, *Reality and Empathy*, 160–61, 43.
9. Ibid., 106.
10. Nick Herbert, *Quantum Reality: Beyond the New Physics* (New York: Anchor Press/Doubleday, 1985), 220–23.
11. Ibid., 168.
12. AC, *Reality and Empathy*, 4–5, 77. See also Charles W. Misner, Kip S. Thorne, and John Archibald Wheeler, *Gravitation* (New York: W. J. Freeman, 1973).
13. Kurt Gödel, "A Remark about the Relationship between Relativity Theory and Idealistic Philosophy," *Albert Einstein: Philosopher-Scientist*, in P. A. Schilpp, ed. (New York: Harper Brothers, 1959), 55–62.
14. AC, *Reality and Empathy*, 110.
15. Louis H. Kauffman and Francisco J. Varela, "Form Dynamics," *Journal of Social and Biological Structures* 3 (1980); Kauffman, "Special Relativity and a Calculus of Distinctions," 1988, http://homepages.math.uic.edu/~kauffman/Relativity.pdf; interview with Louis H. Kauffman, November 22, 2022.
16. Louis H. Kauffman, email to author, September 12, 2022.

17. Douglas R. Hofstadter, *Gödel, Escher, Bach: An Eternal Golden Braid*, 20th anniversary ed. (New York: Basic Books, 1999), P-2.

18. AC, *Reality and Empathy*, 189.

19. Douglas R. Hofstadter, *Gödel, Escher, Bach*, 559.

20. Ibid., 709.

21. Douglas R. Hofstadter, *I Am a Strange Loop* (New York: Basic Books, 2007).

22. AC, *Reality and Empathy*, 191.

23. Ibid., 21.

24. Ibid., 164.

25. James Jeans, *Physics and Philosophy* (New York: Dover Publications, 1981), 216.

26. AC, *Reality and Empathy*, 196.

27. Ibid., 196–98.

28. Ibid., 25–26, 103.

29. Ibid., 103.

30. AC, "An Invisible College?" *ReVision: A Journal of Consciousness and Change*, Spring 1983.

31. AC, *Reality and Empathy*, 201.

32. Ibid., 217.

33. Ibid., 180, 23.

34. Ibid., 235, 249.

35. Ibid., 32, 30.

36. Fritjof Capra, *The Tao of Physics: An Exploration of the Parallels between Modern Physics and Eastern Mysticism*, Fifth Edition (Boulder: CO: Shambhala Publications, 2010), 320, 340.

37. AC, *Reality and Empathy*, 249, 248.

38. Ibid., 89.

39. Ibid., 244–46.

40. Interview with Louis H. Kauffman, August 30, 2022.

41. Peter Medawar, letter to "Henry," March 29, 1982.

42. Martin Gardiner, "Comfort's Comforts," *Nature*, April 26, 1984.

43. Interview with Louis H. Kauffman, August 30, 2022.

44. AC, letter to Nathan Shock, July 20, 1984.

45. AC, letter to Medic International, September 24, 1985.

46. AC, letter to Robert Maxwell, November 10, 1981.

47. AC, letter to the editor, *World Business News*, July 16, 1981.

48. AC, "Living All Your Life," in *Molecular Biology of Aging*, ed. A. D. Woodhead, A. D. Blackett, and A. Hollaender (Boston: Springer, 1985), 224.

49. Ibid., 225.

50. Ibid., 222–23.

51. Alex Coppen, letter to AC, January 7, 1985.

52. AC, letter to Keith Harrison, September 16, 1984.

53. AC, letter to Harris Seed, February 6, 1985.

54. AC, letter to George Woodcock, December 16, 1990.

55. AC, letter to Roy C. Smith, Comins & Co., September 25, 1986.

56. Alex and Jane Comfort, "Replies to Inland Revenue Questionnaire of 12th February 1987."

57. AC, letter to "Dr. Jolley," February 14, 1985.

58. Duncan Baird, email to author, November 24, 2022.

59. AC, letter to Gordon M. Smith, September 19, 1984.

60. AC, letter to James Mitchell, September 26, 1983.

61. AC, letter to James Mitchell, May 19, 1984.

62. AC, letter to Helene Hahn, Paramount Pictures, September 8, 1981.

63. AC, letter to Helene Kahn, September 28, 1981.

64. Steven X. Rea, "Film: 'Joy of Sex' at the Movies," *Philadelphia Inquirer*, August 4, 1984.

65. AC, letter to Jack Tresidder, September 4, 1985.

66. James Mitchell, letter to AC, March 28, 1984.

67. Jack Tresidder, letters to AC, July 5 and 19, 1985.

68. AC, letter to Jack Tresidder, August 6, 1985.

69. AC, letter to Jack Tresidder, September 4, 1985.

70. Peter Mead, letter to AC, December 18, 1985.

71. Boyce Rensberger, "AIDS Cases in 1985 Exceed Total of All Previous Years," *Washington Post*, January 17, 1986.

72. Interview with Tony Cobb, November 17, 2015.

73. AC, letter to Jack Tresidder, June 21, 1986.

74. AC, *More Joy: A Lovemaking Companion to* The Joy of Sex, rev. and updated ed. (New York: Pocket Books, 1987), 11–14.

75. AC, letter to Alan Mirken, November 29, 1986; Alan Mirken, letter to AC, December 11, 1987.

76. Elizabeth Mehren, "Gallup on Women Book Buyers," *Los Angeles Times*, July 5, 1987.

77. A.M. Chaplin, "Safe Sex a Greater Concern in Updated Edition of 'Joy of Sex.'"

78. Geoffrey Robertson, "A Laundry List Approach to Obscenity," *Guardian*, February 7, 1986.

79. Ruth Westheimer, "Forgot to Say She Had Herpes," *New York Daily News*, May 4, 1986.

80. Ned Barnett, "Technicality Means No Life Term for Convicted Sex Offender," *Tampa Bay Times*, March 26, 1987.

81. A. M. Chaplin, "Safe Sex a Greater Concern in Updated Edition of 'Joy of Sex,'" *Baltimore Sun*, January 12, 1987.

82. Jane Ellison, "Guru Who Is Still Preaching the Virtues of Safe Sex," *Daily Telegraph*, April 29, 1987.

83. John Gaskell, "'Joy of Sex' Manual Warns of Aids—at Last," *Sunday Telegraph*, October 5, 1986.

84. See AC, "AIDS (and STD) Prophylaxis: Urgent Need for an Effective Genital Antiseptic," *Journal of the Royal Society of Medicine* 79 (May 1986).

85. AC, letter to Viscount Whitelaw, November 3, 1986.

86. Jack Tresidder, letter to AC, October 28, 1986.

Chapter 22: Emperors and Philosophers (1984–1991)

1. AC, letter to the secretary, Nuffield Foundation, November 26, 1985; Madhu Kanungo, letter to AC, February 24, 1986.

2. Graham Bennette, letter to AC, August 8, 1986

3. Stewart R. Sutherland, letters to AC, February 13 and April 1, 1987.

4. William Davison et al., letter to AC, June 6, 1986.

5. AC, letter to William Davison, June 14, 1986.

6. Fred Marnau, letters to AC, July 23 and August 7, 1985.

7. AC, letter to Robert Greacen, June 7, 1986.

8. Laurie Crawford, letter to AC, September 14, 1986.

9. Martin Dodd, Emma's Community Book & Coffee Shop, letter to AC, October 1986.

10. Charles Coulé, letter to AC, October 8, 1985.
11. AC, letter to the editor, *Guardian*, September 14, 1985.
12. Daniel Johnson, "She Wore Her Suits Like Armor," *Wall Street Journal*, January 28, 2016.
13. AC, letter to S. K. Biswas, January 10, 1985.
14. AC, "Why not can the Bomb?" *The Guardian*, November 13, 1987.
15. AC, letter to the editor, *New Statesman*, September 19, 1985.
16. AC, letter to the editor, *Guardian*, October 1, 1986.
17. Printed in *The Observer*, February 13, 1987.
18. AC, letter to the editor, *Guardian*, March 29, 1987.
19. Dennis Gould, letters to AC, August 21, September 9, and September 17, 1987.
20. Vernon Richards, letter to AC, October 21, 1987.
21. AC, letter to Vernon Richards, October 23, 1987.
22. AC, letter to "Mr. Rose," BBC Channel 4, August 5, 1985.
23. Jim Reynolds, letter to AC, July 8, 1985.
24. AC, letter to James Brabazon, February 26, 1985; letter to Rupert Hart-Davies, February 26, 1985.
25. AC, letter to the editor, Sotheby's International Poetry Competition, March 18, 1982.
26. AC, letter to Louis H. Kauffman, March 1, 1986; letter to Robert Greacen, June 7, 1986.
27. Christopher Reid, letter to AC, undated, 1986.
28. Jeffrey Levy, "The Very Bohemian Ms Banbridge," *Daily Mail*, January 19, 1994.
29. AC, *Imperial Patient: The Memoirs of Nero's Doctor* (London: Gerald Duckworth, 1987), 47.
30. Ibid., 37.
31. Ibid. 154, 150.
32. Patrick Parrinder, "Unquiet Deaths," *London Review of Books*, September 3, 1987.
33. AC, *Imperial Patient*, 70–71.
34. See Arthur E. Salmon, *Alex Comfort* (Boston: Twayne, 1978).
35. Norman Shrapnel, "Rehabilitating Nero," *Guardian*, July 3, 1987.
36. AC, letter to Jonathan Powell, BBC, August 5, 1985.
37. Jonathan Powell, letter to AC, September 3, 1985.
38. Jonathan Powell, letter to AC, December 5, 1985.
39. Colin Haycraft, letter to AC, June 8, 1987.
40. AC, letter to "Mr. Smith," March 20, 1984.
41. AC, letter to Roger Van Zwaanenberg, May 23, 1987.
42. AC, letter to Ian Stevenson, May 23, 1982.
43. AC, "An Invisible College?"
44. AC, letter to "Graham," January 10, 1983.
45. Interview with Louis H. Kauffman, August 30, 2022.
46. Alison Watson, letter to AC, January 23, 1987.
47. AC, letter to Alison Watson, March 24, 1987.
48. See Ted Bastin, H. Pierre Noyes, and John Amson, "On the Physical Interpretation and the Mathematical Structure of the Combinatorial Hierarchy," *International Journal of Theoretical Physics* 18 (July 1979).
49. AC, letter to Faruq Abdullah, June 10, 1987.
50. AC, letter to Ted Bastin, June 24, 1987.
51. Ted Bastin, letter to AC, July 17, 1987.
52. AC, letter to Frederick Parker-Rhodes, June 10, 1987.

53. AC, letter to Colin Haycraft, May 8, 1988.
54. AC, letter to Colin Haycraft, May 18, 1989.
55. AC, interviewed by David Goodway, March 16, 1989.
56. AC, *The Philosophers* (London: Gerald Duckworth, 1989), 108.
57. Ibid., 176.
58. AC, letter to Colin Haycraft, May 18, 1989.
59. Christopher Wordsworth, "License to Itch," *Guardian*, July 21, 1987.
60. AC, interviewed by David Goodway, March 16, 1989.
61. AC, *The Philosophers*, 169–70.
62. Richard Norton-Taylor, "Blake Files Spoke of Persecution," *Guardian*, June 22, 1991.
63. Barrie Penrose, "Author Knew of Spy Escape Case; Michael Randle and Pat Pottle," *Sunday Times* (London), January 29, 1989.
64. Michael Randle, letter to AC, June 20, 1990.
65. AC, letter to Michael Randle, July 1, 1990.
66. Quentin McDermott, "The State vs Randle and Pottle," *City Limits*, May 17–24, 1990.
67. "Activists Who Helped Free British Double Agent Found Innocent," United Press International, June 26, 1991.
68. AC, letter to Andrew Motion, March 18, 1989; letter to Nicholas Hyman, August 7, 1990.
69. AC, letter to James Brabazon, January 23, 1983.
70. AC, letter to Hugh Lockhart, August 7, 1990.
71. AC, letter to Erica Smith, February 16, 1990.
72. Erica Smith, letter to AC, July 12, 1990.
73. AC, "Science, Religion, and Scientism," lecture to South Place Ethical Society, September 20, 1990.
74. AC, letter to Hilary Davies, November 28, 1987.
75. AC, letter to "Mr. Corkery," April 24, 1982.
76. AC, interviewed by David Goodway, March 16, 1989.
77. AC, letter to Gary J. Panepinto, August 26, 1987.
78. Brian D. Johnson, "Big Bad Movies," *Maclean's*, April 9, 1990.
79. AC, letter to Peter Mead, May 27, 1987; letter to Syd Cappe, May 28 1987; letter to Edith Tolin, May 29, 1987.
80. AC, letter to Syd Cappe, January 13, 1988.
81. AC, letter to Syd Cappe, January 21, 1988.
82. AC, letter to Desmond Morris, June 30, 1988.
83. Interview with Desmond Morris, March 16, 2016.
84. Ibid.
85. Jack Harte, "Censorship," speech delivered at Cork World Book Festival, April 21, 2015.
86. "Poetry Reading by Comfort," *Sunday Tribune*, October 4, 1987.
87. Quoted in Des Nix, "The Joy of Being Comfort," *Sunday Press*, October 4, 1987.
88. Interview with Jack Harte, June 22, 2018.
89. "Joy Is Unconfined," *Guardian*, September 27, 1989.
90. Jack Harte, "Censorship," speech delivered at Cork World Book Festival, April 21, 2015.
91. AC, letter to Jack Harte, October 8, 1987.
92. Interview with Cicely Hill, January 14, 2016.
93. This paragraph and following: AC, interviewed by David Goodway, March 6, March 16, and April 25, 1989.
94. AC, letter to Jean Medawar, March 7, 1988.

95. Jane Comfort, letter to Anthony Colville, October 1, 1991.
96. AC, letter to John Doheny, January 11, 1990.
97. AC, letter to the librarian, University College London, April 5, 1990.
98. Alan Hamilton, "Times Diary, *Times* (London), February 13, 1990.
99. AC, letter to Sarah J. Skinner, May 6, 1990.
100. AC, interviewed by David Goodway, March 16, 1989.
101. Interview with Simon McMurtrie, August 11, 2015.
102. Interview with Tony Cobb, February 17, 2015.
103. Interview with Duncan Baird, February 17, 2021.
104. AC, *The New Joy of Sex: A Gourmet Guide to Lovemaking for the Nineties* (New York: Crown, 1991), 15.
105. Ibid., 6–8.
106. This paragraph and the four following: interviews with Tony Cobb, November 17, 2015; Richard Charkin, February 2, 2921; Simon McMurtrie, August 11, 2015; and Duncan Baird, February 17, 2021.
107. David Behrens, "The Return of Sex: It's Still a Joy," *Newsday*, October 9, 1991.
108. George Woodcock, letter to AC, September 16, 1990.
109. AC, letter to George Woodcock, December 16, 1990.

Chapter 23: Confinement (1991–2000)

1. AC, letter to George Woodcock, December 16, 1990.
2. Interview with Nicholas Comfort, June 25, 2015.
3. Nicholas Comfort, *Copy!*, 444–45.
4. AC, letter to Nick Comfort, January 8, 1985.
5. Interview with Nick Comfort, December 17, 2014.
6. Vivienne Menkes, "Mitchell Beazley Moves, Restructures, Retains Authors," *Publishers Weekly*, August 30, 1991.
7. Megan Tressider, "How Nature Got It Wrong for Women," *Sunday Telegraph*, July 7, 1991.
8. Amit Roy, "The New Joy of Discounting," *Sunday Telegraph*, September 29, 1991.
9. Reported in *Echo* (Loughborough), October 4, 1991, and *Burton Mail*, October 19, 1991.
10. David Gelman, "There's Still Sex to Be Found in 'Joy,'" *Newsweek*, October 21, 1991.
11. "Just the Man to Put You off Sex," *Sunday Telegraph*, September 22, 1991.
12. Quoted in Lisa Faye Kaplan, "The New 'Joy of Sex' Includes Safe Sex," *Lansing (MI) State Journal*, November 17, 1991.
13. David Behrens, "The Return of Sex: It's Still a Joy," *Newsday*, October 9, 1991.
14. Ibid.
15. Adam Gopnik, "Notes and Comment," *New Yorker*, October 7, 1991.
16. "Saucy TV Gift," *Evening Chronicle* (Newcastle-upon-Tyne), December 21, 1991.
17. David Gelman, "There's Still Sex to Be Found in 'Joy."
18. Interview with Tony Cobb, November 17, 2015.
19. Interview with Cicely Hill, January 14, 2016,
20. John Doheny, letter to AC, February 25, 1992.
21. Coroner's attendance note, November 28, 1991.
22. Interview with Nicholas Comfort, November 14, 2021.

23. Nicholas Comfort, email to author, September 22, 2022.
24. Jane Comfort, postcard to H. B. (Tony) Gibson, November 14, 1991.
25. Interview with Nicholas Comfort, July 13, 2015.
26. Nicholas Lezard, "Round Up," *Guardian*, July 19, 1994.
27. AC, *Mikrokosmos* (London: Sinclair-Stevenson, 1994), 40–41.
28. Ibid., 29.
29. Ibid., 37.
30. Ibid., 43.
31. Ibid., 41–42.
32. Ibid., 64.
33. Judith Kendra, letter to AC, January 11, 1994; Judith Kendra, letter to Corinne Reid Comfort, December 2, 1994.
34. Liz Hunt, "Alex Comfort's Joy of … Poetry," *Independent*, November 12, 1996.
35. Ian Parker, "The Grand Old Man of Sex," *Independent*, October 2, 1994.
36. Interview with Nicholas Comfort, December 17, 2014.
37. Quoted in John Illman, "The Sex Files," *Guardian*, November 12, 1996.
38. Liz Hunt, "Alex Comfort's Joy of … Poetry."
39. Interview with Marilyn Yalom, June 9, 2009.
40. Bernard J. Strehler, letter to AC, January 17, 1992.
41. Cindy Babski, letter to AC, March 16, 1992.
42. Robert Eagle, letter to AC, July 6, 1992.
43. Linda Grant, letter to Nicholas Comfort, February 18, 1993,
44. David Peat, letter to AC, February 22, 1993.
45. Jason Massot, letter to AC, February 24, 1995.
46. Roger Gosden, letter to AC, June 12, 1995.
47. Mark Downie, letter to AC, October 10, 1995.
48. Alan Rusbridger, letter to AC, October 16, 1995.
49. Sheila Jones, letters to AC, March 11 and April 17, 1998.
50. Peter Wells, letter to AC, October 24, 1998.
51. Graecen: Robert Greacen, *The Sash My Father Wore: An Autobiography* (Edinburgh: Mainstream Publishing, 1997); letter to Nick Comfort, November 29, 1996; letter to AC, March 21, 1997.
52. Leonard Hayflick, letter to AC, February 5, 1996.
53. Interview with Leonard Hayflick, February 17, 2010.
54. T. B. L. Kirkwood, "Alex Comfort and the Measure of Aging," *Experimental Gerontology* 33, nos. 1–2 (1998).
55. Richard C. Adelman, "The Alzheimerization of Aging: A Brief Update," *Experimental Gerontology* 33, nos. 1–2 (1998).
56. William F. Forbes, "Editorial," *Experimental Gerontology* 33, nos. 1–2 (1998).
57. Caleb Finch, "Alex Comfort: Intellectual Eminence in Science and Humanism," *Experimental Gerontology* 33, nos. 1–2 (1998).
58. AC, *The Novel and Our Time* (London: Phoenix House, 1948).
59. Nicholas Comfort, *Copy!*, 484.

Conclusion: Afterlife

1. Peter Davison, *Lost Orwell: Being a Supplement to* The Complete Works of George Orwell (London: Timewell, 2006), 140–41.
2. Ibid., 142.
3. Interview with Nicholas Comfort, November 21, 2016.
4. Ibid.

5. Paul Flewers, *"I Know How, but I Don't Know Why": George Orwell's Conception of Totalitarianism* (Coventry: New Interventions, 1999), 29.

6. Nicholas Moore, letter to Arthur Salmon, September 29, 1980.

7. Tom Utley, "Orwell Is Revealed in Role of State Informer," *Daily Telegraph*, July 12, 1996.

8. Frances Stoner Saunders, *The Cultural Cold War: The CIA and the World of Arts and Letters* (New York: New Press, 1999), 59.

9. Ibid., 299; Saunders's italics.

10. Timothy Garton Ash, "Orwell's List," *New York Review of Books*, September 25, 2003.

11. AC, "1939 and 1984: George Orwell and the Vision of Judgment." in Peter Stansky, ed., *On Nineteen Eighty-Four* (New York: W.H. Freeman, 1983), 20.

12. Cole Moreton, "Why We Still Need Doctor Love," *Independent*, April 2, 2000.

13. Bart Barnes, "'Joy of Sex' Author Alex Comfort Dies at 80," *Washington Post*, March 27, 2000.

14. Nic North, "Comfort and Joy," *Mirror*, March 28, 2000.

15. John Pilgrim, "Alex Comfort: The Last Positivist?" *Independent*, March 30, 2000.

16. Adrian Mitchell, "Appreciation: Alex Comfort," *Guardian*, date unknown, 2000.

17. "The Malign Legacy of Dr Comfort," *Daily Mail*, March 29, 2000.

18. Julie Burchill. "Why This Book Has Done Such Damage to Women," *Daily Mail*, November 14, 1996.

19. David Frum, "'Joy of Sex'? Real Intimacy Was Too Close for Comfort," *Wall Street Journal*, April 5, 2000.

20. Ruth Westheimer, "Eulogy," *Time*, April 10, 2000.

21. Nicholas Comfort, "The Facts of Life about My Father, His Mistress, and *The Joy of Sex*," *Daily Telegraph*, March 30, 2000.

22. Bridget Harrison, "Old-school Swooning," *New York Post*, January 26, 2003.

23. Kristin Rodine, "Nampa Library Restores 'Joy of Sex' books," *Idaho Statesman*, September 14, 2008.

24. Ariel Levy, "Doing It," *New Yorker*, January 5, 2009.

25. Quoted in Celia Dodd, "Meet the Woman Who Rewrote *The Joy of Sex*," *Times* (London), August 23, 2008.

26. Quoted in Sarah Lyall, "Revising 'Sex' for the 21st Century," *New York Times*, December 18, 2008.

27. Cited in David Rosen, "How the Christian Right Won the Culture Wars," *Counterpunch*, October 15, 2020.

28. See, for example, Daniel Bergner, *What Do Women Want? Adventures in the Science of Female Desire* (New York: Ecco/HarperCollins Publishers, 2013); Rachel E. Gross, "A Blind Spot," *New York Times*, October 18, 2022.

29. Hallie Lieberman, "Broadening Access to Sexual Health," *Wall Street Journal*, January 13, 2022.

30. Kate Zavadski, "Parents Can Lose Custody of Children Just for Being Kinky," *Daily Beast*, June 18, 2015.

31. Charles Blow, "The Decade We Changed Our Minds," *New York Times*, December 30, 2019.

32. Debora L. Spar, "The Poly-Parents Are Coming," *New York Times*, August 16, 2020.

33. Cathy Winks and Anne Semans, *The Good Vibrations Guide to Sex: The Most Complete Sex Manual Ever Written*, 3rd ed. (San Francisco: Cleis Press, 2002), 133.

34. Ibid., xi.

35. Bonnie Rochman, "Rewriting 'The Talk,'" *New York Times Magazine*, March 29, 2015.

36. David Akadjian, "Sex Is Like Pre-chewed Chewing Gum . . . Is That What You Want to Present to Your Husband?" Akadjian.com, August 20, 2015.

37. Sarah Jacoby, "Could birth control be banned? How overturning Rose affects birth control," *Today*, May 3, 2022.

38. JoAnn Wypijewski, "How Capitalism Created Sexual Dysfunction," lithub.com, June 3, 2020.

39. Noreena Hertz, *The Lonely Century: How to Restore Human Connection in a World That's Pulling Apart* (New York: Currency, 2021), 14–15.

40. Jacqueline Rose, *On Violence and On Violence against Women* (New York: Farrar, Straus & Giroux, 2022), 368.

41. Parul Sehgal, "Trouble Grows behind the Walls We Set Up," *New York Times*, May 13, 2021.

42. Jamie Heckert, "Relating Differently," *Sexualities* 13, no. 4 (2010).

43. AC, *The Joy of Sex*, 14.

44. Hayley Phelan, "The #MeToo Effect on Sex," *New York Times*, March 18, 2018.

45. Ariel Levy, "Tables for Two," *New Yorker*, August 6, 2012.

46. Julie Verhoeven, email to author, February 6, 2021.

47. Interview with Nicholas Comfort, June 26, 2015.

48. Interview with Caleb Finch, May 14, 2018.

49. Ashok K. Shetty, Maheedhar Kodali, Raghavendra Upadhya, and Leelavathi N. Madhu, "Emerging Anti-Aging Strategies—Scientific Basis and Efficacy," *Aging and Disease*, December 2018.

50. Sumathi Reddy, "Calculate the Speed of Aging," *Wall Street Journal*, July 14, 2015.

51. Shetty, et al, "Emerging Anti-Aging Strategies—Scientific Basis and Efficacy."

52. Cited in Pagan Kennedy, "No Magic Pill Will get You to 100," *New York Times*, March 11, 2018. See Caleb E. Finch, *Global Air Pollution in Aging and Disease: Reading Smoke Signals* (San Diego: Academic Press, 2018).

53. Tad Friend, "Silicon Valley's Quest to Live Forever," *New Yorker*, April 3, 2017.

54. Sven Bulterijs, Raphaella S. Hull, Victor C. E. Björk, and Avi G. Roy, "It Is Time to Classify Biological Aging as a Disease," *Frontiers in Genetics*, June 18, 2015.

55. AC, "Living All Your Life," in *Molecular Biology of Aging*, A. D. Woodhead, A. D. Blackett, and A. Hollaender, eds. (Boston: Springer, 1985), 213.

56. AC, *Nature and Human Nature*, 214.

57. AC, *A Good Age*, 13–14.

58. Dilip V. Jeste, "Psychiatry of Old Age Is Coming of Age," *American Journal of Psychiatry*, October 1997.

59. Angela J. Beck et al., "Estimating the Distribution of the U.S. Psychiatric Subspecialist Workforce," University of Michigan School of Public Health, Behavioral Health Workforce Research Center, December 2018.

60. Marcy Cottrell Houle, "Lost in the Land of Pink Bibs," *New York Times*, September 23, 2015.

61. Susan Aronson, *Elderhood: Redefining Aging, Transforming Medicine, Reimagining Life* (New York: Bloomsbury Publishing, 2019), 148.

62. AC, "Living All Your Life," in *Molecular Biology of Aging*, A.D. Woodhead, A.D. Blackett, and A. Hollaender, eds. (Boston: Springer, 1985), 223.

63. Quoted in Stuart Jeffries, "David Graeber: People Spend Their Lives Working Jobs They Think Are Unnecessary," *Guardian*, March 23, 2015.

64. AC, "The Art of the Possible," *The Listener*, March 24, 1960.

65. David Goodway, *Anarchist Seeds beneath the Snow*, 247–48.

66. Hugh Kenner, "The Comfort behind *The Joy of Sex*."

67. Walter Tevis, *The Man Who Fell to Earth* (New York: Del Rey Impact/Ballantine Publishing, 1999), 205.

68. Gareth Cook, "Mind Games," *New York Times Magazine*, September 22, 2020.

69. Evan Thompson, *Waking, Dreaming, Being: Self and Consciousness in Neuroscience, Meditation, and Philosophy* (New York: Columbia University Press, 2014), 165.

70. Ibid., xxvi.

71. Melvin Konner, *Believers: Faith in Human Nature* (New York: W.W. Norton, 2019), 138.

72. Ibid., 26.

73. Anil Seth, *Being You: A New Science of Consciousness* (New York: Dutton, 2021), 98.

74. Ibid., 7.

75. John Markoff, "Sorry, Einstein, but 'Spooky Action' Seems Real," *New York Times*, October 21, 2015.

76. AC, *Reality and Empathy*, 147.

77. Sabine Hossenfelder, *Existential Physics: A Scientist's Guide to Life's Biggest Questions* (New York: Viking, 2022), 37.

78. Quoted in Bradford Morrow, "An Afternoon with Kenneth," *Chicago Review*, Autumn 2006.

79. Quoted in H. B. Gibson, letter to the editor, *Freedom*, August 6, 1994.

80. Dannie Abse, *Collected Poems* (University of Pittsburgh Press, 1977), 6.

81. Andrea Wulf, *Magnificent Rebels: The First Romantics and the Invention of the Self* (New York: Alfred A. Knopf, 2022), 133, 150.

82. Andrea Wulf, "Can an Old Philosophy Help Us Solve a New Problem?" *New York Times*, September 17, 2022.

83. Andrea Wulf, *Magnificent Rebels*, 133, 18.

Acknowledgments

ALEX COMFORT SAID THAT his life and work comprised one large project, but that project covered a half-dozen different fields, causes, and professions. For me, each required a discreet mini-research effort, as did identifying the threads that bound them together. Many people have been helpful, not to say vital, to me in telling Alex's story.

My greatest debt is to Nicholas Comfort, who was unfailingly generous with his time, recollections, and archives—no strings attached—and who helped with several needed document and photo scans. Nick's own 2021 memoir, *Copy! A Life in Print, Parliament and Far Flung Places*, supplied vital information about the Comfort, Fenner, and Harris families and about Alex and Ruth Comfort's married life. I am especially grateful to Nick for an enriching tour of Alex Comfort's London and for tracing his father's movements and the progress of his health following his 1991 brain hemorrhage. I sincerely hope this book enriches his and his children's memories of their remarkable forebear.

David Goodway knew Alex Comfort and interviewed him extensively; edited his last collection of essays, *Writings against Power and Death*; and authored the authoritative *Anarchist Seeds beneath the Snow: Left-Libertarian Thought and British Writers from William Morris to Colin Ward* (2006), which helped me at the outset to understand Alex's place in the British anarchist tradition. David generously shared his memories, his collection of books and papers, and recordings of his interviews with Alex and Alex's friend Fred Marnau. He was also an invaluable critical voice as I developed my perspective on Alex's career and creative achievements.

Pagan Kennedy provided valuable background, insights, and wise advice in the very early stages, as well as notes from her interview of Alex's longtime friend, Robert Greacen.

Alex's long and complex publishing history could make up a book by itself. It also encompassed a fascinating period of change for the industry in both the UK and the United States. Alex had a dozen significant book-publishing relationships during his career; the most important were with Mitchell Beazley and its successor companies, Quartet Books and Eyre & Spottiswode, in the UK, and Viking, Crown Publishers, and Simon & Schuster in the United States. I am especially grateful to Peter Kindersley and Max Monserrat for their recollections of working on the original edition of *The Joy of Sex* with Alex, and to Duncan Baird, Simon McMurtrie, Richard Charkin, Tony Cobbe, and Michael Leonard for helping to fill in the later segments of the story. Christopher Foss helpfully answered my questions about the process of illustrating *Joy* and *More Joy*. Allison and Andrew Temple-Smith shared recollections of their father, Maurice Temple-Smith, Alex's editor at Eyre and Spottiswode, and the late John Boothe and the late Carmen Callil provided valuable help regarding the UK publication of *Joy* and its context.

The late Alan Mirken of Crown supplied much of the story of the book's publication in the United States, along with Bruce Harris and Alan Kahn. For the rest, I'm most grateful to the legendary Dick Snyder, then publisher at Simon & Schuster. Charles Silverstein and Edmund White kindly shared their recollections of creating the pioneering *Joy of Gay Sex*.

Among Alex's scientific colleagues, I had the honor and pleasure of interviewing the late Zhores Medvedev, who helped me understand Alex's impact on the development of gerontology in the Soviet Union and the importance of relations between Soviet and Western scientists in the '60s. Leonard Hayflick was one of Alex's best friends, and Alex one of his great champions; Len provided important insights on Alex as a person as well as a scientist, as did Caleb Finch and Cyril Gryfe. Andrew Pomiankowski, professor of genetics and director of the Division of Biosciences at University College London, helped me to link Alex's work at UCL and the Medical Research Council with that of his colleagues and with the work in genetics and gerontology ongoing there. Two other colleagues, the late Robin Holliday and the late Krishna Rao Dronamraju, were also very helpful in contextualizing Alex's accomplishment as a gerontologist, as was Jonathan Weiner. I owe a special debt to Louis H. Kauffman for his very lucid and patient explanation of the iterant and for sharing his recollections and correspondence with Alex.

Alex had few very close friends; among the very closest were the late Marilyn Yalom, her husband Irvin, and their children Ben and Eve, who shared their recollections as well as correspondence with Alex. I'm most grateful for these intimate and insightful glimpses of my subject. Other of Alex's friends, neighbors, and professional colleagues who helped generously were John Mackall, Syd Cappe, the inimitable Cicely

Hill, and the equally inimitable Desmond Morris. Jack Harte supplied the story of Alex's memorable 1987 poetry reading and talk in Dublin. I'm especially grateful to Michael Randle, Alex's comrade in the Direct Action Committee against Nuclear War and the Committee of 100, for his recollections, and to April Carter for suggestions on archival material. Special thanks to Chris Richards for his revealing and detailed tour of Havengore, Alex's childhood home.

Alex was never a member of the Sandstone Foundation for Community Systems Research, but he was always a welcome guest, and when I wanted to find out more about that unique place, ten alumni and guests of the extended Sandstone community stepped up to share their memories with me. Sandstone's cofounder, the one and only Barbara Williamson, was especially generous, as were the indefatigable Marty Zitter, who also put me in touch with much of the rest of the crew, and the very incisive Magi Discoe. Jonathan Dana, the late Betty Dodson, Al Gentry, Peter Lert, Jennifer O'Farrell, Magen O'Farrell, and Lucy Yaney were all extremely helpful as well. Special thanks to Marty and Jonathan for a wonderful tour of the Sandstone property.

Numerous scholars, artists, and writers who understood the context and significance of many aspects of Alex's career and work provided important recollections and insights. First and foremost was Arthur E. Salmon, who wrote the first literary study of my subject, *Alex Comfort* (1978), as well as *Poets of the Apocalypse* (1983), a study of Alex and his poetic contemporaries. Arthur generously opened his papers to me, including interviews and correspondence with Alex and several of his associates in the British poetry world of the '40s, and shared valuable recollections of these individuals and his keen understanding of their work.

My friend and fellow biographer Robert Goff shared sources and insights with me along the way, and I with him. Julie Verhoeven shared the story of her fantastic 2015 video installation, *The Art of the Joy of Sex*. Jay Gertzman provided valuable information and perspective on the twentieth-century dirty book trade, as did C.V.J. Scheiner (M.D., Ph.D). My thanks also to Susan Davis, Timothy Dickinson, Joyce Fleming, Lesley A. Hall, Carissa Honeywell, Erica Jong, Brian McConnachie, Annie Sprinkle, James Strick, Gay Talese, Veronica Vera, Ruth Westheimer, and Paul Willetts for their observations, recollections, and insights, and to Matthew Sweet for details of his 2012 Radio 3 feature on Alex. Special thanks to Judith Legman for sharing correspondence between Alex and her late husband, Gershon Legman.

ALEX COMFORT LED A well-documented life. Most of his papers are in the archives of University College London, while his papers on sex and sexuality are in the collection of the Kinsey Institute for Research in Sex, Gender, and Reproduction at Indiana University. I am grateful to the archivists at both institutions for making their holdings available to me. Other collections that made materials available were the International Institute of Social History, Amsterdam; the New York Public Library; and the Archive of British Printing and Publishing at Reading University. Random House, which now includes Crown Publishing, opened their files relating to *The Joy of Sex* and its successors.

I especially want to thank Stefan Dickers at Bishopsgate Library, London, for making the archives of the Peace Pledge Union available, Julie Perry at the University of Bradford for supplying materials and correspondence from and to the Direct Action Committee and the Committee of 100, and Nicole Gross with the Highgate School Archive. The archivists at the Harry Ransom Center at the University of Texas at Austin were especially helpful during the dark early days of the COVID pandemic, searching their holdings for correspondence between Alex and several of his friends, publishers, and other associates.

At UCL, Wendy Russell, Fiona Williamson, and Katy Makin facilitated my visit to the Medawar Building, where Alex had his offices. Thanks also to Muslima Chowdhury for introducing me to UCL's Institute of Healthy Ageing.

Interlibrary loan is a precious resource, particularly for independent scholars, and especially valuable in the hands of librarians who really know the ropes. I owe a debt to Liz Jacobson-Carroll and Jane Buchanan, formerly of the Buckland Public Library, for their repeated and patient assistance.

In researching this book, I benefited repeatedly from the help of my friend, the supersleuth of twentieth-century British and American literature, Robert Nedelkoff. I hope it meets his expectations and offers him some hints for future detective work. Other friends and family who commented, criticized, supplied sage advice, and generally tolerated my preoccupation with Alex Comfort include Meryl Altman, Mary Baine Campbell, Margery and the late Richard Dearborn, Ruah Donnelly and Steve Dinkelacker, Anne Fadiman, Gayle Feldman, Sam Knox, the late Robert Laursen, Tom Laursen, the late Marian Meade, Chuck Morse, Keith Nightenhelser, Linus Owens, Barry Pateman, Carl Rollyson, Amanda Vaill, Kevin Van Meter, Hugo Vickers, Kristian Williams, David Wyner, and several of the NYPL Cullman Center Fellows, class of 2018–19. Throughout much of this project, members of the Anarchist Studies Network were making new research available that shone new light on Alex's place in the movement.

The Plainfield Biographers' Group, including Lina Bernstein, Heather Clark, Mary V. Dearborn, David Perkins, and Mary and Robert Bagg, read early drafts of some chapters; their comments and criticisms were invaluable. The Autonolistas of New York City, Christopher Cardinale and Melissa Jameson, helped keep me engaged and moving forward, as always. Thanks also to Freedom Book Shop and Publishing House, London, and to Jane Roy Brown and Straw Dog Writers Guild's Writers Read event in Ashfield, Massachusetts, for the opportunity to bring something of Alex's life to an in-person audience.

No grants, awards, fellowships, stipends, subsidies, subventions, or other financial underwriting were received for the research and writing of this book. AK Press gave me the opportunity to tell the story of a remarkable person, of modern English literature, of biology and gerontology, of anarchism and antiauthoritarian struggle, of sexual behavior and liberation, and of the exploration of mind, consciousness, and the self. I am deeply grateful to Zach Blue, Sophia Hussain, and Charles Weigl at AK for their faith and support, and especially to my editor, Chris Dodge.

As always, Mary V. Dearborn supplied editorial advice, criticism, and line editing every step of the way. More fundamentally, her many biographical projects over the past thirty-five years and her incomparable skills in the form provided a master class in how to research and tell a life story and comprehend a writer's artistry, aspirations, and achievement. That, and her constant patience and support, made this book possible.

CPSIA information can be obtained
at www.ICGtesting.com
Printed in the USA
JSHW080833020423
39770JS00002B/6